S0-AEZ-823

Contents

vii

x

A

ABDICATION

1 God grant him peace and happiness but never understanding of what he has lost.
Stanley Baldwin of Edward VIII's abdication.

2 I have found it impossible to carry the heavy burden of responsibility and to discharge my duties as King as I would wish to do, without the help and support of the woman I love.
Edward VIII. Abdication speech 11 Dec 1936.

3 Are they going to chop off Uncle David's head?
Princess Margaret, on hearing of his abdication. Quoted Marion Crawford, THE LITTLE PRINCESSES

4 68 is no age to give up your job.
Queen Mary on hearing of the abdication of Queen Wilhelmina of Holland. Quoted Peter Lane, OUR FUTURE KING

ABILITY

5 The finest plans have always been spoiled by the littleness of them that should carry them out. Even emperors can't do it all by themselves.
Bertolt Brecht, MOTHER COURAGE AND HER CHILDREN 1939

6 Time goes by: reputation increases, ability declines.
Dag Hammarskjöld, MARKINGS 1964

7 Intelligence is quickness to apprehend as distinct from ability, which is capacity to act wisely on the thing apprehended.
A. N. Whitehead, DIALOGUES 1953

ABNORMALITY

8 If it weren't for the fact that all of us are slightly abnormal there wouldn't be any point in giving each person a separate name.
Ugo Betti, THE FUGITIVE 1953

9 *Abnormal, adj.* Not conforming to standard. In matters of thought and conduct, to be independent is to be abnormal, to be abnormal is to be detested.
Ambrose Bierce, THE DEVIL'S DICTIONARY 1906

10 Life is an abnormal business.
Eugene Ionesco, RHINOCEROS 1959

11 She cut off her nipples with garden shears. You call that normal?
Elizabeth Taylor. Line spoken to Marlon Brando in REFLECTIONS IN A GOLDEN EYE *(film)*

ABORTION

12 Abortion leads to an appalling trivialisation of the act of procreation.
Dr Donald Coggan, when Archbishop of York. Speech to Shaftesbury Society 2 Oct 1973

13 You ought to be ashamed, I said, to look so antique / (And her only Thirty-one). / I can't help it she said, pulling a long face / It's them pills I took to bring it off, she said / (She's had five already, and nearly died of young George) / The chemist said it would be all right, but I've never been the same / You're a proper fool, I said.
T. S. Eliot, THE WASTE LAND, *A Game of Chess* 1922

14 Abortion is a step beyond contraception. They both control or interfere with birth. I don't see how anyone who favours contraception or considers it permissible can object to abortion.
Dr Oscar Fasker. Quoted Edward F. Murphy, MACMILLAN TREASURY OF RELEVANT QUOTATIONS

1

1 We cannot treat the human embryo as cheap and worthless without passing judgment on all human life, including our own.
Monica Furlong, CHRISTIAN UNCERTAINTIES 1975

2 If men could get pregnant, abortion would be a sacrament.
Florynce Kennedy. Quoted Barbara Rowe, THE BOOK OF QUOTES

3 Sadie said: 'How does she manage it?' and Aunt Emily said: 'Skiing or hunting, or just jumping off the kitchen table.'
Nancy Mitford, THE PURSUIT OF LOVE 1945

4 It serves me right for putting all my eggs in one bastard.
Dorothy Parker, on having an abortion

5 Those who recommend it always took good care to get themselves born.
Ronald Reagan. Quoted Katherine Whitehorn, Observer, Signs of Life 10 *May* 1983

6 The greatest destroyer of peace is abortion because if a mother can kill her own child what is left for me to kill you and you to kill me? There is nothing between.
Mother Teresa, Nobel Peace Prize Lecture 1979

7 As one priest gloomily admitted, if they really accepted the conception argument, then they ought to spend their time baptising the menstrual flow.
Katharine Whitehorn, Observer, Our bodies, Ourselves and Them 15 *Jul* 1979

8 Abortion is the worst approach to the problem of birth control because it puts all the responsibility on women.
Shirley Williams, interviewed by Miriam Gross, Observer 22 *Mar* 1981

ABSENCE

9 I was courtmartialled in my absence, and sentenced to death in my absence, so I said they could shoot me in my absence.
Brendan Behan, THE HOSTAGE 1959

10 Absence blots people out. We really have no absent friends.
Elizabeth Bowen, DEATH OF THE HEART 1938

11 Absence and letters are the forcing ground of love. What renews it and confirms it is presence and bed.
Gerald Brenan, THOUGHTS IN A DRY SEASON 1979

12 That which you love most in him [a friend] may be clearer in his absence.
Kahil Gibran, THE PROPHET 1923

13 Where you used to be there is a hole in the world which I find myself constantly walking round in the daytime and falling into at night. I miss you like hell.
Edna St Vincent Millay, LETTERS 1952

14 But when he's gone / Me and them lonesome blues collide / The bed's too big / The frying pan's too wide.
Joni Mitchell, MY OLD MAN (*song*)

15 A cry of Absence, Absence in the heart / And in the wood the furious winter blowing.
John Crowe Ransome, SELECTED POEMS, *Winter Remembered* 1945

ABSENTMINDEDNESS

16 That Greek one then is my hero, who watched the bath water / Rise above his navel and rushed out naked. 'I found it / I found it' into the street in all his shining, and forgot / That others would only stare at his genitals.
Dannie Abse, WALKING UNDER WATER, *Letter to Alex Comfort*

17 I liked the store detective who said he'd seen a lot of people who were so confused that they'd stolen things, but never one so confused that they'd paid twice.
Baroness Phillips, Sunday Telegraph 14 *Aug* 1977

18 The Reverend Eli Jenkins finds a rhyme and dips a pen in his cocoa.
Dylan Thomas, UNDER MILK WOOD 1954

ABSTINENCE

19 One reason I don't drink is that I want to know when I am having a good time.
Nancy Astor

1 When a reformed drunkard gives advice you don't just hear it, you see it.
Dr Seldon Bacon, Chairman Connecticut Commission on Alcoholism. Quoted News Review 24 *Jun* 1948

2 *Abstainer:* a weak person who yields to the temptation of denying himself a pleasure.
Ambrose Bierce, THE DEVIL'S DICTIONARY 1906

3 *Total abstainer:* one who abstains from everything but abstention, and especially from inactivity in the affairs of others.
Ibid.

4 Half the vices which the world condemns most loudly have seeds of good in them and require moderate use rather than total abstinence.
Samuel Butler, THE WAY OF ALL FLESH 1903

5 Teetotallers lack the sympathy and generosity of men that drink.
W. H. Davies, Introduction to SHORTER LYRICS OF THE 20TH CENTURY

6 My stories written when sober are stupid.
F. Scott Fitzgerald

7 Abstinence is the thin edge of the pledge.
Graffito. Quoted Nigel Rees, GRAFFITI RULES OK 1979

8 He drank like a fish, if drinking nothing but water could be so described.
A. E. Housman

9 Abstemiousness can be a form of self-indulgence.
Malcolm Muggeridge, CHRONICLES OF WASTED TIME, *The Infernal Grove* 1972

10 An abstainer is the sort of man you wouldn't want to drink with even if he did.
George Jean Nathan

11 It ought to give pause to the most fanatical teetotaller that the only humans worth saving in the Flood were a family of vintners.
Dr Bernard Rudofsky, NOW I LAY ME DOWN TO EAT

12 The people who are regarded as moral luminaries are those who forgo ordinary pleasures themselves and find compensation in interfering with the pleasures of others.
Bertrand Russell, SCEPTICAL ESSAYS

13 Self denial is not a virtue, it is only the effect of prudence on rascality.
George Bernard Shaw, MAN AND SUPERMAN 1905

14 He'll probably never write a good play again.
George Bernard Shaw of Eugene O'Neill on hearing he was giving up drinking.

15 A lady temperance candidate concluded her passionate oration 'I would rather commit adultery than take a glass of beer.' Whereupon a clear voice from the audience asked 'Who wouldn't?'
Adlai Stevenson

ABSTRACT

16 The utmost abstractions are the true weapons with which to control our thought of concrete fact.
A. N. Whitehead, SCIENCE AND THE MODERN WORLD 1925

ABSURD

17 I have a fine sense of the ridiculous, but no sense of humour.
Edward Albee, WHO'S AFRAID OF VIRGINIA WOOLF? 1962

18 There is always something absurd about the past.
Max Beerbohm, AND EVEN NOW

19 The absurd has meaning only in so far as it is not agreed to.
Albert Camus, THE MYTH OF SISYPHUS 1942

20 As an absurdity it was so colossal that it took on the air of a great truth.
William Cooper, SCENES FROM PROVINCIAL LIFE

21 As a man is so's his God; this word / Explains why God's so often absurd.
Giles and Melville Harcourt, SHORT PRAYERS FOR THE LONG DAY 1978

1 The world is so overflowing with absurdity that it is difficult for the humorist to compete.
Malcolm Muggeridge on becoming editor of Punch

2 What I try to do in my plays is to get this recognisable reality of the absurdity of what we do and how we behave and how we speak.
Harold Pinter. Quoted Martin Esslin, THE THEATRE OF THE ABSURD

3 Life is full of infinite absurdities, which strangely enough, do not even need to appear plausible, since they are true.
Luigi Pirandello, SIX CHARACTERS IN SEARCH OF AN AUTHOR 1921

4 The more absurd life is, the more insupportable death is.
Jean-Paul Sartre, WORDS

ABUSE

5 To hell with you. Offensive letter follows.
Anonymous telegram sent to Sir Alec Douglas-Home

6 I very rarely indulge in abusive epithets, and when I used the word stupidity I meant what I said.
Stanley Baldwin, House of Commons 25 Oct 1926

7 Go on, abuse me — your own husband that took you off the streets on a Sunday morning when there wasn't a pub open in the city.
Brendan Behan, THE HOSTAGE 1958

8 To abuse a man is a lover-like thing and gives him rights.
Joyce Cary, HERSELF SURPRISED 1941

9 Abuse is in order, but it is best if it is supported by argument.
Robin Day as chairman of Election Call, BBC Radio 13 Apr 1979

10 No one can be as calculatedly rude as the British, which amazes Americans, who do not understand studied insult and can only offer abuse as a substitute.
Paul Gallico, New York Times 14 Jan 1962

11 Among the working classes one of the unforgivable words of abuse is 'bastard' — because they take bastardy seriously.
Robert Graves, OCCUPATION: WRITER

12 Had your father spent more of your mother's immoral earnings on your education you would not even then have been a gentleman.
Seymour Hicks, VINTAGE YEARS

13 It is not for nothing that, in the English language alone, to accuse someone of trying to be funny is highly abusive.
Malcolm Muggeridge, TREAD SOFTLY FOR YOU TREAD ON MY JOKES 1966

14 A. E. Housman kept a little notebook in which he jotted down hurtful and disparaging phrases as they occurred to him. He applied the phrases later when suitable enemies presented themselves.
Frank Muir, THE FRANK MUIR BOOK 1976

15 When political ammunition runs low, inevitably the rusty artillery of abuse is always wheeled into action.
Adlai Stevenson. Speech, New York 22 Sep 1952

16 'He called me a muddle-headed old ass' he said. 'Well you are a muddle-headed old ass,' I pointed out, quick as a flash, and he seemed to see the justice of this.
P. G. Wodehouse, PIGS HAVE WINGS 1952

ACCENT

17 My mother came from Nashville, Tennessee, and try as she might she couldn't obliterate her accent. Just like Margaret Thatcher. Just like Ted Heath.
Lord Hailsham. Quoted Observer 18 Oct 1981

ACCEPTANCE

18 Ah, when to the heart of man / Was it ever less than a treason / To go with the drift of things / To yield with a grace to reason / And bow and accept at the end / Of a love or season.
Robert Frost, RELUCTANCE 1913

ACCIDENT

1 The lady downstairs did her back in last winter. You have to be careful in the dark. She slipped on the puke.
Anonymous Liverpool youth. Quoted Ian Jack, Sunday Times Magazine 25 Aug 1985

2 An act of God was defined as something which no reasonable man could have expected.
A. P. Herbert, UNCOMMON LAW 1935

3 'I knew a rent collector that fell down in a pub and stabbed himself in the heart with his own pencil' says Dagswood.
Gerald Kersh, THE NINE LIVES OF BILL NELSON 1941

4 so unlucky / that he runs into accidents / which started out to happen / to somebody else.
Don Marquis, ARCHY'S LIFE OF MEHITABEL 1933

5 A hole is nothing at all, but you can break your neck in it.
Austin O'Malley

6 It is the overtakers who keep the undertakers busy.
William Pitts. Quoted Observer 27 Dec 1963

ACCLAIM

7 It took him twenty years to become an overnight sensation.
Milton Berle of Phil Silvers in the show TOP BANANAS

8 I have myself a constitutional dislike to limelight, which often disfigures that which it is intended to adorn.
Viscount Harcourt. Speech, Corona Club 18 Jun 1912

9 Glory is largely a theatrical concept. There is no striving for glory without a vivid awareness of an audience.
Eric Hoffer, THE TRUE BELIEVER 1951

10 They gave me star treatment because I was making a lot of money. But I was just as good when I was poor.
Bob Marley, Radio Times 18 Sep 1981

ACCOMPLISHMENT

11 It is all very well to be able to write books, but can you waggle your ears?

J. M. Barrie, who could, to H. G. Wells, who couldn't. Quoted J. A. Hamerton, BARRIE: THE STORY OF A GENIUS 1929

12 I know a girl who can tie a knot in the stalk of a cherry with her tongue.
A. A. Milne, NOT THAT IT MATTERS, *Golden Fruit* 1919

13 I used to have a cousin who could open a beer bottle with his teeth. That was his only accomplishment, all he could do — he was just a human bottle-opener. And then one day, at a wedding party, he broke his front teeth off!
Tennessee Williams, A STREETCAR NAMED DESIRE 1947

14 One of his [Sir R. Baden-Powell's] accomplishments is to draw a picture with his left hand and shade it at the same time with his right hand.
Marcus Woodward, John o' London's Weekly 1929

ACHIEVEMENT

15 Achievement is the end of endeavour and the beginning of disgust.
Ambrose Bierce, THE DEVIL'S DICTIONARY, 1906

16 The lizard that essayed to become a crocodile burst at the moment of attainment.
Ernest Bramah, KAI LUNG UNROLLS HIS MAT 1928

17 If there are obstacles, the shortest line between two points may be the crooked one.
Bertolt Brecht, GALILEO 1938

18 To reach completion is to return to one's starting point. My instinctive bent takes pleasure in curves and spheres and circles.
Colette, reputed last words 1954

19 Few who reach the summit can be acquitted of vanity or conceit.
Sir John Colville, THE CHURCHILLIANS 1982

20 Happiness is in the imagination. What we perform, is always inferior to what we imagine.
Cyril Connolly, THE UNQUIET GRAVE 1948

1 People love chopping wood. In this activity one immediately sees results.
Albert Einstein. Quoted Carl Seelig, ALBERT EINSTEIN

2 Only the mediocre are always at their best.
Graffito. Quoted BBC Radio 4, Quote Unquote 29 May 1980

3 To stretch the octave twixt the dream and deed. Ah, that's the thrill.
Richard le Gullienne, THE DECADENT TO HIS SOUL

4 Those who believe that they are exclusively in the right are generally those who achieve something.
Aldous Huxley, PROPER STUDIES 1927

5 The achievements which society rewards are won at the cost of diminution of personality.
Carl Jung, PSYCHOLOGICAL REFLECTIONS 1951

6 All struggle has for its end relief or repose.
(Percy) Wyndham Lewis, THE ART OF BEING RULED 1926

7 You can do anything in this world if you are prepared to take the consequences.
W. Somerset Maugham, THE CIRCLE 1921

8 In the past things that men could do were very limited. Bad men, even with the very worst intentions, could do only a very finite amount of harm. Good men, with the very best intentions, could do only a very limited amount of good. But with every increase in knowledge there has been an increase in what men can achieve.
Bertrand Russell, Saturday Evening Post, The Expanding Mental Universe 18 Jul 1959

9 Who are the men that do things? The husbands of the shrew and the drunkard, the men with the thorn in the flesh.
George Bernard Shaw, HEARTBREAK HOUSE 1920

10 There are two things to aim at in life; first to get what you want, and, after that, to enjoy it. Only the wisest of mankind achieve the second.
Logan Pearsall Smith, ALL TRIVIA, *Afterthoughts* 1931

11 I am an American and I have lived half my life in Paris, not the half which made me, but the half in which I made what I made.
Gertrude Stein, AN AMERICAN AND FRANCE 1930

12 There are no gains without pains.
Adlai Stevenson, Democratic Convention acceptance speech 26 Jul 1952

13 Looking back at the age of eighty-eight I see clearly that I achieved practically nothing. The world today and the history of the human anthill during the last fifty-seven years would be exactly the same if I had played ping pong instead of sitting on committees and writing books and memoranda . . . I must have in a long life ground through between a hundred and fifty thousand and two hundred thousand hours of perfectly useless work.
Leonard Woolf, THE JOURNEY NOT THE ARRIVAL MATTERS

ACQUAINTANCE

14 *Acquaintance:* a degree of friendship called slight when the object is poor or obscure, and intimate when he is rich or famous.
Ambrose Bierce, THE DEVIL'S DICTIONARY 1906

15 It was possible to be acquainted with him [Lord Birkenhead] and to dislike him intensely; it was impossible to know him and not to love him.
Sir Austen Chamberlain. Quoted 2nd Earl of Birkenhead, LIFE OF LORD BIRKENHEAD VOL 2

16 The art of life is to keep down acquaintances. One's friends one can manage but one's acquaintances can be the devil.
E. V. Lucas, OVER BEMERTON'S 1908

17 The intimacy of shipboard, which is due to propinquity rather than any community of taste.
W. Somerset Maugham, RAIN 1921

18 The mere process of growing old together will make the slightest acquaintance seem a bosom friend.
Logan Pearsall Smith, ALL TRIVIA 1931

19 Acquaintanceship stands in the same relation to friendship that a flirtation does to a love affair – exciting but unsatisfying.
Alec Waugh, ON DOING WHAT ONE LIKES

ACTING

20 The most precious things in speech are the pauses.

Advice given by Ralph Richardson in an interview.

1 A year or two ago Ralph Richardson had the habit of acting all his parts with his buttocks. I cured him of this and his Henry V had no backside at all, though it reappeared, and rightly, in his next comic part.
James Agate, EGO 1 1935

2 Mr Ainley played the old codger (Prospero) like a toastmaster celebrating his golden wedding.
James Agate, Sunday Times 1 Aug 1934

3 Julie Andrews is like a nun with a switchblade.
Anon. Quoted Leslie Halliwell, FILMGOER'S BOOK OF QUOTES 1973

4 Television is for making one famous, films are for making money, and an actor's proper place is the theatre.
Alan Badel. Quoted David Gillard, Radio Times 19 May 1984

5 There are lots of methods. Mine involves a lot of talent, a glass, and some cracked ice.
John Barrymore. Quoted Leslie Halliwell, FILMGOER'S BOOK OF QUOTES 1973

6 In *Casablanca* there was often nothing in my face. But the audience put into my face what they thought I was giving.
Ingrid Bergman, MY STORY

7 Shoes are the key to character. From them develop the walk, the stance, the sag or spead of the shoulders, the breath.
Dirk Bogarde, SNAKES AND LADDERS 1978

8 An actor is a guy who, if you aren't talking about him, isn't listening.
Marlon Brando. Quoted Observer Jan 1956

9 Mr Cooke knows all the tricks, but I regret to say can perform none of them.
Alistair Cooke, quoting a critic in the Cambridge Review of his performance with the Cambridge University Mummers TV Times 11 Mar 1977

10 On a fine December day in 1924, as I walked down Hollywood Boulevard towards nowhere in particular, I was down to that essential starting place for all actors. I was broke.
Gary Cooper, Saturday Evening Post, Well, It Was This Way 7 Apr 1956

11 The general consensus seems to be that I don't act at all.
Ibid.

12 Acting is not a matter of being somebody else, it's a matter of seeming to be somebody else. — I'd have been a murderess, a suicide and a drunkard if I'd lived all my parts. You've got to stay outside what you're doing.
Gladys Cooper. Quoted Sheridan Morley, Sunday Times 15 Dec 1968

13 I've always thought I'd be particularly good in Romeo — as the nurse.
Noël Coward. Quoted William Marchant, THE PLEASURE OF HIS COMPANY

14 Gertie has an astounding sense of the complete reality of the moment and her moments, dictated by the extreme variability of her moods, change so swiftly that it is frequently difficult to discover what, apart from eating, sleeping and acting, is true of her at all.
Noël Coward of Gertrude Lawrence, PRESENT INDICATIVE 1931

15 Why make the effort to learn long and exquisitely written speeches by good authors when 'I love you, damn you', and 'What about a drink?' succeeded even better among the public and took less time to say?
Daphne Du Maurier, GERALD 1934

16 What are known as 'straight' parts are the most difficult as one has to try to be natural, which is only possible in the bathroom.
Gerald Du Maurier, in a letter to Reginald Pound. Quoted, THEIR MOODS AND MINE 1935

17 The question actors most often get asked is how they can bear saying the same things over and over again, night after night, but God knows what the answer to *that* is, don't we all *anyway*; might as well get paid for it.
Elaine Dundy, THE DUD AVOCADO 1958

18 I may never have been very pretty but I was jolly larky and that's what counts in the theatre. That and being able to act, of course. Nowadays, you know, it's all done by lights and machinery, but I always tell them in film studios that they're not to try to make me look young any more – I just want to look nice.
Dame Edith Evans at 89 in TV Times

1 You spend your life doing something they put people in asylums for.
Jane Fonda. Quoted Leslie Halliwell,
FILMGOER'S BOOK OF QUOTES 1973

2 All actors are darlings backstage.
Bamber Gascoigne, FROM FRINGE TO FLYING CIRCUS, *Preface* 1980

3 The most important thing in acting is honesty. Once you've learned to fake that, you're in.
Sam Goldwyn

4 An actor is an interpreter of other men's words, often a soul which wishes to reveal itself to the world but dare not, a craftsman, a bag of tricks, a vanity bag, a cool observer of mankind, a child, and at best an unfrocked priest who, for an hour or two, can call on heaven and hell to mesmerise a group of innocents.
Sir Alec Guinness, BLESSINGS IN DISGUISE 1985

5 Actors and burglars work better at night.
Sir Cedric Hardwicke

6 Julie Andrews has the wonderful British strength that makes you wonder why they lost India.
Moss Hart

7 It is best in the theatre to act with confidence no matter how little right you have to it.
Lillian Hellman, PENTIMENTO

8 Acting isn't a very high class way of making a living, is it?
Katherine Hepburn. Quoted Observer 26 *Jan* 1979

9 The chief requisite of an actor is the ability to do nothing well, which is by no means so easy as it seems.
Alfred Hitchcock. Quoted François Truffaut, HITCHCOCK 1968

10 He [Rudolf Valentino] had the acting talents of the average wardrobe.
Clyde Jeavons and Jeremy Pascall, A PICTORIAL HISTORY OF SEX IN THE MOVIES

11 Life as an actor is a constant series of equations. You've got to balance your work with how you want to live . . . It's no use playing all the great roles and ending up late

in life living in a poky bedsit in Notting Hill Gate with your wife having left you.
Freddie Jones, Radio Times 24 *Mar* 1979

12 The necessary qualifications for a successful actress are, the face of Venus, the figure of Juno, the brains of Minerva, the memory of Macaulay, the chastity of Diana, the grace of Terpsichore, but above and beyond all the *hide* of a rhinoceros.
Dame Madge Kendal, AUTOBIOGRAPHY

13 I adore not being me. I'm not very good at being me. That's why I adore acting so much.
Deborah Kerr. Quoted Ronald Hayman, The Times 2 *Dec* 1972

14 Joan Crawford is the only actress to read the whole script. Most actresses just read their own lines to find out what clothes they're going to wear.
Anita Loos. Quoted Leslie Halliwell,
FILMGOER'S BOOK OF QUOTES 1973

15 All acting is illusion and the last reward therefore disillusion.
J.P. McEvoy, Stage Jun 1941

16 It's extraordinary how they keep young. Actresses I mean. I think it's because they are always playing different parts.
W. Somerset Maugham, THE CIRCLE 1921

17 I played the part of the mad king in *Beau Brummell* exactly the same way as I played Louis XVI in *Marie Antoinette*, but no one noticed. You see, I wore a different wig.
Robert Morley. Quoted Margaret Morley,
LARGER THAN LIFE

18 Was she a great actress? Yes, I think so. Of course, women act all the time. It is easier to judge a man.
Iris Murdoch, THE SEA, THE SEA 1980

19 Can you imagine being wonderfully over-paid for dressing up and playing games?
David Niven, in an interview

20 When I cry do you want the tears to run all the way, or shall I stop them half way down?
Margaret O'Brien, child actress, to her director. Quoted Leslie Halliwell,
FILMGOER'S BOOK OF QUOTES 1973

21 Acting is not a profession for adults.
Laurence Olivier

1 She ran the whole gamut of the emotions from A to B.
Dorothy Parker of Katherine Hepburn in a Broadway play

2 Alfred Hitchcock was once reported as saying that 'actors are like cattle' but he denied this. 'What I said was, "actors should be *treated* like cattle".'
Nigel Rees, BBC Radio 4, Quote Unquote

3 Actors are the jockeys of literature; they don't ride horses, they ride plays, and make them run.
Sir Ralph Richardson, Observer, Recollections of a Lucky Man 19 Dec 1982

4 Farce is tragedy with the trousers down.
Brian Rix, The Times 3 Apr 1971

5 During a Peter Brook production of *Oedipus* at the National Theatre, a tremendous golden phallus was carried round the stage. 'Nobody we know, dear', confided Coral Browne to actor Charles Gray in a whisper which carried across the stalls.
Bryon Rogers, Sunday Telegraph, Don't Say Browne Say Outrageous, 19 Jan 1986

6 Mr Novello plays the King with all the assurance of a man who has gauged public taste down to the last emotional millimetre.
Milton Shulman, Evening Standard, reviewing King's Rhapsody 1949

7 Some of my best leading men have been dogs and horses.
Elizabeth Taylor in an interview with John Higgins, The Times 18 Feb 1981

8 Last night Cleopatra barged up the Nile and sank.
Frank Thring, Argus (Melbourne)

9 I am quite a good enough critic to know that my performance is not 'quite dreadful'; it is, in fact, only slightly less than mediocre. I do not actually exit through the scenery, or wave to my friends in the audience.
Kenneth Tynan, replying to criticism from Beverley Baxter in the Evening Standard of his performance as the Player King in Alec Guinness's production of Hamlet 1949

10 The actor doesn't mind screaming and crying on the stage, but would sooner not do it on the street.
John Updike. Quoted John Heilpern, Observer 25 Mar 1979

11 I grew a beard for Nero, in *Quo Vadis*, but Metro-Goldwyn-Mayer thought it didn't look real, so I had to wear a false one.
Peter Ustinov, DEAR ME 1977

12 The only emotion excited was a horrible sort of pity . . . for all the people who live by this terrible compulsion to act, to be applauded, living alone in their bed-sitters, knowing nothing and nobody.
Auberon Waugh of Richard Huggett's one-man show A Talent to Abuse, about Evelyn Waugh, The Times 1 Aug 1981

13 Nobody likes my acting except the public.
John Wayne. Quoted obituary, Daily Telegraph 13 Jun 1979

14 I learned two things at RADA: first that I couldn't act; second that it didn't matter.
Wilfred Hyde White. Quoted Richard Murdoch, BBC1 TV, The Old Boy Network 8 Oct 1981

15 Every now and then when you're on the stage, you hear the best sound that a player can hear. It is a sound you can't get in movies or in television. It is the sound of a wonderful deep silence that means you've hit them where they live.
Shelley Winters, Theatre Arts, Jun 1956

16 The scenery was beautiful, but the actors got in front of it.
Alexander Woollcott, New Yorker

ACTION

17 The world can only be grasped by action not by contemplation. The hand is more important than the eye.
Jacob Bronowski, THE ASCENT OF MAN 1973

18 Action is the only reality; not only reality but morality as well.
Abbie Hoffman. Quoted Barbara Rowe, THE BOOK OF QUOTES

19 No action is in itself good or bad, but only such according to convention.
W. Somerset Maugham, A WRITER'S NOTEBOOK 1949

20 Trust the man who hesitates in his speech and is quick and steady in action, but beware of long arguments and long beards.
George Santayana, SOLILOQUIES IN ENGLAND 1922

1 Nothing is ever done in this world until men
are prepared to kill one another if it is not
done.
George Bernard Shaw, MAJOR
BARBARA 1905

2 From the moment of birth we are immersed
in action, and can only fitfully guide it by
taking thought.
A. N. Whitehead, SCIENCE AND THE
MODERN WORLD 1925

3 It does not matter what men say in words, so
long as their activities are controlled by
settled instincts.
Ibid.

ACTIVITY

4 You've been a busy bugger, haven't you?
*George V to Capt. Billy Bishop V C, air ace
of World War I*

5 I got the blues thinking of the future, so I left
off and made some marmalade. It's amazing
how it cheers one up to shred oranges.
D. H. Lawrence, LETTERS 1932

6 He had given, for a time, a tremendously
effective impression, which turned out on
closer inspection to be only activity.
Bernard Levin, of Harold Wilson, THE
PENDULUM YEARS 1976

ADAPTATION

7 Human creatures have a marvellous power
of adapting themselves to necessity.
George Gissing, THE PRIVATE PAPERS OF
HENRY RYECROFT 1903

8 Remember that cartoon of a couple watching a sticky kiss on the silver screen and the
man saying wistfully 'in the book he hits her
with an axe'.
*Katherine Whitehorn, Observer, In Praise of
Shorter Books* 11 *Oct* 1981

ADDICTION

9 It was a shock to discover that Ivor Novello
was addicted to Nescafé.
*Gabriele Annan, Times Literary
Supplement, review of Sandy Wilson's* IVOR
19 *Dec* 1975

10 All sins tend to be addictive, and the
terminal point of addiction is what is called
damnation.
W. H. Auden, A CERTAIN WORLD

11 Cocaine isn't habit-forming. I should know.
I've been using it for years.
*Tallulah Bankhead. Quoted Leslie
Halliwell,* FILMGOER'S BOOK OF
QUOTES 1973

12 I always keep a supply of stimulant handy in
case I see a snake — which I also keep
handy.
W. C. Fields. Quoted Carey Ford, THE TUNE
OF LAUGHTER

13 First you take a drink. Then the drink takes
a drink, then the drink takes you.
F. Scott Fitzgerald. Quoted Jules Feiffer,
ACKROYD

14 Jack London was corporally mature, innerly
a child. He mastered the outward circumstances of life and then played with toys. He
preferred to live in a nursery and blamed his
excess drinking on the fact that no nurse was
there to keep the liquor from his lips.
Waldo Frank. Quoted Joan London, JACK
LONDON

15 Blow your mind — smoke dynamite.
Graffito. Quoted Nigel Rees, GRAFFITI
LIVES — O.K.

16 Every form of addiction is bad, no matter
whether the narcotic be alcohol or morphine
or idealism.
Carl Jung, MEMORIES, DREAMS,
REFLECTIONS

17 Is marijuana addictive? Yes in the sense that
most of the really pleasant things in life are
worth endlessly repeating.
Richard Neville, PLAYPOWER

18 The Koala bears feed, I understand, on
leaves so potent they spend half their time
stoned out of their fur.
Katherine Whitehorn, Observer 25 *Mar* 1979

ADMINISTRATION

19 He thinks that to say something is to do
something, which is an imperfect view of
administration.
*Henry Cabot Lodge, of William Jennings
Bryant in a letter to Sturgis Bigelow* 28 *May*
1913

1 He becomes fussy about filing, keen on seeing that pencils are sharpened, eager to ensure that the windows are open (or shut) and apt to use two or three different-coloured inks.
C. Northcote Parkinson, PARKINSON'S LAW 1957

2 We have so many forms to fill in and the excessive time spent on paper work means there is less time for prayer.
Abbot Leo Smith, of Buckfast Abbey. Quoted Observer 22 Apr 1979

ADMIRATION

3 *Admiration:* our polite recognition of another man's resemblance to ourselves.
Ambrose Bierce, THE DEVIL'S DICTIONARY 1906

4 When we admire somebody we like to hear him praised by others – but not too much.
Gerald Brenan, THOUGHTS IN A DRY SEASON 1979

5 The worst tragedy for a poet is to be admired through being misunderstood.
Jean Cocteau, LE RAPPEL À L'ORDRE

6 No one can make us hate ourselves like an admirer.
Cyril Connolly, ENEMIES OF PROMISE 1938

7 I have been the recipient of excessive admiration and reverence from my fellow beings through no fault and no merit of my own.
Albert Einstein, IDEAS AND OPINIONS

8 Melba's voice stirs me to almost passionate admiration, but admiration isn't joy; admiration doesn't satisfy; there is no ecstasy in admiration.
Selwyn Rider, Triad 10 Mar 1919

ADOLESCENCE

9 Were I to deduce any system from my feelings on leaving Eton, it might be called The Theory of Permanent Adolescence.
Cyril Connolly, ENEMIES OF PROMISE 1938

10 Too chaste an adolescence makes for a dissolute old age.
André Gide, JOURNALS 1939—1950

11 The whole National Youth Movement is being weakened by the failure of those in charge of girls to understand that the natural characteristics of adolescent boys are not the same as those of adolescent girls.
Basil Henriques. Quoted News Review 10 Apr 1947

12 So much adolescence is an ill-defined dying, / An intolerable waiting, / A longing for another place and time, / Another condition.
Theodore Roethke, COLLECTED VERSE, *I'm Here* 1961

13 As a result of all his education, from everything he sees and hears around him, the child absorbs such a lot of lies and foolish nonsense, mixed in with essential truths, that the first duty of the adolescent who wants to be a healthy man is to disgorge it all.
Romain Rolland, JEAN CHRISTOPHE 1912

14 It is the highest creatures who take the longest to mature, and are the most helpless during their immaturity.
George Bernard Shaw, BACK TO METHUSELAH 1922

15 First love is only a little foolishness and a lot of curiosity.
George Bernard Shaw, JOHN BULL'S OTHER ISLAND 1904

16 That toil of growing up. / The ignominy of boyhood: the distress / Of boyhood changing into man: / The unfinished man and his pain.
W. B. Yeats, THE WINDING STAIR AND OTHER POEMS 1929

ADORATION

17 I am a true adorer of life, and if I can't reach the face of it I plant my kiss somewhere lower down.
Saul Bellow, HENDERSON THE RAIN KING 1959

18 I hope you have lost your good looks for while they last any fool can adore you, and the adoration of fools is bad for the soul. No, give me a ruined complexion and a lost figure and sixteen chins on a farmyard of crow's feet and an obvious wig. Then you shall see me come out strong.
George Bernard Shaw, letter to Mrs Pat Campbell

ADULATION

1 That layer of blubber which encases an English peer, the sediment of permanent adulation.
Cyril Connolly, ENEMIES OF PROMISE 1938

2 There is no such thing as a great man or a great woman. People believe in them, just as they used to believe in unicorns and dragons. The greatest man or woman is 99 per cent just like yourself.
George Bernard Shaw, BBC Radio 11 *Jul* 1932

3 Adulation is all right if you don't inhale.
Adlai Stevenson

ADULT

4 If this was adulthood the only improvement she could detect in her situation was that she could now eat dessert without eating her vegetables.
Lisa Alther, KINFLICKS 1976

5 Grown up, and that is a terribly hard thing to do. It is much easier to skip it and go from one childhood to another.
F. Scott Fitzgerald, THE CRACK-UP 1936

6 One of the most obvious facts about grown-ups to a child is that they have forgotten what it is like to be a child.
Randall Jarrell, THIRD BOOK OF CRITICISM 1969

7 The process of maturing is an art to be learned, an effort to be sustained. By the age of fifty you have made yourself what you are and if it is good it is better than your youth.
Marya Mannes, MORE IN ANGER 1958

8 Adults are obsolete children.
Dr Seuss

ADULTERY

9 At her confirmation classes they had worked through the Commandments. At the seventh an evening had been devoted to impure curiosity.
Elizabeth Bowen, TO THE NORTH 1932

10 Sara could commit adultery at one end and

weep for her sins at the other, and enjoy both operations at once.
Joyce Cary, THE HORSE'S MOUTH 1944

11 Throughout history frail women have fascinated men, have confessed their adultery to them, and have been forgiven.
Judge Fraser Harrison. Quoted News Review 10 *Jul* 1947

12 There are few who would not rather be taken in adultery than in provincialism.
Aldous Huxley, ANTIC HAY 1923

13 Time's up for Sir John and for little Lady Jane. Put thy shimmy on, Lady Chatterley.
D. H. Lawrence, LADY CHATTERLEY'S LOVER 1928

14 Accursed from their birth they be / Who seek to find monogamy. / Pursuing it from bed to bed — / I think they would be better dead.
Dorothy Parker, REUBEN'S CHILDREN

15 On a sofa upholstered in human skin / Mona did researches in original sin.
William Plomer, MEWS FLAT MONA

16 The psychology of adultery has been falsified by conventional morals, which assume, in monogamous countries, that attraction to one person cannot coexist with affection for another. Everybody knows that this is untrue.
Bertrand Russell, MARRIAGE AND MORALS 1929

ADVENTURE

17 Adventure is the vitalising element in histories, both individual and social.
William Bolitho, TWELVE AGAINST THE GODS 1929

18 One does not discover new lands without consenting to lose sight of the shore for a very long time.
André Gide, THE COUNTERFEITERS 1926

19 How narrow is the line which separates an adventure from an ordeal.
Harold Nicolson, SMALL TALK

20 Anything, everything, little or big becomes an adventure when the right person shares it. Nothing, nothing, nothing is worthwhile when we have to do it alone.
Katherine Norris, HANDS FULL OF LIVING

1 Had we lived I should have had a tale to tell of the hardihood, endurance and courage of my companions which would have stirred the heart of every Englishman. These rough notes and our dead bodies must tell the tale.
Capt. Robert Falcon Scott, last message 1912

2 Adventure is the result of poor planning.
Col. Blatchford Snell

3 Without adventure civilisation is in full decay.
A. N. Whitehead, ADVENTURES OF IDEAS 1933

ADVERSITY

4 Adversity, if a man is set down to it by degrees, is more supportable with equanimity by most people than any great prosperity arrived at in a single lifetime.
Samuel Butler, THE WAY OF ALL FLESH 1903

5 I'll say this for adversity — people seem to be able to stand it, and that's more'n I kin say fer prosperity.
Kim Hubbard, ABE MARTIN'S BROADCAST

ADVERTISING

6 Parenthesis-proud, bracket-bold, happiest with hyphens / The writers stagger intoxicated by terms, adjective-unsteadied / Describing in graceless phrase fizzling soda-syphon / All things crisp, crunchy, malted, tangy, sugared and shredded.
Anthony Brode, BREAKFAST WITH GERARD MANLEY HOPKINS

7 He [John Snagge] had been against commercial broadcasting ever since he heard a Toscanini radio concert in New York interrupted by the sponsor's slogan 'It may be December outside, ladies; but it is always August under your armpits.'
Evening Standard. Quoted News Review 13 Nov 1947

8 The case cannot stand if it is the process of satisfying the wants that creates the wants.
J. K. Galbraith, THE AFFLUENT SOCIETY 1958

9 In a well-to-do community we cannot be much concerned to buy. The marginal utility of money is low; were it otherwise, people would not be open to persuasion.
J. K. Galbraith, ECONOMICS, PEACE AND LAUGHTER

10 There is little that can be said about most economic goods. A toothbrush does little but clean teeth. Aspirin does little but dull pain. Alcohol is important mostly for making people more or less drunk . . . There being so little to be said, much to be invented.
Ibid.

11 We live surrounded by a systematic appeal to a dream world which all mature, scientific people readily would reject. We quite literally advertise our commitment to immaturity, mendacity and profound gullibility. It is the hallmark of the culture.
Ibid.

12 How can you ever forgive yourself?
Greta Garbo to one who admitted composing for the film NINOTCHKA *the rubric 'Garbo laughs'*

13 With regard to anything that is likely to obsess a society, it is important not to give it too much advertisement.
(Percy) Wyndham Lewis, TIME AND WESTERN MAN 1927

14 Who are these advertising men kidding? Between the tired, sad, gentle faces of the subway riders and the grinning Holy Families of the Ad-Mass, there exists no possibility of even a wishful identification.
Mary McCarthy, ON THE CONTRARY 1961

15 Ads push the principle of noise all the way to the plateau of percussion. They are quite in accord with the procedures of brainwashing.
Marshall McLuhan, UNDERSTANDING MEDIA 1964

16 It isn't advertising *anything,* dammit.
Father to a small boy looking at a rainbow. Caption to a cartoon by Charles H. Martin, in the New Yorker

17 I think that I shall never see / A billboard lovely as a tree / Indeed unless the billboards fall / I'll never see a tree at all.
Ogden Nash, HAPPY DAYS, *The Song of the Open Road*

1 The consumer is not a moron. She is your wife. Don't insult her intelligence.
Angus Ogilvy, OGILVY ON ADVERTISING 1983

2 When I write an ad I don't want you to tell me you find it creative. I want you to find it so interesting that you *buy* the *product*.
Ibid.

3 The Hidden Persuaders.
Vance Packard. Book title

4 Living in an age of advertisement we are perpetually disillusioned. The perfect life is spread before us every day but it changes and withers at a touch.
J. B. Priestley, ALL ABOUT OURSELVES

5 Those who prefer their English sloppy have only themselves to thank if the advertising writer uses his mastery of vocabulary and syntax to mislead their minds.
Dorothy L. Sayers, Spectator 19 Nov 1937

6 I will not permit, while I live, a teleview of 'The Man Born To Be King' punctuated by advertisements. Though, of course, it offers scope: the episode of the Feeding of the Five Thousand presented by Hovis bread and MacFisheries for instance, would be very suitable.
Dorothy L. Sayers. Quoted Janet Hitchman, SUCH A STRANGE LADY

7 Lloyd George said to me that once one had assured oneself of food and shelter, which meant security, the next thing that mattered was advertisement.
A. J. Sylvester, DIARY 27 *Apr* 1933

8 I must say we really enjoy all the commercials in our household, but I always get a tense feeling in case anyone picks the wrong pile of washing in that detergent advertisement.
Letter to TV Times

9 Like! Like! Like! The babble of this subculture is drowning me.
Gore Vidal, MYRA BRECKINRIDGE 1968

10 Half the money I spend on advertising is wasted, and the trouble is, I don't know which half.
John Wanamaker. Quoted David Ogilvy, CONFESSIONS OF AN ADVERTISING MAN

ADVICE

11 To consult is to seek another's advice on a course already decided upon.
Ambrose Bierce, THE DEVIL'S DICTIONARY 1906

12 As a grown man you should know better than to go round advising people.
The Cook to the Chaplain in Bertolt Brecht's MOTHER COURAGE AND HER CHILDREN 1939

13 Friendship will not stand the strain of very much good advice for very long.
Robert Lynd, A PEAL OF BELLS

14 England is, and always has been, a country infested with people who love to tell us what to do, but who very rarely seem to know what's going on.
Colin MacInnes, ENGLAND, HALF ENGLISH

15 A good man giving bad advice is more dangerous than a nasty man giving bad advice.
Conor Cruise O'Brien, Observer, The Pope and the Unwanted Child 2 Oct 1979

16 I hope, for his own sake, that he has younger people than me at his disposal if he wishes to ask for bad advice, especially if he means to follow it.
Marcel Proust, REMEMBRANCE OF THINGS PAST 1913—27

17 Ann will do just exactly what she likes. And what's more, she'll force us to advise her to do it; and she'll put the blame on us if it turns out badly.
George Bernard Shaw, MAN AND SUPERMAN 1905

18 Don't tell your friends their social faults; they will cure the fault and never forgive you.
Logan Pearsall Smith, ALL TRIVIA, Afterthoughts 1931

19 No one wants advice — only corroboration.
John Steinbeck, THE WINTER OF OUR DISCONTENT 1961

20 I have found the best way to give advice to your children is to find out what they want and then advise them to do it.
Harry S Truman, TV interview 27 May 1955

AFFECTION

1 I do not know how it comes about, but if you sit opposite a man every day and you are engaged in fighting him, you cannot help getting a liking for him whether he deserves it or not.
A. J. Balfour. Quoted by his niece, Blanche E. Dugdale, Daily Telegraph 16 *Apr* 1936

2 A mixture of admiration and pity is one of the surest recipes for affection.
André Maurois, ARIEL 1923

3 You can have an affection for a murderer or a sodomite, but you cannot have an affection for a man whose breath stinks — habitually stinks, I mean.
George Orwell, THE ROAD TO WIGAN PIER 1937

4 Human nature is so constructed that it gives affection most readily to those who least demand it.
Bertrand Russell, THE CONQUEST OF HAPPINESS 1930

AFFLUENCE

5 Why not? Isn't God a millionaire?
Frank Buchman, founder of Moral Re-Armament, on being challenged to explain how he could afford to live in the best hotels

6 With increasing well-being all people become aware, sooner or later, that they have something to protect.
J. K. Galbraith, THE AFFLUENT SOCIETY 1958

7 Increase of material comforts, it may be generally laid down, does not in any way whatsoever conduce to moral growth.
Mahatma Gandhi. Quoted obituary, News Chronicle 31 *Jan* 1948

8 The affluent society has made everyone dislike work, and come to think of idleness as the happiest life.
Sir Geoffrey Keynes. Quoted Robert Chesshyre, Observer 25 *Oct* 1981

9 I don't know how much money I've got . . . I did ask the accountant how much it came to. I wrote it down on a bit of paper. But I've lost the bit of paper.
John Lennon. Quoted Hunter Davies, THE BEATLES

10 Most of our people have never had it so good. Go around the country, go to the industrial towns, go to the farms — and you will see a state of prosperity such as we have never had in my lifetime, or indeed ever in the history of this country.
Harold Macmillan. Speech, Bradford 20 *Jul* 1957

11 When I am a rich man with my own bicycle and can have beer for breakfast I shall give up writing poetry altogether and just be absolutely disgusting.
Dylan Thomas and John Davenport, THE DEATH OF THE KING'S CANARY

AFRICAN

12 We have the happiest Africans in the world.
Ian Smith. Quoted Observer, Sayings of the Week 28 *Nov* 1971

AGE

13 Age has its compensations. It is less apt to be brow-beaten by discretion.
Charlie Chaplin, MY AUTOBIOGRAPHY 1962

14 A very old twelve.
Noël Coward's reply when asked how old a certain society lady looked after her most recent facelift

15 My age is 39 plus tax.
Liberace in his TV show

16 Paradoxical as it may seem, to believe in youth is to look backward; to look forward we must believe in age.
Dorothy L. Sayers, STRONG MEAT

17 I'd like to go on being 35 for a long time.
Margaret Thatcher, in 1961

18 He was either a man of about a hundred and fifty who was rather young for his years, or a man of about a hundred and ten who had been aged by trouble.
P. G. Wodehouse

19 If I'd known how old I was going to be I'd have taken better care of myself.
Adolph Zukor, founder of Paramount Pictures, on the approach of his hundredth birthday. Quoted Benny Green, Radio Times 17 *Feb* 1979

AGENT

1 My agent gets ten per cent of everything I get, except my blinding headaches.
Fred Allen, American radio comedian

2 Pimps who . . . don't do anything, don't make anything — they just stand there and take their cut.
Jean Giraudoux, TIIE MADWOMAN OF CHAILLOT 1945

AGGRESSION

3 Pale Ebcnczer thought it wrong to fight / But Roaring Bill (who killed him) thought it right.
Hilaire Belloc, EPIGRAMS

4 One of his minor purposes is to disembowel his enemies who are numerous for the simple reason that he wants them to be numerous. He would be less tiresome if he were more urbane.
Arnold Bennett of (Percy) Wyndham Lewis, Evening Standard 28 Apr 1927

5 A literary aphorism makes a poor defence against a well-propelled battleaxe.
Ernest Bramah, KAI LUNG UNROLLS HIS MAT 1928

6 Fighting is essentially a masculine idea; a woman's weapon is her tongue.
Hermione Gingold. Quoted Barbara Rowe, BOOK OF QUOTES

7 Guns before butter. Guns will make us powerful; butter will only make us fat.
Hermann Goering, German broadcast 1936

8 Nobody ever forgets where he buried the hatchet.
Kim Hubbard, ABE MARTIN'S BROADCAST

9 It is no use speaking in soft, gentle tones if everyone else is shouting.
J. B. Priestley, THOUGHTS IN THE WILDERNESS

10 Of the four wars in my lifetime none came about because the United States was too strong.
Ronald Reagan, Presidential campaign speech 9 Jun 1980

11 Do not hit at all if it can be avoided, but never hit softly.
Theodore Roosevelt, AUTOBIOGRAPHY 1913

12 To knock a thing down, especially if it is cocked up at an arrogant angle, is a deep delight to the blood.
George Santayana, THE LIFE OF REASON, *Reason in Society* 1906

AGNOSTIC

13 John Grubby, who was short and stout / And troubled with religious doubt / Refused about the age of three / To sit upon the curate's knee.
G. K. Chesterton, THE NEW FREETHINKER

14 Those who deny Thee could not deny, if Thou didst not exist; and their denial is never complete, for if it were so, they would not exist.
T. S. Eliot, MURDER IN THE CATHEDRAL 1935

15 The sheer babyhood of the human race against the background of incalculable time makes anything but a questing agnosticism absurdly presumptuous.
L. E. Jones, I FORGOT TO TELL YOU

16 The question most commonly asked by the agnostic is not 'Do you believe in the authenticity of the Holy House at Loreto?' or 'Do you think an individual can justly inherit a right to the labour of another?' but 'Do you believe in Hell?'
Evelyn Waugh, Commonweal 16 Jul 1948

AGREEMENT

17 When you accept our views we shall be in full agreement with you.
Moshe Dayan to Cyrus Vance 10 Aug 1977

ALCOHOL

18 Mona Lisa cocktail — two of them and you can't get the silly grin off your face.
Anon.

19 Reality is a delusion created by an alcohol deficiency.
Anon. Quoted BBC Radio 4 Quote Unquote 7 Jun 1979

1 Always remember, I have taken more out of alcohol than alcohol has taken out of me.
Winston Churchill. Quoted Quentin Reynolds, BY QUENTIN REYNOLDS

2 It smells like gangrene starting in a mil dewed silo, it tastes like the wrath to come, and when you absorb a deep swig of it you have all the sensations of having swallowed a lighted kerosene lamp.
Irvin S. Cobb, defining corn liquor for the Distillers' Code Authority

3 Maybe alcohol picks you up a little bit, but it sure lets you down in a hurry.
Betty Ford, wife of President Ford, on admitting to being an alcoholic

4 Alcohol is the most powerful depressant of the central nervous system available in this country without a doctor's prescription. If it were being introduced now it would be a controlled drug.
Dr John Navard, Secretary British Medical Association. Speech, Jun 1985

5 The sway of alcohol over mankind is unquestionably due to its power to stimulate the mystic faculties of human nature, usually crushed to earth by the cold facts and dry criticisms of the sober hour.
William James. Quoted New York Times 29 Feb 1948

6 Crazy folks shouldn't drink — it's like throwing gasoline on a banked fire.
Donald Newlove, THOSE DRINKING DAYS

7 There is an unbroken testimony of all history that alcoholic liquors have been used by the strongest, wisest, handsomest and in every way best races of all times.
George Saintsbury, NOTES ON A CELLAR BOOK

8 When I do come to town, bang go my plans in a horrid alcohol explosion that scatters all my good intentions like bits of limbs and clothes over the doorsteps and into the saloon bars of the tawdriest pubs in London.
Dylan Thomas in a letter to a friend 1936

9 It was my Uncle George who discovered that alcohol was a food well in advance of modern medical thought.
P. G. Wodehouse, THE INIMITABLE JEEVES

10 Alcohol sobers me. After a few swallows of brandy I no longer think of you.
Margaret Yourcenar, FIRES

ALIMONY

11 You never realise how short a month is until you pay alimony.
John Barrymore, in an interview.

12 The wages of sin is alimony.
Carolyn Wells

13 Judges, as a class, display, in the matter of arranging alimony, that reckless generosity that is found only in men who are giving away somebody else's cash.
P. G. Wodehouse, LOUDER AND FUNNIER

ALTERNATIVE

14 Alternatives, and particularly desirable alternatives, grow only on imaginary trees.
Saul Bellow, DANGLING MAN 1944

15 The weak are always forced to decide between alternatives they have not chosen themselves.
Dietrich Bonhoeffer, LETTERS AND PAPERS FROM PRISON 1951

16 'I have decided that the office cannot continue to hold both you and me. One of us must go. Which shall it be?'
'Well, Mr Wrackham, your name is painted on the door, so I suppose it would be simpler if you stayed.'
F. Scott Fitzgerald, THE CRACK-UP 1936

17 Germany will either be a world power or will not be.
Adolf Hitler, MEIN KAMPF 1924

18 I cannot see who is ahead — it is either Oxford or Cambridge.
John Snagge, commentary on 1949 boat race.

AMATEUR

19 Professionals built the *Titanic* — amateurs the ark.
Anon. Quoted BBC Radio 4, The News Quiz 27 Oct 1979

AMBIGUITY

20 The Government offers no hope and the Labour party offers no sense. The Alliance offers both.
Roy Jenkins. Election speech, Bermondsey, Feb 1983

1 One of the questions was 'Do you think contraceptives are 100 per cent reliable?' Unfortunately the word 'contraceptive' was not always understood so when the answer was 'I don't know' it was not clear if the answer referred to the reliability of contraceptives or merely that the question was not understood.
M. Schofield, THE SEXUAL BEHAVIOUR OF YOUNG PEOPLE

AMBITION

2 A desire is real when the possibility of satisfaction exists for the individual who entertains it — a desire for a Cadillac which may be real for a prosperous American businessman would be fantastic for a Chinese peasant.
W. H. Auden, THE DYER'S HAND 1962

3 I have been absolutely hag-ridden with ambition. If I could wish to have anything in the world it would be to be free of ambition.
Tallulah Bankhead. Quoted Lee Israel, MISS TALLULAH BANKHEAD

4 I have decided to be the stationmaster at Blake Hall on the Ongar branch of the Central Line. There's a lovely wooden Saxon church near there. I'll be able to walk over the fields this springtime to Ongar where 'Twinkle, twinkle little star' was written.
Sir John Betjeman, Observer Magazine 1 *Apr* 1979

5 I've always had a secret ambition to be the master of a tideway tug, either on the Thames or on the Solent, and I'm finally going to try it. Every day you can deal bossily and skilfully with ships of all sizes in every sort of wind and tide. The bridge is easy: the scenery is varied; it's never very rough, and you get home at night.
Sir Hugh Casson, Observer Magazine 1 *Apr* 1979

6 His childhood ambition had been to be a taxidermist, and for a year or two he toddled around in a cloud of formaldehyde.
Alistair Cooke, of Theodore Roosevelt, AMERICA

7 I should like to be a horse.
Queen Elizabeth II, *when a child*

8 My ambition is to live in a hot country and watch someone throw stones in the sea.
Gracie Fields, News Chronicle 9 *Jan* 1932

9 Modern man lives under the illusion that he knows what he wants, while he actually wants what he is supposed to want.
Erich Fromm, ESCAPE FROM FREEDOM 1941

10 If you start acting when you're five there isn't a lot of point in finding something else to do when you're 84 . . . I'd like to go have a look at Saturn now that they seem to have got cameras up there.
Lillian Gish, The Times 19 *Nov* 1980

11 The average girl's ambition is to make some man a good husband.
Chal Herry, Saturday Evening Post 20 *Nov* 1948

12 I can conceive no better fortune when the time comes than to cultivate private rather than public aspirations, to live, love, garden and die deep in the English countryside.
Douglas Jay, CHANGE AND FORTUNE

13 We all want to be famous people, and the moment we want to *be* something we are no longer free.
Krishnamurti, THE PENGUIN KRISHNAMURTI READER

14 Vocational Guide for the Truly Ambitious, or — So You Want to be the Pope.
Fran Lebowitz. Essay title

15 All I want is a room somewhere / Far away from the cold night air / With one enormous chair. / Ooh, wouldn't it be lov-er-ly.
Alan Jay Lerner, MY FAIR LADY 1956

16 The trouble is that really wanting things is so rare. It's a lukewarm world.
E. V. Lucas, 365 DAYS AND ONE MORE

17 You've got a goal. I've got a goal. Now all we need is a football team.
Groucho Marx, A NIGHT AT THE OPERA

18 Men do not heed the rungs by which they climb.
John Masefield, AUTOBIOGRAPHY

19 If men could regard the events of their own lives with more open minds they would frequently discover that they did not really desire the things they failed to obtain.
André Maurois, THE ART OF LIVING

1 [The average man] is always waiting for something to happen to him instead of setting to work to make it happen. For one person who dreams of making fifty thousand pounds a hundred people dream of being left fifty thousand pounds.
A. A. Milne, IF I MAY

2 The end of ambition comes as a great relief.
Malcolm Muggeridge at 78 to John Mortimer, Sunday Times 19 Apr 1981

3 If I had not been born Perón I would have liked to be Perón.
President Juan Perón. Quoted Observer, Sayings of the Week 21 Feb 1960

4 Ambition is the grand enemy of all peace.
John Cowper Powys, THE MEANING OF CULTURE 1930

5 The Palmer family of Camden Town have failed in their great war-time ambition — to breed a red, white and blue mouse before World War II came to an end.
Reynolds News. Quoted Michael Bateman, THIS ENGLAND

6 I want to be another Emma Hamilton. I'm looking for another Lord Nelson, only taller.
Mandy Rice-Davies, at the time of the Profumo scandal 1963

7 The young have aspirations that never come to pass, the old have reminiscences of what never happened.
Saki, REGINALD AT THE CARLTON 1904

8 The indefatigable pursuit of an unattainable perfection, even though it consist in nothing more than in the pounding of an old piano, is what alone gives meaning to our life on this unavailing star.
Logan Pearsall Smith, ALL TRIVIA, *Afterthoughts 1931*

9 Dan Jones was going to compose the most prodigious symphony, Fred James paint the most miraculously meretricious picture, Charles Fisher catch the poshest trout, Vernon Watkins and Young Thomas write the most boiling poems, how they would ring the bells of London and paint it like a tart.
Dylan Thomas, THE RETURN JOURNEY

10 A Spanish writer who was described as the best writer in Spain became angry because he wanted to be told he was the best in the world. I must confess I recognise something of myself in that.
John Updike. Quoted John Heilpern, Observer 25 Mar 1979

11 There are few *Vogue* readers who have never harboured a slinking desire to be thrown across the saddle of a plunging white stallion, galloped to a palmy oasis and stuffed with dates in a striped prison by swarthy warriors.
Vogue

12 We think that what we are doing is for reasons of idealism but people's ambition begins to grow as they feel the attraction of power.
Shirley Williams. Interviewed by Miriam Gross, Observer 22 Mar 1981

13 Caged birds accept each other but flight is what they long for.
Tennessee Williams, CAMINO REAL 1953

14 I would like to be the head of an advertising agency.
The Duchess of Windsor

AMOEBA

15 Amoebas at the start / Were not complex; / They tore themselves apart / And started sex.
Arthur Guiterman, SEX

ANALOGY

16 Though analogy is often misleading it is the least misleading thing we have.
Samuel Butler, NOTEBOOKS, *Music, Pictures and Books* 1912

17 Analogies prove nothing, that is quite true, but they can make one feel more at home.
Sigmund Freud, NEW INTRODUCTORY LECTURES ON PSYCHOANALYSIS 1952

ANARCHY

18 I am a Tory Anarchist. I should like everyone to go about doing just as he pleased — short of altering any of the things to which I have grown accustomed.
Max Beerbohm

1 To a real anarchist a poke in the eye is better than a bunch of flowers. It makes him see stars.
Joyce Cary, THE HORSE'S MOUTH 1944

2 Anarchism is a game at which the Police can beat you.
George Bernard Shaw, MISALLIANCE 1910. *Epigraph to Joe Orton's* LOOT 1967

3 My political opinions lean more and more towards anarchy . . . The most improper job of any man, even saints, is bossing other men.
J. R. R. Tolkien, LETTERS

ANATOMY

4 We tolerate shapes in human beings that would horrify us if we saw them in a horse.
W. R. Inge (Dean of St Pauls), NOTEBOOKS

5 A human being: an ingenious assembly of portable plumbing.
Christopher Morley, HUMAN BEING

6 He [man] is proud that he has the biggest brain of all the primates, but attempts to conceal that he also has the biggest penis.
Desmond Morris, THE NAKED APE

ANCESTRY

7 Genealogy is an account of one's descent from a man who did not particularly care to trace his own.
Ambrose Bierce, THE DEVIL'S DICTIONARY 1906

8 Somewhere back along your pedigree a bitch got over the wall.
Robert Bolt, A MAN FOR ALL SEASONS 1960

9 We all of us may have kings' blood in our veins . . . We tell ourselves that Shakespeare was the son of a wool-peddler and Napoleon of a farmer and Luther of a peasant, and we hold up our hands at the marvel. But who knows what kings and prophets they had in their ancestry?
John Buchan, THE PATH OF THE KING

10 Henry I is in lots of family trees. He was very good at it. He had twenty illegitimate children before he was married and nobody counted them afterwards.
Will Cuppy, THE DECLINE AND FALL OF PRACTICALLY EVERYBODY

11 A study of family portraits is enough to convert a man to the theory of reincarnation.
Sir Arthur Conan Doyle, THE HOUND OF THE BASKERVILLES 1902

12 There is no king who has not had a slave among his ancestors, and no slave who has not had a king among his.
Helen Keller, STORY OF MY LIFE 1947

13 Family trees are often like St Pancras station, the incongruous fruits of the Gothic revival.
Harold Kurtz, Daily Telegraph 18 Aug 1966

14 [Ezra] Pound has spent his life trying to live down a family scandal — he's Longfellow's grand-nephew.
D. H. Lawrence in a letter to Robert Graves

15 i have often noticed that / ancestors never boast / of the descendants who boast / of ancestors; i would / rather start a family than / finish one. blood will tell but often / it tells too much.
Don Marquis, A ROACH OF THE TAVERNS

16 To have an ancestor who was hanged for sheep-stealing gives me a certain social standing, don't you think?
Robert Morley, BBC Radio 4, *Start the Week* 7 Sep 1981

17 Our family didn't exactly come from the wrong side of the tracks but we were certainly always within sound of the train whistles.
Ronald Reagan. Quoted Bill Adler, THE REAGAN WIT

18 Of remote ancestors I can discover only one who did not live to a great age, and he died of a disease now rare, namely, having his head cut off.
Bertrand Russell, of Lord William Russell. Quoted Michael Foot, DEBTS OF HONOUR

19 Every president of the US has somehow been found to descend from Edward II.
Gore Vidal. Quoted John Heilpern, Observer 26 Apr 1981

ANGEL

1 Steel engravings of Protestant angels brought up on milk pudding.
Hilaire Belloc in a letter to Mrs Wansborough 6 Jan 1926

2 God made the angels, to show him splendour.
Robert Bolt, A MAN FOR ALL SEASONS 1960

3 Angels can fly because they take themselves lightly.
G. K. Chesterton, ORTHODOXY 1909

4 An angel whose muscles developed no more power weight for weight than those of an eagle or a pigeon would require a breast projecting for about four feet to house the muscles engaged in working its wings, while to economise in weight, its legs would have to be reduced to mere stilts.
J. B. S. Haldane, POSSIBLE WORLDS 1927

5 If a man is only a little lower than the angels, the angels should reform.
Mary Wilson Little

6 If some angel appeared to me without a carnal body and assured me that it was perfectly happy on prayer and music I should congratulate him, but shouldn't care to emulate him.
George Santayana, LETTERS

7 In heaven, an angel is nobody in particular.
George Bernard Shaw

8 Angels have no private lives.
Stevie Small, Sunday Times 7 Apr 1964

9 There is no reason why good cannot triumph as often as evil. The triumph of anything is a matter of organisation. If there are such things as angels I hope they are organised along the lines of the Mafia.
Kurt Vonnegut, SIRENS OF TITAN

ANGER

10 I was never an Angry Young Man. I am angry only when I hit my thumb with a hammer.
Kingsley Amis, Eton College Chronicle, Jun 1979

11 He [Henry Cabot Lodge] could enrage his antagonists by making them feel their own impotence to enrage him.
Anon.

12 Speak when you are angry and you will make the best speech you will ever regret.
Ambrose Bierce, THE DEVIL'S DICTIONARY 1906

13 Few men can afford to be angry.
Augustin Burell, EDMUND BURKE

14 I know of no more disagreeable sensation than being left generally angry without anybody in particular to be angry at.
Frank Moore Colby, THE COLBY ESSAYS 1926

15 People in a temper often say a lot of terrible, silly things they mean.
Penelope Gilliat. Quoted Katherine Whitehorn, VIEW FROM A COLUMN 1981

16 'I am beside myself.'
'Move over. You're in bad company.'
Groucho Marx, A NIGHT AT THE OPERA

17 It is my rule never to lose my temper till it would be detrimental to keep it.
Sean O'Casey, THE PLOUGH AND THE STARS 1926

18 She struck me as being a shade below par, and she spoke with a good deal of animation about skinning you with a blunt knife.
P. G. Wodehouse, PIGS HAVE WINGS 1952

ANGLING

19 The charm of fishing is that it is the pursuit of what is elusive but obtainable, a perpetual series of occasions for hope.
John Buchan, New York Times 15 Apr 1951

20 Fishing is undoubtedly a form of madness but, happily for the once-bitten, there is no cure.
Alec Douglas-Home, THE WAY THE WIND BLOWS 1976

ANSWER

21 An answer is always a form of death.
John Fowles, THE MAGUS

1 Now I cannot for the life of me pass an Intelligence Test. They ask you questions like this, 'Do you know the answer to 2+2?' To such a question I reply 'Four'. The correct answer is 'Yes'.
Gerald Kersh, CLEAN BRIGHT AND SLIGHTLY OILED 1940

2 If we can really understand the problem the answer will come out of it, because the answer is not separate from the problem.
Krishnamurti, THE PENGUIN KRISHNAMURTI READER

ANTHOLOGY

3 A well chosen anthology is a complete dispensary of medicine for the more common mental disorders, and may be used as much for prevention as cure.
Robert Graves, ON ENGLISH POETRY 1962

4 The thing to do with anecdotes is to tell them; or failing that, to listen to them. To make books out of them is like giving a dinner that consists solely of stuffed olives and after-dinner mints.
Philip Howard, The Times, reviewing the OXFORD BOOK OF AMERICAN LITERARY ANECDOTES 10 *Dec* 1981

ANTICIPATION

5 Talk about the joys of the unexpected, can they compare with the joys of the expected, of finding everything delightfully and completely what you knew it was going to be?
Elizabeth Bibesco, BALLOONS

6 The habit of looking to the future and thinking that the whole meaning of the present lies in what it will bring forth is a pernicious one. There can be no value in the whole unless there is value in the parts.
Bertrand Russell, THE CONQUEST OF HAPPINESS 1930

ANTIQUE

7 An antique is something that's been useless so long it's still in pretty good condition.
Franklin P. Jones, Saturday Evening Post 21 *Feb* 1956

APATHY

8 Science may have found a cure for most evils, but it has found no remedy for the worst of them all — the apathy of human beings.
Helen Keller, MY RELIGION 1927

9 Sit on your arse for fifty years and hang your hat on a pension.
Louis MacNeice, BAGPIPE MUSIC

APHORISM

10 We endeavour to stuff the universe into the gullet of an aphorism.
Paul Eldridge, HORNS OF GLASS

11 An aphorism is never exactly truthful. It is either a half-truth or a truth and a half.
Karl Kraus, APHORISMS

APOLOGY

12 To apologise is to lay the foundation for a future offence.
Ambrose Bierce, THE DEVIL'S DICTIONARY 1906

13 It is a good rule in life never to apologise. The right sort of people do not want apologies, and the wrong sort take a mean advantage of them.
P. G. Wodehouse, THE MAN UPSTAIRS

APPEARANCE

14 Lytton Strachey peered at everyone through thick glasses, looking like an owl in daylight. He is immensely tall, and could be even twice his height if he were not as bent as sloppy asparagus.
Cecil Beaton, DIARY 1923

15 She looks like Lady Chatterley above the waist and the gamekeeper below.
Cyril Connolly of Vita Sackville-West

16 Do I look as if I sold Bentleys in Great Portland Street?
Noël Coward, on being mistaken for Rex Harrison

17 He had grey curly hair and a face like a jubilee bonfire.
Lionel Curtis of Cecil Rhodes, WITH MILNER IN SOUTH AFRICA

1 His hair and teeth were both parted in the middle.
Peter De Vries, CONSENTING ADULTS

2 Why not be oneself? That is the whole secret of a successful appearance. If one is a greyhound why try to look like a Pekinese?
Edith Sitwell, WHY I LOOK AS I DO

3 Small, shrivelled chap. Looks like a haddock with lung trouble.
P. G. Wodehouse, THE INIMITABLE JEEVES 1924

4 A tall, drooping man, looking as if he had been stuffed in a hurry by an incompetent taxidermist.
P. G. Wodehouse, THE MATING SEASON

APPEASEMENT

5 An appeaser is one who feeds a crocodile, hoping it will eat him last.
Winston Churchill after Munich 1938

6 If war is so easily averted as all this it does seem a pity no PM has thought of it before . . . Peace without Honour seems to be what we have got. I'm glad. One can't expect *both*.
Rose Macaulay in a letter to Daniel George (Bunting) on the Munich crisis 1938

APPETITE

7 Other people's appetites easily appear excessive when one doesn't share them.
André Gide, THE COUNTERFEITERS 1926

APPLAUSE

8 Applause is the echo of a platitude.
Ambrose Bierce, THE DEVIL'S DICTIONARY 1906

9 When I hear a man applauded by the mob I feel sorry for him. All he has to do to be hissed is to live long enough.
H. L. Mencken, MINORITY REPORT

APPLE

10 The apple was the first fruit of the world,

according to Genesis, but it was no Cox's Orange pippin. God gave the crab apple and left the rest to man.
JANE GRIGSON'S FRUIT BOOK

APPRECIATION

11 The power of appreciating is worth any amount of the power of despising.
A. C. Benson, FROM A COLLEGE WINDOW 1906

APPREHENSION

12 Even in slight things the experience of the new is rarely without some stirring of foreboding.
Eric Hoffer, THE ORDEAL OF CHANGE 1964

ARCHITECTURE

13 It has all the earmarks of an eyesore.
American tourist of the Albert Memorial

14 Ee, but it would make a grand Co-op.
Anon. Said of All Souls, Oxford

15 What is proposed is like a monstrous carbuncle on the face of a much loved and elegant friend.
Charles, Prince of Wales. Speech to RIBA on the proposed extension to the National Gallery 30 *May* 1984

16 Architecture is pre-eminently the art of significant forms in space – that is, forms significant of their functions.
Claud Bragdon, Outlook 27 *May* 1931

17 Architecture is inhabited sculpture.
Constantin Brancusi. Quoted Igor Stravinsky, THEMES AND EPISODES 1966

18 We shape our buildings; thereafter they shape us.
Winston Churchill, Time 12 *Sep* 1960

19 French Classical architecture . . . was the work not of craftsmen but of wonderfully gifted civil servants.
Kenneth, Lord Clark, CIVILISATION 1969

20 Architecture, of all the arts, is the one which acts the most slowly, but the most surely, on the soul.
Ernest Dimnet, WHAT WE LIVE BY

1 A courageous and partly successful attempt to disguise a gasworks as a racquets court.
Peter Fleming, of the Shakespeare Memorial Theatre. Sunday Times 1951

2 Large buildings in London and elsewhere today are too often designed in the lift going down to lunch.
Sir William Holford. Quoted Observer 5 Jun 1960

3 A seventeenth-century palace was totally without privacy. Architects had not yet invented the corridor . . . One simply walked through a succession of other people's rooms in which literally anything could be going on.
Aldous Huxley, THEME AND VARIATIONS 1950

4 A hundred and fifty accurate reproductions of Anne Hathaway's cottage each complete with garage and central heating.
Osbert Lancaster, PILLAR TO POST, Stockbroker's Tudor

5 The materials of city planning are: sky, space, trees, steel and cement; in that order and that hierarchy.
Le Corbusier

6 There is nothing in which the birds differ more from man than the way they can build and yet leave a landscape as it was before.
Robert Lynd, THE BLUE LION

7 I thought it looked as if it was something that had crawled out of the sea and was up to no good. It reminds me of one of those films where giant ants and things take over.
Beverley Nichols, of the Sydney Opera House. Sydney Sun News Pictorial 5 Feb 1968

8 The challenge for the modern architect is the same as the challenge for all of us in our lives, to make out of the ordinary something out-of-the-ordinary.
Patrick Nuttgens, BBC TV, Architecture for Everyman, Feb 1979

9 Architecture is the most inescapable of the higher arts.
Anthony Quinton, The Times, Romantic Crying Wolfe 25 Mar 1982

10 One might regard architecture as history arrested in stone, the movement of time congealed . . . at every point a building

expresses the needs, the character of its age.
A. L. Rowse, THE USE OF HISTORY

11 Its shoulders break the clouds apart / A concrete stake in the city's heart.
Richard Usborne, FOUR STAR HOTEL

12 From Tromso to Angora the horrible little architects crept about — curly-headed, horn-spectacled, volubly explaining their 'machines for living'. Villas like sewage farms, mansions like half-submerged Channel steamers, offices like vast beehives or cucumber frames sprang up round their feet, furnished with electric fires that blistered the ankles, windows that blinded the eyes, patent 'sound proof' partitions which resounded with the rattle of a hundred typewriters and the buzzing of a hundred telephones.
Evelyn Waugh, Country Life 20 Feb 1936

13 One of the best warehouses I ever saw was the Vatican in Rome.
Arnold Wesker, CHIPS WITH EVERYTHING 1962

14 The modern buildings that you see / Are often most alarming / But I am sure that you'll agree / A ruin / can be charming.
Sandy Wilson, THE BOY FRIEND

15 One of those mid-Victorian jobs in glazed red brick which always seem to bob up in these olde worlde hamlets and do so much to encourage the drift to the towns.
P. G. Wodehouse, THE MATING SEASON 1949

16 The physician can bury his mistakes, but the architect can only advise his client to plant vines.
Frank Lloyd Wright, New York Times Magazine 4 Oct 1953

ARGUMENT

17 Most of the arguments to which I am a party fall somewhat short of being impressive owing to the fact that neither I nor my opponent knows what we are talking about.
Robert Benchley, BENCHLEY — OR ELSE

18 It is no use arguing with a prophet; you can only disbelieve him.
Winston Churchill of Prof. Lindemann. Quoted John Colville, THE CHURCHILLIANS 1981

1 It is only damned fools who argue. Never contradict, never explain, never apologise. These are the secrets of a happy life.
Lord Fisher. Letter to The Times 5 Sep 1919

2 A disagreement may be the shortest cut between two minds.
Kahil Gibran, SAND AND FOAM 1927

3 A stigma is good enough to beat a dogma with.
Philip Guedella. Speech to Cambridge Union. Quoted H. Montgomery Hyde, PRIVATE PAPERS OF NORMAN BIRKETT

4 By the very act of arguing, you awake the patient's reason; and once it is awake, who can foresee the result?
C. S. Lewis, THE SCREWTAPE LETTERS 1942

5 'Yes, but not in the South' with slight adjustments will do for any argument about any place, if not about any person.
Stephen Potter, LIFEMANSHIP 1950

6 Partisanship is our great curse. We too readily assume that everything has two sides and that it is our duty to be on one or the other.
James Harvey Robinson, THE MIND IN THE MAKING

7 The most savage controversies are those about matters as to which there is no good evidence either way.
Bertrand Russell, UNPOPULAR ESSAYS 1950

ARISTOCRACY

8 The great and very obvious merit of the English aristocracy is that nobody could possibly take it seriously.
G. K. Chesterton, ORTHODOXY 1908

9 The point about the aristocracy is that they all know each other.
Jilly Cooper, CLASS 1980

10 If human beings could be propagated by cutting, like apple trees, aristocracy would be biologically sound.
J. B. S. Haldane, THE INEQUALITY OF MAN

11 A society without an aristocracy, without an élite minority, is not a society.
José Ortega y Gasset, MEDITATIONS ON QUIXOTE 1914

12 The aristocratic rebel, since he has enough to eat, must have other causes of discontent.
Bertrand Russell, HISTORY OF WESTERN PHILOSOPHY 1945

13 Unlike the male codfish, which, suddenly finding itself the parent of three and a half million little codfish, cheerfully resolves to love them all, the British aristocracy is apt to look with a somewhat jaundiced eye on its younger sons.
P. G. Wodehouse, The Listener 30 May 1963

ARMAMENTS

14 The demon scientists and rulers of the land / Pile the bombs like fiddler crabs pile balls of sand.
Roy Fuller COLLECTED POEMS 1985

15 It is not armaments that cause war, but war that causes armaments.
Salvador de Madariaga, MORNING WITHOUT NOON

16 All this about 'the burden of armaments' is rubbish; the cost of the biggest armies at present is not worth counting beside the cost of idle property holding.
George Bernard Shaw. Letter to John Galsworthy 1911. Quoted H.V. Marrot, LIFE AND LETTERS OF JOHN GALSWORTHY

ARMOUR

17 Armour is the kind of clothing worn by a man whose tailor was a blacksmith.
Ambrose Bierce, THE DEVIL'S DICTIONARY 1906

ARMY

18 This is the army, Mr Jones / No private baths or telephones.
Irving Berlin, THIS IS THE ARMY *(song)*

19 It is characteristic of the military mind that non-human factors are held essential while the human being, his desires and thoughts — in short the psychological factors — are considered unimportant and secondary.
Albert Einstein, OUT OF MY LATER LIFE

1 At Toronto a major saw me at Movement Control. He wore no Intelligence green flash, but the faint aroma of lunacy and the fierce but vague eyes identified him as a member of the Intelligence Corps.
Sir Alec Guinness BLESSINGS IN DISGUISE 1985

2 What is unique about this regiment? It is the only one in which the Colonel is legally married to the Colonel in Chief.
Philip, Duke of Edinburgh, when being entertained to dinner by the Welsh Guards

ARROGANCE

3 A good way to deal with arrogance is simply to allow it to exhaust itself.
Noël Coward. Quoted William Marchant, THE PRIVILEGE OF HIS COMPANY 1980

4 In any imaginable society he [Sinclair Lewis] would be as noticeable as a bashful cyclone. He enters a room with diffident insolence, bracing himself against what lies in wait for him.
Carl Van Doren, SINCLAIR LEWIS

ART

5 Paintings, like people, are prone to diseases. They break out in boils, and crack under the strain of exposure.
Harold Acton, The Times, Saturday Review 18 Sep 1970

6 Millais once confessed that the only thing he enjoyed about portrait painting was putting the highlights on the boots of his subjects.
James Agate, EGO 1935–48

7 The object of art is to give life shape.
Jean Anouilh, THE REHEARSAL 1950

8 It [art] grows out of me like my toenails. I have to cut it off and then it grows again.
Jean Arp. Quoted The Times 8 Jun 1966

9 Klee's pictures seem to me to resemble, not pictures, but a sample book of patterns of linoleum.
The Hon. Sir Cyril Asquith in a letter to Alfred Munnings

10 Art is born of humiliation.
W. H. Auden. Quoted Humphrey Carpenter, AUDEN: A BIOGRAPHY

11 The lower one's vitality, the more sensitive one is to great art.
Max Beerbohm, SEVEN MEN 1919

12 Art and Religion are two roads by which men escape from circumstance to ecstasy.
Clive Bell, ART 1914

13 I mistrust violence in almost any art. It is often an easy way out. It's much more difficult to draw a beautiful face than an ugly one.
Quentin Bell, in an interview with Sarah Howell, Observer Magazine 18 Mar 1979

14 Art attempts to find in the universe, in matter as well as in the facts of life, what is fundamental, enduring, essential.
Saul Bellow. Nobel Prize speech 1970

15 I wanted to become a work of art myself, and not an artist.
Bernard Berenson, SUNSET AND TWILIGHT, *Diaries* 1947—58

16 A work of art is no good if it doesn't provoke a furore.
Sir Isaiah Berlin, Observer 2 Nov 1980

17 The drawing is on the level of that of an untaught child of seven or eight years old, the sense of colour that of a tea-tray painter, the method that of a schoolboy who wiped his fingers on a slate after spitting on them.
Wilfred Scawen Blunt, on Post Impressionists, MY DIARIES 1920

18 Surrealism was successful in its details and a failure in its essentials.
Luis Buñuel, MY LAST BREATH 1984

19 Artists, who get no end of kicks out of the trade they practise, are always eager to say what hell it is.
Anthony Burgess, HOMAGE TO QWERT YUIOP 1986

20 Most of those who call themselves artists are in reality picture dealers, only they make the pictures themselves.
Samuel Butler, NOTEBOOKS 1912

21 Art is what is deposited behind glass in galleries and museums and in the rooms of rich people: but it does not move about live in the streets, it does not twinkle from the handsome cornices of windows, it does not take up its stand at the street corner like a statue.
Karel Čapek, LETTERS FROM ENGLAND

1 Abstract art? A product of the untalented, sold by the unprincipled to the utterly bewildered.
Al Capp, Li'l Abner cartoonist, National Observer 1 *Jul* 1963

2 Remember I'm an artist. And you know what that means in a court of law. Next worse to an actress.
Joyce Cary, THE HORSE'S MOUTH 1944

3 To have an *avant garde* you have to have a *garde*.
Sir Hugh Casson, Daily Telegraph 13 *Jan* 1974

4 What was any art but an effort to make a sheath, a mould, in which to imprison for a moment the shining, elusive element which is life itself.
Willa Cather, THE SONG OF THE LARK 1915

5 In matters of art it is more blessed to respond than to judge.
Lord David Cecil in a radio programme

6 Art is the unceasing effort to compete with the beauty of flowers — and never succeeding.
Marc Chagall 1977

7 The artistic temperament is a disease that afflicts amateurs.
G. K. Chesterton, HERETICS 1905

8 Art is not a pastime, but a priesthood.
Jean Cocteau, New York Times 8 *Sep* 1982

9 That is what the title of artist means; one who perceives more than his fellows, and who records more than he has seen.
Gordon Craig, ON THE ART OF THE THEATRE 1911

10 He made a last desperate coup to persuade the world he was an artist by marrying a model. But this device deceived nobody.
Aleister Crowley, of Sir Gerald Kelly, CONFESSIONS

11 If a cloud is going to support a lady of substantial proportions you must make it fairly solid.
Mr Justice Darling, Edwards Huntingdon v. Lewis and Simmons, May 1917

12 Artists hate the enlightened amateur unless he buys.
Ernest Dimnet, WHAT WE LIVE BY

13 In our daily lives — eating, dressing, working, or seeking amusement — art, good or bad, is always with us. For most of us, most of the time, it is bad art.
R. L. Duffus, North American Review, Sep 1936

14 Every master knows that the material teaches the artist.
Ilya Ehrenburg, Saturday Review 30 *Sep* 1967

15 The more perfect the artist the more completely separate in him will be the man who suffers and the mind which creates.
T. S. Eliot. Quoted Cyril Connolly, THE UNQUIET GRAVE 1945

16 The reputation of the Academy has got to a point where election should be positively distressing to a serious painter.
Evening Standard 22 *Feb* 1961

17 Artists can colour the sky red because they *know* it is blue. Those of us who aren't artists must colour things the way they really are or people might think we were stupid.
Jules Feiffer, CRAWLING ARNOLD

18 Art is significant deformity.
Roger Fry

19 A work of art is part of nature seen through a temperament.
André Gide, PROTESTS

20 I do not think abstract art can ever be as good as the art of a religious age. It stands on a different level of human aspiration.
Sir Ernest Gombrich. Quoted D.A.N. Jones, Radio Times 9 *Feb* 1979

21 The history of art in this century is seen, partly, as a history of revulsion. Artists have tried to *avoid* something, to *not* do something. But in *generic* primitive art they are not trying to *avoid* anything.
Ibid.

22 All men are creative but few are artists.
Paul Goodman, GROWING UP ABSURD 1960

23 No artist is ahead of his time. He *is* his time; it is just that others are behind the times.
Martha Graham. Quoted John Heilpern, Observer Magazine, The Amazing Martha 8 *Jul* 1979

1 It is not puritanism to affirm that the activity of the artist differs from the activity of the sanitary inspector.
Geoffrey Grigson. Quoted News Review 20 *Mar* 1947

2 Great art is the expression of a solution of the conflict between the demands of the world without and that within.
Edith Hamilton, THE GREEK WAY 1930

3 If they [artists] do see fields blue they are deranged, and should go to an asylum. If they only pretend to see them blue, they are criminals and should go to prison.
Adolf Hitler. Speech in Munich

4 The finest works of art are precious, among other reasons, because they make it possible for us to know, if only imperfectly and for a little while, what it actually feels like to think subtly and feel nobly.
Aldous Huxley, ENDS AND MEANS 1937

5 Recognisableness is an artistic quality which most people find profoundly thrilling.
Aldous Huxley, MUSIC AT NIGHT 1931

6 Art is one of the means whereby man seeks to redeem a life which is experienced as chaotic, senseless and largely evil.
Aldous Huxley, THEME AND VARIATIONS 1950

7 The artist, like the God of creation, remains within or behind or beyond or above his handiwork, invisible, refined out of existence, indifferent, paring his fingernails.
James Joyce, A PORTRAIT OF THE ARTIST AS A YOUNG MAN 1916

8 In a free society art is not a weapon.
John F. Kennedy. Speech at dedication of Robert Frost Library, Nov 1962

9 Artists are not engineers of the soul.
Ibid.

10 Drawing is the art of taking a line for a walk.
Paul Klee

11 Art does not reproduce what we see. It makes us see.
Paul Klee, CREATIVE CREDO

12 Art is art and there is nothing can be done to prevent it, but there is the Mayoress's decency to be considered.

A Lancashire Mayor on the display of nude figures in the Town Hall

13 Art is not a special sauce applied to ordinary cooking; it is the cooking itself if it is good.
W. R. Lethaby, FORM IN CIVILIZATION

14 The goitrous, torpid and squinting husks provided by Matisse in his sculpture are worthless except as tactful decorations for a mental home.
(Percy) Wyndham Lewis, THE ART OF BEING RULED

15 If you want to know what actually is occurring inside, underneath, at the centre, at any given moment, art is a truer guide than politics more often than not.
(Percy) Wyndham Lewis, TIME AND WESTERN MAN 1927

16 In other countries art and literature are left to a lot of shabby bums living in attics and feeding on booze and spaghetti, but in America the successful writer or picture-painter is indistinguishable from any other decent business man.
Sinclair Lewis, BABBITT 1922

17 The poet should believe in art for its own sake, but the draughtsman inevitably moralises. Artists always preach, if it is nothing more than their school of art. Art is pre-eminently didactic.
Vachel Lindsay. Quoted Edgar Lee Masters, VACHEL LINDSAY, A POET IN AMERICA

18 Art enlarges experience by admitting us to the inner life of others.
Walter Lippmann, A PREFACE TO POLITICS, *The Golden Rule and After* 1914

19 Every artist has his own distorting mirror; it is his method of making reality fresh and therefore recognisably real.
Robert Lynd, John o'London's Weekly 10 *Apr* 1930

20 The whole of art is an appeal to a reality which is not without us but in our minds.
Desmond McCarthy, THEATRE 1940

21 A good rocking horse has often more of the true horse about it than an instantaneous photograph of a Derby winner.
Desmond McCarthy, MANET AND HIS CONTEMPORARIES

1 Our feeling for a work of art is rarely independent of the place it occupies in art history.
André Malraux, THE VOICES OF SILENCE 1951

2 All art is a revolt against man's fate.
Ibid.

3 All works of art are successful because of, not in spite of, the limitations that form places upon them . . . the sense of triumph lies not merely in the humanity of the subject or the story, but also in the skill with which the artist moves freely within his self-imposed limits.
Roger Manvell, FILM

4 It is wrong to try to make art too life-like; it becomes released from its limitations and so loses its sense of form and proportion.
Ibid.

5 In those days, as a little child, I was living in Paradise and had no need of the arts, which at best are only a shadow of Paradise.
John Masefield, SO LONG TO LEARN

6 The worst sin that can be committed against the artist is to take him at his word, to see in his work a fulfilment instead of a horizon.
Henry Miller, THE COSMOLOGICAL EYE 1939

7 The artist does not tinker with the universe; he re-creates it out of his own experience and understanding of life.
Ibid.

8 An artist is always alone — if he *is* an artist; the artist needs loneliness.
Henry Miller, TROPIC OF CANCER 1934

9 After Matisse and Picasso there is nothing more to be done.
John Minton to John Moynihan 1957.
Quoted Dan Farson, OUT OF STEP

10 We are all heirs to the loveliness of the visible world, but only by the process of art can we be inducted into possession of this large estate.
C. E. Montague, A WRITER'S NOTES ON HIS TRADE 1930

11 To be aristocratic in art one must avoid polite society.
George Moore. Quoted Cyril Connolly, ENEMIES OF PROMISE 1938

12 She [Chanel] exemplified the unwelcome truth that a good artist can be a shocking bad lot.
Raymond Mortimer, TRY ANYTHING ONCE

13 People don't learn to enjoy pictures because they seldom look at them; and they seldom look at pictures because they have never learnt to enjoy them.
Ibid.

14 Communication is the purpose of all art, though a man may write or paint from a desire for self expression. The result does not function as a work of art until somebody receives a communication from it.
Ibid.

15 The [modern] painter plumes himself upon an independence such as was never dreamed of by Piero della Francesca or Titian or Watteau. To paint the subjects that people relish is, he thinks, below his dignity. In fact it is above his capacity — not because he lacks the accomplishment, but because he lacks the impulse.
Ibid.

16 A work of art has no importance whatever to society. It is only important to the individual.
Vladimir Nabokov, STRONG OPINIONS

17 Great art is as irrational as great music. It is mad with its own loveliness.
George Jean Nathan, HOUSE OF SATAN

18 Art is a form of catharsis.
Dorothy Parker, ART

19 Painting is a blind man's profession. He paints not what he sees, but what he feels, what he tells himself about what he has seen.
Pablo Picasso. Quoted Jean Cocteau, JOURNALS

20 There are painters who transform the sun into a yellow spot, but there are others who, with the help of their art and their intelligence, transform a yellow spot into the sun.
Attributed to Pablo Picasso by Edith Sitwell, RHYMES AND REASON

21 If your man says of some picture 'Yes but what does it mean?' ask him and keep on asking him, what his carpet means, or the circular patterns on his rubber shoe-soles. Make him lift up his foot to look at them.
Stephen Potter, ONE-UPMANSHIP 1952

1 Thanks to art, instead of seeing a single world, our own, we see it multiply until we have before us as many worlds as there are original artists.
Marcel Proust, MAXIMS 1948

2 Artistic genius in its reactions is like those extremely high temperatures which have the power to disintegrate combinations of atoms which they proceed to combine afresh in a diametrically opposite order.
Marcel Proust, REMEMBRANCE OF THINGS PAST 1913—27

3 Right now we're into creative groups. That's where taxidermy turns into an art form.
Jonathan Raban, OLD GLORY

4 Half of art is knowing when to stop.
Arthur William Radford

5 A work of art is good if it has sprung from necessity.
Rainer Maria Rilke, LETTER TO A YOUNG POET 1903

6 We walk in the dark — we do what we can — we give what we have. Our doubt is our passion and our passion is our task. The rest is the madness of art.
Philip Roth, THE GHOST WRITER

7 What garlic is to salad, insanity is to art.
Augustus Saint-Gandens, REMINISCENCES 1913

8 Nothing is so poor and melancholy as art that is interested in itself and not in its subject.
George Santayana, THE LIFE OF REASON, *Reason in Art* 1905

9 If it is art it is not for all, and if it is for all it is not art.
Arnold Schoenberg. Quoted Nat Shapiro, ENCYCLOPEDIA OF QUOTATIONS ABOUT MUSIC

10 The true artist will let his wife starve, his children go barefoot, his mother drudge for her living at seventy, sooner than work at anything but his art.
George Bernard Shaw, MAN AND SUPERMAN 1905

11 The artist, like the idiot or clown, sits on the edge of the world, and a push may send him over it.
Sir Osbert Sitwell, THE SCARLET TREE 1945

12 The vitality of a new movement in art or letters can be pretty accurately gauged by the fury it arouses.
Logan Pearsall Smith, of Impressionism, ALL TRIVIA, *Afterthoughts* 1931

13 A portrait is a picture in which there is something wrong with the mouth.
Eugene Speicher. Quoted Frank Muir, THE FRANK MUIR BOOK 1976

14 The naked truth about me is to the naked truth about Salvador Dali as an old ukulele in the attic is to a piano in a tree, and I mean a piano with breasts.
James Thurber, THE THURBER MERRY-GO-ROUND 1945

15 The arts are an even better barometer of what is happening in our world than the stock market or debates in Congress.
Henrik Willem Van Loon, THE ARTS

16 I was so desirous of getting it [a picture] right that I did it with my shoes off.
G. F. Watts. Quoted Christopher Hassall, EDWARD MARSH

17 I took Art at College as my second subject one semester. I'd have taken it as my first subject only Dad lost his money in religion so I had to learn a trade.
Evelyn Waugh, THE LOVED ONE 1948

18 A work of art has an author and yet, when it is perfect, it has something which is anonymous about it.
Simone Weil, GRAVITY AND GRACE 1927

19 He [Sinclair Lewis] is a master of that species of art to which belong glass flowers, imitation fruit, Mme Tussaud's waxworks, and barnyard symphonies which aims at deceiving the spectator into thinking that the work in question is not an artificial product but the real thing.
T. K. Whipple, SPOKESMAN

20 Art flourishes where there is a sense of adventure, a sense of nothing having been done before.
A. N. Whitehead, DIALOGUES 1953

21 Art is the imposing of a pattern on experience, and our aesthetic enjoyment in recognition of the pattern.
Ibid.

1 Art for art's sake is a philosophy of the well-fed.
Cao Yu, Chinese playwright, Observer 13 *Apr* 1980

ASPIRATE

2 J. H. Thomas: I've got an 'orrible 'eadache. Birkenhead: Why not try a couple of aspirates?
Quoted 2nd Earl Birkenhead in his biography of his father

HERBERT HENRY ASQUITH

3 He brought to Cabinet meetings the cool calculation that he displayed at the bridge table.
Robert Cecil, LIFE IN EDWARDIAN ENGLAND 1969

4 Arthur [Balfour] is wicked and moral. Asquith is good and immoral.
Winston Churchill. Quoted Ernest Raymond, MR BALFOUR

5 His mind opened and shut smoothly and exactly, like the breech of a gun.
Winston Churchill, GREAT CONTEMPORARIES 1937

6 Asquith worries too much about small points. If you were buying a large mansion he would come to you and say 'Have you thought there is no accommodation for the cat?'
David Lloyd George. Letter to Lord Riddell 1915

MARGOT ASQUITH

7 A *café chantant* attached to a cathedral.
Anon.

8 Beneath a bony, witch-like hand, with a big hooked nose and sharp, dark eyes moved and attitudinised a small skinny body dressed usually in the height of fashion.
Lord David Cecil, Observer, Staying with Margot 20 *Dec* 1981

9 That gifted entertainer, the Countess of Oxford and Asquith, author of The Auto-biography of Margot Asquith (four volumes, ready boxed, suitable for throwing purposes).
Dorothy Parker, (Constant Reader) New Yorker, Re-enter Margot Asquith, A Masterpiece from the French 22 *Oct* 1927

10 I think it must be pleasanter to be Margot Asquith than to be any other living human being . . . Her perfect confidence in herself is a thing to which monuments should be erected . . . The affair between Margot Asquith and Margot Asquith will live as one of the prettiest love stories in all literature.
Ibid.

11 Her face, except her forehead, is wrinkled past makeup; she uses a vivid orange lipstick not perhaps as an expression of her vitality but as a gesture to it. Her voice is the unfaltering instrument of moods that still seem to be as varying as a debutante's.
Reginald Pound, THEIR MOODS AND MINE 1937

ASSASSINATION

12 Assassination — an accident of my trade.
Alfonso XIII of Spain, after the attempt on his life on his wedding day 31 *May* 1906

13 If someone is going to shoot you there is nothing much you can do about it. If you're going to start worrying about it, it's time to give up.
Prince Charles, on Australian TV 1974

14 Assassination should be used as the vote should ideally be used, that is, bearing in mind only the public good and regardless of personal interest.
Edward Hyams, KILLING NO MURDER

15 If someone wants to shoot me from a window with a rifle, nobody can stop it, so why worry about it?
John F. Kennedy to his wife Jacqueline, before starting for Dallas the day he was assassinated 22 *Nov* 1963

16 I live each day under a threat of death. I know that I can meet a violent end.
Martin Luther King, in an interview with Gerald Priestland, broadcast by the BBC the day he was shot 4 *Apr* 1968

17 But how did you enjoy the *play* Mrs Lincoln?
Tom Lehrer

1 He was a liar, and he was nothing but a damned demagogue. It didn't surprise me when they shot him. These demagogues, the ones that live by demagoguery, they all end up the same way.
Harry S Truman, of Huey Long. Quoted Merle Miller, PLAIN SPEAKING

ASSURANCE

2 . . . on whom assurance sits / As a silk hat on a Bradford millionaire.
T. S. Eliot, THE WASTE LAND 1922

FRED ASTAIRE

3 He is the nearest we are ever likely to get to a human Mickey Mouse.
Graham Greene. Quoted Leslie Halliwell, FILMGOER'S BOOK OF QUOTES 1973

4 The audience meets Mr Astaire and the film at their best when he is adjusting his cravat to an elaborate dance routine or saying delicious things with his flashing feet that a lyricist would have difficulty putting into words.
André Sennwald reviewing THE GAY DIVORCE

LORD ASTOR

5 He would, wouldn't he?
Mandy Rice-Davies, at the trial of Stephen Ward 29 Jun 1963, when told that Lord Astor had denied her allegations

NANCY ASTOR

6 Lady Astor, canvassing for her first parliamentary seat in Plymouth, because of her status and also because she was new to the town, was allotted a senior naval officer as a minder and together they went round knocking at doors. 'Is your mother home?' asked Lady Astor imperiously when one door was opened by a small girl. 'No,' replied the child 'but she said if a lady comes with a sailor they're to use the upstairs room and leave ten bob.'
Sue Arnold, Observer Magazine 16 Jun 1985

7 Nobody wants me as a Cabinet Minister and they are perfectly right. I am an agitator, not an administrator.
Nancy Astor. Speech 1929

8 When you come into the Debating Chamber, Nancy, I feel as though you had come into my bathroom and I had only a sponge to cover myself with.
Winston Churchill to Lady Astor. Quoted John Beavers, Sunday Referee 19 Feb 1939

9 Her uncompromising Protestantism was tenuous but unyielding, like a strand of barbed wire in a hedge.
Walter Eliot. Quoted Christopher Sykes, NANCY

10 Viscount Waldorf Astor owned Britain's two most influential newspapers, *The Times* and the *Observer*, but his American wife, Nancy, had a wider circulation than both papers put together.
Emery Kelen, PEACE IN THEIR TIME

11 Nancy was a devout Christian Scientist, but not a good one. She kept confusing herself with God. She didn't know when to step aside and give God a chance.
Mrs Gordon Smith. Quoted Elizabeth Langhorne, NANCY ASTOR AND HER FRIENDS

ASTROLOGY

12 If Leo your own birthday marks / You will lust until forty, when starts / A new pleasure in stamps / Boy Scouts and their camps / And fondling nude statues in parks.
Anon. Quoted Frank Muir, FRANK MUIR GOES INTO SUPERSTITION 1981

13 If you had been born two days later you would have been kind, generous and witty.
Cartoon caption by Hoest

14 As soon as man began to realise his own insignificance astrology died an instant, natural and inevitable death.
Sir James Jeans. Quoted The People

ASTRONOMY

15 *Observatory:* A place where astronomers conjecture among the guesses of their predecessors.
Ambrose Bierce, THE DEVIL'S DICTIONARY 1906

1 A thousand million years before you were born a parcel of light was sent off from a distant star. Yesterday it was delivered at Mount Palomar in California.
Ritchie Calder, News Chronicle 8 Mar 1948

2 I have loved the stars too fondly to be fearful of the night.
Epitaph of unknown astronomer; epigraph to Len Deighton's TWINKLE, TWINKLE, LITTLE SPY 1976

3 Astronomy teaches the correct use of the sun and the planets.
Stephen Leacock, LITERARY LAPSES 1910

ATHEIST

4 Man without God risks his life for impure causes and cannot avoid doing so . . . Atheist-humanism can define itself only by accepting the limits of human existence.
Raymond Aron, SELECTED ESSAYS

5 I am an atheist still, thank God.
Luis Buñuel. Quoted Ado Kyrou, LUIS BUÑUEL: AN INTRODUCTION

6 An atheist is a man with no visible means of support.
H. E. Fosdick. Attributed by Jonathan Hunt, DICTIONARY OF QUOTATIONS. *Also attributed to John Buchan,* MEMORY HOLD THE DOOR 1940

7 There seems to be a terrible misunderstanding on the part of a great many people to the effect that when you cease to believe you may cease to behave.
Louis Kronenberger, COMPANY MANNERS, *The Spirit of the Age* 1954

8 She calls herself an atheist, though she has a somewhat inconsistent regard for Quakers.
Observer, Profile of Pat Arrowsmith 13 *May* 1982

9 The sort of atheist who does not so much disbelieve in God as personally dislike Him.
George Orwell, DOWN AND OUT IN PARIS AND LONDON 1933

10 God can stand being told by Professor Ayer and Marghanita Laski that he doesn't exist.
J. B. Priestley, THE BBC'S DUTY TO SOCIETY

11 The highest praise of God consists in the denial of Him by the atheist, who finds creation so perfect that he can dispense with a creator.
Marcel Proust, REMEMBRANCE OF THINGS PAST 1913—27

12 I was told that the Chinese said they would bury me by the Western Lake and build a shrine to my memory. I have some slight regret that this did not happen as I might have become a god, which would have been very *chic* for an atheist.
Bertrand Russell, AUTOBIOGRAPHY 1967

13 My atheism, like Spinoza's, is true piety towards the universe and denies only gods made by men in their own image to be servants of their human interests.
George Santayana, SOLILOQUIES IN ENGLAND 1927

14 When the atheist is confronted with one of the natural outrages against the dignity and decency of life he is tempted to act for the moment as if God existed simply in order to have something on which to unloose his outraged feelings.
Philip Toynbee, Observer, Death of a Mother 17 *Apr* 1968

ATHLETICS

15 The popular belief in athletics is grounded upon the theory that violent exercise makes for bodily health and that bodily health is necessary to mental vigour. Both halves of this theory are highly dubious. Athletes, as a class, are not above the normal in health, but below it.
H. L Mencken, American Mercury, Jun 1951

ATOM

16 We have grasped the mystery of the atom and rejected the Sermon on the Mount.
Gen. Omar Bradley. Speech 11 *Nov* 1948

17 That is how the atom is split. But what does it mean? To us who think in terms of practical use it means — Nothing!
Ritchie Calder, Daily Herald, 27 *Jun* 1932

18 It was in 1909 at the Cavendish laboratory, Cambridge, that they drank a toast 'to the electron. May it never be of use to anybody.'
Cyril Connolly, Observer, Turned to Dust and Ashes 2 *Oct* 1977

1 One of the things which distinguishes ours from all earlier generations is this, that we have seen our atoms.
Karl Kelchner Darrow, THE RENAISSANCE OF PHYSICS

2 There is no evil in the atom — only in men's souls.
Adlai Stevenson. Speech, Harvard 18 Sep 1952

ATOM BOMB

3 And the criminal, multi-coloured flash / Of an H-bomb is no more beautiful / Than an autopsy when the belly's opened / To show cathedral windows never opened.
Dannie Abse, POEMS, GOLDER'S GREEN, *Pathology of Colours*

4 Let us not deceive ourselves; we must elect world peace or world destruction.
Bernard Baruch. Address to UN Atomic Energy Commission 14 Jun 1946

5 From now on every generation will be aware that it could be the last generation on earth.
Stuart Blanche, Archbishop of York. Church of England synod, Church and the Bomb debate 10 Feb 1983

6 World War died, and lies for ever buried at Nagasaki.
Group Captain Leonard Cheshire, BBC 1 TV 29 Jul 1985

7 Atomic energy might be as good as our present day explosives but it is unlikely to produce anything much more dangerous.
Winston Churchill in 1939. Quoted Chris Morgan and David Langford, FACTS AND FALLACIES

8 No country without an atom bomb could properly consider itself independent.
Charles de Gaulle. Quoted New York Times Magazine 12 May 1968

9 We've got to take the atom bomb seriously. It's dynamite.
Sam Goldwyn. Quoted Alva Johnson, THE GREAT GOLDWYN

10 My God! It worked.
M. Griesen, observer at first test

11 The bomb that fell on Hiroshima fell on America, too.
Hermann Hagedorn, THE BOMB THAT FELL ON AMERICA

12 Aside from being tremendous it was one of the most aesthetically beautiful things I have ever seen.
Donald Hornig, THE DECISION TO DROP THE BOMB

13 The atom bomb will never go off, and I speak as an expert on explosives.
Admiral William Leahy to President Truman 1943. Quoted Chris Morgan and David Langford, FACTS AND FALLACIES

14 Surely if all the human race is obliterated the Creator will look rather foolish. But to whom?
George Lyttelton

15 The atom bomb is a paper tiger with which the Americans try to frighten people.
Mao Tse Tung. Speech 1946

16 And all because mankind would persist in tinkering with atoms.
George F. Morrell, This and That 2 Aug 1930

17 I am become Death, the shaker of worlds.
Dr Robert Oppenheimer, quoting a Hindu poem, after the Los Alamos test explosion 16 July 1945

18 The genius of Einstein leads to Hiroshima.
Pablo Picasso. Quoted Françoise Gilot and Carlton Lake, LIFE WITH PICASSO

ATOMIC ENERGY

19 The release of atomic power has changed everything except our way of thinking and thus we are being driven unarmed towards a catastrophe.
Albert Einstein. Quoted Carl Seilig's biography of him

20 We cannot control atomic energy to an extent which would be of any value commercially, and I believe we are not likely ever to be able to do so.
Prof. Ernest Rutherford. Speech to British Association for the Advancement of Science 1933

1 The terror of the atom age is not the violence
of the new power but the speed of man's
adjustment to it — the speed of his
acceptance.
E. B. White, THE SECOND TREE FROM THE
CORNER, *Notes On Our Time* 1953

ATROCITY

2 The greatest horrors in our world, from the
executions in Iran to the brutalities of the
IRA, are committed by people who are
totally sincere.
John Mortimer. Quoted Observer 5 Aug
1979

ATTENTION

3 I have always suffered from the diverted
attention of the two distinct general com-
partments of my mind. The one into which
the sun most rarely shines is the one
reserved for soul-stirring impressions. If a
monkey and a minaret were competing for
my attention, the monkey would always
win.
Stella Benson, THE LITTLE WORLD 1925

CLEMENT ATTLEE

4 An empty taxi drew up outside No. 10 and
out got Clem Attlee.
Anon.

5 Few thought him ever a starter / There were
many who thought themselves smarter / But
he ended PM, CH and OM / An Earl and a
Knight of the Garter.
Attlee, on himself

6 He seems determined to make a trumpet
sound like a tin whistle.
Aneurin Bevan, writing in Tribune 1945

7 He brings to the fierce struggle of politics
the tepid enthusiasm of a lazy summer
afternoon at a cricket match.
Ibid.

8 He is a sheep in sheep's clothing.
Winston Churchill

9 He is a modest little man with much to be
modest about.
Ibid.

10 He abandoned his visit to Australia for fear

that when the mouse was away the cats
would play.
*Winston Churchill, Quoted James Lee-
Milne*, DIARIES 1946-7 1983

11 Mr Attlee combines a limited outlook with
strong qualities of resistance.
Winston Churchill. Speech 27 Apr 1951

12 Mr Attlee touches nothing that he does not
dehydrate.
The Economist 16 *Aug* 1947

13 Labour's greatest triumph was scored under
Attlee who had the charisma of an average
building society branch manager.
*Eric Hobsbawm, Observer, Sayings of the
Week* 9 *Oct* 1983

14 He is a bourgeois who is strangling the
British bourgeoisie out of existence with a
smile.
Peter Howard, Daily Mail 28 May 1947

15 His capacity for saying nothing was absolutely pre-eminent and he avoided all the
traps which other people fell into. We used
to say he would never use one syllable where
none would do.
*Douglas Jay, Thames TV, The Day Before
Yesterday* 1970

16 I usually suggested a precise course of action
to which he need only reply 'Yes' or 'No'.
Among the longest comments I ever
extracted from him was 'Wouldn't serve any
useful purpose'.
Douglas Jay, CHANGE AND FORTUNE 1980

17 Charisma? He did not recognise the word,
except as a clue in his beloved *Times*
crossword.
James Margach, THE ABUSE OF POWER 1981

18 He succeeded in presiding over the biggest
social, political and economic revolutions of
the century. He never lost a single by-
election and after five years of ceaseless
press harassment he polled the highest
popular vote at any election before or since.
Ibid.

19 He was a man who tucked his personality
behind a pipe and left colleagues and public
to make what they could of the smoke
signals.
*Frederick Newman, in the Daily Sketch.
Quoted James Margach*, THE ABUSE OF
POWER 1981

1 Attlee is a charming man, but as a public speaker he is, compared to Winston, like a village fiddler after Paganini.
Harold Nicolson, DIARIES 10 *Nov* 1947

2 He reminds me of nothing so much as a dead fish before it has had time to stiffen.
George Orwell

3 He must have been pretty shrewd because he managed to escape from three conspiracies to throw him out.
Lord Shinwell, Thames TV, The Day Before Yesterday 1970

ATTRACTION

4 Men of every age flocked around her like gulls round a council tip.
John Carey, of Diana Cooper. Sunday Times 20 *Sep* 1981

5 They became, and remained, lovers for over 10 years. He said he was attracted to her 'hard mind'. She said she was attracted to him because he smelt of walnut.
Of Rebecca West and H. G. Wells, Guardian obituary 16 *Mar* 1983

ATTRIBUTION

6 I had far far rather that people should attribute my verses to you than yours to me.
A. E. Housman, to his brother Laurence, LETTERS *(edited by Henry Maas)*

W. H. AUDEN

7 We have one poet of genius in Auden who is able to write prolifically, carelessly and exquisitely, nor does he seem to have to pay any price for his inspiration. It is as if he worked under the influence of some mysterious drug, which presents him with a private vision, a mastery of form and vocabulary.
Cyril Connolly, ENEMIES OF PROMISE 1938

8 Auden is something of an intellectual jackdaw, picking up bright pebbles of ideas so as to fit them into exciting conceptual patterns.
Richard Hoggart, W. H. AUDEN 1951

9 One never steps twice into the same Auden.
Randall Jarrell, THE THIRD BOOK OF CRITICISM 1969

10 An engaging, bookish, American talent, too verbose to be memorable and too intellectual to be moving.
Philip Larkin. Quoted George T. Wright, W. H. AUDEN

11 He is all ice and woodenfaced acrobatics.
(Percy) Wyndham Lewis, BLASTING AND BOMBARDIERING 1937

12 The high watermark, so to speak, of Socialist literature is W. H. Auden, a sort of gutless Kipling.
George Orwell, THE ROAD TO WIGAN PIER 1937

AUDIENCE

13 Long experience has taught me that in England nobody goes to the theatre unless he or she has bronchitis.
James Agate, EGO 1935

14 Of the type of audience at a chamber-music concert an Oxford don once remarked 'They look like the sort of people who go to the English Church abroad'.
W. H. Auden, A CERTAIN WORLD

15 To go back to *Punch and Judy* — what acting could add anything to that tremendous drama? What a relief to think that the audience standing there in the Tottenham Court Road did not go away saying: 'She was very good, but that's not my idea of Judy'.
Maurice Baring. Quoted Dame Ethel Smyth, MAURICE BARING

16 You look as if you have lived on grass for three years, like the King in the Bible. On the whole I would prefer to conduct for people in deepest Africa who beat tom-toms and live on nuts.
Sir Thomas Beecham. Quoted Charles Reid, THOMAS BEECHAM

17 Audiences don't know anybody writes a picture. They think the actors make it up as they go along.
William Holden. Lines from film, SUNSET BOULEVARD

1 Those in the cheaper seats, clap; the rest of you rattle your jewellery.
John Lennon, at Royal Command Performance, Nov 1963

2 If one talks to more than four people it is an audience, and one cannot really exchange thoughts with an audience.
Anne Morrow Lindbergh, NORTH TO THE ORIENT 1935

3 The audience is not the least important actor in the play and if it will not do its allotted share the play falls to pieces.
W. Somerset Maugham, THE SUMMING UP 1938

4 If all the world's a stage, and all the men and women merely players, where do all the audiences come from?
Denis Norden, BBC Radio 4, *My Word* 30 *Feb* 1977

5 I never fully understood the need for a 'live' audience. My music, because of its extreme quietude, would be happiest with a dead one.
Igor Stravinsky, London Magazine, Mar 1967

6 There have been more complaints about our inaudible actors. Perhaps they do not wish to interrupt the conversation in the stalls and boxes.
Sunday Express 5 *Nov* 1933

7 In England they cough all the time and they don't know they're doing it. In America all you see is a sea of disappearing backs as they rush out, and in Australia they're always so hungry that they eat right through the performance.
Googie Withers at a Foyles Literary Lunch 12 *Jun* 1979

8 The audience strummed their catarrhs.
Alexander Woollcott, WHILE ROME BURNS 1934

AUNT

9 *Everyone* has an aunt in Tunbridge Wells.
Brian Johnston, BBC Radio 4, *Down Your Way* 24 *Mar* 1981

10 Why is it that the sudden mention of an aunt is so deflating to a poem?
Edward Marsh, AMBROSIA AND SMALL BEER

11 By the time one has educated them to an appreciation of the fact that one does not wear red woollen mittens in the West End, they die, or quarrel with the family, or do something equally inconsiderate.
Saki, REGINALD ON CHRISTMAS PRESENTS

12 Aunt Agatha . . . the Pest of Pont Street, the human snapping turtle.
P. G. Wodehouse, CARRY ON JEEVES 1925

13 It is no use telling me there are bad aunts and good aunts. At the core they are all alike. Sooner or later, out pops the cloven hoof.
P. G. Wodehouse, THE CODE OF THE WOOSTERS 1938

14 Aunt Agatha, who eats broken bottles and wears barbed wire next the skin.
Ibid.

15 Aunt Agatha's demeanour was now rather like that of one who, picking daisies on the railway, has just caught the down express in the small of the back.
P. G. Wodehouse, THE INIMITABLE JEEVES 1924

16 In this life it is not aunts that matter, but the courage one brings to them.
P. G. Wodehouse, THE MATING SEASON 1949

AUSTRALIA

17 Australia got me over my shyness.
Charles, Prince of Wales. Quoted Noël St George, ROYAL QUOTES

18 I couldn't imagine a better place for making a film on the end of the world.
Attr. Ava Gardner, of Melbourne. Quoted Keith Dunstan, KNOCKERS

19 The Sydney opera house looks like a typewriter full of oyster shells . . . like a broken Pyrex casserole dish in a brown cardboard box.
Clive James, Observer 23 *Oct* 1983

20 It was deathly still. Even the few birds seemed to be swamped in silence. Waiting — waiting — the bush seemed to be warily waiting. And he could not penetrate into its secret. He couldn't get at it. Nobody could get at it. What was it waiting for?
D. H. Lawrence, KANGAROO 1923

1 It's so empty and featureless, like a newspaper that has been entirely censored. We
used to drive for miles, always expecting
that round the next corner there would be
something to look at, and there never was.
That's the charm of Australia.
Robert Morley, RESPONSIBLE GENTLEMAN

AUTHOR

2 Is the bedroom door open or shut?
*Ruby M. Ayres, asking for editorial
instructions on being commissioned to write
a serial*

3 When I decided to write I didn't have any of
the background or equipment that was
considered necessary then. I thought all
authors were Englishmen.
*Rex Beach. Quoted in his obituary notice,
Reuters 8 Dec 1949*

4 When I am dead I hope it may be said / 'His
sins were scarlet, but his books were read.'
Hilaire Belloc, EPIGRAMS

5 Bad authors are those who write with
reference to an inner context which the
reader cannot know.
Albert Camus, NOTEBOOKS 1935—1942

6 Yes, I am exactly like the characters in my
books. I am very tough and have been
known to break a Vienna roll with my bare
hands. I am very handsome, have a powerful
physique and change my shirt every Mon-
day.
Raymond Chandler, RAYMOND CHANDLER
SPEAKING

7 A good novel tells us the truth about its
hero; but a bad novel tells us the truth about
its author.
G. K. Chesterton, HERETICS 1905

8 An author arrives at a good style when his
language performs what is required of it
without shyness.
Cyril Connolly, ENEMIES OF PROMISE 1938

9 Authors are sometimes like tomcats: they
distrust all the other toms but they are kind
to kittens.
Malcolm Cowley, WRITERS AT WORK 1958

10 I killed myself off at the end of my book
because it was high time.
*Bruce Frederick Cummings (W. N. P.
Barbellion) writing of his* JOURNAL OF A
DISAPPOINTED MAN

11 An author ought to write for the youth of his
own generation, the critics of the next, and
schoolmasters of ever after.
*F. Scott Fitzgerald. Quoted the Guardian 13
Nov 1964*

12 It does seem to me very bad to spend months
writing a book and then months constantly
being asked what you meant by it.
*Sir John Gielgud at a Foyles Literary Lunch
8 Feb 1979*

13 Authors are easy enough to get on with — if
you are fond of children.
*Michael Joseph. Quoted Observer 29 May
1949*

14 Being a novelist I consider myself superior
to the saint, the scientist, the philosopher
and the poet, who are all great masters of
different bits of life but never get the whole
hog.
D. H. Lawrence, PHOENIX 1936

15 Authors and uncaptured criminals are the
only people free from routine.
Eric Linklater, POET'S PUB 1925

16 I write for no other purpose than to add to
the beauty that now belongs to me. I write a
book for no other reason than to add three
or four hundred acres to my magnificent
estate.
*Jack London. Quoted Charles Child
Walcutt,* JACK LONDON

17 Almost anyone can be an author; the
business is to collect money and fame from
this state of being.
A. A. Milne, NOT THAT IT MATTERS 1919

18 I am the kind of writer that people think
other people are reading.
V. S. Naipaul, Radio Times 24 Mar 1979

19 In this country it is rare for anyone, let alone
a publisher, to take writers seriously.
*Anthony Powell, Daily Telegraph 8 Feb
1979*

20 Any man who becomes a novelist forfeits all
the rights to scholarship.
Anthony Powell, BBC Radio 3 6 Oct 1980

1 Real men do things. They don't just write about them.
Frederic Raphael, Sunday Times 8 Oct 1978

2 Everybody writes a book too many.
Mordecai Richler, Observer, Sayings of the Week 9 Jun 1985

3 Writing is not a profession, but a vocation of unhappiness.
Georges Simenon. Quoted John Heilpern, Observer 25 Mar 1979

4 I would never read a book if it were possible to talk for half an hour with the man who wrote it.
President Woodrow Wilson in a speech to students at Princeton University 1910

AUTHORITY

5 Anything you make a mistake about, I will get you out of, and anything you do well, I will take credit for.
Ernest Bevin to a subordinate. Quoted Alan Bullock, LIFE AND TIMES OF ERNEST BEVIN

6 There is one thing about being a president — nobody can tell you when to sit down.
President Dwight Eisenhower to an interviewer, Jul 1953

AUTOBIOGRAPHY

7 Autobiography is now as common as adultery and hardly less reprehensible.
Lord Altrincham. Quoted Leon Harris, THE FINE ART OF POLITICAL WIT

8 Autobiography is the outcome of a struggle in the author's brain between the desire to be truthful and the desire to be interesting.
Vernon Bartlett, I KNOW WHAT I LIKED

9 Autobiography, to be any good, must be largely untrue.
Patricia Beer, The Listener

10 Just as there is nothing between the admirable omelette and the intolerable, so with autobiography.
Hilaire Belloc, A CONVERSATION WITH A CAT

11 One learns little more about a man from the feats of his literary memory than from the feats of his alimentary canal.
F. M. Colby. Quoted C. Fadiman, READING I HAVE LIKED

12 An autobiography is an obituary in serial form with the last instalment missing.
Quentin Crisp, THE NAKED CIVIL SERVANT

13 Twenty-five seems to me the latest age at which anybody should write an autobiography. It has an air of finality about it, as though one had clambered to the summit of a great hill, and were waving goodbye to some distant country which can never be revisited.
Beverley Nichols, TWENTY-FIVE 1925

14 I have a certain hesitation in starting my biography too soon for fear of something important having not yet happened. Suppose I should end my days as President of Mexico; the biography would seem incomplete if it did not mention this fact.
Bertrand Russell. Letter to Stanley Unwin, Nov 1930

15 You'll want to know . . . all that David Copperfield type of crap. But I don't feel like going into it.
J. D. Salinger, CATCHER IN THE RYE 1951

16 Autobiographies ought to begin with Chapter Two.
Ellery Sedgwick, THE HAPPY PROFESSION

AUTOGRAPH

17 He seemed such a nice old gentleman I thought I would give him my autograph as a souvenir.
Adolf Hitler, of Austen Chamberlain after Munich

AUTUMN

18 Fallen leaves lying on the grass in November bring more happiness than daffodils.
Cyril Connolly, THE UNQUIET GRAVE 1945

19 Now it is autumn and the falling fruit / And the long journey to oblivion. / The apples falling like great drops of dew / To bruise themselves an exit from themselves.
D. H. Lawrence, THE SHIPS OF DEATH 1932

AVARICE

1 The trouble is, Mr Goldwyn, that you are only interested in art, and I am only interested in money.
George Bernard Shaw. Quoted Alva Johnson, THE GREAT GOLDWYN

AVERAGE

2 Most people are such fools that it is really no great compliment to say that a man is above the average.
W. Somerset Maugham, A WRITER'S NOTEBOOK 1949

AVIATION

3 It felt as if angels were pushing.
Adolf Galland, on flying a jet aircraft, THE FIRST AND THE LAST

4 The aeroplane will never fly.
Lord Haldane, Secretary for War 1907.
Quoted Chris Morgan and David Langford, FACTS AND FALLACIES

5 I don't know how old the plane was, but Lindbergh's lunch was still on the seat. The path to the washroom was outside.
Bob Hope, I OWE RUSSIA 1200 DOLLARS 1963

6 Concorde is great. It gives you three extra hours to find your luggage.
Bob Hope, to reporters at Heathrow

7 In the space age, man will be able to go around the world in two hours – one hour for the flying and the other to get to the airport.
Neil McElroy, Look Magazine 18 *Feb* 1958

8 The aeroplane has unveiled for us the true face of the earth.
Antoine de Saint-Exupéry, WIND, SAND AND STARS 1939

B

BABY

1 A baby is an alimentary canal with a loud voice at one end and no responsibility at the other.
E. Adamson

2 Save trouble and tiredness. Put the baby in a D-Baby Cot which folds up flat in a second and can be carried like an attache case.
Advertisement in Kent newspaper

3 There is no finer investment for any community than putting milk into babies.
Winston Churchill in a radio broadcast 21 *Mar* 1943

4 When Baby's cries grew harder to bear / I popped him in the Frigidaire / I never would have done so if / I'd known he'd be frozen stiff. / My wife said 'George I'm so unhappy / Our darling's now completely frappé'.
Harry Graham, MORE RUTHLESS RHYMES

5 We all of us wanted babies — but did we want children?
Eda J. Leshan. Quoted Katharine Whitehorn, HOW TO SURVIVE CHILDREN

6 A bit of talcum / Is always walcum.
Ogden Nash, REFLECTIONS ON BABIES

7 I can see that it is a very homely baby, indeed. Still I never see many babies that I consider rose geraniums for looks, anyway.
Damon Runyon, GUYS AND DOLLS 1932

8 How to fold a diaper depends on the size of the baby and the diaper.
Dr Benjamin Spock, BABY AND CHILD CARE 1941

9 There was in his possession a photograph of himself at the same early age, in which he, too, looked like a homicidal fried egg.
P. G. Wodehouse, SONNY BOY

BALDNESS

10 The only thing that can stop hair falling is the floor.
Will Rogers, AUTOBIOGRAPHY 1949

STANLEY BALDWIN

11 It is medicine man talk . . . Murmurs of admiration break out as this second-rate orator trails his tawdry wisps of mist over the parliamentary scene.
Aneurin Bevan, Tribune 1947

12 The candle in that great turnip has gone out.
Winston Churchill, on Baldwin's retirement. Quoted Harold Nicolson, DIARIES 17 *Aug* 1950

13 At times I could have murdered S.B. but I would always have voted him a state funeral.
Colin R. Coote, Daily Telegraph, A New Judgment on Baldwin 15 *Nov* 1973

14 Not even a public figure. A man of no experience. And of the utmost insignificance.
Lord Curzon, when passed over in favour of Baldwin as Prime Minister. Quoted Harold Nicolson, CURZON, THE LAST PHASE

15 Baldwin was never quite sure that anybody was right, especially himself.
Harold Macmillan, THE PAST MASTERS

16 As a man he was unattractive, with unpleasant habits, always scratching himself.
Diana Mosley, THE DUCHESS OF WINDSOR

17 Stanley Baldwin always hits the nail on the head, but it doesn't go in any further.
G. M. Young. Quoted G. W. Lyttelton, THE LYTTELTON HART-DAVIS LETTERS 2 *May* 1951

A. J. BALFOUR

18 He played politics in the same spirit as he played golf.
Robert Cecil, LIFE IN EDWARDIAN ENGLAND 1969

19 A lay priest seeking a secular goal.
Winston Churchill, GREAT CONTEMPORARIES 1937

1 A powerful, graceful cat, walking delicately and unsoiled across a rather muddy street.
Ibid.

2 He was eminently one of the Cole Porter school of famous men, who only fell to rise again. Picking himself up and brushing himself down became a minor art form, ruefully admired by his contemporaries.
Peter Clarke, Observer 12 May 1985

3 When Arthur Balfour launched his scheme for peopling Palestine with Jewish immigrants, I am credibly informed that he did not know there were Arabs in the country.
W. R. Inge (Dean of St Pauls), The Evening Standard

BANK

4 Banks lend you money as people lend you an umbrella when the sun is shining and want it back when it starts to rain.
Sir Edward Beddington-Behrens, LOOK BACK—LOOK FORWARD

TALLULAH BANKHEAD

5 Tallulah is always skating on thin ice. Everyone wants to be there when it breaks.
Mrs Patrick Campbell, The Times obituary 13 Dec 1968

J. M. BARRIE

6 When I began writing novels people said they were not real novels. When I began writing plays folk said they were not real plays. I expect they are going about now saying I am not a real baronet.
J. M. Barrie on receiving a knighthood. Quoted J. A. Hammerton, BARRIE: THE STORY OF A GENIUS

7 The cheerful clatter of Sir James Barrie's cans as he went round with the milk of human kindness.
Philip Guedella, SOME CRITICS

BATH

8 Whenever I have a bath I make a list of the things I am going to need and check it carefully before entering the water.
Patrick Campbell, Sunday Times

9 If you don't lock the bathroom some people are taking baths every day.
J. Glenton, speaking to Morecambe Hotels and Caterers' Association. Reported Morecambe Guardian

10 I test my bath before I sit / And I'm always moved to wonderment / That what chills the finger not a bit / Is so frigid upon the fundament.
Ogden Nash, SAMSON AGONISTES

11 MPs are protesting about a Gas Board advertisement urging couples to share a bath to save fuel. It shows a couple sharing a bath with the comment 'Put a bit of romance in your bath'. Mrs Ida Jones in an interview said 'I cannot understand what all the fuss is about. There's nothing wrong in it. It's better than a rubber duck.'
The Times 29 Jan 1974

12 I have had a good many more uplifting thoughts, creative and expansive visions, while soaking in comfortable baths or drying myself after bracing showers in well-equipped American bathrooms than I have ever had in any cathedral.
Edmund Wilson, A PIECE OF MY MIND 1956

BEARD

13 He had a thin vague beard, or rather he had a chin on which large numbers of hairs weakly curled and clustered to cover its retreat.
Max Beerbohm. Quoted S. C. Roberts, THE INCOMPARABLE MAX

14 Shaw's wife . . . implored Nancy [Astor] to look after him and make him wash his beard. These instructions Nancy carried out faithfully, to the point of washing Shaw's beard personally, in the Metropole Hotel, Moscow, watched by the fascinated hotel staff.
Geoffrey Bocca, Sunday Express, The Lady and the Commissar 5 Feb 1956

15 It always seemed to me that men wore their beards like they wore their neckties, for show.
D. H. Lawrence, ST. MAWR 1925

16 An irregular greying beard was a decoration to a face which badly needed assistance.
Edgar Wallace, AGAIN SAUNDERS 1931

THE BEATLES

1 Q. How do you rate your music?
   A. We're good musicians. Just adequate.
   Q. Then why are you so popular?
   A. Maybe people like adequate music.
   *The Beatles, in an interview. Quoted Nat
   Shapiro,* ENCYCLOPEDIA OF QUOTATIONS
   ABOUT MUSIC

2 Four in many ways ordinary young men
   subjected to unprecedented pressures and
   granted unprecedented freedoms. They
   could have anything money could buy, but
   they couldn't walk down the street.
   Peter Brown and Steven Gaines, THE LOVE
   YOU MAKE 1983

3 When you get to the top there is nowhere to
   go but down, but the Beatles could not get
   down. There they remain, unreachable,
   frozen, fabulous.
   Philip Larkin, Observer, Fighting the Fab
   9 Oct 1983

4 Their vulgar prodigality is impossible to
   summarise.
   Ibid.

5 Lots of people who complained about us
   receiving the MBE received theirs for
   heroism in war — for killing people. We
   received ours for entertaining other people.
   I'd say we deserve ours more.
   John Lennon, BEATLES ILLUSTRATED
   LYRICS

6 Do you remember when everyone began
   analysing Beatle songs? I don't think I
   understood what some of them were supposed to be about.
   Ringo Starr. Quoted Nat Shapiro,
   ENCYCLOPEDIA OF QUOTATIONS ABOUT
   MUSIC

BEAUTY

7 She looked very beautiful with some red
   roses in her hat and the dainty red rouge in
   her cheeks looking quite the thing.
   Daisy Ashford (aged 9), THE YOUNG
   VISITERS 1919

8 Her beauty sweetens her wit like honey on
   the tip of a dagger.
   Raymond Asquith of Lady Diana Manners,
   LIFE AND LETTERS

9 Only in romantic novels are the beautiful
   guaranteed happiness.
   Lady Cynthia Asquith, DIARIES

10 Incredibly, inordinately, devastatingly,
   immortally, calamitously, hearteningly,
   adorably beautiful.
   *Rupert Brooke of the actress Kathleen
   Nesbitt*

11 It is hard, if not impossible, to snub a
   beautiful woman — they remain beautiful
   and the snub recoils.
   Winston Churchill

12 Beauty often starts small and becomes
   immense.
   *Jean Cocteau in an interview with Derek
   Prouse, Sunday Times 20 Oct 1963*

13 Beautiful women must think about their
   beauty as capitalists think about their
   investments or politicians about their
   majorities; it is all they have to ensure their
   places in the world.
   Cyril Connolly, Sunday Times 21 Apr 1968

14 She was often underrated because she was
   so beautiful.
   *George Cukor, of Vivien Leigh. Quoted
   Gavin Lambert,* ON CUKOR

15 Only with beauty wake wild memories — /
   Sorrow for where you are, for where you
   would be.
   Walter De La Mare, THE CAGE

16 After a certain degree of prettiness, one
   pretty girl is as pretty as another.
   F. Scott Fitzgerald, THE CRACK-UP 1936

17 Nonsense and beauty have close connec-
   tions.
   E. M. Forster, THE LONGEST JOURNEY
   1907

18 Think of all the beauty still left around you
   and be happy.
   Anne Frank, DIARY OF A YOUNG GIRL 1952

19 Beauty is intrinsically edifying.
   Aldous Huxley, TIME MUST HAVE A
   STOP 1944

20 I'm tired of all this nonsense about beauty
   only being skin deep. That's deep enough.
   What do you want — an adorable
   pancreas?
   Jean Kerr, THE SNAKE HAS ALL THE LINES

1 Beauty is an *experience*, nothing else. It is not a fixed pattern or an arrangement of features. It is something *felt*.
D. H. Lawrence, ESSAYS

2 Beauty you lifted up my sleeping eye / And filled my heart with longing with a look.
John Masefield, SONNETS

3 Beauty is perfect, and perfection (such is human nature) holds our attention for but a little while . . . Let us face it, beauty is a bit of a bore.
W. Somerset Maugham, CAKES AND ALE 1930

4 The beautiful should be defined as that of which the admiring contemplation is good in itself.
G. E. Moore, PRINCIPIA ETHICA 1903

5 Beauty is everlasting / And dust is for a time.
Marianne Moore, IN DISTRUST OF MERITS 1951

6 Beauty is a sequence of hypotheses which ugliness cuts short when it bars the way that we could already see opening into the unknown.
Marcel Proust, REMEMBRANCE OF THINGS PAST 1913—1927

7 Beauty is all very well at first, but who ever looks at it when it has been in the house three days?
George Bernard Shaw, MAN AND SUPERMAN 1905

8 All ugliness passes and beauty endures; except of the skin.
Edith Sitwell, LETTERS

9 Use harms and even destroys beauty. The noblest function of an object is to be contemplated.
Miguel de Unamuno, MIST

10 The beauty of the world has two edges, one of laughter, one of anguish, cutting the heart asunder.
Virginia Woolf, A ROOM OF ONE'S OWN 1929

LORD BEAVERBROOK

11 Beaverbrook is so pleased to be in the Government that he is like the town tart who has finally married the Mayor.
Beverley Baxter. Quoted Henry Channon, DIARY 12 *Jun* 1940

12 The Beaver is not a bad man; he is a bad boy.
John Buchan. Quoted Observer 29 *May* 1949

13 David Lloyd George called at Chertley Court near Leatherhead where Beaverbrook lived, to consult his friend about a current political conspiracy.
'Is the lord at home?' he asked the butler.
'No sir, the lord is out walking.'
'Ah', said Lloyd George. 'On the water, I presume.'
Hugh Cudlipp, WALKING ON THE WATER 1976

SAMUEL BECKETT

14 You either like Samuel Beckett's plays or you think they are a heap of twaddle. They remind me of something Sir John Betjeman might do if you filled him up with benzedrine and then force-fed him Guinness intravenously.
Tom Davis, Observer 17 *Jun* 1979

15 He believed in this kind of literature being a kind of murmur, out of which sense gradually should emerge.
Martin Esslin on Samuel Beckett's radio work, The Listener 25 *Nov* 82

BED

16 The cool kindness of sheets that soon smooth away trouble; and the rough male kiss of blankets.
Rupert Brooke, THE GREAT LOVER

17 Personally I am a great believer in bed, in constantly keeping horizontal. The heart and everything else goes slower and the whole system is refreshed.
Sir Henry Campbell-Bannerman. Letter to Mrs Whiteley 11 *Sep* 1900

18 I am surprised that none of your correspondents has proposed the obvious solution [to reading in bed] — the provision of a series of slits in the bedclothes through which the hands may be projected in the manner of the old-fashioned Turkish bath box. When not in use the slits may be closed by zips or buttons.
H. Malcolm Carter. Letter to The Times 10 *Jan* 1962

1 No civilised person ever goes to bed the same day he gets up.
Richard Harding Davis, GALLAGHER

2 Dr Marie Stopes could not and would not sleep unless her bed was aligned north to south. If unable to move it she would lie across it slantwise, correctly orientated.
Mary Eden and Richard Carrington, THE PHILOSOPHY OF THE BED

3 When my husband reads in bed on warm nights he puts a colander over his head. He says it keeps off the flies, shades his eyes from the light, and lets in air at the same time.
Letter to Good Shopping. Quoted New Statesman

4 No human being believes that any other human being has a right to be in bed when he himself is up.
Robert Lynd, RAIN, RAIN GO TO SPAIN

5 I forget who it was that recommended men for their souls' sake to do each day two things they disliked. It is a precept that I have followed scrupulously; for every day I have got up and I have gone to bed.
W. Somerset Maugham, THE MOON AND SIXPENCE 1919

6 It was such a lovely day I thought it was a pity to get up.
W. Somerset Maugham, OUR BETTERS 1923

7 He really is a hero for his bed. I have known him often being *tired* of laying in bed, get up to have a rest, and after he had rested get back into bed again like a martyr.
Henry Moat. Quoted Sir Osbert Sitwell, THE SCARLET TREE 1945

8 So we switched on the emotion heater and went to bed.
Overheard. Quoted Mary Malcolm, BBC Radio, Quote Unquote 4 Feb 1981

9 To prevent bedtime from becoming monotonous my husband gets into bed at the right side on Mondays and Tuesdays, the left side on Wednesdays and Thursdays, and climbs the footboard on Fridays, Saturdays and Sundays.
Letter to Reveille. Quoted New Statesman.

10 Rose is a wonderful hand for making up beds, although several times, when she is in a hurry to get off, I hear she makes up beds with guests still in them.
Damon Runyon, MORE THAN SOMEWHAT 1937

BEE

11 And bees will stand / Upon their hands in fragrant deeps.
W. H. Davies, COMPLETE POEMS, *Days Too Short* 1943

12 Forget not bees in winter though they sleep.
Vita Sackville-West, THE LAND 1926

13 A German general claims that bees can now be enrolled as spies. They have strong homing instincts and can carry messages by means of varying colours painted on their backs.
Titbits 14 Mar 1936

14 According to the theory of dynamics and as may be readily demonstrated through wind-tunnel experiments, the bumble-bee is unable to fly. This is because the size, weight and shape of his body in relation to the total wingspread makes flying impossible. But the bumble bee, being ignorant of these scientific facts, goes ahead and flies anyway — and makes a little honey every day.
War-time sign in General Motors factory

15 A dark Assyrian beard began to grow on one of the topmost twigs of the elm. The bees were clustering about the new queen.
Henry Williamson, LIFE IN A DEVON VILLAGE 1935

SIR THOMAS BEECHAM

16 I was always touched by the friendliness and humility beneath the brilliant exterior. Remember he always bowed first to the *orchestra* and only secondly to the audience.
Richard Arnell, BEECHAM REMEMBERED *(edited by Humphrey Proctor-Gregg)*

17 There was a break in the recording session of an opera in the Kingsway Hall. Sir Thomas was alone when some recording engineers entered and one asked how things were progressing.
'Reasonably well,' said Sir Thomas, 'But I sometimes long for the days of the old castrati. You knew where you were with them.'
Harold Atkins and Archie Norman, BEECHAM STORIES

1 Beecham was deeply rooted in provincial England. In this respect he resembled Arnold Bennett. One from Lancashire, one from the Potteries. Both enjoyed being thought of as 'cards' which indeed they were.
Lord Boothby, MY YESTERDAY, YOUR TOMORROW 1962

2 A complex character — Falstaff, Puck and Malvolio all mixed up, each likely to overwhelm the others. Witty, then waggish, supercilious, then genial, kindly and sometimes cruel, an artist in affectation, yet somehow always himself. Lancashire in his bones, yet a man of the world.
Neville Cardus, SIR THOMAS BEECHAM

BEGGING

3 Once I built a railroad, now its done / Brother can you spare a dime.
Edgar Y. Harburg (song) 1932

BEGINNING

4 With the possible exception of the equator, everything begins somewhere.
Peter Fleming, ONE'S COMPANY

5 You're searching, Joe / For things that don't exist. I mean beginnings. / Ends and beginnings — there are no such things / There are only middles.
Robert Frost, IN THE HOME STRETCH

BEHAVIOUR

6 He neither drank, smoked, nor rode a bicycle. Living frugally, saving his money, he died early, surrounded by greedy relatives. It was a great lesson to me.
John Barrymore. Quoted J. P. McEvoy, Stage, Jan 1941

7 There is no surer way of calling the worst out of anyone than that of taking their worst as being their true selves; no surer way of bringing out the best than by only accepting that as being true of them.
E. F. Benson, REX

8 You must never do that! That's what little French boys do.
Sir Hugh Casson and Joyce Grenfell, NANNY SAYS 1972

9 Sit up straight at the table so there's room for a mouse at the front and a cat at the back.
Ibid.

10 Shoddy table manners have broken up many a happy bond.
Colette, GIGI 1945

11 I like to eat with nice people, drink with nice people, and sleep with a clear conscience.
Lord Denning, Observer, Sayings of the Week 18 Jul 1982

12 A man's ethical behaviour should be based effectually on sympathy, education and social ties and needs; no religious basis is necessary. Man would indeed be in a poor way if he had to be restrained by fear of punishment and hope of reward after death.
Albert Einstein, New York Times Magazine, Religion and Science 9 Nov 1930

13 If you live among wolves you have to act like a wolf.
Nikita Khrushchev, Observer, Sayings of the Week 1964

14 Many things — such as loving, going to sleep or behaving unaffectedly — are done worst when we try hardest to do them.
C. S. Lewis, STUDIES IN MEDIEVAL AND RENAISSANCE LITERATURE

15 He is Harrow and Oxford, and often behaves like Borstal and Parkhurst.
Reginald Pound of Beachcomber (J. B. Morton), THEIR MOODS AND MINE 1935

16 I never observe rules of conduct, and therefore have given up making them.
George Bernard Shaw. Quoted Hesketh Pearson, BERNARD SHAW 1942

17 If people behaved in the way nations do they would all be put into straitjackets.
Tennessee Williams on BBC Radio

BEHAVIOURISM

18 Behaviourism has substituted for the erstwhile anthropomorphic view of the rat a ratomorphic view of man.
Arthur Koestler, THE GHOST IN THE MACHINE

19 Behaviourism is a kind of flat-earth view of the mind.
Ibid.

1 If 'mind' acts on body, then all physical laws are invalid.
John Broadus Watson, BEHAVIOURISM

BELIEF

2 What matters to me is not whether it is true or not but that I believe it to be true, or rather not that I *believe* it, but that *I* believe it — I trust I make myself obscure?
Robert Bolt, A MAN FOR ALL SEASONS 1960

3 If people stop believing in religion they don't then believe in nothing, they believe in everything.
G. K. Chesterton. Quoted Katherine Whitehorn, Observer 16 *Sep* 1979

4 The majority of people live below the level of belief or doubt. It takes application and a kind of genius to believe anything.
T. S. Eliot, THE ENEMY

5 A man must not swallow more beliefs than he can digest.
Havelock Ellis, THE DANCE OF LIFE 1923

6 My dear child, you must believe in God in spite of what the clergy tell you.
Dr Benjamin Jowett on his death bed.
Quoted Margot Asquith,
AUTOBIOGRAPHY 1936

7 The constant assertion of belief is an indication of fear.
Krishnamurti, THE PENGUIN KRISHNAMURTI READER

8 No amount of manifest absurdity could deter those who wanted to believe from believing.
Bernard Levin, THE PENDULUM YEARS 1976

9 The world goes on because a few men in each generation believe in it utterly, accept it unquestioningly, they underwrite it with their lives.
Henry Miller, THE AIR-CONDITIONED NIGHTMARE 1945

10 You're not free / Until you have been made captive by / Supreme belief.
Marianne Moore, COLLECTED POEMS, *Spencer's Ireland* 1951

11 In view of the widespread silliness of the majority of mankind a widespread belief is more likely to be foolish than sensible.
Bertrand Russell, MARRIAGE AND MORALS 1929

12 The brute necessity of believing something so long as life lasts does not justify any belief in particular.
George Santayana, SCEPTICISM AND ANIMAL FAITH 1923

13 I confused things with their names. That is belief.
Jean-Paul Sartre, WORDS

14 When Cardinal Newman was a child he 'wished he could believe the Arabian Nights were true'. When he came to be a man his wish seems to have been granted.
Lytton Strachey, EMINENT VICTORIANS 1918

15 To believe in God is to yearn for His existence and furthermore, it is to act as if He did exist.
Miguel de Unamuno, THE TRAGIC SENSE OF LIFE 1913

16 You don't have to believe in witches to admire Macbeth.
David Willcocks. Quoted Geoffrey Wansell, *Sunday Telegraph Magazine* 18 *Jun* 1985

BELLS

17 I heard the church bells hollowing out the sky, / Deep beyond deep, like never-ending stars, / And turned to Archibald, my safe old bear, / Whose woollen eyes looked sad or glad at me.
Sir John Betjeman, SUMMONED BY BELLS 1960

TONY BENN

18 He is the Bertie Wooster of Marxism.
Reported by Malcolm Bradbury in BBC Radio 4, Quote Unquote 13 *Sep* 1979

19 He led the left, not through any rigorous approach, but through dazzling rhetoric and an instinctive popularism, owing much of his appeal to his ability to always appear thoroughly English, reasonable and Christian.
Anthony Sampson, THE CHANGING ANATOMY OF BRITAIN 1982

1 Tony Benn proposed to his beloved while sitting on an Oxford park bench. She said yes. Benn was so carried away by that golden moment that he wrote to the City Council pleading with it to let him buy the bench. The council agreed and Benn had it placed in the garden of his London home as a permanent reminder of his love.
The Times, Diary, 8 Aug 1985

2 I have always said about Tony that he immatures with age.
Sir Harold Wilson, THE CHARIOT OF ISRAEL

ARNOLD BENNETT

3 Bennett — a sort of pig in clover.
D. H. Lawrence, letter to Aldous Huxley 27 Mar 1928

4 He never outgrew the provincialism that made the Savoy Hotel in his eyes the Earthly Paradise.
S. P. B. Mais, ALL THE DAYS OF MY LIFE

BEREAVEMENT

5 She revealed such a depth and intensity of suffering as made me feel one could never be happy while she was alive. She regards the remainder of her life as a bad debt to be discharged.
Lady Cynthia Asquith of her widowed sister-in-law, DIARIES 1915

6 Not the least hard thing to bear when they go away from us, these quiet friends [dogs] is that they carry away with them so many years of our own lives.
John Galsworthy, MEMOIRS

7 Life after 35 is one long memorial service.
Lady Hartwell. Quoted Roy Strong, The Times 8 Oct 1983

8 It was sea and islands now. Atlantis had sunk.
C. S. Lewis on the death of his mother, SURPRISED BY JOY, The Shape of My Early Life 1965

9 Passionate grief does not link us with the dead but cuts us off from them.
C. S. Lewis, A GRIEF OBSERVED

10 I am not resigned to the shuttering away of loving hearts in the hard ground. / So it is,

and so it will be, for so it has been, time out of mind. / Into the darkness they go, the wise and the lovely. Crowned / With lilies and with laurel they go; but I am not resigned.
Edna St Vincent Millay, DIRGE WITHOUT MUSIC 1928

11 One reason you are stricken when your parents die is that the audience you've been aiming at all your life — shocking it, pleasing it — has suddenly left the theatre.
Katharine Whitehorn, Observer, Act Your Self 4 Dec 1983

SIR JOHN BETJEMAN

12 He has a passion for Victoriana / Nostalgia flows like lava from his quill / How lovely the remembered dreams of Cornwall! / How long the golden days of Muswell Hill.
Roger Woddis, Radio Times, Far more than freckled girls 12 Feb 1983

BETRAYAL

13 All a man can betray is his conscience.
Joseph Conrad, UNDER WESTERN EYES 1911

14 If I had to choose between betraying my country and betraying my friend I hope I should have the guts to betray my country.
E. M. Forster, WHAT I BELIEVE

15 Greater love hath no man than this, that he lay down his friends for his life.
Jeremy Thorpe, of Selwyn Lloyd's dismissal as Chancellor of the Exchequer by Harold Macmillan 13 Jul 1962

ANEURIN BEVAN

16 That squalid nuisance and Welsh soapbox buccaneer.
James Robertson Armstrong, founder of the Vermin Club. Quoted News Review 19 Aug 1948

17 If thy Nye offend thee, pluck it out.
Clement Attlee to Labour NEC, Mar 1955

18 He will be as great a curse to this country in peace as he was a squalid nuisance in time of war.
Winston Churchill. Quoted Robert Lewis Taylor, THE AMAZING MR CHURCHILL

1 A merchant of discourtesy.
Winston Churchill. Quoted Michael Foot,
ANEURIN BEVAN, VOL. 1

2 Nye wasn't cut out to be a leader. He was cut
out to be a prophet. It's no joke being leader
of the Labour Party, and Nye didn't want
the bother; he just wanted to have it all led
for him.
*Richard Crossman, Thames TV, The Day
Before Yesterday* 1970

3 He was like a fire in a room on a cold day.
*Constance Cummings. Quoted Michael
Foot,* ANEURIN BEVAN 1897—1945

4 Repent, for the kingdom of Bevan is Nye.
Election slogan, Northampton 1959

5 He should have been a poet, political parties
only chain such spirits.
Michael Foot, ANEURIN BEVAN 1945—1960

6 Aneurin Bevan was a true orator in the
sense that even on quite important issues he
did not know what he was going to say until
he had said it.
*Paul Johnson, Daily Telegraph, Searching
for a Phrase* 27 Jul 1979

7 He could boil blood with the evidence of
misery, split sides with his jests, and make
spirits soar with his visions.
Neil Kinnock, The Times 3 May 1982

8 Nye was born old and died young.
Jennie Lee. Quoted Michael Foot, ANEURIN
BEVAN 1897—1945

9 An ideal Welsh type, the Prophet Aneurin;
fatal charm, magic voice, exquisite sensi-
tiveness to beauty, and a liability to break
loose at any moment and create 15 different
kinds of roaring hell.
Timothy Shy, News Chronicle 1946

ERNEST BEVIN

10 A speech from Ernest Bevin on a major
occasion had all the horrific fascination of a
public execution. If the mind was left
immune, eyes and ears and emotions were
riveted.
Michael Foot, ANEURIN BEVAN

11 Bevin always treated the Soviet Union as if
it were a breakaway faction of the Transport
and General Workers Union.
Kingsley Martin, HAROLD LASKI

12 He objected to ideas only when others had
them.
A. J. P. Taylor, ENGLISH HISTORY 1914–1945

13 Bevin thought he was Palmerston wearing
Keir Hardie's cloth cap, whereas he was
really the Foreign Office's Charlie McCar-
thy.
Konni Zilliacus. Quoted Kingsley Martin,
HAROLD LASKI

BIBLE

14 Had the Bible been in clear straightforward
language, had the ambiguities and contradictions been edited out, and had the
language been constantly modernised to
accord with contemporary taste it would
almost certainly have been, or become, a
work of lesser influence.
J. K. Galbraith, ECONOMICS, PEACE AND
LAUGHTER

15 THE NUMBER ONE BOOK OF THE
AGES WAS WRITTEN BY A COMMIT-
TEE, AND IT WAS CALLED THE Bible.
Louis B. Mayer. Quoted Leslie Halliwell,
FILMGOER'S BOOK OF QUOTATIONS 1973

16 A lady's husband seeks compensation by
reading the lessons in church with great
gusto, particularly such passages as deal
with fornication.
Douglas Sutherland, THE ENGLISH
GENTLEMAN'S WIFE 1979

BIGAMY

17 Sometimes people commit bigamy to please
the landlady.
*Sir Gerald Dodson. Quoted Observer,
Sayings of the Week* 18 Oct 1942

18 'That's bigamy.'
'Yes and its big of me, too. It's big of all of
us. I'm sick of these conventional marriages.
One woman and one man was good enough
for your grandmother, but who wants to
marry your grandmother? Nobody, not
even your grandfather.'
Groucho Marx, ANIMAL CRACKERS

19 The plural of spouse is spice.
Robert Morley

1 My wife is going to be very nervous when she hears about this. My wife is very strict with me. My wife does not allow me to go around marrying people.
Damon Runyon, MORE THAN SOMEWHAT 1937

BIGOTRY

2 We call a man a bigot or a slave of dogma because he is a thinker who has thought thoroughly and to a definite end.
G. K. Chesterton, ALL THINGS CONSIDERED 1908

3 The more you are right, the more natural that everyone else should be bullied into thinking likewise.
George Orwell, SELECTED ESSAYS 1968

4 How it infuriates a bigot when he is forced to drag into the light his dark convictions.
Logan Pearsall Smith, ALL TRIVIA, *Afterthoughts* 1931

5 Bigotry tries to keep truth safe in its hand with a grip that kills it.
Rabindranath Tagore, FIREFLIES 1928

6 Human beings are perhaps never more frightening than when they are convinced beyond doubt that they are right.
Laurens Van Der Post, THE LOST WORLD OF THE KALAHARI 1958

BIOGRAPHY

7 A biography without humour is almost too great a burden to be endured.
Peter Ackroyd, Sunday Times, 13 Oct 1985

8 Biography should be written by an acute enemy.
A. J. Balfour. Quoted S. K. Ratcliffe, Observer 30 Jan 1927

9 The art of Biography / Is different from Geography / Geography is about maps / Biography is about chaps.
E. C. Bentley, BIOGRAPHY FOR BEGINNERS

10 I read biographies to see how other people handled problems like mine.
James Callaghan, interview with Kenneth Harris, Observer 3 Dec 1976

11 I enjoy reading biographies because I want to know about the people who messed up the world.
Marie Dressler, Passing Show 3 Feb 1934

12 Not all the secrets of the human heart are known to official biographers.
Lord Francis-Williams, A PATTERN OF RULERS

13 Literary biography is a progressive disease. As one predator leaves the host another arrives. What authorised biographies eschew can be made the basis of another, better-selling version.
Germaine Greer. Speech to Folio Society 30 Jan 1986

14 Biography, like big-game hunting, is one of the recognised forms of sport, and it is as unfair as only sport can be.
Philip Guedella, SUPERS AND SUPERMAN

15 It simplifies even while seeking to enrich.
Henry James. Quoted Leon Edel, HENRY JAMES, THE MASTER 1901—1916

16 It is by no means true that the major figures of history are the most interesting. Indeed, in a sense, the opposite is the case. Those who take the leading roles in the world of action are so obvious that there is really nothing to say about them, and vice versa.
Malcolm Muggeridge, TREAD SOFTLY FOR YOU TREAD ON MY JOKES 1966

17 Biography, if it is to enhance understanding, add to history or interpret character, must be constructive and not destructive.
Harold Nicolson, The Times 20 Mar 1949

18 It is perhaps as difficult to write a good life as to live one.
Lytton Strachey. Quoted as epigraph to John Gunther's ROOSEVELT IN RETROSPECT

19 After you have traced a man down to the last munched bath bun you are still left with the whole mystery of art of "the madness of art".
Tony Tanner, reviewing Leon Edel's, HENRY JAMES, THE MASTER 1901—1916, *The Times* 3 Aug 1972

20 The primary duty of a serious biographer is to illuminate his subject's life work, not to play the spy in his bedroom.
Philip Toynbee, reviewing Vincent Broome's HAVELOCK ELLIS, PHILOSOPHER OF SEX, *Observer* 18 Mar 1979

1 The best sort of book to start with is biography. If you want to make a success of it, choose as a subject someone very famous who has had plenty of books written about him quite recently. Many young writers make the mistake of choosing some forgotten Caroline clergyman or eighteenth-century traveller.
Evelyn Waugh, Passing Show, The Way to Fame 2 Feb 1929

2 A biographical account of a person is like an embalmed body with the organs and guts taken out.
H. G. Wells

3 There is so little information about Marshal Louis Nicolas Davout, one of the leaders of Napoleon's army, that a Huddersfield man is writing his biography.
Yorkshire Post. Quoted Punch 23 Feb 1972

BIRD

4 And hear the pleasant cuckoo loud and long / The simple bird that thinks two notes a song.
W. H. Davies, APRIL CHARMS

5 All thrushes (not only those in this neck of the Glyndebourne woods) sooner or later sing the tune of the first subject of Mozart's G Minor Symphony (K. 550) — and what's more phrase it a sight better than most conductors. The tempo is always dead right and there is no suggestion of an unauthorised accent on the ninth note of the phrase.
Spike Hughes, letter to The Times 15 Jun 1962

6 Cuckoos, like noise falling in drops off leaves.
D. H. Lawrence, FANTASIA OF THE UNCONSCIOUS 1922

7 A fly can't bird, but a bird can fly.
A. A. Milne, WINNIE THE POOH 1926

LORD BIRKENHEAD (F. E. SMITH)

8 Lord Birkenhead is very clever but sometimes his brains go to his head.
Margot Asquith, AUTOBIOGRAPHY 1936

9 'Who is this Effie Smith?' asked an old lady when the country was ringing with his maiden speech. 'She can't be a modest girl to be talked about so much.'
2nd Earl of Birkenhead, F.E. — THE LIFE OF F.E. SMITH, FIRST EARL OF BIRKENHEAD

10 He was an orator in an age of mutterers.
Ibid.

BIRTH

11 When Lady Louise Moncrieff's last [sixteenth] child was born her sister, Lady Elizabeth Arthur was present and called out, 'It's all right, Louise, and you have got another little boy!' And the reply of the poor tired lady was: 'My dear, I really don't care if it is a parrot.'
Lord Ormathwaite, WHEN I WAS AT COURT

12 Congratulations. We all knew you had it in you.
Dorothy Parker, telegram to a friend who had just become a mother. Quoted Alexander Woollcott, WHILE ROME BURNS, *Our Mrs Parker* 1934

13 I was born because it was a habit in those days. People didn't know any different.
Will Rogers, AUTOBIOGRAPHY 1949

14 He is always breaking the law. He broke the law when he was born. His parents were not married.
George Bernard Shaw, MAJOR BARBARA 1905

15 What a perfect escape the return to the womb was. Better by far than Religion or Art or the South Sea Islands. It was so snug and warm there, and the feeding was automatic. Everything perfect in that hotel. No wonder the memory of those accommodations lingered in the blood and nerves of everyone. It was dark, yes, but what a warm, rich darkness. The grave wasn't in it. No wonder one fought so desperately against being evicted when the nine months' lease was up.
Nathanael West, THE DAY OF THE LOCUST 1939

BIRTHDAY

16 It's strange how I seem to spend my birthdays away from home. I must subcon-

sciously arrange these trips so the dagger of time pierces an empty bed.
John Updike. Quoted John Heilpern, Observer 25 Mar 1979

BIRTH-RATE

1 Despite the efforts of Mussolini and the Pope, the birthrate of Italy is declining.
Nancy Astor. Quoted John Beevers, Sunday Referee 19 Feb 1939

OTTO VON BISMARCK

2 If the sole duty of a statesman is to do the best he can for his country, then Bismarck did his duty. If, between nations, honour and justice count for anything, then Bismarck was a bandit.
Kenneth Bell, Teacher's World, The Iron Chancellor, Sep 1929

3 If he was never foolish enough to say 'power transcends right' that, nevertheless, was his belief.
Emil Ludwig, BISMARCK, THE STORY OF A FIGHTER

BLAME

4 Her whole life was governed by her desire not to be blamed, so she never did anything, and got blamed for that.
Gerald Brenan, THOUGHTS IN A DRY SEASON 1979

BLASPHEMY

5 Blasphemy itself could not survive religion; if anyone doubts that let him try to blaspheme Odin.
G. K. Chesterton, Daily News 25 Jun 1904

6 Beware of the community in which blasphemy does not exist; underneath, atheism runs rampant.
Antonio Machado, JUAN DE MAIRENA 1943

BLINDNESS

7 A picture gallery is a dull place for a blind man.
George Bernard Shaw, MAN AND SUPERMAN 1905

BLOOMSBURY

8 An article in *Harper's* by Duncan Grant's granddaughter explained how he'd taught her to roast an egg in a bonfire.
Frances Donnelly, The Listener, Bloomsbury Boom 5 Aug 1982

BOASTFULNESS

9 Christianity will go. We're more popular than Jesus now.
John Lennon 1966

10 A boaster is not always a liar.
Eric Partridge, John o'London's Weekly 7 Oct 1938

11 The Hon. Mrs Ronald Greville likes to boast that in a single morning three kings had been sitting on her bed; presumably not all at the same time.
Kenneth Rose, KINGS, QUEENS AND COURTIERS 1985

BOAT

12 Believe me my young friend there is nothing — absolutely nothing — half so much worth doing as simply messing about in boats.
Kenneth Grahame, WIND IN THE WILLOWS 1908

BOGNOR

13 Bugger Bognor!
Reputedly George V's last words (he had recently been there for his health and it was suggested he might return)

BOOK

14 This book tells more about penguins than I am interested in knowing.
Attr. to unknown schoolchild's essay

15 A best-seller is a book which somehow sells well because it is selling well.
Daniel Boorstin, THE IMAGE 1962

16 Books most of all resemble us in their precarious hold on life.
Joseph Conrad, NOTES ON LIFE AND LETTERS 1921

1 A book is not harmless merely because no one is consciously offended by it.
T. S. Eliot, RELIGION AND LITERATURE

2 One always tends to overpraise a long book because one has got through it.
E. M. Forster, ASPECTS OF THE NOVEL 1927

3 I know every book of mine by its scent, and I have but to put my nose between its pages to be reminded of all sorts of things.
George Gissing, THE PRIVATE PAPERS OF HENRY RYECROFT 1903

4 Even bad books are books and therefore sacred.
Günther Grass, THE TIN DRUM 1962

5 Books of poems lying around are handy / For killing persistent irritating flies.
Geoffrey Grigson, HISTORY OF HIM 1951

6 All good books are alike in that they are truer than if they really happened and after you are finished reading one you will feel that all that happened to you, and afterwards it all belongs to you.
Ernest Hemingway

7 The mortality of all inanimate things is terrible to me, but that of books most of all.
William Dean Howells. Letter to Charles Eliot Norton 6 Apr 1903

8 The proper study of mankind is books.
Aldous Huxley, CROME YELLOW 1921

9 The librarian gave Geordie 'Mother Goose's Nursery Rhymes'. Geordie read it from cover to cover, and when I asked him how he liked it he said 'It's nowt but a pack of lies.'
Gerald Kersh, THE NINE LIVES OF BILL NELSON 1941

10 Few books today are forgivable.
R. D. Laing, THE POLITICS OF EXPERIENCE

11 Books are a load of crap.
Philip Larkin, A STUDY OF READING HABITS

12 My books are not scandalous, not sexy, and the story waves about from place to place — and yet, much to my surprise, they are still in print.
Laurie Lee in an interview with Philip Radcliffe, Observer 8 Jan 1979

13 Book — the noblest sound that man has yet uttered.
Bernard Levin, TAKING SIDES

14 It's not a dirty book, it's an earthy book, which is a very different thing.
Librarian to borrower. Cartoon caption in the New Yorker

15 Books have no value in themselves. They are valuable because they make more real, more interesting, more effective the other things that readers are doing, thinking, feeling and enjoying.
Lionel McColvin, THE PERSONAL LIBRARY

16 Many of those who make insufficient use of books neglect them because they mistakenly regard books as something separate and apart from life; because they think of 'books' as synonymous with literature.
Ibid.

17 In the main there are two sorts of books; those that no one reads, and those that no one ought to read.
H. L. Mencken, PREJUDICES 1919

18 If good books did good, the world would have been converted long ago.
George Moore, HAIL AND FAREWELL 1914

19 There are some books which cannot be adequately reviewed for twenty or thirty years after they come out.
John Morley, RECOLLECTIONS 1917

20 Booksellers' returns and the computer have freed the modern bookbuyer from the agonies of decision making. Once a book has been declared a bestseller, its sales accelerate — like the freshwater polyp, the best seller breeds from itself — and the book-buyer can happily accept the judgment of the great majority.
Frank Muir, THE FRANK MUIR BOOK 1976

21 An anthologist is a lazy fellow who likes to spend a quiet evening at home raiding good books.
Dorothy Parker

22 This is not a novel to be tossed aside lightly. It should be thrown with great force.
Ibid.

23 Surely there's enough happiness in life without having to go to books for it.
Ibid.

1 At last, an unprintable book that is readable.
Ezra Pound of Henry Miller's TROPIC OF CANCER

2 You might think the least important thing about a book is its title. Surely what matters is the content. And yet one fusses over the title for hours, as if, like the figurehead of some romantic merchantman, it conferred magic properties on the ship and all who sailed in her.
Gerald Priestland, PRIESTLAND'S PROGRESS 1982

3 We all know that books burn — yet we have the greater knowledge that books cannot be killed by fire. People die, but books never die.
Franklin D. Roosevelt, to American Booksellers Association 23 *Apr* 1942

4 A best seller is the gilded tomb of a mediocre talent.
Logan Pearsall Smith, ALL TRIVIA, *Afterthoughts* 1931

5 Give me a bed and a book and I am happy.
Ibid.

6 Much is written of the power of the Press, a power which may last but a day; by comparison little is heard of the power of books, which may endure for generations.
Sir Stanley Unwin, THE TRUTH ABOUT PUBLISHING

7 Books, I don't know what you see in them . . . I can understand a person reading them, but I can't for the life of me see why people have to write them.
Peter Ustinov, PHOTO-FINISH

8 One book's very like another — after all what is it? Something to read and be done with. It's not a thing that matters like print dresses and serviettes — where you either like 'em or don't, and people judge you by them.
H. G. Wells, KIPPS 1905

BORE

9 For *deliberate* and *intentional* boring you must have a man of some ability to practise it well, as you must practise any art well.
Hilaire Belloc, CONVERSATION WITH A CAT

10 *Bore*: a person who talks when you wish him to listen.
Ambrose Bierce, THE DEVIL'S DICTIONARY 1906

11 The English sent all their bores abroad and acquired the empire as a punishment.
Edward Bond, NARROW ROAD TO THE DEEP NORTH

12 Tony was a first class bore. He had a habit of choosing a subject and then droning round and round it like an inaccurate bomb-aimer round his target, ever unable to hit.
Nancy Mitford, THE PURSUIT OF LOVE 1945

13 He's an old bore. Even the grave yawns for him.
H. Beerbohm Tree, of Israel Zangwill. Quoted by Hesketh Pearson, BEERBOHM TREE

14 A healthy male bore consumes, *each year* one and a half times his own weight in other people's patience.
John Updike, ASSORTED PROSE 1965

15 Rather inclined to collar the conversation and turn it in the direction of his home town's water supply.
P. G. Wodehouse, MY MAN JEEVES 1919

BOREDOM

16 Millions long for immortality who do not know what to do with themselves on a rainy Sunday afternoon.
Susan Ertz, ANGER IN THE SKY

17 Boredom, which would engulf whole towns in the Middle Ages, and which, because it was a denial of life itself, was made an offence against God by the Church.
Ian Fleming. Quoted John Pearson, LIFE OF IAN FLEMING

18 It is not surprising that boredom — in human beings so often the mask of fear — is a problem in marriage as it is a problem in prayer.
Monica Furlong, CHRISTIAN UNCERTAINTIES 1975

19 No society seems ever to have succumbed to boredom. Man has developed an obvious capacity for surviving the pompous reiteration of the commonplace.
J. K. Galbraith, THE AFFLUENT SOCIETY 1958

1 Living in Coventry is about as interesting as watching a plank warp.
Graffito. Quoted Nigel Rees GRAFFITI 2 1980

2 Boredom seemed to swell like a balloon inside the head; it became a pressure inside the skull; sometimes I feared this balloon would burst and I would lose my reason.
Graham Greene, A SORT OF LIFE

3 The effect of boredom on a large scale in history is underestimated. It is a main cause of revolutions, and would soon bring to an end all the static Utopias and the farmyard civilisation of the Fabians.
W. R. Inge (Dean of St Pauls), THE END OF AN AGE 1948

4 The average male gets his living by such depressing devices that boredom becomes a sort of natural state to him.
H. L. Mencken, IN DEFENCE OF WOMEN

5 Boredom is a vital problem for the moralist, since half the sins of mankind are caused by the fear of it.
Bertrand Russell, THE CONQUEST OF HAPPINESS 1930

6 One can be bored until boredom becomes a mystical experience.
Logan Pearsall Smith, ALL TRIVIA 1931

7 Somebody's boring me, and I think it's me.
Attr. Dylan Thomas, BBC Radio 4, Quote Unquote 21 Jun 1980

BOURGEOIS

8 I call bourgeois anyone who says no to himself, who gives up struggle and renounces love in favour of his security. I call bourgeois anyone who places anything above feeling.
Léon-Paul Farque, SOUS LA LAMPE

9 The bourgeois prefers comfort to pleasure, convenience to liberty, and a pleasant temperature to the deathly inner consuming fire.
Hermann Hesse, TREATISE ON THE STEPPENWOLF 1927

10 How beastly the bourgeois is / Especially the male of the species.
D. H. Lawrence, HOW BEASTLY THE BOURGEOIS IS 1929

11 The British Bourgeoisie / Is not born / And does not die / But if it is ill / It has a frightened look in its eyes.
Osbert Sitwell, AT THE HOUSE OF MRS KINFOOT

BOXING

12 Because a boxer gets hurt, should they stop boxing? That would be crazy. More people die in bath tubs.
Muhammad Ali, Observer, Sayings of the Week 23 Sep 1984

13 He [Muhammad Ali] stings like a bee but lives like a WASP.
Eamonn Andrews, Punch 23 Feb 1972

14 There is nothing bellicose about boxing. It is fully in keeping with the principles of the United Nations Organisation.
Field-Marshal Montgomery. Quoted News Review 20 May 1948

15 Among the boxing fraternity there is an adage — first the timing goes, then the legs, then the mind and then the friends. That is the history of many people who thought boxing an easy way to riches.
Lord Taylor of Gryfe, introducing the defeated Boxing Bill, House of Lords 26 Nov 1981

16 Boxing is glamorised violence.
Ibid.

BOY SCOUT

17 I have seen thousands of boys and young men, narrow-chested, hunched-up, miserable specimens, smoking endless cigarettes, many of them betting.
Sir Robert Baden-Powell, explaining his reasons for starting the Boy Scout movement 1907

18 The Boer War was obviously a good thing in the end because it was the cause of Boy Scouts and of their remarkable Chief Scout, General Baden Powell (known affectionately as BOP.)
W. C. Sellar and R. J. Yeatman, 1066 AND ALL THAT 1930

BRAIN

1 My brain; it's my second favourite organ.
Woody Allen and Marshall Brickman,
SLEEPER *(film)*

2 Brain – an apparatus with which we think we
think.
Ambrose Bierce, THE DEVIL'S
DICTIONARY 1906

3 Never trust men with short legs. Brains too
near their bottoms.
Noël Coward. Quoted Nancy McPhee,
BOOK OF INSULTS

4 The brain is a wonderful organ; it starts
working the moment you get up in the
morning, and does not stop until you get to
the office.
Robert Frost

5 If the human brain was simple enough for us
to understand we'd be so simple we
couldn't.
Graffito. Quoted Nigel Rees, GRAFFITI 2

6 So this gentleman said a girl with brains
ought to do something with them besides
think.
Anita Loos, GENTLEMEN PREFER
BLONDES 1925

7 What good are brains to a man? They only
unsettle him.
P. G. Wodehouse, ADVENTURES OF
SALLY 1920

BRAVERY

8 There is no such thing as bravery; only
degrees of fear.
*John Wainwright. Quoted Philippa
Toomey, The Times* 30 *Jul* 1980

BREAD

9 You can travel fifty thousand miles in
America without once tasting good bread.
Henry Miller, REMEMBER TO REMEMBER,
The Staff of Life 1947

10 How important bread is to a nation and how
utterly are we betrayed in this country. If
Mother's proud she must be the only one.
Robert Morley, MORLEY MARVELS,
Sloshing and Noshing 1976

11 Bread is an emotive substance. Shortage of
it has traditionally been a sign of dangerous
irritation among those prone to riot.
Daily Telegraph leader 9 *Nov* 1978

BREAKFAST

12 He was the old buster who, a few years later,
came down to breakfast one morning, lifted
the first cover he saw, said 'Eggs! Eggs!
Eggs! Damn all eggs' in an overwrought sort
of voice and instantly legged it for France,
never to return to the bosom of his family.
P. G. Wodehouse, JEEVES TAKES CHARGE

13 I hadn't the heart to touch my breakfast. I
told Jeeves to drink it himself.
P. G. Wodehouse, MY MAN JEEVES 1919

BERTOLT BRECHT

14 He could make a horse act.
Lotte Lenya, BBC1 TV 24 *May* 1979

15 It [the Days of the Commune] has . . . the
eloquence of a conversation between a
speak-your-weight machine and a whoopee
cushion.
Bernard Levin, Sunday Times 6 *Nov* 1977

BRIBERY

16 When their lordships asked Bacon / How
many bribes he had taken / He had at least
the grace / To get very red in the face.
Hilaire Belloc, BASELESS BIOGRAPHY

17 Unlike the alleged Good Woman of the
Bible, I'm not above rubies.
Saki, REGINALD ON CHRISTMAS PRESENTS

BRITISH EMPIRE

18 Britain is necessarily the world's worst
offender as a colonial power. She may be
said to be the best of the worst.
*Nnamdi Azikiwe, Nigerian politician, News
Review* 24 *Jul* 1947

19 When we speak of Empire it is in no spirit of
flag-wagging. We feel that in this great
inheritance of ours, separated as it is by the
seas, we have yet one home and one people.
Stanley Baldwin. Speech 5 *Dec* 1924

1 The British Empire has done so much harm to so many nations and peoples that it deserves to perish.
William Scawen Blunt, MY DIARIES 1889–1914

2 Learn to think imperially.
Joseph Chamberlain. Speech, London Guildhall 19 Jan 1904

3 I have not become the King's First Minister in order to preside over the liquidation of the British Empire.
Winston Churchill, Lord Mayor's Banquet 10 Nov 1942

4 It may well be that Britain will be more honoured by the historian for the way in which she disposed of an empire than for the way she acquired it.
Sir David Ormsby Gore. Press interview 28 Oct 1962

5 You know why the sun never sets on the British Empire, don't you? It doesn't trust it.
Gilbert Harding. Quoted Wallace Reyburn, GILBERT HARDING : A CANDID PORTRAYAL 1979

6 A great Empire will be destroyed which it was never my intention to destroy or even to harm.
Adolf Hitler. Speech 19 Jul 1940

7 Britain was led by adventurers when she built her empire. Today she is ruled merely by incompetents.
Adolf Hitler. Quoted Alan Bullock, HITLER

8 It took God longer to write the Bible than it has taken him to build the British Empire.
William C. MacDonald, MODERN EVANGELISM

9 Providence is on the side of the British Empire after all.
Lord Northcliffe, on hearing how Kitchener had drowned when HMS Hampshire was sunk by a mine. Quoted A. J. P. Taylor, ENGLISH HISTORY 1914–1945

10 The so-called British Empire is in reality an *English* empire, of which Ireland, Scotland and Wales formed the original colonies.
F. A. Ridley, Socialist Leader, Feb 1948

11 The British Empire is one of the greatest enslavers of human beings in the world.
Paul Robeson. Quoted News Review 3 Oct 1946

12 Gentlemen like to hoard relics of the great days of the British Empire — assegais from the Matabele campaign, daggers from China and a solar topee with a hole in the brim where great-uncle George tried to shoot himself in Pondicherry and missed.
Douglas Sutherland, THE ENGLISH GENTLEMAN 1978

13 From the day it broke away from the British Empire the United States has been living in large measure under the protection of that Empire, and in particular of the British Fleet.
President Harry S Truman. Quoted News Review 20 Mar 1947

14 Other nations use 'force'; we Britons alone use 'might'.
Evelyn Waugh, SCOOP 1938

BENJAMIN BRITTEN

15 I may not be the best living composer, but I'm certainly the busiest.
Benjamin Britten of himself to William Plomer, ELECTRIC DELIGHTS

BROADCASTING

16 Of all the things that are broadcast, the thing which gives me the greatest delight and to which I can listen however tired I am, is the sound of Big Ben.
Stanley Baldwin, BBC dinner 16 Dec 1926

17 *ITMA* is the average man's equivalent of *Finnegan's Wake*
Arthur Calder-Marshall, Tribune

18 If I possessed the power of conveying unlimited sexual attraction through the potency of my voice I would not be reduced to accepting a miserable pittance from the BBC for interviewing a faded female in a damp basement.
Gilbert Harding on being asked to sound more sexy when interviewing Mae West. Quoted in his biography

19 I consider radio to be an advanced form of television. The pictures on TV are very drab and mundane compared to the mental pictures produced by radio.
Miles Kington, The Times 6 Mar 1986

1 We have got to the stage where, both in radio and television news, agonising over auxiliaries is a prevalent malaise. There is a feeling among newsreaders that they are enhancing their own importance and giving the impression of midden journalistic subtlety by perpetuating the same solecisms. Readers should be taught to discern and stick to the facts and to avoid shaded, argumentative or opinionated inflections.
Alvar Lidell, The Listener 7 *Apr* 1979

2 The BBC to me is like democracy – a good thing that those who run it do their best to spoil.
G. W. Lyttelton, THE LYTTELTON HART-DAVIS LETTERS 30 *Nov* 1955

3 It is a sobering thought that eighty per cent of listeners are doing something else while they are listening to the radio.
Aubrey Singer, director BBC Radio, at a press interview 5 *Mar* 1979

BROADMINDEDNESS

4 Human beings never shocked him, never surprised him. He viewed them like the priest in the confessional whose penitent said 'I have committed murder' and who merely enquired 'How many times?'
Charles Curran MP of Sir Beverley Baxter, The Times 4 *May* 1964

BUCKINGHAM PALACE

5 You've got a smashing house here for a matinee.
Bud Flanagan to the Duke of Edinburgh on being invested with the OBE 1959

6 This isn't ours. It's a tied cottage.
Philip, Duke of Edinburgh. Quoted Noël St George, ROYAL QUOTES

7 We live in what virtually amounts to a museum — which does not happen to a lot of people.
Ibid.

BULLFIGHTING

8 Bullfighting is the only art in which the artist is in danger of death and in which the degree of brilliance in the performance is left to the fighter's honour.

Ernest Hemingway, DEATH IN THE AFTERNOON 1932

BUREAUCRACY

9 The perfect bureaucrat everywhere is the man who manages to make no decisions, and escape all responsibility.
Brooks Atkinson, ONCE AROUND THE SUN 1951

10 Some civil servants are neither servants nor civil.
Winston Churchill. Quoted Walter H. Toms in a letter to the Observer 8 *Apr* 1979

11 Though park railings in Manchester are being removed for scrap, the park gates will be retained and locked at night to indicate that the parks are officially shut.
Daily Despatch

12 In the Nuts (unground) (other than groundnuts) Order, the expression nuts will have relevance to such nuts other than groundnuts as would but for this amending order not qualify as nuts (unground) (other than groundnuts) by reason of their being nuts (unground).
Government amendment

13 Official dignity tends to increase in inverse ratio to the importance of the country in which the office is held.
Aldous Huxley, BEYOND THE MEXIQUE BAY 1934

14 A civil servant doesn't make jokes.
Eugene Ionesco, THE KILLER 1958

15 The perfect civil servant is the man who has a valid objection to any possible solution.
A. H. Keates. Speech to Institute of Hospital Management, Connaught Rooms 16 *May* 1965

16 He picked up a slip of paper and a blue pencil, intending to write the word *Balls*. But the pencil broke and as he sharpened it the gentleman remembered where he was; he compromised, wrote *Round Objects*, inserted the slip and pushed the file aside. Many weeks later the file came back to him with a note from the Director General which said 'Who is Mr Round, and why does he object?'
Gerald Kersh, CLEAN, BRIGHT AND SLIGHTLY OILED 1946

1 For the purpose of this part of the schedule a person over pensionable age, not being an insured person, shall be treated as an employed person if he would be an insured person were he under pensionable age and would be an employed person were he an insured person.
National Insurance Bill, first schedule

2 It will be observed that air travel, considered as a retirement-accelerator, has the advantage of including a fair amount of form-filling.
C. Northcote Parkinson, PARKINSON'S LAW 1957

3 An Edinburgh doctor raised money to get a television set for a disabled patient. He then asked the post office if the man's licence fee could be reduced. 'Only,' said an official, 'if the disabled man was also blind.'
Kenneth Robinson, Punch 9 Feb 1972

4 The exercise of power is agreeable, especially when it is an obscure individual who exercises power over a prominent one.
Bertrand Russell, American Mercury, May 1940

5 The working of great institutions is mainly the result of a vast mass of routine, petty malice, self interest, carelessness and sheer mistake. Only a residual fraction is thought.
George Santayana, THE CRIME OF GALILEO

6 There is something about a bureaucrat that does not like a poem.
Gore Vidal, SEX, DEATH AND MONEY *(Preface)*

BURGLAR

7 A burglar who respects his art always takes his time before he takes anything else.
O. Henry, MAKES THE WHOLE WORLD KIN

BUSINESS

8 Always let the man you are doing business with make some money.
Jarvis Astaire, TACTICS: THE ART AND SCIENCE OF SUCCESS. (*ed. Edward de Bono*) 1985

9 The gambling known as business looks with austere disfavour on the business known as gambling.
Ambrose Bierce. Quoted H. L. Mencken.

10 A business that makes nothing but money is a poor kind of business.
Henry Ford. Interview 1919

11 Chaplin is no business man — all he knows is that he can't take any less.
Sam Goldwyn. Quoted Charles Chaplin, MY AUTOBIOGRAPHY 1964

12 The aim of all legitimate business is service, for profit, at a risk.
Benjamin C. Leeming, IMAGINATION

13 Few have heard of Fra Luca Parioli, the inventor of double-entry book-keeping; but he has probably had more influence on human life than has Dante or Michelangelo.
Herbert J. Muller, USES OF THE PAST

14 The secret of business is to know something that nobody else knows.
Aristotle Onassis

15 The trouble with senior management, I notice as an outsider, is that there are too many one-ulcer men holding down two-ulcer men's jobs.
Philip, Duke of Edinburgh. Speech 7 May 1963

16 Business only contributes fully to society if it is efficient, successful, profitable and socially responsible.
Lord Sieff, Observer, Sayings of the Week 30 *Aug* 1981

R. A. BUTLER

17 His great failing is that he likes to be a don among politicians and a politician among dons.
Iain Macleod. Quoted Patrick Cosgrave, R. A. BUTLER, AN ENGLISH LIFE

BUTTERFLY

18 The butterfly counts not months but moments, and has time enough.
Rabindranath Tagore, FIREFLIES 1928

C

CALIFORNIA

1 California is a fine place to live in — if you happen to be an orange.
Fred Allen, American Radio Show

2 I met a Californian who would / Talk California – a state so blessed / He said, in climate, none had ever died there / A natural death, and Vigilance Committees / Had had to organise to stock the graveyards / And vindicate the state's humanity.
Robert Frost, NEW HAMPSHIRE 1923

3 California is a great spot for meeting people who come from some place else.
Christopher Isherwood. Quoted Michael Davie, Observer Magazine 12 Aug 1984

JAMES CALLAGHAN

4 If Hugh Gaitskell's motto was 'fight, fight and fight again' then Jim Callaghan's is 'manœuvre, manœuvre and manœuvre again'.
Ian Bradley, The Times 16 Oct 1980

5 There is nobody in politics I can remember, and no case I can think of in history where a man combined such a powerful political personality with so little intelligence.
Roy Jenkins. Quoted Richard Crossman, DIARIES 5 Sep 1969

6 He's inordinately ambitious and inordinately weak. So weak that as Chancellor he used to weep on my shoulder and then go away and intrigue against me. That's a pretty fair analysis.
Harold Wilson. Ibid. 4 Sep 1969

7 That fellow is getting above himself. We must teach him a lesson. I'll do so after Cabinet tomorrow.
Harold Wilson. Ibid. 29 May 1969.

8 I'm having to hold his hand. His nerve isn't very good these days.
Harold Wilson of James Callaghan as Chancellor of the Exchequer 1964

CAMBRIDGE

9 For Cambridge people rarely smile, / Being urban, squat and packed with guile.
Rupert Brooke, THE OLD VICARAGE, GRANTCHESTER 1912

10 There, much is good because so little is new.
J. K. Galbraith, A LIFE IN OUR TIMES 1982

11 I find Cambridge an asylum, in every sense of the word.
Attr. A. E. Housman

12 Cambridge — the romantic dream of those who never went there.
Malcolm Muggeridge, BBC TV 26 Feb 1981

13 Cambridge is the city of perspiring dreams.
Frederic Raphael, THE GLITTERING PRIZES

14 Trinity is like a dead body in a high state of putrefaction. The only interest of it is the worms that come out of it.
Lytton Strachey. Quoted Michael Holroyd, LYTTON STRACHEY

CAMEL

15 The trouble with camels is that they expel foul smells — from both ends at once.
Charles, Prince of Wales, after riding one at Olympia 13 Dec 1979

16 Our camels sniff the evening and are glad.
James Elroy Flecker, THE GOLDEN JOURNEY TO SAMARKAND 1913

17 'Humph yourself'
And the camel humphed himself.
Rudyard Kipling, HOW THE CAMEL GOT ITS HUMP 1902

1 The camel has a single hump / The dromed-
ary two / Or else the other way around / I'm
never sure. Are you?
Ogden Nash, THE CAMEL

CANADA

2 Canada is a country so square that even the
female impersonators are women.
Richard Benner, OUTRAGEOUS *(film script)*

3 You have to know a man awfully well in
Canada to know his surname.
John Buchan. Quoted Observer 24 *May*
1950

4 I don't even know what street Canada is on.
Al Capone

CANARY

5 The song of canaries / Never varies / And
when they're molting / They're revolting.
Ogden Nash, CUSTARD AND CO.

CANDIDATE

6 Any American who is prepared to run for
President should automatically, by defini-
tion, be disqualified from ever doing so.
Gore Vidal

CANNIBAL

7 A cannibal is a guy who goes into a
restaurant and orders the waiter.
Jack Benny, radio script

8 They were inclined to cook their captives
alive, as we do lobsters, to improve their
flavour.
Rose Macaulay, THE TOWERS OF
TREBIZOND 1956

9 If cannibals should ever catch me I hope
they will say 'We have eaten Dr Schweitzer
and he was good to the end — and the end
wasn't bad'.
Dr Albert Schweitzer

CAPABILITY

10 I do not think thinking about a situation
does much good. One knows by instinct
what one can do.
A. C. Benson, letter to M.E.A.

CAPITALISM

11 Capitalism without bankruptcy is like
Christianity without hell.
*Frank Borman, chief of Eastern Airways,
Observer, Sayings of the Week, 6 Mar* 1986

12 History suggests that capitalism is a necessary condition for political freedom. Clearly
it is not a sufficient condition.
Milton Friedman, CAPITALISM AND
FREEDOM

13 The system of private property is the most
important guarantee of freedom, not only
for those who own property but scarcely less
for those who do not.
Friedrich August von Hayek, THE ROAD TO
SERFDOM

14 It is the unacceptable face of capitalism but
one should not suggest that the whole of
British industry consists of practices of this
kind.
Edward Heath of the Lonrho Affair 1973

15 The forces of a capitalist society, if left
unchecked, tend to make the rich richer and
the poor poorer.
Jawaharlal Nehru, CREDO

16 Capitalism inevitably and by virtue of the
very logic of its civilisation creates, educates
and subsidises a vested interest in social
unrest.
Joseph Alois Schumpeter, CAPITALISM,
SOCIALISM AND DEMOCRACY

17 There is in the capitalist system a tendency
towards self-destruction.
Ibid.

CAREER

18 A dictionary definition of career is 'A
head-long rush, usually downhill'. Not a bad
description really.
Michael Bentine, THE LONG BANANA SKIN

CARELESSNESS

19 Carelessness about our security is dangerous; carelessness about our freedom is also
dangerous.
Adlai Stevenson. Speech, Detroit 7 *Oct* 1952

CARICATURE

1 I seemed to have mislaid my gift for dispraise. Pity crept in. So I gave up caricaturing, except privately.
Max Beerbohm. Quoted S. N. Behrens, CONVERSATION WITH MAX 1960

2 Caricature shows society, sometimes quite literally, the arse of history.
William Feaver, MASTERS OF CARICATURE

3 Caricature shows society, not as it would choose to be shown, but with its breeches down.
George Melly, Observer magazine, Irreverent Images 16 *Aug* 1981

JIMMY CARTER

4 He is the only man since my dear husband died, to have the effrontery to kiss me on the lips.
Queen Elizabeth, the Queen Mother. Quoted Peter Hillman, Observer 13 *Feb* 1983

5 I don't know what people have got against Jimmy Carter. He's done nothing.
Bob Hope. Election campaign speech for Ronald Reagan 2 *Nov* 1980

CAT

6 A cat that lives with a good family is used to being talked to all the time.
Lettice Cooper, PARKIN

7 You always ought to have tom cats arranged, you know — it makes 'em more companionable.
Noël Coward, CAT'S CRADLE

8 Within that porch, across the way / I see two naked eyes this night / Two eyes that neither shut nor blink / Searching my face with a green light / But cats to me are strange, so strange / I cannot sleep if one is near; / And though I'm sure I see those eyes / I'm not so sure a body's there!
W. H. Davies, THE CAT

9 What cats most appreciate in a human being is not the ability to produce food which they take for granted but his or her entertainment value.
Geoffrey Household, ROGUE MALE

10 The cat — He walked by himself and all places were alike to him.
Rudyard Kipling, JUST SO STORIES 1902

11 A black cat dropped soundlessly from a high wall, like a spoonful of dark treacle, and melted under a gate.
Elizabeth Lemarchand, ALIBI FOR A CORPSE

12 I would never wound a cat's feelings, no matter how downright aggressive I might be to humans.
A. L. Rowse, THREE CORNISH CATS

13 A. L. Rowse is the only person I know who used to ring up one of his cats from the United States. They apparently had lively interchanges.
Roy Strong, The Times 5 *Nov* 1983

14 'We have cats the way other people have mice. (signed) Mrs C. L. Footloose'
'I see you have. I can't tell from your communication whether you wish advice or are just boasting'.
James Thurber, MY LIFE AND HARD TIMES 1933

15 I have just been given a very engaging Persian Kitten . . . and his opinion is that *I* have been given to *him*.
Evelyn Underhill, LETTERS

CATHEDRAL

16 Cathedrals, / Luxury liners laden with souls, / Holding to the east their hulls of stone.
W. H. Auden, ON THIS ISLAND XVII

CAUTION

17 As carefully as an out of work showgirl uses her last good pair of stockings.
Raymond Chandler, THE BIG SLEEP 1939

18 Didn't you hear me keeping still?
Sam Goldwyn. Quoted Alva Johnson, THE GREAT GOLDWYN

19 When one finds oneself in the middle of a minefield it is seldom wise to get up and run.
Michael Howard, reviewing PROTEST AND SURVIVE, *by E. P. Thomson and Dan Smith, Sunday Times* 9 *Nov* 1980

1 Set the foot down with distrust on the crust
of the world – it is thin.
Edna St Vincent Millay, HUNTSMAN, WHAT
QUARRY?, *Underground System*
1939

2 If we shake hands with icy fingers it is
because we have burnt them so horribly
before.
Logan Pearsall Smith, ALL TRIVIA,
Afterthoughts 1931

3 Closing the door with the delicate caution of
one brushing flies off a sleeping Venus, he
passed out of my life.
P. G. Wodehouse, VERY GOOD JEEVES,
Jeeves and the Old School Chum

CELIBACY

4 If every man gave up women in God's
name / Where in God's name would be the
men / To give up women in a generation's
time?
Christopher Fry, CARTMANTLE 1962

5 Celibacy is not an inherited characteristic.
Graffito. Quoted Nigel Rees, GRAFFITI
LIVES OK

CENSORSHIP

6 What the country wants in its police is that
they should be the guardians of law and
order and not, as there is a tendency for
them now to try to be, censors of public
morals.
*Lord Balfour of Burleigh on the Savidge
Case* 1928

7 This film is apparently meaningless, but if it
has any meaning it is doubtless objection-
able.
*British Board of Film Censors, banning Jean
Cocteau's* THE SEASHELL AND THE
CLERGYMAN 1956

8 Lord Longford is against us reading or
seeing things that keep our minds below the
navel.
William Hardcastle, Punch 1 *Dec* 1972

9 I shall judge films as I would horseflesh or a
dog. I shall look for clean lines.
*Major Harding de Fontlangue Cox. Quoted
Sunday Express*

10 The trouble with censors is they worry if a
girl has cleavage. They ought to worry if she
hasn't any.
Marilyn Monroe. Quoted Leslie Halliwell,
FILMGOER'S BOOK OF QUOTES 1973

11 Censors are paid to have dirty minds.
John Trevelyan, British film censor 1970

CEREMONY

12 I am unaccustomed to unveiling busts of
any sort, but . . . I now complete the
process of helping my father to expose
himself.
*Prince Charles, unveiling a sculpture of the
Duke of Edinburgh at the Royal Thames
Yacht Club*

13 Middle-aged men dressing up like refugees
from a pack of cards.
Philip Howard, The Times 4 *Nov* 1981

14 A lot of time and energy has been spent in
arranging for you to listen to me take a long
time to declare open a building which
everyone knows is open already.
*Philip, Duke of Edinburgh. Speech in
Chesterfield* 21 *Nov* 1958

15 I declare this thing open – whatever it is.
*Philip, Duke of Edinburgh, opening an
annex to Vancouver City Hall*

16 Ceremonial is an art form that embodies the
continuation of the nation, and the deposit
of history.
Sir Arthur Wagner. Quoted ibid.

AUSTEN CHAMBERLAIN

17 He is more loyal to his friends than to his
convictions.
Margot Asquith, AUTOBIOGRAPHY 1936

18 He always plays the game, And he always
loses it.
Winston Churchill

JOSEPH CHAMBERLAIN

19 Like many successful organisers he has an
uninteresting mind.
Margot Asquith, AUTOBIOGRAPHY 1936

NEVILLE CHAMBERLAIN

1 It was like a visit to Woolworths. Everything in its place and nothing over sixpence.
Aneurin Bevan, of a speech by Neville Chamberlain

2 That old town clerk, looking at foreign affairs through the wrong end of a municipal drain pipe.
Attr. Winston Churchill, after Munich, by R. L. Taylor, THE AMAZING MR CHURCHILL; *but also attr. to David Lloyd George by Leon Harris,* THE FINE ART OF POLITICAL WIT

3 In the depths of that dusty soul there is nothing but abject surrender.
Winston Churchill

4 The people of Birmingham have a specially heavy burden for they have given the world the curse of the present British Prime Minister.
Sir Stafford Cripps. Speech, Birmingham 18 *Mar* 1938

5 An unremarkable figure; gaunt, with bushy eyebrows and old-fashioned moustache, but no democratically endearing features.
Robert Graves and Alan Hodge, THE LONG WEEKEND 1940

6 He seemed such a nice old gentleman that I thought I would give him my autograph as a souvenir.
Adolf Hitler after Munich

7 He did not know the language of war.
Lord Home, LETTERS TO A GRANDSON 1983

8 He was a meticulous housemaid, great at tidying up.
A. J. P. Taylor, ENGLISH HISTORY 1916—1945

9 Praise be to God and to Mr Chamberlain. I find no sacrilege, no bathos, in coupling those two names.
Godfrey Winn, Daily Express, after Munich

CHAMBERPOTS

. 10 Pots, chamber, plain. Pots, chamber, with Admiralty monogram in blue, for hospital. Pots, chamber, fluted, with royal cypher in gold, for flag officers only. Pots, chamber, round, rubber, lunatic.
Classification of chamber pots on an Admiralty stores list

CHANCE

11 Random my bottom! A true miracle say I. / For who is not certain that he was meant to be.
W. H. Auden

12 Who knows how much turns on whether a Prime Minister's pipe is clean or foul, or the head of the Foreign Office has had sufficiency of sleep?
Lord Horder, THE LITTLE GENIUS

CHANGE

13 Most of the change we think we see in life / Is due to truths being in and out of favour.
Robert Frost, THE BLACK COTTAGE 1914

14 Every institution not only carries within it the seeds of its own dissolution but prepares the way for its most hated rival.
W. R. Inge (Dean of St Pauls), OUTSPOKEN ESSAYS, *The Victorian Age* 1922

15 We do not succeed in changing things according to our desire, but gradually our desire changes.
Marcel Proust, REMEMBRANCE OF THINGS PAST, *The Fugitive* 1925

CHAOS

16 Chaos often breeds life, when order breeds habit.
Henry Brooks Adams, THE EDUCATION OF HENRY ADAMS 1918

17 The whole world's in a state o' chassis.
Sean O'Casey, JUNO AND THE PAYCOCK 1924

CHARLIE CHAPLIN

18 I remain one thing and one thing only, and that is a clown. It places me on a far higher plane than any politician.
Charlie Chaplin, AUTOBIOGRAPHY 1964

19 Chaplin's genius was in comedy. He had no sense of humour.
Lita Grey, ex-wife. Quoted Richard Lamparski, WHATEVER BECAME OF—? 1983

1 He pitied everything that stumbled or whimpered or wagged a tail, particularly he pitied himself. There has never been a portrait of self pity so vivid or so shocking as Charlie with a rose in his hand.
Robert Hatch, Reporter 25 Nov 1952

2 . . . somehow importing to the peeling of a banana the elegant nonchalance of a duke drawing a monogrammed cigarette from a platinum case.
Alexander Woollcott, WHILE ROME BURNS 1934

CHARACTER

3 He is a very hard guy indeed. In fact I hear the softest thing about him is his front teeth.
Damon Runyon, MORE THAN SOMEWHAT 1937

CHARITY

4 In common with many Christians of the classic type he felt sincerely safer and more at ease when he had given away all he had, like a man passing a ball in a game.
Margery Allingham, TIGER IN THE SMOKE 1957

5 A man who sees another man on the street corner with only a stump for an arm will be so shocked the first time he'll give him sixpence. But the second time it'll only be a threepenny bit. And if he sees him a third time he'll cold-bloodedly have him handed over to the police.
Bertolt Brecht, THE THREEPENNY OPERA 1928

6 Too many people have decided to do without generosity in order to practise charity.
Albert Camus, THE FALL 1956

7 Philanthropy is commendable, but it must not cause the philanthropist to overlook the circumstances of economic injustice which make philanthropy necessary.
Martin Luther King, STRENGTH TO LOVE 1963

8 Lots of people think they are charitable if they give away their old clothes and things they don't want.
Myrtle Reed, OLD ROSE AND SILVER

9 The dignity of the individual demands that he be not reduced to vassalage by the largesse of others.
Antoine de Saint-Exupéry, FLIGHT TO ARRAS 1942

10 No one would remember the Good Samaritan if he had only good intentions. He had money as well.
Margaret Thatcher. Quoted Rt Revd Kenneth Skelon, Bishop of Lichfield, at a diocesan synod 5 Mar 1983

CHARM

11 [Charm] is a sort of bloom on a woman. If you have it you don't need anything else; and if you don't have it, it doesn't much matter what else you have.
J. M. Barrie, WHAT EVERY WOMAN KNOWS 1908

12 Charm is a way of getting the answer yes, without having asked any clear question.
Albert Camus, THE FALL 1956

13 All charming people have something to conceal, usually their total dependence on the appreciation of others.
Cyril Connolly, ENEMIES OF PROMISE 1938

14 History is bright and fiction dull with homely men who have charmed women.
O. Henry, ROADS OF DESTINY, *Next to Reading Matter* 1909

15 Oozing charm from every pore / He oiled his way across the floor.
Alan Jay Lerner, MY FAIR LADY 1956

16 She whose body's young and cool / Has no need of dancing school.
Dorothy Parker, SALOME'S DANCING LESSON

CHASTITY

17 Chastity; the most unnatural of the sexual perversions.
Aldous Huxley, EYELESS IN GAZA 1936

18 Many citizens claim it is a great shame that such a beautiful doll is wasting her time being good.
Damon Runyon, GUYS AND DOLLS 1932

1 A well-preserved virginity *may* signify a limited capacity for love.
Robert Shields, Observer 13 *Jun* 1965

CHEATING

2 It is almost always worth while to be cheated; people's little frauds have an interest which more than repays what they cost us.
Logan Pearsall Smith, ALL TRIVIA, *Afterthoughts* 1931

CHEESE

3 Ah, Wensleydale! The Mozart of cheeses.
T. S. Eliot. Quoted Roy Perrot, Observer 10 *Jan* 1965

4 Cheese — milk's leap towards immortality.
Clifton Fadiman, ANY NUMBER CAN PLAY 1957

5 How can you have a one-party system in a country that has two hundred varieties of cheese?
General de Gaulle, BBC Radio 4, *Quote Unquote* 18 *Jul* 1979

CHESS

6 Chess — a game in the playing of which there is no element of chance.
Opening words of international rules

G. K. CHESTERTON

7 Remote and ineffectual don / That dared attack my Chesterton.
Hilaire Belloc, LINES TO A DON

8 G.K.Chesterton had a multiplicity of talents, not least among them the almost invariable capacity, when throwing buns in the air, to catch them in his mouth.
A. N. Wilson, Sunday Telegraph 16 *Jun* 1985

CHICAGO

9 You can say this for Chicago — there's no hypocrisy problem there. There's no *need* for hypocrisy. Everyone's *proud* of being a bastard.
Saul Bellow. Quoted Martin Amis, Observer 11 *Dec* 1983

10 Pentonville is joyous to Chicago, Manchester is a paradise to it, Wapping, Whitechapel and Deptford are gardens to it.
John Masefield, in a letter to his wife, Constance 1916

11 Here is the difference between Dante, Milton and me. They wrote about hell and never saw the place. I wrote about Chicago after looking the place over for years and years.
Carl Sandburg. Quoted Harry Golden, CARL SANDBURG

CHILDREN

12 It is no wonder people are so horrible when they start life as children.
Kingsley Amis, ONE FAT ENGLISHMAN 1963

13 'We don't know what to make of him' said his mother (of a badly behaved child). 'How about a nice rug?'
Tallulah Bankhead. Quoted David Frost and Anthony Jay, TO ENGLAND WITH LOVE

14 Childhood is measured out by sounds and smells / And sights before the dark of reason grows.
John Betjeman, SUMMONED BY BELLS 1960

15 Boys do not grow up gradually. They move forward in spurts like the hands of clocks in railway stations.
Cyril Connolly, ENEMIES OF PROMISE 1938

16 The trouble with children is that they are not returnable.
Quentin Crisp, THE NAKED CIVIL SERVANT

17 Anybody who hates children and dogs can't be all bad.
W. C. Fields. Quoted Radio Times 12 *Aug* 1965

18 Nervous breakdowns are hereditary. We get them from our children.
Graffito. Quoted Nigel Rees, GRAFFITI 2

19 There is always one moment in childhood when the door opens and lets in the future.
Graham Greene, THE POWER AND THE GLORY 1940

20 It's a lovely silver star, and you are going to put up your hand and point to it. And what are you going to say when you do that? —

No Sidney, he *isn't* going to say 'Please may I go to the bathroom'.
Joyce Grenfell, GEORGE DON'T DO THAT, *The Nativity Play*

1 Let's put on our thinking caps shall we and think what flowers we are going to be . . . A horse isn't a flower Sidney . . . No a *carrot* isn't a flower Sidney . . . No Sidney you can't be a super jet — all right you can be a cauliflower, but be it *gently.*
Ibid., Flowers

2 Jenny, when we have paid a visit to the littlest room what do we do? — We pull our knickers up again.
Ibid., Going Home Time

3 Thank you Dicky, for closing the cupboard door for me. — Dicky, is there someone *in* that cupboard? – Well let her out at once.
Ibid.

4 The business of being a child interests a child not at all. Children very rarely play at being other children.
David Holloway, Daily Telegraph, As We Grow Up 15 Dec 1966

5 You Americans do not rear children, you *incite* them, you give them food and shelter and applause.
Randall Jarrell, PICTURES FROM AN INSTITUTION 1954

6 Never have ideas about children — and never have ideas *for* them.
D. H. Lawrence, FANTASIA OF THE UNCONSCIOUS 1922

7 Even when freshly washed and relieved of all obvious confections, children tend to be sticky.
Fran Lebowitz. Quoted Frank Muir, ON CHILDREN

8 This would be a better world for children if parents had to eat the spinach.
Groucho Marx, ANIMAL CRACKERS

9 My mother loved children — she would have given anything if I had been one.
Groucho Marx. Quoted Frank Muir, ON CHILDREN

10 Childhood is the kingdom where no one dies.
Edna St Vincent Millay, WINE FROM THESE GRAPES 1934

11 A child's spirit is like a child, you can never catch it by running after it; you must stand still, and, for love, it will soon itself come back.
Arthur Miller, THE CRUCIBLE 1953

12 Some people do not make good children. They should spring upon the world fully grown, preferably with a gin and tonic in hand, and conversation in full swing, a camera equipped with sound on the premises to record the event.
Margaret Morley, LARGER THAN LIFE — A BIOGRAPHY OF ROBERT MORLEY

13 The entry of a child into any situation changes the whole situation.
Iris Murdoch. Quoted Rachel Billington, The Times, Profile, Iris Murdoch 15 Apr 1983

14 Grown-ups never understand anything for themselves, and it is tiresome for children to be always and forever explaining things to them.
Antoine de Saint-Exupéry, THE LITTLE PRINCE 1943

15 Affection between adults (if they are really adult in mind and not really grown-up children) and creatures so relatively selfish and cruel as children necessarily are without knowing it, cannot be called natural.
George Bernard Shaw. Quoted Hesketh Pearson, BERNARD SHAW 1942

16 Nothing would induce me to go over my childhood days again. I thought I was happy because my mother said I was.
Rev. H. R. L. Sheppard. Quoted Carolyn Scott, DICK SHEPPARD

CHINA

17 Very big, China.
Noël Coward, PRIVATE LIVES 1930

CHOICE

18 Every act is an act of self sacrifice. When you choose anything, you reject everything else.
G. K. Chesterton, ORTHODOXY 1908

19 Man must choose whether to be rich in things or in the freedom to use them.
I. D. Illich, DESCHOOLING SOCIETY

1 To choose is to reject, an action painful to
those greedy for experience.
Yehudi Menuhin, UNFINISHED
JOURNEY 1977

JESUS CHRIST

2 A man who called himself the son of God is
either a madman or telling the truth.
Nobody ever said that Christ was mad,
therefore Christ was the son of God.
G. K. Chesterton. Quoted Lynette Hunter,
G. K. CHESTERTON'S EXPLORATIONS IN
ALLEGORY 1979

3 Jesus Christ was not a Conservative.
Eric Heffer, Observer, Sayings of the Week
20 Feb 1983

4 He might be described as an underpri-
vileged, colonial, working-class victim of
political and religious persecution.
Philip, Duke of Edinburgh, A QUESTION OF
BALANCE 1982

5 Whether you think Jesus was God or not,
you must admit that he was a first-rate
political economist.
George Bernard Shaw, ANDROCLES AND
THE LION, *Preface* 1912

CHRISTIANITY

6 It is our business, as readers of literature, to
know what we like. It is our business as
Christians as *well* as readers of literature, to
know what we ought to like. It is our
business as honest men not to assume that
what we like is what we ought to like.
T. S. Eliot, SELECTED ESSAYS

7 The Gospel is essentially a message of
spiritual redemption, not of social reform.
W. R. Inge (Dean of St Pauls), FREEDOM,
LOVE AND TRUTH 1936

8 Christianity is a revolutionary idealism
which estranges revolutionaries by its idealism and conservatives by its drastic revalua-
tion of earthly goods.
Ibid.

9 Christianity promises to make men free; it
never promises to make them independent.
W. R. Inge (Dean of St Pauls), THE
PHILOSOPHY OF PLOTINUS 1929

10 It is a Christian's duty to get on with doing
the will of God, and not to waste time
tinkering with his own psychology. To know
how bad we are is an excellent recipe for
becoming much worse.
C. S. Lewis. Quoted Humphrey Carpenter,
THE INKLINGS 1978

11 I wonder when Christianity will have
sufficiently decayed for the fact to be driven
out of men's heads that pleasure is not
hurtful nor pain beneficial.
W. Somerset Maugham, A WRITER'S
NOTEBOOK 1949

12 Christianity is not tied to any ideology.
*Dr Hugh Montefiore (Bishop of
Birmingham). Church of England Synod,
The Church and the Bomb debate* 10 Feb
1983

13 Christianity was not founded by clergymen.
Norman Vincent Peale, FAITH FOR TODAY

14 The worst of the idealistic education most of
us have had under Christian authority is that
it makes us so ashamed of our real feelings
towards human beings that we indulge in a
constant process of self deception.
John Cowper Powys, THE MEANING OF
CULTURE

15 I submit that Christians ought not to be
scared of a moral issue just because
someone has stuck a political flag on it.
*Gerald Priestland, BBC Radio 4, Yours
Faithfully* 5 Sep 1978

16 In the ethic of Christianity it is the relation of
the soul to God that is important not the
relation of man to his fellow man.
Bertrand Russell, MARRIAGE AND
MORALS 1929

17 'The fashion just now is a Roman Catholic
frame of mind with an Agnostic conscience:
you get the mediaeval picturesqueness of
the one with the modern convenience of the
other.'
The Duchess suppressed a sniff. She was one
of those people who regard the Church of
England with patronizing affection, as if it
were something that had grown up in their
kitchen garden.
Saki, REGINALD AT THE THEATRE

18 People may say what they like about the
decay of Christianity; the religious system

that produced green Chartreuse can never really die.
Saki, REGINALD ON CHRISTMAS PRESENTS

1 Civilisation is perhaps approaching one of those long winters that overtake it from time to time. Romantic Christendom — picturesque, passionate, unhappy episode — may be coming to an end. Such a catastrophe would be no reason for despair.
George Santayana, CHARACTER AND OPINION IN THE UNITED STATES 1920

2 Popular Christianity has for its emblem a gibbet, for its chief sensation a sanguinary execution after torture, for its central mystery an insane vengeance brought off by a trumpery expiation. But there is a nobler and profounder Christianity which affirms the sacred mystery of equality and forbids the glaring futility and folly of vengeance.
George Bernard Shaw, MAJOR BARBARA, *Preface* 1905

3 The nearest he gets to being a Christian is stirring his tea with an apostle spoon.
Peter Spence, BBC TV, To the Manor Born 25 Dec 1979

4 The Christian believes that he was created to know, love and serve God in this world and to be happy with him in the next. That is the sole reason for his existence.
Evelyn Waugh, Month, Nov 1949

5 Christianity is pre-eminently the religion of slaves, slaves cannot help belonging to it, and I am among them.
Simone Weil, THE NEED FOR ROOTS

CHRISTMAS

6 I'm dreaming of a white Christmas / Just like the ones I used to know.
Irving Berlin, HOLIDAY INN 1942

7 This most tremendous tale of all / Seen in a stained glass window's hue / A baby in an ox's stall.
John Betjeman, CHRISTMAS

8 My mother-in-law has come round to our house at Christmas seven years running. This year we're having a change. We're going to let her in.
Les Dawson, BBC TV, Pebble Mill 27 Dec 1979

9 A woman who is insidiously ostentatious about the flower-like and impersonal quality of her beauty can be given a hot water bottle or a small biscuit-coloured Shetland shawl to wear in bed or a tin of patent food which announces clearly on the front label that it has been specially treated to make it more easily digestible . . . Thrown in with the rest somebody can give her a cheap lipstick, smelling of lard.
Stephen Potter, ONE-UPMANSHIP 1952

10 Poor relations may be maddened by giving them useful [Christmas] presents like scissors, or bradawls.
Ibid.

11 Fall back on the general suggestion that all this being tremendously nice at Christmas is redolent of somebody covering up a tendency to be tremendously nasty all the rest of the year. Suggest that for you, personally, it makes no difference.
Stephen Potter, SUPERMANSHIP 1952

12 It always seems such a mixing of this world and the next — but that, after all, is the idea.
Evelyn Underhill, LETTERS

13 Xmas is a good time with all those presents and good food and i hope it will never die out or at any rate not until i am grown up and hav to pay for it.
Geoffrey Willans and Ronald Searle, HOW TO BE TOPP

CHURCH

14 There is little good in filling churches with people who go out just exactly the same as they come in; the call of the Church is not to fill churches but to fill heaven.
Father Andrew, THE WAY OF VICTORY

15 What an amazing capacity for disappointment the Church has.
Nigel Balchin, LORD, I WAS AFRAID

16 The Church's Restoration / In eighteen eighty three / Has left for contemplation / Not what there used to be.
Sir John Betjeman, HYMN

17 The British churchman goes to church as he goes to the bathroom, with the minimum of fuss and no explanation if he can help it.
Ronald Blythe, THE AGE OF ILLUSION

1 The Church of England, that finest flower of our Island genius for compromise; that system, peculiar to these shores, which deflects the currents of religious passion down the canals of moderation.
Robert Bolt, A MAN FOR ALL SEASONS 1960

2 There would never be any stigma attached to a young man going into the Church because the upper classes have to believe in God.
Jilly Cooper, CLASS

3 The hippopotamus's day / Is passed in sleep, at night he hunts. / God works in a mysterious way — / The church can sleep and feed at once.
T. S. Eliot, THE HIPPOPOTAMUS 1920

4 The greatest mistake the bishops make is in thinking they are the Church. The Church is the laity.
Lord Hailsham. Quoted Susan Barnes,
BEHIND THE IMAGE

5 People expect the clergy to have the grace of a swan, the friendliness of a sparrow, the strength of an eagle and the night-hours of an owl — and some people expect such a bird to live on the food of a canary.
Rev. Edward Jeffrey. Quoted Observer 14 Jun 1964

6 The Church must be reminded that it is not the master or the servant of the state but rather the conscience of the state.
Martin Luther King, STRENGTH TO LOVE 1963

7 There are many who stay away from church these days because you hardly ever mention God any more.
Arthur Miller, THE CRUCIBLE 1953

8 The churches grow old, but do not grow up.
Doris Langley Moore, THE VULGAR HEART

9 He preaches a remarkably good sermon. It is so hard to avoid offending people like us.
Man to Wife, cartoon caption in the New Yorker 1938

10 The Church of England is the perfect church for those who don't go to church.
Gerald Priestland, BBC Radio 4, Priestland's Progress 19 Nov 1981

11 The Catholic church is a church of sinners in

the sense that the Quaker church is a church of saints.
Shirley Williams, interviewed by Miriam Gross, Observer 22 Mar 1981

RANDOLPH CHURCHILL

12 Someone, I don't know who, hearing that Randolph Churchill was on the *Queen Mary* with Eden said 'I suppose he's the camel to break the straw's back'.
Rupert Hart-Davis, THE LYTTELTON HART-DAVIS LETTERS 5 Mar 1950

WINSTON CHURCHILL

13 Trouble with Winston; nails his trousers to the mast and can't climb down.
Clement Attlee. Quoted Sir Harold Wilson,
A PRIME MINISTER ON PRIME MINISTERS

14 Then comes Winston with his hundred horse-power mind and what can I do?
Stanley Baldwin. Quoted G. M. Young,
STANLEY BALDWIN

15 Churchill has the habit of breaking the rungs of any ladder he puts his foot on.
Lord Beaverbrook, letter to Arthur Brisbane 20 Oct 1932

16 Churchill, on top of the wave, has in him the stuff of which tyrants are made.
Lord Beaverbrook, POLITICIANS AND THE WAR 1959

17 He never spares himself in conversation. He gives himself so generously that hardly anybody else is permitted to give anything in his presence.
Aneurin Bevan

18 He always refers to a defeat or a disaster as though it came from God, but to a victory as though it came from himself.
Aneurin Bevan. Quoted Leon Harris, THE FINE ART OF POLITICAL WIT

19 He is a man suffering from petrified adolescence.
Aneurin Bevan. Quoted Vincent Brome,
ANEURIN BEVAN

20 [He is] a wholesaler in disaster.
Aneurin Bevan. Quoted Michael Foot,
ANEURIN BEVAN VOL. 1

1 Winston has devoted the best years of his life to preparing his impromptu speeches.
Lord Birkenhead

2 Englishman, 25 years old, about five feet eight inches tall, indifferent build, walks with a forward stoop, pale appearance, reddish brown hair, small and hardly noticeable moustache, talks through his nose and cannot pronounce the letter 'S' properly.
Boer description of Churchill after his escape from them

3 Churchill had no objection to us kicking poor old Chamberlain, but he didn't like being hurt himself.
Hugh Cudlipp, WALKING ON THE WATER

4 For a very short period in history Churchill was a necessary shit. He didn't like the upper classes and the upper classes didn't like him. He managed to combine tremendous egalitarianism with being a roaring old snob.
Osbert Lancaster. Quoted Duncan Fallowell, Times Profile 11 *Oct* 1982

5 He has spoilt himself by reading about Napoleon.
David Lloyd George. Quoted Frances Stevenson, DIARIES 19 *May* 1917

6 Winston would go up to his Creator and say that he would very much like to meet His Son, about Whom he had heard a great deal and, if possible, would like to call on the Holy Ghost. Winston *loves* meeting people.
David Lloyd George. Quoted A. J. Sylvester, DIARY 2 *Jan 1937*

7 Churchill's part in World War II reduces the classic figures of Rome and Greece to the relatively inconsequent stature of actors in drama of minor scope.
Mark Sullivan, New York Herald Tribune 11 May 1975

8 By his father he is an Englishman, by his mother an American. Behold the perfect man.
Attr. Mark Twain when Churchill was on a lecture tour in the United States

CINEMA

9 Cinema managers are nice and let you pop in to see a film without telling. My mother has seen quite a few films that way recently.
Princess Anne. Quoted Noël St George, ROYAL QUOTES

10 Movie music is noise. It is even more painful than my sciatica.
Sir Thomas Beecham, Time magazine 24 *Feb* 1958

11 Cecil B. de Mille / Rather against his will / Was persuaded to leave Moses / Out of 'The Wars of the Roses'.
E. C. Bentley, CLERIHEWS

12 The most positive thing in the motion picture business is the negative.
Steve Broidy, President of Monogram Pictures

13 All I need to make a comedy is a park, a policeman and a pretty girl.
Charlie Chaplin, MY AUTOBIOGRAPHY 1964

14 A film is a petrified fountain of thought.
Jean Cocteau, Esquire, Feb 1961

15 In Westerns you were permitted to kiss your horse but never your girl.
Gary Cooper, Saturday Evening Post, Well It was This Way 17 *Mar* 1958

16 Film music is like a small lamp that you place below the screen to warm it.
Aaron Copland. Quoted Nat Shapiro, AN ENCYCLOPEDIA OF QUOTATIONS ABOUT MUSIC

17 An affair between a mad rockinghorse and a rawhide suitcase.
Noël Coward, of Jeanette MacDonald and Nelson Eddy in Technicolor version of BITTER SWEET

18 Valentino silently acted out the fantasies of women all over the world. Valentino and his world were a dream. A whole generation of females wanted to ride off into a sandy paradise with him. At thirteen I had been such a female.
Bette Davis, THE LONELY LIFE

19 The cinema has become more and more like the theatre. It's all mumbling and muttering.
Shelagh Delaney, A TASTE OF HONEY 1958

1 A film musician is like a mortician — he can't bring the body back to life, but he is expected to make it look better.
Adolph Deutsch. Quoted Tony Thomas,
MUSIC FOR THE MOVIES 1973

2 When I asked her where she had learnt to read so quickly she replied 'On the screens at cinemas'
Ronald Firbank, THE FLOWER BENEATH THE FOOT 1923

3 Hollywood is a Jewish holiday, a Gentile tragedy.
F. Scott Fitzgerald. Quoted Matthew J. Bruccoli, SOME SORT OF EPIC GRANDEUR

4 No music has ever saved a bad picture, but a lot of good pictures have saved a lot of bad music.
Jerry Goldsmith. Quoted Irwin Bazedon,
KNOWING THE SCORE 1975

5 God makes stars. I just produce them.
Sam Goldwyn. Quoted Paul Holt, Daily Express 16 *May* 1939

6 Who in hell wants to see a picture about a herring?
Sam Goldwyn, on its being suggested that he make a film on the life of Bismarck. Quoted Reginald Pound, THEIR MOODS AND MINE 1937

7 Why should people go out and pay to see bad movies when they can stay at home and see bad television for nothing?
Sam Goldwyn, Observer 9 *Sep* 1956

8 It's greater than a masterpiece — it's mediocre.
Attr. Sam Goldwyn. Quoted Alva Johnson,
THE GREAT GOLDWYN

9 Take away the essentials and what have you got?
Sam Goldwyn. Ibid.

10 Every director bites the hand that lays the golden egg.
Ibid.

11 I want a movie that starts with an earthquake and works up to a climax.
Ibid.

12 'But Mr. Goldwyn, what is the *message* of this film?'
'I am just planning a movie. I am not interested in messages. Messages are for Western Union.'
Sam Goldwyn at a script conference. Ibid.

13 The cinema serves the proletariat as well as the middle classes. So long as we have the cinema and commercialised football the proletariat will give no trouble to their masters in England.
Rev. I. C. Hardwick at the conference of Modern Churchmen, quoted Morning Post

14 There's a lot of nice guys walking around Hollywood but they aren't eating.
Henry Hatheway, producer. Quoted Charles Hamblett, The Times 22 *Mar* 1969

15 The maidens who haunt picture palaces / Know nothing of psycho-analysis / And Sigmund Freud / Would be greatly annoyed / As they cling to their long-standing phalluses.
A. P. Herbert

16 The cinema is not a slice of life but a piece of cake.
Alfred Hitchcock, Sunday Times Magazine 6 *Mar* 1977

17 Folks, you ain't heard nothing yet.
Al Jolson, THE JAZZ SINGER, *Oct* 1927

18 The cinema, like the detective story, makes it possible to experience without danger all the excitement, passion and desirousness which must be repressed in a humanitarian ordering of life.
Carl Jung. Quoted Roger Manvell, FILM

19 God made the fine arts, but man made the film.
Roger Manvell, FILM

20 How I dislike Technicolor, which suffuses everything with stale mustard.
Edward Marsh, AMBROSIA AND SMALL BEER

21 Saddest movie I've ever seen — I cried all the way through. It's sad when you're 82.
Groucho Marx of LAST TANGO IN PARIS

22 Theda Bara made voluptuousness a common American commodity, as accessible as chewing gum.
Lloyd Morris, NOT SO LONG AGO

1 For a time Henry Luce was on the Board of Directors of Paramount. Hoped to learn something of cinema, heard nothing discussed but banking, resigned sadly.
The New Yorker 28 Nov 1936

2 Every film is launched like a squid, in an obscuring cloud of spectacular publicity.
Dudley Nichols, Introduction to Lewis Tacobe, ART OF THE MOVIES

3 Hollywood — the city of dreadful day.
S. J. Perelman. Quoted Joe Adamson, GROUCHO, HARPO, CHICO AND SOMETIMES ZEPPO 1973

4 I've done an awful lot of stuff that is a monument to public patience.
Tyrone Power. Quoted David Shipman, THE GREAT MOVIE STARS

5 If you're not very careful I'll play this scene as you want it.
Claude Rains to producer Pascal, during making of JULIUS CAESAR. *Quoted BBC Radio 4, Quote Unquote*

6 The cinema in the hands of the Soviet power represents a great and priceless force.
Joseph Stalin. Quoted Roger Manvell, FILM

7 You can seduce a man's wife there [Hollywood], attack his daughter and wipe your hands on his canary, but if you don't like his movie you're dead.
Attr. Joseph von Sternberg

8 Film music should have the same relationship to the film drama that somebody's piano playing in my living room has to the book I am reading.
Igor Stravinsky, Music Digest, Sep 1946

9 The fault in our Hollywood musical credo lies in the simple truth that it is not possible to write real music about an unreal emotion.
Virgil Thomson, New York Herald Tribune 10 *Apr* 1949

10 I wouldn't say when you've seen one Western you've seen the lot; but when you've seen the lot you get the feeling that you've seen one.
Katherine Whitehorn, SHOUTS AND MURMURS, *Decoding the West*

11 The way things are going I'd be more interested in seeing Cleopatra play the life of Elizabeth Taylor.
Earl Wilson. Quoted Radio Times, Nov 1962

CITY

12 Cities, like cats, will reveal themselves at night.
Rupert Brooke, LETTERS FROM AMERICA 1916

13 As a remedy to life in society I would suggest the big city. Nowadays it is the only desert within our means.
Albert Camus, NOTEBOOKS 1935—1942

14 No city should be too large for a man to walk out of in a morning.
Cyril Connolly, THE UNQUIET GRAVE 1945

15 A large city cannot be experientially known; its life is too manifold for any individual to be able to participate in it.
Aldous Huxley, BEYOND THE MEXIQUE BAY 1941

16 The city is not a concrete jungle. It is a human zoo.
Desmond Morris, THE HUMAN ZOO

CIVILISATION

17 Civilised people can talk about anything. For them no subject is taboo.
Clive Bell, CIVILISATION, AN ESSAY 1928

18 All great civilisations, in their early stages, are based on success in war.
Kenneth, Lord Clark, CIVILISATION 1969

19 Civilisation is an active deposit which is formed by the combustion of the present and the past.
Cyril Connolly, ENEMIES OF PROMISE 1938

20 No man who is in a hurry is quite civilised.
Will Durant, WHAT IS CIVILISATION?

21 Civilised men arrived in the Pacific, armed with alcohol, syphilis, trousers, and the Bible.
Havelock Ellis, THE DANCE OF LIFE 1923

22 The people of Europe, before they were touched by modern civilisation, had much in common with the people of the East.
Mahatma Gandhi. Quoted obituary, News Chronicle 31 Jan 1948

23 There is precious little in civilisation to appeal to a yeti.
Sir Edmund Hillary. Quoted Observer 3 Jun 1960

1 Compassion is not enough. Civilisation depends upon the cultivation of excellence, and therefore of superiority and inequality.
Philip Howard reviewing John Sparrow's WORDS ON THE AIR

2 Any hopefulness for the future of civilisation is based on the reasonable expectation that humanity is still only beginning its course.
W. R. Inge (Dean of St Pauls), THE CHURCH AND THE AGE 1911

3 The nineteenth century regarded European civilisation as mature and late, the final expression of the human spirit. We are only now beginning to realise that it is young and childish.
C. E. M. Joad, GUIDE TO MODERN THOUGHT 1933

4 Human history, if you read it right, is the record of the efforts to tame Father . . . the greatest triumph of what we call civilisation was the domestication of the human male.
Max Lerner, THE UNFINISHED COUNTRY, *The Revolt of the American Father* 1959

5 Civilisation — by which I here mean barbarism made strong and luxurious by mechanical power.
C. S. Lewis, A PREFACE TO PARADISE LOST, *being the Ballard Mattheus Lectures, delivered at University College, North Wales* 1941

6 The civilisation of man might be measured by the manner in which he sets about planning and interpreting the flow of sense experiences which constitutes physical life.
Roger Manvell, FILM

7 *Teddie*: England seems to me full of people doing things they don't want to because other people expect it of them.
Elizabeth: Isn't that what you call a high degree of civilisation?
W. Somerset Maugham, THE CIRCLE 1921

8 Collectivism is the ancient principle of savagery. A savage's whole existence is ruled by tribal leaders. Civilisation is the process of freeing man from men.
Ayn Rand, THE MORAL BASIS OF INDIVIDUALISM

9 All civilised people are in some way what would be thought abnormal, and they suffer because they don't know that really ever so many people are just like them.
Bertrand Russell, letter to Ottoline Morrell. Quoted in his AUTOBIOGRAPHY VOL. II 1967

10 Our laws make law impossible, our liberties destroy all freedom, our property is organised robbery, our morality is an impudent hypocrisy, our wisdom is administered by inexperienced or mal-experienced dupes, our power wielded by cowards and weaklings, and our honour false in all its points. I am an enemy of the existing order for good reasons.
George Bernard Shaw, MAJOR BARBARA, *Preface* 1905

11 Civilisation has made the peasantry a pack animal.
Leon Trotsky, HISTORY OF THE RUSSIAN REVOLUTION 1932

12 Civilisation advances by extending the number of important operations which we can perform without thinking about them.
A. N. Whitehead, AN INTRODUCTION TO MATHEMATICS 1911

13 Civilisation is hooped together, brought / Under a rule, under the semblance of peace / By manifold illusion.
W. B. Yeats, A FULL MOON IN MARCH, *Supernatural Songs, Meru* 1934

14 Civilisation is an exercise in self-restraint.
W. B. Yeats

CLASS

15 We have barely noticed that the leisured class has been replaced by another and much larger class to which work has none of the old connotations of pain, fatigue, or other mental or physical discomfort.
J. K. Galbraith, THE AFFLUENT SOCIETY 1958

16 The one class you *do* not belong to and are not proud of at all is the lower-middle class. No one ever describes himself as belonging to the lower-middle class.
George Mikes, HOW TO BE INIMITABLE

17 Folkestone was refined, genteel, tidy and, for a child, exciting. The West End . . . was full of PLUs (People Like Us — a phrase used by the gentry of the period to distinguish the U from the non-U).
Margaret Morley, LARGER THAN LIFE — A BIOGRAPHY OF ROBERT MORLEY

1 I can't help feeling wary when I hear anything said about the masses. First you take their faces from 'em, calling them the masses, and then you accuse 'em of not having any faces.
J. B. Priestley, SATURN OVER THE WATER

2 You can be in the Horseguards and still be common, dear.
Terence Rattigan, SEPARATE TABLES 1954

3 Marx sought to replace natural antagonism by class antagonisms.
H. G. Wells, SHORT HISTORY OF THE WORLD 1922

CLEANLINESS

4 Bath twice a day to be really clean, once a day to be passably clean, once a week to avoid being a public nuisance.
Anthony Burgess, INSIDE MR ENDERBY 1966

5 Look at your dirty fingernails. Are we in mourning for the cat?
Sir Hugh Casson and Joyce Grenfell, NANNY SAYS 1972

GEORGES CLEMENCEAU

6 There the old Tiger would be sitting, in his grey gloves and grey skullcap, usually wearing grey slippers, looking like a great grey cat.
Bernard Baruch, THE PUBLIC YEARS

CLERGY

7 The average curate at home was something between a eunuch and a snigger.
Ronald Firbank, THE FLOWER BENEATH THE FOOT 1923

8 He had been a bishop so long that no one knew now what he thought about death, or indeed about anything except the Prayer Book, any change in which he deprecated with determination.
John Galsworthy, MAID IN WAITING

9 The clergy should regard themselves as physicians of the soul.
W. R. Inge (Dean of St Pauls). Quoted Ray Giles, CHRISTIAN HERALD, *Jul* 1941

10 Heaven may be for the laity, but this world is certainly for the clergy.
George Moore, HAIL AND FAREWELL 1914

11 The world would be the poorer without the antics of clergymen.
V. S. Pritchett, IN MY GOOD BOOKS, *The Dean*

12 A parson should light fires in dark rooms and go on lighting them all his life.
Rev. H. R. L. Sheppard. Quoted Carolyn Scott, DICK SHEPPARD

13 There is a species of person called a 'Modern Churchman', who draws the full salary of a beneficed clergyman and need not commit himself to any religious belief.
Evelyn Waugh, DECLINE AND FALL 1928

CLEVERNESS

14 When I have to listen to somebody from one of those American 'think tanks' I cannot help remembering the verdict of Tao Te Ching. 'Extreme cleverness is as bad as stupidity'.
J. B. Priestley, OUTCRIES AND ASIDES

CLICHÉ

15 Let's have some new clichés.
Sam Goldwyn. Quoted Observer 9 *Sep* 1956

16 The truths of the past are the clichés of the present.
Ned Rorem, MUSIC FROM INSIDE OUT, *Listening and Hearing* 1967

CLIMATE

17 Let us blame the climate for it; we pass, the climate remains.
John Masefield, SO LONG TO LEARN

18 People get a bad impression of it [the English climate] by continually trying to treat it as if it was a bank clerk, who ought to be on time on Tuesday next, instead of philosophically seeing it as a painter, who may do anything so long as you don't try to predict what.
Katherine Whitehorn, Observer 7 *Aug* 1966

CLOTHES

1 Old age has released me from at least one
absurdity — an excessive worry about
clothes, which came less from a desire to
look smart than from a fear of being
conspicuous. More parties have been spoilt
for me than for most people because I had
on the wrong clothes.
Vernon Bartlett, I KNOW WHAT I LIKED

2 A bit of black material to reduce Old Adam
to the Common Man.
Robert Bolt, A MAN FOR ALL SEASONS 1960

3 From the cradle to the coffin, underwear
comes first.
Bertolt Brecht, THE THREEPENNY
OPERA 1928

4 Clothes seem to suffer a sea-change when
they get on to me. They look quite
promising in the shop, and not entirely
without hope when I get them back into my
wardrobe. But then, when I put them on
they tend to deteriorate with a very strange
rapidity and one feels so sorry for them.
Joyce Grenfell, STATELY AS A GALLEON

5 You walk into your tailor's and ask for the
cheapest suit in the shop, and he says, you're
wearing it.
Trevor Griffiths, THE COMEDIANS *(play)*

6 You have got to be a Queen to get away with
a hat like that.
Anita Loos, GENTLEMEN PREFER
BLONDES 1925

7 Where is the man could ease a heart / Like a
satin gown?
Dorothy Parker, ENOUGH ROPE 1926

8 All dress is fancy dress, is it not, except our
natural skins.
George Bernard Shaw, SAINT JOAN 1927

9 The trouble with most Englishwomen is that
they *will* dress as if they had been a mouse in
some previous incarnation.
Edith Sitwell, HOW TO WEAR DRAMATIC
CLOTHES

10 The people who have a suit for every day of
the week and even, one is reluctantly led to
believe, more expansive wardrobes, are
parvenus of the worst sort. A gentleman
generally has two suits.
Douglas Sutherland, THE ENGLISH
GENTLEMAN 1978

11 [A gentleman] always buys his underwear at
Marks and Spencer and always tells his
friends about it as an indication that he is
democratic about clothes. In fact a lot of
time is taken up at cocktail parties by
gentlemen telling each other where they buy
their underwear.
Ibid.

12 All ladies dress like the Queen, which is
much the same as dressing like the Queen
Mother. By and large they are at their best
dressed for a brisk walk in the rain but they
can look awe-inspiring at Hunt Balls and
above all at weddings.
Douglas Sutherland, THE ENGLISH
GENTLEMAN'S WIFE 1979

13 We still buy cotton frocks in April as a folk
magic to bring on summer, forgetting that
the golden afternoon of the Edwardian era
was due, as much as anything, to the fact
that they never (well almost never), abandoned their petticoats and stays and waist-
coats.
Katherine Whitehorn, Observer 7 Aug 1966

CLOUD

14 Bright towers of silence.
Walter de la Mare, ENGLAND

15 every cloud / has its silver / lining but it is /
sometimes a little / difficult to get it to / the
mint.
Don Marquis, CERTAIN MAXIMS OF
ARCHY 1935

16 . . . carven towers / Stiff sculpted like a
heap of marble flowers.
Edward Shanks, CLOUDS

CLUB

17 On his [Sir James Barrie] first visit to the
Athenaeum Club he asked an octogenarian
biologist the way to the dining room. The
biologist burst into tears. He had been a
member for fifty years. No one had ever
spoken to him before.
Anon.

18 Clubs are places where men spend all their
time thinking angrily about nothing.
*Viscount Castlerosse. Quoted George
Malcolm Thompson*, LORD CASTLEROSSE,
HIS LIFE AND TIMES

1 Please accept my resignation. I don't want to belong to any club that would accept me as a member.
Attr. Groucho Marx by Bennett Cerf and others

2 Members can amuse themselves by sitting at the window and 'watching the demned people getting wet outside'.
Douglas Sutherland, THE ENGLISH GENTLEMAN 1978

3 Most clubs have the atmosphere of a Duke's house with the Duke lying dead upstairs.
Ibid.

4 A club is a kind of transport café for the upper classes.
The Times Diary, of Pratts, owned by the Duke of Devonshire 13 Jun 1984

COALMINING

5 In other trades there are a thousand diversions to break the monotony of work — the passing traffic, the morning newspaper, above all, the sky, the sunshine, the wind, the rain. The miner has none of these. Every day for eight hours he dies, gives up a slice of life, literally drops out of life and buries himself.
Aneurin Bevan. Quoted Michael Foot, ANEURIN BEVAN 1897—1945

COCOA

6 Half past nine high time for supper / 'Cocoa love?' 'Of course my dear.' / . . . For they've stumbled on the secret / Of a love that never wanes / Rapt beneath the tumbled bedclothes / Cocoa coursing through their veins.
Stanley J. Sharpless, CUPID'S NIGHTCAP, *New Statesman and Nation 7 Nov 1953*

COFFEE

7 Coffee in England is just toasted milk.
Christopher Fry, New York Post 29 Nov 1962

COINCIDENCE

8 What a marvellous coincidence. You're writing a book and I'm reading one.
Leo Garel. Caption to cartoon of a blonde at a party, Saturday Evening Post 1960

9 Although we talk so much about coincidence we do not really believe in it. In our heart of hearts we think better of the universe, we are secretly convinced that it is not such a slipshod, haphazard affair, that everything in it has meaning.
J. B. Priestley, A COINCIDENCE

COLLECTING

10 One of the silliest questions you can ask a book collector is, 'Have you read all these?' Of course he hasn't. Some books are bought to look at, not to read.
Sir John Betjeman, Daily Herald. Quoted News Review 28 Nov 1946

COLOUR

11 I know the colour rose and it is lovely / but not when it ripens in a tumour / and healing greens, leaves and grass so springlike, / in limbs that fester are not springlike . . . / So in the simple blessing of a rainbow / in the bevelled edge of a sunlit mirror, / I have seen visible, Death's artifact / like a soldier's ribbon on a tunic tacked.
Dannie Abse, GOLDERS GREEN, *Pathology of Colours*

12 Grey is a colour that always seems on the verge of changing to some other colour.
G. K. Chesterton, ALARMS AND DISCURSIONS 1916

13 I don't want the Legion d'honneur — I'd love it if it were pink, but red is vulgar.
Marie Laurencin. Quoted René Gimpel, DIARY OF AN ART DEALER

14 I've been forty years discovering that the queen of all colours is black.
Auguste Pierre Renoir. Quoted Ambrose Vollard, RECOLLECTIONS OF A PICTURE DEALER

COMEDY

15 All comedians are anarchists.
Ken Dodd, Radio Times 24 Mar 1979

1 The first thing any comedian does on getting an unscheduled laugh is to verify the state of his buttons; the second is to look around to see if a cat has walked out on the stage.
W. C. Fields. Quoted Robert Lewis Taylor,
W. C. FIELDS, ROWDY KING OF COMEDY

2 Comedy is an escape, not from truth but from despair; a narrow escape into faith.
Christopher Fry, Time 22 Nov 1950

3 Our comedies are not to be laughed at.
Sam Goldwyn. Quoted Alva Johnson, THE GREAT GOLDWYN

4 Comedy takes place in a world where the mind is always superior to the emotions.
Joseph Wood Krutch, THE MODERN TEMPER 1929

5 The test of a real comedian is whether you laugh at him before he opens his mouth.
George Jean Nathan, American Mercury, Sep 1929

6 Comedy is the last refuge of the non-conformist mind.
Gilbert Seldes, New Republic 20 Dec 1954

7 The only rules comedy can tolerate are those of taste, and the only limitations those of libel.
James Thurber, LANTERNS AND LANCES 1961

8 Comedy can slide the knife in with more deadly effect than tragedy.
Claire Tomlin, Sunday Times, Miss Austen's Confinement 29 Oct 1978

9 Comedy is the clash of character. Eliminate character from comedy and you get farce.
W. B. Yeats, DRAMATIS PERSONAE

COMFORT

10 Comfort came in with the middle classes.
Clive Bell, CIVILISATION 1928

COMMERCE

11 The myth that holds that the great corporation is the puppet of the market, the powerless servant of the consumer, is in fact, one of the devices by which its power is perpetuated.
J. K. Galbraith, AGE OF UNCERTAINTY 1977

COMMITMENT

12 That this round O of faithfulness / We swear / May never wither to an empty nought / Nor petrify into a square.
W. H. Auden, MODERN CANTERBURY PILGRIMS

13 For I have promises to keep / And many miles to go before I sleep.
Robert Frost, STOPPING BY WOODS ON A SNOWY EVENING 1923

COMMITTEE

14 If Moses had operated through committees the Israelites never would have got across the Red Sea.
Gen. William Booth, Salvation Army founder. Quoted Edward Morello, New York World-Telegram 28 Jul 1965

15 A committee is a group of the unwilling, picked from the unfit, to do the unnecessary.
Richard Harkness, New York Herald Tribune 15 Jun 1960

16 A committee is an animal with four back legs.
John Le Carre, TINKER, TAILOR, SOLDIER, SPY

COMMONSENSE

17 Commonsense appears to be only another name for the thoughtlessness of the unthinking. It is made of the prejudices of childhood, the idiosyncrasies of individual character and the opinion of the newspapers.
W. Somerset Maugham, A WRITER'S NOTEBOOK 1949

COMMUNICATION

18 Trying to talk to the government is like trying to hold a conversation with the Talking Clock.
Alan Fisher, TUC Conference 7 Sep 1981

19 In spite of life, in spite of intelligence and intuition and sympathy, one can never really communicate anything to anybody . . . our life is a sentence of perpetual solitary confinement.
Aldous Huxley, COLLECTED ESSAYS 1960

1 The electric age establishes a global network that has much of the character of our central nervous system.
Marshall McLuhan, UNDERSTANDING MEDIA 1964

2 Verbal communication about music is impossible, except among musicians.
Virgil Thomson, THE STATE OF MUSIC 1939

COMMUNISM

3 I would not mind sitting on a platform with a Russian communist, but I would not be seen dead with a British communist.
Lady Astor 1942

4 The Communist Party is not a party, it is a conspiracy.
Aneurin Bevan in an article in Tribune

5 A communist should be tidier, and not make work for the servants.
Caryl Brahms and Ned Sherrin, THE MITFORD GIRLS 1982

6 Communism is the new religion which denies original sin, though seldom do we meet a real communist who seems either complete or happy.
Cyril Connolly, THE UNQUIET GRAVE 1945

7 Communism has never come to power in a country that was not disrupted by war or corruption, or both.
John F. Kennedy. Speech to NATO 3 Jul 1963

8 Were I a communist, the type of person whom I should most wish to attack would not be the millionaire or the imperialist, but the soft, reasonable, tolerant, secure, self-satisfied intellectual like Vita and myself.
Harold Nicolson, DIARY 4 Aug 1932

9 The Catholic and the Communist are alike in assuming that an opponent cannot be both honest and intelligent.
George Orwell, SELECTED ESSAYS, *The Prevention of Literature* 1968

10 It is one of the weaknesses of Communism, though it has virtues we too often refuse to acknowledge, that it does seem to create a general scene that is altogether too damnably drab.
J. B. Priestley, New Statesman, Dandy Days

11 The sturdy young Nazis of Germany (are) Europe's guardians against the Communist danger.
Lord Rothermere, owner of Daily Mirror and Mail 1933

12 Communism is the corruption of a dream of justice.
Adlai Stevenson. Speech, Urbana 1951

13 The crusade against Communism was even more imaginary than the spectre of Communism.
A. J. P. Taylor, ORIGINS OF THE SECOND WORLD WAR 1962

COMMUNITY

14 Our most basic common link is that we all inhabit this planet.
John F. Kennedy. Speech 10 Jun 1963

COMPARISON

15 There is no need to worry about mere size. We do not necessarily respect a fat man more than a thin man. Sir Isaac Newton was very much smaller than a hippopotamus, but we do not on that account value him less.
Bertrand Russell, Saturday Evening Post, The Expanding Mental Universe 2 Jul 1959

COMPASSION

16 One cannot weep for the entire world, it is beyond human strength. One must choose.
Jean Anouilh, CÉCILE 1949

17 You don't have to be poor to have a heart. Women who have got money are just as interested in the welfare of another as other women.
Lady Astor, House of Commons 1939

18 Billy in one of his nice new sashes / Fell in the fire and was burnt to ashes / Now, although the room grows chilly / I haven't the heart to poke poor Billy.
Harry Graham, RUTHLESS RHYMES

19 Compassion is the albatross of the Liberal.
J. B. Priestley. Quoted Vernon Bartlett, I KNOW WHAT I LIKED

COMPETITION

1 Competitions are for horses, not artists.
Béla Bartók, Saturday Review 25 *Aug* 1962

2 I dislike it [competition] in real life and I do
not see why it should be introduced into
one's amusements. If it amuses me to do a
thing I do not see that it much matters
whether I do it better than another person.
A. C. Benson, FROM A COLLEGE
WINDOW 1906

COMPLIMENT

3 Nothing is so silly as the expression of a man
who is being complimented.
André Gide, JOURNALS 1939—1950

COMPOSING

4 Composing is like driving down a foggy road
towards a house. Slowly you see more
details of the house — the colour of the
slates and bricks, the shape of the windows.
The notes are the bricks and mortar of the
house.
Benjamin Britten. Quoted Nat Shapiro, AN
ENCYCLOPEDIA OF QUOTATIONS ABOUT
MUSIC

5 Good music resembles something. It resembles the composer.
Jean Cocteau, COCK AND HARLEQUIN 1918

6 It is a good thing [Sir Hubert] Parry died
when he did; otherwise he might have set
the whole Bible to music
Frederick Delius. Quoted Philip Heseltine,
DELIUS

7 Composers shouldn't think too much — it
interferes with their plagiarism.
*Howard Dietz. Letter to Goddard
Lieberson, Nov* 1974

8 Why should I write a fugue or something
that won't appeal to anyone, when the
people yearn for things that will stir them.
Sir Edward Elgar. Quoted Nat Shapiro, AN
ENCYCLOPEDIA OF QUOTATIONS ABOUT
MUSIC

9 Things take shape without my knowing it. I
am only the lead pencil and cannot foresee.
Sir Edward Elgar. Quoted Basil Maine,
ELGAR, HIS LIFE AND WORKS

10 There is music in the air, music all round us:
the world is full of it, and you simply take as
much as you require.
Ibid.

11 I have no use at all for those composers who
cannot write without being surrounded by
stained glass windows for the sake of
atmosphere.
Ibid.

12 I have no opinion of the composer who can
think only in terms of the keyboard.
Ibid.

13 A nation creates music — the composer only
arranges it.
Mikhail Glinka, Theatre Arts magazine, Jun
1958

14 Never compose anything unless the not
composing of it becomes a positive nuisance
to you.
*Gustav Holst. Letter to W. G.
Whittaker* 1921

15 The contemporary composer is a gate-
crasher trying to push his way into a
company to which he has not been invited.
Arthur Honegger, JE SUIS COMPOSITEUR

16 Strauss remembers. Beethoven dreams.
Charles Ives, ESSAYS BEFORE A
SONATA 1920

17 A composer is unable to hide anything — by
his music you shall know him.
Yehudi Menuhin, THEME AND
VARIATIONS 1972

18 With many composers you gradually
become aware that they have the defects of
their qualities. With [Sir Hubert] Parry the
process is reversed; it is only by degrees that
you discover him to possess the qualities of
his defects.
R. O. Morris, Music and Letters, Mar 1920

19 Every great composer, without exception,
has been appreciated, admired, applauded
and loved in his own time. Even those who
died miserably, died famous.
Henry Pleasants, THE AGONY OF MODERN
MUSIC 1955

20 If a composer could state in words what
being a composer means he would no longer
need to be a composer.
Ned Rorem, CRITICAL AFFAIRS 1970

1 The performer may have a responsibility towards the composer, but the composer has none towards the performer beyond the practical one of making his music performable on some terms.
Ned Rorem, THE FINAL DIARY 1974

2 Every composer's music reflects in its subject matter and in its style the source of the money the composer is living on while writing the music.
Virgil Thomson, THE STATE OF MUSIC 1939

COMPREHENSION

3 Thoroughly worldly people never understand even the world: they rely on a few cynical maxims which are not true.
G. K. Chesterton, ORTHODOXY 1908

COMPROMISE

4 The English — or at least those who are in positions of power — like to believe in the efficiency of negotiation, compromise, reconciliation, give-and-take. They would never dream of setting fire to an embassy.
William Davis, Punch 9 *Feb* 1972

5 Compromise is never anything but an ignoble truce between the duty of a man and the terror of a coward.
Reginald Wright Kauffman, THE WAY OF PEACE

6 If one cannot catch a bird of paradise, better take a wet hen.
Nikita Khrushchev. Quoted Time 1 *Jun* 1958

7 I offer my opponents a bargain; if they will stop telling falsehoods about us, I will stop telling the truth about them.
Adlai Stevenson. Campaign speech 1952

COMPULSION

8 I find I always have to write *something* on a steamed mirror.
Elaine Dundy, THE DUD AVOCADO 1958

COMPUTER

9 To err is human, but to really foul things up requires a computer.
Anon. Quoted BBC Radio 4, *Quote Unquote* 22 *Feb* 1982

10 Man is still the most extraordinary computer of all.
John F. Kennedy. Speech 21 *May* 1963

COMRADESHIP

11 War is too terrible a price to pay even for the advantages of comradeship.
W. H. Nevinson, John o' London's Weekly, reviewing Edmund Blunden's UNDERTONES OF WAR 22 *Dec* 1928

CONCEIT

12 Harold [Robbins] could be the best conversationalist in the world – if he ever found anyone he thought worth talking to.
Herbert Alexander. Quoted Alan Whicker in TV interview

13 No poet or novelist wishes he were the only one who ever lived, but most of them wish they were the only one alive, and quite a number fondly believe their wish has been granted.
W. H. Auden, THE DYER'S HAND, *Writing* 1962

14 One of my chief regrets during my years in the theatre is that I couldn't sit in the audience and watch me.
John Barrymore, in an interview

15 Conceit is God's gift to little men.
Bruce Barton, CONCEIT

16 To say that a man is vain means merely that he is pleased with the effect he produces on other people. A conceited man is satisfied with the effect he produces on himself.
Sir Max Beerbohm, AND EVEN NOW, *Quia Imperfectum*

17 I conceived at least one great love in my life, of which I was always the object.
Albert Camus, THE FALL 1956

18 He (Thomas E. Dewey) is just about the nastiest little man I've ever known. He struts sitting down.
Mrs Dykstra. Quoted J. T. Patterson, MR REPUBLICAN

19 He thinks he knows as much as Leonardo da Vinci. The trouble is, a lot of things have happened since da Vinci's time.
Peter Hillmore quoting an anonymous MP, Observer 1 *Apr* 1984

1 Try not to despise yourself too much — it is
only conceit.
P. J. Kavanagh, A SONG AND DANCE

2 If you think you are not conceited you are
very conceited indeed.
C. S. Lewis, MERE CHRISTIANITY

3 He [Arnold Bennett] has described how,
when as a young dramatic critic, he went to a
Lyceum first night, he would saunter into
the stalls and 'glancing at the front row of the
pit with cold and aloof disdain' would think
'don't you wish you were me?'
*Robert Lynd. Arnold Bennett obituary,
News Chronicle* 28 *Mar* 1931

4 Tomorrow every Duchess in London will be
wanting to kiss me.
*Ramsay MacDonald, on forming the
National Government. Quoted Viscount
Snowden*, AUTOBIOGRAPHY

5 It's about time the piano realised it did not
write the concerto.
Joseph L. Mankiewicz, ALL ABOUT EVE
(*film*)

6 The affair between Margot Asquith and
Margot Asquith will live as one of the
prettiest love stories in all literature.
*Dorothy Parker, reviewing Margot
Asquith's autobiography, New Yorker* 1936

7 She had the expression of someone who
would not be surprised to find her portrait
on a postage stamp.
*Penny Patrick, The Times, On the crest of a
wave* 14 *Sep* 1983

8 A lot of men who have accepted — or had
imposed upon them in boyhood — the old
English public school styles of careful
modesty in speech, with much understate-
ment, have behind their masks an appalling
and impregnable conceit of themselves. If
they do not blow their own trumpets it is
because they feel you are not fit to listen to
the performance.
J. B. Priestley, OUTCRIES AND ASIDES

9 No person loving or admiring himself is
alone.
Theodore Reik, OF LOVE AND LUST 1957

10 If I were a medical man I would prescribe a
holiday to any patient who considered his
work important.
Bertrand Russell, THE CONQUEST OF
HAPPINESS 1930

11 We believe, first and foremost, what makes
us feel we are fine fellows.
Bertrand Russell, UNPOPULAR ESSAYS 1950

12 In America everybody is of the opinion that
he has no social superiors, but he does not
admit that he has no social inferiors.
Ibid.

13 If I ever felt inclined to be scared going into a
room full of people I would say to myself
'You're the cleverest member of one of the
cleverest families in the cleverest class of the
cleverest nation in the world, so what have
you got to be frightened of?'
*Beatrice Webb. Quoted David A. Shannon,
introduction to Beatrice Webb's* AMERICAN
DIARY

14 I am not conceited. It is just that I have a
fondness for the good things in life and I
happen to be one of them.
Kenneth Williams, in a TV interview

15 It's the greatest love story since Tristan and
Isolde, and Ed Koch plays both parts.
Daniel Wolf, reviewing MAYOR, *by Ed
Koch, Mayor of New York, Daily Telegraph*
1 *Feb* 1984

CONCERT

16 Of the type of audience at a chamber music
concert an Oxford don once remarked
'They look like the sort of people who go to
the English Church abroad.'
W. H. Auden, A CERTAIN WORLD

17 Even before the music begins there is that
bored look in people's faces. A polite form
of self-imposed torture, the concert.
Henry Miller, TROPIC OF CANCER 1934

18 A concert is like a bullfight — the moment of
truth.
Artur Rubenstein. Quoted Robert Jacobson,
REVERBERATIONS 1974

CONDESCENSION

19 When he greeted one, one always felt like a
delicate monkey being put through tricks.
*Cyril Connolly of Ian Fleming. Quoted John
Pearson*, LIFE OF IAN FLEMING 1966

CONDUCTOR

1 There was one respect in which Landon Ronald outshone all other conductors. This was in the gleam of his shirtfront and the gloss of his enormous cuffs, out of which peeped tiny, fastidious fingers. He made music sound as if it, too, had been laundered.
James Agate, EGO 4 1940

2 I spend up to six hours a day waving my arms about and if everyone else did the same they would stay much healthier.
Sir Malcolm Sargent. Quoted Leslie Ayre, THE WIT OF MUSIC

3 Conductors must give unmistakable and suggestive signals to the orchestra — not choreography to the audience.
George Szell, Newsweek 28 Jan 1963

CONFESSION

4 The Roman Catholic Church, by using confession, makes people interested in themselves, and, feeling it right to be interested, it makes everyone form a kind of romantic picture of himself or herself.
A. C. Benson, DIARIES 1920

5 It was reading Rousseau's 'Confessions' that first determined me to write mine and at the same time to have a more satisfactory life to make a record of.
William Scawen Blunt, MY DIARIES 1888–1914

6 We confess our bad qualities to others out of fear of appearing naïve or ridiculous by not being aware of them.
Gerald Brenan, THOUGHTS IN A DRY SEASON 1979

7 There was really no joy in pouring out one's sins while he sat assiduously picking his nose.
Ronald Firbank, VALMOUTH 1919

8 Should we all confess our sins to one another we would all laugh at one another for our lack of originality.
Kahil Gibran, SAND AND FOAM 1927

9 Before confession, be perfectly sure that you do not wish to be forgiven.
Katherine Mansfield. Quoted Anthony Helpen, KATHERINE MANSFIELD

10 Confession may be good for my soul, but it sure plays hell with my reputation.
Mark Twain. Quoted Janet Wells, Observer, The Diarists 3 Jan 1982

CONFIDENCE

11 I envy people who have the confidence to open and shut train windows without asking if I mind, who can read road maps, or join without inhibition in community singing and applaud themselves afterwards.
Basil Boothroyd, Punch 10 May 1972

12 I wasn't lucky. I deserved it.
Margaret Thatcher on receiving school prize, aged 9. Quoted Observer 6 May 1979

CONFORMITY

13 For one man who thanks God that he is not as other men there are a few thousand to offer thanks that they are as other men, sufficiently as others to escape attention.
John Dewey, HUMAN NATURE AND CONFLICT

CONFUSION

14 Confusion is a word we have invented for an order which is not understood.
Henry Miller, TROPIC OF CANCER 1934

JOSEPH CONRAD

15 The first mate is a Pole called Conrad, and is a capital chap though queer to look at; he is a man of travel and experience in many parts of the world, and has a fund of yarns on which I draw freely.
John Galsworthy in a letter written at age 26, when travelling home in a clipper from Australia. Quoted Dudley Barker, JOHN GALSWORTHY, MAN OF PRINCIPLE

16 What is Conrad but the wreck of Stevenson floating about in the slip-slop of Henry James?
George Moore. Quoted G. W. Lyttelton, THE LYTTELTON HART-DAVIS LETTERS 8 Mar 1950

17 One of the surest signs of his genius is that women dislike his books.
George Orwell, New English Weekly 23 Jul 1936

CONSCIENCE

1 You cannot make yourself feel something
you do not feel, but you can make yourself
do right in spite of your feelings.
Pearl S. Buck, TO MY DAUGHTER, WITH
LOVE, *My Neighbour's Son* 1967

2 The wings of a beautiful but ineffectual
conscience beating vainly in a vacuum jar.
T. S. Eliot. Quoted J. C. Levenson, THE
MIND AND ART OF HENRY ADAMS 1957

3 Conscience is the internal perception of the
rejection of a particular wish operating
within us.
Sigmund Freud, TOTEM AND TABOO 1918

4 The paradoxical   and tragic — situation of
a man is that his conscience is weakest when
he needs it most.
Erich Fromm, MAN FOR HIMSELF 1947

5 I cannot and will not cut my conscience to
suit this year's fashions.
*Lillian Hellman to the Unamerican Activities
Committee* 1952

6 When one has a conscience it is generally a
bad one.
Eugene Ionesco, FRAGMENTS OF A JOURNAL

7 Conscience was the barmaid of the Victorian soul . . . [It] would permit, rather
ungraciously perhaps, the indulgence of a
number of carefully selected desires. Once
the appointed limit was reached conscience
would rap on the bar of the soul. 'Time's up,
gentlemen' she would say.
C. E. M. Joad, UNDER THE FIFTH RIB

8 The Anglo-Saxon conscience does not
prevent the Anglo-Saxon from sinning. It
merely prevents him from enjoying it.
*Salvador de Madariaga. Quoted David Frost
and Anthony Jay,* TO ENGLAND WITH
LOVE 1981

9 There is only one way to achieve happiness
on this terrestrial ball, / And that is to have a
clear conscience, or none at all.
Ogden Nash, I'M A STRANGER HERE MYSELF

CONSEQUENCE

10 In nature there are neither rewards nor
punishments — there are consequences.
Robert G. Ingersoll, SOME REASON WHY

CONSERVATION

11 Having to save the old that's worth saving,
whether in landscape, houses, manners,
institutions or human types, is one of our
greatest problems, and the one we bother
least about.
John Galsworthy, OVER THE RIVER

12 Save trees — eat a beaver.
Graffito. Quoted Nigel Rees, GRAFFITI
LIVES OK 1979

13 Such prosperity as we have known up to the
present is the consequence of rapidly
spending the planet's irreplaceable capital.
Aldous Huxley, THEME AND
VARIATIONS 1950

14 We face the question whether a still higher
'standard of living' is worth its cost in things
natural, wild and free. For us of the
minority, the opportunity to see geese is
more important than television.
Aldo Leopold, A SAND COUNTY ALMANAC

15 People gush and moan too much about the
loss of ancient buildings of no special
note . . . In towns, as in human bodies, the
only state of health is one of rapid wasting
and repair.
C. E. Montague, THE RIGHT PLACE

16 To wear the arctic fox / You have to kill it.
Marianne Moore, COLLECTED POEMS, *The
Arctic Ox (or Goat)* 1951

17 Here is the Earth, don't spend it all at once.
Barty Phillips, Observer, Mind Your Planet
8 *Jul* 1979

18 The nation that destroys its soil destroys
itself.
Franklin D. Roosevelt 26 *Feb* 1937

19 Shooting is a great contribution to conservation.
*Richard Tracey, British Field Sports Society.
Quoted Observer, Sayings of the Week*
20 *Aug* 1981

CONSERVATISM

20 So far as I am concerned the Tory party are
lower than vermin.
Aneurin Bevan. Speech, Manchester 4
Jul 1949

1 The conservative has little to fear from the man whose reason is the servant of his passions, but let him beware of him in whom reason has become the greatest and most terrible of his passions.
J. B. S. Haldane, DAEDALUS OR SCIENCE AND THE FUTURE

2 The Conservatives know there are books to read, pictures to look at, music to listen to — and grouse to shoot.
Harold Macmillan. Quoted Nigel Nicholson, Thames TV, The Day Before Yesterday 1970

CONSISTENCY

3 Consistency is contrary to nature, contrary to life. The only completely consistent people are the dead.
Aldous Huxley, COLLECTED ESSAYS 1960

CONSOLATION

4 Nobody can have the consolation of religion or philosophy unless he has first experienced their desolations.
Aldous Huxley, COLLECTED ESSAYS 1960

CONSUMERISM

5 The first enslaving illusion is the idea that people are born to be consumers and that they can attain any of their goals by purchasing goods and services.
Ivan Illich, DISABLING PROFESSIONS

CONTACT

6 The meeting of two personalities is like the contact of two chemical substances; if there is any reaction both are transformed.
Carl Jung, MODERN MAN IN SEARCH OF A SOUL

CONTENTMENT

7 *Contentment* who had known youth as a child and never seen him since.
Rupert Brooke, THE FUNERAL OF YOUTH

8 Being 'contented' ought to mean in English

as it does in French, being pleased. Being content with an attic ought not to mean being unable to move from it and resigned to living in it; it ought to mean appreciating all there is in such a position. For true contentment is a real, even an active virtue — not only affirmative, but creative. It is the power of getting out of a situation all there is in it.
G. K. Chesterton, A MISCELLANY OF MEN 1912

9 A householder, whose lawn needed cutting, saw Mose scuffling along the dusty road and called out 'Hey Moses! Want to make a quarter?' Mose paused only long enough to reply, 'No, suh. Ah got one.'
Alexander Woollcott, WHILE ROME BURNS, *Colossal Bronze* 1934

CONTRACEPTION

10 I would as soon condemn the use of soap as the practice of birth control.
Ernest William Barnes (Bishop of Birmingham), RISE OF CHRISTIANITY

11 He [Pope Paul] could have spared a paragraph in his long encyclical to assist the people who will be left holding the baby.
Lady Antonia Fraser. Quoted Bernard Levin, THE PENDULUM YEARS 1976

12 Most Catholic parents feel that they know more about the practical problems of married life than an elderly bachelor in Rome.
Paul Johnson, New Statesman, of Pope Paul's encyclical forbidding all artificial forms of contraception

13 A vast trade is being done in contraceptives. I would like to make a bonfire of them and dance round it.
The Bishop of London, House of Lords

14 Where are the children I might have had? . . . Drowned to the accompaniment of the rattling of a thousand douche bags.
Malcolm Lowry, UNDER THE VOLCANO 1947

15 Contraceptives should be used on all conceivable occasions.
Spike Milligan, THE LAST GOON SHOW OF ALL

1 Birth control would be far more convincing as a scientific argument if it could be guaranteed to improve and not merely thin out our race.
Reginald Pound, THEIR MOODS AND MINE 1935

2 Few will now bother to ask whether the Pope is infallible, they are more concerned with whether the Pill is infallible.
John Robinson (Bishop of Woolwich) of Pope Paul's encyclical forbidding artificial contraception

3 We want far better reasons for having children than not knowing how to prevent them.
Dora Russell, HYPATIA

4 Skullion placed contraceptives in the lower social category of things along with elastic-sided boots and made-up bow ties. Not the sort of attire for a gentleman.
Tom Sharpe, PORTERHOUSE BLUES

CONTRACT

5 A verbal contract isn't worth the paper it is written on.
Sam Goldwyn. Quoted Alva Johnson, THE GREAT GOLDWYN

CONTRAST

6 Active happiness depends to some extent on contrast — a lover's meeting would not be the same without the days of deprivation.
Graham Greene, A SORT OF LIFE

CONVENTION

7 The fact that a convention exists indicates that a way of living has been devised capable of maintaining itself.
George Santayana, PERSONS AND PLACES 1953

CONVERSATION

8 They had no conversation, properly speaking. They made use of the spoken word in much the same way as the guard of a train makes use of his flags or lantern.
Samuel Beckett, MALONE DIES 1951

9 Good talkers, when they have run down, are miserable; they know they have betrayed themselves.
Cyril Connolly, ENEMIES OF PROMISE 1938

10 Apart from theology and sex there is really nothing to talk about.
Harold J. Laski, HOLMES—LASKI LETTERS

11 Good communication is as stimulating as black coffee and just as hard to sleep after.
Anne Lindbergh, GIFT FROM THE SEA 1955

12 Uncle Albert made a list of conversational openings. Among the earliest items was: 'Are you aware that the heaviest eater in the zoo is the gnu?'
G. W. Lyttelton, THE LYTTELTON HART-DAVIS LETTERS 15 Nov 1955

13 Conversation is one of the greatest pleasures of life. But it wants leisure.
W. Somerset Maugham, THE TREMBLING OF A LEAF 1921

14 Beware of the conversationalist who adds 'in other words'. He is merely starting afresh.
Robert Morley. Quoted Observer 6 Dec 1964

CONVERSION

15 Sudden conversion, a belief which may be right, but which is peculiarly attractive to the half-baked mind.
E. M. Forster, HOWARD'S END 1918

16 Why do born-again people so often make you wish they'd never been born the first time?
Katherine Whitehorn, Observer 20 May 1979

CONVICTION

17 At eighteen our convictions are hills from which we look; at forty-five they are caves in which we hide.
F. Scott Fitzgerald, BERNICE BOBS HER HAIR

COOKERY

18 Be content to remember that those who can make omelettes properly can do nothing else.
Hilaire Belloc, A CONVERSATION WITH A CAT

1 The turtle must be put in straw in the cellar and given water every two to three hours. It should be beheaded at night and left hanging neck downwards.
The Cookery Book of Lady Clark of Tillyponce 1909

2 An unwatched pot boils *immediately*.
H. F. Ellis, Punch, For Men in Aprons

3 The speed with which boiling milk rises from the bottom of the pan to any point beyond the top is greater than the speed at which the human brain and hand can combine to snatch the wretched thing off.
Ibid.

CALVIN COOLIDGE

4 He looks as if he had been weaned on a pickle.
Alice Roosevelt Longworth

5 He had one really notable talent. He slept more than any other president.
H. L. Mencken, obituary of Coolidge

6 How could they tell?
Dorothy Parker, on being told that ex-President Coolidge had died

CORNWALL

7 O the harbour of Fowey / Is a beautiful spot / And it's there I enjowey / To sail in a yot / Or to race in a yacht / round a marker or buoy / Such a beautiful spacht / Is the harbour of Fuoy.
Sir Arthur Quiller-Couch

CORRESPONDENCE

8 'Christ Almighty — another letter from my father' said the Earl of Chesterfield's son.
Caryl Brahms and S. J. Simon, NO NIGHTINGALES

9 Why it should be such an effort to write to the people one loves I can't imagine. It's none at all to write to those who don't really count.
Katherine Mansfield, JOURNALS 1954

10 An intention to write never turns into a letter. A letter must happen to one like a surprise, and one may not know where in the day there was room for it to come into being.
Rainer Maria Rilke, LETTERS 1892—1910

11 The letter which merely answers another letter is no letter at all.
Mark Van Doren. Quoted Clifton Fadiman, ANY NUMBER CAN PLAY 1957

12 His courtesy was somewhat extravagant. He would write and thank people who wrote to thank him for wedding presents and when he encountered anyone as punctilious as himself the correspondence ended only with death.
Evelyn Waugh, Life 8 Apr 1946

COSMETICS

13 Most women are not so young as they are painted.
Max Beerbohm, A DEFENCE OF COSMETICS 1922

14 Waits at the window wearing the face that she keeps in a jar by the door.
John Lennon and Paul McCartney, ELEANOR RIGBY *(song)*

15 A girl whose cheeks are covered with paint / Has an advantage with me over one whose ain't.
Ogden Nash, BIOLOGICAL REFLECTION

COSMOS

16 The cosmos is about the smallest hole that a man can hide his head in.
G. K. Chesterton, ORTHODOXY 1908

COUNTRY LIFE

17 The country is laid out in a haphazard, sloppy fashion, offensive to the tidy, organised mind.
Alan Brien, Punch 22 Mar 1979

18 I have always felt a faint scepticism, a mild horror about the country. One goes for quiet and a gang of rooks is at work, murderously tearing at the furrows.
Fanfarlo (L. M. Storier), SHAVING THROUGH THE BLITZ

1 No country home is complete without a surly figure seated in the kitchen like Rodin's Thinker, wishing she was back in a hot little room under the Third Avenue Elevator.
S. J. Perelman, ACHES AND PAINS 1947

2 The pleasure of country life lies really in the eternally renewed evidences of the will to live.
Vita Sackville-West, COUNTRY NOTES

3 I'm not a country man; I'd like to believe in the wide open spaces as the wrapping around walls, the windy boredom between house and house . . . man made his house to keep the world and weather out, making his own weathery world inside. That's the trouble with the country; there's too much public world between the private ones.
Dylan Thomas, letter to Vernon Watkins 2 *Apr* 1936

4 The average countryman mistrusts trees and has a fear of anything large and alive, and not easily tamed or destroyed.
J. R. R. Tolkien, LETTERS

5 A lovely house where an aged colonel plays wireless music to an obese retriever.
Evelyn Waugh, Country Life 26 *Feb* 1938

COURAGE

6 Until the day of his death, no man can be sure of his courage.
Jean Anouilh, BECKET 1959

7 The fearless man is his own salvation.
Robert Bridges, THE FIRST SEVEN DIVISIONS

8 Courage is almost a contradiction in terms. It means a strong desire to live taking the form of a readiness to die.
G. K. Chesterton, ORTHODOXY 1908

9 The people I respect must behave as if they were immortal and as if society was eternal.
E. M. Forster, TWO CHEERS FOR DEMOCRACY 1951

10 If the creator had a purpose in equipping us with a neck, he surely meant us to stick it out.
Arthur Koestler, ENCOUNTER 1970

11 One has to be seventy before one is full of courage. The young are always half hearted.
D. H. Lawrence, SELECTED LETTERS 1962

12 It takes a good deal of physical courage to ride a horse. This, however, I have. I get it at about forty cents a flask and take it as required.
Stephen Leacock, LITERARY LAPSES 1910

13 Courage is not simply *one* of the virtues but the form of every virtue at the testing point, which means at the point of highest reality.
C. S. Lewis. Quoted Cyril Connolly, THE UNQUIET GRAVE 1945

14 What meditation on human fate requires so much courage as stepping into a cold bath?
C. S. Lewis. Quoted Humphrey Carpenter, THE INKLINGS 1978

15 Life shrinks or expands in proportion to one's courage.
Anaïs Nin, DIARY, *Jun* 1941

16 The man who is courageous in any matter except physical danger is thought ill of.
Bertrand Russell, THE CONQUEST OF HAPPINESS 1930

17 She wasn't courageous, if by courage is meant mastery of fear, for she did not know about fear. She was fearless of physical danger, of criticism, of people.
The Times, obituary of Nancy, Viscountess Astor 4 *May* 1964

COURTESY

18 It is wise to apply the oil of refined politeness to the mechanism of friendship.
Colette, EARTHLY PARADISE

19 There can be no defence like elaborate courtesy.
E. V. Lucas, READING, WRITING AND REMEMBERING

COURTSHIP

20 Let us now bask under the spreading trees said Bernard in a passionate tone.
Oh yes lets said Ethel and she opened her dainty parasole and sank down upon the long grass. She closed her eyes but was far from asleep.
Daisy Ashford (aged 9), THE YOUNG VISITERS 1919

1 And I shall find some girl perhaps / And a better one than you / With eyes as wise, but kinder / And lips as soft, but true / And I daresay she will do.
Rupert Brooke, THE CHILTERNS

2 As soon as I get hold of a hand they sort of disconnect it from the rest of them.
F. Scott Fitzgerald, THIS SIDE OF PARADISE 1920

3 'We might be brother and sister' said Jennie [Lee] the first time they really talked together.
'Aye' said Nye [Aneurin Bevan] with an appraising mischievous grin, 'but with a tendency to incest.'
Michael Foot, ANEURIN BEVAN 1897—1945

4 Kissing your hand may make you feel very good but a diamond and sapphire bracelet lasts forever.
Anita Loos, GENTLEMEN PREFER BLONDES 1929

5 I'm sorry, Sigmund, you frighten me, but that isn't enough for marriage.
Cartoon caption in the New Yorker

6 Men seldom make passes / At girls who wear glasses.
Dorothy Parker, ENOUGH ROPE 1927

7 She will never win him whose / Words showed that she feared to lose.
Dorothy Parker, DEATH AND TAXES 1931

8 Gattling-Fenn was getting bald in a curious way. Yet he was always falling in love with horrifyingly pretty girls of vacant mind.
Stephen Potter, LIFEMANSHIP 1950

9 Throw away your little bedsocks and your Welsh wool knitted jacket. I will warm the sheets like an electric toaster. I will lie by your side like the Sunday roast.
Dylan Thomas, UNDER MILK WOOD 1954

10 . . . watching the moon come up lazily out of the old cemetery in which nine of his daughters were lying, and only two of them were dead.
James Thurber, BATEMAN COMES HOME

COW

11 The cow is of the bovine ilk / One end is moo, the other milk.
Ogden Nash, THE COW

NOËL COWARD

12 Edna Ferber turned up sporting a tailored suit similar to one Noël Coward was wearing. 'You look almost like a man' Coward said. 'So' Miss Ferber replied, 'do you'.
Robert E. Brennan, WIT'S END 1968

13 Noël Coward should be used as a cabaret, not as a guest. The deserts of pomposity between the oases of wit are too vast.
Ann Fleming, LETTERS 1985

14 I can't bear another moment of Noël's inane chatter. If he wags his silly finger at me once more, I'll hit him.
Ernest Hemingway. Quoted Alec Guinness, BLESSINGS IN DISGUISE 1985

15 He was his own greatest invention.
John Osborne. Quoted William Marchant, THE PLEASURE OF HIS COMPANY

16 If his face suggested an old boot it was unquestionably hand made.
Kenneth Tynan, THE SOUND OF TWO HANDS CLAPPING

17 He was once Slightly in Peter Pan, and has been wholly Peter Pan ever since.
Kenneth Tynan. Quoted BBC Radio 4, Quote Unquote 13 Sep 1979

COWARDICE

18 The last thing a woman will consent to discover in a man whom she loves, or on whom she simply depends, is want of courage.
Joseph Conrad, VICTORY 1915

19 He was just a coward, and that is the worst luck any man can have.
Ernest Hemingway, FOR WHOM THE BELL TOLLS 1940

20 Cowardice, as distinguished from panic, is almost always simply a lack of ability to suspend the functioning of the imagination.
Ernest Hemingway, MEN AT WAR

21 I'm a hero with coward's legs.
Spike Milligan, PUCKOON

1 As an old soldier I admit the cowardice. It's as universal as seasickness and matters just as little.
George Bernard Shaw, MAN AND SUPERMAN 1905

CREATION

2 The attempt to impose upon man, a creature of growth and capable of sweetness, to ooze juicily at the last round the bearded lips of God, to attempt to impose, I say, laws and conditions appropriate to a mechanical creation, against this I raise my sword pen.
Anthony Burgess, A CLOCKWORK ORANGE 1962

3 Gabriel: How about cleanin' up de whole mess of 'em and startin' all over ag'n wid some new kind of animal?
God: An' admit I'm licked?
Marc Connelly, THE GREEN PASTURES 1930

4 The presence in Nature of so many phenomena requiring intelligence for their appreciation implied a kindred intelligence to produce them.
Sir Ambrose Fleming, presidential address Victoria Institute 18 *Mar* 1936

5 I can't help feeling sceptical about the Bible's claim that God made man in his own image . . . He could have achieved that simply by creating a couple of mirrors, or a closed-circuit television.
Michael Frayn, CONSTRUCTIONS

6 The universe seems to have been designed by a pure mathematician.
Sir James Jeans, THE MYSTERIOUS UNIVERSE 1930

7 And God stepped out on space / And he looked around and said / 'I'm lonely — / I'll make me a world'.
J. W. Johnson, GOD'S TROMBONES 1927

8 God is really only another artist. He invented the giraffe, the elephant and the cat. He has no real style. He just goes on trying other things.
Pablo Picasso. Quoted Françoise Gilot and Carlton Lake, LIFE WITH PICASSO

CREATIVENESS

9 In search of ideas I spent yesterday morning in walking about, and went to the stores and bought things in four departments. A wonderful and delightful way of spending time and money. Better than most theatres . . . I think this sort of activity does stimulate creative ideas.
Arnold Bennett, JOURNALS 1911—1921

10 Every animal leaves traces of what it was; only man leaves traces of what he created.
Jacob Bronowski, THE ASCENT OF MAN 1973

11 'I like,' she once confided to me, 'to have creative beings around me. I like to live always within the possibility that someone in my house may at this moment be attempting to cut off his ears.' She did, however, insist that her violence should be, so to speak, house-trained: screaming and blood on the chair-covers were quite unforgiveable.
William Trevor, A STANDARD OF BEHAVIOUR

CREDIT

12 Never in the history of human credit has so much been owed.
Margaret Thatcher. Quoted Observer, Sayings of the Week 12 *Oct* 1975

CREDULITY

13 He had been kicked in the head when young and believed everything he read in the Sunday papers.
George Ade, THE SLIM GIRL

CRICKET

14 I would rather see the whole village dead at my feet than a man bowling in braces.
Adrian Allington, THE AMAZING TEST MATCH CRIME 1984

15 There is more to life than cricket.
Ian Botham, on playing football for Scunthorpe United reserves 1980

16 His off drives are like a white owl flying.
Neville Cardus of Frank Woolley, DAYS IN THE SUN

1 Cricket, like music, has its slow movements, especially when my native county of Lancashire is playing.
Neville Cardus, AUTOBIOGRAPHY

2 What are the butchers for?
Pauline Chase, an American actress, asking about the umpires at Lords. Quoted Bertie Hollander, BEFORE I FORGET

3 It is not the mere presence of the clergy at Lords that is impressive but rather the twin stamp of English and Anglican which they bear. You can be sure they are cricketers all, and because cricket is of the very soul of England it is in England's Church that they have found their vocation.
The Church Times

4 If Stalin had learned to play cricket the world might now be a better place to live in.
Dr R. Downey (Bishop of Liverpool), News Review 22 Apr 1948

5 My wife had an uncle who could never walk down the nave of his abbey without wondering whether it would take spin.
Lord Home, BBC 1 TV, The Twentieth Century Revisited 13 Jul 1982

6 Whenever I saw him bat I felt sorry for the ball.
Sir Leonard Hutton of Walter Hammond. Quoted Patrick Murphy, THE CENTURIANS 1983

7 The flannelled fool's at the wicket.
Rudyard Kipling, THE ISLANDERS 1902

8 Herbert Strudwick used to recommend to wicket-keepers 'Rinse your hands in the chamber pot every day. The urine hardens them wonderfully'.
David Lemmon, THE GREAT WICKET KEEPERS 1984

9 I don't think it at all polite the way bowlers rub the ball all over themselves at cricket.
Letter to the Manchester Evening News

10 Many continentals think life is a game, the English think cricket is a game.
George Mikes, HOW TO BE AN ALIEN 1946

11 The English are not a very spiritual people, so they invented cricket to give them some idea of eternity.
George Bernard Shaw

12 I have always looked upon cricket as organised loafing.
William Temple, when Headmaster of Repton, addressing parents

13 It felt like having Menuhin playing second fiddle to my lead.
Frank Tyson, of partnering J. B. Statham, WISDEN ANTHOLOGY 1963—1982

14 Why are the umpires, the only two people on the field who aren't going to get grass stains on their knees, the only ones allowed to wear dark trousers?
Katherine Whitehorn, VIEW FROM A COLUMN 1981

CRIME

15 It is not a fragrant world.
Raymond Chandler. Quoted Colin Watson, Radio Times 21 Apr 1979

16 A broad definition of crime in England is that it is any lower-class activity that is displeasing to the upper class.
David Frost and Anthony Jay, TO ENGLAND WITH LOVE

17 Crime doesn't pay, but the hours are good.
Graffito. Quoted Nigel Rees, GRAFFITI 2

18 It was beautiful and simple, as all truly great swindles are.
O. Henry, THE GENTLE GRAFTER 1908

19 A burglar who respects his art always takes his time before taking anything else.
O. Henry, MAKES THE WHOLE WORLD KIN

20 Crime is a logical extension of the sort of behaviour that is often considered perfectly respectable in legitimate business.
Robert Rice, THE BUSINESS OF CRIME 1956

21 Much as he is opposed to law-breaking he is not bigoted about it.
Damon Runyon, MORE THAN SOMEWHAT 1937

22 People who go to prison are not just criminals but, by definition, unsuccessful criminals.
The Times 13 Apr 1981

23 Almost all crime is due to the repressed desire for aesthetic expression.
Evelyn Waugh, DECLINE AND FALL 1928

SIR STAFFORD CRIPPS

1 He has a brilliant mind, until he makes it up.
Margot Asquith, AUTOBIOGRAPHY 1936

2 There, but for the grace of God, goes God.
Winston Churchill

3 Sir Stafford has built a high stone wall
around his mind, as though it were an
intellectual nudist colony.
Tribune. Quoted News Review 18 *Mar* 1948

4 No one likes Cripps. He does not allow it.
Alain Verney, Tribune des Nations (Paris),
Nov 1947

CRISIS

5 I felt as if the Suez Canal was flowing
through my drawing room.
Lady Eden, recalling the Suez Crisis

6 When written in Chinese the word crisis is
composed of two characters. One represents danger and the other represents
opportunity.
John F. Kennedy. Speech 12 *Apr* 1959

7 If you can keep your head when all about
you are losing theirs, it is just possible that
you haven't grasped the situation.
Jean Kerr, PLEASE DON'T EAT THE DAISIES

8 There can't be a crisis next week. My
schedule is already full.
Henry Kissinger. Quoted BBC Radio 4,
Quote Unquote 2 *Feb* 1982

CRITICS

9 Critics always want to put you into pigeon
holes, which can be very uncomfortable
unless you happen to be a pigeon.
Max Adrian. Quoted Barry Norman, The
Times 4 *Jul* 1972

10 The one thing I most emphatically do not
ask of a critic is that he tells me what I *ought*
to approve or condemn. I have no objection
to his telling me what works and authors he
likes and dislikes.
W. H. Auden, THE DYER'S HAND 1962

11 Pleasure is by no means an infallible critical
guide, but it is the least fallible.
Ibid.

12 Attacking bad books is not only a waste of
time but bad for the character . . . One
cannot attack a bad book without showing
off.
Ibid.

13 There is less in this than meets the eye.
Tallulah Bankhead. Quoted Alexander
Woolcott, SHOUTS AND MURMURS 1922

14 A critic was a man with a wee foot-rule who
measured plays with it, and if it was five by
four it was a good play, and if it was no' five
by four it was no' a play.
Sir James Barrie. Speech to the Critics'
Circle. Quoted Hamilton Fyfe, John
o'London's Weekly 2 *Jul* 1937

15 Because a critic is never criticised he passes
through the world without knowing what
the world thinks of him.
Clifford Bax, John o'London's Weekly, Mr
Agate keeps egoing on 2 *Sep* 1940

16 Criticism of the arts in London, taken by
and large, ends in a display of suburban
omniscience which sees no further than the
next door garden.
Sir Thomas Beecham. Quoted Neville
Cardus, SIR THOMAS BEECHAM

17 The trouble with music critics is that they so
often have the score in their hands and not in
their heads.
Sir Thomas Beecham. Quoted Harold
Atkins and Archie Newman, BEECHAM
STORIES

18 I will try to account for the degree of my
aesthetic emotion. That, I conceive, is the
function of a critic.
Clive Bell, ART 1914

19 My mother — who was an alertly respectable woman — told me at an early age that I
was not to play with critics.
Robert Bolt

20 'They're very noisy at night. You can't
sleep . . . because of them.'
Mel Brooks interviewed by Maurice
Zolotow, New York Times 30 *Mar* 1975

21 In art, rebellion is consummated and
perpetuated in the art of real creation, not in
criticism or commentary.
Albert Camus, THE REBEL 1951

1 I do not resent criticism, even when, for the sake of emphasis, it parts for the time with reality.
Winston Churchill, House of Commons 22 Jan 1941

2 I am the only critic in London who is too small for his boots.
Alan Dent. Quoted James Agate, EGO 4 1939

3 Critics never change; I'm still getting the same notices I used to get as a child. They tell me I play very well for my age.
Mischa Elman, in his seventies. Quoted Anthony Hopkins, MUSIC ALL ROUND ME

4 There is no more absolutely thrilling experience in dramatic criticism than to be absolutely certain that all the others are wrong.
Harold Hobson, INDIRECT JOURNEY

5 The best critic will be the epitome of the best part of any audience, its head, heart and soul.
Philip Hope-Wallace. Quoted The Times obituary 17 Dec 1979

6 No critic has ever settled anything.
James Huneker, PATHOS OF DISTANCE

7 The critic should describe and not prescribe.
Eugene Ionesco, IMPROVISATION

8 Never trust the artist. Trust the tale. The proper function of a critic is to save the tale from the artist who created it.
D. H. Lawrence, STUDIES IN CLASSIC AMERICAN LITERATURE

9 The only way to escape misrepresentation is never to commit oneself to any critical judgment that makes an impact — that is never *say* anything.
F. R. Leavis, THE GREAT TRADITION 1948

10 I cried all the way to the bank.
Liberace's retort to adverse criticism

11 People ask you for criticism, but they only want praise.
W. Somerset Maugham, OF HUMAN BONDAGE 1915

12 The savage review is a too easy form of fun . . . Far too many worthless books are published every year; why pick out one for attack, unless it is likely to win more respect than it deserves?
Raymond Mortimer, REVIEWING

13 Woollcott's reviews resemble either a gravy bomb, a bursting gladiolus, a palpitating *orissa cantata*, an attack of psychic hydrophobia, or a Roman denunciation.
George Jean Nathan, SMART SET 1921

14 The greater part of critics are parasites, who, if nothing had been written, would find nothing to write.
J. B. Priestley, OUTCRIES AND ASIDES

15 I never read anything concerning my work. I feel that criticism is a letter to the public which the author, since it is not directed to him, does not have to open and read.
Rainer Maria Rilke, LETTERS

16 The golden rule in criticism is for the critic to be on a level with the author — that is why the eighteenth-century Dr. Johnson is still the grandest critic of Shakespeare, and also why we can ignore 99 per cent of the production of the critical industry.
A. L. Rowse, PORTRAITS AND VIEWS 1979

17 Pay no attention to what critics say. No statue has ever been put up to a critic.
Attr. Jean Sibelius

18 I doubt that art needed Ruskin any more than a moving train needs one of its passengers to shove it.
Tom Stoppard, Times Literary Supplement 3 Jun 1977

19 I had another dream the other day about music critics. They were small and rodent-like with padlocked ears, as if they had stepped out of a painting by Goya.
Igor Stravinsky, Evening Standard 20 Oct 1969

20 They criticised Henry James as they might criticise a cat for not being a dog.
James Thurber, THE WINGS OF HENRY JAMES

21 A good drama critic is one who perceives what is happening in the theatre of his time. A great drama critic is one who perceives what is not happening.
Kenneth Tynan, TYNAN RIGHT AND LEFT

22 Writing criticism is to writing fiction as hugging the shore is to sailing in the open sea.
John Updike, HUGGING THE SHORE 1984

1 Most writers in the course of their careers, become thick-skinned and learn to accept vituperation, which in any other profession would be unimaginably offensive, as a healthy counterpoise to unintelligent praise.
Evelyn Waugh, New York Times Magazine 30 *Nov* 1952

2 A year to write a play, a year before it's produced, then those unassailable reviews, claiming the right to be unfair. Two years of work wiped out, two more years to wait.
Arnold Wesker, The Listener 27 *Aug* 1983

RICHARD CROSSMAN

3 He is a man of many opinions, most of them of short duration.
Bessie Braddock, THE BRADDOCKS

CRUELTY

4 The impulse to cruelty is, in many people, almost as violent as the impulse to sexual love — almost as violent and much more mischievous.
Aldous Huxley, BEYOND THE MEXIQUE BAY 1944

5 My mother used to pull my ears and it never did get that much attention.
Lyndon B. Johnson, after the protests caused by a press photograph of him lifting his dog by the ears.

6 The infliction of cruelty with a good conscience is a delight to moralists.
Bertrand Russell, SCEPTICAL ESSAYS 1928

7 Cruelty would be delicious if one could only find some sort of cruelty that didn't hurt.
George Bernard Shaw, HEARTBREAK HOUSE 1920

CRYING

8 Tears were to me what glass beads are to African traders.
Quentin Crisp, THE NAKED CIVIL SERVANT

9 Many tears are joyful.
Tom Stoppard, JUMPERS

10 Only those who still have hopes can benefit from tears.
Nathanael West, THE DAY OF THE LOCUST 1939

CULTURE

11 Culture is far more dangerous than Philistinism, because it is more intelligent and more pliant; it has a specious air of being on the side of the artist.
Clive Bell, ART 1914

12 And what is culture but palaver and swank. I turn up my nose at culture.
Idris Davies, THE LAY PREACHER PONDERS

13 A man of one idea — that all civilisation was the printed fungus of rottenness. He hated any sign of culture.
D. H. Lawrence, THE WHITE PEACOCK 1911

14 Every man with a belly full of culture is an enemy of the human race.
Henry Miller, TROPIC OF CANCER 1934

15 Culture is not life in its entirety, but just the moment of security, strength and clarity.
Jose Ortega y Gasset, MEDITATIONS ON QUIXOTE 1914

16 Culture would not be culture if it were not an acquired taste.
John Cowper Powys, THE MEANING OF CULTURE

17 Culture is on the horns of this dilemma; if profound and noble it must remain rare, if common it must become mean.
George Santayana, THE LIFE OF REASON 1906

18 Mrs Bullinger is one of the ladies who pursue Culture in bands, as though it were dangerous to meet it alone.
Edith Wharton, XINGU

CURIOSITY

19 Curiosity is free-wheeling intelligence.
Alistair Cooke, Vogue, Jan 1953

20 The great thing in life is to be simple and the perfectly simple thing is to look through keyholes.
George Bernard Shaw, GREAT CATHERINE 1918

21 He that breaks a thing to find out what it is has left the path of wisdom.
J. R. R. Tolkien, FELLOWSHIP OF THE RING 1956

1 Disinterested intellectual curiosity is the
lifeblood of real civilisation.
G. M. Trevelyan, ENGLISH SOCIAL HISTORY,
Preface 1944

LORD CURZON

2 I met Curzon in Downing Street, from
whom I got the sort of greeting a corpse
would give to an undertaker.
*Stanley Baldwin, after being chosen Prime
Minister in preference to Curzon, May* 1923

CYNIC

3 *Cynic:* a blackguard whose faulty vision sees
things as they are, and not as they ought to
be.
Ambrose Bierce, THE DEVIL'S
DICTIONARY 1906

4 The temptation shared by all forms of
intelligence: cynicism.
Albert Camus, NOTEBOOKS 1935—1942

5 Cynicism, that corrosive acid of the spirit.
Reginald Pound, THEIR MOODS AND
MINE 1935

D

DANCING

1 Dancing is a perpendicular expression of a
horizontal desire.
Anon.

2 I have no desire to prove anything by
dancing. I have never used it as an outlet or a
means of expressing myself. I just dance.
Fred Astaire. Quoted Leslie Halliwell,
FILMGOER'S BOOK OF QUOTES 1973

3 I just put my feet in the air and move them
around.
Ibid.

4 Dancing is the body made poetic.
Ernst Bacon, NOTES ON THE PIANO 1963

5 Wasn't it Nietzsche who said he wouldn't
believe in a God who could not dance?
Neither could I.
Isadora Duncan. Quoted Lon Tellegan,
WOMEN HAVE BEEN KIND

6 Dancing is the loftiest, the most moving and
the most beautiful of the arts, because it is
no mere translation or abstraction from life,
it is life itself.
Havelock Ellis, THE DANCE OF LIFE 1923

7 She clapped me to her bosom like a
belladonna plaster.
Richard Gordon, DOCTOR AT SEA

8 It is not important that you should know
what a dance means. It is only important
that you should be stirred. If you can write
the story of your dance, it is a literary thing,
but it is not dancing.
Martha Graham. Quoted John Heilpern,
Observer Magazine, The Amazing Martha
8 Jul 1979

9 I refuse to admit that the dance has
limitations that prevent its acceptance and
understanding. The reality of the dance is its
truth to our inner life. Therein lies its power
to move and communicate experience.

We are a visually stimulated world today.
The eye is not to be denied.
Martha Graham 1930

10 Sometimes I think that dancing, like youth,
is wasted on the young.
Max Lerner, THE UNFINISHED
COUNTRY 1959

11 I could dance with you till the cows come
home. Better still, I'll dance with the cows
and *you* come home.
Groucho Marx, DUCK SOUP

12 Fat wet bodies go waddling by / Girded with
satin though God knows why / Gripped by
satyrs in white and black / With a fat wet
hand on a fat wet back.
Alfred Noyes, COLLECTED POEMS, *A*
Victory Dance 1947

13 George M. Cohen always dances interes-
tingly; he has sardonic legs.
Gilbert Seldes, THE SEVEN LIVELY ARTS

14 In the next round the first couple will be
proper, the second couple improper. Couples will be alternately proper and improper
throughout the movement.
Cecil Sharpe, COUNTRY DANCE BOOK

15 Dancing is a very crude attempt to get into
the rhythm of life.
George Bernard Shaw, BACK TO
METHUSELAH 1922

16 O body swayed to music, O brightening
glance / How can we know the dancer from
the dance?
W. B. Yeats, THE TOWER, *Among School*
Children 1928

DANGER

17 Mortal danger is an effective antidote for
fixed ideas.
Field Marshal Erwin Rommel, THE ROMMEL
PAPERS

1 Confront a child, a puppy and a kitten with a sudden danger; the child will turn instinctively for assistance, the puppy will grovel in abject submission, the kitten will brace its tiny body for a frantic resistance.
Saki, THE ACHIEVEMENT OF THE CAT

DARKNESS

2 The darkness declares the glory of the light.
T. S. Eliot, MURDER IN THE
CATHEDRAL 1935

DAWN

3 The morning breaks like a pomegranate / In a shining crock of red.
D. H. Lawrence, WEDDING MORN

4 An owl flies home past Bethesda, to a chapel in an oak. And the dawn inches up.
Dylan Thomas, UNDER MILK WOOD 1954

5 The town ripples like a lake in the waking haze.
Ibid.

6 I hate the dawn. The grass always looks as though it has been left out all night.
Clifton Webb, THE DARK CORNER *(film)*

7 For what human ill does not dawn seem to be an alternative?
Thornton Wilder, THE BRIDGE OF SAN LUIS
REY 1927

DEATH

8 'Are you sure he is dead?'
'He seemed dead. I did my imitation of Maurice Chevalier and it usually gets a big hand. This time, nothing.'
Woody Allen, New Yorker, The Condemned
21 *Nov* 1977

9 Life has its appropriate rewards, whereas when you're dead it's hard to find the light switch.
Woody Allen, WITHOUT FEATHERS

10 On the plus side, death is one of the few things that can be done as easily lying down.
Ibid.

11 It's not that I'm afraid to die. I just don't want to be there when it happens.
Ibid.

12 My family has always been into death. My father, the Major, used to insist on having an ice pick next to his placemat at meals so that he could perform an emergency tracheotomy when one of us strangled on a piece of meat. Even now, by running my index fingers along my collarbones to the indentation where the bones join, I can locate the optimal site for a tracheal puncture with the same deftness as a junky a vein.
Lisa Alther, KINFLICKS, *opening paragraph 1976*

13 Death is nature's way of telling you to slow down.
Anon.

14 Death is the only solution to life which has not so far been definitely proved to be the wrong one.
Raymond Asquith, LIFE AND LETTERS

15 To die will be an awfully big adventure.
J. M. Barrie, PETER PAN 1904

16 He has gone to that Bourne from which no Hollingsworth returns.
Beachcomber (J. B. Morton). Quoted Daily Telegraph obituary 12 *May* 1979

17 It is time for me to become an apprentice once more.
Lord Beaverbrook in his last public speech

18 Death is the dark backing a mirror needs if we are to see anything.
Saul Bellow, Quoted Martin Amis, Observer
11 *Dec* 1983

19 Who now dies at home? Who sees death? We sicken and fade in a hospital ward, and dying is for doctors, with a phone call to the family.
Alan Bennett, FORTY YEARS ON

20 She was always very composed. Now she's decomposed.
Ambrose Bierce. Quoted Richard Connor,
AMBROSE BIERCE

21 Nought broken save this body, lost but breath; / Nothing to shake the laughing heart's long peace there / But only agony, and that has ending / And the worst friend and enemy is but Death.
Rupert Brooke, PEACE

1 Worn hides that scarcely clothe the soul /
They are so rotten, old and thin / Or firm
and soft and warm and full / Fellmonger
Death gets every skin.
Basil Bunting, VILLON

2 To die is to leave off dying and do the thing
once and for all.
Samuel Butler, NOTEBOOKS 1912

3 While other people's deaths are deeply sad,
one's own is surely a bit of a joke.
James Cameron, Observer, Sayings 17 *Jan*
1982

4 Men are never convinced of your reasons, of
your sincerity, of the seriousness of your
sufferings, except by your death.
Albert Camus, THE FALL 1956

5 I am ready to meet my Maker. Whether my
Maker is prepared for the ordeal of meeting
me is another matter.
*Winston Churchill in an interview on his 75th
birthday*

6 The problem is not life after death, which I
regard as absurd, but life before death. That
is urgent, real and earnest.
Hugh Cudlipp, WALKING ON THE WATER

7 When I die I want to decompose in a barrel
of porter and have it served in all the pubs in
Dublin.
J. P. Donleavy, THE GINGER MAN 1955

8 Phlebas the Phoenician, a fortnight dead /
Forget the cry of gulls and the deep sea
swell.
T. S. Eliot, THE WASTE LAND 1922

9 Why should the dead be wiser than the
living? The dead know only this — that it
was better to be alive.
James Elroy Flecker, HASSAN 1923

10 I am afraid to think about my death, / When
it shall be and whether, in great pain / I shall
rise up and fight the air for breath / Or
calmly wait the bursting of my brain.
Ibid.

11 Our final experience, like our first, is
conjectural. We move between two dark-
nesses.
E. M. Forster, ASPECTS OF THE NOVEL 1927

12 The goal of all life is death.
*Sigmund Freud. Quoted New York Times
Magazine* 6 *May* 1966

13 Why fear death? It is the most beautiful
adventure in life.
*Charles Frohman, last words before going
down on the Lusitania* 7 *May* 1915

14 The idea of having to die without having
lived is unbearable.
Erich Fromm, MAN FOR HIMSELF 1947

15 The nearest friends can go / With anyone to
death, comes so far short / They might as
well not try to go at all.
Robert Frost, NORTH OF BOSTON, *Home
Burial* 1914

16 Death's a new interest in life.
Christopher Fry, A PHOENIX TOO
FREQUENT 1949

17 Maintenant elle est comme les autres.
*Charles de Gaulle, at the funeral of his
handicapped daughter*

18 Death is the next step after the pension — it
is perpetual retirement without pay.
Jean Giraudoux, THE ENCHANTED 1933

19 As life's span lengthens more time is allowed
for the encounter with germs or other
accidents. We do not die. We are killed.
George W. Grey, Harper's, Feb 1941

20 I should like to die at the last possible
moment not only of old age but even more
slowly, for never having had the time to live
I should at least like to have time to die. Yes,
I ask for a slow death and every possible
infirmity. That is essential if I am to go
without too much regret.
Sacha Guitry. Quoted Sunday Graphic 13
Nov 1933

21 In the last analysis it is our conception of
death which decides the answers to all the
questions life puts to us.
Dag Hammarskjöld, DIARIES

22 I am not afraid of death. I am afraid of
dying. I should be very glad to be dead, but I
don't look forward to the actual process of
dying.
*Gilbert Harding to John Freeman, BBC TV,
Face to Face*

23 Turn up the lights. I don't want to go home
in the dark.
O. Henry, last words

1 Death is the only thing we haven't succeeded in completely vulgarising.
Aldous Huxley, EYELESS IN GAZA 1936

2 Ignore death until the last moment; then when it can't be ignored any longer have yourself squirted full of morphia and shuffle off in a corner.
Aldous Huxley, TIME MUST HAVE A STOP 1944

3 Every man his price. Well preserved fat corpse, gentleman, epicure, invaluable for fruit garden. A bargain. By carcass of William Wilkinson, auditor and accountant, lately deceased, three pounds thirteen and six. With thanks.
James Joyce, ULYSSES

4 Death is the only pure, beautiful conclusion of a great passion.
D. H. Lawrence, FANTASIA OF THE UNCONSCIOUS 1922

5 I detest life-insurance agents. They always argue that I shall some day die, which is not so.
Stephen Leacock, LITERARY LAPSES 1910

6 When bees swarm in your nostrils / And honey drips from the sockets / Of eyes that today are frantic / With love that is frustrated.
Alun Lewis, TO A COMRADE IN ARMS

7 This is the Black Widow death.
Robert Lowell, MR EDWARDS AND THE SPIDER

8 The only religious way to think of death is as a part and parcel of life.
Thomas Mann, THE MAGIC MOUNTAIN 1924

9 A man's dying is more the survivor's affair than his own.
Ibid.

10 Either he's dead or my watch has stopped.
Groucho Marx, A DAY AT THE RACES *(film) script by Robert Pirosh, George Seaton and George Oppenheim* 1937

11 Death opens unknown doors. It is most grand to die.
John Masefield, POMPEY THE GREAT 1910

12 Dying is a very dull dreary affair and my advice to you is to have nothing whatever to do with it.
W. Somerset Maugham, last words

13 Life is a great surprise. I do not see why death should not be an even greater one.
Vladimir Nabokov, PALE FIRE 1962

14 George Gershwin is dead. I don't have to believe it if I don't want to.
John O'Hara. Quoted Alistair Cooke, BBC Radio 4, Letter from America 31 May 1974

15 All victory ends in the defeat of death. That's sure. But does defeat end in the victory of death? That's what I wonder.
Eugene O'Neill, MOURNING BECOMES ELECTRA 1931

16 I don't mind dying; the trouble is you feel so bloody stiff the next day.
Overheard. Quoted George Axlerod, BBC Radio 4, Quote Unquote 13 Sep 1979

17 In the happy no-time of his sleeping / Death took him by the heart.
Wilfred Owen, POEMS, *Asleep* 1920

18 It costs me never a stab nor squirm / To tread by chance upon a worm / 'Aha my little dear', I say / 'Your clan will pay me back one day.'
Dorothy Parker, SUNSET GUN, *Thought for a Sunshiny Morning* 1928

19 What I look forward to is not a violent death, but dying in the normal way, with my head in the gas oven.
Leo Pavia. Quoted James Agate, EGO 4 *9 Oct* 1938

20 Dying / Is an art, like everything else. / I do it exceptionally well.
Sylvia Plath, ARIEL, *Lady Lazarus*

21 Death is the least we have to fear.
Peter Porter, YOUR ATTENTION PLEASE

22 The people who pretend that dying is rather like strolling into the next room always leave me unconvinced. Death like birth, must be a tremendous event.
J. B. Priestley, OUTCRIES AND ASIDES

23 I have a rendezvous with death / At some disputed barricade.
Alan Seeger, I HAVE A RENDEZVOUS WITH DEATH

1 Life levels all men; death reveals the
eminent.
*George Bernard Shaw, MAN AND
SUPERMAN 1905*

2 I was much further out than you thought /
And not waving but drowning.
Stevie Smith, NOT WAVING BUT DROWNING

3 If there wasn't death I think you couldn't go
on.
Stevie Smith, Observer 9 Nov 1969

4 Death is all in the mind, really. Once you're
dead you forget all about it.
*Jack Trevor Storey, ITV, Jack on the Box 19
Jan 1979*

5 A beautiful death is for people who have
lived like animals to die like angels.
*Mother Teresa, FOR THE BROTHERHOOD OF
MAN*

6 And death shall have no dominion / Dead
men naked they shall be one / With the man
in the wind and the west morn.
*Dylan Thomas, AND DEATH SHALL HAVE
NO DOMINION 1943*

7 Do not go gently into that good night / Old
age should burn and rave at close of day /
Rage rage against the dying of the light.
*Dylan Thomas, DO NOT GO GENTLY INTO
THAT GOOD NIGHT 1952*

8 After the first death there is no other.
*Dylan Thomas, A REFUSAL TO MOURN THE
DEATH OF A CHILD 1946*

9 Death, the only immortal who treats us all
alike, whose peace and whose refuge are for
all. The soiled and the pure, the rich and the
poor, the loved and the unloved.
Mark Twain, on his deathbed

10 The great thing about the dead, they make
space.
John Updike, RABBIT IS RICH

11 We are secretly more terrified of death now
than in medieval times. It is the one aspect of
life, so to speak, that civilisation has not
improved.
Peter Watson, The Times Diary 6 Aug 1981

12 The experiment will be over, the rinsed
beaker returned to its shelf, the crystals
gone dissolving down the wastepipe; the
duster sweeps the bench.
H. G. Wells, FIRST AND LAST THINGS

13 You're old when most people would rather
have you dead.
William Wharton, DAD 1981

14 One of us must go.
*Oscar Wilde, of himself and the wallpaper in
his room. Reputed last words 1900*

15 Death is one moment, life is so many of
them.
*Tennessee Williams, THE MILK TRAIN
DOESN'T STOP HERE ANY MORE 1962*

DEBT

16 The National Debt is a very Good Thing and
it would be dangerous to pay it off for fear of
Political Economy.
*W. C. Sellar and R. J. Yeatman, 1066 AND
ALL THAT 1930*

17 In the midst of life we are in debt.
Sunday Express 11 Sep 1932

18 I may be a chump, but it's my boast that I
don't owe a penny to a single soul — except
tradesmen of course.
*P. G. Wodehouse, JEEVES AND THE HARD-
BOILED EGG*

DECEIT

19 O what a tangled web we weave / When first
we practise to deceive / But when we've
practised quite a while / How vastly we
improve our style.
J. R. Pope, A WORD OF ENCOURAGEMENT

DECISIONS

20 Academic staff rather enjoy coming to a
conclusion, but they don't like coming to
decisions at all.
Lord Annan, Observer 8 Feb 1981

21 I always have one golden rule for such
occasions — I ask myself what Nanny would
have expected me to do.
*Lord Carrington. Quoted Observer, Last of
the Tory Grandees 23 Jan 1983*

22 Impelled by a state of mind which is destined
not to last, we make our irrevocable
decisions.
*Marcel Proust, REMEMBRANCE OF THINGS
PAST 1913—27*

DECORUM

1 Their marriage customs when we first settled in the islands were so shocking that I couldn't possibly tell you about them. But I'll tell Mrs. MacPhail and she'll tell you.
W. Somerset Maugham, RAIN 1921

DEDICATION

2 To my daughter Leonora without whose never failing sympathy and encouragement this book would have been finished in half the time.
P. G. Wodehouse

DEFENCE

3 The bomber will always get through. The only defence is an offence, which means you have to kill women and children more quickly than the enemy if you want to save yourselves.
Stanley Baldwin, House of Commons, Nov 1932

DEFERENCE

4 There are only two people you should ever call 'Sir' — God and the King.
Ian Fleming to Philip Brownrigg. Quoted John Pearson, LIFE OF IAN FLEMING 1966

DEFIANCE

5 We shall defend our island whatever the cost may be. We shall fight on the beaches, we shall fight on the landing grounds, we shall fight on the fields and in the streets, we shall fight in the hills; we shall never surrender.
Winston Churchill, House of Commons 4 Jun 1940

6 But I, despite expert advice / Keep doing things I think are nice, / And though to good I never come — / Inseparable my nose and thumb.
Dorothy Parker, NEITHER BLOODY NOR UNBOWED

DEFINITION

7 To define a thing is to substitute the definition for the thing itself.
Georges Braque, The Times 12 May 1962

DEMOCRACY

8 Democracy means government by discussion, but it is only effective if you can stop people talking.
Clement Attlee, ANATOMY OF BRITAIN

9 The leadership of the privileged has passed away; but it has not been succeeded by that of the eminent. We have entered the region of mass effects.
Winston Churchill, GREAT CONTEMPORARIES 1937

10 What concerns everyone can only be resolved by everyone.
Friedrich Durrenmatt, THE PHYSICISTS, 21 *Points* 1962

11 In every dictatorship wealth is a sacred thing; in democracies it is the *only* sacred thing.
Anatole France, PENGUIN ISLAND 1908

12 Democracy used to be wonderful but now it has got into the wrong hands.
Graffito. Quoted BBC Radio 4, News Quiz 13 Jan 1980

13 Even though counting heads is not an ideal way to govern, at least it is better than breaking them.
Judge Learned Hand. Speech to US Federal Bar Association 8 Mar 1932

14 I swear to the Lord / I still can't see / Why democracy means / Everybody but me.
Langston Hughes, THE BLACK MAN SPEAKS

15 Democracy is only an experiment in government and it has the obvious disadvantage of merely counting votes instead of weighing them.
W. R. Inge (Dean of St Pauls), POSSIBLE RECOVERY

16 A democracy is a state which recognises the subjecting of the minority to the majority.
V. I. Lenin, THE STATE AND THE REVOLUTION

17 I am a democrat because I believe in the Fall and therefore think men too wicked to be trusted with more than the minimum of power over other men.
C. S. Lewis. Quoted Humphrey Carpenter, THE INKLINGS 1978

1 Democracy which began by liberating man politically has developed a dangerous tendency to enslave him through the tyranny of majorities and the deadly power of their opinion.
Ludwig Lewisohn, THE MODERN DRAMA

2 The democratic movement loves a crowd and fears the individuals who compose it.
Walter Lippmann, A PREFACE TO POLITICS 1914

3 Popular government has not yet been proved to guarantee, always and everywhere, good government.
Walter Lippmann, THE PUBLIC PHILOSOPHY 1955

4 In England it is bad manners to be clear, to assert something confidently. It may be your personal view that two and two make four, but you must not state it in a self-assured way because this is a democratic country and others may be of a different opinion.
George Mikes, HOW TO BE AN ALIEN 1946

5 The blind lead the blind. It's the democratic way.
Henry Miller, THE AIR CONDITIONED NIGHTMARE 1945

6 Democracy functions effectively only in its natural unity, the nation-state; the rest is clouds of gas, excuses, abdication and Euro-waffle.
Austin Mitchell, THE CASE FOR LABOUR 1983

7 Man's capacity for justice makes democracy possible, but man's inclination to injustice makes democracy necessary.
Reinhold Niebuhr, THE CHILDREN OF LIGHT AND THE CHILDREN OF DARKNESS 1944

8 Democracy is clearly most appropriate for countries which enjoy an economic surplus and least appropriate where there is an economic insufficiency.
David Morris Potter, PEOPLE OF PLENTY

9 Envy is the basis of democracy.
Bertrand Russell, THE CONQUEST OF HAPPINESS 1930

10 We must be thoroughly democratic and patronise everybody without distinction of class.
George Bernard Shaw, JOHN BULL'S OTHER ISLAND 1904

11 Democracy substitutes election by the incompetent many for appointment by the corrupt few.
George Bernard Shaw, MAN AND SUPERMAN 1905

12 People who want to understand democracy should spend less time in the library with Aristotle and more time on the buses and in the subway.
Simeon Strunsky, NO MEAN CITY

13 There is a limit to the application of democratic methods. You can enquire of all the passengers as to what kind of car they like to ride in, but it is impossible to question them as to whether to apply the brakes when the train is at full speed and an accident threatens.
Leon Trotsky, HISTORY OF THE RUSSIAN REVOLUTION 1932

14 Democracy is supposed to give you the feeling of choice, like Painkiller X and Painkiller Y. But they're both just aspirin.
Gore Vidal. Quoted Martin Amis, Observer 7 Feb 1982

15 The person most to be feared in modern society is the Common Man.
C. V. Wedgwood, VELVET STUDIES

16 Democracy is the recurrent suspicion that more than half of the people are right more than half the time.
E. B. White, THE WILD FLAG 1946

17 That a peasant may become a king does not render the kingdom a democracy.
Woodrow Wilson. Speech, Chattanooga 31 *Aug* 1910

18 The world must be made safe for democracy.
Woodrow Wilson. Speech to US Congress 2 *Apr* 1917

DENTIST

19 The thought of dentists gave him just the same sick horror as the thought of socialism.
H. G. Wells, BEALBY

DEPRESSION

20 It is a bad sign when people are depressed by their own good fortune.
Robert Bolt, A MAN FOR ALL SEASONS 1906

1 In a real dark night of the soul it is always
three in the morning, day after day.
F. Scott Fitzgerald, THE CRACK-UP 1931

2 Noble deeds and hot baths are the best cures
for depression.
Dodie Smith, I CAPTURE THE CASTLE 1948

DESPAIR

3 I turned to speak to God / About the world
in despair / But to make bad matters worse /
I found God wasn't there.
Robert Frost, NOT ALL THERE

4 Despair is the price one pays for setting
oneself an impossible aim.
Graham Greene, THE HEART OF THE
MATTER 1948

5 He who has never hoped can never despair.
George Bernard Shaw, CAESAR AND
CLEOPATRA 1906

6 She gave a sort of despairing gesture, like a
vicar's daughter who has discovered Eras-
tinism in the village.
P. G. Wodehouse, LAUGHING GAS 1957

DESTINY

7 We are not permitted to choose the frame of
our destiny. But what we put into it is ours.
Dag Hammarskjöld, MARKINGS 1964

DESTRUCTION

8 The ridiculous empires break like biscuits.
Roy Fuller, THE MIDDLE OF A WAR

EAMON DE VALERA

9 Lloyd George once remarked that negotiat-
ing with De Valera was like picking up
mercury with a fork. De Valera replied
'Why doesn't he try a spoon?'
Bernard Baruch, THE PUBLIC YEARS

DEVIL

10 An apology for the Devil: It must be
remembered that we have only heard one
side of the case. God has written all the
books.
Samuel Butler, NOTEBOOKS 1912

11 Few people now believe in the devil; but
many enjoy behaving as their ancestors
behaved when the Fiend was a reality as
unquestionable as his opposite number.
Aldous Huxley, THE DEVILS OF
LOUDUN 1952

12 The Devil usually speaks a language called
Bellsybabble, which he makes up himself as
he goes along but when he is very angry he
can speak bad French very well though some
who have heard him say that he has a strong
Dublin accent.
James Joyce, THE CAT AND THE DEVIL

13 It is so stupid of modern civilisation to have
given up belief in the devil when he is the
only explanation of it.
Ronald Knox, LET DONS DELIGHT

14 It is no use casting out devils. They belong to
us, we must accept them and be at peace
with them.
D. H. Lawrence, PHOENIX 1936

15 I used to think the Devil hid / In women's
smiles and wine's carouse, / I called him
Satan, Beelzebub / But now I call him dirty
louse.
Isaac Rosenberg, THE IMMORTALS

16 The Devil can quote Shakespeare for his
own purpose.
George Bernard Shaw

DIALECT

17 Gag me with a spoon!
The Guardian, *Valspeak: dialect of Valley
Girls, San Fernando Valley, California* 26
Oct 1982

DIARY

18 Only good girls keep diaries. Bad girls don't
have the time.
Attr. Tallulah Bankhead

19 I do not keep a diary. Never have. To write a
diary every day is like returning to one's own
vomit.
Enoch Powell, Sunday Times 6 *Nov* 1977

1 Part secret vice, part safety valve, the daily diary entry was also a sort of verbal acrobatic routine, or what Virginia Woolf called 'a fidget round'.
Hilary Spurling, Observer, Verbal acrobatics 24 *Jun* 1984

2 I always say, keep a diary and one day it will keep you.
Mae West. Quoted Janet Watts, Observer, The Diarist 3 *Jan* 1982

3 Nothing has really happened until it has been recorded.
Virginia Woolf. Quoted Harold Nicolson, DIARIES

4 I got out this diary and read, as one always reads one's own writing, with a kind of guilty intensity.
Virginia Woolf, A WRITER'S DIARY 1953

5 Should you wish to make sure that your birthday will be celebrated three hundred years hence, your best course undoubtedly, is to keep a diary.
Virginia Woolf, THE COMMON READER 1925

6 The good diarist writes either for himself alone or for a posterity so distant that it can safely hear every secret and justly weigh every motive.
Ibid.

11 The people must be led, but only at a pace with which they can keep up. To lead them we must give a lot of power to a very few men, and the success of such an experiment depends upon the choice of exceptional men.
Dr Salazar, dictator of Portugal. Quoted Vernon Bartlett, I KNOW WHAT I LIKED

DICTION

12 She is the great lady of the American stage. Her voice is so beautiful that you won't understand a word she says.
Mrs Pat Campbell of an unnamed actress. Quoted James Agate, EGO 3 6 *May* 1937

13 Oh my God. Remember you're in Egypt. The *skay* is only seen in Kensington.
Sir H. Beerbohm Tree, to an actress at rehearsal. Quoted Hesketh Pearson, BEERBOHM TREE

DICTIONARY

14 The responsibility of a dictionary is to record a language, not set its style.
Philip Gove, editor in chief of WEBSTER'S THIRD NEW INTERNATIONAL DICTIONARY, *in a letter to Life* 17 *Nov* 1961

DICTATORSHIP

7 Dictators ride to and fro on tigers which they dare not dismount. And the tigers are getting hungry.
Winston Churchill, WHILE ENGLAND SLEPT

8 I suspect that in our loathing of totalitarianism there is infused a good deal of admiration for its efficiency.
T. S. Eliot, THE IDEA OF A CHRISTIAN SOCIETY 1939

9 So long as men worship the Caesars and Napoleons, Caesars and Napoleons will arise to make them miserable.
Aldous Huxley, ENDS AND MEANS 1937

10 The identification of one person with a country is always fragile, even if it does not seem so at the time.
Adam Mars-Jones, Sunday Times 8 *Sep* 1985

DIET

15 The right diet directs sexual energy into the parts that matter.
Barbara Cartland. Quoted Observer 11 *Jan* 1981

16 Don't eat too many almonds. They add weight to the breasts.
Colette, GIGI 1945

17 Unlike Americans, the English do not take their digestions seriously.
Oswald Greene (advertising agent for Colman's Mustard). Quoted Janet Hitchman, SUCH A STRANGE LADY

18 There was only one occasion in my life when I put myself on a strict diet and I can tell you, hand on heart, it was the most miserable afternoon I have ever spent.
Denis Norden, OH, MY WORD

DIFFERENCE

1 'Vot' asked George I courteously, 'is the difference between a public nuisance and a public convenience?'
Caryl Brahms and S. J. Simon, NO NIGHTINGALES

DIGNITY

2 It is only people of small stature who need to stand on their dignity.
Arnold Bennett, JOURNALS 1928

3 It is terrifying to see how easily, in certain people, all dignity collapses. Yet when you think about it, this is quite normal since they only maintain this dignity by constantly striving against their own nature.
Albert Camus, NOTEBOOKS 1935—1942

4 The English are, on the whole, much more concerned with dignity than with passion. They resent nothing so much as to be made to look foolish.
William Davies, Punch 9 Feb 1972

5 Dignity is something you are born with or without. Too many people confuse dignity with pomposity.
Mary Margaret McBride

DIPLOMACY

6 [John Foster Dulles] invented Brinkmanship, the most popular game since Monopoly.
Richard Armour, IT ALL STARTED WITH COLUMBUS 1961

7 Let us not be deceived — we are today in the midst of a cold war.
Bernard Baruch. Speech South Carolina Legislature 16 *Apr* 1947

8 The ability to get to the verge without getting into the war is the necessary art. If you try to run away from it, if you are scared to go to the brink, you are lost.
John Foster Dulles. Quoted James Shepley, Life, How Dulles Avoided War 16 *Jan* 1956

9 Diplomats never ask. They make representations.
J. K. Galbraith, ECONOMICS, PEACE AND LAUGHTER

10 Diplomacy is to do and say / The nastiest thing in the nicest way.
Isaac Goldberg, THE REFLEX

11 Diplomacy is the art of fishing tranquilly in troubled waters.
J. Christopher Harold, BONAPARTE IN EGYPT

12 Megaphone diplomacy leads to a dialogue of the deaf.
Geoffrey Howe, Observer, Sayings of the Week 29 *Sep* 1985

13 Forever poised between a cliche and an indiscretion.
Harold Macmillan. Quoted Newsweek 30 *Apr* 1956

14 At vast expense the Ambassadors offer up their livers almost every night in the service of their country.
Patrick O'Donovan, A JOURNALIST'S ODYSSEY 1985

15 Diplomats are just as essential to starting a war as soldiers are to finishing it. You take Diplomacy out of war and the thing would fall flat in a week.
Will Rogers, AUTOBIOGRAPHY 1949

16 A nation does not have to be cruel to be tough.
F. D. Roosevelt. Radio speech 13 *Oct* 1940

17 Speak softly and carry a big stick.
Theodore Roosevelt. Speech 2 *Sep* 1901

18 One of the defects of the summit meeting is that if it doesn't come off there's nowhere else to go.
Lord Sheffield, Thames Television, The Day Before Yesterday 1970

19 Brinkmanship — the art of bringing us to the edge of the nuclear abyss.
Adlai Stevenson. Speech 25 *Feb* 1952

20 A diplomat is a person who can tell you to go to hell in such a way that you actually look forward to the trip.
Caskie Stinnet, OUT OF THE RED

21 A diplomat these days is nothing but a head waiter who's allowed to sit down occasionally.
Peter Ustinov, ROMANOFF AND JULIET

1 Moral power is probably best when it is not used. The less you use it the more you have.
Andrew Young in an interview with Jonathan Power, Observer 8 *Sep* 1979

DISAGREEMENT

2 The history of scholarship is a history of disagreements.
Charles Evans Hughes. Speech to American Law Institute 7 *May* 1936

DISAPPROVAL

3 Disapproval from persons whose approval is as weightless as a man in space, is no worse than bouquets from them.
William Plomer, London Magazine, Oct 1963

DISARMAMENT

4 We are discussing the end of the world — or how to delay it.
Stuart Blanche (Archbishop of York), Church of England Synod, The Church and the Bomb debate 10 *Feb* 1983

DISBELIEF

5 If faith can move mountains, disbelief can deny them existence and faith is impotent against such importance.
Arnold Schoenberg, preface to Anton Webern's SIX BAGATELLES FOR STRING QUARTET 1908

DISCIPLINE

6 Historically, those people that did not discipline themselves had discipline thrust upon them from the outside.
Alistair Cooke, AMERICA

DISCOMFORT

7 How did the Greeks stand marble benches in their theatres?
Aldous Huxley, ANTIC HAY 1923

DISCONTENT

8 Sir Humphry Davy / Detested gravy / He died in the odium / Of having discovered sodium.
E. C. Bentley, BIOGRAPHY FOR BEGINNERS 1921

9 While not exactly disgruntled, he was far from feeling gruntled.
P. G. Wodehouse, CODE OF THE WOOSTERS 1938

DISCRETION

10 Drawing on my fine command of language, I said nothing.
Robert Benchley, CHIPS OFF THE OLD BENCHLEY 1949

11 If you don't say anything you won't be called on to repeat it.
Calvin Coolidge

DISGUST

12 I had something of the feeling that one has when one looks into a sink without holding one's nose.
John Galsworthy of serving on a Grand Jury, MEMORIES

DISILLUSION

13 The coach has turned into a pumpkin and the mice have all run away.
Lady Bird Johnson on leaving the White House on the election of Richard Nixon. Quoted Lyndon B. Johnson, THE VANTAGE POINT

14 There aren't any big, brave causes left.
John Osborne, LOOK BACK IN ANGER 1957

15 Nothing can be more deeply wounding than the disillusionments of a child or adolescent, but the disillusionments of an old man are old scars, slowly formed over the wounds of a long lifetime.
William Plomer, BBC broadcast on Leonard Woolf 14 *Dec* 1969

DISLIKE

1 You really have to get to know Dewey to dislike him.
James T. Patterson, MR REPUBLICAN, A BIOGRAPHY OF ROBERT A. TAFT

WALT DISNEY

2 Soft little faces turned stony when I dealt out books by such counterfeit authors as Barrie, Collodi or Salten. Was I really too dumb, their withering looks asked plainly, to know that Walt Disney had written 'Peter Pan' and 'Pinocchio' and 'Bambi'?
Wanda Burgan, Punch, Librarian 12 *Sep* 1962

3 I love Mickey Mouse more than any woman I've every known.
Walt Disney. Quoted Walter Wagner, YOU MUST REMEMBER THIS

4 He can make an endlessly amusing operetta out of some old razor blades, a needle and thread, and perhaps a few soft-shelled crabs.
Otis Ferguson, THE FILM CRITICISM OF OTIS FERGUSON

5 Disney . . . an artist who uses his brains, the most significant figure in graphic art since Leonardo.
David Low. Quoted R. Schickel, WALT DISNEY

DISPARAGEMENT

6 Lord Montague of Beaulieu . . . has a splendid motor museum. My husband refers cattily to him and his collection as 'Edward and his Garage'.
Duchess of Bedford, NICOLE NOBODY

DISRESPECT

7 I suggest that speakers in 'Children's Hour' should not use the word 'Hello' when addressing children. Country children now invariably greet their elders with this word, spoken in anything but a respectful tone.
Letter to Radio Times

DIVERSITY

8 Every divergence deserves to be cherished, simply because it widens the bounds of life. Let us be united by everything that divides us.
Karel Čapek, LETTERS FROM SPAIN

DIVORCE

9 Divorce of one's parents is said to be disturbing, but I don't know that I want sympathy. I might otherwise have been a factory hand in Leeds.
Paul Ableman in an interview, The Times 11 *Jul* 1970

10 You can make divorce as easy to obtain as a dog licence, but you can't burn away the sense of shame and waste.
A. Alvarez, LIFE AFTER MARRIAGE 1982

11 She blamed me for cruelty and flagrant infidelity. I spent a whole weekend in Brighton with a lady called Vera Williams. She had the nastiest-looking hair brush I have ever seen.
Noël Coward, PRIVATE LIVES 1930

12 Divorce is America's great contribution to marriage.
Edmund Fawcett and Tony Thomas, AMERICA, AMERICANS 1983

13 A woman's career, particularly if it is successful, is often blamed for the break-up of a marriage, but never a man's.
Eva Figes, PATRIARCHAL ATTITUDES 1970

14 You never really know a man until you have divorced him.
Zsa-Zsa Gabor

15 The trouble is, Jane is still young enough to think one man may be better than another.
Jennie Lee. Quoted Jill Craigie, The Times 13 *Nov* 1980

DOCTOR

16 My dear old friend George V always told me he would never have died but for that vile doctor [Dawson of Penn].
Margot Asquith, AUTOBIOGRAPHY 1936

1 Physicians of the utmost fame / Were called at once; but when they came / They answered as they took their fees, / 'There is no cure for this disease.'
Hilaire Belloc, CAUTIONARY TALES 1907

2 They leave it to Nature to cure in her own time, but they take the credit. As well as very fat fees.
Anthony Burgess, NOTHING LIKE THE SUN 1964

3 I went to my doctor and asked for something for persistent wind. He gave me a kite.
Les Dawson, BBC TV, The Good Old Days 24 *Apr* 1979

4 The doctor was puzzled by the fact that it wasn't quite jaundice. If it became jaundice they could treat it. If it didn't become jaundice and went away they could discharge him. But this just being short of jaundice all the time confused them.
Joseph Heller, CATCH 22 1961

5 Medicine's real triumphs lie in improving the quality of life for everyone not in death-defying heroics that benefit or torment a few.
New York Times, on the first artificial heart implant 16 *Dec* 1982

6 One finger in the throat and one in the rectum makes a good diagnostician.
Sir William Osler. Quoted Philip Howard, The Times 16 *Nov* 1985

7 When treating a cold a Doctor can go rather mechanically through a list of prescriptions, remedies and a routine which the patient 'must' follow and then say 'I've got just the same sort of cold myself. They're about everywhere. What do I do about it? Well personally I do nothing whatever. Absolutely nothing — I'm sorry to say. Just go on as if nothing has happened. What? Bed — that is my order to you.'
Stephen Potter, ONE-UPMANSHIP 1952

8 If Patient turns out to be really ill after all, it is always possible to look grave at the same time and say 'You realise, I suppose, that twenty-five years ago you'd have been dead'.
Ibid.

9 Doctors really must get typewriters. This lady is suffering from something unreadable.
Judge Tudor Rees, Brentford County Court. Quoted News Review 27 *Nov* 1947

10 Let no one suppose that the words doctor and patient can disguise from the parties the fact that they are employer and employee.
George Bernard Shaw, DOCTOR'S DILEMMA, *preface* 1906

DOG

11 The woman who is really kind to dogs is always one who has failed to inspire sympathy in men.
Max Beerbohm, ZULEIKA DOBSON 1911

12 The great pleasure of a dog is that you may make a fool of yourself with him and not only will he not scold you, he will make a fool of himself too.
Samuel Butler, NOTEBOOKS 1912

13 It's a rough-haired canary.
Mrs Pat Campbell, to a customs officer who found her pet pekinese smuggled in her muff

14 The dog is the public enemy of a large and increasing proportion of men. What dear Fido does when he goes out for his constitutional seems to be quite out of the realm of ordinary jurisprudence.
Dr O. P. Clark, Medical World, Mar 1947

15 Anybody who hates children and dogs can't be all bad.
W. C. Fields. Quoted Robert Lewis Taylor, W. C. FIELDS, ROWDY KING OF COMEDY

16 To his dog, every man is Napoleon, hence the constant popularity of dogs.
Aldous Huxley

17 If you go out for a walk with a friend, don't say a word for hours; if you go out for a walk with your dog, keep chatting to him.
George Mikes, HOW TO BE AN ALIEN 1946

18 The censure of a dog is something no man can stand.
Christopher Morley, THE HAUNTED BOOKSHOP 1919

19 A dog gladly admits the superiority of his master over himself, accepts his judgment as final, but, contrary to what many dog-lovers believe, he does not consider himself as a slave. His submission is voluntary, and he expects his own small rights to be respected.
Axel Munthe, THE STORY OF SAN MICHELE

1 A door is what a dog is always on the wrong side of.
Ogden Nash, THE PRIVATE DINING ROOM, *A Dog's Best Friend is His Illiteracy* 1953

2 Dogs display reluctance and wrath / If you try to give them a bath / They bury bones in hideaways / And half the time they trot sideaways.
Ogden Nash, I'M A STRANGER HERE MYSELF, *An Introduction to Dogs* 1938

3 The dogs had eaten the upholstery of a Packard convertible that afternoon, and were consequently somewhat subdued.
S. J. Perelman, THE LAST LAUGH

4 In the case of the gentleman the worship of his dogs reaches its apotheosis when they are so old and cantankerous that they are deaf and blind and smell of blocked drains. Then they enjoy the best chair in the drawing room, from which point of vantage they enjoy their last remaining pleasure of biting anyone who comes near them.
Douglas Sutherland, THE ENGLISH GENTLEMAN 1978

5 He was always sorry, mother said, after he bit someone, but we could not understand how she figured this out. He didn't act sorry.
James Thurber, THE DOG THAT BIT PEOPLE

6 It is a terrible thing for an old lady to outlive her dogs.
Tennessee Williams, CAMINO REAL 1953

7 I can train any dog in five minutes. It's training the owner that takes longer.
Barbara Woodhouse

8 The poor dog had a distressing malady. Mrs (Dorothy) Parker issued bulletins about his health. Confidential bulletins, tinged with scepticism. 'He *said* he got it from a lamp post.'
Alexander Woollcott, WHILE ROME BURNS, *Our Mrs Parker* 1935

DOGMATISM

9 When people are least sure, they are often the most dogmatic.
J. K. Galbraith, THE GREAT CRASH 1955

10 The greater the ignorance the greater the dogmatism.
Sir William Osler, *Montreal Medical Journal* 1902

DOUBT

11 Your doubt may be a good quality if you train it.
Rainer Maria Rilke, LETTERS TO A YOUNG POET 1903

12 The trouble with the world is that the stupid are cocksure and the intelligent full of doubt.
Bertrand Russell, AUTOBIOGRAPHY 1969

13 Doubt is part of all religion. All the religious thinkers were doubters.
Isaac Bashevis Singer. Quoted Richard Burgen, New York Times Magazine 3 Dec 1978

DRAMA

14 Drama is a synthetic and not an analytical art. Very few novelists grasp the fact that a tone of voice and a slight change of facial expression may suggest more than pages of analysis and description.
E. A. Baughan, John o'London's Weekly, Galsworthy: The Plays 8 Dec 1928

15 A play should give you something to think about. When I see a play and understand it the first time, then I know it can't be much good.
T. S. Eliot, New York Post 22 Sep 1963

16 In my plays I want to look at life — at the commonplace of existence — as if we had just turned a corner and run into it for the first time.
Christopher Fry, Time 20 Nov 1952

17 The theatre, so called, can flourish on barbarism, but any *drama* worth speaking of can develop but in the air of civilisation.
Henry James, letter to C. E. Wheeler 2 Apr 1911

18 All playwrights should be dead for three hundred years.
Joseph L. Mankiewicz, ALL ABOUT EVE *(film)*

19 The drama is make-believe. It does not deal with truth but with effect.
W. Somerset Maugham, THE SUMMING UP 1938

20 The structure of a play is always the story of how the birds came home to roost.
Arthur Miller, Harper's, Aug 1958

1 Drama — what literature does at night.
George Jean Nathan, TESTAMENT OF A
CRITIC

2 Drama is action, sir, action and not con-
founded philosophy.
Luigi Pirandello, SIX CHARACTERS IN
SEARCH OF AN AUTHOR 1921

3 A play isn't a text. It's an event.
*Tom Stoppard. Quoted Pendennis,
Observer 30 Aug* 1981

4 The unencumbered stage encourages the
truth operative in everyone. The less seen,
the more heard. The eye is the enemy of the
ear in real drama.
Thornton Wilder, New York Times 6 Nov
1961

DREAM

5 Last night I dreamt I went to Manderley
again.
Daphne du Maurier, REBECCA, *opening
words* 1938

6 I'm one of those people given to dreaming
about the Queen. In one, I remember, I was
just getting on very well with the Queen
when Prince Charles came in, dressed in
Boy Scout uniform.
*Graham Greene, in an interview with J. W.
Lambert, Sunday Times 5 Mar* 1978

7 To say that, when you dream, you are not
conscious is to speak loosely; one is only
conscious, only lucid in dreams.
Eugene Ionesco, FRAGMENTS OF A JOURNAL

8 I was never able to agree with Freud that the
dream is a 'façade' behind which its meaning
was hidden — a meaning already known but
maliciously, so to speak, withheld from
consciousness. To me dreams are a part of
nature, which harbours no intention to deceive but expresses something
as best it can, just as a plant grows or an
animal seeks its food as best it can.
Carl Jung, MEMORIES, DREAMS,
REFLECTIONS

9 It is on the whole probable that we
continually dream, but that consciousness
makes such a noise that we do not hear it.
Carl Jung. Quoted Charles Rycroft, THE
INNOCENCE OF DREAMS

10 If you can dream, and not make dream your
master.
Rudyard Kipling, IF 1910

11 All men dream; but not equally. Those who
dream by night in the dusty recesses of their
minds wake in the day to find it was vanity;
but the dreamers of the day are dangerous
men, for they may act their dream with open
eyes, to make it possible.
T. E. Lawrence, SEVEN PILLARS OF
WISDOM 1926

12 The boys are dreaming wicked or of the
bucking ranches of the night and the
jollyrodgered sea.
Dylan Thomas, UNDER MILK WOOD 1954

13 One can write, think and pray exclusively of
others; dreams are all egocentric.
Evelyn Waugh, DIARIES 5 *Oct* 1962

14 I have spread my dreams under your feet; /
Tread softly because you tread on my
dreams.
W. B. Yeats, HE WISHES FOR THE CLOTHS OF
HEAVEN 1950

DRESS

15 It was necessary to abolish the fez, which sat
on the heads of our nation as an emblem of
ignorance, negligence, fanaticism and
hatred of progress and civilisation; to accept
in its place the hat, the headgear worn by all
the civilised world.
*Kemal Ataturk, addressing the Turkish
Assembly, Oct* 1927

16 I prefer the clothes I wear in Worcestershire
to those I wear in London.
Stanley Baldwin. Speech 5 May 1925

17 There is invariably something odd about
women who wear ankle socks.
Alan Bennett, THE OLD COUNTRY

18 One cannot say she was dressed. She was
clothed. And so uncertainly that it was
unsure she would remain even that.
*Ivy Compton-Burnett. Quoted Julian
Mitchell, BBC Radio 4, Quote Unquote 5
Feb* 1982

19 Edith Sitwell, in that great Risorgimento
cape of hers, looks as if she were covering a
teapot, or a telephone.
Noël Coward. Quoted William Merchant,
THE PRIVILEGE OF HIS COMPANY 1980

1 His clothes were pressed, like pretty leaves,
when they / Are found in Bibles closed for
many a day.
W. H. Davies, ONE POET VISITS ANOTHER

2 An overcoat of a plaid so loud that when it
was removed and shut in a closet a hush
seemed to fall over the house.
Peter De Vries, CONSENTING ADULTS

3 Contrary to popular belief, English women
do not wear tweed nightgowns.
Hermione Gingold, Saturday Review 10 *Apr*
1955

4 The pull-over, of subfusc colouring and
worn by daring young men over a soft-
collared shirt, with a coloured tie and no
tie-pin . . . was the first garment that could
be used interchangeably by men and
women.
Robert Graves and Alan Hodge, THE LONG
WEEKEND 1940

5 The main difference between the upper and
lower orders in Britain is that the upper
orders wear fancy dress once or twice a year,
and the lower orders wear it all the time.
Clive James, BRILLIANT CREATURES 1983

6 When I was a boy they were so covered up
that I thought all women were solid down to
the ankles, where they branched out into a
pair of feet.
C. E. M. Joad. Quoted News Review 16 *Jan*
1947

7 He [Marlon Brando] dressed himself up so
nattily for his first audition that none of the
people there took him for an actor. 'From
that time on I determined to become the
messiest dresser of them all' he says. Thus
was the torn T-shirt launched.
Roderick Mann, Sunday Express 16 *Jul* 1961

8 There was a young belle of old Natchez /
Whose garments were always in patchez /
When comment arose / On the state of her
clothes / She drawled: When Ah itchez Ah
scratchez.
Ogden Nash, I'M A STRANGER HERE
MYSELF, *Requiem* 1938

9 Disgraceful, I know, but I can't help
choosing my underwear with a view to it
being seen.
Barbara Pym, A VERY PRIVATE EYE 1984

10 His socks compelled one's attention without
losing one's respect.
Saki, MINISTERS OF GRACE

11 We cannot congratulate Mr. Churchill on
his wedding outfit. It was not a success. The
sleeves were too short and too backward
hanging, and consequently creased badly
when the arms were brought forward. It was
too long and heavy for a morning coat, and
too skimpy for a 'frock'.
Tailor and Cutter 1908

12 Gloves have always been in some sense a
symbol of gentility.
The Times. *Quoted News Review* 24 *Jul* 1947

DRINK

13 The point about white Burgundies is that I
hate them myself. They so closely resemble
a blend of cold chalk soup and alum cordial
with an additive or two to bring it to the
colour of children's pee.
Kingsley Amis, THE GREEN MAN 1969

14 Some years ago a couple of friends of mine
stopped drinking suddenly and died in
agony. I swore then that such a thing should
never happen to me.
*John Barrymore. Quoted J. P. McEvoy,
Stage, Jan* 1941

15 'Do you realise that those martinis you keep
drinking are slow poison?'
'I'm in no hurry.'
*Retort, variously attributed but believed
originated by Robert Benchley at a party*

16 Note in the barracks: 'Drink drives out the
man and brings out the beast'. Which makes
men understand why they like it.
Albert Camus, NOTEBOOKS 1935—1942

17 Lord Carson: Do you drink?
Witness: That's my business.
Carson: Any other?
Lord Carson. Quoted Edward Bell, THESE
MEDDLESOME ATTORNEYS

18 By the end of five days I had completely
overcome my repugnance for the taste of
whisky.
Winston Churchill, MY EARLY LIFE 1930

19 Swill champagne but sip claret.
*Winston Churchill. Quoted John Boyd
Carpenter*, WAY OF LIFE 1982

1 You can no more keep a martini in the refrigerator than you can keep a kiss there. The proper union of gin and vermouth . . . is one of the happiest marriages on earth and one of the shortest lived.
Bernard De Voto, THE HOUR 1951

2 When he buys his ties he has to ask if gin will make them run.
F. Scott Fitzgerald, NOTEBOOKS

3 Never have a small glass of port, my lad. It just goes wambling around looking for damage to do. Have a large glass. It settles down and does you good.
Attr. Lord Goddard, advising a young member at his club

4 I'd rather have a full bottle in front of me than a full-frontal lobotomy.
Grafitto. Quoted BBC Radio 4, Quote Unquote

5 You might make that a double.
Neville Heath, when offered a drink by the prison governor before being executed for a double murder, Oct 1946

6 Champagne is the right drink for politics. It stimulates at the time and does not deaden afterwards. In the nineteenth century it was prized for its medicinal qualities. It is a pity that most twentieth-century politicians have abandoned champagne for other drinks which are heavier and just as expensive.
Douglas Hurd, AN END TO PROMISES: A SKETCH OF GOVERNMENT 1970—74

7 Champagne has the taste of an apple peeled with a steel knife.
Aldous Huxley, TIME MUST HAVE A STOP 1944

8 I have never been able to drink except when I am thirsty, then it is most enjoyable.
Geoffrey Keynes, THE GATES OF MEMORY 1981

9 The Spanish wine, my God it is foul, catpiss is champagne compared, this is the sulphurous urination of some aged horse.
D. H. Lawrence. Letter to Rhys Davis 25 Apr 1929

10 Two inches to the north-west is written a word full of meaning — the most purposeful word that can be written on a map — 'Inn'.
A. A. Milne, IF I MAY

11 Three highballs and I think I'm St Francis of Assisi.
Dorothy Parker, JUST A LITTLE ONE

12 Champagne and orange juice is a great drink. The orange improves the champagne. The champagne definitely improves the orange.
Philip, Duke of Edinburgh. Quoted Noël St George, ROYAL QUOTES

13 Beer drinking don't do half the harm of lovemaking.
Eden Philpotts, THE FARMER'S WIFE

14 I can't drink Guinness out of a thick mug. I only like it out of a thin glass.
Harold Pinter, THE CARETAKER 1959

15 A good general rule is to say the bouquet is better than the taste, and vice versa.
Stephen Potter, ONE-UPMANSHIP 1952

16 I am only a beer teetotaller, not a champagne teetotaller.
George Bernard Shaw, CANDIDA 1904

17 I must get out of these wet clothes and into a dry martini.
Alexander Woollcott. Quoted Howard Techmann, SMART ALEC 1976

DRUNKENNESS

18 . . . a drunken, ridiculous air, like solemn men in paper hats.
J. G. Farrell, TROUBLES

19 Pubs make you as drunk as they can, as soon as they can, and turn nasty when they succeed.
Colin MacInnes, ENGLAND HALF-ENGLISH

20 You are not drunk if you can lie on the floor without holding on.
Dean Martin. Quoted Peter Dickson, THE OFFICIAL RULES

21 Philip Toynbee had an unfortunate disposition to collapse under drink as though a sniper had picked him off.
Jessica Mitford, THE FACE OF PHILIP 1984

22 I am as drunk as a lord, but then, I am one, so what does it matter?
Bertrand Russell. Quoted Ralph Schoenmann, BERTRAND RUSSELL, PHILOSOPHER OF THE CENTURY

1 I think I am the only one of His Majesty's
Ministers who has drunk a Soviet Minister
under the table.
*Harold Wilson, when President of the Board
of Trade. Quoted News Review 13 May 1948*

DUKE

2 The advantages of being a Duke may be
completely undeserved, but they are numerous and enormous.
Duke of Bedford, BOOK OF SNOBS

3 I am the rock-and-roll version of Pomp and
Circumstance.
*Duke of Bedford. Quoted David
MacDonald, Saturday Evening Post 11 Jul
1959*

4 Lord Lucky, by a curious fluke / Became a
most important duke / From living in a vile
hotel / A long way east of Camberwell / He
rose in less than half an hour / To riches,
dignity and power.
Hilaire Belloc, MORE PEERS

5 A fully equipped duke costs as much to keep
up as two dreadnoughts. They are just as
great a terror, and last longer.
*David Lloyd George at Newcastle upon
Tyne 1909*

6 Of course, in these days, Russian Dukes are
about as useful as dandruff.
*Damon Runyon, MORE THAN SOMEWHAT,
Broadway Financier 1937*

DUTY

7 There are a lot of things in life which need
doing which you may not like the idea of
doing. This is the whole idea of duty.
Charles, Prince of Wales. Quoted Time

8 Let us therefore brace ourselves to our
duties, and so bear ourselves that, if the
British Empire and its Commonwealth last
for a thousand years, men will say 'This was
their finest hour.'
*Winston Churchill, House of Commons 18
Jun 1940*

9 When a duty ceases to be a pleasure then it
ceases to exist.
*Norman Douglas, GOODBYE TO WESTERN
CULTURE*

10 Duty largely consists of pretending that the
trivial is critical.
John Fowles, THE MAGUS 1965

11 The dull, leaden, soul-depressing sensation
known as the sense of duty.
O. Henry, NO STORY

12 Do your duty. Fear God. Honour the King.
*Lord Kitchener. Message in soldier's
paybooks 1914–1918 war*

13 If we believe a thing to be bad, and if we
have a right to prevent it, it is our duty to try
to prevent it, and damn the consequences.
*Alfred, Lord Milner. Speech, Glasgow 26
Nov 1909*

14 O Duty / Why has thou not the visage of a
sweetie or a cutie? / Why glitter thy
spectacles so ominously? / Why art thou
clad so abominously? / Why art thou so
different from Venus? / And why do you
and I have so few interests in common
between us?
Ogden Nash, KIND OF AN ODE TO DUTY

15 A sense of duty is useful in work, but
offensive in personal relations. People wish
to be liked, not endured with patient
resignation.
*Bertrand Russell, THE CONQUEST OF
HAPPINESS 1930*

16 When a stupid man is doing something he is
ashamed of, he always declares that it is his
duty.
*George Bernard Shaw, CAESAR AND
CLEOPATRA 1906*

17 The worst of doing one's duty was that it
apparently unfitted one for doing anything
else.
*Edith Wharton, THE AGE OF
INNOCENCE 1920*

E

EAR

1 Miss Penny laughed and rattled the miniature gallows of her ears.
Aldous Huxley, MORTAL COILS 1922

EAST

2 The mysterious East, perfumed like a flower, silent like death, dark like a grave.
Joseph Conrad, YOUTH 1902

EATING

3 The last man in the world whose opinion I would take on what to eat would be a doctor. It is far safer to consult a waiter, and not a bit more expensive.
Robert Lynd, SOLOMON IN ALL HIS GLORY

4 On the Continent people use a fork as though a fork were a shovel: in England they turn it upside down and push everything — including peas — on top of it.
George Mikes, HOW TO BE AN ALIEN 1946

5 In England – whether the meal is divine or foul – you eat it as if you did not notice the difference.
Ibid.

6 The man in evening clothes dining with the napkin in his lap will eat only half as much food as a diner in evening clothes with his napkin in his collar. The former will not only be worrying about spotting his shirt bosom but about the remarks his wife will make if he does.
Damon Runyon, MORE THAN SOMEWHAT 1937

7 I eat merely to put food out of my mind.
N. F. Simpson, THE HOLE

8 The Russians in the late war were enormously impressed by Churchill at the table. His appetite for caviar and vodka convinced them that they were fighting on the right side.
Robert Lewis Taylor, THE AMAZING MR CHURCHILL

9 'If you don't mind' said Colonel Blount, 'I prefer not to talk at meals.' He popped a morocco-bound volume of *Punch* before his plate against a vast silver urn from which grew a small castor-oil plant.
'Give Mr Symes a book,' he said.
Mrs Florin put another volume of *Punch* beside Adam.
'If you come across anything really funny, read it to me,' said Colonel Blount.
Then they had luncheon.
Evelyn Waugh, VILE BODIES 1930

ECCENTRICITY

10 She used to eat chops in the small hours and sleep in a hat. Once she arrived home at seven a.m. carrying a gate. Who am I to say there was anything wrong with her?
Alan Coren, THE SANITY INSPECTOR 1974

11 The individual rebel, no matter how unspotted from the world he may keep himself, is bound to be tainted by idiosyncrasy and eccentricity; he is likely to be a prig and a faddist.
Eric Gill. Quoted Malcolm Yorke, ERIC GILL : MAN OF FLESH AND SPIRIT 1981

12 I am not going to be quite as reclusive as I have been because it has apparently attracted so much attention that I have just got to live a somewhat modified life in order not to be an oddity.
Howard Hughes, last public statement 1972

ECONOMICS

13 Man will never be enslaved by machinery *if* the man tending the machine be paid enough.
Karel Čapek. Quoted in obituary by Guy Ramsay, News Chronicle 27 Dec 1938

1 Economics, whether you like it or not, are here to stay.
Charles, Prince of Wales, BBC Radio London 14 Nov 1980

2 There is no such thing as a free lunch.
Economists' aphorism. Quoted Richard Rose and Gay Peters, CAN GOVERNMENTS GO BANKRUPT?

3 Everyone is always in favour of general economy and specific expenditure.
Sir Anthony Eden. Quoted Observer 17 Jun 1958

4 Economics as a positive science is a body of tentatively accepted generalisations about economic phenomena that can be used to predict the consequences of changes in circumstances.
Milton Friedman, ESSAYS ON POSITIVE ECONOMICS

5 Just as there must be balance in what a community produces, so there must also be a balance in what the community consumes.
J. K. Galbraith, THE AFFLUENT SOCIETY 1958

6 Economists are economical, among other things, of ideas. They make those they acquire as graduate students do for a lifetime. Changes in economics come only with changing generations.
J. K. Galbraith, AGE OF UNCERTAINTY 1977

7 What is wholly mysterious in economics is not likely to be important.
J. K. Galbraith, ECONOMICS, PEACE AND LAUGHTER

8 Economists have vanities of expression and an accomplished practitioner can often get the words parameter, stochastic and aggregation into a single sentence.
Ibid.

9 The individual serves the industrial system not by supplying it with savings and the resulting capital; he serves it by consuming its products.
J. K. Galbraith, THE NEW INDUSTRIAL STATE 1967

10 The economists who are most highly regarded in their own time have almost always been those who confined themselves

to abstract speculation unmarred by social purpose.
J. K. Galbraith, A LIFE IN OUR TIMES 1982

11 There is little point in producing more food if the hungry cannot afford to buy it.
Geoffrey Lean, Observer 20 Aug 1978

12 There are in the field of economic events no constant relations, and consequently no measurement is possible.
Ludwig Elder von Mises, HUMAN ACTION

13 Recession is when your neighbour loses his job; depression is when you lose yours.
Ronald Reagan, Presidential campaign speech, Oct 1980

14 Thanks to Keynes, with his cocksure advice, his pseudo-scientific rigour, his political influence, social position and philosophical air, economics became the teacher of politics, and the professor of this newfangled subject became the master of those who govern us.
Roger Scruton, The Times 11 Feb 1986

15 What economic history needs at present is not more documents but a pair of stout boots.
R.H. Tawney. Quoted A.L. Rowse, THE USE OF HISTORY

16 The government is paying peanuts and getting monkeys.
Richard Wainwright MP, BBC Radio 4, The Week in Westminster 10 Jul 1982

17 One man's pay rise is another man's price increase.
Sir Harold Wilson

ECSTASY

18 The ecstasy of religion, the ecstasy of art and the ecstasy of love are the only things worth thinking about and experiencing.
Don Marquis, THE ALMOST PERFECT STATE

ANTHONY EDEN

19 He is more pathetic than sinister. Beneath the sophistication of his appearance and manner he has all the unplumbable stupidities and unawareness of his class and type.
Aneurin Bevan, Tribune 15 Jan 1943

1 The charming milksop who became the blood-lusting monster.
Brendan Bracken. Quoted David Carlton, ANTHONY EDEN 1981

2 That's Anthony for you — half mad baronet, half beautiful woman.
R. A. Butler. Ibid.

3 . . . his unfortunate propensity to offer cliches and platitudes on a scale unusual even for a politician.
David Carlton, ANTHONY EDEN 1981

4 He had antennae in all directions, but no brains.
Gladwin Jebb. Quoted Hugh Dalton Diary 1940—45 1986

5 He is an overripe banana, yellow outside, squishy in.
Reginald Paget

6 He will be the worst prime minister since Lord North.
Lord Swinton to Winston Churchill. Quoted J. A. Cross, LORD SWINTON 1983

7 The best advertisement the Fifty Shilling Tailors ever had.
Bonar Thompson. Quoted Michael Foot, DEBTS OF HONOUR 1981

EDINBURGH

8 . . . a dignified spinster with syphilis.
Charles Higham, THE ADVENTURES OF CONAN DOYLE

EDUCATION

9 'Whom are you?' he said, for he had been to night school.
George Ade, BANG! BANG!, *The Steel Box*

10 More will mean worse.
Kingsley Amis, Encounter

11 My degree was a kind of inoculation. I got just enough education to make me immune from it for the rest of my life.
Alan Bennett, FORTY YEARS ON

12 If education is considered as an industry then it is the most extravagant and inefficient I know.
Lord Bowden, Observer, Sayings of the Year 1964

13 Education bewildered me with knowledge and facts in which I was only mildly interested.
Charles Chaplin, MY AUTOBIOGRAPHY 1964

14 I learn the way the monkey learns — watching its parents.
Charles, Prince of Wales. Quoted Graham and Heather Fisher, CHARLES: THE MAN AND THE PRINCE

15 The prolonged education indispensable to the progress of society is not natural to mankind.
Winston Churchill, MY EARLY LIFE 1930

16 She has set herself an extremely low standard, which she has failed to maintain.
Quoted from her school report by Jilly Cooper, Sunday Times 16 Jul 1978

17 The one real object of education is to leave a man in the condition of continually asking questions.
Bishop Creighton. Quoted C. A. Alington, THINGS ANCIENT AND MODERN

18 It is nothing short of a miracle that modern methods of instruction have not yet strangled the holy curiosity of enquiry.
Albert Einstein, AUTOBIOGRAPHY

19 Discussion in all higher education, is the vacuum which is used to fill a vacuum.
J. K. Galbraith, A LIFE IN OUR TIMES 1981

20 Yesterday I couldn't spell engineer. Now I are one.
Graffito. Quoted Nigel Rees, GRAFFITI 2

21 Until all teachers are geniuses and enthusiasts, nobody will learn anything, except what they teach themselves.
Aldous Huxley, ANTIC HAY 1923

22 The urge to do something for the young is strong only in parents, and in them only for the few years during which their children are at school.
Aldous Huxley, THE DOORS OF PERCEPTION 1954

23 The aim of education is the knowledge not of facts, but of values.
W. R. Inge (Dean of St Pauls), THE CHURCH IN THE WORLD

1 At a time when this country is supposed to be bankrupt they spend money on semi-education of the lower classes who will merely learn to be dissatisfied.
James Lees-Milne, MIDWAY ON THE WAVES 1985

2 Ruth's grandchildren are at that fashionable school in Dorset, and can already change wheels, top batteries and milk cows. They are going to learn to read next year you say. At ten and twelve? Isn't that a little soon?
Rose Macaulay, PERSONAL PLEASURES

3 Education must have an end in view, for it is not an end in itself.
Sybil Marshall, AN EXPERIMENT IN EDUCATION

4 Today nearly everyone can read, but only a few people can think.
Cardinal Alfredo Ottaviani. Speech 1956

5 Barnsley Grammar School did for education what myxamatosis did for rabbits.
Michael Parkinson, BBC TV 31 *Jan* 1981

6 Learning against a background of no experience means that there is no way of assessing the importance or the relevance of what is being taught.
Philip, Duke of Edinburgh, A QUESTION OF BALANCE 1982

7 The so-called method of co-education is false in theory and harmful to Christian training.
Pope Pius XI, Divini illius magistri 31 *Dec* 1929

8 Real education must ultimately be limited to one who really insists on knowing; the rest is merely sheep-herding.
Ezra Pound, ABC OF READING 1934

9 Of all human activities education is the most likely to give rise to cant, pomposity and fraudulent expertise.
John Rae, Head Master of Westminster School. Speech, Jun 1983

10 A man who has never gone to school may steal from a freight car, but if he has a university education he may steal the whole railroad.
Franklin D. Roosevelt

11 We are faced with the paradox that education has become one of the chief obstacles to intelligence and freedom of thought.
Bertrand Russell, SCEPTICAL ESSAYS 1928

12 Children with Hyacinth's temperament don't know better as they grow older, they merely know more.
Saki, THE JOYS OF PEACE

13 *Educ:* during the holidays from Eton.
Sir Osbert Sitwell, entry in WHO'S WHO

14 Education is what survives when what has been learnt has been forgotten.
B. F. Skinner, New Scientist 21 *May* 1964

15 If I were asked when I received the best part of my education I should reply, not at school or college, but in the days when, as a young, inexperienced and conceited teacher of Tutorial Classes, I underwent week by week, a series of friendly but effective deflations at the hands of the students composing them.
Professor R. H. Tawney THE RADICAL TRADITION 1960

16 Samuel Beckett once taught briefly at Campbell College, Belfast. When he was told that he was teaching the cream of Ulster he replied, 'Yes. Rich and thick.'
The Times Diary 21 *Feb* 1984

17 Socrates gave no diplomas or degrees and would have subjected any disciple who demanded one to a disconcerting catechism on the nature of true knowledge.
G. M. Trevelyan, HISTORY OF ENGLAND 1926

18 Education has produced a vast population able to read, but unable to distinguish what is worth reading.
Ibid.

19 I always tell students that it is what you learn after you know it all that counts.
Harry S Truman

20 The overthrow of the public school system would be most welcome as it would put more money in the pockets of middle-class parents.
Auberon Waugh, IN THE LION'S DEN

21 It really doesn't matter what children learn, so long as they learn something.
Auberon Waugh, Sunday Telegraph 3 *Nov* 1985

1 By introducing a uniform system of education and by seeking to make it universal and compulsory the State is attempting to minimise natural superiorities. The precocious child is regarded as a problem and his development is, when possible, stunted.
Evelyn Waugh, commentary to T. A. MacInery's THE PRIVATE MAN

2 An educated man should know everything about something, and something about everything.
Dame C. V. Wedgwood. Address, Birkbeck College 1963

3 Human history becomes more and more a race between education and catastrophe.
H. G. Wells, THE OUTLINE OF HISTORY 1920

EDWARD VII

4 The leader writer on a great Northern Daily said on the morning after King Edward died that if he had not been a king he would have been the best type of sporting publican.
James Agate, EGO 1 1935

5 I wouldn't know the King from the Knave.
Nancy Astor, declining an invitation to play bridge with Edward VII. Quoted Geoffrey Bocca, NANCY, THE INCREDIBLE ASTOR, *Sunday Express* 8 Jan 1956

6 A capable, amiable, but very crafty man, with a remarkably sinister look in his eyes — *not* our friend.
Prince Eulenberg, to Kaiser Wilhelm II. Quoted Dr Johannes Haller, PRINCE EULENBERG, THE KAISER'S FRIEND

7 He wasn't clever, but he always did the right thing, which is better than brains.
Lord Fisher. Letter to Reginald McKenna 14 May 1910

8 He had many romantic occupations. He went betting and visited Paris and was sometimes late for dinner; in addition he was merry with actresses and kind to gipsies.
W. C. Sellar and R. J. Yeatman, 1066 AND ALL THAT 1930

9 Edward VII smoked cigars and was addicted to entente cordials, married a Sea King's daughter and invented appendicitis.
Ibid.

10 Edward VII, who was not quite a gentleman, but let that pass, was among the first to spread around the rumour that the young ladies of Paris threw off their clothes more readily than their English sisters and the French named a boulevard after him in recognition of his researches on that subject.
Douglas Sutherland, THE ENGLISH GENTLEMAN 1978

11 We shall not pretend that there is nothing in his long career which those who respect and admire him would wish otherwise.
The Times, leader on Edward VII's accession 23 Jan 1901

12 You cannot imagine what a Satan he is.
Kaiser Wilhelm II. Quoted Robert Cecil, LIFE IN EDWARDIAN ENGLAND 1969

EDWARD VIII

13 As a prince, as a King, as a man, he was at his best only when the going was good.
Alistair Cooke, SIX MEN

14 He was born to be a salesman. He would be an admirable representative of Rolls Royce. But an ex-King cannot start selling motor cars.
Duchess of Windsor. Quoted Harold Nicolson, DIARIES 28 May 1947

EEC

15 It reminds me of a huge hamster cage where creatures of various size and importance spin round in wheels which give enormous traction but no forward movement.
David Haworth and Andrew Mulligan, Observer, The dream that faded 2 Jan 1981

EFFICIENCY

16 Efficiency . . . should possess a sweeping gesture — even if that gesture may at moments sweep the ornaments off the mantelpiece.
Harold Nicolson, SMALL TALK

17 There are only two qualities in the world, efficiency and inefficiency; and only two sorts of people, the efficient and the inefficient.
George Bernard Shaw, JOHN BULL'S OTHER ISLAND 1904

EFFORT

1 All struggle has for its end relief and repose.
(Percy) Wyndham Lewis, THE ART OF BEING
RULED 1926

2 The world is an oyster but you don't crack it
open on a mattress.
Arthur Miller, DEATH OF A SALESMAN 1949

EGG

3 It was obvious that the egg had come first.
There was something dignified about a
silent passive egg, whereas Aunt Irene
found it difficult to envisage an angel
bearing a hen — which despite its
undoubted merits, was a foolish and largely
intractable bird.
Alice Thomas Ellis, THE 27TH KINGDOM
1982

EGO

4 One may understand the cosmos, but never
the ego; the self is more distant than any
star.
G. K. Chesterton, ORTHODOXY 1908

EGOTISM

5 Only the insane take themselves seriously.
Max Beerbohm. Quoted S. N. Behren,
CONVERSATIONS WITH MAX

6 *Egotist*: a person of low taste, more
interested in himself than me.
Ambrose Bierce, THE DEVIL'S
DICTIONARY 1906

7 Egotism is the anaesthetic that dulls the pain
of stupidity.
Frank Leary, Look Magazine 10 *Jan* 1955

8 No egotism is so insufferable as that of the
Christian with regard to his soul.
W. Somerset Maugham, A WRITER'S
NOTEBOOK 1969

9 He fell in love with himself at first sight and
it is a passion to which he has always
remained faithful. Self-love seems so often
unrequited.
Anthony Powell, THE ACCEPTANCE
WORLD 1955

10 The man who loves only himself cannot, it is
true, be accused of promiscuity in his
affections, but he is bound in the end to
suffer intolerable boredom from the inevitable sameness of his affections.
Bertrand Russell, AUTOBIOGRAPHY 1967

11 Interest in oneself leads to no activity of a
progressive kind. It may lead to the keeping
of a diary, to getting psycho-analysed, or
perhaps to becoming a monk.
Bertrand Russell, THE CONQUEST OF
HAPPINESS 1930

EGYPT

12 I dare say you can't judge Egypt by Aida.
Ronald Firbank, THE ECCENTRICITIES OF
CARDINAL PIRELLI 1926

ALBERT EINSTEIN

13 If my theory of relativity is proved successful
Germany will claim me as a German and
France will declare I am a citizen of the
whole world. Should my theory prove
untrue, France will say I'm a German and
Germany will say I am a Jew.
Albert Einstein. Quoted News Review 8 *May*
1947

14 Einstein — the greatest Jew since Christ.
J. B. S. Haldane, DAEDALUS OR SCIENCE
AND THE FUTURE

DWIGHT D. EISENHOWER

15 The best clerk I ever fired.
*General MacArthur. Quoted Marquis
Childs*, EISENHOWER, CAPTIVE HERO

ELECTION

16 Elections are won by men and women
chiefly because most people vote against
somebody rather than for somebody.
Franklin P. Adams, NODS AND BECKS 1944

17 The Labour candidate represents the shirk-
ing classes but I represent the working
classes.
Lady Astor. Election speech 1919

1 Minorities are valuable people, and on the whole those who are opposed to you are more likely to vote than those who support you.
Richard Crossman, DIARIES 5 *Feb* 1970

2 No matter who you vote for, the Government always gets in.
Graffito. Quoted, BBC South West 30 *Apr* 1979

3 Anyone who votes Labour ought to be locked up.
Field Marshal Montgomery. Speech at Woodford, Essex 1959

4 Many immigrants vote Labour because they think the labour exchanges at which they sign on belong to the Labour Party.
Frank Muir, BBC Radio 22 *Apr* 1979

ELECTRICITY

5 Electrical force is defined as something which causes motion of electrical charge; an electrical charge is something which exerts electrical force.
Sir Arthur Eddington, THE NATURE OF THE PHYSICAL WORLD

6 Pylons, those pillars / Bare like nude giant girls that have no secret.
Stephen Spender, THE PYLONS

ELEGANCE

7 To achieve harmony in bad taste is the height of elegance.
Jean Genet, THE THIEF'S JOURNAL 1949

8 Tom [Mix] was as elegant on a horse as Fred Astaire on a dance floor, and that's the elegantest there is.
Adela Rogers St Johns, THE HONEYCOMB

ELEPHANT

9 'Where are elephants found?'
'Elephants are so large that they are rarely lost.'
Anonymous schoolchild. Quoted Cecil Hunt, HOWLERS

10 Elephants in the circus / Have aeons of weariness round their eyes / Yet they sit up / And show vast bellies to the children.
D. H. Lawrence, COLLECTED POEMS 1928

11 Did I ever tell you how I shot a wild elephant in my pyjamas? How he got into my pyjamas I'll never know. Getting his tusks off was quite a problem. In Alabama the Tuscaloosa.
Groucho Marx, ANIMAL CRACKERS *(film)*

EDWARD ELGAR

12 Elgar's A flat symphony is the musical equivalent of St Pancras Station.
Sir Thomas Beecham. Quoted Neville Cardus, SIR THOMAS BEECHAM

13 Elgar's *Gerontius* has been rightly described by George Moore as holy water in a German beer barrel.
Sir Thomas Beecham. Quoted Lord Boothby, MY YESTERDAY, YOUR TOMORROW

T. S. ELIOT

14 As a poet Eliot could more easily achieve intensity than extension, and the same thing was true of his prose writing.
Bernard Bergonzi, T. S. ELIOT

15 How unpleasant to meet Mr Eliot / With his features of clerical cut / And his brow so grim / And his mouth so prim / And his conversation so nicely / Restricted to What Precisely / And If and Perhaps and But.
T. S. Eliot, SELF PORTRAIT

16 Smell . . . was Eliot's special sense, his special delicacy.
Geoffrey Grigson, THE PRIVATE ART

QUEEN ELIZABETH II

17 It always frightens me that people should love her so much.
Queen Elizabeth the Queen Mother, of her daughter as a child

18 The Queen is a very pleasant middle to upper-class type of lady, with a talkative, retired Navy husband.
Malcolm Muggeridge, Saturday Evening Post

EMOTION

1 Lord Lundy from his earliest years / Was far too easily moved to tears.
Hilaire Belloc, CAUTIONARY TALES 1907

2 Amanda: I sort of melted like snow in the sunlight.
Elyot: That must have been an edifying spectacle.
Noël Coward, PRIVATE LIVES 1930

3 An intimate friend and a hated enemy have always been indispensable to my emotional life.
Sigmund Freud. Quoted Helen Walker Pinner, FREUD, HIS LIFE AND HIS MIND

4 What we feel and think and are is to a great extent determined by the state of our ductless glands and viscera.
Aldous Huxley, MUSIC AT NIGHT, *Meditation on El Greco* 1931

5 One of the effects of a safe and civilised life is an immense oversensitiveness which makes all the primary emotions seem somewhat disgusting.
George Orwell, COLLECTED ESSAYS 1968

6 She ran the gamut of the emotions from A to B.
Dorothy Parker, Life Magazine, of Katherine Hepburn in THE LAKE

7 She entered his life under his fingernail and prised it up until he screamed.
Peter Townsend, HORSE'S NECK 1985

8 Intellect is to emotion as our clothes are to our bodies; we could not very well have civilised life without clothes, but we would be in a poor way if we had only clothes without bodies.
A. N. Whitehead, DIALOGUES

9 He groaned slightly and winced, like Prometheus watching his vulture dropping in for lunch.
P. G. Wodehouse. Quoted R. Usborne, WODEHOUSE AT WORK 1961

10 It is so many years before one can believe enough in what one feels even to know what that feeling is.
W. B. Yeats, AUTOBIOGRAPHIES 1955

EMPIRE

11 The day of small nations has long passed away. The day of Empires has come.
Joseph Chamberlain. Speech, Birmingham 12 May 1904

12 The empires of the future are empires of the mind.
Winston Churchill. Address, Harvard University 1945

ENCOURAGEMENT

13 It is always pleasant to be urged to do something on the ground that one can do it well.
George Santayana, LETTERS

ENDEAVOUR

14 In such a heart as Robert Falcon Scott's it was human endeavour that mattered, not mere ambition to achieve.
Herbert G. Pouting, THE GREAT WHITE SOUTH

ENDURANCE

15 The manner in which one endures what must be endured is more important than the thing that must be endured.
Dean Acheson. Quoted Merle Miller, PLAIN SPEAKING: AN ORAL BIOGRAPHY OF HARRY S. TRUMAN

ENEMY

16 If I have enemies — perhaps to have enemies is as great an honour as my friendships.
Stanley Baldwin. Speech at Unionist Conference 11 Feb 1924

17 You shall judge of a man by his foes as well as by his friends.
Joseph Conrad, LORD JIM 1900

18 One loves him for the enemies he has made.
Bernard Crick of A. J. P. Taylor, Sunday Times 9 Nov 1980

1 All enemies, except those fighting for the strictly limited food supply of a given territory, may be described as artificial enemies.
Aldous Huxley, BEYOND THE MEXIQUE BAY 1944

2 There is nothing ignoble in loving one's enemies; but much that is dangerous.
Bernard Levin, THE PENDULUM YEARS 1976

ENGLISH

3 That typically English characteristic for which there is no English name — *esprit de corps.*
Sir Frank Adcock

4 Think of what our nation stands for / Books from Boots and country lanes. / Free speech, free passes, class distinction, / Democracy and proper drains.
Sir John Betjeman, IN WESTMINSTER ABBEY 1940

5 Ever since Sherlock Holmes most Englishmen have been born with a detective novel attached to their umbilical cords.
Tristan Bisch, SECRET SERVICE UNMASKED

6 The English sent all their bores abroad and acquired the empire as a punishment.
Edward Bond, NARROW ROAD TO THE DEEP NORTH

7 Personal relationships, colour-coded by sex and not placed or framed by any clear sense of economic realities have been, too much, the English preoccupation.
Elizabeth Bowen. Quoted Hemione Lee, ELIZABETH BOWEN: AN ESTIMATION 1982

8 No Englishman could pass for an American.
Heywood Brown, PIECES OF HATE 1922

9 It seems to me that you can go sauntering along for a certain period telling the English some interesting things about themselves, and then all at once it feels as if you have stepped on the prongs of a rake.
Patrick Campbell, LIFE IN THIN SLICES

10 The English never draw a line without blurring it.
Winston Churchill, House of Commons 16 *Nov* 1948

11 At twelve noon / The natives swoon / And no further work is done / But mad dogs and Englishmen / Go out in the noonday sun.
Noël Coward, MAD DOGS AND ENGLISHMEN

12 I have never met an Englishman who did not speak of his countrymen as if he was quite unlike them.
Pierre Daninos, MAJOR THOMPSON AND I

13 England is the single country where patriotism does not represent a threat or challenge to the rest of the world.
Wilhelm Dibelius, ENGLAND

14 It is said, I believe, that to behold the Englishman at his best one should watch him play tip and run.
Ronald Firbank, THE FLOWER BENEATH THE FOOT 1923

15 [An Englishman] must not express great joy or sorrow, or even open his mouth too wide when he talks — his pipe might fall out if he did.
E. M. Forster, ABINGER HARVEST 1936

16 The Englishman is unable to like anyone who cannot knock him down.
E. M. Forster. Quoted Raymond Mortimer, TRY ANYTHING ONCE

17 René Gimpel's definition of an English gentleman — a man with a passion for horses, playing with a ball, probably many a broken bone in his body and in his pocket a letter to *The Times.*
Gimpel fils, letter to The Times 31 *Jan* 1970

18 The Englishman never enjoys himself except for a noble purpose.
A. P. Herbert, UNCOMMON LAW 1935

19 The place was so English I wouldn't be surprised if the mice wore monocles.
Bob Hope, I OWE RUSSIA 1200 DOLLARS

20 This man looked English! . . . He *is* an Englishman, she decided with queer mounting excitement, for only an Englishman would have ridden so spirited a mount without the help of spurs.
Elizabeth Hoy, TO WIN A PARADISE

21 If it is good to have one foot in England it is still better, or at least as good, to have the other out of it.
Henry James. Quoted F. O. Mattheissen, THE JAMES FAMILY 1946

1 It will be said of this generation that it found England a land of beauty and left it a land of beauty spots.
C. E. M. Joad. Quoted Observer 31 May 1953

2 An Englishman's way of speaking absolutely classifies him. The moment he talks he makes some other Englishman despise him.
Alan Jay Lerner, MY FAIR LADY *(film)* 1956

3 England is only a little island where one cannot go far out of one's way.
Eric Linklater, POET'S PUB 1929

4 Here is one of the points about the planet which should be remembered; into every penetrable corner of it, and into most of the impenetrable corners, the English will penetrate.
Rose Macaulay, CREWE TRAIN 1926

5 The Englishman is naturally wasteful, especially of public money. It is a question of a blunted sense of life, a dullness towards a bright design, an apathy. Let us blame the climate for it; we pass, the climate remains.
John Masefield, SO LONG TO LEARN 1952

6 Be on your guard against an Englishman who speaks French perfectly; he is very likely to be a card-sharper or an attaché in the diplomatic service.
W. Somerset Maugham, THE SUMMING UP 1936

7 An Englishman, even if he is alone, forms an orderly queue of one.
George Mikes, HOW TO BE AN ALIEN 1946

8 When people say England, they sometimes mean Great Britain, sometimes the United Kingdom, sometimes the British Isles, – but never England.
Ibid.

9 Continental people have a sex life, the English have hot water bottles.
Ibid.

10 Englishmen know instinctively that what the world needs most is whatever is best for Great Britain.
Ogden Nash, ENGLAND EXPECTS

11 I always suspect Englishmen who admire Arabs, and who put on fancy dress when entertaining parties in Sussex.
Harold Nicolson. Reviewing WILFRED

SCAWEN BLUNT, *by the Earl of Lytton,* Observer 11 *Jun* 1961

12 Remember that you are an Englishman and have consequently won first prize in the lottery of life.
Cecil Rhodes. Quoted Peter Ustinov, DEAR ME 1977

13 The English react to things slowly. This produces an effect of self-mastery or strength in repose. Their unhurried habit gives them time to stoke up the fire of decision.
Ranjee Shahani, Illustrated Weekly of India. Quoted News Review 23 Oct 1947

14 Do you think the laws of God will be suspended in favour of England because you were born in it?
George Bernard Shaw, HEARTBREAK HOUSE 1920

15 An Englishman thinks he is moral when he is only uncomfortable.
George Bernard Shaw, MAN AND SUPERMAN 1905

16 You English are an extraordinary people. You think war is a joke. Yet you take this [*Chu Chin Chow*] seriously.
Unknown French Lady. Quoted Richard Prentis, John o' London's Weekly 4 Apr 1936

17 You never find an Englishman among the underdogs — except in England of course.
Evelyn Waugh, THE LOVED ONE 1948

ENJOYMENT

18 I'm all for rational enjoyment, and so forth, but I think a fellow makes himself conspicuous when he throws soft-boiled eggs at the electric fan.
P. G. Wodehouse, JEEVES AND THE UNBIDDEN GUEST

ENTERPRISE

19 Buying and selling securities on the Stock Exchange do not start new industries. Big business never starts anything new. It merely absorbs, consolidates and profits at the expense of others.
Franklin D. Roosevelt. Quoted Harold L. Ickes, MY TWELVE YEARS WITH F. D. R.

ENTERTAINMENT

1 What the mass media offer is not popular art, but entertainment which is intended to be consumed like food, forgotten, and replaced by a new dish.
W. H. Auden, THE DYER'S HAND 1962

2 Give the public what they want. Most people don't want works of art. They want cups of tea and donkey rides.
Duke of Bedford. Quoted David MacDonald, Saturday Evening Post 11 *Jul* 1959

3 [David N. Martin] received a telegram stating 'Show stopped by flying ants.' He is supposed to have replied by cable: 'Book them for a further week.'
Michael Bentine, THE LONG BANANA SKIN

4 There's no business like show business.
Irving Berlin, ANNIE GET YOUR GUN *(film)* 1946

5 Night clubs are places where the tables are reserved and the guests aren't.
Frank Caspar, American radio comedian 1942

6 I am interested in everything so long as it is well done. I would rather see a good juggler than a bad Hamlet.
C. B. Cochran, SECRETS OF A SHOWMAN

7 Comedy, like sodomy, is an unnatural act.
Marty Feldman, The Times 9 *Jun* 1969

8 We're an institution. And our staunchest supporters are the intellectuals — like the Queen Mother and Princess Margaret.
Bud Flanagan. Quoted in his obituary, Daily Express 21 *Oct* 1968

9 All my shows are great. Some of them are bad. But they are all great.
Sir Lew Grade. Quoted George Brook and Tony Lyons, Observer 6 *Sep* 1981

10 I've always felt England was a great place to work in. It's an island and the audience can't run very far.
Bob Hope, I OWE RUSSIA 1200 DOLLARS

11 To the music of Rimsky-Korsakoff / I could never take my corset off / And where are the sailors who would pay / To see me strip to Massenet?

Gypsy Rose Lee. Quoted N. Shapiro, AN ENCYCLOPEDIA OF QUOTATIONS ABOUT MUSIC

12 We are more popular than Jesus.
John Lennon, of the Beatles, in an interview in 1966

13 What else is the tale of Dick Whittington but a glorification of private enterprise and bourgeois ideals?
Observer. Quoted News Review 23 *Jan* 1947

14 The interval can be filled by a ballet *Six Who Pass While the Concrete Boils* in which half a dozen stocky Bryn Mawr girls in grey jerseys stride compulsively from one end of the stage to the other tugging at a veil. This symbolises the forces of water, sand and Portland cement at first refusing to work harmoniously, then uniting for the common good.
S. J. Perelman, CRAZY LIKE A FOX 1944

15 So Silk becomes a Ziegfeld dancer and she is quite a sensation with the dramatic critics on the night she opens because she dances with all her clothes on which is considered a very big novelty indeed.
Damon Runyon, MORE THAN SOMEWHAT, *Broadway Financier* 1937

16 A unique evening! I wouldn't have left a turn unstoned.
A. Wimperis. Quoted E. Short, FIFTY YEARS OF VAUDEVILLE

ENVIRONMENT

17 We are the children of our landscape; it dictates behaviour and even thought, in the measure to which we are responsive to it.
Lawrence Durrell, JUSTINE 1957

18 Dr Karl Pearson has said that the influence of environment is 'possibly not one tenth that of heredity'. This is an absurdity. Shakespeare, born among the Esquimaux, could not have written ninety per cent of *Hamlet*.
G. A. Studdart-Kennedy, ENVIRONMENT 1928

ENVY

19 I go about looking at horses and cattle. They eat grass, make love, work when they have to, bear their young. I am sick with envy of them.
Sherwood Anderson, LETTERS 1953

1 Envy is everywhere / Who is without envy?
And most people / Are unaware or
unashamed of being envious.
T. S. Eliot, THE ELDER STATESMAN

2 There is a strong disposition in youth, from
which some individuals never escape, to
suppose that everyone else is having a more
enjoyable time than we are ourselves.
Anthony Powell, A BUYER'S MARKET 1952

3 Beggars do not envy millionaires, though of
course they will envy other beggars who are
more successful.
Bertrand Russell, THE CONQUEST OF
HAPPINESS 1930

4 The man with toothache thinks everyone
happy whose teeth are sound.
George Bernard Shaw, MAN AND
SUPERMAN 1905

EPIDEMIC

5 The Black Death started under the armpits
and spread all over Europe.
*Schoolboy howler. Quoted Christopher
Matthews, BBC Radio 4, Quote Unquote* 17
Jul 1980

EPIGRAM

6 An epigram is only another word for a
platitude on its night out.
*Philip Guedella, speech to Cambridge
Union.*

7 *Epigram:* a wisecrack that played Carnegie
Hall.
Oscar Levant, Coronet Magazine, Sep 1968

8 Anyone can tell the truth but only very few
of us can make epigrams.
W. Somerset Maugham, A WRITER'S
NOTEBOOK 1949

9 Such is epigram, requiring / Wit, occasion,
and good luck.
Christopher Morley, The Epigram

EPITAPH

10 Let us honour if we can / The vertical man /
Though we value none / But the horizontal
one.
W. H. Auden, EPIGRAPH FOR POEMS 1930

11 I've played everything but the harp.
*Lionel Barrymore on being asked what
words he would like on his tombstone*

12 'What would you like your epitaph to be?'
'I'll be right back.'
*Johnny Carson at a press conference. Quoted
Kenneth Tynan, New Yorker* 20 *Feb* 1978

13 The best you can expect is a few daffodils in
a jam-jar and a rough-hewn stone bearing
the legend 'He came and he went.'
*Tony Hancock, BBC Radio, Hancock's
Half Hour* 1964

14 At last God caught his eye.
*Harry Secombe, Punch, epitaph for a head
waiter* 17 *May* 1962

JACOB EPSTEIN

15 They are a form of statuary which no careful
father would wish his daughter, or no
discerning young man his fiancee, to see.
Evening Standard and St James Gazette 1908

16 The Epstein . . . makes me feel physically
sick. The wretched woman has two sets of
breasts and a hip joint like a merrythought.
John Galsworthy

EQUALITY

17 From the point of view of sexual morality
the aeroplane is valuable in war in that it
destroys men and women in equal numbers.
*Ernest William Barnes (Bishop of
Birmingham),* RISE OF CHRISTIANITY

18 The social process requires the standardisation of man, and this standardisation is
called equality.
Erich Fromm, THE ART OF LOVING 1956

19 Equality is a mortuary word.
Christopher Fry, VENUS OBSERVED 1950

20 We clamour for equality chiefly in matters in
which we ourselves cannot hope to obtain
excellence.
Eric Hoffer, THE PASSIONATE STATE OF
MIND 1954

21 That all men are equal is a proposition to
which, in ordinary times, no sane individual
has ever given his assent.
Aldous Huxley, PROPER STUDIES 1927

1 Be careful that mindless clichés about élitism and the cult of personality are not back to front ways of attacking excellence.
Prof. J. Jones in a lecture at Oxford 19 Feb 1979

2 All men are created equal — until they prove otherwise.
Ben Kuroki, New York Herald Tribune 4 Nov 1945

3 No man who says 'I am as good as you' believes it. The St Bernard never says it to the toy dog, nor the scholar to the dunce, nor the employable to the bum, nor the pretty woman to the plain. The claim to equality is made only by those who feel themselves to be in some way inferior.
C. S. Lewis, SCREWTAPE PROPOSES A TOAST

4 All animals are equal, but some animals are more equal than others.
George Orwell, ANIMAL FARM 1945

5 The idea of taking away property from other people has much more appeal if one has none of one's own.
Philip, Duke of Edinburgh, A QUESTION OF BALANCE 1982

6 True education makes for inequality; the inequality of individuality, the inequality of success; the glorious inequality of talent, of genius; for inequality, not mediocrity, individual superiority, not standardisation, is the measure of progress in the world.
Felix E. Schelling, PEDAGOGICALLY SPEAKING

EROTICISM

7 — the rather refined young man who preferred sex dreams to visiting brothels because he met a much nicer type of girl that way.
Vivian Mercier, PERSPECTIVES ON PORNOGRAPHY

ESCAPE

8 We don't even talk of an escape from Bristol prison. The word is dematerialisation.
Lord Mancroft. Quoted Observer 5 Aug 1956

ETERNITY

9 We have no guarantee that the afterlife will be any less exasperating than this one, have we?
Noël Coward, BLITHE SPIRIT 1941

10 Eternity is not something that begins after you are dead. It is going on all the time. We are in it now.
Charlotte P. Gilman, THE FORERUNNER

11 Eternity's a terrible thought. I mean, where's it going to end?
Tom Stoppard, ROSENCRANTZ AND GUILDENSTERN ARE DEAD 1967

ETHICS

12 A tailor sold a pair of trousers for thirty shillings which was ten shillings more than he expected to get. He asked himself 'Shall I keep the ten shillings, or shall I be honest — and share it with my partner?' That's ethics.
Lord Hewart, NOT WITHOUT PREJUDICE 1938

13 The inescapable though often dodged fact is that anything, absolutely anything, which may be used to do good may be used to do harm, or worse.
J. W. Lambert, Sunday Times 26 Feb 1978

14 I can only say that while my own opinions as to ethics do not satisfy me, other people's satisfy me still less.
Bertrand Russell, REPLY TO MY CRITICS

15 The first step in the evolution of ethics is a sense of solidarity with other human beings.
Albert Schweitzer, THE TEACHING OF REVERENCE FOR LIFE

ETIQUETTE

16 Whatever your Uncle Bob's failures were, he never tucked his serviette into his dickie.
Noël Coward, THE CAFÉ DE LA PAIX

17 Etiquette can be at the same time a means of approaching people and of staying clear of them.
David Riesman, THE LONELY CROWD 1950

18 Never speak loudly unless the house is on fire.
H. W. Thompson, BODY, BOOTS AND BREECHES

1 He found that a fork in his inexperienced hand was an instrument of chase rather than capture.
H. G. Wells, KIPPS 1905

2 When a girl lit up a cigarette after the soup her hostess said icily 'We seem to have finished' and led the entire party from the room. That was the end of the dinner.
Katherine Whitehorn, Observer 27 Jul 1980

EUPHEMISM

3 You must not use the word 'poor'. They are described as 'the lower income group'.
Winston Churchill. Speech, Cardiff 8 Feb 1950

4 Those extraordinary Australian euphemisms for vomiting — parking the tiger, yodelling on the lawn, the technicolor yawn, the liquid laugh.
Barry Humphries. Quoted FROM FRINGE TO FLYING CIRCUS 1981

5 Any euphemism ceases to be euphemistic after a time and the true meaning begins to show through. It is a losing game but we keep on trying.
Joseph Wood Krutch, IF YOU DON'T MIND MY SAYING SO 1964

EUTHANASIA

6 It is easier to accept the principle of euthanasia than to devise satisfactory plans for putting it into operation.
Lord Devlin. Quoted Observer 23 Aug 1981

EVENING

7 It is in this unearthly first hour of twilight that earth's almost agonised livingness is felt. This hour is so dreadful to some people that they hurry indoors and turn on the lights.
Elizabeth Bowen, THE DEATH OF THE HEART 1938

8 When the evening is spread out against the sky / Like a patient etherised upon a table.
T. S. Eliot, LOVE SONG OF J. ALFRED PRUFROCK 1915

9 Homeward, and brings the sailor home from sea / The typist home at teatime.
T. S. Eliot, THE WASTE LAND 1922

EVENT

10 People to whom nothing has ever happened / Cannot understand the unimportance of words.
T. S. Eliot, THE FAMILY RENUNION 1939

EVIL

11 Good can imagine Evil; but Evil cannot imagine Good
W. H. Auden, A CERTAIN WORLD

12 Evil is unspectacular and always human / And shares our bed and eats at our own table.
W. H. Auden, HERMAN MELVILLE

13 A belief in a supernatural source of evil is not necessary; men alone are quite capable of every sort of wickedness.
Joseph Conrad, UNDER WESTERN EYES 1911

14 He who passively accepts evil is as much involved in it as he who helps to perpetrate it.
Martin Luther King, STRIDE TOWARDS FREEDOM 1958

15 Theologians are always bothering about the origin of evil, but evil is just natural behaviour; it's the origin of human goodness that is really so extraordinary and inexplicable.
Kingsley Martin

16 There is no explanation for evil. It must be looked upon as a necessary part of the order of the universe. To ignore it is childish, to bewail it senseless.
W. Somerset Maugham, THE SUMMING UP 1938

17 Between two evils I always pick the one I have never tried before.
Mae West, KLONDIKE ANNIE *(film)*

EVOLUTION

18 Does Nature care in the least whether we evolve or not? Her instincts are for the gratification of hunger and sex, the destruction of rivals and the protection of offspring. What monster first slipped in the idea of progress?
Cyril Connolly, THE UNQUIET GRAVE 1945

1 It isn't easy to see how the first stages in the development of certain organs could be of survival value. Evolution remains a hypothesis.
I. N. Hawthorne (Professor of Biochemistry, Nottingham), QUESTIONS OF SCIENCE AND FAITH

2 Even without the aid of artificial gadgetry human beings are able to survive and flourish in forests and in deserts, in the tropics and the Arctic . . . no other natural species has this kind of flexibility. So if man evolved from his predecessors by natural selection associated with adaptation to a specialised environment, what kind of environment was that?
Sir Edmund Leach, address to British Association 2 Sep 1981

3 The death of the failure. This is the path by which the beast rose to manhood, by which man goes on to higher things.
H. G. Wells, THE SLEEPER WAKES 1911

4 Descended from the apes? My dear, we will hope it is not true. But if it is, let us pray that it may not become generally known.
Wife of a canon of Worcester Cathedral, on hearing the theory of evolution. Quoted F. Ashley Montagu, MAN'S MOST DANGEROUS MYTH, *The Fallacy of Race*

5 We are all of us guinea-pigs in the laboratory of God. Humanity is just a work in progress.
Tennessee Williams, CAMINO REAL 1953

EXAGGERATION

6 An exaggeration is a truth that has lost its temper.
Kahil Gibran, THOUGHTS AND MEDITATIONS 1961

EXAMINATION

7 I am surprised that in my later life I should have become so experienced in taking degrees when as a schoolboy I was so bad at passing examinations. In fact one might almost say that no one ever passed so few examinations and received so many degrees.
Winston Churchill. Quoted Colin Coote, A CHURCHILL READER

8 Examinations — nature's laxative.
Graffito, City of London Polytechnic. Quoted Nigel Rees, GRAFFITI 2

9 Examinations are harmless when the examinee is indifferent to their result, but as soon as they matter they begin to distort his attitude to education and to conceal its purpose.
Sir Richard Livingstone, ON EDUCATION

10 The defect in the intelligence test is that high marks are gained by those who subsequently prove to be practically illiterate. So much time has been spent in studying the art of being tested that the candidate has rarely had time for anything else.
C. Northcote Parkinson, PARKINSON'S LAW 1957

11 Do not on any account attempt to write on both sides of the paper at once.
W. C. Sellar and R. J. Yeatman, 1066 AND ALL THAT 1930

12 Examinations, thought by the progressives of the last century to be a defence against privilege, are now denounced in the consultations of school-teachers as introducing an unhealthy spirit of competition into education.
Evelyn Waugh, commentary for T. A. MacInerys, THE PRIVATE MAN

EXAMPLE

13 Example moves the world more than doctrine.
Henry Miller, THE COSMOLOGICAL EYE 1934

EXCESS

14 A poet always has too many words in his vocabulary, a painter too many colours in his palette, a musician too many notes on his keyboard.
Jean Cocteau. Quoted Nat Shapiro, ENCYCLOPEDIA OF QUOTATIONS ABOUT MUSIC

15 It would be possible to rob even a healthy beast of prey of its voraciousness if it were possible, with the aid of a whip, to force the beast to devour continuously, even when it was not hungry.
Albert Einstein, AUTOBIOGRAPHY

1 An unrestricted satisfaction of every need presents itself as the most enticing method of conducting one's life, but it means putting enjoyment before caution, and soon brings its own punishment.
Sigmund Freud, CIVILISATION AND ITS DISCONTENTS 1930

2 Excess on occasion is exhilarating. It prevents moderation from acquiring the deadening effect of habit.
W. Somerset Maugham, THE SUMMING UP 1938

EXCUSE

3 I was bold enough to decline an invitation to *Hamlet* on the grounds that I already knew who won.
Quentin Crisp, THE NAKED CIVIL SERVANT

4 Several excuses are always less convincing than one.
Aldous Huxley, POINT COUNTER POINT 1934

5 I'm sorry I'm late. Someone stole my hoop so I had to walk here.
Ted Kavanagh, BBC Radio, ITMA

6 A Shakespearian exit. (I go to look upon a hedge.)
E. Arnot Robertson, FOUR FRIGHTENED PEOPLE 1931

EXERCISE

7 Exercise is bunk. If you are healthy you don't need it, if you are sick you shouldn't take it.
Henry Ford

8 It was Gloria Bristol [Hollywood beauty specialist] who put the Duchess of Windsor wise to the benefits of standing on her head.
Sheila Graham. Quoted News Review 16 Jan 1947

9 Little good can come of regular exercise which reduces life to a monotonous machine.
E. V. Knox, GORGEOUS TIMES

10 I have always said that exercise is a short cut to the cemetery.
John Mortimer, RUMPOLE OF THE BAILEY 1978

11 The beneficent effects of the regular quarter-hour's exercise before breakfast is more than offset by the mental wear-and-tear in getting out of bed fifteen minutes earlier than one otherwise would.
Simeon Strunsky, THE PATIENT OBSERVER

EXISTENCE

12 Common sense tells us that our existence is but a brief crack of light between two eternities of darkness.
Vladimir Nabokov, SPEAK, MEMORY 1967

EXPEDIENCY

13 No man is justified in doing evil on the ground of expediency.
Theodore Roosevelt, THE STRENUOUS LIFE 1900

EXPENDITURE

14 Expenditure rises to meet income. Individual expenditure not only rises to meet income but tends to surpass it.
C. Northcote Parkinson, THE LAW AND THE PROFITS

EXPERIENCE

15 One should try everything once, except folk dancing and incest.
Arnold Bax, FAREWELL TO MY YOUTH

16 You will think me lamentably crude; my experience of life has been drawn from life itself.
Max Beerbohm, ZULEIKA DOBSON 1911

17 There is no unique image of our whole world of experience.
Niels Bohr

18 You cannot acquire experience by making experiments. You cannot create experience. You must undergo it.
Albert Camus, NOTEBOOKS 1935—1942

19 You have not had thirty years of experience. You have had one year's experience thirty times.
J. L. Carr, THE HARPOLE REPORT

1 No one over thirty-five is worth meeting who has not something to teach us, something more than we could learn for ourselves, from a book.
Cyril Connolly, THE UNQUIET GRAVE 1945

2 What one has not experienced one will never understand in print.
Isadora Duncan, MY LIFE 1927

3 We had the experience but missed the meaning / And approach to the meaning restores the experience / In a different form, beyond any meaning / We can assign to happiness.
T. S. Eliot, FOUR QUARTETS 1942

4 What a man knows he has by experience / But what a man is precedes experience.
Christopher Fry, CURTMANTLE 1961

5 The most important lesson is to understand life, not to make *a priori* judgments about it.
David Garnett, GREAT FRIENDS

6 We cannot afford to forget any experiences, even the most painful.
Dag Hammarskjöld, MARKINGS 1964

7 Experience is never limited, and it is never complete; it is an immense sensibility, a kind of huge spider-web of the finest silk threads suspended in the chamber of consciousness, and catching every air-borne particle in its tissue.
Henry James, THE ART OF FICTION 1934

8 Welcome, O life! I go to encounter for the millionth time the reality of experience and to forge in the smithy of my soul the uncreated conscience of my race.
James Joyce, A PORTRAIT OF THE ARTIST AS A YOUNG MAN 1916

9 Mythology, religion and philosophy are alike in that each has as its function the interpretation of experience in terms which have human value.
Joseph Wood Krutch, THE MODERN TEMPER 1929

10 Judgement comes from experience — and experience comes from bad judgement.
Brig. Gen. J. W. Lang

11 How different the new order would be if we could consult the veteran instead of the politician.
Henry Miller, THE WISDOM OF THE HEART 1941

12 Experience is a fruit-tree fruitless / Experience is a shoe-tree bootless. / For sterile wearience and drearience / Depend, my boy, upon experience.
Ogden Nash, EXPERIENCE TO LET

13 When I was young I was told 'You'll see when you are fifty'. I am fifty and I haven't seen a thing.
Erik Satie. Quoted Pierre-Daniel Templier, ERIK SATIE

14 Men are wise in proportion, not to their experience, but to their capacity for experience.
George Bernard Shaw, MAN AND SUPERMAN 1905

15 Experience is the comb life brings you after you have lost your hair.
Judith Stern. Quoted BBC Radio 4, *Quote Unquote*

16 What a man knows at 50 which he didn't know at 20 is, for the most part, incommunicable.
Adlai Stevenson

17 We live in reference to past experience and not to future events, however inevitable.
H. G. Wells, MIND AT THE END OF ITS TETHER 1946

EXPERIMENT

18 One disadvantage of being a hog is that at any moment some blundering fool may try to make a silk purse out of your wife's ear.
Beachcomber (J. B. Morton), Daily Express, By the Way

19 There is always more chance of hitting upon something valuable when you aren't too sure what you want to hit upon.
A. N. Whitehead, DIALOGUES

EXPERT

20 An expert is a man who has made all the mistakes that can be made in a very narrow field.
Niels Bohr. Quoted A. L. Mackay, THE HARVEST OF A QUIET EYE

21 An expert is one who knows more and more about less and less.
Nicholas Murray Butler

1 An expert is someone who knows some of the worst mistakes that can be made in his subject, and how to avoid them.
Werner Heisenberg, PHYSICS AND BEYOND

2 [Experts are] pundits of the technological age who can't put a fresh ribbon in their typewriters, and resounding authorities on the problems of the farmer who has never grown a geranium in a pot.
Westbrook Pegler. Quoted Alistair Cooke, BBC Radio 4, Letter from America 29 Jun 1969

3 In the matter of leaking tunnels and their designers, Mr J.A. Bush wonders about the meaning of the word 'expert'. The derivation in the circumstances seems both obvious and opposite. It is from 'ex' a has-been, and 'spurt', a drip under pressure.
Nicholas Radcliffe. Letter to Daily Telegraph 24 Sep 1985

4 Even when all the experts agree, they may well be mistaken.
Bertrand Russell, AUTOBIOGRAPHY 1967

EXPLANATION

5 A little inaccuracy sometimes saves tons of explanation.
Saki, THE SQUARE EGG

EXPLOITATION

6 When you are skinning your customers you should leave some skin on to grow, so that you can skin them again.
Nikita Khrushchev. Speech to British Industrialists, May 1961

7 Round all the Arts there is a vast exploitation fringe.
J. B. Priestley. Quoted News Review 12 Dec 1946

EXPLORATION

8 Polar exploration is at once the cleanest and most isolated way of having a bad time which has been devised.
Apsley Cherry-Gerard, THE WORST JOURNEY IN THE WORLD

EXPRESSION

9 Ethel pulled her hair and looked very sneery.
Daisy Ashford (aged 9), THE YOUNG VISITERS 1919

10 A short man with a hard red face like a book of rules.
Anthony Carson, New Statesman 22 Nov 1964

11 She looks at other women as though she would inhale them.
Ronald Firbank, THE FLOWER BENEATH THE FOOT 1923

12 I do not think I have ever seen a nastier looking man. Under the black hat, when I had first seen them, the eyes were those of an unsuccessful rapist.
Ernest Hemingway of (Percy) Wyndham Lewis, A MOVEABLE FEAST 1964

13 When I look into a girl's eyes I can tell just what she thinks of me. It's pretty depressing.
Bob Hope, MY FAVOURITE SPY *(film)*

14 His mouth shut like the two halves of a muffin.
Rosamond Lehmann, INVITATION TO THE WALTZ 1932

15 He hung his mouth open as though he were an animal in a zoo inviting buns.
(Percy) Wyndham Lewis of Ford Maddox Ford, RUDE ASSIGNMENT 1950

EXTRAVAGANCE

16 He [Lord Birkenhead] had no idea of the value of money. He refused to attend to his income tax returns and incurred an enormous overdraft. When remonstrated with he would buy another car or a new motor launch.
Second Earl of Birkenhead, LIFE OF LORD BIRKENHEAD

17 A policy of buying a biscuit early in the morning and walking about all day looking for a dog to give it to.
Winston Churchill, House of Commons, Budget debate 1929

18 We're too poor to economise. Economy is a luxury: our only salvation is extravagance.
F. Scott Fitzgerald. Quoted Paul Sann, THE LAWLESS DECADE

1 I have saved nothing and shall die on straw.
Storm Jameson, JOURNEY FROM THE NORTH
VOL1 1969

2 She not only worships the Golden Calf, she
barbecues it for lunch.
Oscar Levant, of Zsa-Zsa Gabor

3 My candle burns at both ends; / It will not
last the night / But oh my foes, and oh my
friends / It gives a lovely light.
Edna St Vincent Millay, A FEW FIGS FROM
THISTLES 1923

4 Tories as well as Socialists should question
the wisdom of granting to the three-year old
Prince Charles an income of £10,000. It is
never good for a small boy to have too much
money to spend.
Daily Telegraph

5 It takes only one gramme of explosive to kill
a man, so why waste five tons?
Solly Zuckerman, FROM APES TO WAR
LORDS

EYE

6 Her eyes are like I do not know what, except
that they are one hundred per cent eyes in
every respect.
Damon Runyon, GUYS AND DOLLS 1932

7 Her eyes are big, and as black as doughnuts,
and she has a look in them that somehow
makes me think she may know more than
she lets on, which I afterwards find out is
very true indeed.
Ibid.

F

FACE

1 I do not say that I was ever what is called
'plain' but I have the sort of face that bores
me when I see it on other people.
Margot Asquith, Countess of Oxford,
Lilliput 1938

2 My face looks like a wedding cake that has
been left out in the rain.
*W. H. Auden. Quoted Humphrey
Carpenter,* AUDEN, A BIOGRAPHY

3 He has a face like a police identikit
photograph.
*Richard Baker of Roger Daltrey, BBC 1 TV
Omnibus 23 Oct* 1983

4 After a certain age every man is responsible
for his face.
Albert Camus, THE FALL 1956

5 A blank helpless sort of face, rather like a
rose just before you drench it with DDT.
*John Carey, of a photograph of Diana
Cooper, Sunday Times 20 Sep* 1981

6 Her face returned to childhood because it
wore that expression of inhuman innocence,
of angelic hardness which ennobles children's faces.
Colette, THE OTHER ONE

7 What will this face be like twenty years from
now? At the moment it isn't so much a face
as a pre-face.
*Noël Coward, of a photograph of Truman
Capote. Quoted William Marchant,* THE
PRIVILEGE OF HIS COMPANY 1980

8 He has a face like a bagful of maggots.
*Jim Crace, of comedian Phil Cool, Radio
Times 24 Aug* 1985

9 . . . that half-melted vanilla face.
Brad Darrack, of Elvis Presley, Life 1974

10 Glenda Jackson has a face to launch a
thousand dredgers.
Jack De Manio. Quoted Diana Rigg, NO
TURN UNSTONED 1982

11 Not so much a face as part of her person that
she happened to leave uncovered so that her
friends might recognise her.
E. V. Lucas, THE OLDEST JOKE

12 Faces, like buildings, are very much the
product of their times. Prewar faces don't
look like postwar faces.
David Mendel, Observer 21 *Jan* 1979

13 He had a face, even in his twenties, which
looked as though he had rented it on a long
lease and had lived in it so long he didn't
want to move out.
David Niven, of George Sanders, BRING ON
THE EMPTY HORSES

14 At fifty everyone has the face he deserves.
George Orwell, last entry in his notebook

15 He had a queer, puckered, grimacing face as
if he had been born in blazing sunshine and
had never got over it.
Reginald Pound, THEIR MOODS AND
MINE 1935

16 She had one of those faces to which
distance . . . gives form and outline and
which, seen close at hand, dissolve back into
dust.
Marcel Proust, REMEMBRANCE OF THINGS
PAST 1913—1927

17 The human face is indeed like the faces of
the God of some oriental theogony, a whole
cluster of faces, crowded together but on
different surfaces so that one does not see
them all at once.
Ibid.

18 A woman whose face looked as if it had been
made of sugar and someone had licked it.
*George Bernard Shaw of Isadora Duncan.
Quoted Hesketh Pearson,* BERNARD
SHAW 1961

1 He had a face that faintly resembled a large wad of cotton wool.
Joseph von Sternberg of Charles Laughton

2 He has features that always look slightly (if he will forgive me) as though he had been photographed through a fish-eye lens.
Paul Vaughan of Dr Jonathan Miller, Radio Times 17 Feb 1979

3 A face like a carving abandoned as altogether too unpromising for completion.
H. G. Wells, FOOD OF THE GODS 1904

4 Time had removed the hair from the top of his head and distributed a small dividend of plunder in little bunches carelessly and impartially over the rest of his features.
H. G. Wells, HISTORY OF MR POLLY 1910

5 He had the face of a saint but he had rendered this generally acceptable by growing side-whiskers.
H. G. Wells, THE LAST TRUMP

FACT

6 The trouble with facts is that there are so many of them.
Samuel McChord Crothers, THE GENTLE READER

7 Facts are only the material of thought.
Ernest Dimnet, THE ART OF THINKING 1928

8 You can't alter facts by filming them over with dead romances.
John Drinkwater, MARY STUART 1921

9 Facts do not cease to exist because they are ignored.
Aldous Huxley, A NOTE ON DOGMA

10 Facts are ventriloquists' dummies. Sitting on a wise man's knee they may be made to utter words of wisdom; elsewhere they say nothing or talk nonsense.
Aldous Huxley, TIME MUST HAVE A STOP 1944

FAILURE

11 The worst of failure of this kind is that it spoils the market for more competent performers.
James Agate, of the bungled attempt to assassinate Hitler, EGO 7 21 *Jul* 1944

12 In a game, just losing is almost as satisfying — in life the loser's score is always zero.
W. H. Auden, THE DYER'S HAND 1962

13 I find failure endearing, don't you?
Max Beerbohm. Quoted S. N. Behren, CONVERSATIONS WITH MAX 1960

14 There is much to be said for failure. It is more interesting than success.
Max Beerbohm, MAINLY ON THE AIR 1946

15 Meet success like a gentleman and disaster like a man.
Lord Birkenhead

16 He was totally used to failure and he did not easily resign himself to a change of regime.
Jorge Louis Borges, FICCIONES

17 The world is made up of people who never quite get into the first team and who just miss the prizes at the flower show.
Jacob Bronowski, THE FACE OF VIOLENCE

18 Everything works out for the best. Even failure.
Gp Captain Leonard Cheshire, THE FACE OF VICTORY

19 If the failures of this world could realise how desperate half the present-day geniuses once felt, they would take heart and try again.
Fay Compton, MEMOIRS

20 I'm a connoisseur of failure. I can smell it, roll it round my mouth, tell you the vintage and the side of the hill that grew it.
Giles Cooper, UNMAN, WITTERING AND ZIGO *(radio play)*

21 Failure must be but a challenge to others.
Amelia Earhart, LAST FIGHT

22 Don't write about my successes. My failures are much more interesting.
Sir John Gielgud. Quoted John Mortimer, IN CHARACTER 1983

23 He was a self-made man who owed his lack of success to nobody.
Joseph Heller, CATCH 22 1961

24 Failure is always more attractive than success.
Anthony Howard, Observer, Labour's Lost Leader 21 *Oct* 1979

1 His failures are priceless experiences in that they not only open up the way to a deeper truth, but force him to change his views and methods.
Carl Jung, MODERN MAN IN SEARCH OF HIS SOUL 1933

2 There is something distinguished about even his [Eugene O'Neill] failures; they sink not trivially but with a certain air of majesty, like a great ship, its flags flying, full of holes.
George Jean Nathan, AMERICAN DRAMA AND ITS CRITICS *(edited Alan S. Downs)*

3 A living failure is better than a dead masterpiece.
George Bernard Shaw, THE ADVENTURES OF THE BLACK GIRL IN HER SEARCH FOR GOD

4 He [Senator W. E. Borah] was always winding himself up, but never struck twelve.
John Chalmers Vinson, WILLIAM E. BORAH AND THE OUTLAWING OF WAR

FAITH

5 I do not pretend to see light, but I do see gleams and I know I am right to follow those gleams.
Father Andrew, LIFE AND LETTERS

6 I am one of those who would rather sink with faith than swim without it.
Stanley Baldwin. Speech, Leeds 12 *Oct* 1923

7 Faith is belief without evidence in what is told by one who speaks without knowledge of things without parallel.
Ambrose Bierce, THE DEVIL'S DICTIONARY 1906

8 It has been said that faith can move mountains, but no one has seen it done, save by the faith that man has in himself, in the steam shovels and the dynamite he has invented in the face of a hostile Nature.
Louis Bromfield, THE STRANGE CASE OF MISS ANNIE SPRAGG 1928

9 One may not doubt that, somehow, good / Shall come of water and of mud. / And, sure, the reverent eye must see / A purpose in liquidity.
Rupert Brooke, HEAVEN 1913

10 You can do very little with faith, but you can do nothing without it.
Samuel Butler, NOTEBOOKS 1912

11 We derive our inspiration from God, but we are grateful to *The Times* for the strengthening of our convictions.
Bishop of Carlisle. Speech to a diocesan conference

12 Faith has need of the whole truth.
Pierre Teilhard de Chardin, THE APPEARANCE OF MAN

13 No faith is our own that we have not arduously won.
Havelock Ellis, THE DANCE OF LIFE 1923

14 The contradictions of the Old Testament mean that with a little effort anyone can find a faith that accords with his preferences and a moral code that is agreeable to his tastes, even if fairly depraved.
J. K. Galbraith, ECONOMICS, PEACE AND LAUGHTER

15 If you have abandoned one faith, do not abandon all faith. There is always an alternative to the faith we lose. Or is it the same faith under another mask?
Graham Greene, THE COMEDIANS 1966

16 Where there is the necessary technical skill to move mountains there is no need for the faith that moves mountains.
Eric Hoffer, THE PASSIONATE STATE OF MIND 1954

17 Faith in a holy cause is to a considerable extent a substitute for the lost faith in ourselves.
Eric Hoffer, THE TRUE BELIEVER 1951

18 A faith cannot be a faith against but *for.*
Archibald MacLeish, Survey Graphic, *Feb* 1941

19 . . . an illogical belief in the occurrence of the improbable.
H. L. Mencken, PREJUDICES 1922

20 I respect faith, but doubt is what gets you an education.
Wilson Mizner

21 Nothing true or beautiful or good makes complete sense in any immediate context of history; therefore we must be saved by faith.
Reinhold Niebuhr, THE IRONY OF AMERICAN HISTORY 1952

1 Faith is a quality which the scientist cannot dispense with.
Max Planck, WHERE IS SCIENCE GOING? 1932

2 It is at night that faith in light is admirable.
Edmond Rostand, CHANTICLEER 1907

3 Faith, even when profound, is never complete.
Jean-Paul Sartre, WORDS 1964

4 I do not believe I know anything about faith. Jesus is my God. I don't think I have any faith but that. But I have a love for men; somewhere in me I have love. I hang on to that.
Rev. H. R. L. Sheppard, IMPATIENCE OF A PARSON 1929

5 Faith which does not doubt is dead faith.
Miguel de Unamuno, THE AGONY OF CHRISTIANITY

6 People are going mad and talking balls to psychiatrists not because of accidents to the chamberpot in the nursery but because there is no logical structure to their beliefs.
Evelyn Waugh, letter to John Betjeman 22 Dec 1946

7 Such lapses from knowledge to faith are perhaps necessary that human heroism may be possible.
H. G. Wells, MR BRITLING SEES IT THROUGH 1946

8 I am more harassed by doubt, insecurity, ambivalence and rebelliousness than ever, and to be once more in St Peter's boat is to be subject to such violent seasickness that every few months I am tempted to throw myself overboard.
Antonia White, THE HOUND AND THE FALCON

FALSENESS

9 That which has been believed by everyone, always and everywhere, has every chance of being false.
Paul Valéry, TELQUEL 1943

FAME

10 There is no future in being an ordinary person.
Susan Mary Alsop on BBC Radio 4

11 I find in London I am getting known by sight. I saw two very rough-looking men on the pavement the other day and one said to the other 'That's the old bloke.'
Stanley Baldwin. Speech, Worcester 10 Aug 1926

12 A friend of mine once said to me 'Everybody is famous for something, and you are famous for living opposite Bernard Shaw.'
J. M. Barrie, Presidential address to the Society of Authors 28 Nov 1928

13 Fame always brings loneliness. Success is as ice cold and lonely as the north pole.
Vicki Baum, GRAND HOTEL

14 It took me fifteen years to discover I had no talent for writing but I couldn't give it up because by that time I was too famous.
Robert Benchley, CHIPS OFF THE OLD BENCHLEY 1949

15 The celebrity is a person who is known for his well-knownness.
Daniel Boorstin, THE IMAGE 1962

16 A sign of a celebrity is often that his name is worth more than his services.
Ibid.

17 There is a lot to be said for not being known to the readers of the *Daily Mirror.*
Anthony Burgess, INSIDE MR ENDERBY 1966

18 Fame is being asked to sign your autograph on the back of a cigarette packet.
Billy Connolly

19 We like to appear in the newspapers, so long as we are in the right column.
T. S. Eliot, THE FAMILY REUNION 1939

20 Once you're dead you're made for life.
Jimi Hendrix

21 Fame is delightful, but as collateral it does not rank high.
Elbert Hubbard, EPIGRAMS 1915

22 Those who are created by publicity will eventually be destroyed by it.
Bernard Levin, THE PENDULUM YEARS 1976

23 Fame, like a drunkard, consumes the house of the soul.
Malcolm Lowry, of the reception given to UNDER THE VOLCANO 1947

1 It stirs up envy, fame does.
Marilyn Monroe. Quoted Richard Schickel,
COMMON FAME: THE CULTURE OF
CELEBRITY 1985

2 It is strange how the memory of a man may
float to posterity on what he would have
himself regarded as the most trifling of his
works.
Sir William Osler, APHORISMS

3 In opera, as with any performing art, to be in
great demand and to command high fees you
must be good of course, but you must also be
famous. The two are different things.
Luciano Pavarotti, AUTOBIOGRAPHY

4 The transient nature of television fame was
well illustrated when I was buying a ticket
for the Motor Show. The ticket-seller
looked at me closely and said: 'Aren't you
what's 'is name?'. 'Yes,' I said. 'I thought
you were.' she said.
Michael Pertwee, NAME DROPPING

5 There is no second money in the hall of
fame. Take the case of Methuselah's
grandpa, Jared. He lived to be 962 years old
— only seven years younger than his
illustrious grandson. That wasn't good
enough; he remains to this day unknown,
unhonoured and unsung.
M. Pitkin

6 If I was in life for fame and fortune I'd be in
the movies or as Whistler said, jump off
Westminster Bridge with fireworks in my
pockets.
John Romer, BBC 2 TV, Romer's Egypt
4 *Sep* 1981

7 In the future, everyone will be famous for 15
minutes.
Andy Warhol

FAMILIARITY

8 There is probably nothing like living
together for blending people to each other.
Ivy Compton-Burnett, MOTHER AND
SON 1955

9 Familiar things happen, and mankind does
not bother about them. It requires a very
unusual mind to undertake the analysis of
the obvious.
A. N. Whitehead, SCIENCE AND THE
MODERN WORLD 1925

FAMILY

10 We're a very remarkable family, and I wish
to God we weren't.
*Florence Joyce, sister of James Joyce.
Quoted Richard Ellman*, JOYCE 1950

11 I was the seventh of nine children. When
you come from that far down you have to
struggle to survive.
Robert F. Kennedy. Quoted B. G. Clinch,
THE KENNEDY NEUROSIS

12 Far from being the basis of the good society,
the family, with its narrow privacy and
tawdry secrets, is the source of all our
discontents.
*Sir Edmund Leach, BBC Reith
Lectures* 1967

13 However much you dislike a relation, and
whatever ill you may yourself say of him,
you do not like others to say anything which
shows him in a ridiculous or objectionable
light; since the discredit thrown on your
relation reflects upon yourself and wounds
your vanity.
W. Somerset Maugham, A WRITER'S
NOTEBOOK 1949

14 Every man sees in his relations, and
especially in his cousins, a series of grotesque caricatures of himself.
H. L. Mencken, PREJUDICES 1919

15 The secret of neurosis is to be found in the
family battle of wills to see who can refuse
longest to help wash the dishes. The sink is
the great symbol of the bloodiness of family
life. All life is bad but family life is worse.
Julian Mitchell, AS FAR AS YOU CAN GO

16 Every generation revolts against its fathers
and makes friends with its grandfathers.
Lewis Mumford, THE BROWN DECADE 1931

17 One would be in less danger / From the wiles
of the stranger / If one's own kin and kith /
Were more fun to be with.
Ogden Nash, FAMILY COURT

18 The best way to keep children home is to
make the home atmosphere pleasant — and
let the air out of the tyres.
Dorothy Parker. Quoted Frank Muir, ON
CHILDREN

1 When our relatives are at home we have to think of all their good points or it would be impossible to endure them.
George Bernard Shaw, HEARTBREAK HOUSE 1920

2 That dear octopus from whose tentacles we never quite escape, nor in our innermost hearts never quite wish to.
Dodie Smith, DEAR OCTOPUS 1938

FANATIC

3 A fanatic is one who can't change his mind and won't change the subject.
Winston Churchill. Attributed by John Bartlett, FAMILIAR QUOTATIONS

4 A fanatic is a man that does what he thinks the Lord would do, if He knew the facts of the case.
Finley Peter Dunne, MR DOOLEY'S OPINIONS, *Casual Observations* 1900

5 Defined in psychological terms, a fanatic is a man who consciously over-compensates a secret doubt.
Aldous Huxley, PROPER STUDIES 1927

6 The evil is not what they [extremists] say about their cause, but what they say about their opponents.
Robert F. Kennedy, THE PURSUIT OF JUSTICE 1964

7 It is characteristic of all movements and crusades that the psychopathic elements rises to the top.
Robert Linder, MUST YOU CONFORM? 1956

8 The more you are in the right the more natural that everyone else should be bullied into thinking likewise.
George Orwell, THE ROAD TO WIGAN PIER 1937

9 Fanaticism consists in redoubling your effort when you have forgotten your aim.
George Santayana, THE LIFE OF REASON, *Reason in Commonsense* 1906

10 There is nobody as enslaved as the fanatic, the person in whom one impulse, one value, has assumed ascendancy over all others.
Milton B. Saperstein, PARADOXES OF EVERYDAY LIFE 1955

138

FANTASY

11 All fantasy should have a solid base in reality.
Max Beerbohm, ZULEIKA DOBSON, *note to* 1946 *edition*

12 . . . dreams of her lover, tall as the town clock tower, Samson-syrup-gold maned, whacking thighed and piping hot, thunderbolt-bassed and barnacle-breasted, flailing up the cockles with his eyes like blowlamps and scooping low over her lonely loving hotwaterbottled body.
Dylan Thomas, UNDER MILK WOOD 1954

13 The poet is in command of his fantasy, while it is exactly the mark of the neurotic that he is possessed by his fantasy.
Lionel Trilling, THE LIBERAL IMAGINATION, *Freud and Literature* 1950

FARMING

14 I have just read an article complaining that there will be a serious shortage of scientists for agriculture after the war. This is terrible. We may have to use farmers again.
Beachcomber (J. B. Morton), HERE AND NOW

15 The field and wood all bone-fed loam / Shot up a roaring harvest home.
Edmund Blunden, SELECTED POEMS, *Rural Economy* 1957

16 'If you put a bull in a field with a herd of cows you wouldn't expect to see a lot of calves the next morning.'
'No. But you'd expect to see a lot of contented faces.'
James Callaghan, retort to James Prior, Minister of Agriculture

17 Lately, I have taken to farming in a modest way . . . If I had heard about it when I was young I probably should never have gone into politics at all.
Winston Churchill. Speech at Kent Agricultural Show, Maidstone. Quoted News Review 29 Jul 1948

18 But it's useless to argue the why and the wherefore / When a crop is so thin / There's nothing to do but set the teeth / And plough it in.
Cecil Day Lewis, A FAILURE

1 Farming looks mighty easy when your plough is a pencil and you're a thousand miles from the cornfield.
Dwight D. Eisenhower. Speech, Peoria 25 Sep 1956

2 A good farmer needs a strong back and a weak mind.
J. K. Galbraith, A LIFE IN OUR TIMES 1982

3 No one can understand farmers unless it is known that, the rarest exceptions apart, they are afflicted with a serious sense of inferiority . . . Working farmers are always struggling with the thought that they are hicks.
Ibid.

4 No one hates his job so heartily as a farmer.
H. L. Mencken, American Mercury, What is Going On In the World? Nov 1933

5 To expect an average farmer to be not only a sower and a reaper, but an agricultural chemist, an accountant, a meteorologist, a veterinary expert, a merchant, a financier and a resident housekeeper all united in a single Admirable Crichton is ridiculous; yet this is our practice.
George Bernard Shaw. Quoted News Review 10 Apr 1947

6 A farmer was asked what sort of year he had just had. 'Medium,' came the reply. 'What do you mean by "medium" ?' 'Worse than last year but better than next.'
Peter Walker. Speech at Royal Horticultural Society 21 May 1979

FASCINATION

7 You fascinated me; but I loved you; so it was heaven. This sister of yours fascinates me; but I hate her; so it is hell.
George Bernard Shaw, HEARTBREAK HOUSE 1920

FASCISM

8 But for the bold experiment of Fascism the decade has not been fruitful in constructive statesmanship.
John Buchan, Morning Post, Dec 1929

9 Fascism was little more than terrorist rule by corrupt gangsters. Mussolini was not corrupt himself but he did nothing except to rage impotently.
A. J. P. Taylor, Observer, The Cardboard Lion 28 Feb 1982

FASHION

10 [Clothes] play such an intimate part in the delicate business of getting oneself across that it seems impossible to discuss them, for long, objectively.
Elizabeth Bowen, COLLECTED IMPRESSIONS 1950

11 Don't ever wear artistic jewellery. It wrecks a woman's reputation.
Colette, GIGI 1945

12 Most of the change we think we see in life / Is due to truths being in and out of favour.
Robert Frost, NORTH OF BOSTON

13 In the [1914—18] war the shortage of sugar and butter and the popularisation of hockey and tennis, greatly reduced women's weight and when they were freed of their tight corsets the popular "hour-glass" figure gave place to the neatly cylindrical.
Robert Graves and Alan Hodge, THE LONG WEEK-END 1940

14 I find I am not as closely in touch with modern life as I once was; I no longer seem to meet ladies in antique shops who are besotted about antlers.
Joyce Grenfell at 60

15 Brought up in an epoch when ladies apparently rolled along on wheels, Mr Quarles was peculiarly susceptible to calves.
Aldous Huxley, POINT COUNTER POINT 1934

16 The surest way to be out of fashion tomorrow is to be in the forefront of it today.
Derek Marlowe, A DANDY IN ASPIC 1966

17 The reason for all this feminine adornment is that women are indulged just because they are in an alien (male) society. They are like girls in a mining camp being rewarded with gold nuggets. Because they are out of place they must be given a treat.
J. B. Priestley, THOUGHTS IN THE WILDERNESS

1 Her frocks are built in Paris, but she wears them with a strong English accent.
Saki, REGINALD ON WOMEN 1904

2 Fashions, after all, are only induced epidemics.
George Bernard Shaw, DOCTOR'S DILEMMA, *Preface* 1906

3 To call a fashion wearable is the kiss of death. No new fashion worth its salt is ever wearable.
Eugenia Sheppard, New York Herald Tribune 13 *Jan* 1960

4 You cannot be both fashionable and first rate.
Logan Pearsall Smith, ALL TRIVIA, *Afterthoughts* 1931

5 If Botticelli were alive today he'd be working for *Vogue*.
Peter Ustinov. Quoted Observer, Sayings of the Week 21 *Oct* 1968

6 And if you feel exotic and extravagant you *could* have some tiny jewelled nose clips.
Woman and Beauty

7 If a woman wishes to be really smart this winter she must wear a coloured ring on the small toe of her left foot to match the colour of the nail varnish she uses on her fingers.
Yorkshire Telegraph and Star

FATALISM

.8 I go the way that Providence dictates with the assurance of a sleepwalker.
Adolf Hitler. Speech, Munich 26 *Sep* 1938

9 One would think we must needs all complete our destinies, merely by the process of living out our lives to the end.
Rose Macaulay, A CASUAL COMMENTARY

10 Death is a warm cloak and an old friend. I regard death as something that comes up on a roulette wheel once in a while.
Gram Papons, rock musician, on being warned that his drug addiction could prove fatal

FATE

11 There is no return game between a man and his stars.
Samuel Beckett, MURPHY 1938

12 The dead leaf on the highlands / The old tramp on the mill drove / Each whirls on nor understands / God's freezing love.
Edmund Blunden, POEMS 1911—1930

13 Only the fool, fixed in his folly, may think he can turn the wheel on which he turns.
T. S. Eliot, MURDER IN THE CATHEDRAL 1935

14 Human reason needs only to will more strongly than fate, and she *is* fate.
Thomas Mann, THE MAGIC MOUNTAIN 1924

15 Fate is the gunman that all gunmen dread. / Fate stings the stinger for his roll of green; / Fate, Strong-Arm-Worker, on the bean / Of strong-arm-workers bumps his pipe of lead.
Don Marquis, PROVERBS

16 However much we dawdle in the sun / We have to hurry at the touch of Fate.
John Masefield, THE WIDOW IN THE BY STREET 1912

17 Listen son, don't fight your custard.
S. J. Perelman

FATHER

18 The night my father got me / His mind was not on me; / He did not plague his fancy / To muse if I should be / The son you see.
A. E. Housman, LAST POEMS 1922

19 It is easier for a father to have children than for children to have a real father.
Pope John XXIII

20 Happy is the child whose father acquits himself with credit in the presence of his friends.
Robert Lynd, THE BLUE LION

21 The fundamental defect of fathers is that they want their children to be a credit to them.
Bertrand Russell, AUTOBIOGRAPHY 1967

22 No man is responsible for his father. That is entirely his mother's affair.
Margaret Turnbull, ALABASTER LAMPS 1925

23 The time not to become a father is eighteen years before a world war.
E. B. White, THE SECOND TREE FROM THE CORNER 1954

1 A father should know how to flirt with a small daughter without making his wife feel like an old discarded bedsock.
Katherine Whitehorn, HOW TO SURVIVE CHILDREN

FATHER-IN-LAW

2 Well, Betjeman, if you're going to be my son-in-law you needn't go on calling me 'Sir'. Call me 'Field Marshal'.
Field Marshal Lord Chetwode to John Betjeman. Quoted Observer 8 Feb 1959

FAULT

3 There is absolutely nothing wrong with Oscar Levant that a miracle can't fix.
Alexander Woollcott. Quoted Margaret Case Harriman, THE VICIOUS CIRCLE 1951

FAVOUR

4 Never claim as a right what you can accept as a favour.
Churton Collins, APHORISMS

FEAR

5 The wild hound, Fear, black ravenous and gaunt.
Lascelles Abercrombie, COLLECTED POEMS, *Marriage Shy* 1930

6 Fears wide as the night.
Laurence Binyon, WESTWARD

7 Fear tastes like a rusty knife and do not let her into your house.
John Cheever, THE WAPSHOT CHRONICLE 1957

8 I have seen the moment of my greatness flicker / And I have seen the eternal Footman hold my coat and snicker / And, in short, I was afraid.
T. S. Eliot, THE LOVE STORY OF J. ALFRED PRUFROCK 1915

9 I will show you fear in a handful of dust.
T. S. Eliot, THE WASTE LAND 1922

10 Fear born of ignorance is worse than fear born of knowledge.
Dr Charles Hill. Address to Hunterian Society. Quoted News Review 2 Dec 1948

11 I'm a stranger and afraid / In a world I never made.
A. E. Housman, LAST POEMS 1922

12 The one permanent emotion of the inferior man, as of all the simple mammals, is fear — fear of the unknown, the complex, the inexplicable. What he wants beyond everything else is safety.
H. L. Mencken, The Yale Review, Jun 1920

13 When you ask her how she felt inside the cement mixer, she thinks it over and says 'Frightened'.
Observer, profile of Pat Arrowsmith 13 May 1962

14 Modern man is aggressive because he is fearful. Almost all propaganda is designed to create fear. Heads of governments and other officials know that a frightened people is easier to govern, will forfeit rights it would otherwise defend, is less likely to demand a better life, and will agree to millions and millions being spent on 'Defence'.
J. B. Priestley, OUTCRIES AND ASIDES

15 Let me assert my firm belief that the only thing we have to fear is fear itself.
Franklin D. Roosevelt. Speech 2 Jul 1932

16 Fear is the main source of superstition and one of the main sources of cruelty. To conquer fear is the beginning of wisdom.
Bertrand Russell, AN OUTLINE OF INTELLECTUAL RUBBISH 1950

17 Fear will drive men to any extreme; and the fear inspired by a superior being is a mystery which cannot be reasoned away.
George Bernard Shaw, ST JOAN, *Preface* 1927

18 Everybody is afraid for himself, and everybody thinks his neighbours' fears are ridiculous, as they generally are.
J. A. Spender, THE COMMENTS OF BAGSHOT

FEAST

19 Feasts must be solemn and rare, or else they cease to be feasts.
Aldous Huxley, DO WHAT YOU WILL

FEATURES

1 Her features did not seem to know the value of team work.
George Ade

2 She has a Siamese forehead and a mouth like a galosh.
Mrs Pat Campbell of an un-named actress.
Quoted James Agate, EGO 3, 6 *May* 1937

FEET

3 He is a big guy . . . with very funny feet which is why he is called Feet. These feet are extra large feet even for a big guy and Dave the Dude says he wears violin cases for shoes. Of course this is not true, because Feet cannot get either of his feet into a violin case, unless it is a case for a very large violin, such as a cello.
Damon Runyon, GUYS AND DOLLS 1932

FEMINISM

4 The suffragettes were triumphant. Woman's place was in the gaol.
Caryl Brahms and S. J. Simon, NO NIGHTINGALES

5 Nothing would induce me to vote for giving women the franchise. I am not going to be henpecked into a question of such importance.
Winston Churchill. Quoted Robert Lewis Taylor, THE AMAZING MR CHURCHILL

6 The all-male religions have produced no religious imagery . . . The great religious art of the world is deeply involved with the female principle.
Kenneth, Lord Clark, CIVILISATION 1969

7 There are times when even a dedicated feminist needs a chauvinist to lean on.
Clive Cussler, VIXEN 1978

8 Ridicule has pursued the feminist down the corridors of time like some satanic practical joker; it is almost a relief when the hilarity turns to anger.
Helen Dudar, Newsweek 23 *Mar* 1970

9 When a woman behaves like a man, why can't she behave like a nice man?
Dame Edith Evans. Quoted Observer,
Sayings of the Week 30 *Sep* 1957

10 Women fail to understand how much men hate them.
Germaine Greer, THE FEMALE EUNUCH

11 Field Marshal Montgomery: Lady Astor, I must tell you that I do not approve of female politicians.
Lady Astor: That's all right. The only General I approve of is Evangeline Booth.
Quoted John Grigg, NANCY ASTOR, PORTRAIT OF A PIONEER

12 In the eighteenth century, when logic and science were the fashion, women tried to talk like men. The twentieth century has reversed the process.
Aldous Huxley, TWO OR THREE GRACES

13 The homo is the legitimate child of the suffragette.
(Percy) Wyndham Lewis, THE ART OF BEING RULED 1926

14 You cannot trust the interests of one class entirely to another class, and you cannot trust the interests of one sex entirely to another sex.
David Lloyd George. Speech on Suffrage 1911

15 This frenzied search for female identity, this *me, me,* what am *I,* what do *I* want, is the kind of self-preoccupation that can send anyone down the path to complete isolation — which is not a path the wife and mother can follow.
Joyce Lubold, THIS HALF OF THE APPLE IS MINE

16 Women these days do not find it difficult to behave like men; but they often find it extremely difficult to behave like gentlemen.
Compton Mackenzie, ON MORAL COURAGE

17 Women's Liberation is just a lot of foolishness. It's the men who are discriminated against. They can't bear children. And no one's likely to do anything about that.
Golda Meir

18 I just hope other women see me as one of them. My main hope as Prime Minister would be to give women more confidence.
Margaret Thatcher. Quoted Observer,
Sayings of the Week 6 *May* 1979

1 People call me a feminist whenever I express sentiments that differentiate me from a doormat or a prostitute.
Rebecca West 1913

2 Whatever women do they must do twice as well as men to be thought half as good. Luckily this is not difficult.
Charlotte Whitton on becoming mayor of Ottawa

3 The Catholic Church has never really come to terms with women. What I object to is being treated either as Madonnas or Mary Magdalenes.
Shirley Williams. Interview with Miriam Gross, Observer 22 Mar 1981

FICTION

4 A novel is balanced between a few true impressions and the multitude of false ones that make up most of what we call life.
Saul Bellow, Nobel Prize speech 1976

5 A work of fiction should be, for its author, a journey into the unknown, and the prose should convey the difficulties of the journey.
Anthony Burgess, HOMAGE TO QWERT YUIOP 1986

6 Every fine story must leave in the mind of the sensitive reader an intangible residuum of pleasure, a cadence, a quality of voice that is exclusively the writer's own, individual, unique.
Willa Cather, NOT UNDER FORTY, *Miss Jewett* 1936

7 There are only two or three human stories, and they go on repeating themselves as fiercely as if they had never happened before.
Willa Cather, O PIONEER 1913

8 When the plot flags, bring in a man with a gun.
Raymond Chandler, giving advice to an interviewer. Quoted RAYMOND CHANDLER SPEAKING

9 What greater prestige can a man like me (not too greatly gifted, but very understanding) have than to have taken a cheap, shoddy and utterly lost kind of writing, and have made of it something that intellectuals claw each other about?
Ibid.

10 Mr Faulkner, of course, is interested in making your mind rather than your flesh creep.
Clifton Fadiman, New Yorker 21 Apr 1934

11 The novel . . . supplies pictures and evidence from which each reader may take that food which best suits her growth. It is the great fertiliser, the quiet fertiliser of people's imagination.
John Galsworthy, LIFE AND LETTERS 1935

12 The novel supplies revelation . . . browsed upon, brooded over, soaked up into the fibre of the mind and conscience.
Ibid.

13 The novel . . . changes the currents of judgment in a man's mind before he even suspects there is a change going on. The more unaware he is, the more surely he is undermined, for he has no means of mobilising his defences.
Ibid.

14 Cynics have claimed there are only six basic plots. Frankenstein and My Fair Lady are really the same story.
Leslie Halliwell, FILMGOER'S BOOK OF QUOTES 1973

15 Do you abominate detective stories? I read two a week in bed at night; can't concentrate on much else then. To me they are a great solace, a sort of mental knitting where it doesn't matter if you drop a stitch.
Rupert Hart-Davis, THE LYTTELTON HART-DAVIS LETTERS 30 Oct 1955

16 When writing a novel a writer should create living people; people, not characters. A *character* is a caricature.
Ernest Hemingway, DEATH IN THE AFTERNOON 1932

17 All good books are alike in that they are truer than if they really happened. After you are finished reading one you will feel that all that happened to you, and afterwards it all belongs to you.
Ernest Hemingway, Esquire, An Old Newsman Writes, Dec 1934

18 Do your bit to save humanity from lapsing back into barbarity by reading all the novels you can.
Richard Hughes. Speech at a Foyle's Library Lunch, to mark his 75th birthday 1975

1 The novel is the last bastion against barbarity. The archetypal non-reader of fiction was Hitler.
Richard Hughes. Quoted Mary Kay Wilmers, Radio Times 12 Jun 1979

2 The kind of house-brick thick paperback novel which records how the rape of a Choctaw squaw eventually leads to the foundation of a vast empire.
Clive James, BRILLIANT CREATURES 1983

3 She rode the trash-horse hell-for-leather.
Rose Macaulay of Ethel M. Dell

4 Casting my mind's eye over the whole of fiction, the only absolutely original creation I can think of is Don Quixote.
W. Somerset Maugham, NOVELS AND THEIR AUTHORS 1955

5 An autobiography can distort; facts can be realigned. But fiction never lies, it reveals the writer totally,
V. S. Naipaul. Quoted Janet Hitchman, SUCH A STRANGE LADY

6 Mr [John] O'Hara's world is populated by the cheap, vulgar, debased and self-destroyed. His reaction to it is a mixture of sardonic scorn, savage contempt and romantic wonder.
Orville Prescott, IN MY OPINION

7 A short story is always a disclosure, frequently an evocation . . . frequently a celebration of a character at bursting point.
V. S. Pritchett, OXFORD BOOK OF SHORT STORIES, *Introduction*

8 The principle of procrastinated rape is said to be the ruling one in all the great bestsellers.
V. S. Pritchett, THE LIVING NOVEL 1946

9 I like shape very much. A novel has to have shape, and life doesn't have any.
Jean Rhys, SMILE PLEASE: AN UNFINISHED AUTOBIOGRAPHY 1979

10 The central theme of the novel is that they were glad to see each other.
Gertrude Stein. Quoted John Malcolm Brinnin, THE THIRD ROSE

11 My brother-in-law wrote an unusual murder story. The victim got killed by a man from another book.
Robert Sylvester

12 Rockfist was born in the mind of Mr Frank Pepper and he first appeared in the pages of *The Champion*, a boy's comic, in October 1938. He finally left the scene some 1000 chapters and five million words later on May 6, 1961. And considering that Leo Tolstoy used 700,000 words in *War and Peace* that must put Rockfist among the all-time greats of fiction.
Tiverton Gazette. Quoted Punch 22 Mar 1972

13 Religion and immorality are the only things that sell books nowadays. I am going to start a middle course and give them crime and blood and three murders to a chapter; such is the insanity of the age that I do not doubt for one moment the success of the venture.
Edgar Wallace, in a letter to his wife 1905

14 Nothing is more insulting to a novelist than to assume that he is incapable of anything except the mere transcription of what he observes.
Evelyn Waugh, Daily Mail 31 May 1930

15 Dialogue in fiction should be reserved for the culminating moments and regarded as the spray into which the great wave of narrative breaks in curving towards the watcher on the shore.
Edith Wharton, THE WRITING OF FICTION 1925

16 In any really good subject one has only to probe deep enough to come to tears.
Ibid.

17 Fiction is like a spider's web, attached ever so slightly perhaps, but still attached, to life at all four corners.
Virginia Woolf, A ROOM OF ONE'S OWN 1929

FIDELITY

18 Faithful women are all alike. They think only of their fidelity and not of their husbands.
Jean Giraudoux, AMPHITRYON 38, 1929

19 For he was a man of unwearied and prolific conjugal fidelity.
Blasco Ibanez, BLOOD AND SAND 1908

FINANCE

20 A man accustomed to think in millions — other people's millions.
Arnold Bennett, JOURNALS 1933

1 First payments is what made us think we were prosperous and the other nineteen is what showed us we were broke.
Will Rogers, AUTOBIOGRAPHY 1949

2 I go to the bank every morning and when I say 'No' I return home at night without worry. But when I say 'Yes' it's like putting your finger into a machine — the whirring wheels may drag your whole body in after the finger.
Sir Nathan Meyer Rothschild. Quoted Virginia Cowles, THE ROTHSCHILDS: A FAMILY OF FORTUNE

3 The faults of the burglar are the qualities of the financier.
George Bernard Shaw, MAJOR BARBARA, *Preface* 1905

FIRE

4 The fire rose in two branched flames like the golden antlers of some enchanted stag.
Katherine Mansfield, JOURNALS 1954

5 The fire was furry as a bear.
Edith Sitwell, DARK SONG

FISH

6 Fish in the unruffled lakes / The swarming colours wear.
W. H. Auden, FISH IN THE UNRUFFLED LAKES 1936

7 And nigh the toppling reed, still as death / The great pike lies, the murderous patriarch.
Edmund Blunden, THE PIKE

8 Fish say they have their stream and pond / But is there anything beyond?
Rupert Brooke, HEAVEN

9 Fish die belly upwards and rise to the surface. It is their way of falling.
André Gide, JOURNALS 1939—1950

10 The tiny fish enjoy themselves in the sea / Quick little splinters of life / Their little lives are fun to them in the sea.
D. H. Lawrence, COLLECTED POEMS, *Little Fish* 1928

11 The Herring is a lucky fish / From all disease inured / Should he be ill while caught at sea; / *Immediately* — he's cured /
Spike Milligan, SILLY VERSES FOR KIDS

FISHING

12 A canny young fisher named Fisher / Once fished on the edge of a fissure / A fish with a grin / Pulled the fisherman in – Now they're fishing the fissure for Fisher.
Anon.

13 1st Woman: Look at that Nogood Boyo now.
2nd Woman: Too lazy to wipe his snout.
3rd Woman: And going out fishing every day and all he ever brought back was a Mrs Samuels.
1st Woman: Been in the water a week.
Dylan Thomas, UNDER MILK WOOD 1954

F. SCOTT FITZGERALD

14 Mr Fitzgerald is a novelist. Mrs Fitzgerald is a novelty.
Ring Lardner, THE OTHER SIDE

15 Although he could write a bad story he could not write badly.
Dorothy Parker. Quoted Anthony Burgess, *Observer*, *Dollars and Dolours* 2 Dec 1979

16 Of good social standing and addicted to strong liquor, he had neither the stamina of a Hemingway nor the peasant goodness of a Faulkner to withstand the corrupting influences attendant on success in the materialistic USA. He wasted his energies on the glossier magazines, wrote rubbishy film scripts, and died in his forties, a bitter exhausted man.
News Review, reviewing THIS SIDE OF PARADISE 9 *Dec* 1948

FLATTERY

17 You must not stop in front of a painting and say 'That must have cost you a fortune!' But you may stop, nod, examine it carefully and ask if it is an early Rembrandt.
George Mikes, HOW TO BE AN ALIEN 1946

18 Tell me all my faults as man to man. I can stand anything but flattery.
George Bernard Shaw, JOHN BULL'S OTHER ISLAND 1904

1 What really flatters a man is that you think him worth flattering.
Ibid.

2 Flattery is all right so long as you don't inhale.
Adlai Stevenson. Speech 1 Feb 1961. Quoted Roy Jenkins, ADLAI STEVENSON

3 The only man who wasn't spoiled by being lionized was Daniel.
Sir H. Beerbohm Tree. Quoted Hesketh Pearson, BEERBOHM TREE

FLEA

4 The fleas that tease in the High Pyrenees.
Hilaire Belloc, TARANTELLA

5 And I have more power / To upset the world / Than the elephant. / When I think of that / I could die of laughing.
Carmen de Bernos Gazztold, THE BEASTS' CHOIR

6 I could not be more astonished if you told me there were fleas at the Ritz.
Ronald Firbank, THE FLOWER BENEATH THE FOOT 1923

FLIRTATION

7 Men want a woman whom they can turn on and off like a light switch.
Ian Fleming

8 The trouble with Ian [Fleming] is that he gets off with women because he can't get on with them.
Rosamond Lehmann. Quoted John Pearson, THE LIFE OF IAN FLEMING 1966

9 Flirtation is merely an expression of considered desire coupled with an admission of its impracticability.
Marya Mannes, BUT WILL IT SELL? 1964

FLOGGING

10 I am all for bringing back the birch but only between consenting adults.
Gore Vidal in a television interview with David Frost

FLOWER

11 The fairest thing in nature, a flower, still has its roots in earth and manure.
D. H. Lawrence. SELECTED LITERARY CRITICISM *(edited Anthony Beal)* 1956

12 People from a planet without flowers would think we must be mad with joy the whole time to have such things about us.
Iris Murdoch, A FAIRLY HONOURABLE DEFEAT

FLY

13 God in his wisdom made the fly / And then forgot to tell us why.
Ogden Nash, GOOD INTENTIONS

FLYING

14 Today we hear so much musical sound all the time, in trains, in aeroplanes, in restaurants, that we are becoming deadened to it. We are able to turn off television or walk out of a bad motion picture or poor concert. You can't walk out of an aeroplane.
Leopold Stokowski. Quoted Nat Shapiro, ENCYCLOPEDIA OF QUOTATIONS ABOUT MUSIC

15 There are only two emotions in a plane, boredom and terror.
Orson Welles, Observer, Sayings of the Week 12 May 1985

16 Success. Four flights. Thursday morning. All against twenty-one-mile wind.
Wilbur and Orville Wright, telegram from Kitty Hawk 17 Dec 1903

FLYING SAUCER

17 Some people say these objects are due to the excessive consumption in the United States of Scotch whisky. But it is not so. They are due to a Soviet athlete, a discus-thrower, practising for the Olympic Games and quite unconscious of his own strength.
Andrei Gromyko, Soviet Foreign Minister. Quoted Lord Glendurgan, House of Lords 17 Jan 1979

FOG

1 The yellow fog that rubs its back upon the window panes.
T. S. Eliot, LOVE SONG OF J. ALFRED PRUFROCK 1915

2 The fog is in the bones of the drowned.
Norman Nicholson, CAEDMON

FOLLY

3 The follies which a man regrets the most in his life, are those which he didn't commit when he had the opportunity.
Helen Rowland, A GUIDE TO MEN

4 He [Jack London] made many mistakes and committed innumerable follies, but at least he had the satisfaction of knowing that they had been big ones.
Irving Stone, SAILOR ON HORSEBACK: *The Biography of Jack London*

FOOD

5 We know more about what goes into a pair of socks than about what goes into our food.
Jonathan Aitken. Speech, House of Commons, on Food Additives Campaign 13 *Dec* 1985

6 They eat and drank deeply of the charming viands ending up with merangs and chocolates.
Daisy Ashford (aged 9), THE YOUNG VISITERS 1919

7 There is no such thing as a little garlic.
Arthur Baer. Quoted, THE FRANK MUIR BOOK

8 Rightly thought of there is poetry in peaches, even when they are canned.
Granville Barker, THE MADRAS HOUSE 1910

9 It would appear that the Ministry of Food base their standards of our bodily requirements of food on calories alone. Surely this is incorrect? After all there are calories in hay, but how many calories can be absorbed by man?
Dr J. M. Bellamy. letter to Daily Telegraph

10 Huntley and Palmer / Grew calmer and calmer. / When either felt restive / He ate a digestive.
E. C. Bentley, CLERIHEWS

11 I like sandwiches.
Ernest Bevin when asked his choice of menu for dinner. Potsdam Conference, Aug 1945

12 *Edible. Adj.* good to eat and wholesome to digest, as a worm to a toad, a toad to a snake, a snake to a pig, a pig to a man, and a man to a worm.
Ambrose Bierce, THE DEVIL'S DICTIONARY 1906

13 Once at dinner when the menu announced Roast Duck and the scouts [at Merton] brought Roast Lamb, 'La Malade Imaginaire' he [Hugh Dyson] said.
Humphrey Carpenter, THE INKLINGS 1980

14 The turkey has practically no taste except a dry fibrous flavour reminiscent of a mixture of warmed-up plaster of Paris and horsehair. The texture is like wet sawdust and the whole vast feathered swindle has the piquancy of a boiled mattress.
Cassandra (William Connor), Daily Mirror 24 *Dec* 1953

15 Always get up from the table feeling as if you could still eat a penny bun.
Sir Hugh Casson and Joyce Grenfell, NANNY SAYS 1972

16 Why do we have so few blue foods?
Campbell Chalmers. Letter to Daily Telegraph 15 *Jul* 1985

17 Take this pudding away. It has no theme.
Winston Churchill to a waiter at the Savoy Hotel. Quoted Lord Butler, Thames TV, The Day Before Yesterday

18 I poke my braised welly with a fork . . . the food is indescribably dire. Malta is the only place in the world where the local delicacy is the bread.
Alan Coren, Punch 12 *Jan* 1972

19 The food was so abominable that I used to cross myself before I took a mouthful. I used to say 'Ian, it tastes like armpits.'
Noël Coward, of Ian Fleming's hospitality. Quoted John Pearson, THE LIFE OF IAN FLEMING 1966

20 I found out what that white stuff was we had in Taipan — it was rice.
Overheard by Noël Coward from a tourist in Raffles Hotel, Singapore

1 It's a very odd thing / As odd as can be, / That whatever Miss T. eats / Turns into Miss T.
Walter De La Mare, MISS T

2 Bouillabaise is only good because cooked by the French, who, if they cared to try, could produce an excellent and nutritious substitute out of cigar stumps and empty matchboxes.
Norman Douglas, SIREN LANDS 1911

3 With packaging materials in short supply people may have to eat fresh food.
The Economist

4 Luckily for him the average Englishman has no culinary sense at all. His palate is burned by tobacco, cocktails and whisky, and cannot appreciate fine savoury sauces.
L'Epoque (Paris). Quoted News Review 3 Jul 1947

5 The French cook: we open tins.
John Galsworthy

6 'Waiter, I found this in my food. It's a cockroach.'
'Listen. With paella, ingredients vary from place to place.'
Malcolm Gluck, Punch, A Portrait of New York 18 Aug 1976

7 Food is the most primitive form of comfort.
Sheila Graham, A STATE OF HEAT

8 Give me a little ham and egg / And let me be alone I beg / Give me my tea, hot, sweet and weak, / Bring me *The Times* and do not speak.
A. P. Herbert, A BOOK OF BALLADS, *Breakfast*

9 Bring porridge, bring sausage, bring fish for a start, / Bring kidneys and mushrooms and partridge's legs. / But let the foundation be bacon and eggs.
Ibid.

10 To know how to order and enjoy good food is part of a civilised education.
Lady Blanche Hozier, mother of Clementine Churchill. Quoted Mary Soames, CLEMENTINE CHURCHILL 1981

11 To know how to order and enjoy good food is part of a civilised education.
Lady Blanche Hozier, mother of Clementine Churchill. Quoted Mary Soames, CLEMENTINE CHURCHILL 1981

12 What was one day a sheep's hind leg and a handful of spinach was the next part of the hand that wrote, the brain that conceived the slow movement of the Jupiter Symphony.
Aldous Huxley, POINT COUNTER POINT 1928

13 It requires a certain kind of mind to see beauty in a hamburger bun.
Ray Kroc, chairman of McDonalds

14 I am very fond of mushrooms. Often I go out into the country and gather a whole basketful. I carry them part of the way home; then I throw them away.
Stephen Leacock, FOOD FOR THOUGHT

15 Cold soup is a very tricky thing and it is a rare hostess who can carry it off. More often than not the dinner guest is left with the impression that had he only come a little earlier he could have gotten it while it was still hot.
Fran Lebowitz, METROPOLITAN LIFE

16 'What on earth is this?'
'A piece of cod, sir'
'The piece of cod which passeth all understanding.'
Attr. Sir Edwin Lutyens, to a waiter at Brooks'

17 Coffee and rolls took on the nature of an orgy. We positively scintillated. Anecdotes of the High Born were poured out, sweetened and sipped: we gorged on scandals of High Birth generously buttered.
Katherine Mansfield, IN A GERMAN PENSION, *The Sisters of the Baroness*

18 We asked for a square meal and they offered us dog biscuits.
John Marshall, SERGEANT DUNN'S FIGHTING SPORTSMEN 1935

19 To eat well in England you should have breakfast three times a day.
W. Somerset Maugham. Quoted David St John Thomas, THE BREAKFAST BOOK 1981

20 On the continent people have good food; in England people have good table manners.
George Mikes, HOW TO BE AN ALIEN 1946

21 Americans can eat garbage provided you sprinkle it liberally with ketchup.
Henry Miller, REMEMBER TO REMEMBER 1947

1 What is the matter with Mary Jane? / She's perfectly well and she hasn't a pain, / And it's lovely rice pudding for dinner again, / What is the matter with Mary Jane?
A. A. Milne, RICE PUDDING

2 It is impossible to have a failure with chutney; there's nothing to set and no ingredient barred.
Robert Morley, Accustomed as I am to Public Speaking

3 When Captain Cook first arrived in the South Seas the islanders were amazed that his sailors chose to take their meals in public and make love in private; to those simple natives it seemed far more seemly to do things the other way round.
John Mortimer, Observer Magazine, How to Avoid Bad Restaurants 16 *Jul* 1978

4 Restaurants have this in common with ladies: the best are often not the most enjoyable, nor the grandest the most friendly, and the pleasures of the evening are frequently spoiled by the final writing of an exorbitant cheque.
Ibid.

5 Avoid any restaurant where a waiter arrives with a handful of knives and forks just as you reach the punch-line of your best story and says 'Which of you is having the fish?'
Ibid.

6 The golden rule when reading the menu in a restaurant is, if you can't pronounce it, you can't afford it.
Frank Muir, ENGLISH DIGEST

7 Some breakfast food manufacturer hit upon the simple notion of emptying out the leavings of carthorse nosebags, adding a few other things like unconsumed portions of chicken layer's mash, and the sweepings of racing stables, packing the mixture in little bags and selling them in health food shops.
Frank Muir, OH, MY WORD

8 Parsley / Is gharshley.
Ogden Nash, FURTHER REFLECTIONS

9 I never see any home cooking. All I get is fancy stuff.
Philip, Duke of Edinburgh in a speech. Quoted Observer, Dec 1962

10 The effect of eating too much lettuce is 'soporific'.
Beatrix Potter, FLOPSY BUNNIES 1902

11 If one were to set up a series of electrodes in a field and pass a current from one electrode to another all the worms would come to the surface and be harvested for food. An average acre contains a ton of worms. There's nothing wrong with worms as food. Fish eat them every day.
Magnus Pyke, BUTTER SIDE UP

12 He orders a Bismarck herring with sliced onions to come along, which is a dish that is considered most invigorating.
Damon Runyon, MORE THAN SOMEWHAT 1937

13 There is no love sincerer than the love of food.
George Bernard Shaw, MAN AND SUPERMAN 1905

14 We are, literally, what we eat.
Terence Stamp

15 Gentlemen do not like food that has been 'messed about with'. Continental cookery gives them diarrhoea.
Douglas Sutherland, THE ENGLISH GENTLEMAN 1978

16 I always have smoked salmon and cheese when I eat at the National Liberal Club because they don't have to cook anything.
Jeremy Thorpe

17 Cider and tinned salmon are the staple diet of the agricultural classes.
Evelyn Waugh, SCOOP 1938

18 'Turbot, sir' said the waiter, placing before me two fishbones, two eyeballs on a bit of wet mackintosh.
Thomas Earle Welby, THE DINNER KNELL

19 You breed babies and you eat chips with everything.
Arnold Wesker, CHIPS WITH EVERYTHING 1962

20 A food is not necessarily essential just because your child hates it.
Katherine Whitehorn, HOW TO SURVIVE CHILDREN

21 One cannot think well, love well, sleep well, unless one has dined well.
Virginia Woolf, A ROOM OF ONE'S OWN 1929

FOOL

1 Why is it that fools always have the instinct to hunt out the unpleasant secrets of life, and the hardiness to mention them?
Emily Eden, THE SEMI-ATTACHED COUPLE

MICHAEL FOOT

2 A good man fallen among politicians.
Daily Mirror, leader 20 Feb 1983

FOOTBALL

3 Like sex, the movements in football are limited and predictable.
Peter Ackroyd, The Times, Football Fantasy 21 Jun 1982

4 Team spirit is an illusion that you only glimpse when you win.
Steve Archibald. Quoted Simon Barnes, The Times 27 Jul 1985

5 It was a bad day for me when I blew my top and spat my chewing gum at my boss.
Alan Brazil, Tottenham Hotspur player, The Times 30 Jun 1984

6 Becoming promotions consultant to Wolverhampton Wanderers is like being asked to join the Titanic in mid-voyage.
Rachel Heyhoe Flint, The Times 13 Apr 1985

7 . . . miry gladiators whose sole purpose in life is to position a surrogate human head between two poles.
Elizabeth Hogg, Daily Telegraph, The Games People Play 7 Sep 1979

8 I loathed the game . . . it was very difficult for me to show courage at it. Football, it seemed to me, is not really played for the pleasure of kicking a ball about, but is a species of fighting.
George Orwell, SUCH, SUCH WERE THE JOYS

9 I am convinced that the greatest contribution Britain has made to the national life of Uruguay was teaching the people football.
Philip, Duke of Edinburgh, on a visit to Montevideo

10 Soccer has elements of both ballet and chess.
Vidal Sassoon, Observer 10 Aug 1979

11 Football's not a matter of life and death. It's much more serious than that.
Bill Shankly. Quoted Peter Ball and Bill Shaw, THE BOOK OF FOOTBALL QUOTATIONS 1984

12 Association football is no longer considered a gentlemanly game. The practice of footballers kissing each other after a goal is scored has lowered the tone. Kissing in public, even between consenting gentlemen, is not considered the done thing.
Douglas Sutherland, THE ENGLISH GENTLEMAN 1978

13 I know more about football than politics.
Harold Wilson 1974

GERALD FORD

14 Jerry Ford is so dumb that he can't fart and chew gum at the same time.
Lyndon B. Johnson

FOREIGNER

15 'Frogs,' he would say, 'are slightly better than Huns or Wops, but abroad is unutterably bloody and foreigners are fiends.'
Nancy Mitford, THE PURSUIT OF LOVE 1945

FORGETFULNESS

16 Not the power to remember, but its very opposite, the power to forget is a necessary condition for our existence.
Sholem Asch, THE NAZARENE 1939

17 A yeomanry colonel introducing his officers to an inspecting general stopped before one of them shaking his head and snapping his fingers. 'This is Captain — Captain — memory like a sieve. I'll be forgetting the names of me hounds next.'
Max Hastings, OXFORD BOOK OF MILITARY ANECDOTES 1985

FORGIVENESS

18 I have looked on a lot of women with lust. I've committed adultery in my heart many times. God recognises I will do this and forgives me.
Jimmy Carter during American Presidential campaign 1976

1 Forgive, O Lord, my little jokes on Thee /
And I'll forgive Thy great big one on me.
Robert Frost, FROM IN THE CLEARING 1962

2 If you forgive people enough you belong to
them, and they to you, whether either
person likes it or not — squatters' rights of
the heart.
James Hilton, TIME AND TIME AGAIN 1953

3 Forgiveness needs to be accepted, as well as
offered, before it is complete.
C. S. Lewis, THE PROBLEM OF PAIN 1940

4 A woman can forgive a man the harm he
does her; but she can never forgive him for
the sacrifices he makes on her account.
*W. Somerset Maugham, THE MOON AND
SIXPENCE 1919*

5 It is by forgiving that one is forgiven.
*Mother Teresa, FOR THE BROTHERHOOD OF
MAN 1980*

E. M. FORSTER

6 When Forster met a BBC executive who had
just rejected a friend's script on the ground
that it didn't give a general picture of China,
Forster was quick to attack on the writer's
behalf. 'Give me a general picture of
England' he asked the Head of the Third
Programme.
Sylvia Clayton, Daily Telegraph 28 Jun 1985

7 Leonard [Woolf] said he thought *Passage to
India* much the best of Morgan Forster's
books, but remarked that on re-reading it he
had been struck anew by the oppressively
feminine influences under which M. had
grown up. I said if one grew up with a lot of
old women it must do a good deal to one's
outlook. 'But Morgan *is* an old woman,' he
said. 'He always has been.'
William Plomer, ELECTRIC DELIGHTS

FRANCE

8 France may be the only country in the world
where the rich are sometimes brilliant.
*Lillian Hellman, AN UNFINISHED
WOMAN 1969*

9 The French never allow a distinguished son
of France to lack a statue.
*E. V. Lucas, WANDERINGS AND
DIVERSIONS 1926*

10 France is a country where the money falls
apart and you can't tear the toilet paper.
*Billy Wilder. Quoted Leslie Halliwell, THE
FILMGOER'S BOOK OF QUOTES 1973*

GENERAL FRANCO

11 We met General Franco. I think he is a very
nice man. He is a keen golfer with a
handicap of two. He is received with great
enthusiasm whenever he appears.
*P. Dunne, MP for Stalybridge and Hyde,
reported Sunday Despatch*

FRAUD

12 There are no new forms of financial fraud; in
the last several hundred years there have
only been small variations on a few classical
designs.
J. K. Galbraith

FREEDOM

13 None who have always been free can
understand the terrible fascinating power of
the hope of freedom on those who are not
free.
*Pearl S. Buck, WHAT AMERICA MEANS TO
ME 1943*

14 I do not believe in freedom in the philosophical sense. Everybody acts not only
under external compulsion but also in
accordance with inner necessity.
Albert Einstein, IDEAS AND OPINIONS

15 Freedom does not guarantee masterpieces.
*E. M. Forster, CULTURE AND FREEDOM,
BBC broadcast 1940*

16 I ought to feel free, yet I cannot keep my hat
on in church, even if no one is looking.
*E. M. Forster. Quoted Raymond Mortimer,
TRY ANYTHING ONCE*

17 A society in which men recognise no check
upon their freedom soon becomes a society
where freedom is a possession of only a
savage few.
Judge Learned Hand, Life 1 Jul 1944

18 What good is freedom if you've not got the
money for it? It's all very fine to go on about
Nora's escape at the end of *A Doll's House*
but just how was she planning to eat that
night?
Lillian Hellman

151

1 Unless a man has the talents to make something of himself, freedom is an unknown burden.
Eric Hoffer, THE TRUE BELIEVER 1951

2 There can be no freedom without the freedom to fail.
Eric Hoffer, THE ORDEAL OF CHANGE 1963

3 Sexual freedom? It's an 'orrible 'ideous slavery. That's what it is.
Aldous Huxley, ANTIC HAY 1923

4 Christianity promises to make men free; it never promises to make them independent.
W. R. Inge (Dean of St Pauls), THE PHILOSOPHY OF PLOTINUS 1929

5 It is often safer to be in chains than to be free.
Franz Kafka, THE CASTLE 1926

6 All free men, wherever they may live, are citizens of Berlin. And therefore, as a free man, I take pride in the words *Ich bin ein Berliner*.
John F. Kennedy. Speech at City Hall, West Berlin 26 *Jun* 1963

7 Freedom has many flaws and our democracy is imperfect, but we have never had to put up a wall to keep our people in.
Ibid.

8 The free way of life proposes ends, but it does not prescribe means.
Robert F. Kennedy, THE PURSUIT OF JUSTICE 1964

9 Freedom is never voluntarily given by the oppressor; it must be demanded by the oppressed.
Martin Luther King, WHY WE CAN'T WAIT 1964

10 Men are freest when they are most unconscious of freedom.
D. H. Lawrence, STUDIES IN CLASSIC AMERICAN LITERATURE 1923

11 People should be compelled to be freer and more individualistic than they naturally desire to be.
(Percy) Wyndham Lewis, TIME AND WESTERN MAN 1927

12 The saddest thing in my life was when I discovered that people can get their freedom

from colonial masters and find themselves unfree.
Joshua Nkomo, *Observer*, *Sayings of the Week* 22 *Apr* 1984

13 Freedom is the right to tell people what they do not want to hear.
George Orwell, THE ROAD TO WIGAN PIER 1937

14 Freedom cannot be bestowed. It must be achieved.
Franklin D. Roosevelt. Speech 16 *Sep* 1936

15 In the future days, which we seek to make secure, we look forward to a world founded on four essential freedoms. The first is freedom of speech and expression — everywhere in the world. The second is freedom of every person to worship God in his own way — everywhere in the world. The third is freedom from want. The fourth is freedom from fear.
Franklin D. Roosevelt. Message to Congress 6 *Jan* 1941

16 Englishmen never will be slaves; they are free to do whatever the Government and public opinion allows them to do.
George Bernard Shaw, MAN AND SUPERMAN 1905

17 You took my freedom away a long time ago and you can't give it back because you haven't got it yourself.
Alexander Solzhenitsyn, THE FIRST CIRCLE 1964

18 The dangers of freedom are appalling.
Lytton Strachey, *letter to Duncan Grant* 12 *Apr* 1907

19 Freedom does not always win. This is one of the bitterest lessons of history.
A. J. P. Taylor

20 I blame Rousseau, myself. 'Man is born free', indeed! Man is *not* born free, he is born attached to his mother by a cord and is incapable of looking after himself for at least seven years, (seventy in some cases).
Katherine Whitehorn, HOW TO SURVIVE CHILDREN

21 Freedom exists only where people take care of the government.
Woodrow Wilson. Speech, New York 22 *Sep* 1912

FREE SPEECH

1 Everybody favours free speech in the slack
moments when no axes are being ground.
Heywood Brown, COLLECTED WORKS 1941

2 The right to be heard does not automatically
include the right to be taken seriously.
*Hubert H. Humphrey. Speech, National
Student Association, Wisconsin* 22 *Aug* 1965

3 Freedom of speech does not include freedom to cry 'Fire' in a crowded theatre.
William Rusher, American TV commentary
10 *Dec* 1979

FREE-WILL

4 Only two possibilities exist; either one must
believe in determinism and regard free-will
as a subjective illusion, or one must become
a mystic, and regard the discovery of natural
laws as a meaningless intellectual game.
*Max Born, Bulletin of the Atomic
Scientists*, *Jun* 1957

5 The human will is free *only* within the
bounds of a determined cosmic system.
Albert Einstein, THE WORLD AS I SEE IT 1934

6 We have to believe in free-will. We've got
no choice.
Isaac Bashevis Singer. Quoted Times Diary
21 *Jun* 1982

SIGMUND FREUD

7 Our rational voice is dumb; over a grave /
The household of Impulse mourns one
dearly loved / Sad is Eros, builder of cities /
And weeping anarchic Aphrodite.
W. H. Auden, IN MEMORY OF SIGMUND
FREUD 1940

8 Tranquillity comes with years, and that
horrid thing which Freud calls sex is
expunged.
E. F. Benson, MAPP AND LUCIA 1935

9 'Why are you looking like that?' asked
Kyril.
'I was wondering why people put ferrets in
their trousers,' said Aunt Irene.
'*Thanatos*,' said Kyril. 'An illustration of the
death wish.'

'What I wish,' said Aunt Irene, 'is that you'd
never read Freud. It's had a very leaden
effect on your conversation.'
Alice Thomas Ellis, THE 27TH
KINGDOM 1982

10 He has shown us all how awful we really are,
for ever nursing grudges we felt in childhood.
*Rebecca West. Quoted Jill Craigie, The
Times* 6 *Dec* 1982

FRIEND

11 One friend in a lifetime is much, two are
many, three are hardly possible.
Henry Brooks Adams, THE EDUCATION OF
HENRY ADAMS 1916

12 A friend in power is a friend lost.
Ibid.

13 I have the best friends any man ever had. If I
have any enemies — perhaps to have
enemies is as great an honour to me as the
friendships of these men.
Stanley Baldwin, Unionist conference 11 *Feb*
1924

14 Old friends are generally the refuge of
unsociable persons.
Max Beerbohm. Quoted C. S. Roberts, THE
INCOMPARABLE MAX

15 When friendship disappears then there is a
space left open to that awful loneliness of
the outside world which is like the cold space
between the planets. It is an air in which men
perish utterly.
Hilaire Belloc, THE FOUR MEN 1912

16 In love one has need of being believed; in
friendship of being understood.
Abel Bonnard, THE ART OF FRIENDSHIP

17 He was a man who liked his friends, yet
whenever one of them was mentioned he
said something disparaging about him.
Gerald Brenan, THOUGHTS IN A DRY
SEASON 1979

18 A good friend can tell you what is the matter
with you in a minute. He may not seem such
a good friend after the telling.
Arthur Brisbane, THE BOOK OF TODAY

1 Churchill's devotion to Beaverbrook always puzzled him [Ernest Bevin]. In the end he decided that Churchill was 'like a man who's married to a whore; he knows she's a whore but he loves her just the same.'
Alan Bullock, LIFE AND TIMES OF ERNEST BEVIN

2 A man's friendships are, like his will, invalidated by his marriage — but they are no less invalidated by the marriages of his friends.
Samuel Butler, THE WAY OF ALL FLESH 1903

3 The friendships which last are those wherein each friend respects the other's dignity to the point of not really wanting anything from him.
Cyril Connolly, THE UNQUIET GRAVE 1945

4 The tragedy of war is that the sense of fellowship it engenders seems to be unable to survive the coming of peace.
Harold Dearden, THE WIND OF CIRCUMSTANCE

5 It is in the thirties that we want friends. In the forties we know they won't save us any more than love did.
F. Scott Fitzgerald, NOTE-BOOKS 1945

6 Never apologise for your terrible friends. We are all *somebody's* terrible friends.
J. Gallagher, Dean of Trinity

7 Friendship needs no words — it is solitude delivered from the anguish of loneliness.
Dag Hammarskjöld, MARKINGS 1964

8 I have no trouble with my enemies — but my goddam friends, they are the ones that keep me walking the floor at night.
Warren Harding to William A. White

9 Friends are God's apology for relations.
Hugh Kingsmill. Quoted Michael Holroyd, THE BEST OF KINGSMILL

10 If you want to make a dangerous man your friend let him do you a favour.
Lewis E. Lawes (warden of Sing-Sing prison), 20,000 YEARS IN SING-SING

11 [Friendship] has no survival value; rather it is one of the things that gives value to survival.
C. S. Lewis, THE FOUR LOVES

12 Many a person has held close, throughout their entire lives, two friends to him that always remained strange to each other, because one of them was attracted by virtue of similarity and the other by virtue of difference.
Emil Ludwig, OF LIFE AND LOVE

13 I always felt that the great high privilege, relief and comfort of friendship was that one had to explain nothing.
Katherine Mansfield. Quoted Antony Alpen, KATHERINE MANSFIELD 1954

14 I am treating you as my friend, asking you to share my present *minuses* in the hope that I can ask you to share my future *pluses.*
Katherine Mansfield, MEMORIES

15 She's been my greatest friend for fifteen years. I know her through and through and I tell you that she hasn't got a single redeeming quality.
W. Somerset Maugham, OUR BETTERS 1923

16 I know a woman who, whenever one of her intimates is attacked in her presence, merely states: 'She is my friend' and refuses to say more.
André Maurois, THE ART OF LIVING

17 One of the most mawkish of human delusions is the notion that friendship should be lifelong. The fact is that a man of resilient mind outwears his friendships just as certainly as he outwears his love affairs and his politics.
H. L. Mencken, SELECTED PREJUDICES

18 The golden period when I had not a single friend.
Henry Miller, TROPIC OF CANCER 1934

19 Money can't buy friends, but you can get a better class of enemy.
Spike Milligan, PUCKOON

20 Two buttocks of one bum.
T. Sturge Moore, of Hilaire Belloc and G. K. Chesterton

21 Soustelle, who had just returned from a visit to Algeria, remarked that all his friends there were bitterly opposed to the General's present policy. 'Alors mon vieux,' de Gaulle said, 'Changez vos amis.'
Malcolm Muggeridge, TREAD SOFTLY FOR YOU TREAD ON MY JOKES 1966

1 Each friend represents a world in us, a world possibly not born until they arrive, and it is only by this meeting that a new world is born.
Anaïs Nin, DIARY, *Mar* 1937

2 The sacrifices of friendship were beautiful in her eyes so long as she was not asked to make them.
Saki, BEASTS AND SUPERBEASTS

3 To win a friend is success, but if you can snatch the friend of a friend, then blow your trumpet.
Logan Pearsall Smith, ALL TRIVIA, *Afterthoughts* 1931

4 I do not believe that friends are necessarily the people you like best; they are merely the people who got there first.
Peter Ustinov, DEAR ME 1977

5 Whenever a friend succeeds a little something in me dies.
Gore Vidal. Quoted Susan Barnes, BEHIND THE IMAGE

6 There was a definite process by which one made people into friends, and it involved talking to them and listening to them for hours at a time.
Rebecca West, THE THINKING REED 1936

7 Comprehension must be the soil in which grow all the fruits of friendship.
Woodrow Wilson. Speech, Mobile Alabama 1913

8 I have lost friends, some by death — others by sheer inability to cross the street.
Virginia Woolf, THE WAVES 1931

FRIGIDITY

9 She [Maureen O'Hara] looks as though butter wouldn't melt in her mouth — or anywhere else.
Elsa Lanchester. Quoted Leslie Halliwell, THE FILMGOER'S BOOK OF QUOTES 1973

FRONTIER

10 When you think about the defence of England you no longer think of the chalk cliffs of Dover. You think of the Rhine. That is where our frontier is today.
Stanley Baldwin, House of Commons 30 *Jul* 1934

ROBERT FROST

11 If it were thought that anything I wrote was influenced by Robert Frost I would take that particular work of mine, shred it and flush it down the toilet, hoping not to clog the pipes.
James Dickey, WRITERS AT WORK *(Fifth Series)*

FULFILMENT

12 I drive along the lanes in my Rolls and I pass some old bloke out walking his dog, and I wonder which of us has got it right.
Paul McCartney, Observer 24 *Jun* 1972

FUNERAL

13 In the city a funeral is just an interruption of traffic. In the country it is a form of entertainment.
George Ade, Cosmopolitan, Feb 1928

14 Her funeral sermon (which was long / And followed by a sacred song) / Mentioned her virtues it is true / But dwelt upon her vices too.
Hilaire Belloc, CAUTIONARY TALES, *Rebecca* 1907

15 To those left behind memorial services serve as a sort of surrogate encounter with death.
Hugh Casson, DIARY 1981

16 If you don't go to other people's funerals they won't come to yours.
Clarence Day, LIFE WITH FATHER 1935

17 I remember Sarah Bernhardt's funeral perfectly. I have never had to wait so long to cross the street.
Eric Dunston. Quoted James Agate, EGO 9 14 *Oct* 1946

18 It is a pity they should have chosen the day of the Eton and Harrow match for the funeral.
Aldous Huxley, THE GIOCONDA SMILE

19 A mortician's life is full of flowers, flowers and beauty.
Eric Linklater, JUAN IN AMERICA 1931

20 There is no sign of depression among us morticians. Our parlours, I'm happy to say, are never empty.
Ibid.

1 There is nothing like a morning funeral for sharpening the appetite for lunch.
Arthur Marshall, Observer, Sayings of the Week 23 Sep 1984

2 One of the crying needs of the time is for a suitable Burial Service for the admittedly damned.
H. L. Mencken, PREJUDICES 1927

3 I have nothing against undertakers personally. It's just that I wouldn't want one to bury my sister.
Jessica Mitford, Saturday Review 1 Feb 1968

4 I can't think of a more wonderful thanksgiving for the life I have had than that everyone should be jolly at my funeral.
Lord Mountbatten in a TV interview shown after his death

5 It gives me a kind of trespassin' joy.
Sean O'Casey at his son's funeral. Quoted Eileen O'Casey, SEAN

6 It only goes to prove that the public will still come if you give them what they want.
Onlooker at funeral of Harry Cohn, head of Columbia Pictures. Quoted Benny Green, Radio Times 17 Feb 1979

7 I wants to arrive up there so grand that the Almighty just won't have the heart to turn me back.
John Quigley, TO REMEMBER WITH TEARS

8 I want Bach's Toccata and Fugue in` D played at my funeral. If it isn't I shall jolly well want to know why.
Dame Sybil Thorndike. Quoted English Digest, Mar 1965

9 The best undertaker in Brooklyn respected, esteemed. He knew all the best people well — knew them well enough even before they died.
Thornton Wilder, THE MATCHMAKER 1955

10 You just came home in time for the funerals, Stella. And funerals are pretty compared to deaths.
Tennessee Williams, A STREETCAR NAMED DESIRE 1947

FURNITURE

11 Lady Kitty: I think it's a beautiful chair. Hepplewhite?

Arnold: No, Sheraton.
Lady Kitty: Oh I know. *The School for Scandal.*
W. Somerset Maugham, THE CIRCLE 1921

12 Gentlemen do not buy furniture. They inherit it. The last time any furniture was bought by any gentlemanly family was in the Victorian era with the result that their drawing-rooms are still filled with under-stuffed sofas, high-backed chairs, and little tables which fall over when you put anything on them.
Douglas Sutherland, THE ENGLISH GENTLEMAN 1978

13 The chair was upholstered in one of those flagrant chintzes, designed, apparently, by the art editor of a seed catalogue.
Alexander Woollcott, WHILE ROME BURNS 1934

FUTILITY

14 Getting the costumes right in *The Cleopatras* [a TV series] was like polishing the fish-knives on the *Titanic.*
Julian Barnes, Observer, Quite Beggaring All Description 13 Mar 1983

15 If you board the wrong train it is no good running along the corridor in the other direction.
Dietrich Bonhoeffer, THE WAY TO FREEDOM

16 A man might as well chain himself to the railings of St Thomas's Hospital and say he wouldn't move until he has a baby.
Winston Churchill. Quoted Robert Lewis Taylor, THE AMAZING MR CHURCHILL

17 A man who has pedalled twenty-five thousand miles on a stationary bicycle has not circled the globe. He has only garnered weariness.
Paul Eldridge, HORNS OF GLASS

18 Carrying bricks to Babel is neither a duty nor a privilege; it seems to be a necessity built into the chromosomes of our species.
Arthur Koestler, BRICKS TO BABEL, Epilogue 1983

19 Figure it out. Work a lifetime to pay off a house. You finally own it, and there's no one to live in it.
Arthur Miller, DEATH OF A SALESMAN 1949

1 At last the ultimate in television party political broadcasts. The programmes no one wants, are to be shown on Channel 4, the channel no one watches. There hasn't been such a brilliant idea since the *Daily Express* offered a trip to the Antarctica as the prize in a competition and only three readers entered for it.
Daily Mirror, leader 16 *Feb* 1983

FUTURE

2 The energies of our system will decay, the glory of the sun will be dimmed, and the earth, tideless and inert, will no longer tolerate the race which has for a moment disturbed its solitude. Man will go down into the pit, and his thoughts will perish.
A. J. Balfour, THE FOUNDATIONS OF BELIEF

3 The composer of the future may well be a combination physicist—mathematician, architect—electronic-engineer—musician.
Irwin Bazelon, KNOWING THE SCORE

4 I never think of the future. It comes soon enough.
Albert Einstein, in an interview, Dec 1930

5 When even lovers find their peace at last / And Earth is but a star that once had shone.
James Elroy Flecker, THE GOLDEN JOURNEY TO SAMARKAND 1913

6 I go to school in youth to learn the future.
Robert Frost, WEST RUNNING BROOK, *What Fifty Said* 1928

7 The future is not what it was.
Bernard Levin, The Sunday Times 22 *May* 1977

8 The future is something which everyone reaches at the rate of sixty minutes an hour, whatever he does, whoever he is.
C. S. Lewis, SCREWTAPE LETTERS 1941

9 To most of us the future seems unsure; but then it always has been; and we who have seen great changes must have great hopes.
John Masefield, GRACE BEFORE PLOUGHING

10 We cannot always build the future for our youth, but we can build our youth for the future.
Franklin D. Roosevelt. Speech, University of Pennsylvania 20 *Sep* 1940

11 Time enough to think of the future when you haven't any future to think of.
George Bernard Shaw, PYGMALION 1913

12 Time and space — time to be alone, space to move about — these may well become the greatest scarcities of tomorrow.
Edwin Way Teale, AUTUMN ACROSS AMERICA 1956

13 Human history becomes more and more a race between education and catastrophe.
H. G. Wells, OUTLINE OF HISTORY 1919

14 The future is the most expensive luxury in the world.
Thornton Wilder, THE MATCHMAKER 1955

G

GAIN

1 There are no gains without pains.
Adlai Stevenson. Speech, Chicago 26 Jul 1952

HUGH GAITSKELL

2 That desiccated calculating machine.
Aneurin Bevan. Quoted Philip M. William, HUGH GAITSKELL: A POLITICAL BIOGRAPHY

3 Gaitskell has a Wykehamistical voice and manner and a 13th-century face.
Henry Channon, DIARY 10 *Apr* 1951

4 An intellectual highbrow who is naturally anxious to impress British labour with the fact that he learnt Latin at Winchester.
Winston Churchill

5 Morally, he was the bravest of all categories; he flinched, but he always went on.
Roy Jenkins. Quoted W. T. Rodgers, HUGH GAITSKELL

JOHN GALSWORTHY

6 Among literary reputations Galsworthy is a corpse that will not lie down.
Cyril Connolly, Sunday Times 27 Jan 1963

7 The author of the *Forsyte Saga* must be the most widely read Harrovian since Byron.
David Williams, Daily Telegraph 4 Oct 1968

GAMBLING

8 The gambling known as business looks with austere disfavour upon the business known as gambling.
Ambrose Bierce. Quoted H. L. Mencken

9 He who can predict winnning numbers has no need to let off fire-crackers.
Ernest Bramah, KAI LUNG UNROLLS HIS MAT 1928

10 No wife can endure a gambling husband unless he is a steady winner.
Lord Dewar. Speech

11 The strength of Monaco is the weakness of the world.
H. A. Gibbons, RIVIERA TOWNS: MONTE CARLO

12 It is a serious indictment of society if gambling is the only way to raise money for certain good causes.
Rev. Dr Stanley Heavenor

13 Lose as if you like it; win as if you were used to it.
Jonas Hitchcock's advice to his son Tommy Hitchcock Jr. Quoted Newsweek

14 Gambling is a disease of barbarians, superficially civilised.
W. R. Inge (Dean of St Pauls), OUTSPOKEN ESSAYS 1919

15 If you can make one heap of all your winnings / And risk it on one turn of pitch-and-toss / And lose, and start again at your beginnings / And never breathe a word about your loss.
Rudyard Kipling, REWARDS AND FAIRIES, *If—,* 1910

16 . . . the apparent desire to accept the certainty of losing money in the long run in return for the remote possibility of winning it in the short.
Bernard Levin, THE PENDULUM YEARS 1976

17 At the Treasury I introduced Premium Bonds and the Archbishop of Canterbury complained that I had 'debauched the people'. I suppose there must have been some confusion with the lotteries which they hold at Church bazaars.
Harold Macmillan (Lord Stockton). Speech, House of Lords 14 Nov 1984

1 The race is not always to the swift, nor the battle to the strong — but that's the way to bet.
Damon Runyon, MORE THAN SOMEWHAT 1937

2 The reason he is called Sky is because he goes so high when it comes to betting on any proposition whatever. He will bet all he has, and nobody can bet any more than that.
Damon Runyon, GUYS AND DOLLS 1932

3 Time spent in a casino is time given to death, a foretaste of the hour when one's flesh will be diverted to the purposes of the worm and not the will.
Rebecca West. Quoted Peter Wolfe,
REBECCA WEST: ARTIST AND THINKER

4 Britain's strength, freedom and solvency apparently depend on the proceeds of a squalid raffle.
Harold Wilson on the introduction of Premium Bonds

GAMEKEEPER

5 Ever since (and possibly before) D. H. Lawrence immortalised the gamekeeper, ladies have liked them a lot . . . As a result many gentlemen say that if they were not gentlemen they would have liked to be gamekeepers.
Douglas Sutherland, THE ENGLISH GENTLEMAN'S WIFE 1979

GAMES

6 There is a vast difference between games and play. Play is played for fun, but games are deadly serious and you do not play them to enjoy yourself.
Maurice Baring, THE PUPPET SHOW OF MEMORY 1922

7 There's something wrong with a young chap who doesn't play games. Not even snooker.
Bernard Hollowood, SCOWLE IN THE SIXTIES

8 It may well be that all games are silly. But then — so are human beings.
Robert Lynd

9 Almost any game with any ball is a good game.
Robert Lynd, THE PEAL OF BELLS

10 It is only children who are irresponsible and ill-educated enough to make a game of games.
Stephen Potter, SENSE OF HUMOUR 1954

11 Games always cover something deep and intense, else there would be no excitement in them, no pleasure, no power to stir us.
Antoine de Saint-Exupéry, AIRMAN'S ODYSSEY

12 Proficiency at billiards is proof of a misspent youth.
Herbert Spencer to a young member of the Athaeneum

INDIRA GANDHI

13 Extraordinarily imaginative, and self-centred or subjective, remarkably selfish, she lives in a world of dreams and vagaries and floats about on imaginary clouds full, probably, of all manner of brave fancies.
Pandit Nehru (her father). Quoted Observer, PROFILE, *The Last Empress of India* 21 Mar 1982

14 A woman who has mastered the art of adapting her demeanour to the occasion, but whose true self is rigorously concealed, and whose look, if you happen to catch her unawares, is often one of cold disdain.
Observer, Profile, The Last Empress of India 21 Mar 1982

15 It is a measure of her iron will that private grief has never been allowed to mar her public appearances except, perhaps, when tears could be expected to yield a dividend.
Ibid.

MAHATMA GANDHI

16 . . . a dear old man, with his bald pate and spectacles, beaky nose and bird-like lips and benign but somewhat toothless smile.
Rodney Bennett, Teacher's World 7 *May* 1930

17 It is . . . nauseating to see Mr Gandhi, a seditious Middle Temple lawyer, now posing as a fakir of a type well known in the East, striding half naked up the steps of the Viceregal Palace, while he is still organising and conducting a defiant campaign of civil disobedience, to parley on equal terms with the representative of the King Emperor.
Winston Churchill. Speech, Epping 23 *Feb* 1931

1 Behind the simplicity and mischievous smile was a very complex man whose conception of life and death was different from those of lesser mortals. He had learned that non-violence provoked violence. He perhaps knew that he would be murdered by a religious fanatic.
Louis Heren, The Times 4 *Dec* 1982

2 You've no idea what it costs to keep the old man in poverty.
Lord Mountbatten. Quoting a colleague, BBC 1 *TV, Lord Mountbatten Remembers* 12 *Nov* 1980

3 It costs a great deal of money to keep Gandhi in poverty.
Sarojini Naidu, Indian poetess. Quoted Woodrow Wyatt, Sunday Times 27 *Nov* 1977

4 The greatest Indian since Buddha.
Edward Thompson, Gandhi's obituary, News Chronicle 31 *Jan* 1948

5 Gandhi was very keen on sex. He renounced it when he was 36, so therefore it was never very far from his thoughts.
Woodrow Wyatt, Sunday Times, Homage to India's Strange Saint 27 *Nov* 1977

GRETA GARBO

6 There is no doubt she can act, if by acting is meant the power to suggest that she is feeling emotion and giving it out again in terms of her own personality.
James Agate of Greta Garbo, AROUND CINEMAS

7 People who know that we both appeared in *Grand Hotel* ask me 'Is Garbo as strange a person as the newspapers say she is?' To which I answer 'I don't know. I've never seen her. Though I have been on the same lot with her for four years I have never met her. She goes between her dressing room and her seat in a car, or closely guarded and in disguise. She never visits other actors or allows them to visit her.'
Wallace Beery, MY UGLY MUG

8 What, when drunk, one sees in other women, one sees in Garbo sober.
Kenneth Tynan, Sunday Times 25 *Aug* 1963

GARDEN

9 After his death the gardener does not become a butterfly, intoxicated by flowers, but a garden worm tasting all the dark nitrogenous and spicy delights of the soil.
Karel Čapek, THE GARDENER'S YEAR

10 The more help a man has in his garden, the less it belongs to him.
W. H. Davies

11 Oh Adam was a gardener and God who made him sees / That half a proper gardener's work is done upon his knees.
Rudyard Kipling, THE GLORY OF THE GARDEN 1911

12 Observing the ancient housekeeper wrestling with the plantlife in the garden, I occasionally point out a weed, and encourage her from the deck chair.
Arthur Marshall, Radio Times 23 *Jul* 1977

13 You must not praise the elegance of an Englishman's house — though you may always be impressed by the garden.
George Mikes, HOW TO BE AN ALIEN 1946

14 My garden will never make me famous / I'm a horticultural ignoramus / I can't tell a stringbean from a soy bean / Or even a girl bean from a boy bean.
Ogden Nash, HE DIGS, HE DUG, HE HAS DUG

15 It is not the business of the botanist to eradicate the weeds. Enough for him if he can just tell us how fast they grow.
C. Northcote Parkinson, PARKINSON'S LAW 1957

16 We have descended into the garden and caught 300 slugs. How I love the mixture of the beautiful and the squalid in gardening. It makes it so lifelike.
Evelyn Underhill, LETTERS

GENERAL DE GAULLE

17 I have every sympathy with General de Gaulle and his violent tantrums but let us conquer some of his country before we start squabbling about how it is to be governed. Yes, let's give him a bit of land to govern first.
Winston Churchill at an invasion conference

1 Intelligent — brilliant — resourceful, he spoils his undoubted talents by his excessive assurance, his contempt for other people's point of view, and his attitude of a king in exile.
Report of French War College 1922

GENEROSITY

2 We cannot win the weak by sharing our wealth with them. They feel our generosity as oppression.
Eric Hoffer, THE ORDEAL OF CHANGE 1962

3 The overpaying instinct is a generous one; better than the underpaying instinct, and not so common.
George Bernard Shaw, CANDIDA 1903

4 Generosity is a two-edged virtue for an artist — it nourishes his imagination but has a fatal effect on his routine.
Alexander Solzhenitsyn, THE FIRST CIRCLE 1964

GENIUS

5 We will always admire, but can never emulate, Genius; and though there is much that can be done with talent there is little you can do with Genius. In essence Genius is not a degree of kind, but a variation in type, and to how few can we apply that word?
Margot Asquith, obituary of Lord Birkenhead, News Chronicle 1 Oct 1930

6 Genius takes many shapes and colours. You have genius of one sort in Jerome Kern. Why deny it?
John Barbirolli, Observer 6 *Jul* 1947

7 Genius does what it must and talent does what it can.
Maurice Baring

8 I have known no man of genius who had not to pay in some affliction or defect, either physical or spiritual, for what the gods had given him.
Max Beerbohm, NO 2 THE PINES

9 Genius-worship is the inevitable sign of an uncreative age.
Clive Bell, ART 1914

10 We define genius as the capacity for productive reaction against one's training.
Bernard Berenson, THE DECLINE OF ART

11 Where a human being has contributed something of genius to human thought and human art he is entitled to claim that the generations which follow shall extirpate from their minds recollections, however grave and painful, of any human infirmity which may have disfigured his career. For art is one thing and morals are quite another.
Lord Birkenhead addressing Scott Society, Edinburgh

12 The most vulgar of art's temptations; to be a genius.
Jorge Luis Borges, FICCIONES 1945

13 There are dancing motes or elements in genius which are impossible to pin down. One can only note their action, marvel at what they leave behind.
Elizabeth Bowen, COLLECTED IMPRESSIONS 1950

14 His genius has open arms.
George Brandes, of Björnstjerne Björnson. Quoted Oliver Edwards, The Times 4 *Aug* 1966

15 It might be more fitly described as a supreme capacity for getting its possessors into trouble of all kinds and keeping them therein so long as the genius remains.
Samuel Butler, NOTEBOOKS 1912

16 Genius, meaning by that an original creative power, is both much more common than we suppose and much more fragile. It is certainly more fragile than talent. For talent belongs to the capable and intelligent who understand their own powers and know how to manage them. Genius is sensitive and impressionable.
Joyce Cary, ART AND REALITY

17 In the presence of a masterpiece something of the artist's intention seems to pass into one's possession.
Hugh Casson, DIARY 1981

18 A genius she may be, but talent she hasn't got.
Mike Curtis, on viewing a screen test. Quoted Jan Peerce (singer)

19 But the genius, as with the birds, discovers within himself that which never need be sought. 'I do not seek, I find' Picasso says, and before him, Cézanne spoke 'I am the primitive of my way.'
Louis Danz, DYNAMIC DISSONANCE

1 Mediocrity knows nothing higher than itself, but talent instantly recognises genius.
Sir Arthur Conan Doyle, THE VALLEY OF FEAR

2 It keeps repeating itself / In this world so fine and honest / The parson alarms the populace / The genius is executed.
Albert Einstein, of the campaign against Bertrand Russell in America 1940

3 In every man of genius a new strange force is brought into the world.
Havelock Ellis, SELECTED ESSAYS

4 It is a sign of real genius that it remains unspoiled by success.
Martin Esslin, THE THEATRE OF THE ABSURD

5 Simply because I have no seniors / The literati will raise the cry / Ewart's a genius.
Gavin Ewart. THE COLLECTED EWART

6 You can see how good things are done, but about the great you can only wonder how the devil he did it.
Charles Fisher, apropos Keats' La Belle Dame Sans Merci. Quoted G. W. Lyttelton, THE LYTTELTON HART-DAVIS LETTERS 30 *Nov* 1959

7 At the heart of genius is mystery. If this were not so then the secret of genius would be uncovered and made accessible to all. Thus genius is beyond science, for science is concerned with behaviour and that which repeats itself with sufficient frequency to form a pattern which we call laws.
Michael Foot, LIFE OF ANEURIN BEVAN 1962

8 The most gifted members of the human species are at their creative best when they cannot have their own way.
Eric Hoffer, THE ORDEAL OF CHANGE 1963

9 Some men come by the name of genius in the same way as an insect comes by the name of centipede — not because it has a hundred feet but because most people can't count above fourteen.
George Lichtenberg

10 Genius is talent provided with ideals.
W. Somerset Maugham, A WRITER'S NOTE-BOOK 1949

11 Genius is an African who dreams up snow.
Vladimir Nabokov, THE GIFT 1963

12 The heart and soul of genius may be mad, but the mind of true genius is ever as clear as the heavens seen through pine trees.
George Jean Nathan, MATERIA CRITICA

13 One of the surest signs of his [Joseph Conrad's] genius is that women dislike his books.
George Orwell, New English Weekly 23 Jul 1936

14 Before I was a genius I was a drudge.
Paderewski

15 To the question 'Do you think genius is hereditary?' he [James McNeil Whistler] replied, 'I can't tell you; heaven has granted me no offspring.'
Hesketh Pearson, LIVES OF THE WITS

16 The genius of Einstein leads to Hiroshima.
Pablo Picasso. Quoted Françoise Gilot and Carlton Lake, LIFE WITH PICASSO

17 The concept of genius as akin to madness has been carefully fostered by the inferiority complex of the public.
Ezra Pound, THE ABC OF READING 1934

18 Genius is the capacity to see ten things where the ordinary man sees one, and where the man of talent sees two or three, *plus* the ability to register that multiple perception in the material of his art.
Ezra Pound, JEFFERSON AND/OR MUSSOLINI

19 Everything great in the world is done by neurotics; they alone founded our religions and created our masterpieces.
Marcel Proust, REMEMBRANCE OF THINGS PAST 1913—1927

20 The man of genius, to shelter himself from the ignorant contempt of the world, may say to himself that since one's contemporaries are incapable of the necessary detachment, works written for posterity should be read by posterity alone, like certain pictures which one cannot appreciate when one stands too close to them.
Ibid.

21 Genius doesn't necessarily wear a beard and have neurotic love affairs, but may be found in a Kensington churchwarden who discusses cheese with the scholarly taste of a connoisseur.
James Reeves, T. S. ELIOT: A SYMPOSIUM

1 Addicts of nonsense haven't the sense to see that men and women of genius educate themselves.
A. L. Rowse, PORTRAITS AND VIEWS, *Jane Austen as Social Realist* 1979

2 All the men of genius that we have ever heard of have triumphed over adverse circumstances, but there is no reason for supposing that there were not innumerable others who succumbed in youth.
Bertrand Russell, THE CONQUEST OF HAPPINESS 1930

3 The essential definition of a genius, I think, is that he is a man who not only knows the laws of things, but experiences them in himself with self-evident certainty. This experience of pure being transcends even love.
Oswald Schwartz, THE PSYCHOLOGY OF SEX

4 There is a certain characteristic common to all those whom we call geniuses. Each of them has a consciousness of being a man apart.
Miguel de Unamuno, ESSAYS AND SOLILOQUIES 1924

5 He is the only genius with an IQ of 60.
Gore Vidal, ANDY WARHOL

6 Genius is in the planet's blood / You are either a poet or a Lilliputian.
Andrei Voznesensky, WHO ARE WE? 1960

7 The man's a genius. From the collar upwards he stands alone.
P. G. Wodehouse, JEEVES TAKES CHARGE

8 When a country produces a man of genius he never is what it wants or believes it wants; he is always unlike its idea of itself.
W. B. Yeats, AUTOBIOGRAPHY 1955

GENTILITY

9 I keep picturing poor dear Nancy Mitford as a house guest in some baronial estate in Wiltshire or Norfolk, having been shown all the blue-ribbon cattle and praising them later to her hostess, unable to use the taboo word 'cows' for fear of causing offence and opting instead for 'the bulls and their wives'.
Noël Coward. Quoted William Marchant, THE PRIVILEGE OF HIS COMPANY 1980

10 I don't want to talk grammar. I want to talk like a lady.
George Bernard Shaw, PYGMALION 1913

GENTLEMAN

11 He [Evelyn Waugh] was very conscious of what a gentleman should or should not do; no gentleman looks out of a window; no gentleman wears a brown suit.
Cecil Beaton, THE STRENUOUS YEARS

12 Jim thought that doing nothing meant being a gentleman.
Louis Bromfield, THE STRANGE CASE OF MISS ANNIE SPRAGG 1928

13 To be born a gentleman is an accident, to die one is an achievement.
Bob Goddard, St Louis Globe-Democrat

14 We are all esquires now, and none of us are gentlemen any more.
Sir Ernest Gowers, Introduction to the revised edition of FOWLER'S MODERN ENGLISH USAGE

15 This is the final test of a gentleman: his respect for those who can be of no possible service to him.
William Lyon Helps

16 I was brought up to believe that a gentleman appears in the papers three times: when he is born, when he gets married, and when he dies. With good behaviour — and a little bit of luck — that can be managed even today.
Michael Hogg, Daily Telegraph 2 Dec 1978

17 The criterion of a gentleman is that however poor he may be he still refuses to do useful work.
George Mikes, HOW TO BE AN ALIEN 1946

18 A gentleman does not utter everything he thinks.
Nigel Nicholson, ALEX: THE LIFE OF FIELD MARSHAL EARL ALEXANDER OF TUNIS

19 A gentleman never heard a story before.
Austin O'Malley, KEYSTONES OF THOUGHT

20 Anyone can be heroic from time to time, but a gentleman is something you have to be all the time.
Luigi Pirandello, THE PLEASURE OF HONESTY 1917

1 A gentleman never eats. He breakfasts, he lunches, he dines — but he never eats.
Cole Porter, quoting advice given by his tutor

2 Of course Miss Missouri Martin is not in a position to argue about gentlemen, because she meets so very few.
Damon Runyon, MORE THAN SOMEWHAT

3 A gentleman is a man whose grandfather earned more than £1000 a year.
Bertrand Russell. Quoted Rupert Crawshay-Williams, RUSSELL REMEMBERED

4 The concept of the gentleman was invented by the aristocrats to keep the middle classes in order.
Ibid.

5 I am a gentleman. I live by robbing the poor.
George Bernard Shaw, MAN AND SUPERMAN 1905

6 A gentleman is someone who gets out of the bath to go to the toilet.
Freddie Trueman. Quoted Jilly Cooper, CLASS

7 A gentleman is a man whose principal ideas are not connected with his personal needs and his personal services.
W. B. Yeats, AUTOBIOGRAPHY 1955

GEOGRAPHY

8 Geography is everywhere.
Graffito. Nigel Rees, GRAFFITI 2

GEORGE V

9 The 700 pages [of Eden's memoirs] contain only one joke — by King George V apropos Sir Samuel Hoare's resignation. 'No more coals to Newcastle; no more Hoares to Paris.'
Malcolm Muggeridge, TREAD SOFTLY FOR YOU TREAD ON MY JOKES 1966

10 He had a gruff, blue-water approach to all human problems.
Duke of Windsor, A KING'S STORY

GEORGE VI

11 Constant tact from others had the effect of making him far too modest and he had quite lost sight of his own merits, if he ever knew them. He was, in fact, ideally suited for the British Throne.
Ronald Blythe, THE AGE OF ILLUSION

12 George VI in the conventional parlance was a Good King who sacrificed his life to his sense of duty. If we are to have monarchs it would be hard to find a better one.
A. J. P. Taylor, Observer, A Dutiful Monarch 24 Oct 1982

13 I am sure it will in no way detract from the prestige of my kingly brother when I say that when we were young I could always manage him.
Duke of Windsor. Quoted News Review 11 Dec 1947

GERIATRICS

14 Most treatment of the old requiring professional intervention not only tends to heighten their pain but, if successful, also protracts it.
Ivan D. Illich, MEDICAL NEMESIS

GERMANY

15 As goes Germany, so goes Europe.
V. Holston, Moscow conference 1947

16 Germany is a machine for producing geniuses. Its crowning product was the German Jew which in suitably dramatic style it then tried to destroy.
Michel Tournier. Quoted Theodore Zeldin, Observer, The Prophet of Unisex 30 Jan 1983

GESTICULATION

17 *Gesticulation*: Any movement made by a foreigner.
Beachcomber (J. B. Morton)

GESTURE

18 The gesture is the thing truly expressive of the individual — as we think so will we act.
Martha Graham. Quoted John Heilpern, Observer Magazine, The Amazing Martha 8 Jul 1979

1 She plucked from my lapel the invisible strand of lint — the universal act of woman to proclaim ownership.
O. Henry, STRICTLY BUSINESS, *A Ramble in Aphasia*

PAUL GETTY

2 . . . who had always been vastly, immeasurably wealthy, and yet went about looking like a man who cannot quite remember whether he remembered to turn the gas off before leaving home.
Bernard Levin, THE PENDULUM YEARS 1976

GIVING

3 You never want to give a man a present when he's feeling good. You want to do it when he's down.
Lyndon B. Johnson. Quoted Doris Kearns, LYNDON JOHNSON AND THE AMAZING DREAM

4 In choosing presents people should remember that the whole point of a present is that it is an extra.
E. V. Lucas, READING, WRITING AND REMEMBERING

5 One should, I think, always give children money, for they will spend it for themselves far more profitably than we can ever spend it for them.
Rose Macaulay, A CASUAL COMMENTARY

6 Send two dozen roses to Room 424 and put 'Emily I love you' on the back of the bill.
Groucho Marx, A NIGHT IN CASABLANCA

7 If somebody gives you one of those de luxe editions of Jane Austen in a stand-up cardboard case, immediately buy any old nineteenth-century copy of a George Eliot novel and tell the Jane Austen giver that you have hunted for years for this example 'of the Bristol edition' (you call it a Bristol First) and that when you found it six months ago you knew he would be the person to appreciate it.
Stephen Potter, ONE-UPMANSHIP 1952

8 The first rule in buying Christmas presents is to select something shiny . . . the wariest person will often mistake shininess for expensiveness.
P. G. Wodehouse, LOUDER AND FUNNIER

GLAMOUR

9 It was a sumpshous place all done up in gold with plenty of looking glases.
Dairy Ashford (aged 9), THE YOUNG VISITERS 1919

10 My grandfather Frank Lloyd Wright wore a red sash on his wedding night. That is glamour.
Anne Baxter, Time Magazine 5 May 1952

11 It was a blonde. A blonde to make a bishop kick a hole in a stained glass window.
Raymond Chandler, FAREWELL MY LOVELY 1940

12 Any girl can be glamorous; all you have to do is stand still and look stupid.
Hedy Lamarr. Quoted Leslie Halliwell, THE FILMGOER'S BOOK OF QUOTES 1978

13 Glamour is when a man knows a woman is a woman.
Gina Lollobrigida. Quoted Observer 15 Jul 1956

GLUTTONY

14 My boy you are not an MP, you are a gastronomic pimp.
Aneurin Bevan, to a colleague he accused of attending too many public dinners. Quoted Michael Foot, ANEURIN BEVAN 1897—1945

15 Gluttony is an emotional escape, a sign that something is eating us.
Peter De Vries, COMFORT ME WITH APPLES 1956

16 'What I like about gluttony' a bishop I knew used to say, 'is that it doesn't hurt anyone else.'
Monica Furlong, CHRISTIAN UNCERTAINTIES

17 There is no love sincerer than the love of food.
George Bernard Shaw, MAN AND SUPERMAN 1905

18 The sin comes in with the determination to refuse food and the self-disgust that follows having, on the contrary, just eaten a whole bar of chocolate all by yourself in the middle of the afternoon. It's worse than going to the pictures in the morning.
Katherine Whitehorn, Punch 10 May 1972

ELINOR GLYN

1 Would you like to sin / With Elinor Glyn /
On a tiger skin / Or would you prefer / To
err with her / On some other fur?
Anon.

2 Elinor Glyn, fortified with coffee and
brandy, took to her bed to write a 90,000
word novel in three weeks, and did it in 18
days.
Laurence Wright, WARM AND SNUG

GOD

3 Every man thinks God is on his side. The
rich and powerful know he is.
Jean Anouilh, THE LARK 1953

4 Does God ever judge us by appearances? I
suspect that he does.
W. H. Auden. Quoted New Yorker 21 Nov
1977

5 What is the prose for God?
H. Granville Barker, WASTE

6 I cannot be angry at God, in whom I do not
believe.
Simone de Beauvoir. Quoted Observer 7 Jan
1979

7 To my mind the most poignant mystical
exhortation ever written is 'Be Still and
know that I am God.'
Arnold Bennett, JOURNALS, *Dec* 1929

8 A God who let us prove his existence would
be an idol.
Dietrich Bonhoeffer, NO RUSTY SWORDS

9 Immense, of fishy form and mind /
Squamous, omnipotent and kind; / And
under that Almighty Fin / The little fish may
enter in.
Rupert Brooke, HEAVEN 1913

10 An honest God: the noblest work of man.
Samuel Butler, NOTEBOOKS 1912

11 God is love — I dare say. But what a
mischievous devil Love is.
Ibid.

12 The Lord will provide, dear, but you must
give him some help.
Sir Hugh Casson and Joyce Grenfell, NANNY
SAYS 1972

13 When God shuts a door he opens a window.
Ibid.

14 There can only be fairy godmothers because
there are godmothers, and there can only be
godmothers because there is God.
G. K. Chesterton, AUTOBIOGRAPHY

15 I took it completely for granted that God
had never spoken anything but the most
dignified English.
Clarence Day, LIFE WITH FATHER 1935

16 It is the final proof of God's omnipotence
that He need not exist in order to save us.
Peter De Vries, THE MACKEREL PLAZA 1958

17 God does not play dice.
Albert Einstein, a favourite axiom,
frequently used

18 God is subtle, but he is not malicious.
Albert Einstein

19 God is an unutterable sign in the Human
Heart, said the old German mystic. And
therewith said the last word.
Havelock Ellis, IMPRESSIONS AND
COMMENTS

20 At bottom God is nothing more than an
exalted father.
Sigmund Freud, TOTEM AND TABOO 1918

21 I turned to speak to God / About the world's
despair; / But to make bad matters worse / I
found God wasn't there.
Robert Frost, COLLECTED POEMS, *Not All*
There 1951

22 God is a verb / Not a noun.
R. Buckminster Fuller, NO MORE SECOND-
HAND GOD 1963

23 The Mister God Light inside us is so's we can
see the Mister God Light outside us and the
Mister God Light outside us is so we can see
the Mister God Light inside us.
Fynn, MISTER GOD, THIS IS ANNA 1974

24 Mister God ain't got no bum.
Ibid.

25 God has no religion.
Mahatma Gandhi

26 God depends on us. It is through us that God
is achieved.
André Gide, JOURNALS 1939–1950

1 God is alive and well but considering a less ambitious project.
Graffito. Quoted Patrick Moore, Observer 18 *Mar* 1979

2 How much reverence can you have for a Supreme Being who finds it necessary to include such phenomena as phlegm and tooth decay in this divine system of creation?
Joseph Heller, CATCH 22 1961

3 The change in our conception of God necessitates the stressing of religious experience as such, as against belief in particular dogma, or in the efficacy of special ritual.
Julian Huxley, ESSAYS OF A BIOLOGIST 1933

4 Operationally, God is beginning to resemble not a ruler but the last fading smile of a cosmic Cheshire cat.
Julian Huxley, RELIGION WITHOUT REVOLUTION

5 The God whom science recognises must be a God of universal laws exclusively . . . He cannot accommodate his processes to the convenience of individuals.
William James, THE VARIETIES OF RELIGIOUS EXPERIENCE 1902

6 One cannot expect to be conscious of God's presence when one has only a bowing acquaintance with Him.
Mme Chiang Kai-shek, I CONFESS MY FAITH

7 The only God that is of use is a being who is personal, supreme and good, and whose existence is as certain as that two and two make four.
W. Somerset Maugham, THE SUMMING UP 1938

8 When men make gods there is no God.
Eugene O'Neill, LAZARUS LAUGHED 1927

9 God is really only another artist. He invented the giraffe, the elephant and the cat. He has no real style. He just goes on trying other things.
Pablo Picasso. Quoted Françoise Gilot and Carlton Lake, LIFE WITH PICASSO

10 Polite Society believed in God so that it need not talk of Him.
Jean-Paul Sartre, WORDS

11 God ain't said nothing for years, He ain't.
Johnny Speight, BBC 1 TV, Till Death Us Do Part

12 Her [Florence Nightingale] conception of God was certainly not orthodox. She felt towards him as she might have felt towards a glorified sanitary engineer; and in some of her speculations she seems hardly to distinguish between the Deity and the Drains.
Lytton Strachey, EMINENT VICTORIANS 1918

13 By and large gentlemen believe in God because, by and large, they are confident God believes in them.
Douglas Sutherland, THE ENGLISH GENTLEMAN 1978

14 It is a mistake to suppose that God is only, or even chiefly, concerned with religion.
William Temple (Archbishop of Canterbury). Quoted R.V.C. Bodley, IN SEARCH OF SERENITY

15 God in his whirlwind silence save, who marks the sparrow's hail / For their souls' song.
Dylan Thomas, OVER ST JOHN'S HILL

16 Thou canst see all the time, O God, man, you're like a bloody cat.
Dylan Thomas, THE PREACHER

17 God is a sort of burglar. As a young man you knock him down; as an old man you try to conciliate him, because he may knock you down.
Sir H. Beerbohm Tree. Quoted Hesketh Pearson, BEERBOHM-TREE

18 'Let God do it all,' someone will say; but if man folds his arms, God will go to sleep.
Miguel de Unamuno, TRAGIC SENSE OF LIFE 1913

19 I don't care what other people say about God. He has been very sweet to me.
Godfrey Winn. Quoted Cyril Fletcher, NICE ONE CYRIL

HERMANN GOERING

20 He may be a blackguard, but he is not a dirty blackguard.
Sir Neville Henderson. Speech, Sleaford, Lancs

GOLDFISH

21 He pasted picture postcards around goldfish bowls to make the goldfish think they were going places.
Fred Allen, American radio comedian

SAM GOLDWYN

1 You always knew where you were with
Goldwyn — nowhere.
F. Scott Fitzgerald. Quoted Matthew J.
Bruccoli, SOME SORT OF EPIC GRANDEUR

GOLF

2 Met her [Celia Johnson's] uncle on the first
tee of a golf course recently. He said 'Is my
niece as good as you say she is?' I said 'No',
drove off and walked away. I will *not* be
talked to about the theatre when I am
playing golf.
James Agate, EGO 1 1935

3 Golf seems to me an arduous way to go for a
walk. I prefer to take the dogs out.
Princess Anne. Quoted Noël St George,
ROYAL QUOTES

4 'What do you go round in, Miss Champion?'
enquired one of the men. 'My ordinary
clothes.' replied Jane.
Florence L. Barclay, THE ROSARY 1909

5 Golf is a game whose aim is to hit a very
small ball into an even smaller hole, with
weapons singularly ill-designed for the
purpose.
Winston Churchill. Quoted Alistair Cooke,
BBC Radio 4 27 Dec 1974

6 Golf has given me an understanding of the
futility of human effort.
Ebra Eban. Quoted Milton Gross,
EIGHTEEN HOLES IN MY HEAD

7 Golf always makes me so damned angry.
George V. Quoted Peter Ross, Sunday
Referee 28 Dec 1938

8 I find it more satisfying to be a bad player at
golf. The worse you play, the better you
remember the occasional good shot.
Nubar Gulbenkian. Quoted in his obituary,
Daily Telegraph 12 Jan 1972

9 Golf may be played on Sunday, not being a
game within the view of the law, but being a
form of moral effort.
Stephen Leacock, OTHER FANCIES, *Why I*
Refuse to Play Golf

10 I do much of my creative thinking while
golfing. If people know you are working at
home they think nothing of walking in for a

cup of coffee. But they wouldn't dream of
interrupting you on the golf course.
Harper Lee, author of TO KILL A MOCKING
BIRD. *Quoted Bruce and Mark Fowler,*
WRITER'S DIGEST

11 Few people are sensible about holidays.
Many play golf, and one odd effect of that
pursuit is that they return to work *manifestly*
stupider than they were. It is, I think, the
company of other golfers.
G. W. Lyttelton, THE LYTTELTON HART-
DAVIS LETTERS 18 *May* 1956

12 Golf – hockey at the halt.
Arthur Marshall, Quoting an unnamed
Cambridge don, Sunday Telegraph 6 Oct
1985

13 The uglier a man's legs are, the better he
plays golf. It is almost a law.
H. G. Wells, BEALBY 1915

14 'What is your handicap?' Lady Cunard
asked Lord Castlerosse on the golf course.
'Drink and debauchery', he answered sadly
but truthfully.
Philip Ziegler, DIANA COOPER 1981

GOODNESS

15 Goodness is easier to recognise than to
define.
W. H. Auden.

16 Good is that which makes for unity. Evil is
that which makes for separateness.
Aldous Huxley, ENDS AND MEANS 1937

17 When I'm good I'm very very good, but
when I'm bad I'm better.
Mae West, I'M NO ANGEL *(film)*

18 'Goodness, what beautiful diamonds.'
'Goodness had nothing to do with it.'
Mae West, NIGHT AFTER NIGHT *(film)*

GOSSIP

19 There are many who dare not kill themselves for fear of what the neighbours will
say.
Cyril Connolly, THE UNQUIET GRAVE 1945

20 I'd love to stay chatting all day, but you
know what it's like.
Diana, Princess of Wales, during an
Australian walkabout 26 Mar 1983

1 To tell me he doesn't like gossip is like someone telling me he doesn't like Queen's Pudding. I simply cannot understand it, nor do I approve.
Robert Morley, MORLEY MARVELS 1976

2 And what she did *next* summer was even worse. I'll tell you when the music starts.
Overheard at Festival Hall, London. Quoted Pendennis, Observer 26 Apr 1959

3 Miss Missouri Martin tells everything she knows as soon as she knows it, which is often before it happens.
Damon Runyon, MORE THAN SOMEWHAT 1937

GOURMET

4 A gourmet is just a glutton with brains.
Philip W. Haberman, Jr, Vogue 1 May 1961

GOVERNMENT

5 Attended Cabinet — I forget what about.
Leo Amery, DIARIES

6 If the King asks you to form a government you say 'Yes' or 'No' not 'I'll let you know later.'
Clement Attlee. Quoted Kenneth Harris, ATTLEE

7 A statesman wants courage and a statesman wants vision; but believe me, after six months' experience, he wants first, second, third and all the time — patience.
Stanley Baldwin. Speech, Plymouth 26 Oct 1923

8 This island is almost made of coal and surrounded by fish. Only an organising genius could produce a shortage of both in Great Britain at the same time.
Aneurin Bevan. Quoted Vincent Broome, ANEURIN BEVAN

9 The object of government in peace and in war is not the glory of rulers or of races, but the happiness of the common man.
William, Lord Beveridge, SOCIAL INSURANCE

10 The only good government is a bad one in the hell of a fright.
Joyce Cary, THE HORSE'S MOUTH 1944

11 I've never regretted being in the government. I love responsibility and I don't mind unpopularity.
Barbara Castle. Quoted Peter Dunn, Sunday Times 2 Jul 1967

12 All governments are pretty much alike, with a tendency on the part of the last to be the worst.
Austen Chamberlain, House of Commons 1919

13 Democracy means government by the uneducated, while aristocracy means government by the badly educated.
G. K. Chesterton, New York Times 1 Feb 1931

14 Few things are more mischievous to good government and to 'domestic tranquillity' than splendid rhetoric that doesn't pay off.
Alistair Cooke, AMERICA

15 Everything goes wrong for a government which is going wrong.
Richard Crossman, DIARIES 1 Dec 1968

16 A Royal Commission is a broody hen sitting on a china egg.
Michael Foot

17 Governments never learn. Only people learn.
Milton Friedman. Quoted Observer 30 Mar 1980

18 A government that is big enough to give you all you want is big enough to take it all away.
Barry Goldwater. Speech, Westchester 21 Oct 1964

19 Mr Callaghan blamed them on strikes and the weather, implying that a government was in varying degrees powerless against both. Strikes, he presumably felt, were acts of God, although a government might one day be able to do something about the weather.
Frank Johnson, Daily Telegraph 16 Mar 1979

20 Amendments are (a) The afterthoughts of law-makers, (b) A method of defeating a resolution by improvement.
Emery Kelen, Christian Science Monitor. Quoted News Review 27 May 1948

1 When we got into office the thing that surprised me most was to find that things were just as bad as we'd been saying they were.
John F. Kennedy. Quoted Barbara Rowe, BOOK OF QUOTES

2 The title [A Distant Mirror, by Barbara W. Tuchman] suggests that the fourteenth and twentieth centuries are directly comparable. I doubt it. Governments now understand their problems even if they cannot cure them.
John Kenyon, Observer, Death of Chivalry 4 *Mar* 1979

3 The first thing [for a government] to do in a crisis is to set up a committee.
Bernard Levin, THE PENDULUM YEARS 1976

4 In a free society the state does not administer the affairs of men. It administers justice among men who conduct their own affairs.
Walter Lippmann, AN ENQUIRY INTO THE PRINCIPLES OF A GOOD SOCIETY

5 The paradox of British politics; the moment one appropriates power one becomes impotent.
Ramsay MacDonald, to Charles Chaplin. Quoted MY AUTOBIOGRAPHY 1964

6 It is the duty of HM Government neither to flap nor falter.
Harold Macmillan. The remark made when Prime Minister which earned him the epithet 'unflappable'

7 After a few months learning geography, now I've got to learn arithmetic.
Harold Macmillan, on moving from the Foreign Office to the Treasury, to Harold Wilson. Quoted A PRIME MINISTER ON PRIME MINISTERS 1977

8 The worst government is the most moral. One composed of cynics is often very tolerant and humane. But when fanatics are on top there is no limit to oppression.
H. L. Mencken, NOTEBOOKS

9 All government, in its essence, is a conspiracy against the superior man.
H. L. Mencken, SMART SET, *Dec* 1919

10 It is much easier being Prime Minister than Lord President of the Council. All you have to do is delegate the work to somebody else.
Herbert Morrison. Quoted News Review, 19 *Aug* 1948

11 The government of England is a limited mockery.
Extract from child's essay. Quoted, THE NELSONIAN

12 I like to operate like a submarine or sonar. When I am picking up noise from both the left and the right I know my course is correct.
President Ordaz of Mexico. Inaugural speech

13 It is said that every people has the government it deserves. It is more to the point that every Government has the electorate it deserves; for the orators of the front bench can edify or debauch an ignorant electorate at will.
George Bernard Shaw, HEARTBREAK HOUSE, *Preface* 1920

14 Down with government by the grey-haired.
George Bernard Shaw, MAN AND SUPERMAN 1905

15 The art of government is the organisation of idolatry.
Ibid. Maxims for Revolutionists.

16 It would be desirable if every government, when it comes to power, should have its old speeches burnt.
Philip Snowden. Quoted in the biography of him by C. E. Bechofer Roberts (Ephesian)

17 Any woman who understands the problems of running a home will be nearer to understanding the problems of running a country.
Margaret Thatcher. Quoted Observer 8 *May* 1979

18 In the whole course of history there's been no government that could alter the laws of nature.
E. Temple Thurston, MR BOTTLEBY DOES SOMETHING

19 To govern is to choose how the revenue from taxes is to be spent.
Gore Vidal, HOMAGE TO DANIEL SHAYS

20 Prime ministers are dispensable, but private secretaries are not.
John Vincent, Observer, The health of the nation 25 *Oct* 1981

1 Theoretically there is a vast difference between the United States and the United Kingdom. My country is not a democracy. It is a monarchy, aided by two houses of parliament, one of which, of lesser importance, is predominantly hereditary and therefore richly representative of the 'private man' in all his idiosyncrasics.
Evelyn Waugh, commentary for T. A. MacInery's THE PRIVATE MAN

2 My reading of history convinces me that most bad government has grown out of too much government.
John Sharp Williams, THOMAS JEFFERSON

3 I was not going to play every position myself, administer to the wounded, and bring on the lemon at half time, but would be a deep-lying centre half, concentrating on defence, distributing the ball and moving upfield only for set-piece occasions.
Harold Wilson, FINAL TERM: THE LABOUR GOVERNMENT 1974—1976

4 No man ever saw a government. I live in the midst of the Government of the United States but I never saw the Government of the United States.
Woodrow Wilson. Speech, Pittsburgh 29 Jan 1916

GRAFFITO

5 Popular education was bringing the graffito lower on the walls.
Oliver St John Gogarty, AS I WAS GOING DOWN SACKVILLE STREET 1937

6 If God had not meant us to write on walls he would never have set us an example.
Graffito. Quoted Nigel Rees, GRAFFITO 2 1980

7 He [Ernest Thesiger] was in Moscow on a theatrical tour. He went into one of the public conveniences and finding himself alone, wrote on the wall "Burgess loves Maclean."
Michael Pertwee, NAME DROPPING

GRANDMOTHER

8 Everyone should try to have a granny, especially those who have no TV. Grannies are the only grown-ups who always have time.
Child quoted by Annejet Campbell, LISTEN TO THE CHILDREN

9 They can answer questions like 'Why do dogs hate cats?' and 'Why isn't God married?' They never mind reading the same story over and over again.
Ibid.

10 They are usually fat but not too fat to tie your shoelaces. They wear glasses and sometimes they can take their teeth out.
Ibid.

GRATITUDE

11 The obligation of gratitude may easily become a trap, and the young are often caught and maimed in it.
Eric Gill, AUTOBIOGRAPHY

12 Gratitude is a sickness suffered by dogs.
Joseph Stalin. Quoted Nikolai Tolstoy, STALIN'S SECRET WAR

GRAVE

13 For rain it hath a friendly sound / To one who's six feet underground; / And scarce the friendly voice or face; / A grave is such a quiet place.
Edna St Vincent Millay, RENASCENCE 1912

14 All roads end at the grave, which is the gate to nothingness.
George Bernard Shaw, THE ADVENTURES OF A BLACK GIRL IN HER SEARCH FOR GOD

GREATNESS

15 You don't have to be a good man to be a great man.
Marquis of Bath in an interview with Tim Heald, Daily Express 4 Apr 1968

16 There is a great man who makes every man feel small. But the really great man is the man who makes every man feel great.
G. K. Chesterton, CHARLES DICKENS 1906

17 Mrs Asquith remarked indiscreetly that if Kitchener was not a great man, he was, at least, a great poster.
Sir Philip Magnus, KITCHENER: PORTRAIT OF AN IMPERIALIST 1958

GREECE

1 The most un-Greek thing we can do is copy the Greeks. For emphatically they were not copyists.
A. N. Whitehead, ADVENTURES OF IDEAS 1933

GREED

2 We take what we want and God sends the bill.
Dr Rhodes Boyson MP, Daily Telegraph 20 Feb 1979

3 Greed, like the love of comfort, is a kind of fear.
Cyril Connolly, THE UNQUIET GRAVE 1945

4 There is enough for the needy but not for the greedy.
Mahatma Gandhi

5 Believe me, of all the people in the world, those who want the most are those who have the most.
David Grayson, THE FRIENDLY ROAD

6 The instinct of acquisitiveness has more perverts, I believe, than the instinct of sex. At any rate people seem to me to be odder about money than about even their amours.
Aldous Huxley, POINT COUNTER POINT 1934

7 Something better than Freedom from Want is Freedom from Wanting
J. P. McEvoy, Travel Magazine, Jun 1946

GREETING

8 I step over to his table and give him a medium hello, and he looks up and gives me a medium hello right back for, to tell the truth, Maury and I are never bosom friends.
Damon Runyon, MORE THAN SOMEWHAT 1937

9 He [John Cartwright MP] seized the newcomers by the hand. Either he was pleased to see them or they owed him money.
Michael White, Guardian, reporting SDP Conference at Bradford 8 Oct 1981

GRIEF

10 Happiness is beneficial for the body but it is grief that develops the powers of the mind.
Marcel Proust, REMEMBRANCE OF THINGS PAST, Time Regained 1927

GRIEVANCE

11 To have a grievance is to have a purpose in life.
Eric Hoffer, THE PASSIONATE STATE OF MIND 1954

GUARANTEE

12 Behold the guarantee — the bold print giveth, and the fine print taketh away.
Anon. Farmer's Digest

GUEST

13 First impressions mean a lot so always have good luggage.
Sir Hugh Casson and Joyce Grenfell, NANNY SAYS 1972

14 I entertained on a cruising trip that was such fun that I had to sink my yacht to make my guests go home.
F. Scott Fitzgerald, NOTEBOOKS

15 Some people can stay longer in an hour than others can in a week.
William Dean Howells. Quoted John Bartlett, FAMILIAR QUOTATIONS

16 Go — and never darken my towels again.
Groucho Marx, DUCK SOUP

17 My father used to say 'Superior people never make long visits'.
Marianne Moore, BLACK EARTH

GUILT

18 I too am a reluctant puritan, feel uneasy / Sometimes as if I travelled without a ticket. / Yet here I am in England, way out in the centre.
Dannie Abse, WAY OUT IN THE CENTRE

19 All those saints covered in blood and the harping on guilt. It's macabre and futile.
Federico Fellini, Observer, Profile 26 Aug 1963

1 True guilt is guilt at the obligation one owes
to oneself to be oneself.
R. D. Laing, SELF AND OTHERS

2 I don't want to forgive myself. That's why I
hate psychoanalysis. I think if you're guilty
of something you should live with it. Get rid
of it — how can you get rid of real guilt? I
think people should live with it — face up to
it.
Orson Welles. Quoted Barbara Leaming,
ORSON WELLES 1985

GUITAR

3 Electric guitars are an abomination. Whoever heard of an electric violin? Or for that
matter an electric singer?
Andres Segovia, THE BEATLES, WORDS
WITHOUT MUSIC 1968

4 The turning point in the history of western
civilisation was reached with the invention
of the electric guitar.
Leni Sinclair. Quoted John Sinclair, GUITAR
ARMY 1972

H

HABIT

1 Violet Trefusis always has a delightfully insouciant way of putting her cigarette out in a pat of butter.
Cecil Beaton. Caption to drawing in Eileen Hope's collection, Salisbury.

2 Habit is a great deadener.
Samuel Beckett, WAITING FOR GODOT 1952

3 'Music' she said dreamily, and such is the force of habit that 'I don't' she added, 'know anything about music really, but I know what I like.'
Max Beerbohm, ZULEIKA DOBSON 1911

4 I take a decided pleasure in forming habits and re-forming old ones . . . The pleasure of doing the same thing in the same way at the same time each day should be noted.
Arnold Bennett, JOURNALS 1911—1921

5 Widget takes a nicotine-stained forefinger out of his nostril which he had been exploring with perseverance worthy of a better object.
Gerald Kersh, CLEAN, BRIGHT AND SLIGHTLY OILED 1946

6 I've grown accustomed to the trace / Of something in the air, / Accustomed to her face.
Alan Jay Lerner, MY FAIR LADY 1956

7 Every afternoon at 4.30 for the past five months I had fallen into an exact routine. First off, I'd tap the dottle from my pipe by knocking it against the hob. I never smoke a pipe, but I like to keep one with a little dottle in it and an inexpensive hob to tap it against. When you're in the writing game these are the little accessories you need.
S. J. Perelman, CRAZY LIKE A FOX 1944

8 To fall into a habit is to begin to cease to be.
Miguel de Unamuno, TRAGIC SENSE OF LIFE 1913

9 She stamped Kipps so deeply with the hat-raising habit that he would uncover if he found himself in the same railway ticket office with a lady, and so stand ceremoniously until the difficulties of change drove him to an apologetic provisional oblique resumption of his headgear.
H. G. Wells, KIPPS 1905

DOUGLAS, EARL HAIG

10 With the publication of his Private Papers in 1952, he committed suicide 25 years after his death.
Lord Beaverbrook, MEN AND POWER

LORD HAILSHAM

11 When I'm sitting on my woolsack I amuse myself saying 'Bollocks' *sotto voce* to the bishops.
Lord Hailsham in an interview with John Mortimer, Sunday Times 25 Aug 1985

12 When self indulgence has reduced a man to the shape of Lord Hailsham, sexual continence involves no more than a sense of the ridiculous.
Reginald Paget MP, House of Commons 16 Jun 1963

13 Sitting on the woolsack in the Lords recently Lord Hailsham, the Lord Chancellor, sneezed most massively. When silence ensued he turned to the 12 bishops in their adjacent seats and exclaimed: 'Aren't any of you going to say "Bless you"?'
The Times, Diary 31 Jul 1985

HAND

14 Old hands soil, it seems, whatever they caress, but they too have their beauty when they are joined in prayer. Young hands were made for caresses and the sheathing of love. It is a pity to make them join too soon.
André Gide, JOURNALS 21 Jan 1929

1 The hand that signed the paper felled a city /
Five sovereign fingers taxed the breath /
Doubled the globe of dead and halved a
country / These five kings did a king to
death.
Dylan Thomas, THE HAND THAT SIGNED
THE PAPER 1930

HANDICAP

2 It is, of course, a bit of a drawback that
science was invented after I left school.
*Lord Carrington. Quoted Observer, Last of
the Tory Grandees* 23 *Jan* 1983

HANGOVER

3 His mouth has been used as a latrine by
some small animal of the night.
Kingsley Amis, LUCKY JIM 1954

4 A mouth like the inside of a zoo-keeper's
welly.
Peter Watson, The Times Diary 27 *Nov* 1981

HAPPINESS

5 Only in romantic novels are the beautiful
guaranteed happiness.
Lady Cynthia Asquith, DIARIES

6 One should never let one's happiness
depend on other people.
H. Granville Barker, THE VOYSEY
INHERITANCE 1905

7 Happy people are failures because they are
on such good terms with themselves that
they don't give a damn.
Agatha Christie, SPARKLING CYANIDE

8 What we call happiness in the strictest sense
of the word comes from the (preferably
sudden) satisfaction of needs which have
been dammed up to a high degree.
Sigmund Freud, CIVILISATION AND ITS
DISCONTENTS

9 Happiness makes up in height what it lacks
in length.
Robert Frost, title of poem 1942

10 Nothing is more fatal to happiness than the
remembrance of happiness.
André Gide, THE IMMORALIST 1902

11 Happiness is the sublime moment when you
get out of your corsets at night.
Joyce Grenfell, in a luncheon club speech

12 It's pretty hard to tell what does bring
happiness; poverty and wealth have both
failed.
Kim Hubbard, ABE MARTIN 1930

13 There is something curiously boring about
somebody else's happiness.
Aldous Huxley, LIMBO, *Cynthia*

14 Happiness is like coke — something you get
as a by-product in the process of making
something else.
Aldous Huxley, POINT COUNTER
POINT 1928

15 Many persons have a wrong idea of what
constitutes true happiness. It is not obtained
through self-gratification, but through fidelity to a worthy purpose.
Helen Keller, JOURNAL 1938

16 'Did you have a happy childhood?' is a false
question. As a child I did not know what
happiness was, and whether I was happy or
not. I was too busy *being*.
Alistair Reid, THE WORLD OF CHILDREN

17 Really high-minded people are indifferent
to happiness, especially other people's.
Bertrand Russell, THE CONQUEST OF
HAPPINESS 1930

18 If you wish to be happy yourself you must
resign yourself to seeing others happy.
Ibid.

19 To be without some of the things you want is
an indispensable part of happiness.
Ibid.

20 A happy life must be to a great extent a quiet
life, for it is only in an atmosphere of quiet
that true joy dare live.
Ibid.

21 I do not believe that science *per se* is an
adequate source of happiness, nor do I think
my own scientific outlook has contributed
very greatly to my own happiness which I
attribute to defecating twice a day with
unfailing regularity.
Bertrand Russell, letter to W. W. Norton 27
Jan 1931

1 Happiness is not best achieved by those who seek it directly.
Bertrand Russell, MYSTICISM AND LOGIC 1918

2 Happiness is the only sanction of life; where happiness fails, existence remains a mad and lamentable experiment.
George Santayana, THE LIFE OF REASON, *Reason in Commonsense* 1906

3 We have no more right to consume happiness without producing it than to consume wealth without producing it.
George Bernard Shaw, CANDIDA 1903

4 A man is happy so long as he chooses to be happy and nothing can stop him.
Alexander Solzhenitsyn, CANCER WARD

5 It is not swinish to be happy unless one is happy in swinish ways.
Susan Stebbing, IDEALS AND ILLUSIONS

6 Happiness is an imaginary condition formerly often attributed by the living to the dead, now normally attributed by adults to children, and by children to adults.
Thomas Szasz, THE SECOND SIN, *Emotions*

7 No one shall say of me that I haven't known perfect happiness, but few could put their finger on the moment or say what made it. Even I myself, stirring occasionally in the pool of content, could only say; 'But this is all I want'.
Virginia Woolf, DIARY 1925-30 1982

8 Who never knew the price of happiness will not be happy.
Yevgeny Yevtushenko, BABI YAR 1961

PRESIDENT HARDING

9 He has a bungalow mind.
Woodrow Wilson. Quoted C. W. Thompson, PRESIDENTS I HAVE KNOWN

HARPSICHORD

10 The sound of a harpsichord: two skeletons copulating on a tin roof.
Sir Thomas Beecham. Quoted Nat Shapiro, ENCYCLOPEDIA OF QUOTATIONS ABOUT MUSIC 1978

HAT

11 Eleanor Roosevelt's hats had the look of having been found under the bed.
Joseph Alsop, FDR 1882 / 1945: THE LIFE AND TIMES OF FRANKLIN D. ROOSEVELT

12 That's a hat to go to a concert half an hour late in.
Margot Asquith. Quoted Arnold Bennett, JOURNALS 1932

13 He can't think without his hat.
Samuel Beckett, WAITING FOR GODOT 1952

14 The bowler of Mr Jerome K. Jerome is a perfect preface to all his works.
Max Beerbohm, DANDIES AND DANDIES

15 The top hat [at Eton] was the most useful of items, being a splendid place to keep ice-cream in summer, and white mice in winter.
Michael Bentine, THE LONG BANANA SKIN

16 He is known to often carry a gun in his pants pocket and to shoot people down as dead as doornails with it if he does not like the way they wear their hats — and Rusty Charlie is very critical of hats.
Damon Runyon, MORE THAN SOMEWHAT 1937

HATE

17 One of the reasons people cling to their hates so stubbornly is because they seem to sense, once hate is gone, that they will be forced to deal with pain.
James Baldwin, NOTES OF A NATIVE SON 1955

18 Hatred rarely does any harm to its object. It is the hater who suffers. His soul is warped and his life poisoned by dwelling on past injuries or projecting schemes of revenge. Rancour in the bosom is the foe of personal happiness.
Lord Beaverbrook, THE DIVINE PROPAGANDIST

19 It does not matter much what a man hates, provided he hates something.
Samuel Butler, NOTEBOOKS 1912

20 I tell you there is such a thing as creative hate.
Willa Cather, THE SONG OF THE LARK 1915

1 I hate nobody except Hitler — and that's professional.
Winston Churchill, to John Colville.
Quoted, THE CHURCHILLIANS

2 Hate has what lust entirely lacks — persistence and continuity; the persistence and continuity of purposive spirit.
Aldous Huxley, BEYOND THE MEXIQUE BAY

3 We must hate — hatred is the basis of Communism. Children must be taught to hate their parents if they are not Communists.
V. I. Lenin. Speech to the Commissars of Education, Moscow 1923

4 Any kiddie in school can love like a fool / But hating, my boy, is an art.
Ogden Nash, PLEAS FOR LESS MALICE TOWARDS NONE

5 Enemies are not those who hate us, but rather those whom we hate.
Dagobert Runes, A DICTIONARY OF THOUGHT

6 Few people can be happy unless they hate some other person, nation or creed.
Bertrand Russell, AUTOBIOGRAPHY 1961

7 Hatred is the coward's revenge for being intimidated.
George Bernard Shaw, MAJOR BARBARA 1905

8 Love for the same thing never makes allies. It's always hate for the same thing.
Howard Spring, MY SON, MY SON 1938

9 To be choked with hate / May well be of all evil chances chief.
W. B. Yeats, COLLECTED POEMS, *A Prayer for My Daughter* 1933

10 An intellectual hatred is the worst.
Ibid.

HEALTH

11 Every day and in every way I am getting better and better.
Emile Coué, AUTOSUGGESTION

12 Many Britons a hundred years ago were bursting with good health, and the remarkable thing was that they knew nothing of vitamins.
Lord Horder, THE LITTLE GENIUS

13 Get your room full of good fresh air. Then shut up the windows and keep it in. It will keep for years. Anyway, don't keep using your lungs all the time. Let them rest.
Stephen Leacock, LITERARY LAPSES 1910

14 What is the thing called health? Simply the state in which the individual happens transiently to be perfectly adapted to his environment. Obviously such states cannot be common, for the environment is in constant flux.
H. L. Mencken, American Mercury, Mar 1930

15 There is no human activity, eating, sleeping, drinking or sex which some doctor somewhere won't discover leads directly to cardiac arrest.
John Mortimer, Observer 20 *Aug* 1978

16 Too much health is unhealthy.
Leo Rosten, HOORAY FOR YIDDISH 1983

17 Use your health, even to the point of wearing it out.
George Bernard Shaw, DOCTOR'S DILEMMA, *Preface* 1908

18 *Mens sana in corpore sano* is a foolish saying. The sound body is a product of a sound mind.
George Bernard Shaw, MAN AND SUPERMAN 1905

WILLIAM RANDOLPH HEARST

19 Upon my honour, I saw a Madonna / Hanging within a niche / Above the door of the private whore / Of the world's worst son of a bitch.
Dorothy Parker, of a picture given by William Randolph Hearst to his mistress.
Quoted Joseph Alsop, THE RARE ART TRADITIONS 1983

HEAT

20 When you're hot, anything can happen.
Jimmy Connors. Quoted Observer, Sayings of the Week 27 *Jun* 1976

EDWARD HEATH

1 If only he had lost his temper in public the way he does in private he would have become a more commanding and successful national leader.
William Davis. Quoted James Margach THE ABUSE OF POWER 1981

2 I've only been happy during three periods of my life; when I was at Balliol, when I was at the Foreign Office (which some people say amounts to the same thing) and when I was Prime Minister.
Edward Heath, Observer, Sayings of the Week 10 *Feb* 1985

3 Edward Heath was once news editor of the *Church Times.* It was a part of his career that he kept in the background. As Prime Minister . . . he never expected a good Press and was always wary of journalists.
James Margach, THE ABUSE OF POWER 1981

4 We must kick Ted in the groin. We must be rough with him.
Harold Wilson. Quoted Richard Crossman, DIARIES 20 *Oct* 1969

HEATHEN

5 *Heathen, n.* A benighted creature who has the folly to worship something he can see and feel.
Ambrose Bierce, THE DEVIL'S DICTIONARY 1906

HEAVEN

6 Hell is paved with good intentions, but heaven goes in for something more dependable. Solid gold.
Joyce Cary, THE HORSE'S MOUTH 1944

7 *Heaven:* the Coney Island of the Christian imagination.
Elbert Hubbard. Quoted Evan Esar, TREASURY OF HUMOROUS QUOTATIONS

8 People who believe they are going there often wonder what they will do with themselves in Heaven. They make the mistake of assuming that the place will be all complete, finished to the last bit of gilding, when they get there. But of course it won't.
J. B. Priestley, DELIGHTS

9 If you go to Heaven without being naturally qualified for it you will not enjoy yourself there.
George Bernard Shaw, MAN AND SUPERMAN 1905

10 The human mind is inspired enough when it comes to inventing horrors; it is when it tries to invent a Heaven that it shows itself cloddish.
Evelyn Waugh, PUT OUT MORE FLAGS 1942

11 'It is a curious thing,' he thought 'that every creed promises a paradise which will be absolutely uninhabitable for anyone of civilised taste.'
Ibid.

HELL

12 That's what Hell must be like, small chat to the babbling of Lethe about the good old days when we wished we were dead.
Samuel Beckett, EMBERS 1960

13 They order things so damnably in Hell.
Hilaire Belloc, TO DIVES

14 The religion of Hell is patriotism and the government is an enlightened democracy.
J. B. Cabell, JURGEN 1919

15 What is Hell? Hell is oneself / Hell is alone, the other figures in it / Merely projections.
T. S. Eliot, THE COCKTAIL PARTY 1949

16 The fear of hell is hell itself.
Kahil Gibran, SPIRITUAL SAYINGS 1963

17 If hell is paved with good intentions, it is, among other reasons, because of the impossibility of calculating consequences.
Aldous Huxley, AFTER MANY A SUMMER 1939

18 His brain was simmering and bubbling within the cracking tenement of the skull. Flames burst forth from his skull like a corolla, shrieking like voices: — Hell! Hell! Hell! Hell! Hell!
James Joyce, A PORTRAIT OF THE ARTIST AS A YOUNG MAN

19 There is wishful thinking in Hell as well as on earth.
C. S. Lewis, SCREWTAPE LETTERS 1942

1 It is idle to believe that a stirrup-pump can
extinguish hell.
Henry Reed, A MAP OF VERONA 1946

2 The infliction of cruelty with a good
conscience is a delight to moralists. That is
why they invented Hell.
Bertrand Russell, SCEPTICAL ESSAYS 1928

3 To work hard, to live hard, to die hard, and
then go to hell after all would be too damned
hard.
Carl Sandburg, THE PEOPLE, YES 1936

4 Hell is full of musical amateurs.
George Bernard Shaw, MAN AND
SUPERMAN 1905

5 There is plenty of humbug in Hell.
Ibid.

HELP

6 You can only help one of your luckless
brothers / By trampling down a dozen
others.
Bertolt Brecht, THE GOOD WOMAN OF
SETZUAN 1938

7 If you see anybody fallen by the wayside and
lying in the ditch, it isn't much good
climbing into the ditch and lying by his side.
*Rev. H. R. L. Sheppard. Quoted Carolyn
Scott,* DICK SHEPPARD

8 I've already had medical attention — a dog
licked me when I was on the ground.
Neil Simon, IT HURTS ONLY WHEN I LAUGH

HEREDITY

9 Purity of race does not exist. Europe is a
continent of energetic mongrels.
H. A. L. Fisher, A HISTORY OF EUROPE

HERESY

10 I did try to find a heresy of my own; and
when I had put the last touches to it, I
discovered that it was orthodox.
G. K. Chesterton, ORTHODOXY 1908

11 Heresy is but the bridge between two
orthodoxies.
Francis Hackett, HENRY VIII

12 Collective wisdom is no adequate substitute
for the intelligence of individuals. Individuals who opposed received opinion have
been the source of all progress. Socrates,
Christ and Galileo all equally incurred the
censure of the orthodox.
Bertrand Russell, American Mercury

13 How can what an Englishman says be
heresy? It is a contradiction in terms.
George Bernard Shaw, ST JOAN 1923

14 Heresy is the lifeblood of religions. It is faith
that begets heretics. There are no heresies in
a dead religion.
André Suarès, PÉGNY 1912

HERO

15 Heroes exterminate each other for the
benefit of people who are not heroes.
Havelock Ellis. Quoted Evan Esar,
TREASURY OF HUMOROUS QUOTATIONS

16 As you get older it is harder to have heroes,
but it is sort of necessary.
Ernest Hemingway. Quoted Lillian Ross,
PORTRAIT OF HEMINGWAY 1961

17 Too much has been said of the heroes of
history — the strong men, the troublesome
men; too little of the amiable, the kindly,
the tolerant.
Stephen Leacock, ESSAYS AND LITERARY
STUDIES

18 What is our task? To make Britain a fit
country for heroes to live in.
David Lloyd George. Speech 22 Nov 1918

19 A hero is a man who would argue with the
Gods and awakens devils to contest his
vision.
Norman Mailer, PRESIDENTIAL
PAPERS 1963

20 I'm a hero with coward's legs. I'm a hero
from the waist up.
Spike Milligan, PUCKOON

21 To be a hero, one must give an order to
oneself.
Simone Weil, NOTEBOOKS

22 Lapses from knowledge to faith are perhaps
necessary that human heroism may be
possible.
H. G. Wells, MR BRITLING SEES IT
THROUGH 1916

HESITATION

1 It is all right to hesitate if you then go ahead.
Bertolt Brecht, THE GOOD WOMAN OF
SETZUAN 1938

2 He who hesitates is sometimes saved.
James Thurber, THE THURBER CARNIVAL,
The Glass in the Field 1945

HINDSIGHT

3 We have constantly to check ourselves in
reading history with the remembrance that,
to the actors in the drama, events appeared
very different from the way they appear to
us. We know what they were doing far
better than they knew themselves.
Randolph Bourne, YOUTH AND LIFE

HIRE-PURCHASE

4 A judge has said that all his experience had
been spent on sorting out the difficulties of
people who, upon the recommendation of
people they did not know, signed documents
they did not read, to buy goods they did not
need, with money they had not got.
Gilbert Harding on TV

HISTORY

5 You don't have to be a Marxist to see that
history repeats itself, first as tragedy then as
farce.
Anon.

6 History does not repeat itself. Historians
repeat each other.
*A. J. Balfour. Quoted by his biographer
Kenneth Young*

7 The ideal thing is for the historian to write
his history and then to have a gang of trained
slaves who can go through the proofs for
various aspects. That is why, taking it all in
all, gentlemen have made the best historians.
*Hilaire Belloc, letter to Arthur Pollen.
Quoted Robert Speight,* LIFE OF HILAIRE
BELLOC

8 It is always curious to read as 'history' what
one has experienced oneself.
Max Beloff, Daily Telegraph 5 Apr 1979

9 History must not be written with bias, both
sides should be given, even if there is only
one side.
John Betjeman, FIRST AND LAST LOVES

10 To walk into history is to be free at once, to
be at large among people.
Elizabeth Bowen, THE HOUSE IN PARIS 1935

11 It has been said that though God cannot
alter the past, historians can; it is perhaps
because they can be useful to Him in this
respect that He tolerates their existence.
Samuel Butler, EREWHON REVISITED 1901

12 History portrays everything as if it could not
have come otherwise. History is on the side
of what happened.
Elias Canetti, THE HUMAN PROVINCE 1985

13 History will record it. I know it will because I
shall write it myself.
*Winston Churchill. Quoted John Boyd
Carpenter,* WAY OF LIFE

14 History creates confusion, even in its own
time.
*Jean Cocteau in an interview with Derek
Prouse, Sunday Times* 20 *Oct* 1963

15 All historians, in attempting to recreate the
past, must necessarily in part invent it.
Glyn Daniel, The Times 29 *Jun* 1985

16 History has many cunning passages, cont-
rived corridors and issues.
T. S. Eliot, GERONTION 1920

17 A people without history / Is not redeemed
for time, for history is a pattern / Of timeless
moments. So while the light fails / On a
winter's afternoon, in a secluded chapel /
History is now and England.
T. S. Eliot, FOUR QUARTETS, *Little
Gidding* 1942

18 The historical sense involves a perception,
not only of the pastness of the past, but of its
presence.
T. S. Eliot, TRADITION AND THE
INDIVIDUAL TALENT 1919

19 The future is dark, the present burdensome.
Only the past, dead and buried, bears
contemplation.
G. R. Ellin, THE PRACTICE OF HISTORY

1 Men wiser and more learned than I have discovered in history a plot, a rhythm, a predetermined pattern. These harmonies are concealed from me. I can see only one emergency following upon another, wave on wave.
H. A. L. Fisher, HISTORY OF EUROPE 1934

2 History is bunk.
Henry Ford, as a witness in his libel suit against Chicago Tribune, Jul 1914

3 We want to live in the present and the only history that is worth a tinker's damn is the history we make today.
Henry Ford, Chicago Tribune 25 May 1916

4 The historian must have some conception of how men who are not historians behave. Otherwise he will move in a world of the dead.
E. M. Forster, ABINGER HARVEST 1936

5 History is attractive to the more timid of us [because] we can recover self-confidence by snubbing the dead.
Ibid.

6 History never looks like history when you are living through it. It always looks confusing and messy, and it always feels uncomfortable.
John W. Gardner, NO EASY VICTORIES 1968

7 My argument is that War makes rattling good history, but Peace is poor reading.
Thomas Hardy, THE DYNASTS 1903

8 It is not the neutrals or the lukewarm who make history.
Adolf Hitler. Speech, Berlin 23 Apr 1933

9 The writing of history may be as creative as the making of it. Both are an interpretation of life.
Philip Hope-Wallace. Quoted The Times, obituary 17 *Dec* 1979

10 Historians have a responsibility to make some sense of the past and not simply to chronicle it.
Michael Howard. Reviewing Herbert Butterfield, THE ORIGIN OF HISTORY, *Times Literary Supplement* 7 *Aug* 1981

11 There is no such thing as a neutral or purely objective historian. Without an opinion a historian would be simply a ticking clock, and unreadable besides.
Philip Howard, The Times, review of Barbara Tuchman's PRACTISING HISTORY 4 *Feb* 1982

12 Events in the past may roughly be divided into those which probably never happened and those which do not matter.
W. R. Inge (Dean of St Pauls), ASSESSMENTS AND ANTICIPATIONS 1929

13 Our chief interest in the past is as a guide to the future.
Ibid.

14 History is a relentless master. It has no present, only the past rushing into the future. To try to hold fast is to be swept aside.
John F. Kennedy. Quoted Barbara Rowe, A BOOK OF QUOTES

15 The lessons of history . . . teach the consequences of certain actions, but they cannot force a recognition of comparable situations.
Henry Kissinger, A WORLD RESTORED 1957

16 We cannot afford to make the world our fellow citizens live in historically unintelligible.
Prof. W. H. MacNeil, A DEFENCE OF WORLD HISTORY, *Royal Historical Society Lecture* 1981

17 The history of the world is the history of the privileged few.
Henry Miller, THE SUNDAY AFTER THE WAR 1944

18 History is seldom tidy.
Simon Nowell-Smith, EDWARDIAN ENGLAND

19 History is not a department of *belles lettres* [not] just an elegant, instructive amusing narrative, but a brand of science.
York Powell, Regius Professor at Oxford. Quoted A. L. Rowse, THE USE OF HISTORY

20 A man without a bias cannot write interesting history — if indeed such a man exists.
Bertrand Russell, AUTOBIOGRAPHY VOL II 1967

21 The memories of men are too frail a thread to hang history on.
John Still, THE JUNGLE TIDE

1 It is not the historian's business to be complimentary; it is his business to lay bare the facts of the case, as he understands them . . . dispassionately, impartially and without ulterior motives.
Lytton Strachey, EMINENT VICTORiANS, *Preface* 1918

2 When I write I have no loyalty except to historical truth as I see it and care no more about British achievements and mistakes than any other.
A. J. P. Taylor, POLITICIANS, SOCIALISM, AND HISTORIANS 1980

3 The task of history is to explain the past, neither to justify nor condemn it.
Ibid.

4 Historians are like deaf people who go on answering questions that no one has asked them.
Leo Tolstoy. Quoted Manning Clark, A DISCOVERY OF AUSTRALIA

5 All history is contemporary history. We create our own ideas of the past; and our adulation, or indifference, or irreverence for it affects the way we live now.
Arnold Toynbee, THE GREEKS AND THEIR HERITAGE 1981

6 I love history. It's so old.
Peter Ustinov, ROMANOFF AND JULIET

7 Perhaps one of the most prolific sources of error in contemporary thinking rises precisely from the popular habit of lifting history out of its proper context and bending it to the values of another age and day. In this way history is never allowed to be itself.
Laurens Van Der Post, THE LOST WORLD OF THE KALAHARI 1958

8 The history of the world is the record of a man in quest of his daily bread and butter.
H. W. Van Loon, THE STORY OF MANKIND 1921

9 Human history becomes more and more a race between education and catastrophe.
H. G. Wells, OUTLINE OF HISTORY 1920

10 History, especially Church History, is always written to justify the survivors.
Morris West, THE CLOWNS OF GOD

11 The real history does not get written, because it is not in people's brains but in

their nerves and vitals.
A. N. Whitehead, DIALOGUES 1953

ADOLF HITLER

12 Hitler talks platitudes, but he believes them. The Duce [Mussolini] controls the crowd. Hitler *is* the crowd. Everything it feels, he feels.
Vernon Bartlett, THIS IS MY LIFE 1937

13 It was impossible to converse with him in any normal way . . . he suddenly started shouting . . . I imagine that a man in a trance would behave in much the same way, and while he was shouting I am convinced that I could have walked out of the room and he would not have noticed my departure.
Ibid.

14 I, and many others who had interviews with him, were at first impressed by his sincerity, and later realised that he was sincere only in his belief that he was destined to rule the world.
Vernon Bartlett, I KNOW WHAT I LIKED

15 Mind you, like Churchill he was a very bad artist. Neither of them were any bloody good at it.
Marquis of Bath, of Hitler paintings bought for Longleat, Daily Express 4 *Apr* 1968

16 The moustache of Hitler, / Could hardly be littler / Was the thought that kept recurring / To Field Marshal Goering.
E. C. Bentley, CLERIHEWS

17 Hitler showed surprising loyalty to Mussolini, but it never extended to trusting him.
Alan Bullock, HITLER

18 Hitler has missed the bus.
Neville Chamberlain, of the invasion of Norway, House of Commons 4 *Apr* 1940

19 The German dictator, instead of snatching the victuals from the table, has been content to have them served to him course by course.
Winston Churchill, House of Commons. Speech after Munich 5 *Oct* 1938

20 This wicked man Hitler, the repository and embodiment of many forms of soul-destroying hatred, this monstrous product of former wrongs and shame.
Winston Churchill, BBC broadcast 11 *Sep* 1940

1 That bloodthirsty guttersnipe.
Winston Churchill, House of Commons

2 I have only one purpose, the destruction of
Hitler and my life is much simplified
thereby. If Hitler invaded Hell I would
make at least a favourable reference to the
Devil in the House of Commons.
Winston Churchill, THE GRAND ALLIANCE

3 To reject the world the most effective way is
to act in such a manner as to force the world
to spew one out — in which case Hitler came
'nearer to God' than St Joan, St Theresa or
St Vincent de Paul.
Richard Coe, THE VISION OF JEAN GENET

4 I could not bear it if I ever had to despair of
this man. This man has everything needed to
be king.
Paul Joseph Goebbels, DIARIES

5 German history does not end with Hitler.
Anyone believing that it does, and possibly
even rejoicing in it, does not realise just how
much he is thereby fulfilling Hitler's last will
and testament.
Sebastian Haffner, THE MEANING OF HITLER

6 He disapproved of Adolf Hitler who had
done such a great job combatting unAmerican activities in Germany.
Joseph Heller, CATCH 22 1962

7 If Hitler had put his energies into promoting
nuclear physics instead of persecuting the
Jews, the history of the world might have
been very different. The first atom bomb
could well have exploded over London
instead of Hiroshima.
David Irving, THE VIRUS HOUSE

8 I tell you, as one who has studied the whole
situation I don't think Hitler is a fool — he is
not going to challenge the British Empire.
David Lloyd George. Speech 1937

9 The Führer never was able to understand or
emulate Anglo-Saxon hypocrisy; he said
what he meant, and he meant what he said, a
novelty in international affairs.
Diana Mosley, LOVED ONES 1985

10 It would have been better for the rest of us if,
instead of German Führer, he had been
editor of *The Times* or Director General of
the BBC or Moderator of the Church of
Scotland, or compère of a late-night television show, but so far as he personally was
concerned it would not have made any
appreciable difference.
Malcolm Muggeridge, TREAD SOFTLY FOR
YOU TREAD ON MY JOKES 1966

11 Hitler was a profoundly *uneducated* man of
genius; there could be nothing more dangerous, with such a criminal mentality in a
position of power.
A. L. Rowse, THE USE OF HISTORY

12 I wouldn't believe Hitler was dead, even if
he told me so himself.
Hjalmar Schacht 3 May 1945

13 A racing tipster who only reached Hitler's
level of accuracy would not do well for his
clients.
A. J. P. Taylor, ORIGINS OF THE SECOND
WORLD WAR 1961

14 Hitler, a bilious ascetic, drank next to
nothing and picked at his food like an
anxious raccoon.
Robert Lewis Taylor, THE AMAZING MR
CHURCHILL

15 The most pathetic thing about Adolf Hitler
was his passionate desire to be approved of
by English gentlemen.
Daily Telegraph. Quoted Michael Bateman,
THIS ENGLAND

16 There is nothing yet to show that the new
Chancellor intends to be immoderate in his
foreign policy.
The Times, leader 1933

17 The machine is running away with *him* as it
ran away with *me.*
*Kaiser Wilhelm II, to Sir Robert Bruce
Lockhart at Doorne* 27 Aug 1939

HOBBY

18 Ornithology used to be an arcane hobby for
embittered schoolmasters, dotty spinsters
and lonely little boys but now it is as normal
a weekend occupation as rug-making or
wife-swapping.
Kyril Bonfiglioli, DON'T POINT THAT THING
AT ME

HOLIDAY

1 We've never had a holiday. A week or two at
Balmoral, or ten days at Sandringham, is the
nearest we get.
Princess Anne. Quoted Noël St George,
ROYAL QUOTES

2 I'm not wild about holidays. They always
seem a ludicrously expensive way of proving
there's no place like home.
Jilly Cooper, Sunday Times 16 *Nov* 1977

3 A period of activity so intense that it can
only be undertaken three or four weeks in
the year.
*Miles Kington. The Times, A Guide to Real
Meanings* 7 *Feb* 1983

4 I don't mind doing the bracing British beach
bit, anoraks and gumboots and soggy fish
fingers in the Sun-'n'-Sands Cafe, so long as
no one suggests I am supposed to enjoy it.
Katherine Whitehorn, HOW TO SURVIVE
CHILDREN

HOLLAND

5 Apart from cheese and tulips, the main
product of the country is advocaat, a drink
made from lawyers.
Alan Coren, THE SANITY INSPECTOR 1974

HOLLYWOOD

6 On transatlantic flights I would recite the
Lord's Prayer to myself on take-off and
landing. One day in May 1981 I found
myself murmuring 'Our Father which art in
Heaven, Hollywood be thy name' and
realised it was time I got out.
Steven Bach, FINAL CUT 1985

7 Hollywood is full of genius. All that it lacks
is talent.
Henri Bernstein. Quoted J. B. Priestley,
LITERATURE AND WESTERN MAN 1960

8 Hollywood is too much publicised. There
are too many people here. Some of them
should go back on a slow train.
Sam Goldwyn. Quoted News Review 11 *Dec*
1947

9 Hollywood is a locality where people
without reputation try to live up to it.
Tom Jenk. Quoted Dick Richards, GINGER,
SALUTE TO A STAR

10 Strip the phoney tinsel off Hollywood and
you'll find the real tinsel underneath.
Oscar Levant. Quoted Leslie Halliwell, THE
FILMGOER'S BOOK OF QUOTES 1973

11 Back to the mink-lined rut.
*Anita Loos, on returning to writing film
scripts. Quoted Stanley Reynolds, in his
obituary of her, The Guardian* 20 *Aug* 1981

12 A trip through a sewer in a glass-bottomed
boat.
Wilson Mizner. Quoted A. Johnson,
LEGEND OF A SPORT

13 Hollywood is a sewer with service from the
Ritz Carlton.
Wilson Mizner

14 Hollywood is a place where they'll pay you a
thousand dollars for a kiss and fifty cents for
your soul.
Marilyn Monroe

15 Hollywood is a combination of Heaven,
Hell and a lunatic asylum.
*Salvation Army Gen. Albert William
Thomas Osborn. Quoted News Review*
28 *Nov* 1946

16 We just got here — you can't judge a place
so fast. Besides it's raining. It's probably
beautiful when the sun comes out.
S. J. Perelman, THE LAST LAUGH 1981

17 In Europe an actor is an artist. In Holly-
wood, if he isn't acting, he's a bum.
Anthony Quinn. Quoted Leslie Halliwell,
THE FILMGOER'S BOOK OF QUOTES 1973

18 In Hollywood if you don't have happiness
you send out for it.
Rex Reed. Quoted J. R. Colombo,
HOLLYWOOD THE BAD

19 They know only one word of more than one
syllable here, and that is fillum.
Louis Sherwin

HOME

20 Home is the place where, when you have to
go there / They have to take you in.
Robert Frost, THE DEATH OF THE HIRED
MAN 1914

1 The best / Thing we can do is to make wherever we are lost in / Look as much like home as we can.
Christopher Fry, THE LADY'S NOT FOR BURNING 1950

2 It was a typical old English country house, fifty-six rooms and a bath. It was a strange kind of bath — it went all round the place. It was called a moat.
Bob Hope, I OWE RUSSIA 1200 DOLLARS

3 I want a house that has got over all its troubles; I don't want to spend the rest of my life bringing up a young and inexperienced house.
Jerome K. Jerome, THEY AND I

4 A real English home it is, just like yours or mine or Mr Anthony Eden's, with a Great Dane on the hearthrug, yards of mullion round the windows and Miss Marlene Dietrich sleeping in the best bedroom.
C. A. Lejeune, Observer review of the film ANGEL 1936

5 There was but one thing wrong with the Babbitt house, it was not a home.
Sinclair Lewis, BABBITT 1922

6 Home is the girl's prison and the woman's workhouse.
George Bernard Shaw, MAN AND SUPERMAN 1905

LORD HOME

7 I had to see that Master Alex didn't talk to the servants and that he didn't leave our part of the house.
Mrs Florence Hill, (Alec Douglas-Home's nurse). Quoted Evening Standard

8 I suppose when you come to think of it, Mr Wilson is the 14th Mr Wilson.
Lord Home, BBC TV 21 Aug 1963

9 The only real and distinctive achievement of the fourteenth Earl was to have been born the heir of the thirteenth.
Sunday Express 1960

10 The whole process [of democracy] has ground to a halt with a 14th Earl.
Harold Wilson, Labour Party Conference 1 Aug 1963

HOMESICKNESS

11 Dear People, I am at present in Bethlehem where Jesus Christ was born. I wish to Christ I was in Wigan where I was born.
Soldier writing home in 1917. Quoted Lord Esher, JOURNALS AND LETTERS

HOMOSEXUALITY

12 Nancy Mitford had the distinction of being one of the first 'fag hags', since she revelled in the company of effeminate young men.
Peter Ackroyd, Sunday Times 13 Oct 1985

13 Buggery is spiritually valuable because of its difficulties and torments.
W. H. Auden. Quoted Humphrey Carpenter, AUDEN, A BIOGRAPHY

14 Everything is controlled by the sods. The country is riddled with homosexuals who are teaching the world how to behave — a spectacle of revolting hypocrisy.
Sir Thomas Beecham. Quoted Charles Reed, BEECHAM, AN INDEPENDENT BIOGRAPHY

15 We're here because we're queer / Because we're queer because we're here.
Brendan Behan, THE HOSTAGE 1958

16 The worst part of being gay in the twentieth century is all that damn disco music to which one has to listen.
Quentin Crisp, MANNERS FROM HEAVEN 1984

17 Tchaikovsky thought of committing suicide for fear of being discovered as a homosexual, but today, if you are a composer and *not* homosexual you might as well put a bullet through your head.
Sergei Diaghilev. Quoted Vernon Duke, LISTEN HERE!

18 Nature's attempt to get rid of the soft boys by sterilising them.
F. Scott Fitzgerald, THE CRACK-UP 1936

19 It is a perfectly ordinary little case of a man charged with indecency with four or five guardsmen.
Mervyn Griffiths-Jones, prosecuting counsel. Reported in the Guardian. Quoted Michael Bateman, THIS ENGLAND

1 'Fundamentally, unconsciously, I believe he's a homosexualist.' 'Perhaps,' said Irene gravely. She knew her Havelock Ellis.
Aldous Huxley, BARREN LEAVES 1925

2 There is probably no sensitive heterosexual alive who is not preoccupied with his latent homosexuality.
Norman Mailer, ADVERTISEMENTS FOR MYSELF 1959

3 This sort of thing may be tolerated by the French — but we are British, thank God.
Viscount Montgomery, House of Lords 26 *May* 1965

4 It is a hard fate to love the untouchable.
David Newsome, A. C. BENSON, DIARIST

5 'I am not your fader but your moder,' quoth he. 'Your father was a rich merchant in Stamboul.'
Ezra Pound, CANTOS 1925

6 . . . the woman whom a mistake on the part of nature had enshrined in the body of M de Charlus.
Marcel Proust, REMEMBRANCE OF THINGS PAST, *Cities of the Plain* 1921–2

7 The middle age of buggers is not to be contemplated without horror.
Virginia Woolf

HONESTY

8 I will have no locked cupboards in my life.
Gertrude Bell. Quoted Janet E. Courtney, AN OXFORD PORTRAIT GALLERY

9 Honesty is incompatible with amassing a large fortune.
Mahatma Gandhi, NON-VIOLENCE IN PEACE AND WAR 1948

10 I am afraid we must make the world honest before we can honestly say to our children that honesty is the best policy.
George Bernard Shaw, BBC Radio 11 *Jul* 1932

HONEYMOON

11 Honeymoons do not seldom end worse than they began and to recover from them may take quite a long time.
Arnold Bennett, HOW TO MAKE THE BEST OF LIFE

12 You mustn't be blase about honeymoons just because this is your second.
Noël Coward, PRIVATE LIVES 1930

13 Here we are on the first night of our honeymoon, with the moon coming up and the music playing, and all you can do is talk about my first husband. It's downright sacrilegious.
Ibid.

14 Honeymooning is a very overrated occupation.
Ibid.

15 The honeymoon wasn't such a ghastly experience really; it was afterwards that was so awful.
Ibid.

HONOURS

16 Literature is always a good card to play for Honours. It makes people think that Cabinet Ministers are educated.
Arnold Bennett, THE TITLE 1918

17 Why should I accept the Garter from His Majesty when his people have just given me the boot?
Winston Churchill after losing the 1945 *election*

18 Members rise from CMG (known sometimes in Whitehall as Call Me God) to KCMG (Kindly Call Me God) to GCMG (God calls me God.)
Anthony Sampson, ANATOMY OF BRITAIN 1962

19 M. Ravel refuses the Legion of Honour, but all his music accepts it.
Erik Satie. Quoted Nat Shapiro, ENCYCLOPEDIA OF QUOTATIONS ABOUT MUSIC

20 Titles distinguish the mediocre, embarrass the superior and are disgraced by the inferior.
George Bernard Shaw, MAN AND SUPERMAN 1905

21 I have been offered titles, but I think they get one into bad company.
George Bernard Shaw, at 90, *on becoming a freeman of Dublin, News Review* 5 *Sep* 1946

1 What harm did I ever do the Labour party?
   R. H. Tawney on being offered a peerage by
   Ramsay MacDonald.

2 How justly we can refer to the Tories as the
   party of dreadful knights.
   Jeremy Thorpe, Liberal assembly 1963

HOPE

3 Hope is a risk that must be run.
   Georges Bernanos, LAST ESSAYS 1955

4 There is some comfort in the thought that in
   the universe we are not alone, but surrounded by our elders and betters.
   Arthur Koestler, BRICKS TO BABEL,
   Epilogue 1983

5 There are no hopeless situations; there are
   only men who have grown hopeless about
   them.
   Clare Boothe Luce, EUROPE IN THE SPRING

6 To face life without hope can mean to live
   without despair.
   Terence Rattigan, THE DEEP BLUE SEA 1952

7 He who has never hoped can never despair.
   George Bernard Shaw, CAESAR AND
   CLEOPATRA 1906

HORSE

8 Did you know horses lead to divorces?
   You've no idea how sexually promiscuous
   they are in the shires. It's all that jumping up
   and down on horses that does it. They get
   over-stimulated.
   Lord Arran, Sunday Times 15 Jan 1967

9 I saw him riding in the Row, clinging to his
   horse like a string of onions.
   Margot Asquith of Lord Hugh Cecil,
   AUTOBIOGRAPHY 1936

10 It's awfully bad luck on Diana / Her ponies
   have swallowed their bits; / She fished down
   their throats with a spanner / And frightened them all into fits.
   Sir John Betjeman

11 *J. M. Astbury K.C.*: Mr Bottomley, why did
   you tell me that you never kept racehorses?

Horatio Bottomley: I gave you a correct
answer. I never kept racehorses. They kept
me.
Horatio Bottomley at his examination for
bankruptcy. Quoted Alan Hyman, THE RISE
AND FALL OF HORATIO BOTTOMLEY

12 I say to parents, especially wealthy parents,
   'Don't give your son money. As far as you
   can afford it, give him horses.'
   Winston Churchill, MY EARLY LIFE 1930

13 A horse is dangerous at both ends and
   uncomfortable in the middle.
   Ian Fleming. Quoted Sunday Times 9 Oct
   1966

14 The horse, the horse! The symbol of surging
   potency and power of movement, of action,
   in man.
   D. H. Lawrence, APOCALYPSE 1931

15 You may have my husband but not my
   horse . . . I'll preserve one last male thing in
   the museum of this world if I can.
   D. H. Lawrence, KANGAROO 1923

16 There are no handles to a horse.
   Stephen Leacock, LITERARY LAPSES 1910

17 It takes a good deal of physical courage to
   ride a horse. This, however, I have. I get it at
   about forty cents a flask and take it as
   required.
   Ibid.

18 He flung himself on his horse and rode off
   madly in all directions.
   Stephen Leacock, NONSENSE NOVELS 1911

19 The outside of a horse is good for the inside
   of a man.
   Lt. Col. Harry Llewellyn, Sunday Express
   25 Jun 1956

20 I'd horsewhip you — if I had a horse.
   Groucho Marx, ANIMAL CRACKERS

21 Nobody has any right to go around looking
   like a horse and behaving as if it was all right.
   You don't catch horses going around
   looking like people, do you?
   Dorothy Parker, HORSIE

22 You'll have to hope that all the horses don't
   pee at the same time.
   Philip, Duke of Edinburgh, commenting on
   the shortage of drains for the Moscow
   Equestrian Olympics 7 Mar 1979

1 I don't even like *old* cars . . . I'd rather have a goddam horse. A horse is at least *human*, for God's sake.
J. D. Salinger, THE CATCHER IN THE RYE 1951

2 Horseback Hall, consisting of a prison for horses with an annexe for the ladies and gentlemen who rode them, hunted them, talked about them, bought them and sold them, and gave nine tenths of their lives to them.
George Bernard Shaw, HEARTBREAK HOUSE, *Preface* 1920

3 There are only two classes in good society in England, the equestrian classes and the neurotic classes.
Ibid.

4 Go anywhere in England where there are natural, wholesome, contented and really nice English people, and what do you always find? That the stables are the real centre of the household.
Ibid.

5 The men of the Golden Horde were almost as kind to children as to horses — though naturally they regarded them with less reverence.
Sir Osbert Sitwell, THE SCARLET TREE 1945

6 We attended stables, as we attended church, in our best clothes, thereby no doubt showing the degree of respect due to horses, as to the deity.
Ibid

HORSE RACING

7 How amusing racing would be if it were not for the horses. They take people's minds off conversation.
Viscount Castlerosse, Sunday Express, Londoner's Log

8 I'm getting to be so big on the turf they are calling me the Aga Cohen.
Bud Flanagan. Quoted in his obituary, Daily Express 21 *Oct* 1968

9 My horse was in the lead, coming down the home stretch, but the caddie fell off.
Sam Goldwyn. Quoted Alva Johnson, THE GREAT GOLDWYN

10 I have no intention of watching undersized Englishmen perched on horses with matchstick legs race along courses planned to amuse Nell Gwynne.
Gilbert Harding. Quoted Wynford Vaughan Thomas, GILBERT HARDING BY HIS FRIENDS

11 The 17th Earl of Derby cherished his racehorses no less than his guests. When one promising animal fell ill it was put on a daily diet of a bottle each of port and brandy, and three dozen eggs.
Kenneth Rose, KINGS, QUEENS AND COURTIERS 1985

12 I was a passenger on a very good horse. It was an easy ride.
Walter Swinburn to reporters, on winning the Derby on Shergar 3 *Jun* 1981

HORSE-RIDING

13 That the world is out of balance and lop-sided we know without being reminded of it by the side-saddle.
Lord Brabazon of Tara. Quoted News Review 19 *Jun* 1947

HOSPITAL

14 One of the most difficult things to contend with in a hospital is the assumption on the part of the staff that because you have lost your gall bladder you have also lost your mind.
Jean Kerr, PLEASE DON'T EAT THE DAISIES

15 To be ill, or to undergo an operation is to be initiated into the mystery of nursing and to learn the comforts and discomforts of an invalid's life; the unearthly fragrance of tea at daybreak; the disappointment of rice-pudding when you thought it was going to be orange jelly; and the behaviour of every constituent part of the bedclothes.
Stephen Paget, CONFESSIO MEDICI

HOSPITALITY

16 To mankind in general Macbeth and Lady Macbeth stand out as the supreme type of all that a host and hostess should not be.
Max Beerbohm

1 Hospitality is a wonderful thing. If people really want you they'll have you even if the cook has just died in the house with smallpox.
F. Scott Fitzgerald, NOTEBOOKS

2 Only ask those people to stay with you or to dine with you, who can ask you in return.
W. Somerset Maugham, A WRITER'S NOTEBOOK 1949

3 There's a sort of person who rushes out of his house to shake hands with you in order not to have to take you inside.
Frederick Raphael. Quoted Janet Watts, Observer 15 *Jul* 1979

HOST

4 Nor was he insincere in saying 'Make my house your inn.' Inns are not residences.
Marianne Moore, BLACK EARTH

HOTEL

5 Airport hotels are so alike that the only way you can make sure of where you are is by looking at the book of matches in the ashtray beside your bed.
William Hardcastle, Punch

6 A whiskered cove who looked like a bandit, as no doubt he was, being the proprietor of the hotel.
P. G. Wodehouse, AUNT AGATHA TAKES THE COUNT

HOUSEWORK

7 I would rather lie on a sofa than sweep beneath it.
Shirley Conran, SUPERWOMAN 1975

8 (1) Only iron some things, (2) Only iron the front of things, (3) Don't iron things while you are wearing them.
Jim Douglas, HOW TO LIVE WITH A WORKING WIFE 1983

HOWARD HUGHES

9 It is a tragedy that Hughes had to die to prove that he was alive.
Walter Kane. Quoted Barbara Rowe, A BOOK OF QUOTES

10 The hygiene-conscious multi-millionaire recluse used to be awoken by a servant pinching a toe through eight thicknesses of paper hanky, increasing the pressure each time until Morpheus was banished. Interesting, but my grandfather preferred whisky dripped from a feather.
Peterborough, Daily Telegraph 24 *Feb* 1985

HUMAN BEING

11 Not philosophers but fret-sawyers and stamp collectors compose the backbone of society.
Aldous Huxley, BRAVE NEW WORLD 1932

12 He is a human being and terrible things are happening to him. So attention must be paid.
Arthur Miller, DEATH OF A SALESMAN 1945

13 A human being is an ingenious assembly of portable plumbing.
Robert Morley, HUMAN BEING

14 We are Borrowers — like you're a — a Human Bean, or whatever it's called.
Mary Norton, THE BORROWERS

15 Human beings are the only animals of which I am thoroughly and cravenly afraid.
George Bernard Shaw

HUMANISM

16 If you can't believe in God, Humanism is the next best thing.
Lord Longford, DIARY OF A YEAR

HUMANITY

17 The human race, to which so many of my readers belong.
G. K. Chesterton, THE NAPOLEON OF NOTTING HILL 1904

18 People are only human, but it really doesn't seem much for them to be.
Ivy Compton-Burnett, A FAMILY AND A FORTUNE 1939

19 It is an unproved assumption that the domination of this planet by our own species is a desirable thing, which must give satisfaction to its creator.
W. R. Inge (Dean of St Pauls), OUTSPOKEN ESSAYS 1919

1 It is not the belief in God, but the belief in
man that has been shattered; and it is amid
the ruins not of Christianity, but of humani-
tarianism, that we English live today.
Douglas Jerrold, GEORGIAN
ADVENTURE 1938

2 There are one hundred and ninety-three
living species of monkeys and apes. One
hundred and ninety-two of them are covered
in hair. The exception is the naked ape
self-named *homo sapiens.*
Desmond Morris, THE NAKED APE

3 Fortunate are those who find some good
cause in which they can act as a man for
other men. Their own humanity will be
enriched.
Albert Schweitzer, THE TEACHING OF
REVERENCE FOR LIFE

4 I can think of no more stirring symbol of
man's humanity to man than a fire engine.
Kurt Vonnegut, THE SIRENS OF TITAN 1959

HUMBUG

5 He was a man after my own heart — the
greatest humbug I have ever known.
*Horatio Bottomley to Arnold Bennett, of Dr
Parker of City Temple*

HUMILIATION

6 Lyndon Johnson humiliated his underlings
by dictating letters while he sat on the
lavatory.
Robert A Caro, THE PATH TO POWER 1983

7 The one thing to do is to do nothing.
Wait . . . You will find that you survive
humiliation and that's an experience of
incalculable value.
T. S. Eliot, THE COCKTAIL PARTY 1949

HUMILITY

8 It is difficult to be humble. Even if you aim
at humility there is no guarantee that when
you have attained the state you will not be
proud of the feat.
Bonamy Dobrée, JOHN WESLEY 1933

9 The only wisdom we can hope to acquire / Is
the wisdom of humility, humility is endless.
T. S. Eliot, FOUR QUARTETS, *East
Coker* 1940

10 Humility is the most difficult of all virtues to
achieve, nothing dies harder than the desire
to think well of oneself.
T. S. Eliot, SHAKESPEARE AND THE
STOICISM OF SENECA

11 The virtue of pride, which was once the
beauty of mankind, has given place to that
fount of all ugliness, Christian humility.
Max Ernst. Quoted John Russell, MAX
ERNST, HIS LIFE AND WORK

12 Turning the other cheek is a kind of moral
ju-jitsu.
Gerald Stanley Lee, CROWDS

13 Archbishop Ullathorne, lecturing on humility, was asked by a student, 'Your Grace,
what is the best book on humility?' He
replied, 'There is only one. I wrote it
myself.'
Lord Longford, HUMILITY

14 Christian humility is preached by the clergy,
but practised only by the lower classes.
Bertrand Russell, AUTOBIOGRAPHY 1967

15 To expect us to feel humble in the presence
of astronomical dimensions merely because
they are big is a sort of cosmic snobbery.
What is significant is mind.
Lord Samuel, BELIEF AND ACTION

16 The Church must learn humility, as well as
teach it.
George Bernard Shaw, ST JOAN,
Preface 1923

17 I detest the humility I should have, and am
angry when I am humble. I appreciate the
social arrogance I have in the face of my
humility.
Dylan Thomas. Quoted Andrew Sinclair,
DYLAN THOMAS, POET OF HIS PEOPLE

18 In the intellectual order, the virtue of
humility is nothing more nor less than the
power of attention.
Simone Weil, GRAVITY AND GRACE 1947

19 The rest of us are like the small boy at my
son's school who was had up before the head
for being a cocky little beast and urged to
adopt humility. So he did, for a bit; then he
lapsed into his old self. 'So how about the
humility then?' asked the Head. 'I *was*
humble for a fortnight' he said, 'but nobody
noticed.'
Katherine Whitehorn, VIEW FROM A
COLUMN 1981

HUMOUR

1 I have a fine sense of the ridiculous but no sense of humour.
Edward Albee, WHO'S AFRAID OF VIRGINIA WOOLF 1962

2 Though the English pride themselves on their sense of humour, they distrust humorous men.
Lord Annan, Observer 2 *Nov* 1980

3 When Nehru invaded Goa I called him a Goa Constrictor! Wasn't that funny? I find all my jokes funny. They're so good. But I only expect one out of six to go down well.
Earl of Arran, Sunday Times 15 *Jan* 1967

4 The marvellous thing about a joke with a double meaning is that it can only mean one thing.
Ronnie Barker, SAUCE

5 Humour undiluted is the most depressing of all phenomena. Humour must have its background of seriousness. Without this contrast there comes none of that incongruity which is the mainspring of laughter.
Max Beerbohm, AROUND THEATRES

6 It is a good deed to forget a poor joke.
Brendan Bracken. Quoted Observer 17 *Oct* 1943

7 To appreciate nonsense requires a serious interest in life.
Gelert Burgess, THE ROMANCE OF THE COMMONPLACE 1916

8 Humorists are not happy men. Like Beachcomber and Saki and Thurber, they burn while Rome fiddles.
Cyril Connolly, ENEMIES OF PROMISE 1938

9 A joke isn't a joke until someone laughs.
Michael Crawford to Alex Coleman in an interview, TV Times 29 *Mar* 1979

10 When you say a friend has a sense of humour do you mean that he makes you laugh, or that he can make you laugh?
Max Frisch, SKETCHBOOK 1966–1971

11 In considering economic behaviour, humour is especially important for, needless to say, much of that behaviour is infinitely ridiculous.
J. K. Galbraith, ECONOMICS, PEACE AND LAUGHTER

12 The essence of humour is surprise; that is why you laugh when you see a joke in *Punch*.
A. P. Herbert. Speech Foyles Literary Lunch, Dec 1948

13 I have never understood why it should be considered derogatory to the Creator to suppose that He has a sense of humour.
W. R. Inge (Dean of St Pauls)

14 It has been discovered experimentally that you can draw laughter from an audience anywhere in the world, of any class or race, simply by walking on to a stage and uttering the words 'I am a married man'.
Ted Kavanagh, News Review 10 *Jul* 1947

15 Fun is fun but no girl wants to laugh all of the time.
Anita Loos, GENTLEMEN PREFER BLONDES 1925

16 One matter Englishmen don't think in the least funny is their happy consciousness of possessing a deep sense of humour.
Marshall McLuhan, THE MECHANICAL BRIDE 1951

17 Impropriety is the soul of wit.
W. Somerset Maugham, THE MOON AND SIXPENCE 1919

18 English humour resembles the Loch Ness Monster in that both are famous but there is a strong suspicion that neither exists.
George Mikes, ENGLISH HUMOUR FOR BEGINNERS 1981

19 Humour must be a by-product of either profound or vivid interest in persons and events, however much this interest be clothed in levity. The impression is made that Miss Macaulay is amused by, but not deeply interested in, people.
New Statesman. Reviewing Rose Macaulay's THEY WERE DEFEATED

20 Instead of doing 'I say, I say, my mother-in-law' you could do 'I say, I say, Harold Macmillan' and it could be the same joke — and very often *was* the same joke.
Bill Oddie, of BBC TV's That Was The Week That Was. Quoted FROM FRINGE TO FLYING CIRCUS 1980

1 There is no more dangerous literary symptom than a temptation to write a book about wit and humour. It indicates the total loss of both.
George Bernard Shaw. Quoted Neville Hildii̇ch, IN PRAISE OF HUMOUR

2 Mark Twain and I are very much in the same position. We have to put things in such a way as to make people, who would otherwise hang us, believe that we are joking.
George Bernard Shaw. Quoted Justin Wintle and Richard Kenin, DICTIONARY OF BIOGRAPHICAL QUOTATIONS

3 There has never been a book on humour written by a funny man. George Meredith's essay on comedy was so dreary I don't think anybody but the proof reader ever got through it all.
Arthur Sheekman, script-writer to the Marx Brothers

4 If a person desires to be a humorist it is necessary that the people around him shall be at least as wise as he is, otherwise his humour will not be comprehended.
James Stephens, THE DEMI-GODS 1914

5 Humour is a serious thing. I like to think of it as one of our greatest and earliest national resources which must be preserved at all costs.
James Thurber, CBS television 4 Mar 1956

6 Humour is emotional chaos remembered in tranquillity.
James Thurber, New York Post 29 Feb 1960

7 The difficulty with humorists is that they will mix what they believe with what they don't; whichever seems likelier to win an effect.
John Updike, RABBIT, RUN 1960

HUNGER

8 A man with money to pay for a meal can talk about hunger without demeaning himself. But for a man with no money hunger is a disgrace.
Vicki Baum, MARTIN'S SUMMER

9 Nobody wants to kiss when they are hungry.
Dorothy Dix. Quoted Burton Stevenson, BOOK OF QUOTATIONS

10 An empty stomach is not a good political adviser.
Albert Einstein, COSMIC RELIGION

11 A hungry man is not a free man.
Adlai Stevenson. Speech 6 Sep 1952

12 No one can worship God or love his neighbour on an empty stomach.
Woodrow Wilson. Speech 23 May 1912

13 We sprang at the black pudding like wolves at a Russian peasant.
P. G. Wodehouse, PERFORMING FLEA 1953

HUNTING

14 Without foxes there would be no fox-hunting and without fox-hunting many would find it impossible to live through an English winter.
Anon. Horse and Hound

15 Hi! Handsome hunting man / Fire your little gun. / Bang! / Now the animal / Is dead and dumb and done / Nevermore to peep again, creep again, leap again / Eat or sleep or drink again, oh what fun.
Walter De La Mare, THE HUNTSMAN

16 I am alarmed to learn from your leading article today that the Duke of Beaufort rides in a car bearing the registration number MFH 1. At these works we travel in FOX 1. May I be assured that, should we happen to meet his Grace on the road, no unseemly incident will occur?
H. P. Forder. Samuel Fox & Co. Ltd., letter to The Times

17 If there is one word in the English language I hate, it is 'game'. It seems to imply that other creatures are about for our sport.
William Holden. Quoted Robert Ottaway, TV Times 24 Aug 1972

18 I have known a fox that was absolutely devoted to fox hunting . . . after we had hunted him many seasons I regret to say we killed him.
Col. Sir Lancelot Rolleston DSO, Daily Mail. Quoted Michael Bateman, THIS ENGLAND

19 If foxes, like women, had a vote I think they would vote unanimously for the keeping up of fox hunting.
Ibid.

1 It isn't mere convention. Everyone can see that the people who hunt are the right people and the people who don't are the wrong ones.
George Bernard Shaw, HEARTBREAK HOUSE 1920

2 The gentleman must realise that once he is in the saddle he must be as rude as possible to anyone who crosses his path.
Douglas Sutherland, THE ENGLISH GENTLEMAN 1978

HUSBAND

3 I never married because there was no need. I have three pets at home which answer the same purpose as a husband. I have a dog which growls every morning, a parrot which swears all the afternoon and a cat that comes home late at night.
Marie Corelli. Quoted James Crichton-Browne, WHAT THE DOCTOR THOUGHT

4 It is ridiculous to think you can spend your entire life with one person. Three is about the right number. Yes, I imagine three husbands would do it.
Claire Booth Luce, Observer, Sayings of the Week 10 Jul 1981

5 A husband is a man who two minutes after his head / Touches the pillow is snoring like an overloaded / Omnibus.
Ogden Nash, MARRIAGE LINES

6 A husband is what is left of the lover after the nerve has been extracted.
Helen Rowland, A GUIDE TO MEN

7 A man ought to be able to be fond of his wife without making a fool of himself about her.
George Bernard Shaw, CANDIDA 1903

8 Chumps always make the best husbands. When you marry, Sally, grab a chump. Tap his head first, and if it rings solid, don't hesitate.
P. G. Wodehouse, ADVENTURES OF SALLY 1920

HYGIENE

9 Clean-shaven, with that mien of scrupulously shampooed and almost medical cleanliness and freshness which is so typical of the hygienic American.
Harold Begby, describing Frank Buchman in LIFE CHANGERS

10 Sybil: I feel smirched and unclean, as if slimy things have been crawling all over me.
Edgar: Maybe they have. That's a very old sofa.
Noël Coward, PRIVATE LIVES 1930

11 I've never had a great many baths and . . . it does not make a great difference to health . . . As for appearance, most of that is underneath and nobody sees it.
Hugh Gaitskell, Minister for Fuel and Power, speaking at an economy drive in 1947, which drew from Winston Churchill in the Commons — When a Minister advocates the policy of fewer baths, is it surprising that the Government gets into increasingly bad odour?

12 Henry IV's feet and armpits enjoyed an international reputation.
Aldous Huxley, THE DEVILS OF LOUDUN 1952

13 With many people, women especially, bacilli have taken the place of spirits. Microbes for them are the personification of evil. They live in terror of germs.
Aldous Huxley, PROPER STUDIES, *The Substitute for Religion* 1927

14 'I see an article where it says mice cause fevers' says somebody else. 'Don't be silly', says Monk. 'They don't get near enough to you to breathe on you or anything.'
Gerald Kersh, CLEAN, BRIGHT AND SLIGHTLY OILED 1946

15 How is it we wash our faces with hot water and our teeth with cold water?
Miles Kington, The Times, Great Mysteries of Our Time 9 Aug 1983

16 Of nothing are you allowed to get the real odour or savour. Everything is sterilized and wrapped in cellophane. The only odour which is recognised and admitted as an odour is halitosis and of this all Americans live in mortal dread.
Henry Miller, THE AIR-CONDITIONED NIGHTMARE 1942

17 On the day there was a full chamber pot under the breakfast table I decided to leave.
George Orwell, THE ROAD TO WIGAN PIER 1937

18 Epstein is a great sculptor. I wish he would wash, but I understand Michelangelo *never* did, so I suppose it is part of the tradition.
Ezra Pound. Quoted Charles Norman, EZRA POUND

1 There were never more bathrooms in England than there are today and never so many dirty necks and fingernails. Countless (girls) should be sent to bed supperless.
Evelyn Waugh, Daily Mail 1961

2 If men cannot live on bread alone, still less can they do so on disinfectant.
A. N. Whitehead. Quoted Peter Viereck, THE UNADJUSTED MAN

HYPOCHONDRIA

3 The man who wants to subject himself to regular examination is the equivalent of the fussy owner-driver, who wants to take excessive care of his car and is perpetually taking the engine down to discover the origin of some supposed abnormality or even to reassure himself all is well.
Dr Adolphe Abrahams, THE HUMAN MACHINE, *lecture to Guild of Public Pharmacists* 22 *Jan* 1930

4 None of my patients are hypochondriacs but you should see some of the owners.
Anonymous veterinary surgeon, Saturday Evening Post, I've Never Lost an Owner 10 *Jul* 1948

5 — and he *baffled* the surgeons. They had Mr Venables look at him — he's one of the top people — he looked at Ulford's stomach and he said 'Well, it could go either way' — Frankly, I think it's *nerves*.
Alan Bennett. Quoted Roger Wilmut, FROM FRINGE TO FLYING CIRCUS 1981

6 She says her blood is nothing but rose-water.
Ronald Firbank, VALMOUTH 1918

7 Everyone has a body and many, revelling in its disorders, really enjoy bad health. There are those who divide their lives into two parts – 'before my operation' and 'since my operation'.
Lord Hill of Luton (The Radio Doctor), BOTH SIDES OF THE HILL

8 All interest in disease and death is only another expression of interest in life.
Thomas Mann, THE MAGIC MOUNTAIN 1934

9 Some people can act as Boswell to their own bowels.
Dr Jonathan Miller, THE BODY IN QUESTION

10 The desire to take medicine is perhaps the greatest feature which distinguishes man from animals.
Sir William Osler, SCIENCE AND IMMORTALITY

11 Neurotic subjects are perhaps less addicted than any, despite the time-honoured phrase, to 'listen to their insides'. They can hear so many things going on inside themselves by which they realise later that they did wrong to let themselves be alarmed, that they end by paying no attention to any of them.
Marcel Proust, REMEMBRANCE OF THINGS PAST 1913–1927

12 He complained about his ribs and told him [the doctor] that they seemed to be giving him claustrophobia.
N. F. Simpson, THE HOLE

HYPOCRISY

13 No man is a hypocrite in his pleasures.
Albert Camus, THE FALL 1956

14 We ought to see far enough into a hypocrite to see even his sincerity.
G. K. Chesterton, HERETICS 1905

15 Other nations may sneer at the hypocritical English but only we can carry it off in the grand manner.
Daily Sketch. Quoted Michael Bateman, THIS ENGLAND

16 There is always a type of man who says he loves his fellow men and expects to make a living at it.
Edgar Watson Howe, VENTURES IN COMMON SENSE

17 The most grave and awful denunciations of obscenity in literature are to be found precisely in those periodicals whose directors are most notoriously alcoholic.
Aldous Huxley, BARREN LEAVES 1925

18 Hypocrisy is the most difficult and nerve-racking vice that a man can pursue; it needs an increasing vigilance and a rare detachment of spirit. It cannot, like adultery or gluttony, be practised at spare moments; it is a whole-time job.
W. Somerset Maugham, CAKES AND ALE 1930

1 Hypocrisy is the homage paid by vice to virtue. It is the conscious assumption of virtue by the unvirtuous.
Gustav Renier, THE ENGLISH – ARE THEY HUMAN?

2 If there is one thing hypocrites hate, it's hypocrisy.
Jack Rosenthal, DEAR ANYONE *(radio play)*

3 Our morality is an impudent hypocrisy.
George Bernard Shaw, MAJOR BARBARA, *Preface* 1905

4 In my day there were things that were done, and things that were not done, and there was even a way of doing things that were not done.
Peter Ustinov, PHOTO-FINISH

HYSTERIA

5 Hysteria, a snake whose scales are tiny mirrors in which the dead world takes on a semblance of life.
Nathanael West, MISS LONELY HEARTS 1933

I

IDEA

1 Man is ready to die for an idea, provided that idea is not quite clear to him.
Paul Eldridge, HORNS OF GLASS

2 At first it is difficult to recognise an idea as original. Nearly any notion, whether old, banal, spurious, novel or brilliant may pop up with a flutter of excitement. How is one to distinguish? Notice, after three days, whether it still quivers.
Kenneth Fisher, THE GURU THERAPIST'S NOTEBOOK

3 Very simple ideas lie within the reach only of complex minds.
Rémy de Gourmont. Quoted Evan Esar, TREASURY OF HUMOROUS QUOTATIONS

4 Men die but an idea does not.
Alan Jay Lerner, THE STREET WHERE I LIVE 1978

5 A man must let his ideas grow, not be continually rooting them up to see how they are getting on.
William McFee, HARBOURS OF MEMORY 1921

6 An idea isn't responsible for the people who believe in it.
Don Marquis, ARCHY DOES HIS PART 1935

7 Men who have thought much have often more to tell than men who have done much.
Allan Massie, The Times 8 Aug 1985

8 A powerful idea communicates some of its strength to him who challenges it.
Marcel Proust, REMEMBRANCE OF THINGS PAST 1913–1927

9 This creature man, who in his own selfish affairs is a coward to the backbone, will fight for an idea like a hero.
George Bernard Shaw, MAN AND SUPERMAN 1905

10 Ideas that enter the mind under fire remain there securely and for ever.
Leon Trotsky, MY LIFE 1930

11 He had ideas about everything. He could no more help having ideas about everything than a dog can resist smelling at your heels.
H. G. Wells, MR BRITLING SEES IT THROUGH 1916

12 Ideas won't keep. Something must be done about them. When the idea is new its custodians have fervour, live for it, and, if need be, die for it.
A. N. Whitehead, DIALOGUES 1953

13 Whenever I hear, as I sometimes do, one of my colleagues say that there are no ideas which cannot be expressed clearly in simple language, I think 'Then your ideas must be very superficial.'
Ibid.

14 I pressed down the mental accelerator. The old lemon throbbed fiercely. I got an idea.
P. G. Wodehouse, JEEVES TAKES CHARGE

IDEALISM

15 Idealism may be defined as well as in any other way, by calling it that spirit which impels an individual or group of individuals to a loftier standard of conduct than that which ordinarily prevails around him or them.
Lord Birkenhead, Rectorial address, Glasgow University, on Idealism in International Politics

16 Positive ideals are becoming a curse, for they can seldom be achieved without someone being killed or maimed or interned.
E. M. Forster, TWO CHEERS FOR DEMOCRACY 1941

1 Idealism is the noble toga that political
gentlemen drape over their will to power.
Aldous Huxley, New York Herald Tribune
25 *Nov* 1963

2 A man has no right to live until he has found
something to die for.
Martin Luther King. Quoted BBC Radio 4
26 *Jul* 1981

3 Away with all ideals. Let each individual act
spontaneously from the for ever incalculable prompting of the creative well-head
from within him. There is no universal law.
D. H. Lawrence, PHOENIX 1936

4 'Dying for an idea' sounds well enough, but
why not let the idea die instead of you?
(Percy) Wyndham Lewis, THE ART OF BEING
RULED 1926

5 Few people are so terrible as frustrated
idealists, who begin to despise or hate
ordinary human nature because it insists
upon behaving like ordinary human nature.
J. B. Priestley, OUTCRIES AND ASIDES

6 Idealism, even subjective idealism, did not
prevent great philosophers from still having
hearty appetites or from presenting themselves with untiring perseverance for election to the Academy.
Marcel Proust, REMEMBRANCE OF THINGS
PAST 1913–1927

7 I am an idealist. I don't know where I'm
going, but I'm on my way.
Carl Sandburg. Quoted Laurence J. Peter,
PETER'S QUOTATIONS

IDLENESS

8 Idleness, that is the curse of other men, is
the muse of poets.
D'Arcy Cresswell, THE POET'S PROGRESS

9 You can tell a British workman by his hands.
They are always in his pockets.
Graffito reported on BBC Radio 4, *Quote
Unquote* 26 *Jun* 1980

IDOLATRY

10 He who slays a king and he who dies for him
are alike idolaters.
George Bernard Shaw, MAN AND
SUPERMAN 1905

11 The savage bows down to idols of wood and
stone; the civilised man to idols of flesh and
blood.
Ibid.

IGNORANCE

12 'Tis ignorance makes the child sublime.
George Barlow, POETRY AND SCIENCE

13 The full area of ignorance is not yet mapped.
We are at present only exploring its fringes.
J. D. Bernal, THE PERPETUAL PESSIMIST

14 *Ignoramus, n.* A person unacquainted with
certain kinds of knowledge familiar to
yourself, and having certain other kinds that
you know nothing about.
Ambrose Bierce, THE DEVIL'S
DICTIONARY 1906

15 The evil that is in the world almost always
comes of ignorance, and good intentions
may do as much harm as malevolence if they
lack understanding.
Albert Camus, THE PLAGUE 1947

16 The most incorrigible vice being that of an
ignorance which fancies it knows everything.
Ibid.

17 It is the tragedy of the world that no one
knows what he doesn't know – and the less a
man knows, the more sure he is that he
knows everything.
Joyce Cary, ART AND REALITY

18 all ignorance toboggans into know / and
trudges up to ignorance again.
e. e. cummings, ONE TIMES ONE 1944

19 The pleasures of ignorance are as great, in
their way, as the pleasures of knowledge.
Aldous Huxley, COLLECTED ESSAYS 1960

20 The greater our knowledge increases the
more our ignorance unfolds.
John F. Kennedy. Address, Rice University
12 *Sep* 1962

21 It is surprising how few of one's friends are
really sure where Carinthia is.
Philip Lewis, THE LADY, *Summer in
Carinthia* 24 *Jun* 1953

1 In expanding the field of knowledge we but increase the horizon of ignorance.
Henry Miller, THE WISDOM OF THE HEART 1941

2 His ignorance was an Empire State Building of ignorance. You had to admire it for its size.
Dorothy Parker, of Harold Ross

3 Our knowledge can only be finite while our ignorance must necessarily be infinite.
Sir Karl Popper, CONJECTURES AND REFUTATIONS

4 Everybody is ignorant, only on different subjects.
Will Rogers, AUTOBIOGRAPHY 1949

5 Somebody else's ignorance is bliss.
Jack Vance, STAR KING

6 Ignorance is not bliss — it is oblivion.
Philip Wylie, GENERATION OF VIPERS 1942

ILLEGITIMACY

7 There are no illegitimate children – only illegitimate parents.
Judge Leon R. Yankwich, decisions in Californian court, Jun 1978

ILLNESS

8 'Ye can call it influenza if ye like,' said Mrs Machin 'there was no illness in my young days. We called a cold a cold.'
Arnold Bennett, THE CARD 1911

9 My father invented a cure for which there was no disease and unfortunately my mother caught it and died of it.
Victor Borge, IN CONCERT

10 Ill health from early youth brings advantages in its train; it disciplines the human spirit and economises its resources.
Lord Curzon. Quoted Edward Marjoribanks, LIFE OF LORD CURZON

11 Men make use of their illnesses at least as much as they are made use of by them.
Aldous Huxley, COLLECTED ESSAYS 1960

12 Illness is not something a person *has*; it's another way of *being*.
Dr Jonathan Miller, THE BODY IN QUESTION

13 Illness can be an insult and a degradation. Pain can reduce a man to the level of an animal creeping into a corner.
Patrick O'Donovan, A JOURNALIST'S ODYSSEY 1985

14 I have Bright's disease and he has mine.
S. J. Perelman. Quoted Bennet Cerf, SHAKE WELL BEFORE USING 1948

15 Illness is the doctor to whom we pay most heed; to kindness, to knowledge, we make promise only; pain we obey.
Marcel Proust, REMEMBRANCE OF THINGS PAST 1913 1927

16 When you were ill you behaved like a true philosopher; every time that you came to yourself you made a joke.
Bertrand Russell, quoting his doctor, AUTOBIOGRAPHY 1967

17 I enjoy convalescence. It is the part that makes illness worth while.
George Bernard Shaw, BACK TO METHUSELAH 1922

ILLUSION

18 Every age is fed on illusions, lest men should renounce life early and the human race come to an end.
Joseph Conrad, VICTORY 1915

19 It is characteristic of the illusion that it derives from men's wishes . . . It need not necessarily be false, that is to say, unrealisable or incompatible with reality.
Sigmund Freud, THE FUTURE OF AN ILLUSION 1928

20 An illusion is not the same as an error . . . Aristotle's belief that vermin are evolved out of dung was an error . . . it was an illusion on the part of Columbus that he had discovered a new sea route to India.
Ibid.

21 If only we can give them faith that mountains can be moved they will accept the illusion that mountains are moveable, and thus an illusion may become a reality.
Benito Mussolini. Quoted Denis Mack Smith, MUSSOLINI

IMAGINATION

1 To treat your facts with imagination is one thing, to imagine your facts is another.
John Burroughs, THE HEART OF BURROUGHS' JOURNALS

2 The most imaginative people are the most credulous, for to them everything is possible.
Alexander Chase, PERSPECTIVES 1966

3 Only in men's imagination does every truth find an effective and undeniable existence. Imagination, not invention, is the supreme master of art as of life.
Joseph Conrad, SOME REMINISCENCES 1912

4 Imagination is more important than knowledge.
Albert Einstein, ON SCIENCE

5 There is no better way of exercising the imagination than studying law.
Jean Giraudoux, TIGER AT THE GATES 1935

6 [Man] does not see the real world. The real world is hidden from him by the wall of imagination.
George Gurdjieff. Quoted P. D. Ouspensky, IN SEARCH OF THE MIRACULOUS

7 Imagination grows by exercise and contrary to common belief is more powerful in the mature than in the young.
W. Somerset Maugham, THE SUMMING UP 1938

8 A rock pile ceases to be a rock pile the moment a single man contemplates it, bearing within him the image of a cathedral.
Antoine de Saint-Exupéry, FLIGHT TO ARRAS 1942

9 It is the spirit of the age to believe that any fact, however suspect, is superior to any imaginative exercise, no matter how true.
Gore Vidal, Encounter, Dec 1967

10 Imagination and fiction make up more than three quarters of our real life.
Simone Weil, GRAVITY AND GROUSE 1947

IMITATION

11 What gives the artist real prestige is his imitators.
Igor Stravinsky, London Magazine, Mar 1967

IMMIGRANT

12 The immigrant, no matter how illiterate or ignorant he may be, always learns too soon.
Henry Frick (partner of Andrew Carnegie). Quoted Alistair Cooke, AMERICA

13 America is not to be made a polyglot boarding house for money-hunters of twenty different nationalities who have changed their former countries for this country only as farmyard beasts change one feeding trough for another.
Theodore Roosevelt. Speech, Bridgeport, Connecticut

14 Some Americans need hyphens in their names because only half of them has come over.
Woodrow Wilson. Speech, Washington 16 *May* 1914

IMMORALITY

15 The only immorality is not to do what one has to do when one has to do it.
Jean Anouilh, BECKET 1959

IMMORTALITY

16 I don't want to achieve immortality through my work, I want to achieve it through not dying.
Woody Allen. Quoted E. Lax, WOODY ALLEN AND HIS COMEDY

17 We are not made to rest in this world. It is not our true native land.
Father Andrew, IN THE SILENCE

18 One cannot live for ever by ignoring the price of coffins.
Ernest Bramah, KAI LUNG UNROLLS HIS MAT 1928

19 The belief in immortality rests not very much on the hope of going on. Few of us want to do that, but we would like very much to begin again.
Heywood Brown, PIECES OF HATE

199

1 I recently visited an Eastern sage and asked him 'Is it possible to live for ever?' 'Certainly', he replied, 'You must undertake to do two things'. 'What are they?' 'Firstly, you must never again make any false statements.' 'That's simple enough. What is the second thing I must do?' 'Every day you must utter the statement "I will repeat this statement tomorrow". If you follow these instructions faithfully you are certain to live for ever.'
Jacqueline Harman. Letter to Daily Telegraph 8 Oct 1985

2 Man is the only animal that contemplates death, and also the only animal that shows any sign of doubt of its finality.
William Ernest Hocking, THE MEANING OF IMMORTALITY IN HUMAN EXPERIENCE 1957

3 God needs immortality to vindicate his ways to man.
W. Somerset Maugham, THE SUMMING UP 1938

4 Either the soul is immortal and we shall not die, or it perishes with the flesh, and we shall not know that we are dead. Live, then, as if you were eternal.
André Maurois. Quoted W. J. Durant, ON THE MEANING OF LIFE

5 I am a temporary enclosure for a temporary purpose; that served, my skull and teeth, my idiosyncrasy and desire, will disperse, I believe, like the timbers of a booth after a fair.
H. G. Wells, FIRST AND LAST THINGS

IMPARTIALITY

6 You must not miss Whitehall. At one end you will find a statue of one of our kings who was beheaded; at the other the monument to the man who did it. This is just an example of our attempts to be fair to everybody.
Sir Edward Appleton. Speech, Stockholm. Quoted News Review 1 Jan 1948

7 I decline utterly to be impartial as between the Fire Brigade and the Fire.
Winston Churchill when editing the British Gazette during the General Strike of 1926

8 The only impartiality possible to the human mind is that which arises from understanding neither side of the case.
Lord Hewart, NOT WITHOUT PREJUDICE 1938

IMPERFECTION

9 We are always glad when a great man reassures us of his humanity by possessing a few peculiarities.
André Maurois, THE ART OF LIVING

IMPERMANENCE

10 There is nothing at all that remains, nor any house; nor any castle; however strong; nor any love, no matter how tender and sound; nor any comradeship among men, however hardy.
Hilaire Belloc, THE FOUR MEN

11 Anything that calls itself new is doomed to a short life.
Tom Wolfe, IN OUR TIMES

IMPOSSIBILITY

12 You can't make souffle rise twice.
Alice Roosevelt Longworth. Quoted James T. Patterson, MR REPUBLICAN, *a biography of Robert A. Taft*

IMPROPRIETY

13 Impropriety is the soul of wit.
W. Somerset Maugham, THE MOON AND SIXPENCE 1919

IMPULSE

14 The most decisive actions of our life — I mean those that are most likely to decide the whole course of our future — are more often than not, unconsidered.
André Gide, THE COUNTERFEITERS 1926

15 Most of us stifle enough good impulses during the course of a day to change the current of our lives . . . The mistakes of inaction, flanked by heavy reasoning, are likely to be worse than the mistakes of genuine impulse.
William Moulton Martin in a CBS broadcast 18 Mar 1941

16 Impulse has more effect than conscious purpose in moulding men's lives.
Bertrand Russell, AUTOBIOGRAPHY 1967

IMPULSIVENESS

1 You are always taking the bull between your teeth.
Sam Goldwyn. Quoted Alva Johnson, THE GREAT GOLDWYN

2 When a prisoner sees the door of his dungeon open he dashes for it without stopping to think where he shall get his dinner.
George Bernard Shaw, BACK TO METHUSELAH, *Preface* 1922

INADEQUACY

3 Who ever is adequate? We all create situations each other can't live up to, then break our hearts at them because they don't.
Elizabeth Bowen, THE DEATH OF THE HEART 1938

4 Our accepting what we are must always inhibit our being what we ought to be.
John Fowles, THE MAGUS 1965

5 Like Brighton pier, all right as far as it goes, but inadequate for getting to France.
Neil Kinnock. Speech, House of Commons 2 Feb 1981

INATTENTION

6 Organ Morgan, you haven't been listening to a word I said. It's organ, organ all the time with you.
Dylan Thomas, UNDER MILK WOOD 1954

INCENTIVE

7 To force myself to earn more money I determined to spend more.
James Agate, EGO

8 If there hadn't been women we'd still be squatting in a cave eating raw meat because we made civilisation in order to impress our girlfriends.
Orson Welles. Quoted Barbara Rowe, A BOOK OF QUOTES

INCOME TAX

9 The hardest thing in the world to understand is income tax.
Albert Einstein. Quoted Barbara Rowe, A BOOK OF QUOTES

10 I decided to turn myself into a company. In those days it was a fashionable tax ploy. It didn't work of course; no tax ploy ever really works. If it did it would mean the end of chartered accountants.
Robert Morley, MORLEY MARVELS 1976

INCOMPETENCE

11 Henry, who can't even strike a match.
Margot Asquith of her husband. Quoted J. A. Spender and Cyril Asquith, LIFE OF LORD OXFORD AND ASQUITH

12 I was dressed by a man who evidently had read his instructions in Braille.
Bette Davis, of her first screen test in THE LONELY LIFE

13 The Organisation of American States couldn't pour piss out of a boot if the instructions were written on the heel.
Lyndon Johnson. Quoted Eric Goldman, THE TRAGEDY OF LYNDON JOHNSON 1969

INCOMPREHENSIBILITY

14 The advantage of the incomprehensible is that it never loses its freshness.
John Weightman. Quoting Paul Varley, Observer 5 Aug 1979

INDECENCY

15 You have left your hero and heroine tied up in a cavern for a week, and they are not married.
G. K. Chesterton quoting, in his autobiography, an editor's complaint to his sister-in-law, Mrs Cecil Chesterton, about a serial story

INDECISION

16 The Right Honourable Gentleman [Sir John Simon] has sat so long on the fence that the iron has entered his soul.
David Lloyd George, House of Commons 1931

1 Like King Solomon, when confronted by an enterprising buyer who showed him 271 new wives in a new harem, he knew perfectly well what was expected of him but did not quite know where to begin. I am in the same position.
Lord Mancroft. Speech, Buyers Benevolent Association, Grosvenor House, London 9 Mar 1954

2 Nothing is so exhausting as indecision, and nothing is so futile.
Bertrand Russell, THE CONQUEST OF HAPPINESS 1930

INDEPENDENCE

3 It's the man who dares to take who is independent, not he who gives.
D. H. Lawrence, SELECTED LETTERS 1962

INDIA

4 There was so much sculpture that I should certainly have missed the indecencies if Major Poonby hadn't been considerate enough to point them out.
J. R. Ackerley, HINDOO HOLIDAY

5 If the British had not been in India that woman Mrs Pandit would have been burnt on her husband's funeral pyre.
Nancy Astor. Quoted John Grigg, NANCY ASTOR: PORTRAIT OF A PIONEER

6 India is a geographical term. It is no more a united nation than the Equator.
Winston Churchill. Speech, Royal Albert Hall 18 May 1931

7 India is materialistic rather than mystical, as the bank managers of gurus testify.
Trevor Fishlock, INDIAN FILE 1983

INDIGNATION

8 Hate is a kind of passive suffering, but indignation is a kind of joy.
W. B. Yeats, LETTERS 1954

INDISCRETION

9 Dentopedology is the science of opening your mouth and putting your foot in it. I've been practising it for years.
Philip, Duke of Edinburgh

INDOLENCE

10 It behoves you for your own well-being not to suffer the grass to grow around your tardy ankles in the matter.
Ernest Bramah, KAI LUNG UNROLLS HIS MAT 1928

11 Alas! The hours we waste in work / And similar inconsequence, / Friends, I beg you do not shirk / Your daily task of indolence.
Don Marquis, THE ALMOST PERFECT STATE

12 Loafing needs no explanation and is its own excuse.
Christopher Morley, MINCE PIE 1919

13 The right to laziness is one of the rights that sensible humanity will learn to consider as something self-evident.
Dr Wilhelm Stekel, THE DEPTHS OF THE SOUL

14 There is a case, and a strong case, for that particular form of indolence that allows us to move through life knowing only what immediately concerns us.
Alec Waugh, ON DOING WHAT ONE LIKES

INDULGENCE

15 Unrestrained indulgence kills not merely passion, but, in the end, even amusement.
Aldous Huxley, COLLECTED ESSAYS 1960

INDUSTRIOUSNESS

16 By working faithfully eight hours a day you may eventually get to be a boss and work twelve hours a day.
Robert Frost. Quoted Barbara Rowe, A BOOK OF QUOTES

INEQUALITY

17 The only inequalities that matter begin in the mind. It is not income levels but differences in mental equipment that keep people apart, breed feelings of inferiority.
Jacquetta Hawkes, New Statesman, Jan 1957

18 We need inequality in order to eliminate poverty.
Sir Keith Joseph. Quoted Audrey Hillar, THIS ENGLAND

1 There is always inequality in life. Some men are killed in a war and some men are wounded and some men never leave the country — Life is unfair.
John F. Kennedy, at a press conference 21 *Mar* 1962

INEVITABILITY

2 Nothing is inevitable until it happens.
A. J. P. Taylor. Quoted George Hutchinson, Daily Telegraph 7 *Jan* 1980

3 The inevitability of gradualness.
Sidney Webb. Presidential address to the annual conference of the Labour Party 1920

INEXPERIENCE

4 She had to confess to inexperience: her personality was still too much for her, like a punt pole.
Elizabeth Bowen, FRIENDS AND RELATIONS 1931

5 Inexperience is what makes a young man do what an older man says is impossible.
Herbert V. Prochow, Saturday Evening Post 4 *Dec* 1948

INFERIORITY

6 No one can make you feel inferior without your consent.
Eleanor Roosevelt. Quoted Don Peretz Elkins, GLAD TO BE ME

INFIDELITY

7 Marriage without love means love without marriage.
Kenneth, Lord Clark, CIVILISATION 1969

8 It is the fear of middle age in the young, and of old age in the middle-aged, which is the prime cause of infidelity, Man's infallible rejuvenator.
Cyril Connolly, THE UNQUIET GRAVE 1945

9 Husbands are chiefly good lovers when they are betraying their wives.
Marilyn Monroe. Quoted Barbara Rowe, A BOOK OF QUOTES

10 One man's folly is another man's wife.
Helen Rowland, A GUIDE TO MEN

INFINITY

11 All finite things reveal infinitude.
Theodore Roethke, THE FAR FIELD

INFLATION

12 Nothing so weakens governments as persistent inflation.
J. K. Galbraith, THE AFFLUENT SOCIETY 1958

13 I don't think one can spend oneself rich.
George Humphrey. Quoted Rhoda Thomas Tripp, INTERNATIONAL THESAURUS OF QUOTATIONS

14 Governments are the chief culprit in inflation because, wishing to avoid unpopularity, they spend too much and tax too little.
Prof. Lord Kaldor, MEMORANDA ON MONETARY POLICY 17 *Aug* 1980

15 The best way to destroy the capitalist system is to debauch the currency. By a continuing process of inflation governments can confiscate, secretly and unobserved, an important part of the wealth of their citizens.
J. M. Keynes, ESSAYS IN PERSUASION 1931

16 Inflation is like sin; every government denounces it and every government practises it.
Sir Frederick Leith-Ross, Observer 30 *Jun* 1957

17 Inflation is bringing us true democracy. For the first time in history luxuries and necessities are selling at the same price.
Robert Orben. Quoted Barbara Rowe, A BOOK OF QUOTES

18 Just about the time you think you can make both ends meet, somebody moves the ends.
Pansy Penner. Quoted Reader's Digest, Dec 1944

19 Inflation sooner or later makes more extensive unemployment inevitable . . . by drawing more and more workers into kinds of jobs which depend on continuing or even accelerating inflation.
F. A. Von Hayek, New York Times 15 *Nov* 1974

1 The disease is painless; it's the cure that hurts.
Katherine Whitehorn, Observer, Deckchair Economics 21 *Aug* 1966

2 From now on the pound abroad is worth 14% or so less in terms of other currencies. It does not mean, of course, that the pound here in Britain, in your pocket, or purse, or in your bank, has been devalued.
Harold Wilson, broadcast 18 *Nov* 1967

INFLUENCE

3 One of the things a man has to fight most bitterly is the influence of those who love him.
Sherwood Anderson, LETTERS 1953

4 Influence is neither good nor bad in an absolute manner, but only in relation to the one who experiences it.
André Gide, PRETEXTS 1903

INFORMALITY

5 He watched her [Lady Astor] fan herself with a dinner plate and push back her tiara like an old hat.
Ernesta Barlow. Quoted Christopher Sykes, NANCY

INFORMATION

6 Information is not culture. In the mind of a truly educated man, facts are organised and they make up a living world in the image of the world of reality.
André Maurois, THE ART OF LIVING

INGRATITUDE

7 Somebody who puts 10p in a blind beggar's tray and gets thanked for it thinks no more about it; but if the beggar spits in his eye he'll probably remember it for the rest of his life. Gratitude, you see, is a pleasant thing, but unexciting; it is *ingratitude* which fascinates us.
Christopher Mayhew, Punch 16 *May* 1973

INHUMANITY

8 A man can only live by absolutely / Forgetting he's a man like other folk.
Bertolt Brecht, THE THREEPENNY OPERA 1928

INJUSTICE

9 Injustice anywhere is a threat to justice everywhere.
Martin Luther King, Atlantic Monthly, Aug 1963

INNOCENCE

10 Innocence with ignorance is not worth having.
Lucilla Andrews, HIGHLAND INTERLUDE

11 'Tis e'er the lot of the innocent in the world to fly to the wolf for succour from the lion.
John Barth, THE SOT-WEED FACTOR 1960

12 Your innocence is on at such a rakish angle / It gives you quite an air of iniquity.
Christopher Fry, THE LADY'S NOT FOR BURNING 1949

13 Innocence is like a dumb leper who has lost his bell, wandering the world, meaning no harm.
Graham Greene, THE QUIET AMERICAN 1955

14 Girls remained an unknown species. I grew up to regard sexual recreation as a socially remote thing, like baccarat or clog dancing.
Philip Larkin, REQUIRED WRITING 1983

15 She [Ellen Terry] was an extremely beautiful girl and as innocent as a rose. When Watts kissed her she took it for granted that she was going to have a baby.
George Bernard Shaw. Quoted Stephen Winston, DAYS WITH BERNARD SHAW

INNOVATION

16 Any new thing must find a new shape, then afterwards one can call it art.
Frieda Lawrence, letter to Edward Garnett 1912

INQUISITIVENESS

1 My advice to you is not to inquire why or whether, but just enjoy your ice cream while it is on your plate — that's my philosophy.
Thornton Wilder, THE SKIN OF OUR TEETH 1942

INSIGHT

2 Insight — the titillating knack for hurting!
Colette, EARTHLY PARADISE, *The Pure and Impure* 1966

3 All men enjoy flashes of insight beyond meanings already established in etymology and grammar.
A. N. Whitehead, ADVENTURES OF IDEAS 1933

INSOMNIA

4 I ain't sleeping. I'm just taking a good look at the insides of my eyelids.
Jonathan Raban, OLD GLORY

INSPIRATION

5 Inspiration is like matter that must be expelled, and ease only comes when it has been expelled in the form of a poem.
T. S. Eliot. Quoted Harold Nicolson, DIARY 19 *Nov* 1953

6 My sole inspiration is a telephone call from a director.
Cole Porter in a press interview 8 *Feb* 1955

7 Inspiration could be called inhaling the memory of an act never experienced.
Ned Rorem, MUSIC FROM INSIDE OUT 1967

8 Work brings inspiration, if inspiration is not discernible at the beginning.
Igor Stravinsky, CHRONICLES OF MY LIFE 1935

9 When I was writing *The Shadow of the Glen* I got more aid than any learning could have given me from a chink in the floor of the old Wicklow House where I was staying, that let me hear what was being said by the servant girls in the kitchen.
J. M. Synge, PLAYBOY OF THE WESTERN WORLD, *Preface* 1907

INSULT

10 Duplicitous bastard. European fiends — just plain cowardly. British, lying through their teeth.
Alexander Haig of Lord Carrington 1982

11 [James Whitcomb Riley] the unctuous, over-cheerful, word-mouthing, flabby-faced citizen who condescendingly tells Providence, in flowery and well-rounded periods, where to get off.
Hewlett Howland. Quoted Richard Crowder, THOSE INNOCENT YEARS

12 He [Drew Pearson] is not a sunnavabitch. He is only a filthy brain child, conceived in ruthlessness and dedicated to the proposition that Judas Iscariot was a piker.
Senator William Jenner of Indiana. Quoted Morris A. Beale, ALL AMERICAN LOUSE

13 . . . has all the depth and glitter of a worn dime.
Dorothy Parker, of Margot Asquith's LAY SERMONS

14 Westbrook Pegler, a guttersnipe, is a gentleman compared to you. You can take that as more of an insult than a reflection of your ancestry.
Harry S Truman, protesting against a criticism of his daughter Margaret's singing by Paul Hume of the Washington Post

INSURANCE

15 If it were not for the insurance companies there would be little litigation of any sort today.
A. P. Herbert, MORE MISLEADING CASES

INTEGRITY

16 I never truckled; I never took off the hat to Fashion and held it out for pennies. By God, I told them the truth.
Frank Norris, THE RESPONSIBILITIES OF A NOVELIST 1903

INTELLECT

17 Since it is seldom clear whether intellectual activity denotes a superior mode of being or a vital deficiency, opinion swings between considering intellect a privilege and seeing it as a handicap.
Jacques Barzun, THE HOUSE OF INTELLECT 1959

1 Intellect has nothing to do with equality except to respect it as a sublime convention.
Ibid.

2 We should take care not to make the intellect our god; it has, of course, powerful muscles, but no personality.
Albert Einstein, OUT OF MY LATER LIFE 1950

3 Little minds are interested in the extraordinary; great minds in the commonplace.
Elbert Hubbard

4 His mind was like a soup dish, wide and shallow; it could hold a small amount of nearly everything, but the slightest jarring spilt the soup into somebody's lap.
Irving Stone of William Jennings Bryant, THE ALSO RAN

5 I rank the wide thinker far above the ready writer. Goethe knew twice as much about the human scene as Shakespeare but could not put it on paper half as well.
Wilfred Whitten, John o' London's Weekly, A Priest of Thought 21 *Jul* 1939

6 The grinding of the intellect is for most people as painful as a dentist's drill.
Leonard Woolf, Observer 28 *Jun* 1959

INTELLECTUAL

7 An intellectual is a man who doesn't know how to park a bike.
Spiro Agnew

8 To the man-in-the-street who I'm sorry to say / Is a keen observer of life / 'Intellectual' suggests straight away / A man who's untrue to his wife.
W. H. Auden, NEW YEAR LETTER

9 The intellectuals' chief cause of anguish are one another's works.
Jacques Barzun, THE HOUSE OF INTELLECT 1959

10 Intellectuals are people who believe that ideas are of more importance than values. That is to say, their own ideas and other people's values.
Gerald Brenan, THOUGHTS IN A DRY SEASON 1979

11 An intellectual is someone whose mind watches itself. I am happy to be both halves, the watcher and the watched.
Albert Camus, NOTEBOOKS 1935–1942

12 Berenson said to Bauer, the antique dealer, 'A man as scholarly as yourself shouldn't be a dealer. It is horrible to be a dealer.' To which Bauer replied 'Between you and me there is no great difference; I am an intellectual dealer and you're a dealing intellectual.' Berenson never forgave him.
René Gimpel, DIARY OF AN ART DEALER

13 Intellectuals can tell themselves anything, sell themselves any bill of goods, which is why they are so often patsies for the ruling classes in nineteenth-century France and England, or twentieth-century Russia and America.
Lillian Hellman, AN UNFINISHED WOMAN 1969

14 A highbrow is the kind of person who looks at a sausage and thinks of Picasso.
A. P. Herbert, THE HIGHBROW

15 A highbrow is a person educated beyond his intelligence.
Attr. Brander Matthews, STEVENSON'S BOOK OF QUOTATIONS

16 Every man with a bellyful of the classics is an enemy of the human race.
Henry Miller, TROPIC OF CANCER 1934

17 I do not know a single person whose intellect I respect deeply who enjoys good health.
Sir Peter Chalmers Mitchell, MY FILL OF DAYS

18 Intellectuals incline to be individualists, or even independents, are not team conscious and tend to regard obedience as a surrender of personality.
Harold Nicolson, Observer 12 *Oct* 1958

19 Intellectuals have the same problems as other people. But they do not bear their sufferings so nobly.
Rev. D. Edward Norman, REITH LECTURES 1978

20 Annabel was accounted a beauty and intellectually gifted; she never played herring, and was reputed to have read Maeterlinck's *Life of the Bee.* If you abstain from tennis *and* read Maeterlinck in a small country village, you are of necessity intellectual.
Saki, REGINALD AT THE THEATRE

1 The trouble with me is, I belong to a vanishing race. I'm one of the intellectuals.
Robert E. Sherwood, THE PETRIFIED FOREST 1935

2 The British don't like intellectuals, except for those with good foreign names like Bronowski, Berlin, Gombrich and Steiner.
Roy Strong. Quoted D. J. Enright, Observer, Word-watching 24 *Jun* 1984

3 A highbrow is a man who has found something more interesting than women.
Edgar Wallace to a Hollywood reporter, Dec 1931

4 A man or woman of thoroughbred intelligence galloping across country in pursuit of an idea.
Virginia Woolf. Quoted Kenneth Tynan, CURTAINS

INTELLIGENCE

5 The intelligent are to the intelligentsia what a man is to a gent.
Stanley Baldwin. Quoted his biographer, G. M. Young

6 Intelligence is the faculty of making artificial objects, especially tools, to make tools.
Henri Bergson, CREATIVE EVOLUTION 1907

7 Intelligence is not to make no mistakes / But quickly to see how to make them good.
Bertolt Brecht, THE MEASURES TAKEN 1930

8 There may be an optimum level of intelligence and perhaps we have already exceeded it. Our brains may be too big — dooming us as Triceratops was doomed by his armour.
Arthur C. Clarke, THE LOST WORLDS OF 2001

9 The greatest intelligence is precisely the one that suffers most from its own limitations.
André Gide, THE COUNTERFEITERS 1926

10 Military Intelligence is a contradiction in terms.
Graffito on Ministry of Defence building. Quoted Nigel Rees, GRAFFITI RULES OK

11 It takes brains not to make money. Any fool can make money. But what about people with talent and brains?
Joseph Heller, CATCH 22 1961

12 You cannot fashion a wit out of two half-wits.
Neil Kinnock, The Times, Past Principles, Future Views 18 *Jul* 1983

13 A child of five would understand this. Send somebody to fetch a child of five.
Groucho Marx, DUCK SOUP

14 Simplicity of character is no hindrance to subtlety of intellect.
John Morley, LIFE OF GLADSTONE 1963

15 There are three kinds of intelligence — the intelligence of man, the intelligence of animals, and the intelligence of the military, in that order.
Gottfried Reinhardt. Quoted Lillian Ross, PICTURE

INTEREST

16 There is no such thing on earth as an uninteresting subject; the only thing that can exist is an uninterested person.
G. K. Chesterton, HERETICS 1905

INTERVIEW

17 I'm notorious for giving a bad interview. I'm an actor and I can't help but feel I'm boring when I'm on as myself.
Rock Hudson. Quoted Alan Martin, TV Times 19 *Oct* 1972

18 'Mr. Coward, have you anything to say to the Sun?' a lady interviewer once asked him. 'Shine.' Noël said pleasantly.
William Marchant, THE PRIVILEGE OF HIS COMPANY 1980

INTOLERANCE

19 What is objectionable, what is dangerous about extremists is not that they are extreme but that they are intolerant.
Robert F. Kennedy, THE PURSUIT OF JUSTICE

20 Intolerance itself is a form of egoism and to condemn egoism intolerantly is to share it.
George Santayana, WORDS OF DOCTRINE

INTRUSION

1 Bloody hell, Ma'am, what's he doing here?
Elizabeth Andrew, the Queen's Chambermaid, faced with Michael Fagan, intruder in the Queen's bedroom 1982

2 Miss Twye was soaping her breasts in the bath / When she heard behind her a meaning laugh / And to her amazement she discovered / A wicked man in the bathroom cupboard.
Gavin Ewart, THE COLLECTED EWART

INTUITION

3 Whereas the mind works in possibilities, the intuitions work in actualities, and what you *intuitively* desire, that is possible to you.
D. H. Lawrence, SELECTED ESSAYS

4 Some of the finest moral intuitions come to quite humble people. The visiting of lofty ideas doesn't depend on formal schooling. Think of those Galilean peasants.
A. N. Whitehead, DIALOGUES 1953

INVECTIVE

5 He [Aneurin Bevan] was the only man I knew who could make a curse sound like a caress.
Michael Foot, ANEURIN BEVAN 1897–1945

INVENTION

6 The Doctor is said to have invented an extraordinary weapon which will make war less brutal. It is described as a very powerful liquid which rots braces at a distance of a mile.
Beachcomber (J. B. Morton), Daily Express, By The Way

7 I don't think necessity is the mother of invention — invention, in my opinion, arises directly from idleness, possibly also from laziness. To save oneself trouble.
Agatha Christie, AUTOBIOGRAPHY

8 The English are not an inventive people; they don't eat enough pie.
Thomas A. Edison, GOLDEN BOOK, *Apr* 1931

9 Inventions that are not made, like babies that are not born, are not missed.
J. K. Galbraith, THE AFFLUENT SOCIETY 1958

10 The means by which we live have outdistanced the ends for which we live.
Martin Luther King, STRENGTH TO LOVE

11 His absent minded scientist, Dr Strabismus (whom God Preserve) of Utrecht, had to his credit a list of inventions that included 'a leather grape', 'a revolving wheelbarrow', 'a hollow glass walking stick for keeping very small flannel shirts in', 'waterproof onions', 'a bottle with its neck in the middle', 'false teeth for swordfish', and 'a foghorn sharpener'.
Bernard Levin, obituary of J. B. Morton (Beachcomber), Observer 13 *May* 1979

12 We live in a time when a man believes himself fabulously capable of creation, but he does not know what to create.
José Ortega y Gassett, THE REVOLT OF THE MASSES 1930

13 Innovation depends on invention and inventors should be treated as the pop stars of industry.
Philip, Duke of Edinburgh. Quoted Noël St. George, ROYAL QUOTES

14 At Elm he [Sir George Sitwell] invented a musical toothbrush which played 'Annie Laurie' as you brushed your teeth, and a small revolver for killing wasps.
Sir Osbert Sitwell, THE SCARLET TREE 1945

IRELAND

15 Anyone who isn't confused here doesn't really understand what is going on.
Belfast man 1970. *Quoted Nigel Rees,* QUOTE UNQUOTE

16 Stone-walled cabin thatched with reeds / Where a Stone Age people breeds / The last of Europe's stone-age race.
Sir John Betjeman, IRELAND WITH EMILY

17 It is not necessary to climb the painful stairs of Irish history, that treadmill of a nation whose labours are as vain for her own uplifting as the convict's are for his own redemption.
Roger Casement, at the end of his trial for high treason

1 In so far as Lloyd George can link his
political misfortunes with this Irish story, he
may be content. In falling through Irish
difficulties he may fall with Essex and with
Strafford, with Pitt and with Gladstone; and
with a line of sovereigns and statesmen,
great or small, spread across the English
history books of seven hundred years.
Winston Churchill, THE WORLD CRISIS,
Aftermath 1929

2 By yesterday morning British troops were
patrolling the streets of Belfast. I fear that
once Catholics and Protestants get used to
our presence they will hate us more than
they hate each other.
Richard Crossman, DIARIES 17 *Aug* 1969

3 I never met anyone in Ireland who understood the Irish question, except one
Englishman who had only been there a
week.
Sir K. Fraser MP, House of Commons, May
1919

4 Ireland is the old sow that eats her farrow.
James Joyce, A PORTRAIT OF THE ARTIST AS
A YOUNG MAN 1914

5 The Irish don't know what they want and are
prepared to fight to the death to get it.
Sir Sidney Littlewood, President of the Law
Society. Speech 13 *Apr* 1961

6 I am troubled, I'm dissatisfied. I'm Irish.
Marianne Moore, SPENSER'S IRELAND 1941

7 The Irish do not want anyone to wish them
well; they want them to wish their enemies
ill.
Harold Nicolson, SMALL TALK

8 Dublin is a city where you can see a sparrow
fall to the ground and God watching it.
Conor Cruise O'Brien

9 The English should give Ireland home rule
— and reserve the motion picture rights.
Will Rogers, AUTOBIOGRAPHY 1949

10 An Irishman's heart is nothing but his
imagination.
George Bernard Shaw, JOHN BULL'S OTHER
ISLAND 1904

11 Every Irishman who felt that his business
was on the higher planes of the cultural
professions felt that his first business was to
get out of Ireland. I felt the same.
George Bernard Shaw. Quoted Hesketh
Pearson, BERNARD SHAW 1942

IRON CURTAIN

12 From Stettin in the Baltic to Trieste in the
Adriatic, an iron curtain has descended
across the continent.
Winston Churchill. Speech, Fulton,
Missouri, Mar 1946

ISOLATION

13 Anything sufficiently isolated, like an egg
cup in an art gallery, cannot avoid acquiring
significance.
Hugh Casson, DIARY 1981

14 We're all of us sentenced to solitary
confinement inside our own skins.
Tennessee Williams, ORPHEUS
DESCENDING 1956

ISOLATIONISM

15 Personally I can't see that foreign stories are
ever news — not real news.
Evelyn Waugh, SCOOP 1938

ITALY

16 Venice is like eating an entire box of
chocolate liqueurs at one go.
Truman Capote. Quoted Observer 26 *Nov*
1961

17 Italy is a poor country full of rich people.
Richard Gardner, ex-US Ambassador in
Rome. Quoted Observer 16 *Aug* 1981

18 Italy is so tender — like cooked macaroni —
yards and yards of soft tenderness ravelled
round everything.
D. H. Lawrence, SEA AND SARDINIA 1923

19 She said that all the sights in Rome were
called after London cinemas.
Nancy Mitford, PIGEON PIE 1940

J

HENRY JAMES

1 Henry James was one of the nicest old ladies I ever met.
William Faulkner

2 Many readers cannot get interested in James. They cannot grant his premise, which is that most of human life has to disappear before he can do us a novel.
E. M. Forster, ASPECTS OF THE NOVEL 1927

3 Sargent's portrait of Henry James is nearly finished, and I hear is a masterpiece. There is a plaid waistcoat in it, like a sea in a storm, which is said to be prodigious.
Edmund Gosse, letter to Thomas Hardy 1913

4 The work of Henry James has always seemed divisible by a simple dynastic arrangement into three reigns: James I, James II and the Old Pretender.
Philip Guedella, MEN OF LETTERS

5 He was a great American writer who came to Venice and looked out of the window and smoked his cigar and thought.
Ernest Hemingway, SELECTED LETTERS 1917–1961

6 Mr James' cosmopolitanism is, after all, limited; to be really cosmopolitan, a man must be at home even in his own country.
Thomas Wentworth Higginson, SHORT STUDIES OF AMERICAN AUTHORS

7 He did not live, he observed life from a window, and too often was inclined to content himself with no more than what his friends told him they saw when *they* looked out of a window.
W. Somerset Maugham, A WRITER'S NOTEBOOK 1949

8 Leviathan retrieving pebbles . . . a magnificent but painful hippopotamus resolved at any cost, even at the cost of its dignity, upon picking up a pea.
H. G. Wells, BOOR

JAPAN

9 The Japs have done nothing for thousands of years but write the wrong way round and paint unrecognisable pictures of red mullet on bits of scented paper.
Raymond Asquith, LIFE AND LETTERS

10 While we spend energy and imagination on inventing new ways of cleaning the floors of our houses, the Japanese solve the problem by not dirtying them in the first place.
Bernard Rudofsky, THE KIMONO HIND

11 The Japanese have perfected good manners and made them indistinguishable from rudeness.
Paul Theroux, THE GREAT RAILWAY BAZAAR

JARGON

12 You and I come by road or rail, but economists travel on infrastructure.
Margaret Thatcher, Observer 26 May 1985

JAZZ

13 Down South where I come from you don't go around hitting too many white keys.
Eubie Blake, centenarian Negro pianist and composer, on being asked on TV why his compositions contained so many sharps and flats 1983

14 Jazz is the only music in which the same note can be played night after night but differently each time.
Ornette Coleman. Quoted Wilfred Mellars, MUSIC IN A NEW FOUND LAND 1964

15 Playing 'bop' is like playing Scrabble with all the vowels missing.
Duke Ellington, Look 10 Aug 1954

16 Jazz without the beat is a telephone yanked from the wall; it just can't communicate.
Leonare Feather, Show Magazine, Jan 1962

1 A jazz musician is a juggler who uses harmonics instead of oranges.
Benny Green, THE RELUCTANT ART

2 It was the first time that I had ever clearly seen a jazz band. The spectacle was positively terrifying.
Aldous Huxley, DO WHAT YOU WILL 1929

3 Jazz is playin' from the heart, you don't lie.
William Geary (Bunk) Johnson. Quoted Nat Shapiro, ENCYCLOPEDIA OF QUOTATIONS ABOUT MUSIC

4 Jazz has never existed in Africa, and it doesn't exist there today.
Max Kaminsky, MY LIFE IN JAZZ 1963

5 If you're in jazz, and more than ten people like you, you're labelled commercial.
Herbie Mann. Quoted Henry Pleasante, SERIOUS MUSIC — AND ALL THAT JAZZ 1919

6 I want to hear screaming and hollering and kicking and biting. That's what the world's about today . . . Life is a bit chaotic, and I think jazzmen should express something of the way life is lived.
Charlie Mariano, DOWNBEAT YEARBOOK 1967

7 During the early years of the century jazz became fortuitously identified with brothels.
Frank Muir, THE FRANK MUIR BOOK 1976

8 What a terrible revenge by the culture of the Negroes on that of the whites.
Ignacy Paderewski. Quoted Nat Shapiro, ENCYCLOPEDIA OF QUOTATIONS ABOUT MUSIC

9 The basic difference between classical music and jazz is that in the former the music is always greater than its performance — whereas the way jazz is performed is always more important than what is being played.
André Previn. Quoted Miles Kington, The Times 1967

10 Jazz is either a thrilling communication with the primitive soul, or an ear-splitting bore.
Winthrop Sargent. Quoted Nat Shapiro, ENCYCLOPEDIA OF QUOTATIONS ABOUT MUSIC

11 Jazz will endure just as long as people hear it through their feet instead of their brains.
John Philip Sousa. Ibid.

JEALOUSY

12 Jealousy is no more than feeling alone among smiling enemies.
Elizabeth Bowen, THE HOUSE IN PARIS 1935

13 It is not love that is blind, but jealousy.
Lawrence Durrell, JUSTINE 1957

14 Jealousy, that dragon which slays love under the pretence of keeping it alive.
Havelock Ellis, ON LIFE AND SEX

15 To jealousy, nothing is more frightful than laughter.
Françoise Sagan, LA CHAMADEN 1966

JEW

16 It's their own silly fault — they ought to have left God alone.
Hilaire Belloc. Quoted Robert Speight, LIFE OF HILAIRE BELLOC

17 The pursuit of knowledge for its own sake, an almost fanatical love of justice and the desire for personal independence — these are the features of the Jewish tradition which make me thank my stars that I belong to it.
Albert Einstein, THE WORLD AS I SEE IT

18 How odd / Of God / To choose / The Jews.
William Norman Ewer, HOW ODD

19 You call me a damned Jew. My race was old when you were all savages. I am proud to be a Jew.
John Galsworthy, LOYALTIES 1922

20 Pessimism is a luxury that a Jew never can allow himself.
Golda Meir. Quoted Observer 29 Dec 1974

21 A Jewish man with parents alive is a fifteen year old boy, and will remain a fifteen year old boy until they die.
Philip Roth, PORTNOY'S COMPLAINT 1969

22 If a Jew is fascinated by Christians it is not because of their virtues, which he values little, but because they represent anonymity, humanity without race.
Jean-Paul Sartre, ANTI-SEMITE AND JEW

23 The Jews generally give good value. They make you pay; but they deliver the goods. In my experience the men who want something for nothing are invariably Christians.
George Bernard Shaw, ST JOAN 1923

JEWELLERY

1 Have you ever noticed that many jewels make women either incredibly fat or incredibly thin?
J. M. Barrie, THE TWELVE POUND LOOK 1912

LYNDON B. JOHNSON

2 Let's face it, Mr President, you're not a very likeable man.
Dean Acheson, when Johnson asked why he wasn't popular. Quoted Robert A. Caro, THE YEARS OF LYNDON JOHNSON: THE PATH TO POWER 1983

JOKE

3 A good joke is not an invention, but a discovery.
E. H. Gombrich, TRIBUTES 1984

4 Readers of *Punch* have much the same attitude to their jokes as port-drinkers have to port. They like them laid down in a cellar to mature. Then, on special occasions they can bring them up, encrusted with cobwebs and savour again their rich, familiar bouquet.
Malcolm Muggeridge, TREAD SOFTLY FOR YOU TREAD ON MY JOKES 1966

JOURNALISM

5 The world really isn't any worse. It's just that the news coverage is so much better.
Anon. English Digest, Mar 1965

6 On the whole the British don't believe what they read in their tabloids. They trust the sports pages; the rest is assumed to be saucy nonsense, lightly seasoned with souped-up fact.
Neal Ascherson, Observer 15 *Sep* 1985

7 'The fact is, Mr Balfour, all the faults of the age come from Christianity and journalism.' 'Christianity, of course. But why journalism?'
Conversation between A. J. Balfour and Frank Harris. Quoted, AUTOBIOGRAPHY OF MARGOT ASQUITH

8 What the proprietorship of these newspapers is aiming at is power, and power without responsibility, the privilege of the harlot throughout the ages.
Stanley Baldwin at a by-election meeting 1931

9 I run the *Daily Express* purely for propaganda and for no other purpose.
Lord Beaverbrook to the Royal Commission on the Press 1948

10 If you want to make mischief come and work on my papers.
Lord Beaverbrook inviting Anthony Howard to join his staff. Quoted Radio Times 27 *Jun* 1981

11 Journalists say a thing that they know isn't true, in the hope that if they keep on saying it long enough it *will* be true.
Arnold Bennett, THE TITLE 1918

12 I can write about anything, from gee-gees to Jesus.
Horatio Bottomley. Quoted Alan Hyman, THE RISE AND FALL OF HORATIO BOTTOMLEY

13 Journalism is the only job that requires no degrees, no diplomas and no specialised knowledge of any kind.
Patrick Campbell, MY LIFE AND EASY TIMES

14 A free press can, of course, be good or bad, but, most certainly, without freedom it will never be anything but bad.
Albert Camus, RESISTANCE, REBELLION AND DEATH 1961

15 Journalism largely consists of saying 'Lord Jones is dead' to people who never knew Lord Jones was alive.
G. K. Chesterton

16 *The Times* is speechless, and takes three columns to express its speechlessness.
Winston Churchill. Speech on Irish Home Rule, Dundee, 14 *May* 1908

17 The journalist is partly in the entertainment business and partly in the advertising business.
Claud Cockburn, IN TIME OF TROUBLE

18 Literature is the art of writing something that will be read twice and journalism what will be grasped at once.
Cyril Connolly, ENEMIES OF PROMISE 1938

1 The more national newspapers there are, the more difficult it is to tell them apart.
Paul Foot, New Statesman, Aug 1985

2 Media is a word that has come to mean bad journalism.
Graham Greene, WAYS OF ESCAPE

3 He put words into my mouth which I had to look up in the dictionary.
Graham Greene of Anthony Burgess interviewing him in the Observer 28 Nov 1982

4 Good taste is, of course, an utterly dispensable part of any journalist's equipment.
Michael Hogg, Daily Telegraph 2 Dec 1978

5 My motto is publish and be sued.
Richard Ingrams, editor of Private Eye, BBC Radio 4, 4 May 1977

6 The secret of successful journalism is to make your readers so angry that they will write half your paper for you.
C. E. M. Joad. Quoted News Review 17 Apr 1947

7 An editor is a man who takes a French poodle, and clips him into the shape of a lion.
Emery Kelen, American cartoonist. Quoted News Review 27 May 1948

8 The best headlines never fi
Bernard Levin, The Times 5 Jul 1980

9 A good newspaper, I suppose, is a nation talking to itself.
Arthur Miller. Quoted Observer 26 Nov 1961

10 It is *hard* news that catches readers. Features hold them.
Lord Northcliffe. Quoted Tom Clarke, THE NORTHCLIFFE DIARY

11 I operate by a sense of smell. If something smells wrong, I go to work.
Drew Pearson. Quoted Oliver Pilat, DREW PEARSON

12 In America journalism is apt to be regarded as an extension of history, in Britain as an extension of conversation.
Anthony Sampson, ANATOMY OF BRITAIN 1962

13 Comment is free but facts are sacred.
Charles Prestwich Scott, Manchester Guardian 6 May 1921

14 [Journalists are] nameless men and women whose scandalously low payment is a guarantee of their ignorance and their servility to the financial department.
George Bernard Shaw, COMMONSENSE ABOUT THE WAR 1914

15 Newspapers are unable, seemingly, to discriminate between a bicycle accident and the collapse of civilisation.
George Bernard Shaw, TOO TRUE TO BE GOOD, *Preface*

16 An editor is one who separates the wheat from the chaff and prints the chaff.
Adlai Stevenson. Quoted Leon Harris, THE FINE ART OF POLITICAL WIT

17 A foreign correspondent is someone who . . . flies around from hotel to hotel and thinks the most interesting thing about any story is the fact that he has arrived to cover it.
Tom Stoppard, NIGHT AND DAY

18 Facing the press is more difficult than bathing a leper.
Mother Teresa. Quoted Eileen Egan, SUCH A VISION OF THE STREET 1985

19 *Punch* — the official journal of dentists' waiting rooms.
The Times 7 Oct 1981

20 Their prose was convulsive, they foamed at the headlines.
H. G. Wells, THE WAR IN THE AIR

21 Journalism — an ability to meet the challenge of filling the space.
Rebecca West, New York Herald Tribune 22 Apr 1956

JOY

22 Pleasure without joy is as hollow as passion without tenderness.
Alan Jay Lerner, THE STREET WHERE I LIVE 1978

JAMES JOYCE

1 Joyce, in effect, was saying that the depiction of life as it is really lived cannot be achieved in neat, periodic sentences and the puppetry of an author (like Thackeray) smugly in control.
Anthony Burgess, Observer Magazine 20 *May* 1979

2 We cannot, I suppose, finally judge *Ulysses* as a work of fiction at all. It is a kind of magical codex of the same order as Dante's *Divine Comedy* (in which hell, heaven and purgatory go on for ever and nothing changes).
Ibid.

3 *Ulysses* is a dogged attempt to cover the universe with mud.
E. M. Forster, ASPECTS OF THE NOVEL 1927

4 My God, what a clumsy *alla patrida* James Joyce is! Nothing but old fags and cabbage stumps of quotations from the Bible and the rest, stewed in the juice of deliberate, journalistic dirty-mindedness.
D. H. Lawrence in a letter to Aldous Huxley 1928

5 There are passages in *Ulysses* which can be read only in the toilet — if one wants to extract the full flavour of their content.
Henry Miller, BLACK SPRING 1936

6 Joyce has freed us from the superstition of syntax.
Dorothy L. Sayers, CLOUD OF WITNESSES 1926

7 The latest acquisition to her library is *Ulysses*. 'It cost me thirty-five shillings, and I got stuck on the first page. I think that's disgusting, don't you? No, not the content. I mean writing a book so that people can't understand it.'
Russell Twisk. Quoting Cilla Black, Radio Times 25 *Jan* 1968

JUDGMENT

8 Don't let your opinion sway your judgment.
Sam Goldwyn. Quoted Sidney Skolsky

9 For when the One Great Scorer comes / To write against your name, / He marks — not that you won or lost — / But how you played the game.
Grantland Rice, ALUMNUS FOOTBALL

JUSTICE

10 Justice must not only be seen to be done. It must be seen to be believed.
Beachcomber (J. B. Morton)

11 The price of justice is eternal publicity.
Arnold Bennett, THINGS THAT HAVE INTERESTED ME

12 You can live without kindness; you can't live without justice.
Edward Bond, SUMMER *(play)*

13 Justice is being allowed to do whatever I like. Injustice is whatever prevents my doing it.
Samuel Butler, NOTEBOOKS 1912

14 Absolute freedom mocks at justice. Absolute justice denies freedom.
Albert Camus, THE REBEL 1951

15 Moderation in the pursuit of justice is no virtue.
Senator Barry Goldwater. Acceptance speech, Republican National Convention, San Francisco 16 *Jul* 1964

16 Justice should not only be done, but manifestly and undoubtedly seen to be done.
Lord Hewart, Justius, Rex v. Sussex 9 *Nov* 1923

17 Your justice would freeze beer.
Arthur Miller, THE CRUCIBLE 1953

18 Justice is so subtle a thing, to interpret it one has only need of a heart.
José Garcia Oliver. Quoted Hugh Thornes, THE SPANISH CIVIL WAR

19 I would rather be British than just.
Rev. Ian Paisley. Quoted Desmond Boal, Sunday Times 12 *Dec* 1971

K

EDWARD KENNEDY

1 Every country needs at least one King
Farouk.
Gore Vidal. Quoted John Heilpern,
Observer 26 Apr 1981

NIKITA KHRUSHCHEV

2 Khrushchev's greatest work, outweighing
all his idiocies and major howlers, was his
destruction of the Stalin legend and the
emptying of the labour camps, returning to
their homes millions of survivors and
formally rehabilitating millions who were
dead.
Edward Crankshaw reviewing Roy
Medvedev's KHRUSHCHEV, *Observer 9 Jan*
1983

KINDNESS

3 When kindness has left people, even for a
few moments, we become afraid of them as
if their reason has left them.
Willa Cather, MY MORTAL ENEMY 1926

4 As the car drove in at the gate we struck a
bumpy patch, and I could hear the milk of
human kindness sloshing about inside him.
P. G. Wodehouse, PIGS HAVE WINGS 1947

KING

5 When in the green lanes I muse / Alone and
hear birds sing / God's pity then, say I, / On
some Poor King.
W.H. Davies, POOR KINGS

6 Scratch a King and find a fool.
Dorothy Parker, SALOME'S DANCING
LESSON

7 Kings are not born, they are made by mass
hallucination.
George Bernard Shaw, MAN AND
SUPERMAN 1905

RUDYARD KIPLING

8 One of the greatest literary geniuses of the
Anglo-Saxon race, and when time has
winnowed away all the vulgarity, lack of
taste, jingoism and cocksure brassiness, the
residue will be read and enjoyed without
end.
Rupert Hart-Davis, THE LYTTELTON HART-
DAVIS LETTERS 13 *Nov* 1958

KISS

9 You have to kiss an awful lot of frogs before
you find a prince.
Graffito. Quoted BBC Radio 4, Quote
Unquote 7 Jun 1979

10 She gave me a sisterly kiss. Older sister.
Norman Mailer, THE DEER PARK 1955

11 Lips that taste of tears, they say / Are the
best for kissing.
Dorothy Parker, THRENODY

12 Blondes have the hottest kisses. Red-heads
are fair-to-middling torrid, and brunettes
are the frigidest of all. It's something to do
with the hormones, no doubt.
Ronald Reagan. Quoted News Review 20
May 1947

13 He gets his kiss, and it is a very large kiss
indeed, with the cut-out open.
Damon Runyon, MORE THAN
SOMEWHAT 1937

14 There is always one who kisses and one who
only allows the kiss.
George Bernard Shaw, MAN AND
SUPERMAN 1905

15 I kissed my first woman and smoked my first
cigarette on the same day. I have never had
time for tobacco since.
Arturo Toscanini. Quoted Evan Esar,
TREASURY OF HUMOROUS QUOTATIONS

LORD KITCHENER

1 He is rather like one of those revolving lighthouses which radiate momentary gleams of revealing light far out into the surrounding gloom, and then relapse into complete darkness.
David Lloyd George. Quoted John Grigg, Sunday Times 4 Sep 1977

KNOWLEDGE

2 There is no absolute knowledge. Those who claim it . . . open the door to tragedy. All information is imperfect. We have to treat it with humility.
Jacob Bronowski, THE ASCENT OF MAN 1973

3 Thorstein Veblen made a distinction between esoteric knowledge, which enjoys the greatest academic prestige but is without economic or industrial effect, and esoteric learning, which, in contrast, has negligible academic prestige, but is very useful.
J. K. Galbraith, A LIFE IN OUR TIMES 1981

4 All genuine knowledge originates in direct experience.
Mao Tse-Tung. Address, Tenan, Jul 1937

5 It is a great nuisance that knowledge can be acquired only by hard work.
W. Somerset Maugham, CAKES AND ALE 1930

6 Sin, guilt, neurosis — they are one and the same, the fruit of the tree of knowledge.
Henry Miller, THE WISDOM OF THE HEART, *Creative Death* 1941

7 You can know more and more about one thing but you can never know everything about one thing; it's hopeless.
Vladimir Nabokov, STRONG OPINIONS

8 I am sufficiently proud of my knowing something to be modest about my not knowing it at all.
Vladimir Nabokov, LOLITA 1955

9 Apart from the known and the unknown, what else is there?
Harold Pinter, THE HOMECOMING 1965

10 His had been an intellectual decision founded on his conviction that if a little knowledge was a dangerous thing, a lot was lethal.
Tom Sharpe, PORTERHOUSE BLUES

11 The right to know is like the right to live. It is fundamental and unconditional in its assumption that knowledge, like life, is a desirable thing.
George Bernard Shaw, DOCTOR'S DILEMMA, *Preface* 1906

12 Supreme knowledge of one subject presupposes as supreme an ignorance of others.
Alec Waugh, ON DOING WHAT ONE LIKES

L

LADY

1 I have defined ladies as people who did not do things for themselves.
Gwen Raverat, PERIOD PIECE

LANDLADY

2 The landlady can be reduced to her lowest terms by a series of propositions.
Stephen Leacock, LITERARY LAPSES 1910

LANGUAGE

3 The root function of language is to control the universe by describing it.
James Baldwin, NOTES OF A NATIVE SON 1955

4 A piece dear, a piece; a bit is what goes in a horse's mouth.
Sir Hugh Casson and Joyce Grenfell, NANNY SAYS 1972

5 Language is a uniquely human characteristic. Each person has programmed into his genes a faculty called universal grammar.
Noam Chomsky. Speech to the Royal Society

6 I got into my bones the essential structure of the ordinary British sentence — which is a noble thing.
Winston Churchill, MY EARLY LIFE 1935

7 If English was good enough for Jesus Christ it's good enough for me.
Dr David Edwards. Quoting an unnamed American Senator, Sunday Telegraph 5 May 1985

8 A physician, at least in the United States, does not tell you that a patient is dying. He says that the prognosis as of this time is without significant areas of encouragement.
J. K. Galbraith, ECONOMICS, PEACE AND LAUGHTER 1971

9 Language always keeps pace with the social development of its users.
John Honey, THE LANGUAGE TRAP 1983

10 The word makes men free; whoever cannot express himself is a slave. Speaking is an act of freedom in itself.
Reggie Kray. Quoted James Fox, Observer Magazine 14 Mar 1986

11 The language that can with the greatest ease make the finest and most numerous distinctions of meaning is the best.
C. S. Lewis. Quoted Sir Ernest Gower, MODERN ENGLISH USAGE *(revised)*

12 The sum of human wisdom is not contained in any one language, and no single language is *capable* of expressing all forms and degrees of human comprehension.
Ezra Pound, THE ABC OF READING 1934

13 Learn Greek, it is the language of wisdom.
George Bernard Shaw, THE ADVENTURES OF THE BLACK GIRL IN HER SEARCH FOR GOD

14 I am often told that I look like Winston Churchill and speak English like Charles Boyer. But I wish it were the other way round.
M. Paul-Henri Spaak

15 Perhaps of all the creations of man language is the most astonishing.
Lytton Strachey, WORDS AND POETRY

16 The limits of my language stand for the limits of my world.
Ludwig Wittgenstein. Quoted Harry Zohn, KARL KRAUS

LAUGHTER

17 Of all the countless people who have lived before our time on this planet, not one is known in history or legend as having died of laughter.
Max Beerbohm, LAUGHTER

1 Genuine laughter is the physical effect produced in the rational being by what suddenly strikes his immortal soul as being damned funny.
Hilaire Belloc, A CONVERSATION WITH AN ANGEL

2 He laughed like an irresponsible foetus.
T. S. Eliot, MR APOLLINAX 1917

3 His laughter tinkled among the teacups.
Ibid.

4 Laugh for the time is brief, a throw the length of a span / Laugh and be proud to belong to the old proud pageant of man.
John Masefield, LAUGH AND BE MERRY

5 Philip Toynbee's laugh was like the hiss of a soda syphon.
Jessica Mitford, THE FACES OF PHILIP 1984

6 The stimulus of a laugh is an intellectual event, yet it quickly goes on to block out all else. There are only two other phenomena that so completely take over your awareness — the orgasm and the sneeze.
Dr Howard Pollio. Quoted Observer 24 Dec 1978

7 We are in the world to laugh. In purgatory or hell we shall no longer be able to do so. And in heaven it would not be proper.
Jules Rénard, Journal, Jun 1907

8 She has a face the size of a town clock and a laugh so hearty it knocks the whipped cream off an order of strawberry shortcake on a table fifty feet away and arouses the indignation of a customer by the name of Goldstein who is about to consume same.
Damon Runyon, GUYS AND DOLLS 1935

9 I have a great desire to make people smile — not laugh. Laughter is too aggressive. People bare their teeth.
Muriel Spark. Quoted Nicholas Shakespeare, The Times, Suffering and the vital Spark 21 Nov 1983

10 The world loved man when he smiled. The world became afraid of him when he laughed.
Rabindranath Tagore, STRAY BIRDS 1916

11 She had a penetrating sort of laugh. Rather like a train going into a tunnel.
P. G. Wodehouse, THE INIMITABLE JEEVES 1924

12 Honoria is one of those robust, dynamic girls with the muscles of a welterweight and a laugh like a squadron of cavalry charging over a tin bridge. A beastly thing to have to face over the breakfast table.
P. G. Wodehouse, THE RUMMY AFFAIR OF OLD BIFFY

13 I haven't laughed so much since my husband died.
Woman complimenting Victor Borge

LAVATORY

14 Here I sit, alone and sixty / Bald and fat and full of sin / Cold the seat and loud the cistern / As I read the Harpic tin.
Alan Bennett

15 'Vot', asked George I courteously 'is ze difference between a public nuisance and a public convenience?'
Caryl Brahms and S. J. Simon, NO NIGHTINGALES

16 Though the pipes that supply the bathroom burst / And the lavatory makes you fear the worst / It was used by Charles the First / Quite informally / And later by George the Fourth / On a journey North.
Noël Coward, THE STATELY HOMES OF ENGLAND

17 The water-closet like the harp is essentially a solo instrument.
Graffito. Quoted Robert Reisner, GRAFFITI

18 A place where even the King goes on foot — *enfin*, the toilet cabinet.
Aldous Huxley, TIME MUST HAVE A STOP 1946

19 You must know that it is by the state of the lavatory that a family is judged.
Pope John XXIII, LETTERS TO HIS FAMILY 1970

20 A very pious man in Prague, a certain K, knew a great deal of the worldly sciences. He had studied them all in the toilet.
Franz Kafka, DIARIES 1914–1923

21 I boast of being the only man in London who has been bombed off a lavatory seat while reading Jane Austen. She went into the bath: I went through the door.
Kingsley Martin, New Statesman 1940

1 And Willy Nilly, rumbling, jockeys out again to the three-seated shack called the House of Commons in the back where the hens weep.
Dylan Thomas, UNDER MILK WOOD 1954

2 When the war broke out she took down the signed photograph of the Kaiser and, with some solemnity, hung it in the servants' lavatory.
Evelyn Waugh, VILE BODIES 1930

LAW

3 Law is merely the expression of the will of the strongest for the time being, and therefore laws have no fixity, but shift from generation to generation.
Henry Brooks Adams, THE LAW OF CIVILISATION AND DECAY 1955

4 Nobody has a more sacred obligation to obey the law than those who make the law.
Jean Anouilh ANTIGONE 1942

5 If a cow with handlebars is a bicycle within the meaning of the Act, then a bicycle with four legs instead of two wheels is a cow.
Beachcomber (J. B. Morton), Daily Express, By the Way

6 It is illegal to make liquor privately or water publicly.
Lord Birkett

7 A witness cannot give evidence of his age unless he remembers being born.
Judge Blagden. Quoted Observer 29 Jan 1950

8 The law is a causeway upon which, so long as he keeps to it, the citizen may walk safely.
Robert Bolt, A MAN FOR ALL SEASONS 1960

9 This case bristles with simplicity.
Mr Justice Comyn, The Old Bailey 11 Feb 1980

10 The Law of England is a very strange one: it cannot compel anyone to tell the truth; but what it can do is to give you seven years for not telling the truth.
Lord Darling. Quoted in the biography of him by D. Walker-Smith

11 Most lawyers are conservative. That's what's wrong with them. They seem to have a vested interest in not changing the law.
Lord Denning. Quoted John Mortimer, IN CHARACTER 1983

12 My husband keeps telling me to go to hell. Have I a legal right to take the children?
Letter to Dorothy Dix. Quoted Denys Parsons, FUNNY AMUSING FUNNY AMAZING

13 Nothing is more destructive of respect for the government and the law of the land than passing laws which cannot be enforced.
Albert Einstein, IDEAS AND OPINIONS

14 A man who applied for a job as gardener at Hampton Court was asked to sign Form E74 in case he gave away information about watering begonias.
Clement Freud, MP for Isle of Ely speaking in support of his bill for repeal of part of the Official Secrets Act, House of Commons 19 Jan 1979

15 Public opinion is always in advance of the law.
John Galsworthy, WINDOWS

16 There is no better way of exercising the imagination than the study of law. No poet ever interpreted nature as freely as a lawyer interprets truth.
Jean Giraudoux, TIGER AT THE GATES 1935

17 The language of the law must not be foreign to the ears of those who are to obey it.
Judge Learned Hand. Speech, Washington DC 11 May 1929

18 The meanest citizen, actuated by the meanest motives, is entitled to insist upon the enforcement of the law. The question is, 'What is the law?' a question which frequently arises in our Courts and sometimes receives a satisfactory answer.
A. P. Herbert, MORE MISLEADING CASES

19 The Common Law of England has been laboriously built up about a mythical figure — the figure of 'the reasonable man'.
A. P. Herbert, UNCOMMON LAW 1935

20 I have come to regard the Law Courts not as a cathedral, but as a casino.
Richard Ingrams, The Guardian 30 Jul 1977

1 Whenever men take the law into their own hands, the loser is the law. And when law loses, freedom languishes.
Robert Kennedy. Quoted Barbara Rowe, A BOOK OF QUOTES

2 Morality cannot be legislated but behaviour can be regulated. Judicial decrees may not change the heart, but they can restrain the heartless.
Martin Luther King, STRENGTH TO LOVE 1963

3 People starting with the idea that certain things are right and are the law, come to believe that others are right because they are the law.
W. Somerset Maugham, A WRITER'S NOTEBOOK 1949

4 The law is nature. The law is only a word for what has a right to happen.
Arthur Miller, A VIEW FROM THE BRIDGE 1955

5 No brilliance is needed in law. Nothing but common sense and relatively clean finger nails.
John Mortimer, A VOYAGE ROUND MY FATHER

6 A judge is not supposed to know anything about the facts of life until they have been presented in evidence and explained to him at least three times.
Lord Chief Justice Parker, Observer 12 Mar 1961

7 Mr Justice Ridley was known as Mr Justice Necessity, since necessity knows no law.
Francis Pearson, MEMORIES OF A KC'S CLERK

8 The law must be stable, but it must not stand still.
Roscoe Pound, INTRODUCTION TO THE PHILOSOPHY OF LAW

9 A man's respect for law and order exists in precise relationship to the size of his pay cheque.
Adam Clayton Powell, KEEP THE FAITH BABY

10 No man is above the law and no man is below it; nor do we ask any man's permission when we require him to obey it.
Theodore Roosevelt. Speech, Jan 1905

11 Government can easily exist without law, but law cannot exist without government.
Bertrand Russell, UNPOPULAR ESSAYS 1950

12 It is a very salutary check for a judge to realise that if he does say something silly it is liable to get into the papers.
Mr Justice Templeman, Observer 20 Aug 1978

13 Presumably any person on a bicycle who charges into an old lady is neither parking nor overtaking her but merely striking her and would not be guilty of an offence.
Robin Turton MP on the Countryside Bill

14 There is presumably nothing to prevent someone setting up as a freelance brain surgeon; though the police might well bring a charge of manslaughter if things went awry.
Alan Watkins, Observer 3 Dec 1978

ANDREW BONAR LAW

15 It is fitting that we should have buried the Unknown Prime Minister by the side of the Unknown Warrior.
H. H. Asquith after Bonar Law's funeral, Westminster Abbey 5 Nov 1923

D. H. LAWRENCE

16 [He is] one of the great denouncers, the great missionaries the English send to themselves to tell them they are crass, gross, lost, dead, mad and addicted to unnatural vices.
Kingsley Amis, WHAT BECAME OF JANE AUSTEN?

17 This pictorial account of the day-to-day life of an English gamekeeper is full of considerable interest to outdoor-minded readers . . . Unfortunately one is obliged to wade through many pages of extraneous material . . . in this reviewer's opinion, the book cannot take the place of J. R. Miller's *Practical Gamekeeping.*
Anon. Field and Stream, review of LADY CHATTERLEY'S LOVER

18 Lawrence seemed to me sometimes to suffer from a delusion similar to the delusion of the sick man who thinks that if a given quantity of medicine will do him good, twice the quantity will do him twice as good.
Arnold Bennett, Evening Standard 12 Apr 1930

1 *The Rainbow*, a novel by Mr D. H. Lawrence, is more hideous than any imaginable reality. The thing is done so coldly, so pompously, so gravely that it is like a savage rite. There is not a gleam of humour in the fog of eloquent lubricity. The thud, thud, thud of hectic phrases is intolerably wearisome.
James Douglas, The Star, reviewing THE RAINBOW 22 *Oct* 1915

2 Interesting, but a type I could not get on with. Obsessed with self. Dead eyes and a red beard, long narrow face. A strange bird.
John Galsworthy, LIFE AND LETTERS *(ed. H. V. Marrot)* 1935

3 Is it [*Lady Chatterley's Lover*] a book you would leave lying around your own house? Is it a book that you would wish your wife or even your servant to read?
Mervyn Griffith-Jones, prosecuting in the obscenity case against Penguin Books 1961

4 For Lawrence, existence was one continuous convalescence; it was as though he were newly reborn from a mortal illness every day of his life.
Aldous Huxley, THE OLIVE TREE

5 You mustn't think I advocate perpetual sex. Far from it. Nothing nauseates me more than promiscuous sex in and out of season.
D. H. Lawrence, on LADY CHATTERLEY'S LOVER, *in a letter to Lady Ottoline Morrell* 22 *Dec* 1928

6 I sincerely believe in restoring the phallic consciousness into our lives because it is the source of all real beauty and all real gentleness. And those are the two things, tenderness and beauty which will save us from the horrors.
D. H. Lawrence, letter to Harriet Monroe 15 *Mar* 1928

7 *Lady Chatterley's Lover* is an extremely dull and portentously silly and pretentious book.
G. W. Lyttelton, THE LYTTELTON HART-DAVIS LETTERS 22 *Dec* 1955

8 Capable of an occasional joke in his letters, he is consistently without humour in his books, a failing rarely, if ever, to be found in novelists of the highest class, from Petronius to Proust.
Anthony Powell, THE STRANGERS ARE ALL GONE, VOL. 4, *The Memoirs*

9 No other writer in the twentieth century, except Freud, has been subject to so much abuse from so many otherwise intelligent people.
Philip Rieff, THE TRIUMPH OF THE THERAPEUTIC

10 *Lady Chatterley's Lover* is a book that all Christians might read with profit.
John Robinson (Bishop of Woolwich) speaking for the defence in the obscenity case against Penguin books 1961

11 His descriptive powers were remarkable, but his ideas cannot too soon be forgotten.
Bertrand Russell, AUTOBIOGRAPHY 1967

T. E. LAWRENCE

12 [He was] a bore, a bounder and a prig. He was intoxicated with his own youth and loathed any milieu which he couldn't dominate. Certainly he had none of a gentleman's instincts, strutting about Peace Conferences in Arab dress.
Henry Channon, DIARY 25 *May* 1935

13 There are those who have tried to dismiss his story with a flourish of the Union Jack, a psycho-analytical catchword or a sneer; it should move our deepest admiration and pity. Like Shelley and like Baudelaire, it may be said of him that he suffered, in his own person, the neurotic ills of an entire generation.
Christopher Isherwood, EXHUMATIONS

14 If he hides in a quarry he puts red flags all round.
George Bernard Shaw. Quoted The Guardian 22 *Jan* 1963

15 He had a genius for backing into the limelight.
Lowell Thomas, LAWRENCE OF ARABIA

16 They only got two things right, the camels and the sand.
Lowell Thomas of the film. Quoted The Times, obituary 29 *Aug* 1981

LAZINESS

17 He has his law degree and a furnished office. It's just a question now of getting him out of bed.
Cartoon caption by Peter Arno, The New Yorker 1938

LEADER

1 People, like sheep, tend to follow a leader — occasionally in the right direction.
Alexander Chase, PERSPECTIVES 1960

2 To be a leader of men one must turn one's back on men.
Havelock Ellis

3 There is a kind of person who out of the very certainty of his purpose, right or wrong, both assumes leadership and is conceded leadership. No quality so assures public success.
J. K. Galbraith, THE AGE OF UNCERTAINTY 1977

4 All of the great leaders have had one characteristic in common; it was the willingness to confront unequivocally the major anxiety of their people in their time. This, and not much else, is the essence of leadership.
Ibid.

5 The leader of genius must have the ability to make different opponents appear as if they belonged to one category.
Adolf Hitler, MEIN KAMPF 1924

6 The art of leadership consists in consolidating the attention of the people against a single adversary and taking care that nothing will split that attention.
Ibid.

7 The English soldiers fight like lions . . . but they are lions led by donkeys.
Max Hoffman. Quoted A. Clark, THE DONKEYS

8 I must follow them, I am their leader.
Andrew Bonar Law. Quoted Ernest Raymond, MR BALFOUR

9 It is not necessary to have original ideas to be quite a successful leader.
Lord Longford, DIARY OF A YEAR

10 Only one man in a thousand is a leader of men — the other 999 follow women.
Groucho Marx. Quoted News Review 10 *Jul* 1947

11 The most important quality in a leader is to be acknowledged as such. All leaders whose fitness is questioned are clearly lacking in force.
André Maurois, THE ART OF LIVING

12 The real leader has no need to lead — he is content to point the way.
Henry Miller, THE WISDOM OF THE HEART 1941

13 Leadership appears to be the art of getting others to want to do something you are convinced should be done.
Vance Packard, THE HIDDEN PERSUADERS

14 I never came to this through driving personal ambition. A combined opportunity and duty presented itself and I took it.
Margaret Thatcher on becoming leader of the Conservative Party, May 1975

15 No amount of learning will make a man a leader unless he has the natural qualities of one.
Gen. Archibald Wavell, The Times 17 *Feb* 1941

LEARNING

16 They know enough who know how to learn.
Henry Brooks Adams, THE EDUCATION OF HENRY ADAMS 1918

17 I learned just by going around. I know all about Kleenex factories, and all sorts of things.
Princess Anne. Quoted Noël St George, ROYAL QUOTES

18 I am always ready to learn although I do not always like being taught.
Winston Churchill. Quoted Observer 9 *Nov* 1952

19 In the traditional method the child must say something that he has merely learned. There is all the difference in the world between having something to say, and having to say something.
John Dewey, DEWEY ON EDUCATION

20 It is a very grave mistake to think that the enjoyment of seeing and searching can be promoted by means of coercion and a sense of duty.
Albert Einstein. Quoted George B. Leonard, EDUCATION AND ECSTASY

21 It is the true nature of mankind to learn from mistakes, not from example.
Fred Hoyle, INTO DEEPEST SPACE

1 A learned man is an idler who kills time by study.
George Bernard Shaw, MAN AND SUPERMAN, *Maxims for Revolutionists* 1905

LEISURE

2 We are closer to the ants than to the butterflies. Very few people can endure much leisure.
Gerald Brenan, THOUGHTS IN A DRY SEASON 1979

3 What is this life if full of care / We have no time to stand and stare?
W. H. Davies, LEISURE

4 I am interested in leisure in the way that a poor man is interested in money. I can't get enough of it.
Philip, Duke of Edinburgh. Quoted Noël St George,

5 To be able to fill leisure intelligently is the last product of civilisation.
Bertrand Russell, THE CONQUEST OF HAPPINESS 1930

6 Leisure is time at personal risk.
A. M. Sullivan, THE THREE DIMENSIONAL MAN

V. I. LENIN

7 Their [the Russian people's] worst misfortune was his birth; their next worst — his death.
Winston Churchill, THE WORLD CRISIS 1929

LIBEL

8 I'd like to see judges in libel cases sitting without juries. Juries hate newspapers.
Lord Denning. Quoted John Mortimer, IN CHARACTER 1983

LIBERALISM

9 If God had been a Liberal there wouldn't have been ten commandments, there would have been ten suggestions.
Malcolm Bradbury and Christopher Bigsby, AFTER DINNER GAME (*TV play*)

10 You Liberals think that goats are just sheep from broken homes.
Ibid.

11 The theory that one race can be superior to another, but that no race can ever be inferior to another.
Miles Kington, The Times, A Guide to Real Meanings 7 Feb 1983

12 Liberalism, in one variation or another, the egghead's credo, may be strategically sound, but it is tactically fallacious, and as such highly misleading as well as highly distinctive. Indeed in my opinion it is *the* destructive force of the age.
Malcolm Muggeridge, TREAD SOFTLY FOR YOU TREAD ON MY JOKES 1966

13 The fallacy of the liberal mind is to see good in everything. This has been of great assistance to the devil.
Malcolm Muggeridge. Quoted John Mortimer, IN CHARACTER 1983

LIBERTY

14 Freeing oppressed nationalities is perhaps the most dangerous of all philanthropic enterprises.
William Bolitho, TWELVE AGAINST THE GODS 1929

15 Liberty is the way, and the only way, of perfectibility. Without liberty, heavy industry can be perfected, but no justice or truth.
Albert Camus, RESISTANCE, REBELLION AND DEATH 1961

16 Liberty is a different kind of pain from prison.
T. S. Eliot, THE FAMILY REUNION 1939

17 Extremism in the defence of liberty is not a vice.
Senator Barry Goldwater. Acceptance speech, Republican National Convention, San Francisco 16 Jul 1964

18 Liberty is so much latitude as the powerful choose to accord to the weak.
Judge Learned Hand. Speech, University of Pennsylvania Law School 21 May 1944

19 Political liberty's a swindle because a man doesn't spend his time being political. He spends it sleeping, eating, amusing himself a little and working — mostly working.
Aldous Huxley, ANTIC HAY 1923

223

1 'Liberty, Mr Gumboil?' he said, 'you don't suppose any serious minded person imagines a revolution is going to bring liberty, do you?'
Ibid.

2 A just society would be one in which liberty for one person is constrained only by the demands created by equal liberty for another.
Ivan Illich, TOOLS FOR CONVIVIALITY

3 The deadliest foe of democracy is not autocracy, but liberty frenzied. Liberty is not fool-proof. For its beneficent working it demands self-restraint.
Otto Kahn, Wisconsin University 14 *Jan* 1918

4 In a state worthy of the name there is no liberty. The people want to exercise power but what on earth would they do with it if it were given to them?
V. I. Lenin, THE STATE AND REVOLUTION 1917

5 It is true that liberty is precious, so precious that it must be rationed.
Ibid.

6 There is always a danger that human beings will lose interest in liberty as soon as they have achieved it or — worse still perhaps — use their new-found liberty to destroy the liberty of others.
Robert Lynd, John o'London's Weekly 30 *Jun* 1939

7 What good is an excess of liberty if individuals are afraid to leave their homes or walk the streets?
Sir David McNee, Metropolitan Police Commissioner, Observer 27 *Aug* 1978

8 My government will protect all liberties but one — the liberty to do away with other liberties.
President Ordaz of Mexico, inaugural speech

9 If liberty means anything at all it means the right to tell people what they do not want to here.
George Orwell. Quoted Peter Lewis, THE ROAD TO 1984 1981

10 Too little liberty brings stagnation, and too much brings chaos.
Bertrand Russell, AUTHORITY AND THE INDIVIDUAL

11 Liberty means responsibility. That is why most men dread it.
George Bernard Shaw, MAN AND SUPERMAN 1905

12 We have confused the free with the free and easy.
Adlai Stevenson, PUTTING FIRST THINGS FIRST

13 Liberty is the hardest test that one can inflict on a people. To know how to be free is not given equally to all men and all nations.
Paul Valéry, REFLECTIONS ON THE WORLD TODAY, *On the Subject of Dictatorship* 1931

14 Liberty does not consist in mere declarations of the rights of man. It consists in the translation of those declarations into definite action.
Woodrow Wilson. Speech 4 *Jul* 1914

LIBRARY

15 I've been drunk for about a week now and I thought it might sober me up to sit in library.
F. Scott Fitzgerald, THE GREAT GATSBY 1925

16 We welcome sleepers here. A sleeping reader is less of a menace to the books than a waking one.
Librarian at Cambridge University. Quoted The Times

17 A library is thought in cold storage.
Lord Samuel

LIE

18 She tells enough white lies to ice a cake.
Margot Asquith, AUTOBIOGRAPHY 1936

19 Matilda told such Dreadful Lies / It made one Gasp and Stretch one's Eyes.
Hilaire Belloc, CAUTIONARY TALES 1907

20 For every time she shouted 'Fire' / They only answered 'Little Liar' / And therefore when her Aunt returned / Matilda, and the House, were Burned.
Ibid.

21 The moment a man talks to his fellows he begins to lie.
Hilaire Belloc, THE SILENCE OF THE SEA

1 Never to lie is to have no lock to your door.
Elizabeth Bowen, THE HOUSE IN PARIS 1935

2 The best liar is he who makes the smallest amount of lying go the longest way.
Samuel Butler, THE WAY OF ALL FLESH 1903

3 I do not mind lying, but I hate inaccuracy.
Samuel Butler, NOTEBOOKS 1912

4 A lie can be half way round the world before the truth has got its boots on.
James Callaghan. Speech 1 Nov 1976

5 It cannot in the opinion of His Majesty's Government be classified as slavery in the extreme acceptance of the word without some risk of terminological inexactitude.
Winston Churchill, House of Commons 22 Feb 1906

6 Without lies humanity would perish of despair and boredom.
Anatole France, THE BLOOM OF LIFE 1922

7 The great masses of the people will more easily fall victims to a great lie than a small one.
Adolf Hitler, MEIN KAMPF 1924

8 A lie goes by the Marconi route, while Truth goes by slow freight and is often ditched at the first water tank.
Elbert Hubbard, EPIGRAMS 1915

9 Nature cannot tell lies, but human beings can and do . . . our ability to tell lies is perhaps our most striking human characteristic.
Sir Edmund Leach. Address to the British Association, York 2 Sep 1981

10 She's too crafty a woman to invent a new lie when an old one will serve.
W. Somerset Maugham, THE CONSTANT WIFE 1926

11 I have never but once succeeded in making him [George Edward Moore] tell a lie and that was by a subterfuge. 'Moore,' I said, 'Do you *always* tell the truth?' 'No', he replied. I believe this to be the only lie he ever told.
Bertrand Russell, AUTOBIOGRAPHY 1967

12 Ellie: But how can you love a liar?
Mrs Hushabye: I don't know. But you can, fortunately. Otherwise there wouldn't be much love in the world.
George Bernard Shaw, HEARTBREAK HOUSE 1920

13 We are all liars to people we don't care for.
George Bernard Shaw, LETTERS

14 The liar's punishment is not in the least that he is not believed, but that he cannot believe anyone else.
George Bernard Shaw

15 A lie is an abomination unto the Lord and a very present help in trouble.
Adlai Stevenson. Speech, Springfield, Jan 1951

16 He will lie even when it is inconvenient: the sign of the true artist.
Gore Vidal, TWO SISTERS 1970

17 Lies are the mortar that binds the savage individual man into the social masonry.
H. G. Wells, LOVE AND MR LEWISHAM 1900

LIFE

18 Life is rather like a tin of sardines — we are all looking for the key.
Alan Bennett, BEYOND THE FRINGE

19 Human beings are designed for paradise. How is it our lives are such hell?
Edward Bond, RESTORATION *(play)*

20 To live is like love, all reason is against it, and all healthy instinct for it.
Samuel Butler, NOTEBOOKS 1912

21 Life is a dusty corridor, I say, / Shut at both ends.
Roy Campbell, THE FLAMING TERRAPIN

22 What is life? It is the flash of a firefly in the night. It is the breath of a buffalo in the wintertime. It is as the little shadow that runs across the grass and loses itself in the sunset.
Truman Capote, IN COLD BLOOD 1965

23 Life was a funny thing that occurred on the way to the grave.
Quentin Crisp, THE NAKED CIVIL SERVANT

24 The man who regards his own life and that of his fellow creatures as meaningless is not merely unfortunate but almost disqualified for life.
Albert Einstein, THE WORLD AS I SEE IT 1934

1 I have measured out my life with coffee spoons.
T. S. Eliot, THE LOVE SONG OF J. ALFRED PRUFROCK 1917

2 The most important lesson is to understand life, not to make *a priori* judgement about it.
David Garnett, GREAT FRIENDS

3 Welcome O Life! I go to encounter for the millionth time the reality of experience and to forge in the smithy of my soul the uncreated conscience of my race.
James Joyce, A PORTRAIT OF THE ARTIST AS A YOUNG MAN *(final words)* 1916

4 Life is a sexually transmitted disease and there is a 100% mortality rate.
R. D. Laing. *Quoted Peter Hillmore*, *Observer* 17 Mar 1985

5 Life is first boredom, then fear / Whether or not we use it, it goes.
Philip Larkin, DOCKERY AND SON 1964

6 Life is something to do when you can't get to sleep.
Fran Lebowitz. *Quoted John Heilpern*, *Observer* 21 Jan 1979

7 Life is like a sewer. What you get out of it depends on what you put into it.
Tom Lehrer, WE WILL ALL GO TOGETHER WHEN WE GO

8 The four stages of man are infancy, childhood, adolescence and obsolescence.
Art Linklater, A CHILD'S GARDEN OF MISINFORMATION 1965

9 A man's life is made up of a few intense moments, and the time spent in between is just packing and doesn't count.
F. W. Lister, THE WIND THAT BLOWS

10 Life to me is like boarding-house wallpaper. It takes a long time to get used to it, but when you finally do, you never notice that it's there. And then you hear the decorators are arriving.
Derek Marlowe, A DANDY IN ASPIC 1966

11 Life's a long headache in a noisy street.
John Masefield, THE WIDOW IN THE BYE STREET 1912

12 For the complete life, the perfect pattern includes old age as well as youth and maturity.

W. Somerset Maugham, THE SUMMING UP 1938

13 Life to me has been like one of those sections of the autostrada on the Italian Riviera on which there are lots of tunnels, some long, some short, with sunlit open spaces of varying lengths between them for which the darkness leaves one dazzled and unprepared.
Eric Newby, A TRAVELLER'S LIFE 1982

14 Life is perhaps best regarded as a bad dream between two awakenings.
Eugene O'Neill, MARCO MILLIONS 1928

15 The length of life is generally in inverse proportion to the rate of living — the more rapid the pace the shorter the time that life endures.
Raymond Pearl. *Quoted George W. Gray*, *Harper's*, Feb 1941

16 Real life is, to most men, a long second-best, a perpetual compromise between the ideal and the possible.
Bertrand Russell, STUDY OF MATHEMATICS

17 When we have found how the nuclei of atoms are built-up we shall have found the greatest secret of all — except life. We shall have found the basis of everything - of the earth we walk on, of the air we breathe, of the sunshine, of our physical body itself, of everything in the world, however great or however small — except life.
Lord Rutherford. *Quoted Passing Show* 24 Sep 1932

18 There is no cure for birth and death save to enjoy the interval.
George Santayana, SOLILOQUIES IN ENGLAND, *War Shrines* 1922

19 Life is not a spectacle or a feast; it is a predicament.
George Santayana, ARTICLES AND ESSAYS

20 Life is a game at which everybody loses.
Leo Sarkadi-Schuller, WITHIN FOUR WALLS

21 Life is a flame that is always burning itself out; but it catches fire again every time a child is born.
George Bernard Shaw, THE ADVENTURES OF THE BLACK GIRL IN HER SEARCH FOR GOD

1 Life is a disease, and the only difference
between one man and another is the stage of
the disease at which he lives.
George Bernard Shaw, BACK TO
METHUSELAH 1922

2 Don't try to live for ever. You will not
succeed.
George Bernard Shaw, THE DOCTOR'S
DILEMMA, *Preface* 1906

3 Life is a cluster of disappointments made
bearable by the challenges they establish.
Peter Vansittart, PATHS FROM A WHITE
HORSE 1985

4 Tisn't life that matters! 'Tis the courage you
bring to it.
Hugh Walpole, FORTITUDE 1913 *(opening
sentence)*

5 Life is an unanswered question, but let's still
believe in the dignity and importance of the
question.
Tennessee Williams, CAMINO REAL 1953

6 Most people's lives — what are they but
trails of debris, long long trails of debris with
nothing to clean it all up but, finally, death?
Tennessee Williams, SUDDENLY, LAST
SUMMER 1958

7 If you come to think of it, what a queer thing
life is! So unlike anything else, don't you
know, if you know what I mean.
P. G. Wodehouse, MY MAN JEEVES 1919

LIGHT

8 The pale, cold light of the winter sunset did
not beautify — it was like the light of truth
itself.
Willa Cather, MY ANTONIA 1918

LIMITATION

9 Art is limitation; the essence of every
picture is the frame!
G. K. Chesterton, ORTHODOXY 1908

LITERACY

10 The ratio of literacy to illiteracy is constant,
but nowadays the illiterates can read and
write.
*Alberto Moravia. Quoted Mary McCarthy,
Observer, A World Out of Joint* 14 Oct 1979

11 Education has produced a vast population
able to read but unable to distinguish what is
worth reading.
G. M. Trevelyan, ENGLISH SOCIAL
HISTORY 1944

LITERATURE

12 Some books are undeservedly forgotten;
none are undeservedly remembered.
W. H. Auden, THE DYER'S HAND,
Reading 1962

13 Of all fatiguing, futile, empty trades, the
worst, I suppose, is writing about writing.
Hilaire Belloc, THE SILENCE OF THE SEA

14 Literature is not a parlour game. But neither
is it the preserve of a small élite.
John Braine, J. B. PRIESTLEY

15 I've always had enough sense not to try and
bite off more than I can chew; in literature
no As for effort are awarded.
John Braine, THE QUEEN OF A DISTANT
COUNTRY

16 Literature has a way of putting life in a
strait-jacket.
Arthur Calder-Marshall, THE TWO
DUCHESSES

17 The primary object of a student of literature
is to be delighted. His duty is to enjoy
himself, his efforts should be directed to
developing his faculty of appreciation.
David Cecil, THE FINE ART OF
READING 1957

18 He set out seriously to describe the inde-
scribable. That is the whole business of
literature and it is a hard row to hoe.
G. K. Chesterton, ALL I SURVEY 1933

19 Literature would be altogether too tense if it
were written solely by immortal authors.
We must take writers as they are, and not
expect them all to last.
Oliver Edwards, The Times 25 *Apr* 1965

20 Only two classes of books are of universal
appeal. The very best and the very worst.
Ford Maddox Ford, JOSEPH CONRAD

21 It is with noble sentiments that bad literature gets written.
André Gide, JOURNAL 2 *Sep* 1940

1 He knew everything about literature except how to enjoy it.
Joseph Heller, CATCH 22 1961

2 That was the chief difference between literature and life. In books, the proportion of exceptional to commonplace people is high; in reality, very low.
Aldous Huxley, EYELESS IN GAZA 1936

3 The fact that many people should be shocked by what he writes practically imposes a duty upon the writer to go on writing.
Aldous Huxley, MUSIC AT NIGHT, *Vulgarity in Literature* 1931

4 There are two literary maladies — writer's cramp and swelled head. The worst of writer's cramp is that it is never cured; the worst of swelled head is that it never kills.
Coulson Kernahan, lecture

5 Our American professors like their literature clear and cold and pure and very dead.
Sinclair Lewis, on receiving the Nobel prize 12 *Dec* 1930

6 Literature is mostly about having sex and not much about having children; life is the other way round.
David Lodge, THE BRITISH MUSEUM IS FALLING DOWN

7 I'm happy the great ones are thriving / But what puzzles my head / Is the thought that they needed reviving / I had never been told they were dead.
Phyllis McGinley, THE PREVALENCE OF LITERARY REVIVAL

8 Good prose should resemble the conversation of a well-bred man.
W. Somerset Maugham, THE SUMMING UP 1938

9 England produced Shakespeare: the British Empire the six-shilling novel.
George Moore, HAIL AND FAREWELL 1911

10 Books give the kind of comfort one feels when one realises that for all its blunders and boners the inner texture of life is also a matter of inspiration and precision.
Vladimir Nabokov, LECTURES ON LITERATURE

11 Literature is not about something: it is the thing itself, the quiddity.
Ibid.

12 There is no test of literary merit except survival, which is itself, an index to majority opinion.
George Orwell, SELECTED ESSAYS 1968

13 Great literature is simply language charged with meaning to the utmost possible degree.
Ezra Pound, HOW TO READ 1931

14 Literature is news that *stays* news.
Ezra Pound, ABC OF READING 1931

15 The illusion of art is to make one believe that great literature is very close to life, but exactly the opposite is true. Life is amorphous, literature is formal.
Françoise Sagan, WRITERS AT WORK 1958

16 To turn events into ideas is the function of literature.
George Santayana, LITTLE ESSAYS

17 His [Ronald Firbank's] most rational response to my attempts at drawing him out about literature and art was 'I adore italics, don't you?'
Siegfried Sassoon, SIEGFRIED'S JOURNEY 1945

18 For me, Literature with a capital L is rubbish.
Georges Simenon. Quoted Fenton Bresler, THE MYSTERY OF GEORGES SIMENON 1983

19 Few understand the work of cummings / And few James Joyce's mental slummings / And few young Ander's coded chatter / But then it is the few that matter.
Dylan Thomas, letter to Pamela Hansford Johnson

20 The first mistake is to assume that literary works can be seeded like tennis players. Imagine having to choose between 'Huckleberry Finn' and 'Crime and Punishment'. One is an apple, the other is plainly a coconut.
Gore Vidal

21 No writer before the middle of the 19th century wrote about the working classes other than as grotesques or as pastoral decoration. Then when they were given the vote certain writers began to suck up to them.
Evelyn Waugh, PARIS REVIEW 1963

22 Literature must be an analysis of experience and a synthesis of the finding into a unity.
Rebecca West, ENDING IN EARNEST

1 Literature is the orchestration of platitudes.
Thornton Wilder, Time 12 Jan 1953

2 A good essay must have this permanent quality about it: it must draw its curtain round us, but it must be a curtain that shuts us in, not out.
Virginia Woolf, THE COMMON READER 1925

3 The poet gives us his essence, but prose takes the mould of the mind and body entire.
Virginia Woolf, THE CAPTAIN'S DEATH BED

LIVERPOOL

4 This god-forsaken city, with a climate so evil that no self-respecting singer would ever set foot in it! It is a catarrhal place that has been the cause through the centuries of the nasal Liverpool accent.
Sir Thomas Beecham. Quoted Harold Atkins and Archie Newman, BEECHAM STORIES

5 Standing on the bridge, staring down at the dirty, rubbish-clogged river, he cried out: 'The quality of Mersey is not strained'.
Jilly Cooper, THE BRITISH IN LOVE

DAVID LLOYD GEORGE

6 Lloyd George could not see a belt without hitting below it.
Margot Asquith, AUTOBIOGRAPHY 1936

7 He [Lloyd George] spent his whole life in plastering together the true and the false and therefrom extracting the plausible.
Stanley Baldwin. Quoted Leon Harris, THE FINE ART OF POLITICAL WIT

8 He did not care in which direction the car was travelling, so long as he remained in the driver's seat.
Lord Beaverbrook, New Statesman 14 Jun 1963

9 Mr Lloyd George spoke for a hundred and seventeen minutes, in which period he was detected only once in the use of an argument.
Arnold Bennett, THINGS THAT HAVE INTERESTED MEN

10 The vehement, contriving, resourceful, nimble-leaping, Lloyd George.
Winston Churchill, GREAT CONTEMPORARIES 1937

11 The Happy Warrior of Squandermania.
Winston Churchill

12 This syren, this goat-footed bard, this half-human visitor to our age from the hag-ridden magic and enchanted woods of Celtic antiquity.
J. M. Keynes. Quoted R. F. Harrod, LIFE OF J. M. KEYNES

13 The rogue elephant among British prime ministers.
Kenneth Morgan, LIFE OF D. LLOYD GEORGE

14 He is without malice of any kind; without prejudices, without morals. He has many enemies and no friends. He does not understand what friendship means . . . and yet he is the best man we have got.
F. S. Oliver, THE ANVIL OF WAR

15 Of the three parties I find them [Labour] the least painful. My objection to the Tories is temperamental and my objection to the Liberals is Lloyd George.
Bertrand Russell in a letter to Maurice Amos MP 16 Jun 1930

16 A master of improvised speech and improvised policies.
A. J. P. Taylor, ENGLISH HISTORY 1914–1945

LOGIC

17 *Logic, n.* The art of thinking and reasoning in strict accordance with the limitations and incapacities of the human understanding.
Ambrose Bierce, THE DEVIL'S DICTIONARY 1906

18 Logic is like the sword — those who appeal to it shall perish by it.
Samuel Butler, NOTEBOOKS 1912

19 The want of logic annoys. Too much logic bores. Life eludes logic, and everything that logic alone constructs remains artificial and forced.
André Gide, JOURNALS 12 *May* 1927

1 Logic is one thing, the human animal another. You can quite easily propose a logical solution to something and at the same time hope in your heart of hearts that it won't work out.
Luigi Pirandello, THE PLEASURE OF HONESTY 1917

2 Pure logic is the ruin of the spirit.
Antoine de Saint-Exupéry, FLIGHT TO ARRAS 1942

3 A mind all logic is like a knife all blade. It makes the hand bleed that uses it.
Rabindranath Tagore, STRAY BIRDS 1916

4 It is no good saying 'I don't happen to be logical'. Logic is simply the architecture of human reason. If you try to base your life and hopes on logical absurdities *you will go mad.*
Evelyn Waugh, letter to John Betjeman 22 Dec 1946

LONDON

5 London is a splendid place to live in for those who can get out of it.
Lord Balfour of Burleigh

6 I don't know what London's coming to — the higher the buildings the lower the morals.
Noë Coward, LAW AND ORDER

7 If I could choose the place where I die it would be London because then the transition from life to death would hardly be noticeable.
Graffito on a wall in Hammersmith. Quoted Nigel Rees, GRAFFITI RULES OK 1979

8 Buckingham Palace, the Queen's delightful home in the London suburb of Westminster.
Barry Humphries, DAME EDNA'S COFFEE TABLE BOOK

9 I thought of London spread out in the sun / Its postal districts packed like squares of wheat.
Philip Larkin, THE WHITSUN WEDDINGS

10 London seems to me like some hoary, massive underworld, a hoary ponderous inferno. The traffic flows the rigid grey streets like the rivers of hell through their banks of dry, rocky ash.
D. H. Lawrence, SELECTED LETTERS 1962

11 And London Town, of all the towns I'm glad to leave behind.
John Masefield, LONDON TOWN

12 London is chaos incorporated.
George Mikes, DOWN WITH EVERYBODY

13 London is a town of nice surprises and at any moment you may run into the Queen doing some shopping, or see a swan flying over.
Nursery World. *Quoted Michael Bateman*, THIS ENGLAND

LONELINESS

14 The work of a Prime Minister is the loneliest job in the world.
Stanley Baldwin. Speech 9 Jan 1927

15 I am feeling very lonely. I've been married for fifteen years, and yesterday my wife ran off with the chap next door. I'm going to miss him terribly.
Les Dawson, BBC TV, Those Were the Days 24 Apr 1979

16 Pray that your loneliness may spur you into finding something to live for, great enough to die for.
Dag Hammarskjöld, DIARIES

17 Lonely people talking to each other can make each other lonelier.
William Hellman, THE AUTUMN GARDEN *(play)* 1951

18 People speak of the sadness of being in a crowd and knowing no one. There is something pleasurable in it too.
Sir Arthur Helps, COMPANIONS OF MY SOLITUDE

19 All the lonely people where do they all come from? / All the lonely people where do they all belong?
John Lennon and Paul McCartney, ELEANOR RIGBY *(song)*

20 We are born helpless. As soon as we are fully conscious we discover loneliness.
C. S. Lewis, THE FOUR LOVES

21 Don't think you can frighten me by telling me I am alone. France is alone; and God is alone; and what is my loneliness before the loneliness of my country and my God?
George Bernard Shaw, ST JOAN 1923

1 Loneliness can be conquered only by those who can bear solitude.
Paul Tillich, THE ETERNAL NOW 1963

LONGEVITY

2 Longevity is the revenge of talent upon genius.
Cyril Connolly, Sunday Times 19 *Jun* 1966

ANITA LOOS

3 You are the first American to make sex funny.
Said to her by a friend, on reading
GENTLEMEN PREFER BLONDES

LOVE

4 If I ever really love it will be like Mary Queen of Scots, who said of her Bothwell that she could follow him round the world in her nightie.
J. M. Barrie, WHAT EVERY WOMAN KNOWS *(play)* 1908

5 To fall in love is to create a religion that has a fallible God.
Jorge Luis Borges, OTHER INQUISITIONS 1952

6 It is proverbial that from a hungry tiger and an affectionate woman there is no escape.
Ernest Bramah, KAI LUNG UNROLLS HIS MAT 1928

7 Love is also like a coconut which is good while it is fresh, but you have to spit it out when the juice is gone, what's left tastes bitter.
Bertolt Brecht, BAAL 1926

8 Falling in love is one of the activities forbidden that tiresome person, the consistently reasonable man.
Sir Arthur Eddington, News Chronicle 2 *Mar* 1932

9 Love is the great enemy of Christian morality.
Max Ernst. Quoted John Russell, MAX ERNST, HIS LIFE AND WORK

10 Love is a great force in private life; it is indeed the greatest of all things; but love in public affairs does not work . . . We can only love what we know personally.
E. M. Forster, TWO CHEERS FOR DEMOCRACY, *Tolerance* 1951

11 When one loves somebody everything is clear — where to go, what to do — it all takes care of itself and one doesn't have to ask anybody about anything.
Maxim Gorky, THE ZYKOVS 1914

12 I know nothing about platonic love except that it is not to be found in the works of Plato.
Edgar Jepson. Quoted James Agate, EGO 5 24 *Aug* 1940

13 The hardships of living together. Forced upon us by strangeness, pity, lust, cowardice, vanity and only deep down, perhaps, a thin little stream worthy of the name of love, impossible to seek out, flashing once in the moment of a moment.
Franz Kafka, DIARIES 1914–23

14 Many a man in love with a dimple makes the mistake of marrying the whole girl.
Stephen Leacock, LITERARY LAPSES 1910

15 So we must say Goodbye, my darling, / and go, as lovers go, for ever; / Tonight remains, to pack and fix on labels / And make an end of lying down together.
Alun Lewis, GOODBYE

16 The only place outside Heaven where you can be safe from all the dangers and perturbations of love is Hell.
C. S. Lewis, THE FOUR LOVES

17 I loved Kirk so much I would have skied down Mount Everest in the nude with a carnation up my nose.
Joyce McKinney, Mormon missionary trial 11 *Dec* 1977

18 Love is simple to understand if you haven't got a mind soft and full of holes. It's a crutch, that's all, and there isn't any one of us that doesn't need a crutch.
Norman Mailer, BARBARY SHORE 1951

19 Love is like quicksilver in the hand. Leave the fingers open and it stays. Clutch it, and it darts away.
Dorothy Parker

1 Here's my strength and weakness gents, / I
loved them until they loved me.
Dorothy Parker, BALLADE AT THIRTY FIVE

2 Every love is the love before / In a duller
dress.
Dorothy Parker, DEATH AND TAXES 1931

3 Scratch a lover and find a fool.
Dorothy Parker, ENOUGH ROPE 1927

4 By the time you say you're his, / Shivering
and sighing / And he vows his passion is /
Infinite, undying — / Lady, make a note of
this / One of you is lying.
Dorothy Parker, NOT SO DEEP AS A
WELL 1936

5 Whose love is given over-well / Shall look
on Helen's face in hell / Whilst those whose
love is thin and wise / May view John Knox
in paradise.
Dorothy Parker, PARTIAL COMFORT

6 Do young men these days still become
hopelessly enamoured of married women
easily ten years their senior who have
mocking, humorous mouths, eyes filled with
tender raillery, and indulgent husbands?
S. J. Perelman, KEEP IT CRISP

7 Love is always in the mood of believing in
miracles.
John Cowper Powys, THE MEANING OF
CULTURE

8 There can be no peace of mind in love since
the advantage one has secured is never
anything but a fresh starting-point for
further desires.
Marcel Proust, REMEMBRANCE OF THINGS
PAST 1913–1927

9 How absurd and delicious it is to be in love
with somebody younger than yourself.
Everybody should try it.
Barbara Pym, A VERY PRIVATE EYE 1984

10 A lot of different guys are considered very
sensible until they get tangled up with a doll,
and maybe loving her, and the first thing
anybody knows they hop out of windows, or
shoot themselves, or shoot somebody else,
and I can see where even a guy like Dave the
Dude may go daffy over a doll.
Damon Runyon, MORE THAN
SOMEWHAT 1937

11 Of all forms of caution, caution in love is

perhaps the most fatal to true happiness.
Bertrand Russell, AUTOBIOGRAPHY 1967

12 To fear love is to fear life, and those who
fear life are already three parts dead.
Bertrand Russell, MARRIAGE AND
MORALS 1929

13 Loving you is like loving a red hot poker
which is a worse bedfellow than even
Lytton's Umbrella; every caress brings on
agony.
Bertrand Russell, letter to Ottoline Morrell,
Jun 1912

14 I did not know I loved you till I heard myself
telling you so — for one instant I thought
'Good God, what have I said?' and then I
knew it was the truth.
Ibid. Mar 1911

15 When we love animals and children too
much we love them at the expense of men.
Jean-Paul Sartre, THE WORDS 1964

16 First love is only a little foolishness and a lot
of curiosity; no really self-respecting woman
would take advantage of it.
George Bernard Shaw, JOHN BULL'S OTHER
ISLAND 1904

17 The fickleness of the women I love is only
equalled by the infernal constancy of the
women who love me.
George Bernard Shaw

18 Love is the only weapon we need.
Rev. H. R. L. Sheppard, THE HUMAN
PARSON

19 It is never too late to fall in love.
Sandy Wilson, THE BOY FRIEND

20 'Ah, love, love' he said. 'Is there anything
like it? Were you ever in love, Beach?'
'Yes, sir, on one occasion, when I was a
young under-footman. But it blew over.'
P. G. Wodehouse, PIGS HAVE WINGS 1952

21 It is love that I am seeking for / But of a
beautiful unheard of kind / That is not in the
world.
W. B. Yeats, THE SHADOWY WATERS

LOYALTY

22 He is more loyal to his friends than to his
convictions.
Margot Asquith of Austen Chamberlain,
AUTOBIOGRAPHY 1936

LUCK

1 I'm told it brings luck whether one believes in it or not.
Niels Bohr on surprise being expressed at his believing in the luck of rabbits' feet. A rabbit's foot was pinned on his laboratory door

2 Some day my boat will come in, and with my luck I'll be at the airport.
Graffito. Quoted Nigel Rees, GRAFFITI 2 1980

3 I am a great believer in luck, and I find the harder I work the more I have of it.
Stephen Leacock, LITERARY LAPSES 1910

LUST

4 Oh whip the dogs away my Lord / That make me ill with lust.
John Betjeman, SENEX

LUXURY

5 The saddest thing I can imagine is to get used to luxury.
Charlie Chaplin, MY AUTOBIOGRAPHY 1964

6 Every luxury was lavished on you — atheism, breast feeding, circumcision.
Joe Orton, LOOT *(play)*

233

M

RAMSAY MACDONALD

1 He is the greatest living master of falling without hurting himself.
Winston Churchill, House of Commons 21 Jan 1921

2 He, more than any other man, has the gift of compressing the largest amount of words into the smallest amount of thought.
Ibid. 23 Mar 1933

3 He dramatizes his position, as always . . . always there is something histrionic and therefore fraudulent about him. I respect and admire him in many ways. But I do see why many people regard him as a complete humbug.
Harold Nicolson, DIARIES 28 Apr 1935

4 We travelled up in the train with Ramsay MacDonald, who spent the time telling long stories of pawky Scots humour so dull that it was almost impossible to tell when the point had been reached.
Bertrand Russell, AUTOBIOGRAPHY 1967

5 There are no professions he ever made, no pledges he ever gave to the country, and no humiliation to which he would not submit if they would only allow him still to be called Prime Minister.
Viscount Snowden, House of Lords 3 Jul 1934

6 MacDonald owes his pre-eminence largely to the fact that he is the only artist, the only aristocrat by temperament and talent in a party of plebeians and plain men.
Beatrice Webb, DIARY, May 1950

MACHINE

7 One cannot walk through a mass production factory and not feel one is in Hell.
W. H. Auden. Quoted Barbara Rowe, A BOOK OF QUOTES

8 When a machine begins to run without human aid it is time to scrap it — whether it be a factory or a government.
Alexander Chase, PERSPECTIVES

9 Machines, from the Maxim gun to the computer, are for the most part means by which a minority can keep free men in subjection.
Kenneth, Lord Clark, CIVILISATION 1969

10 Machinery is the sub-conscious mind of the world.
Gerald Stanley Lee, CROWDS

11 You cannot endow even the best machine with initiative. The jolliest steam-roller will not plant flowers.
Walter Lippmann, A PREFACE TO POLITICS 1914

12 It is critical vision alone which can mitigate the unimpeded operation of the automatic.
Marshall McLuhan, THE MECHANICAL BRIDE 1951

13 By his very success in inventing labour-saving devices modern man has manufactured an abyss of boredom that only the privileged classes in earlier civilisations have ever fathomed.
Lewis Mumford, THE CONDUCT OF LIFE 1951

14 Machines are worshipped because they are beautiful and valued because they confer power; they are hated because they are hideous and loathed because they impose slavery.
Bertrand Russell, SCEPTICAL ESSAYS 1928

15 The machine does not isolate man from the great problems of nature but plunges him more deeply into them.
Antoine de Saint-Exupéry, WIND, SAND AND STARS 1939

1 The real problem is not whether machines think, but whether men do.
B. F. Skinner, CONTINGENCIES OF REINFORCEMENT

2 If automation keeps up, man will atrophy all his limbs but the push button finger.
Frank Lloyd Wright, New York Times 27 *Nov* 1955

HAROLD MACMILLAN

3 By far the most radical man I've known in politics wasn't on the labour side at all — Harold Macmillan. If it hadn't been for the war he'd have joined the Labour Party. If that had happened Macmillan would have been Labour Prime Minister, and not me.
Clement Attlee. Quoted James Margach, THE ABUSE OF POWER 1981

4 One can never escape the suspicion with Mr Macmillan that all his life was a preparation for elder statesmanship.
Frank Johnson, The Times 30 *Apr* 1981

5 The eyes were *hooded*, they seemed to hover always on the verge of a *wink* at his fantastic good fortune in being set down in the country of the blind, where none could see through him.
Bernard Levin, THE PENDULUM YEARS 1976

6 It was almost impossible to believe that he was anything but a down-at-heel actor resting between engagements at the decrepit theatres of minor provincial towns.
Ibid.

7 I am MacWonder one moment and Mac-Blunder the next.
Of himself. Quoted Colin R. Coote, Daily Telegraph 15 *Nov* 1973

8 Harold Macmillan always struck me as a parody of a Conservative politician in a novel by Trollope.
Malcolm Muggeridge, CHRONICLES OF WASTED TIME, *The Infernal Grove* 1972

9 Macmillan's role as a poseur was itself a pose.
Harold Wilson, A PRIME MINISTER ON PRIME MINISTERS 1977

MADNESS

10 We are all born mad, and some remain so.
Samuel Beckett, WAITING FOR GODOT 1952

11 Madness alone is entirely free from the commonplace. However terrible or twisted or invalid the visions of sick brains, each is individual and new.
William Bolitho, CAMERA OBSCURA

12 What is madness / To those who only observe, is often wisdom / To those to whom it happens.
Christopher Fry, A PHOENIX TOO FREQUENT 1949

13 Should those about us think us mad it would be difficult to keep faith in one's own sanity.
J. F. Spalding, GLIMPSES OF TRUTH

MAJORITY

14 The one pervading evil of democracy is the tyranny of the majority.
Lord Acton, THE HISTORY OF FREEDOM

15 If it has to choose who is to be crucified the crowd will always save Barabbas.
Jean Cocteau, LE RAPPEL À L'ORDRE 1926

16 One with the law is a majority.
Calvin Coolidge. Speech 27 *Jul* 1920

17 When great changes occur in history, when great principles are involved, as a rule the majority are wrong.
Eugene V. Debs. Speech 12 *Aug* 1918

18 The great silent majority.
Richard Nixon. Speech 3 *Nov* 1969

MALICE

19 I have never killed a man, but I have read many obituaries with a lot of pleasure.
Clarence Darrow, MEDLEY

MAN

20 Men are beasts and even beasts don't behave as they do.
Brigitte Bardot. Quoted Barbara Rowe, A BOOK OF QUOTES

1 There are so many kinds of awful men.
Wendy Cope, MAKING COCOA FOR
KINGSLEY AMIS 1986

2 Man is an intelligence in servitude to his
organs.
Aldous Huxley, THEME AND
VARIATIONS 1950

3 Women want mediocre men, and men are
working hard to be as mediocre as possible.
Margaret Mead

4 Man is not *like* an animal. Man *is* an
animal.
Mary Midgley, BEAST AND MAN 1980

5 There was, I think, never any reason to
believe in any innate superiority of the male,
except his superior muscle.
Bertrand Russell, UNPOPULAR ESSAYS 1950

6 A man in the house is worth two in the
street.
Mae West, line spoken in film BELLE OF THE
NINETIES

MANKIND

7 Mankind is not a tribe of animals to which
we owe compassion. Mankind is a club to
which we owe our subscription.
G. K. Chesterton, Daily News 10 *Apr* 1906

8 What is man, when you come to think upon
him, but a minutely set, ingenious machine
for turning, with infinite artfulness, the red
wine of Shiraz into urine?
Isak Dinesen, SEVEN GOTHIC TALES, *The
Dreamers* 1934

9 Man would be otherwise. That is the essence
of the specifically human.
Antonio Machado, JUAN DE
MATRENA 1943

10 Man is the measure of all things, and his
welfare is the sole and single criterion of
truth.
Thomas Mann, THE MAGIC
MOUNTAIN 1924

11 Man, unlike any other thing organic or
inorganic in the universe, grows beyond his
work, walks up the stairs of his concepts,
emerges ahead of his accomplishments.
John Steinbeck, THE GRAPES OF
WRATH 1939

12 If this is God's world there are no unimportant people.
*Rt. Hon. George Thomas, former Speaker
of the House of Commons, to Richard
Baker, BBC TV* 2 *Aug* 1981

MANNERS

13 Phone for the fish knives Norman, / As cook
is a trifle unnerved; / You kiddies have
crumpled the serviettes / And I must have
things daintily served.
Sir John Betjeman, HOW TO GET ON IN
SOCIETY

14 Do up your butterflies.
Sir Hugh Casson and Joyce Grenfell, NANNY
SAYS 1972

15 The great secret is not having bad manners
or good manners or any other particular sort
of manners, but having the same manners
for all human souls.
George Bernard Shaw, PYGMALION 1933

MARRIAGE

16 You can measure the social caste of a person
by the distance between the husband's and
wife's apartments.
*Alfonso XIII of Spain. Quoted Harold
Brooke-Baker, Daily Telegraph* 26 *Jul* 1982

17 When I told my mother of my engagement
she sank upon the settee, put a handkerchief
to her eyes and cried 'You might as well
marry your groom.'
Margot Asquith, AUTOBIOGRAPHY 1936

18 I married beneath me — all women do.
Nancy Astor. Speech, Oldham 1951

19 The state or condition of a community
consisting of a master, a mistress and two
slaves, making two in all.
Ambrose Bierce, THE DEVIL'S
DICTIONARY 1906

20 Marriage is the result of the longing for the
deep, deep peace of the double bed after the
hurly-burly of the chaise-longue.
Mrs Pat Campbell

21 The advantage of being married to an
archaeologist is that the older one grows the
more interested he becomes.
Agatha Christie, MURDER IN
MESOPOTAMIA 1936

1 Actually, I believe in marriage, having done it three times.
Joan Collins in an interview with Miriam Gross, Observer 8 *Oct* 1985

2 Marriage is a wonderful invention; but then again so is a bicycle repair kit.
Billy Connolly, THE AUTHORISED VERSION

3 The dread of loneliness is greater than the fear of bondage, so we get married.
Cyril Connolly, THE UNQUIET GRAVE 1945

4 Most marriages don't add two people together. They subtract one from the other.
Ian Fleming, DIAMONDS ARE FOR EVER 1956

5 I've had a lot of very good friends. I've always liked them too much to want to marry them.
Lillian Gish, The Times 19 *Nov* 1980

6 The trouble with my wife is that she is a whore in the kitchen and a cook in bed.
Geoffrey Gorer, EXPLORING THE ENGLISH CHARACTER

7 When a woman gets married it is like jumping into a hole in the ice in the middle of winter; you do it once and you remember it the rest of your days.
Maxim Gorky, THE LOWER DEPTHS 1902

8 The concept of two people living together for 25 years without having a cross word suggests a lack of spirit only to be admired in sheep.
A. P. Herbert, News Chronicle 1940

9 The critical period in matrimony is breakfast time.
A. P. Herbert, UNCOMMON LAW 1933

10 One of the difficulties of marriage is not that it ties a man to a woman but that it separates her from all others.
Dr Charles Hill. Speech to London Chamber of Commerce 4 *Sep* 1956

11 Seldom, or perhaps never does a marriage develop into an individual relationship smoothly and without crises; there is no coming to consciousness without pain.
Carl Jung, CONTRIBUTIONS TO ANALYTICAL PSYCHOLOGY 1928

12 Marrying a man is like buying something you've been admiring for a long time in a shop window. You may love it when you get it home, but it doesn't always go with everything else in the house.
Jean Kerr, THE SNAKE HAS ALL THE LINES

13 He married a woman to stop her getting away / Now she's there all day.
Philip Larkin, SELF'S THE MAN

14 Only the strong of heart can be well married, since they do not turn to marriage to supply what no other human being can ever get from another – a sure sense of the fortress within himself.
Max Lerner, THE UNFINISHED COUNTRY 1929

15 So they were married — to be the more together — / And found they were never again so much together — / Divided by the morning tea, / By the evening paper, / By children and tradesmen's bills.
Louis MacNeice, LES SYLPHIDES

16 If people waited to know each other before they married, the world wouldn't be so overpopulated as it is now.
W. Somerset Maugham, MRS DOT

17 Marriage is like pleading guilty to an indefinite sentence. Without parole.
John Mortimer, THE TRIALS OF RUMPOLE 1979

18 One doesn't have to get anywhere in a marriage. It's not a public conveyance.
Iris Murdoch, A SEVERED HEAD 1961

19 In every marriage there is a selfish and an unselfish partner. A pattern is set up and soon becomes inflexible, of one person always making the demands and one person always giving way.
Ibid.

20 Perhaps the saddest lot that can fall mortal man is to be the husband of a lady poet.
George Jean Nathan

21 Marriage is rather a silly habit.
John Osborne. Quoted Observer, Sayings of the Week 1 *Jun* 1978

22 A modernist married a fundamentalist wife / And she led him a catechism and dogma life.
Keith Preston, MARITAL TRAGEDY

1 A good marriage is that in which each appoints the other the guardian of his solitude.
Rainer Maria Rilke, LETTERS 1892–1910

2 It takes patience to appreciate domestic bliss, volatile spirits prefer unhappiness.
George Santayana, THE LIFE OF REASON, *Reason in Society* 1906

3 Your aspect is softened. You have been boiled in bread and milk for years and years, like other married men, poor devil!
George Bernard Shaw, HEARTBREAK HOUSE 1920

4 My mother married a very good man . . . and she is not at all keen on my doing the same.
Ibid.

5 The more a man knows, and the farther he travels, the more likely he is to marry a country girl.
George Bernard Shaw, JOHN BULL'S OTHER ISLAND 1904

6 It is a woman's business to get married as soon as possible; and a man's to keep unmarried as long as he can.
George Bernard Shaw, MAN AND SUPERMAN 1905

7 Those who talk most about the blessings of marriage and the constancy of its vows are the very people who declare that if the chain were broken and the prisoners were left free to choose, the whole social fabric would fly asunder. You can't have the argument both ways.
Ibid.

8 Marriage is popular because it combines the minimum of temptation with the maximum of opportunity.
Ibid.

9 What a holler there would be if people had to pay the minister as much to marry them as they have to pay a lawyer to get them a divorce.
Claire Trevor, New York Journal, American 12 *Oct* 1960

10 Take it from me, marriage isn't a word — it's a sentence.
From King Vidor's silent film, THE CROWD 1928

11 It isn't silence you can cut with a knife any more, it's interchange of ideas. Intelligent discussion of practically everything is what is breaking up modern marriage.
E. B. White, EVERY DAY IS SATURDAY

12 London is spattered with couples living in sin whose lives are just as dreary as those of the respectably married.
Katherine Whitehorn, Observer 9 *Dec* 1978

13 People who wish to get married should actually have met before deciding to do so.
William Whitelaw, House of Commons 14 *Nov* 1979

14 Marriage is a bribe to make a housekeeper think she's a householder.
Thornton Wilder, THE MATCHMAKER 1955

15 The best part of marriage is the fights. The rest is merely so-so.
Ibid.

16 All the unhappy marriages came from the husband having brains.
P. G. Wodehouse, ADVENTURES OF SALLY 1920

17 Marriage is the net in which the jade snares the jaded.
P. G. Wodehouse and Guy Bolton, BRING ON THE GIRLS

18 Marriage isn't a process of prolonging the life of love, but of mummifying the corpse.
Ibid.

19 Don't let your marriage go stale. / Change the bag on the Hoover of life.
Victoria Wood, ITV, Wood and Walters 17 *Jan* 1982

MARTYR

20 It is often pleasant to stone a martyr, no matter how much we admire him.
John Barth, THE FLOATING OPERA 1956

21 To die for a religion is easier than to live it absolutely.
Jorge Luis Borges, LABYRINTHS 1962

22 Martyrs, my friend, have to choose between being forgotten, mocked or used. As for being understood — never.
Albert Camus, THE FALL 1956

1 Perhaps there is no happiness in life so perfect as the martyr's.
O. Henry, THE TRIMMED LAMP 1907

2 It is not the least of a martyr's scourges to be canonised by the persons who burned him.
Murray Kempton, PART OF OUR TIME 1955

3 I look on martyrs as mistakes / But still they burned for it at stakes.
John Masefield, THE EVERLASTING MERCY 1911

KARL MARX

4 Karl Marx wasn't a Marxist all the time. He got drunk in the Tottenham Court Road.
Michael Foot. Quoted Susan Barnes, BEHIND THE IMAGE

5 Much of the world's work is done by men who do not feel quite well. Marx is a case in point.
J. K. Galbraith, THE AGE OF UNCERTAINTY 1977

6 He is the apostle of class-hatred, the founder of a Satanic anti-religion, which resembles some religions in its cruelty, fanaticism and irrationality.
W. R. Inge (Dean of St Paul's), ASSESSMENTS AND ANTICIPATIONS 1929

7 There is not one of his predictions that has not been falsified by events, and there is not one of his theories which has not been riddled by hostile criticism.
Ibid.

8 Mrs Karl Marx, at the end of a long and bleak life, remarked 'How good it would have been if Karl had made some capital instead of writing so much about it.'
Will Rogers. Quoted Leon Harris, THE FINE ART OF POLITICAL WIT

MARXISM

9 The Marxist analysis has got nothing to do with what happened in Stalin's Russia; it's like blaming Jesus Christ for the Inquisition in Spain.
Tony Benn. Quoted Observer 27 Apr 1980

10 Marxism is like a classical building that followed the Renaissance; beautiful in its way, but incapable of growth.
Harold Macmillan. Speech to Primrose League 29 Apr 1981

11 Marxism is essentially a product of the bourgeois mind.
Joseph Alois Schumpeter, CAPITALISM, SOCIALISM AND DEMOCRACY

QUEEN MARY

12 Queen Mary looked like the Jungfrau, white, and sparkling in the sun.
Henry Channon, DIARY 22 Jun 1937

MATHEMATICS

13 What is algebra exactly? Is it those three-cornered things?
J. M. Barrie, QUALITY STREET 1901

14 When we reach the sphere of mathematics we are among processes which seem to some the most inhuman of all human activities and the most remote from poetry. Yet it is here that the artist has fullest scope for his imagination.
Havelock Ellis, THE DANCE OF LIFE 1923

15 The mathematician has reached the highest rung on the ladder of human thought.
Ibid.

16 One has to be able to count, if only so that at fifty-one doesn't marry a girl of twenty.
Maxim Gorky, THE ZYKOVS 1914

17 Once I had learnt my twelve times table [at the age of three] it was downhill all the way.
Fred Hoyle

18 The only way I can distinguish proper from improper fractions / Is by their actions.
Ogden Nash, ASK DADDY, HE WON'T KNOW

19 The true spirit of delight, the exaltation, the sense of being more than Man, which is the touchstone of the highest excellence, is to be found in mathematics as surely as in poetry.
Bertrand Russell, MYSTICISM AND LOGIC 1917

20 Mathematics, rightly viewed, possesses not only truth but supreme beauty — a beauty cold and austere like that of sculpture.
Ibid.

1 Mathematics may be defined as the subject in which we never know what we are talking about, nor whether what we are saying is true.
Ibid.

2 I like mathematics because it is *not* human and has nothing particular to do with this planet or with the whole accidental universe — because, like Spinoza's God, it won't love us in return.
Bertrand Russell, letter to Lady Ottoline Morrell, Mar 1912

3 I knew a mathematician who said 'I do not know as much as God. But I know as much as God knew at my age'.
Milton Shulman, BBC Radio 4, Stop The Week 31 Mar 1979

4 Numbers constitute the only universal language.
Nathanael West, MISS LONELY HEARTS 1933

5 The science of pure mathematics, in its modern developments, may claim to be the most original creation of the human spirit.
A. N. Whitehead, SCIENCE AND THE MODERN WORLD 1925

6 Mathematics is thought moving in the sphere of complete abstraction from any particular instance of what it is talking about.
Ibid.

MATURITY

7 The mark of the immature man is that he wants to die nobly for a cause, while the mark of the mature man is that he wants to live humbly for one.
Wilhelm Stekel. Quoted J. D. Salinger, CATCHER IN THE RYE 1951

MAYONNAISE

8 Aunt Irene really inclined to that simplest of all views: the one expressed so cogently in the book of Genesis, which explained everything with appealing clarity. This was the only view that explained, for instance, mayonnaise. It was patently absurd to suppose that mayonnaise had come about through random chance, that anyone could

ever have been silly or brilliant enough to predict what would happen if he slowly trickled oil on to egg yolks and then gone ahead and tried it.
Alice Thomas Ellis, THE 27TH KINGDOM 1982

MEANNESS

9 Is Mr Benny tight? Well a little snug, perhaps. If he can't take it with him, he ain't gonna go.
Eddie Anderson, who played the part of Rochester in Jack Benny's radio programmes. Quoted Irving A. Fein, JACK BENNY

10 I've been in London four days and already I've spent seven pounds. Next time I'll come *alone.*
Jack Benny. Quoted William Marchant, THE PRIVILEGE OF HIS COMPANY

11 Some people have a necessity to be mean, as if they were exercising a faculty which they had to partially neglect since childhood.
F. Scott Fitzgerland, THE CRACK-UP 1936

MEDICINE

12 Stopped at a small chemist's and bought some tablets. Said to Leo 'I just can't bear to run short of Acetylmethyldimethylox-amidphenylhydrazine'
James Agate, EGO 3 9 Apr 1937

13 A miracle drug is any drug that will do what the label says it will do.
Eric Hodgins, EPISODE

14 When you buy a pill and buy peace with it you get conditioned to cheap solutions instead of deep ones.
Max Lerner, THE UNFINISHED COUNTRY 1959

15 Medicine is a noble profession but a damn bad business.
Sir Humphrey Davy Rolleston, physician to George V. Quoted Lore and Maurice Cowan, THE WIT OF MEDICINE

16 When there's a cure, it was only half a disease.
Leo Rosten, HOORAY FOR YIDDISH 1983

1 There is at bottom only one genuinely scientific treatment for all diseases, and that is to stimulate the phagocytes.
George Bernard Shaw, THE DOCTOR'S DILEMMA 1906

2 It should be the function of medicine to have people die young as late as possible.
Ernest L. Wynder

MEDIOCRITY

3 Only mediocrity can be trusted to be always at its best.
Max Beerbohm. Quoted S. N. Behrman, CONVERSATIONS WITH MAX 1960

4 Some men are born mediocre, some men achieve mediocrity, and some men have mediocrity thrust upon them.
Joseph Heller, CATCH 22 1961

5 It isn't evil that is ruining the earth, but mediocrity. The crime is not that Nero played while Rome burned, but that he played badly.
Ned Rorem, THE FINAL DIARY 1974

MEDITATION

6 Meditation is not a means to an end. It is both the means and the end.
Krishnamurti, THE PENGUIN KRISHNAMURTI READER

MEEKNESS

7 We have the highest authority for believing that the meek shall inherit the earth; but I have never found any particular corroboration for this aphorism in the records of Somerset House.
Lord Birkenhead (F. E. Smith). Quoted his son and biographer, 2nd Earl of Birkenhead

8 The meek do inherit the earth, but the modern sceptics are too meek even to claim their inheritance.
G. K. Chesterton, ORTHODOXY 1908

9 The meek shall inherit the earth but not the mineral rights.
Paul Getty

10 The meek shall inherit the earth — if that's all right with you.
Graffito. Quoted Peterborough, Daily Telegraph 12 *Jul* 1979

11 It's going to be fun to watch and see how long the meek can keep the earth when they inherit it.
Kim Hubbard, ABE MARTIN

MEGALOMANIA

12 The megalomaniac differs from the narcissist by the fact that he wishes to be powerful rather than charming and seeks to be feared rather than loved. To his type belong many lunatics and most of the great men of history.
Bertrand Russell, THE CONQUEST OF HAPPINESS 1930

MELODY

13 The heart of the melody can never be put down on paper.
Pablo Casals, CONVERSATIONS 1956

14 Melody is a form of remembrance. It must have a quality of meritability in our ears.
Gian-Carlo Menotti, Time 1 May 1950

MEMORIAL

15 You can keep the things of bronze and stone and give me one man to remember me just once a year.
Damon Runyon, last words

MEMORY

16 Memories are like stones, time and distance crack them like acid.
Ugo Betti, GOAT ISLAND 1946

17 It is all right for beasts to have no memories; but we poor humans have to be compensated.
William Bolitho, CAMERA OBSCURA

18 The charm, one might say the genius, of memory is that it is choosy, chancy and temperamental; it rejects the edifying cathedral and indelibly photographs the small boy outside, chewing a hunk of melon in the dust.
Elizabeth Bowen, Vogue 15 Sep 1955

1 Some memories are realities, and are better than anything that can ever happen to one again.
Willa Cather, MY ANTONIA 1918

2 Memory is the thing you forget with.
Alexander Chase, PERSPECTIVES 1960

3 One learns little more about a man from his feats of literary memory than from the feats of his alimentary canal.
Frank Moore Colby, THE COLBY ESSAYS, *Quotation and Allusion* 1926

4 Our memories are card-indexes consulted and then put back in disorder by authorities whom we do not control.
Cyril Connolly, THE UNQUIET GRAVE 1945

5 I have a memory like an elephant. In fact elephants often consult me.
Noël Coward. Quoted J. K. Galbraith, A LIFE IN OUR TIMES 1981

6 We do not know the true value of our moments until they have undergone the test of memory.
Georges Duhamel, THE HEART'S DOMAIN 1919

7 Do not trust your memory, it is a net full of holes; the most beautiful prizes slip through it.
Ibid.

8 Men live by forgetting — women live on memories.
T. S. Eliot, THE ELDER STATESMAN

9 Midnight shakes the memory as a madman shakes a dead geranium.
T. S. Eliot, RHAPSODY ON A WINDY NIGHT 1917

10 'My name is Eddie Seagoon.'
'Gad, what a memory.'
The Goon Show, BBC Radio

11 Some women'll stay in a man's memory if they once walked down a street.
Rudyard Kipling, TRAFFICS AND DISCOVERIES 1904

12 Only stay quiet while my mind remembers / The beauty of fire from the beauty of embers.
John Masefield, ON GROWING OLD

13 [My memory is] like a broken goldwasher's pan that often holds the mud and lets through the nuggets.
Raymond Mortimer, TRY ANYTHING ONCE

14 What beastly incidents our memories insist on cherishing — the ugly and disgusting — the beautiful things we have to keep diaries to remember.
Eugene O'Neill, STRANGE INTERLUDE 1928

15 Time, which changes people, does not alter the image we have retained of them.
Marcel Proust, REMEMBRANCE OF THINGS PAST 1913—1927

16 Anything processed by memory is a fiction.
Michael Ratcliffe, reviewing Paul Fussell's ABROAD, *The Times* 19 Mar 1931

17 No man, and no force can abolish memory.
Franklin D. Roosevelt 23 Apr 1942

18 The pleasure in music recalled is virtually non-existent. Music must be re-heard to be re-experienced.
Ned Rorem, PURE CONTRAPTION 1974

19 There are three things I always forget. Names, faces and — the third I can't remember.
Italo Svevo

20 The nice thing about having memories is that you can choose.
William Trevor, MATILDA'S ENGLAND, *BBC (play)*

21 In memory everything seems to happen to music.
Tennessee Williams, THE GLASS MENAGERIE 1944

22 Life is all memory, except for the one present moment that goes by you so quick you hardly catch it going.
Tennessee Williams, THE MILK TRAIN DOESN'T STOP HERE ANY MORE 1962

23 All I can recall of the actual poetry is the bit that goes Tum-tum, tum-tum, tum-tumpty-tum
I slew him, tum-tum, tum.
P. G. Wodehouse, JEEVES TAKES CHARGE

24 Memories are like mulligatawny soup in a cheap restaurant. It is best not to stir them.
P. G. Wodehouse and Guy Bolton, BRING ON THE GIRLS

METAPHOR

1 The metaphor is probably the most fertile
power possessed by man.
José Ortega y Gasset, THE
DEHUMANISATION OF ART

METAPHYSICS

2 The unrest which keeps the never stopping
clock of metaphysics going is the thought
that the non-existence of the world is just as
possible as its existence.
William James, SOME PROBLEMS OF
PHILOSOPHY, *The Problem of Being* 1911

MIDDLE-AGE

3 Variously reckoned to suit the reckoner.
*Definition as appears in Chambers
Dictionary*

4 The years between fifty and seventy are the
hardest. You are always being asked to do
things, and you are not yet decrepit enough
to turn them down.
T. S. Eliot, Time 23 *Oct* 1950

5 The long dull monotonous years of middle-
aged prosperity or middle-aged adversity
are excellent campaigning weather for the
Devil.
C. S. Lewis, THE SCREWTAPE LETTERS 1942

6 . . . when a man is always thinking that in a
week or two he will feel as good as ever.
Don Marquis, ARCHY AND
MEHITABEL 1927

MIDDLE CLASS

7 Who is it that exercises social power today?
Who imposes the forms of his own mind on
the period? Without a doubt the man of the
middle class.
José Ortega y Gassett, THE REVOLT OF THE
MASSES, *The Barbarism of
Specialisation* 1930

8 A moderately honest man, with a moderately faithful wife, moderate drinkers
both, in a moderately healthy house; that is
the true middle class unit.
George Bernard Shaw, MAN AND
SUPERMAN 1905

9 I have to live for others and not for myself;
that's middle class morality.
George Bernard Shaw, PYGMALION 1913

MILLIONAIRE

10 All millionaires love a baked apple.
Ronald Firbank, VAINGLORY 1915

11 I would not say millionaires were mean.
They simply have a healthy respect for
money. I've noticed that people who don't
respect money don't have any.
*Paul Getty, interviewed on the TV
programme, This Week*

A. A. MILNE

12 Tonstant Weader fwowed up.
*Constant Reader (Dorothy Parker), of
Winnie the Pooh in book review in the New
Yorker*

MIND

13 His mind was like a Roquefort cheese, so
ripe that it was palpably falling to pieces.
*Van Wyck Brooks of Ford Maddox Ford.
Quoted Douglas Golding*, THE LAST
PRE-RAPHAELITE

14 I am incurably convinced that the object of
opening the mind, as of opening the mouth,
is to shut it on something solid.
G. K. Chesterton, AUTOBIOGRAPHY

15 The mind has its own womb to which,
baffled by speculation, it longs to return.
Cyril Connolly, THE UNQUIET GRAVE 1945

16 Minds are like parachutes; they only function when open.
Lord Dewar in a speech

17 Experience offers proof on every hand that
vigorous mental life may be but one side of a
personality, of which the other is moral
barbarism.
George Gissing, THE PRIVATE PAPERS OF
HENRY RYECROFT 1903

18 It is the mind which creates the world about
us, and even though we stand side by side in
the same meadow, my eyes will never see
what is beheld by yours, my heart will never
stir to the emotions with which yours is
touched.
Ibid.

1 The pendulum of the mind oscillates between sense and nonsense, not between right and wrong.
Carl Jung, MEMORIES, DREAMS, REFLECTIONS

2 The mind is like a richly woven tapestry in which the colours are distilled from the experiences of the senses, and the design drawn from the convolutions of the intellect.
Carson McCullers, REFLECTIONS IN A GOLDEN EYE

3 I have never yet met the cultivated mind that has not its shrubbery. I loathe and detest shrubberies.
Katherine Mansfield, JOURNALS 1954

4 Certainly, in our intellectual behaviour we rarely solve a tricky problem by a steady climb to success.
M. Minsky, Steps Towards Artificial Intelligence, Proc. IRE 1961

5 The discovery that the mind can regulate its thoughts, fostering some and dismissing others, is one of the most important stages in the art of self-culture. It is astonishing how little this art is practised among Westerners.
John Cowper Powys, THE MEANING OF CULTURE 1930

6 The mind is a strange machine which can combine the materials offered to it in the most astonishing ways.
Bertrand Russell, THE CONQUEST OF HAPPINESS 1930

7 The Ghost in the Machine.
Gilbert Ryle, CONCEPT OF MIND

8 Hardly anybody, except perhaps the Greeks at their best, has realised the sweetness and glory of being a rational animal.
George Santayana, CHARACTER AND OPINION IN THE UNITED STATES 1921

9 The mind is the expression of the soul, which belongs to God and must be let alone by Government.
Adlai Stevenson. Speech, Salt Lake City 14 *Oct* 1952

10 The mind is the most capricious of insects — flitting, fluttering.
Virginia Woolf, A WRITER'S DIARY 1953

MINORITY

11 To be in the weakest camp is to be in the strongest school.
G. K. Chesterton, HERETICS 1905

12 Minorities are individuals or groups of individuals especially qualified. The masses are the collection of people not specially qualified.
José Ortega y Gasset, THE REVOLT OF THE MASSES 1930

13 A resolute minority has usually prevailed over an easygoing or wobbly majority whose prime purpose was to be left alone.
James Reston, SKETCHES IN THE SAND 1967

14 The only tyrannies from which men, women and children are suffering in real life are the tyrannies of minorities.
Theodore Roosevelt. Speech 22 Mar 1912

MIRACLE

15 True miracles are created by men when they use the courage and intelligence that God gave them.
Jean Anouilh, THE LARK 1955

16 Miracles are laughed at by a nation that reads thirty million newspapers a day and supports Wall Street.
Finley Peter Dunne, MR DOOLEY'S OPINIONS, *Casual Observations* 1900

17 Everything is miraculous. It is miraculous that one does not melt in one's bath.
Pablo Picasso. Quoted Jean Cocteau

18 Miracles are propitious accidents, the natural causes of which are too complicated to be readily understood.
George Santayana, THE ETHICS OF SPINOZA

19 A miracle is an event which creates faith. Frauds deceive. An event which creates faith does not deceive; therefore it is not a fraud, but a miracle.
George Bernard Shaw, ST JOAN 1927

MIRROR

20 Mirrors should think longer before they reflect.
Jean Cocteau in an interview with Derek Prouse, Sunday Times 20 Oct 1963

1 Mirrors are the windows of the devil, overlooking nothing but a landscape of lies.
Leon Garfield, THE PRISONERS OF SEPTEMBER

2 The mirror usually reflects only the way others see us, the way we are expected to behave — forecast to behave — hardly ever what we really are.
Luigi Pirandello, THE RULES OF THE GAME 1918

3 Almost always it is the fear of being ourselves that brings us to the mirror.
Antonio Porchia, VOICES 1968

4 The walls of an empty room are mirrors that double and redouble our sense of ourselves.
John Updike, THE CENTAUR 1963

MISANTHROPY

5 The misanthropic idea, as in Byron, is not a truth but it is one of the immortal lies. As long as humanity lives, it can be hated.
G. K. Chesterton, USES OF ADVERSITY 1920

6 I've always been interested in people but I've never liked them.
W. Somerset Maugham. Quoted Observer 28 *Aug* 1949

7 A young, earnest American brought up the subject of nuclear warfare which, he said, might well destroy the entire human race. 'I can't wait' P. G. Wodehouse murmured.
Malcolm Muggeridge, TREAD SOFTLY FOR YOU TREAD ON MY JOKES 1966

MISER

8 The miser puts his gold pieces into a coffer, but as soon as the coffer is closed it is as if it were empty.
André Gide, PRETEXTS, *Concerning Influence in Literature* 1903

MISERY

9 If you feel depressed you shouldn't go out on the street because it will show on your face and you'll give it to others. Misery is a communicable disease.
Martha Graham. Quoted John Heilpern, Observer Magazine, The Amazing Martha 8 *Jul* 1979

10 Half the misery in the world is caused by ignorance. The other half is caused by knowledge.
Bonar Thompson, Hyde Park orator, THE BLACK HAT

MISFORTUNE

11 Calamities are of two kinds: Misfortune to ourselves and good fortune to others.
Ambrose Bierce, THE DEVIL'S DICTIONARY 1906

12 Who has not proved the justice of the saying 'She who breaks the lid by noon will crack the dish ere nightfall'?
Ernest Bramah, KAI LUNG UNROLLS HIS MAT 1928

MISSIONARY

13 When the missionaries came to Africa they had the Bible and we had the land. They said 'Let us pray'. We closed our eyes. When we opened them we had the Bible and they had the land.
Bishop Desmond Tutu, Observer, Sayings of the Weeks 16 *Dec* 1984

MISTAKE

14 I see now clearly, / The many, many mistakes I have made / My whole life through, mistake upon mistake / The mistaken attempts to correct mistakes / By methods which proved to be equally mistaken.
T. S. Eliot, THE ELDER STATESMAN

15 For creating a good impression on others there's nothing to beat being totally and catastrophically wrong.
Michael Frayn, SWEET DREAMS

16 The greatest mistake you can make in life is to be continually fearing you will make one.
Elbert Hubbard, THE NOTEBOOK 1927

17 It is a good thing to make mistakes so long as you are found out quickly.
J. M. Keynes

18 To be a victim of one's own mistakes is bad enough, but to be the victim of the other fellow's mistakes as well is too much.
Henry Miller, THE AIR-CONDITIONED NIGHTMARE 1945

1 A life spent in making mistakes is not only more honorable but more useful than a life spent doing nothing.
George Bernard Shaw, DOCTOR'S DILEMMA, *Preface* 1906

2 I have learned throughout my life as a composer chiefly through my mistakes and pursuits of false assumptions, not by my exposure to wisdom and founts of knowledge.
Igor Stravinsky, THEMES AND EPISODES, *Contingencies* 1966

3 If we had more time for discussion we should probably have made a great many more mistakes.
Leon Trotsky, MY LIFE 1930

MISTRESS

4 I've always found it much more dangerous to fool with a man's mistress than his wife.
Harold Robbins, THE INHERITORS 1969

5 A mistress is something that comes between a master and a mattress.
Robyn Wallis, *BBC TV*, *Mistress* 30 *Oct* 1983

MISTRUST

6 Everyone likes a kidder, but no one lends him money.
Arthur Miller, DEATH OF A SALESMAN 1957

MISUNDERSTANDING

7 Once he [my husband] thought I remarked that I liked the plays of Mozart. 'But Mozart didn't write plays. He was strictly a composer,' he said. 'Not Mozart,' I explained. 'Moss Hart.'
Duchess of Bedford, NICOLE NOBODY

8 There is no worse lie than a truth misunderstood by those who hear it.
William James, THE VARIETIES OF RELIGIOUS EXPERIENCE 1902

9 It is a misfortune for Anglo-American friendship that the two countries are supposed to have a common language.
Bertrand Russell, Saturday Evening Post 3 *Jun* 1944

10 When a grammar school boy was asked what he knew about VD he replied 'Nothing, unless you mean vapour density.'
M. Schofield, THE SEXUAL BEHAVIOUR OF YOUNG PEOPLE

NANCY MITFORD

11 Nice cheap girl to take out for the evening. Costs you only eighteen and six for an orangeade in a night club.
Evelyn Waugh of Nancy Mitford. Quoted Maurice Brown, MEMORIES

MODERATION

12 Moderation is a virtue only in those who are thought to have an alternative.
Henry Kissinger, Observer, Sayings of the Week 24 *Jan* 1982

13 The reasonable man adapts himself to the world.
George Bernard Shaw, MAN AND SUPERMAN 1905

MODESTY

14 A nun, asked why she wore a chemise in the bath where no one could see her, replied 'God sees everything.'
Anon.

15 I am not quite a gentleman, but you would hardly notice it.
Daisy Ashford (aged 9), THE YOUNG VISITERS 1919

16 His modesty amounts to a deformity.
Margot Asquith of her husband, H. H. Asquith the Earl of Oxford and Asquith, AUTOBIOGRAPHY 1936

17 I'm a second eleven sort of chap.
J. M. Barrie, THE ADMIRABLE CRICHTON 1902

18 A modest man is usually admired — if people ever hear of him.
Edgar Watson Howe, VENTURES IN COMMON SENSE 1919

19 Reserve is an artificial quality that is developed in most of us as the result of innumerable rebuffs.
W. Somerset Maugham, CAKES AND ALE 1930

1 In some remote regions of Islam it is said, a woman caught unveiled by a stranger will raise her skirt to cover her face.
Raymond Mortimer, COLETTE

2 He was a very modest man, and his most extreme boast was that he did try to have the qualities of his defects.
Bertrand Russell of Prof. A. N. Whitehead, PORTRAITS FROM MEMORY

3 I have often wished I had time to cultivate modesty, but I am too busy thinking about myself.
Edith Sitwell

4 When I pass my name in such huge letters I blush, but at the same time instinctively raise my hat.
Sir H. Beerbohm Tree. Quoted Hesketh Pearson, BEERBOHM TREE

MOLE

5 The houses are blind as moles / (though moles see fine tonight in the snouting, velvet dingles).
Dylan Thomas, UNDER MILK WOOD 1954

MOMENT

6 After all, any given moment has its value; it can be questioned in the light of after-events, but the moment remains.
F. Scott Fitzgerald, THE CRACK-UP 1936

7 In order to be utterly happy the only thing necessary is to refrain from comparing this moment with other moments in the past, which I often did not fully enjoy because I was comparing them with other moments of the future.
André Gide, JOURNALS 1939–1950

8 Florence Farr once said to me, 'If we could say to ourselves, with sincerity "this passing moment is as good as any I shall ever know", we could die upon the instant, and be united with God.'
W. B. Yeats, AUTOBIOGRAPHY 1926

MONARCHY

9 We are a middle-class people and we have a middle-class royal family, hard working, with no aristocratic excesses.

Hector Bolitho. Quoted Reginald Pound, THEIR MOODS AND MINE 1935

10 The monarchy is the oldest profession in the world.
Charles, Prince of Wales. Quoted Noël St George, ROYAL QUOTES

11 On the whole it is wise in human affairs and in the government of men, to separate pomp from power.
Winston Churchill. Speech, Ottawa 1952

12 Monarchy survives because it is out of the arena of political controversy. Nobody blames the Queen for the high price of meat.
William Davis

13 Monarchy is an occupation of considerable drudgery.
Edward, Duke of Windsor

14 Life in Buckingham Palace isn't too bad, but too many formal dinners. Yuk!
Diana, Princess of Wales in a letter to former teaching colleague. Quoted Sunday Times Magazine 26 Jul 1981

15 There will soon be only five kings left — the Kings of England, Diamonds, Hearts, Spades and Clubs.
King Farouk of Egypt 1951

16 Well, what are you socialists going to do about me?
George V to Ramsay MacDonald when he first presented himself at Buckingham Palace

17 We're not a family; we're a firm.
George VI. Quoted Peter Lane, OUR FUTURE KING

18 The strength of the monarchy does not lie in the power it has, but in the power it denies others.
Anthony Jay. Quoted Anthony Sampson, THE CHANGING ANATOMY OF BRITAIN 1982

19 If you find you are to be presented to the Queen, do not rush up to her. She will eventually be brought around to you like a dessert trolley at a good restaurant.
Los Angeles Times. Advice given during visit of Queen Elizabeth II, Mar 1983

20 We sometimes forget that monarchs are just normal people trapped by abnormal circumstances.
Michael MacDonald, letter to Daily Telegraph 23 May 1979

1 As long as our family can produce nicely
brought up young people it will be all right.
Princess Margaret. Quoted Andrew Duncan

2 In this business you can't afford to be a
shrinking violet.
*Lord Mountbatten's advice to Charles,
Prince of Wales. Quoted Anthony Sampson,*
THE CHANGING ANATOMY OF BRITAIN 1982

3 Monarchy is the gold filling in the mouth of
decay.
John Osborne. Quoted Bernard Levin, THE
PENDULUM YEARS 1976

4 I am referred to in that splendid language
[pidgin English] as Feller-belong-Queen.
*Philip, Duke of Edinburgh. Speech, Ottawa
29 Oct 1958*

5 Royalty puts a human face on the operations
of government.
*Dr Runcie (Archbishop of Canterbury),
sermon at St Pauls Cathedral on the occasion
of the Queen Mother's 80th birthday* 16 Jul
1980

6 We have brains enough to know that Kings
do not come as small as this little squirt.
Damon Runyon, MORE THAN
SOMEWHAT 1937

7 Kings are not born, they are made by
artificial hallucination.
George Bernard Shaw, MAN AND
SUPERMAN 1905

8 The monarchy is a labour-intensive industry.
Harold Wilson. Quoted Observer 13 Feb
1977

MONEY

9 Old pennies have a picture on the back of a
lady riding a bicycle. Her name is Ruby
Tanner.
Anonymous schoolgirl

10 A man who has a million dollars is as well off
as if he were rich.
J. J. Astor III

11 Money, it turned out, was exactly like sex.
You thought of nothing else if you didn't
have it and thought of other things if you
did.

James Baldwin, NOBODY KNOWS MY NAME,
*The Black Boy Looks At the White
Boy* 1961

12 My brother down in Texas / Can't even
write his name. / He signs his cheques with
Xs / But they cash 'em just the same.
Irving Berlin, ANNIE GET YOUR GUN

13 *Money, n.* A blessing that is of no advantage
to us excepting when we part with it.
Ambrose Bierce, THE DEVIL'S
DICTIONARY 1906

14 One must choose, in life, between making
money and spending it.
Edouard Bourdet, LES TEMPS
DIFFICILES 1934

15 Life is short and so is money.
Bertolt Brecht, THE THREEPENNY
OPERA 1928

16 When you have told anyone you have left
them a legacy the only decent thing to do is
to die at once.
Samuel Butler. Quoted Festing Jones, SAM
BUTLER, A MEMOIR 1917

17 It is a kind of spiritual snobbery that makes
people think that they can be happy without
money.
Albert Camus, NOTEBOOKS 1935–1942

18 A banker is a man who lends you an
umbrella when the sun is shining and wants
it back the minute it starts raining.
Bennett Cerf, LAUGHTER UNLIMITED 1951

19 To be clever enough to get all the money one
must be stupid enough to want it.
G. K. Chesterton, THE INNOCENCE OF
FATHER BROWN 1911

20 All my available funds are completely tied
up in ready cash.
W. C. Fields. Quoted Bennett Cerf, TRY AND
STOP ME 1947

21 Money is like an arm or leg; use it or lose it.
Henry Ford, New York Times 8 Nov 1931

22 One of the evils of money is that it tempts us
to look at it rather than at the things that it
buys.
E. M. Forster, TWO CHEERS FOR
DEMOCRACY 1951

1 Money is a singular thing. It ranks with love as man's greatest source of joy. And with his death as his greatest source of anxiety.
J. K. Galbraith, THE AGE OF UNCERTAINTY 1977

2 Money differs from an automobile, a mistress or cancer in being equally important to those who have it and those who don't.
Ibid.

3 Maybe money is unreal for most of us, easier to give away than things we want.
Lillian Hellman, AN UNFINISHED WOMAN 1969

4 'To make money', said Mr Porteous, 'one must be really interested in money.'
Aldous Huxley, ANTIC HAY 1923

5 The size of sums of money appears to vary in a remarkable way according as they are being paid in or paid out.
Julian Huxley, ESSAYS OF A BIOLOGIST 1923

6 It is extraordinary how many emotional storms one may weather in safety if one is ballasted with ever so little gold.
William McFee, CASUALS OF THE SEA 1916

7 Money doesn't buy friends, but it allows a better class of enemies.
Lord Mancroft, Punch

8 I must say I hate money but it's the lack of it I hate most.
Katherine Mansfield. Quoted Anthony Alpers, KATHERINE MANSFIELD 1954

9 What's a thousand dollars? Mere chicken feed. A poultry matter.
Groucho Marx, COCONUTS

10 Money is like a sixth sense without which you cannot make complete use of the other five.
W. Somerset Maugham, OF HUMAN BONDAGE 1915

11 If one has an income of five thousand a year, four thousand should be considered as pocket money.
Herbert Morgan. Quoted James Agate, EGO 3 27 Sep 1936

12 Money is like manure. If you spread it around it does a lot of good. But if you pile it up in one place it stinks like hell.

Clint Murchison Jr. Quoted Time 16 *Jun* 1961

13 Some people's money is merited / And other people's is inherited.
Ogden Nash, THE TERRIBLE PEOPLE

14 I can't take it with me I know / But will it last until I go?
Martha F. Newmeyer, SIMULTANEOUS DEPARTURE

15 Silver money is jolly. It dances and hums. Paper money crackles like dead leaves.
Extract from a child's essay. Quoted New York Times Magazine 8 *Sep* 1940

16 If women didn't exist, all the money in the world would have no meaning.
Aristotle Onassis. Quoted Barbara Rowe, A BOOK OF QUOTES

17 Money is good for bribing your way through the inconveniences of life.
Gottfried Reinhardt. Quoted Lillian Ross, PICTURE

18 Money may not buy happiness. But with it you can rent enough.
Dick Richards, GINGER, SALUTE TO A STAR

19 All decent people live beyond their incomes nowadays, and those who aren't respectable live beyond other people's. A few gifted individuals manage to do both.
Saki, THE MATCH-MAKER

20 The surest way to ruin a man who doesn't know how to handle money is to give him some.
George Bernard Shaw, HEARTBREAK HOUSE 1920

21 Not the least of its virtues is that it destroys base people as certainly as it fortifies and dignifies noble people.
George Bernard Shaw, MAJOR BARBARA, *Preface* 1905

22 The universal regard for money is the one hopeful fact in our civilisation. Money is the most important thing in the world. It represents health, strength, honour, generosity and beauty.
Ibid.

23 Lack of money is the root of all evil.
George Bernard Shaw, MAN AND SUPERMAN, *Maxims for Revolutionists* 1905

1 There was a time when a fool and his money were soon parted, but now it happens to everybody.
Adlai Stevenson, THE STEVENSON WIT

2 To have subsidised a Bach or Fullbrighted a Beethoven would have done no good at all. Money may kindle but it cannot, by itself for very long, burn.
Igor Stravinsky. Quoted Barbara Rowe, A BOOK OF QUOTES

3 Nine times out of ten money will do the trick required at the moment.
John Wain, Punch 28 Sep 1960

4 The easiest way for your children to learn about money is for you not to have any.
Katherine Whitehorn, HOW TO SURVIVE CHILDREN

5 Money should circulate like rainwater.
Thornton Wilder, THE MATCHMAKER 1955

6 I'd give a thousand dollars right now to be a millionaire.
Hal Wilton, DOOMED TO THE BIG HOUSE 1935

7 With money I'll throttle the beast-blind world beneath my fingers. Without it I am strapped, weakened, my life is a curse and a care.
Thomas Wolfe, LETTERS 1956

8 A broker is a man who runs your fortune into a shoestring.
Alexander Woollcott. Quoted Samuel Hopkins Adams, THE WORLD OF A. WOOLLCOTT 1945

MONOTONY

9 Life is simply one damn thing after another.
Elbert Hubbard, NOTEBOOKS 1927

10 It is not true that life is one damn thing after another — it is one damn thing over and over.
Edna St Vincent Millay, LETTERS 1952

MARILYN MONROE

11 If she was a victim, she was a victim of friends.
George Cukor. Quoted Gavin Lambert, ON CUKOR

250

12 She was never permitted to mature into a warm, vibrant woman, or fully use her gifts for comedy, despite the signals and flashes she kept sending up. Instead she was turned into a figure of mockery in the parts she played and to the men she played with.
Molly Haskell, FROM REVERENCE TO RAPE

13 She was good at being inarticulately abstracted for the same reason that midgets are good at being short.
Clive James, AT THE PILLARS OF HERCULES

14 A phenomenon of nature, like Niagara Falls and the Grand Canyon.
Nunnally Johnson. Quoted William Manchester, THE GLORY AND THE DREAM

15 . . . a very Stradivarius of sex, so gorgeous, forgiving, humorous, compliant and tender that even the most mediocre musician would relax his lack of art in the dissolving magic of her violin.
Norman Mailer, MARILYN

16 Marilyn's need to be desired was so great that she could make love to a camera.
William Manchester, THE GLORY AND THE DREAM

17 That she withstood the incredible, unknowable pressures of her public legend as long as she did is evidence of the stamina of the human.
Vogue editorial. Quoted Edward Wagen Knecht, SEVEN DAUGHTERS OF THE THEATRE

FIELD MARSHAL MONTGOMERY

18 In defeat he is unbeatable; in victory unbearable.
Winston Churchill. Quoted Edward Marsh, AMBROSIA AND SMALL BEER

MOON

19 The moon is a different thing to each one of us. It looks like a vast, lonely, forbidding place, an expanse of nothing.
Frank Borman, broadcasting from Apollo VIII 24 Dec 1968

20 O the moon shone bright on Mrs Porter / And on her daughter / They wash their feet in soda water.
T. S. Eliot, THE WASTE LAND 1922

1 The moon is nothing / But a circumambulating aphrodisiac / Divinely subsidized to provoke the world / Into a rising birth-rate.
Christopher Fry, THE LADY'S NOT FOR BURNING 1949

2 The moon was a ghostly galleon tossed upon cloudy seas.
Alfred Noyes, COLLECTED POEMS, *The Highwayman* 1947

HENRY MOORE

3 Sculptor Henry Moore has been asked not to leave any holes in which boys could trap their heads when he carves 'Family Group' for Harlow New Town.
News Chronicle. Quoted Michael Bateman, THIS ENGLAND

MORALITY

4 No morality can be founded on authority, even if the authority were divine.
A. J. Ayer, ESSAY ON HUMANISM

5 I am as pure as the driven slush.
Tallulah Bankhead. Quoted Observer 24 *Feb* 1957

6 Fine feelings are as much a luxury as clean gloves.
Granville Barker, THE VOYSEY INHERITANCE 1905

7 She is the kind of girl who will not go anywhere without her mother. And her mother will go anywhere.
John Barrymore, of his ex-wife Elaine. Quoted J. P. McEvoy, Stage, Jan 1941

8 Morality's not practical. Morality's a gesture. A complicated gesture learned from books.
Robert Bolt, A MAN FOR AI L SEASONS 1962

9 It doesn't matter what you do, as long as you don't do it in public and frighten the horses.
Mrs Pat Campbell

10 What is moral is what you feel good after, and what is immoral is what you feel bad after.
Ernest Hemingway, DEATH IN THE AFTERNOON 1932

11 Half, at least, of all morality is negative and consists in keeping out of mischief.
Aldous Huxley, THE DOORS OF PERCEPTION 1926

12 The quality of moral behaviour varies in inverse ratio to the number of human beings involved.
Aldous Huxley, GREY EMINENCE

13 Morality which is based on ideas, or on an ideal, is an unmitigated evil.
D. H. Lawrence, FANTASIA OF THE UNCONSCIOUS 1922

14 There is nothing so bad but it can masquerade as moral.
Walter Lippmann, A PREFACE TO POLITICS, *Some Necessary Iconoclasm* 1914

15 You can't learn too soon that the most useful thing about a principle is that it can always be sacrificed to expediency.
W. Somerset Maugham, THE CIRCLE 1921

16 As soon as one is unhappy one becomes moral.
Marcel Proust, REMEMBRANCE OF THINGS PAST 1917–1927

17 Morality consists in suspecting other people of not being legally married.
George Bernard Shaw, THE DOCTOR'S DILEMMA 1906

18 I don't believe in morality. I am a disciple of Bernard Shaw.
Ibid.

19 The so-called new morality is too often the old immorality condoned.
Lord Shawcross, Observer 17 *Nov* 1963

20 Morals are an acquirement — like music, like a foreign language, like piety, poker, paralysis — no man is born with them.
Mark Twain, SEVENTIETH BIRTHDAY 1907

21 As society is now constituted, a literal adherence to the moral precepts scattered throughout the Gospels would mean sudden death.
A. N. Whitehead, ADVENTURES IN IDEAS 1933

22 What is morality in any given time or place? It is what the majority then and there happen to like and immorality is what they dislike.
A. N. Whitehead, DIALOGUES, *recorded by Lucien Price* 1953

MORNING

1 The principality of the sky lightens now,
over our green hill, into spring morning
larked and crowed and belling.
Dylan Thomas, UNDER MILK WOOD 1954

MOTHER

2 Sweet little old lady wishes to correspond
with six-foot student with brown eyes and
answering to the initials J. D. B. (signed)
His Mother.
*Advert in a student magazine. Quoted
Venture, Aug* 1980

3 Mother love, particularly in America, is a
highly respected and much publicised emotion and when exacerbated by gin and
bourbon it can become extremely formid-
able.
Noël Coward, FUTURE INDEFINITE 1954

4 It's a wise child that knows its own father,
but it's one child in a million who knows his
mother. They're a mysterious mob,
mothers.
Robertson Davies, WHAT'S BRED IN THE
BONE 1986

5 Mother is the dead heart of the family,
spending father's earnings on consumer
goods to enhance the environment in which
he eats, sleeps and watches television.
Germaine Greer, THE FEMALE EUNUCH

6 My mother was dead five years before I
knew that I had loved her very much.
Lillian Hellman, AN UNFINISHED
WOMAN 1969

7 Nobody can have the soul of me. My mother
has had it, and nobody can have it again.
Nobody can come into my very self again,
and breathe me like an atmosphere.
D. H. Lawrence, LETTERS 1936

8 Few misfortunes can befall a boy which
bring worse consequences than to have a
really affectionate mother.
W. Somerset Maugham, A WRITER'S
NOTEBOOK 1949

9 Who has not watched a mother stroke her
child's cheek or kiss her child *in a certain way*
and felt a nervous shudder at the possessive
outrage done to a free solitary human soul?
John Cowper Powys, THE MEANING OF
CULTURE 1930

10 There is only one person an English girl
hates more than she hates her elder sister;
and that is her mother.
George Bernard Shaw, MAN AND
SUPERMAN 1905

11 Motherhood is the most emotional experience of one's life. One joins a kind of
women's mafia.
*Janet Suzman, Observer, Sayings of the
Week*, 19 Jul 1981

12 There's a part of every man which resents
the great big bossy woman that once made
him eat up his spinach and wash behind his
ears.
Katherine Whitehorn, Observer, 16 Jan 1983

MOTHER-IN-LAW

13 The day my mother-in-law called, the mice
threw themselves on the traps.
Les Dawson, BBC TV, Dawson's Watch

14 Mussolini in knickers.
Les Dawson, BBC TV, programme title 18
Oct 1981

15 Nye [Aneurin Bevan] loved telling people
that he had to marry Jennie to get his
mother-in-law.
Michael Foot, ANEURIN BEVAN 1897–1945

MOTORING

16 A pedestrian is a man who has two cars —
one being driven by his wife, the other by
one of his children.
Robert Bradbury, New York Times 5 *Sep*
1962

17 We are nourishing at immense cost a
monster of great potential destructiveness,
and yet we love him dearly.
Prof. Colin Buchanan, INTRODUCTION TO
TRAFFIC IN TOWNS 1963

18 Americans are broad-minded people.
They'll accept the fact that a person can be
an alcoholic, a dope fiend, a wife beater,
and even a newspaperman, but if a man
doesn't drive, there is something wrong with
him.
Art Buchwald, HOW MUCH IS THAT IN
DOLLARS? 1961

252

1 The automobile changed our dress, manners, social customs, vacation habits, the shape of our cities, consumer purchasing patterns, common tastes and positions of intercourse.
John Ketas, THE INSOLENT CHARIOTS

2 When I caught a glimpse of Rita / Filling in a ticket in her little white book / In a cap she looked much older / And the bag across her shoulder / Made her look a little like a military man / Lovely Rita, Meter Maid.
John Lennon and Paul McCartney, LOVELY RITA *(song)*

3 To George F. Babbitt his motor car was poetry and tragedy, love and heroism. The office was his pirate ship, but the car his perilous journey ashore.
Sinclair Lewis, BABBITT 1922

4 The car has become the carapace, the protective and aggressive shell, of urban and suburban man.
Marshall McLuhan, UNDERSTANDING MEDIA 1964

5 . . . an old bullnosed Morris he called God because it moved in a mysterious way.
Lord Mancroft, Punch

6 Very often a gentleman's wife will have her own car, particularly if she can afford to buy it herself. Anything that is small and uncomfortable will do.
Douglas Sutherland, THE ENGLISH GENTLEMAN 1978

7 The most non-gent car of all is the Rolls Royce. If, however, he happens to have been left one by an eccentric aunt it should be very old and not very clean. Some gentlemen carry this further, keeping old sacks on the back seat and leaving bird messes on the roof where the chickens have roosted.
Ibid.

MOUSTACHE

8 The huge laughing cockroaches on his top lip.
Osip Mandelstam, POEMS, *Stalin Epigram*

9 He has a moustache like a mosquito's whiskers across his upper lip.
Damon Runyon, MORE THAN SOMEWHAT 1937

10 His nicotine, egg yellow, weeping walrus Victorian moustache worn thick and long in memory of Doctor Crippen.
Dylan Thomas, UNDER MILK WOOD 1954

MALCOLM MUGGERIDGE

11 The most wonderful deceitful character – saved by his sense of humour.
Osbert Lancaster. Quoted Duncan Fallowell, Times Profile 11 *Oct* 1982

12 He combines the roles of the voice crying in the wilderness and the voice full of the most worldly relish.
Bernard Levin, THE PENDULUM YEARS 1976

13 Muggeridge found himself in the dire situation of a thief crucified between two Christs.
Anthony Powell, THE STRANGERS ARE ALL GONE, VOL 4, *The Memoirs*

14 He thinks he was knocked off his horse by God, like St Paul on the road to Damascus. His critics think he simply fell off from old age.
Katherine Whitehorn, Observer 20 *May* 1979

MURDER

15 No actions are bad in themselves — even murder can be justified.
Dietrich Bonhoeffer, NO RUSTY SWORDS

16 Every murderer is probably somebody's old friend.
Agatha Christie, THE MYSTERIOUS AFFAIR AT STYLES 1920

17 Why murder is the greatest of all crimes is not that the life taken may be that of an Abraham Lincoln, but because it might be yours or mine.
F. Tennyson Jesse, COMMENTS ON CAIN

18 He who bears the brand of Cain shall rule the earth.
George Bernard Shaw, BACK TO METHUSELAH 1922

IRIS MURDOCH

19 She is like a character out of Hieronymus Bosch — the very nicest character.
Rachel Billington, Times profile 25 *Apr* 1983

1 A tousled, heelless, ladder-stockinged little
   lady — crackling with intelligence but
   nothing at all of a prig.
   George Lyttelton, THE LYTTELTON HART-
   DAVIS LETTERS 1959

2 Iris Murdoch writes Hampstead novels *in
   excelsis* (though the setting is rarely Hampstead), that is, books whose characters are
   extensively pre-occupied with their emotions and who pair off and break up with
   operatic intensity.
   Adam Mars-Jones, Sunday Times 29 Sep
   1985

MUSEUM

3 How fortunate we are that the British
   Museum and the National Gallery are full of
   objects that are neither British nor National.
   Russell Chamberlain, LOOT: THE HERITAGE
   OF PLUNDER 1983

MUSIC

4 Delius is all intoxication but it is all the same
   intoxication. Wagner has a hundred ways of
   making you tight.
   Anon. Quoted James Agate, EGO 7, *Sep*
   1944

5 A friend said to Chopin / It would be topin /
   If only yude / Write an étude.
   Anon.

6 There's only two ways to sum up music:
   either it's good or it's bad. If it's good you
   don't mess about with it, you just enjoy it.
   Louis Armstrong. Quoted Nat Shapiro, AN
   ENCYCLOPEDIA OF QUOTATIONS ABOUT
   MUSIC

7 Music is the best means we have of digesting
   time.
   W. H. Auden. Quoted Robert Craft,
   STRAVINSKY: THE CHRONICLE OF A
   FRIENDSHIP 1972

8 Music can be made anywhere, is invisible
   and doesn't smell.
   W. H. Auden, IN PRAISE OF
   LIMESTONE 1941

9 I have played everywhere except in the
   street. I even played in pantomime at the old
   Surrey, and I don't regret a minute of it.
   John Barbirolli, Observer 6 Jul 1947

10 Whether the angels play only Bach praising
   God I am not quite sure. I am sure however
   that *en famille* they play Mozart.
   *Karl Barth. Quoted New York Times
   obituary 11 Dec 1968*

11 The search for a critical vocabulary in which
   we may speak of music by strict notations is
   quite absurd; not even the conventional
   notes and signs of a score can precisely
   denote the sounds that we hear.
   Jacques Barzun, PLEASURES OF MUSIC 1951

12 All Bach's last movements are like the
   running of a sewing machine.
   *Arnold Bax. Quoted Basil Maine, Morning
   Post 21 Aug 1930*

13 The English may not like music but they
   absolutely love the noise it makes.
   Sir Thomas Beecham, A MINGLED
   CHIME 1944

14 Music *per se* means nothing; it is sheer sound
   and the interpreter can do no more with it
   than his own capacities, mental and spiritual
   will allow, and the same applies to the
   listener.
   Ibid.

15 Music first and last should sound well,
   should allure and enchant the ear, never
   mind the inner significance.
   *Sir Thomas Beecham. Quoted Harold
   Atkins and Archie Newman*, BEECHAM
   STORIES

16 Even Beethoven thumped the tub; the
   Ninth Symphony was composed by a sort of
   Mr Gladstone of music.
   Ibid.

17 Too much counterpoint — and what is
   worse, Protestant counterpoint.
   Ibid. (of Bach)

18 What can you do with it? It's like a lot of
   yaks jumping about.
   Ibid. (of Beethoven's seventh symphony)

19 If I were a dictator I should make it
   compulsory for every member of the
   population between the ages of four and
   eighty to listen to Mozart for at least a
   quarter of an hour daily for the coming five
   years.
   Ibid.

1 In the first movement alone I took notice of six pregnancies and at least four miscarriages.
Ibid. (of Bruckner's seventh symphony)

2 Doctors of Music! That means they have sat on their bottoms for six hours and done a paper on harmony, but they can't play the National Anthem.
Ibid.

3 Forget about bars. Look at the phrases, please. Remember that bars are only the boxes in which music is packed.
Ibid.

4 Great music is that which penetrates the ear with facility and quits the memory with difficulty. Magical music never leaves the memory.
Sir Thomas Beecham. Quoted Lord Boothby, MY YESTERDAY, YOUR TOMORROW.

5 Brass bands are all very well in their place — outdoors and several miles away.
Sir Thomas Beecham. Quoted Michael Kennedy, Daily Telegraph 17 Feb 1979

6 There are only two things requisite so far as the public is concerned for a good performance. That is for the orchestra to begin together and end together. In between it doesn't matter much.
Sir Thomas Beecham. Quoted Nigel Rees, QUOTE UNQUOTE

7 A musicologist is a person who can read music but can't hear it.
Sir Thomas Beecham. Quoted Harold C. Schonberg, THE GREAT CONDUCTORS 1967

8 A man cannot make the viola agreeable to me. It is the only instrument which women can play supremely well.
Sir Thomas Beecham. Speech at the Savoy. Reported News Review 22 Aug 1946

9 *Clarionet, n.* An instrument of torture operated by a person with cotton in his ears. There are two instruments worse than a clarionet — two clarionets.
Ambrose Bierce, THE DEVIL'S DICTIONARY 1906

10 Your true music lover does more than admire the music — he sweats a little in her service.
Catherine Drinker Bowen, FRIENDS AND FIDDLERS 1935

11 Music does not exist until it is performed.
Benjamin Britten. Quoted Timothy Green, BENJAMIN BRITTEN'S WORLD OF MUSIC

12 Almost the only thing music can represent unambiguously is the cuckoo — and that it can't differentiate from a cuckoo clock.
Brigid Brophy, A LITERARY PERSON'S GUIDE TO OPERA 1965

13 Music is edifying, for from time to time it sets the soul in operation.
John Cage, FORERUNNER OF MODERN MUSIC 1949

14 Let no one imagine that in owning a recording he has the muse. The very practice of music is a celebration that we own nothing.
John Cage, SILENCE, *Lecture on Something* 1949

15 To make divine things human, and human things divine; such is Bach, the greatest and purest moment in music of all times.
Pablo Casals. Speech, Prades Bach Festival 1950

16 An oboe is an ill-wind that nobody blows good.
Bennett Cerf, LAUGHING STOCK 1952

17 Strange how potent cheap music is.
Noël Coward, PRIVATE LIVES 1930

18 The Detroit Quartet played Brahms last night. Brahms lost.
Anonymous critic. Quoted Bennett Cerf, TRY AND STOP ME 1943

19 When music sounds, gone is the earth I know. / And all her lovely things lovelier grow.
Walter De La Mare, FAREWELL

20 Music was invented to confirm human loneliness.
Lawrence Durrell, CLEA 1960

21 It is a curious thing that the performances which I have hated and loathed as being a caricature of my thoughts are the very ones held up as patterns.
Sir Edward Elgar. Quoted Basil Maine, ELGAR: HIS LIFE AND WORKS

22 The Third Symphony (of Brahms) is an example at the height of music because the work gives no clue to what it means. It is simply a piece of music.
Ibid.

1 I believed at this time that the only real composers were dead ones. I saw it as a sort of posthumous award.
Brian Ferneyhough, interviewed in the Observer 8 *Jun* 1978

2 Beethoven's Fifth Symphony is the most sublime noise that has ever penetrated into the ear of man.
F. M Forster, HOWARDS END 1910

3 Please write music like Wagner, only louder.
Sam Goldwyn, instructing composer for a movie. Quoted Alva Johnson, THE GREAT GOLDWYN

4 This music won't do. There's not enough sarcasm in it.
Sam Goldwyn. Ibid.

5 Music means everything to me when I'm alone. And it's the best way of getting that bloody man Wilson out of my hair.
Edward Heath. Quoted James Margach, THE ABUSE OF POWER 1980

6 I occasionally play works by contemporary composers, and for two reasons. First, to discourage the composer from writing any more, and secondly to remind myself how much I appreciate Beethoven.
Jascha Heifetz, Life 28 *Jul* 1961

7 Music is meaningless noise unless it touches a receiving mind.
Paul Hindemith, A COMPOSER'S WORLD 1961

8 People who make music together cannot be enemies, at least while the music lasts.
Ibid.

9 Never compose anything unless the not composing of it becomes a positive nuisance to you.
Gustav Holst. Quoted from a letter to W. G. Whittaker, N. Shapiro, ENCYCLOPEDIA OF QUOTATIONS ABOUT MUSIC

10 The public doesn't want new music; the main thing it demands of a composer is that he be dead.
Arthur Honegger. Quoted THE FRANK MUIR BOOK 1976

11 Compare the music of 'the Beggar's Opera' with the music of a contemporary revue. They differ as life in the Garden of Eden differed from life in the artistic quarter of Gomorrah.
Aldous Huxley, ALONG THE ROAD

12 After silence, that which comes nearest to expressing the inexpressible is music.
Aldous Huxley, MUSIC AT NIGHT 1931

13 Humphrey Searle writes music that sounds like the theme from *Star Wars* played backwards through a washing machine.
Clive James, Observer, The Sorry Serpent 16 *Mar* 1979

14 All full-time writers, even if they can't tell a tonic solfa from a ton of sulphur should stay in touch with music if they can, if only to remind themselves that compared with musicians they are in a low state of training.
Clive James, Observer 8 *Mar* 1981

15 Of all musicians, flautists are obviously the ones who know something we don't know.
Paul Jennings, JENGUIN PENNINGS

16 Nothing is wrong when done to music.
Jerome Kern. Quoted Nat Shapiro, ENCYCLOPEDIA OF QUOTATIONS ABOUT MUSIC

17 What is the Ninth Symphony compared to a Tin Pan Alley hit played on a hurdy-gurdy and a memory?
Karl Kraus, APHORISMS

18 It is sobering to consider that when Mozart was my age he had been dead a year.
Tom Lehrer. Quoted Nat Shapiro, ENCYCLOPEDIA OF QUOTATIONS ABOUT MUSIC

19 There can no more be a new Beethoven than there can be a new Christopher Columbus.
René Leonormond, ÉTUDE SUR L'HARMONIE MODERNE 1913

20 Having adapted Beethoven's Sixth Symphony for 'Fantasia' Walt Disney commented 'Gee, this'll make Beethoven.'
Marshall McLuhan, CULTURE IS OUR BUSINESS 1970

21 Play 'Somewhere My Love Lies Sleeping' with a male chorus.
Groucho Marx, ANIMAL CRACKERS

22 I am merely a musical bricklayer.
Sir Robert Mayer on his hundredth birthday 4 *Jun* 1979

1 I find that I never lose Bach. I don't know why I have always loved him so. Except that he is so pure, so relentless and incorruptible, like a principle of geometry.
Edna St Vincent Millay, LETTERS 1943

2 Music is a beautiful opiate, if you don't take it too seriously.
Henry Miller, THE AIR CONDITIONED NIGHTMARE 1945

3 Sir Arthur Bliss, Master of the Queen's Music, once described the BBC's pop programme as 'aural hashish', but it's not that good.
Richard Neville, PLAYPOWER 1970

4 During the playing of Rossini's 'William Tell' overture [at the Albert Hall] an American lady said, 'Back home this is known as "The Lone Ranger". '
Peterborough, Daily Telegraph 13 Jul 1979

5 Anybody who loves music has to be worried by the romantic assumption that it contains meanings expressible in words.
Anthony Powell, Observer, Music of the Spheres 13 Feb 1983

6 You can chase a Beethoven symphony all your life and never catch up.
André Previn. Quoted Nat Shapiro, ENCYCLOPEDIA OF QUOTATIONS ABOUT MUSIC 1978

7 The sound of music — as opposed to rustling leaves or words or love — is sensual only secondarily. First it must make sense.
Ned Rorem, MUSIC FROM INSIDE OUT 1967

8 The hardest of all arts to speak of is music, because music has no meaning to speak of.
Ibid.

9 After a rousing performance of 'Rule Britannia' King George VI said to Sir Malcolm Sargent 'You will in future always include that in the programme when I am present'. 'But, Your Majesty, how can I include "Rule Britannia" if I am about to conduct a sacred work like the St Matthew Passion?' 'No problem. I shall not be there.'
Kenneth Roase, KINGS, QUEENS AND COURTIERS 1985

10 Sometimes I think, not so much am I a pianist, but a vampire. All my life I have lived off the blood of Chopin.
Artur Rubenstein at 90

11 It is folly to believe that, because man has invented the aeroplane, music should sound like a factory turning out Spitfires.
Malcolm Sargent. Quoted James Agate EGO 20 Sep 1944

12 The musician is perhaps the most modest of animals, but he is also the proudest. It is he who invented the sublime art of ruining poetry.
Erik Satie. Quoted Pierre-Daniel Templier, ERIK SATIE

13 Sunshine can burn you, food can poison you, words can condemn you, pictures can insult you; music cannot punish — only bless.
Artur Schnabel, MUSIC AND THE LINE OF MOST RESISTANCE 1942

14 I don't think that there was ever a piece of music that changed a man's decision on how to vote.
Artur Schnabel, MY LIFE AND MUSIC

15 I am attracted only to music which I consider to be better than it can be performed.
Ibid.

16 The sonatas of Mozart are unique; they are too easy for children and too difficult for adults.
Ibid.

17 Hell is full of musical amateurs. Music is the brandy of the damned.
George Bernard Shaw, MAN AND SUPERMAN 1905

18 The finale of Mozart's Jupiter Symphony is like the Cathedral of Cologne.
Dmitri Shostakovitch, TESTIMONY

19 If, as is nearly always the case, music appears to express something, this is only an illusion and not a reality.
Igor Stravinsky, CHRONICLES OF MY LIFE 1936

20 If melody were all of music, what could we prize in the various forces that make up the immense work of Beethoven, in which melody is assuredly the least?
Igor Stravinsky, POETICS OF MUSIC 1947

1 The trouble with music appreciation in general is that people are taught to have too much respect for music; they should be taught to love it instead.
Igor Stravinsky, New York Times Magazine 27 Sep 1964

2 I don't write modern music. I only write good music.
Igor Stravinsky to journalists on his first visit to America 1925

3 Conductors' careers are made for the most part with 'romantic' music. 'Classic' music eliminates the conductor; we do not remember him in it.
Igor Stravinsky. Quoted Robert Craft, CONVERSATIONS WITH IGOR STRAVINSKY 1958

4 My music is best understood by children and animals.
Igor Stravinsky, Observer 8 Oct 1961

5 My favourite music is the sound of radio commercials at ten dollars a whack.
Lord Thomson of Fleet

6 God tells me how he wants this music played — and you get in his way.
Arturo Toscanini at rehearsal. Quoted Howard Tubman, Etude, Jun 1940

7 I don't know whether I like it, but it is what I meant.
Ralph Vaughan Williams of his Fourth Symphony. Quoted Sir Adrian Boult, BBC 1 Aug 1945

8 Within limits, any music can be made to fit any situation.
Ralph Vaughan Williams (of composing music for the cinema), FILM MUSIC NOTES 1946

9 Music is natural law as related to a sense of hearing.
Anton Webern, THE PATH TO THE NEW MUSIC 1962

10 It is very odd about George and music. You know his parents were quite normal — liked horses and dogs, and the country.
Duke of Windsor, of George Lascelles, 7th Earl of Harewood. Quoted Shirley Lowe, The Times, Hedgehogs and High Notes 23 Jun 1983

BENITO MUSSOLINI

11 The crafty, cold-blooded, black-hearted Italian.
Winston Churchill, radio broadcast 9 Feb 1941

12 Italy's pinchbeck Caesar.
Winston Churchill. Speech, London Guildhall 30 Jun 1943

13 This whipped jackal . . . is frisking up by the side of the German tiger.
Winston Churchill, House of Commons, Apr 1941

14 Kipling cherished an unworthy admiration for Mussolini — the only journalist so far as I know to become a dictator.
Jan Morris, Daily Telegraph, The Marvel of Kipling 20 Oct 1978

15 Sawdust Caesar.
Gilbert Seldes, book title

MYSTERY

16 Show me a man or woman who cannot stand mysteries and I will show you a fool. A clever fool — perhaps — but a fool just the same.
Raymond Chandler, RAYMOND CHANDLER SPEAKING

17 The most beautiful thing we can experience is the mysterious. It is the source of all true art and science.
Albert Einstein, WHAT I BELIEVE 1934

MYSTICISM

18 The dilemma of the mystic is not so much that of setting down his mystical experience in words as of making his words fully and to their very last echo intelligible to those to whom any such experience is unknown.
Walter De La Mare, PLEASURES AND EXPECTATIONS

19 I have found a perfect description of mysticism — it is the attempt to get rid of mystery.
Roger Fry. Quoted Virginia Woolf

20 The ultimate gift of a conscious life is a sense of the mystery that encompasses it.
Lewis Mumford, THE CONDUCT OF LIFE 1951

1 Mysticism is, in essence, little more than a certain intensity and depth of feeling in regard to what is believed about the universe.
Bertrand Russell, MYSTICISM AND LOGIC 1917

2 Mystics always hope that science will some day overtake them.
Booth Tarkington, LOOKING FORWARD TO THE GREAT ADVENTURE 1926

3 *That* the world is, is the mystical.
Ludwig Wittgenstein

N

NAME

1 The 't' is silent as in Harlow.
*Margot Asquith, on her name being
mispronounced by Jean Harlow*

2 Mr Ball? How very singular.
Sir Thomas Beecham

3 Don't take action because of a name. A
name is an uncertain thing. You can't count
on it.
Bertolt Brecht, A MAN'S A MAN 1927

4 Going to call him 'William'? What kind of a
name is that? Every Tom, Dick and Harry is
called William. Why not call him Bill?
Sam Goldwyn. Quoted Bennett Cerf

5 A self-made man may prefer a self-made
name.
*Judge Learned Hand, when Samuel
Goldwyn changed his name from Goldfish*

6 I [Lorelei Lee] was named after a girl who
became famous for sitting on a rock in
Germany.
Anita Loos, GENTLEMEN PREFER
BLONDES 1925

7 The name of a man is a numbing blow from
which he never recovers.
Marshall McLuhan, UNDERSTANDING
MEDIA 1967

8 Groucho is not my real name. I'm breaking
it in for a friend.
Groucho Marx

9 Each planet, each plant, each butterfly,
each moth, each beetle, becomes doubly
real to you when you know its name. Lucky
indeed are those who from their earliest
childhood have heard all these things
named.
John Cowper Powys, THE MEANING OF
CULTURE 1930

10 The medieval saints would scarcely have
been pleased if they could have foreseen
that their names would be associated
nowadays chiefly with racehorses and the
cheaper clarets.
Saki, REGINALD AT THE CARLTON 1904

NARROW-MINDEDNESS

11 It is better to be narrow-minded than to
have no mind at all, to hold limited and rigid
principles than none at all.
Evelyn Waugh, A LITTLE ORDER

NATIONALISM

12 Nationalism is an infantile disease. It is the
measles of mankind.
Albert Einstein. Quoted Edwin Muller,
EINSTEIN: A STUDY IN SIMPLICITY

NATURE

13 It is an outcome of faith that nature — as she
is perceptible to our five senses – takes the
character of such a well formulated puzzle.
Albert Einstein, OUT OF MY LATER
YEARS 1950

14 How nature loves the incomplete. She
knows / If she drew a conclusion it would
finish her.
Christopher Fry, VENUS OBSERVED 1950

15 The whole of nature is a conjugation of the
verb to eat, in the active and the passive.
W. R. Inge (Dean of St Pauls), OUTSPOKEN
ESSAYS 1919

16 We need for our happiness to feel ourselves
part of Nature, as Wordsworth did,
although few of us can share his belief that
its workings are moral.
Raymond Mortimer, LANDSCAPE

1 A vacuum is a hell of a lot better than some of the stuff that nature replaces it with.
Tennessee Williams, CAT ON A HOT TIN ROOF 1955

NAVY

2 We joined the Navy, to see the world / And what did we see? We saw the sea.
Irving Berlin (song)

3 Don't talk to me of naval tradition. It is all rum, sodomy and the lash.
Winston Churchill, in 1911

NEGRO

4 Only in the case of the Negro has the melting pot failed to bring a minority into the mainstream of American life.
John F. Kennedy, A NATION OF IMMIGRANTS 1958

5 Never forget that two blacks do not make a white.
George Bernard Shaw, THE ADVENTURES OF THE BLACK GIRL IN HER SEARCH FOR GOD

NEIGHBOUR

6 Do not love your neighbour as yourself. If you are on good terms with yourself it is an impertinence; if on bad, an injury.
George Bernard Shaw, MAN AND SUPERMAN 1905

NEPOTISM

7 Nepotism is only kin deep.
Peter Hillmore, *Observer* 20 *Oct* 1985

8 I was president of Fox when I was 22 years old because my father gave me the studio as a birthday present.
Richard Zanuck. Quoted Sue Summers, *Sunday Times* 8 *Sep* 1985

NEUROSIS

9 Modern neurosis began with the discoveries of Copernicus. Science made man feel small by showing him the earth was not at the centre of the universe.
Mary McCarthy, ON THE CONTRARY 1961

10 Neurosis is the way of avoiding non-being by avoiding being.
Paul Tillich, THE COURAGE TO BE 1952

NEWS

11 I want news of peace. Get me some news of peace.
Lord Beaverbrook, on the eve of the outbreak of World War II. Quoted Jonah Barrington, MASTER OF NONE

12 When a dog bites a man that's not news. If a man bites a dog, that's news.
John B. Bogart. Quoted Frank M. O'Brien, THE STORY OF THE NEW YORK SUN

13 Nothing is news until it has appeared in *The Times*.
Ralph Deakin, Foreign News Editor of The Times. Quoted Claud Cockburn, COCKBURN SUMS UP

14 News is what a chap who doesn't care much about anything wants to read. And it's only news until he has read it. After that it's dead.
Evelyn Waugh, SCOOP 1938

NEWSPAPER

15 Have you noticed that life, real honest to goodness life, with murders and catastrophes and fabulous inheritances, happens almost exclusively in newspapers?
Jean Anouilh, THE REHEARSAL 1950

16 The occupational disease among newspaper proprietors is megalomania.
Michael Foot, DEBTS OF HONOUR, *The Case for Beelzebub* 1982

17 A good newspaper, I suppose, is a nation talking to itself.
Arthur Miller, *Observer* 26 *Nov* 1961

18 Produced by office boys for office boys.
Marquis of Salisbury, of the Daily Mail

19 A newspaper, not having to act on its descriptions and reports, but only to sell them to idly curious people, has nothing but honour to lose by inaccuracy and unveracity.
George Bernard Shaw, A DOCTOR'S DILEMMA 1900

1 They were not so much published as carried screaming into the street.
H. G. Wells, WAR IN THE AIR

NEW YORK

2 When an American stays away from New York too long something happens to him. Perhaps he becomes a little provincial, a little dead and afraid.
Sherwood Anderson, LETTERS 1953

3 New York, the hussy, was taken in sin again.
Thomas Beer, THE MAUVE DECADE 1926

4 Long Island represents the American's idea of what God would have done with Nature if he'd had the money.
Peter Fleming in a letter to his brother Rupert
29 Sep 1929

5 Mass is said in 23 different languages in this city.
Edward Koch, mayor of New York, The Times 17 *Feb* 1983

6 New York is, after all, a place of business; it is not constructed to be lived in.
(Percy) Wyndham Lewis, AMERICA AND COSMIC MAN

7 New York has a trip-hammer vitality which drives you insane with restlessness, if you have no inner stabiliser.
Henry Miller, THE COLOSSUS OF MAROUSSI 1941

8 I miss the animal buoyancy of New York, the animal vitality. I did not mind that it had no meaning and no depth.
Anaïs Nin, DIARIES VOL 2 1967

9 New York is like a disco, but without the music.
Elaine Stritch. Quoted Observer 17 *Feb* 1980

10 When I leave it I never dare look back lest I turn into a pillar of salt and the conductor throw me over his left shoulder for good luck.
Frank Sullivan

11 New York's a small place when it comes to the part of it that wakes up just as the rest is going to bed.
P. G. Wodehouse, THE AUNT AND THE SLUGGARD

12 One belongs to New York instantly. One belongs to it as much in five minutes as in five years.
Thomas Wolfe, THE WEB AND THE ROCK 1939

NIGHT

13 Midnight shakes the memory / As a madman shakes a dead geranium.
T. S. Eliot, RHAPSODY ON A WINDY NIGHT

14 In the country the darkness of night is friendly and familiar, but in a city, with its blaze of lights, it is unnatural, hostile and menacing. It is like a monstrous vulture that hovers, biding its time.
W. Somerset Maugham, A WRITER'S NOTEBOOK 1949

15 It is spring, moonless night in the small town, starless and bible-black.
Dylan Thomas, UNDER MILK WOOD 1954

16 It is tonight in Donkey Street, trotting silent, with seaweed on its hooves, along the cockled cobbles, past curtained fernpot, text and trinket, harmonium, holy dresser, watercolours done by hand, china dog and rosy tin teacaddy. It is night neddying among the snuggeries of babies.
Ibid.

17 The lamps of London uphold the dark as upon the points of a bayonet.
Virginia Woolf, JACOB'S ROOM 1922

NIGHTINGALE

18 The nightingales are singing near / The Convent of the Sacred Heart / And sang within the bloody wood / When Agamemnon cried aloud.
T. S. Eliot, SWEENEY AMONG THE NIGHTINGALES 1920

RICHARD M. NIXON

19 President Nixon's motto was, if two wrongs don't make a right, try three.
Norman Cousins. Quoted Christie Davies, Daily Telegraph 17 *Jul* 1979

20 Nixon is the kind of politician who would cut down a redwood tree, then mount the stump for a conservation speech.
Adlai Stevenson. Quoted Leon Harris, THE FINE ART OF POLITICAL WIT 1966

NOBILITY

1 Godolphin Horne was nobly born: / He held the human race in scorn.
Hilaire Belloc, CAUTIONARY TALES 1901

2 Real nobility is based on scorn, courage, and profound indifference.
Albert Camus, NOTEBOOKS 1935–1942

NONSENSE

3 It is a far, far better thing to have a firm anchor in nonsense than to put out on troubled seas of thought.
J. K. Galbraith, THE AFFLUENT SOCIETY 1958

4 Even God has been defended with nonsense.
Walter Lippmann, A PREFACE TO POLITICS, *The Golden Rule and After* 1914

LORD NORTHCLIFFE

5 Have you heard? The Prime Minister has resigned and Northcliffe has sent for the King.
A member of Northcliffe's staff. Quoted Hamilton Fyfe, NORTHCLIFFE, AN INTIMATE BIOGRAPHY

6 He aspired to power instead of influence and as a result forfeited both.
A. J. P. Taylor, ENGLISH HISTORY 1914–1945

NOSE

7 Red noses last a lifetime, red roses but a day.
From a song by Lord Berners

8 Where you get that nose from, Lily? / Got it from my father, silly. / You've got it on upside down! / Oh there's a conk!
Dylan Thomas, UNDER MILK WOOD 1954

NOSTALGIA

9 Nostalgia is like a grammar lesson. You find the present tense and the past perfect.
Anon. New Venture, Jun 1981

10 For the first time in my life I have become a wireless fan. I suppose it is due to being alone in a foreign country. I listen to everything from England, even the cricket matches and the Stock Exchange quotations.
W. H. Auden, LETTERS FROM ICELAND 1937

11 Were we closer to the ground as children, or is the grass emptier now?
Alan Bennett, FORTY YEARS ON

12 Nothing recalls the past so potently as a smell.
Winston Churchill, MY EARLY LIFE 1930

13 Despair abroad can always nurse pleasant thoughts of home.
Christopher Fry, A PHOENIX TOO FREQUENT 1949

14 When I hold my hands as if in prayer and roll a pencil between them I can smell the plasticine snakes I made in Class 1B at Kogarah Infant's School.
Clive James, FALLING TOWARDS ENGLAND 1985

15 . . . the glamour / Of childish days is upon me, my manhood is cast / Down in the flood of remembrance, I weep like a child for the past.
D. H. Lawrence, PIANO

16 They spend their time mostly looking forward to the past.
John Osborne, LOOK BACK IN ANGER 1956

17 The earth's about five thousand million years old. Who can afford to live in the past?
Harold Pinter, THE HOMECOMING 1965

NUDITY

18 We cannot return to Eden by the simple expedient of removing our clothes.
Paul Ableman, ANATOMY OF NAKEDNESS

19 What can you give a nudist on his birthday?
Gracie Fields (song title)

20 If we had been meant to go naked there wouldn't be any fig trees.
A speaker on Newstalk BBC 4 26 May 1979

21 Nudism is a lot of fuss about nothing.
Piccolo Pete, Pictorial Weekly 3 Sep 1932

1 As naked as an ash tree in the moon of May.
J. M. Synge, THE PLAYBOY OF THE WESTERN
WORLD 1907

2 Modesty is a very odd, subtle thing.
Someone, I forget who, said it is all a
matter of beauty. If we were all perfect we
should not mind walking about with no
clothes at all.
Marie Tempest, letter to The Times 5 Jan
1935

3 Many people may be depressed by the
spectacle of naked humanity. Personally I
can't see that an ugly body is any more
offensive than an ugly dress.
Evelyn Waugh, Daily Mail 5 Jul 1930

NUN

4 Monica Baldwin's book 'I leapt over the
wall' strengthened my desire not to become
a nun.
Noël Coward, DIARIES

O

OBEDIENCE

1 The Englishman walks before the law like a trained circus-horse. He has the sense of legality in his bones, in his muscles.
Maxim Gorky, ENEMIES

OBESITY

2 Never get fat, dear child. Fat smothers anyone's vitality.
Margot Asquith to Anita Loos. Quoted KISS HOLLYWOOD GOOD-BYE

3 I had to face the facts, I was pear-shaped. I was a bit depressed because I hate pears.
Charlotte Bingham, CORONET AMONG THE WEEDS

4 I look like an elderly wasp in an interesting condition.
Mrs Pat Campbell. Quoted Alan Dent, MRS PATRICK CAMPBELL

5 Obesity is a mental state, a disease brought on by boredom and disappointment.
Cyril Connolly, THE UNQUIET GRAVE 1945

6 I may be seen any day struggling up Fleet Street in my worsted bonds like a cocktail sausage with hernia, in a hail of lethal buttons that would do credit to a New Orleans cop.
Alan Coren, THE SANITY INSPECTOR 1974

7 That dark day when a man decides he must wear his belt under instead of over his cascading paunch.
Peter De Vries, CONSENTING ADULTS

8 Her age and most of her measurements were forty-four — not, you would have thought, much of a date for anyone but a cannibal planning a long voyage in a canoe.
Katherine Whitehorn, VIEW FROM A COLUMN 1981

9 She fitted into my largest armchair as if it had been built round her by someone who knew they were wearing armchairs tight round the hips this season.
P. G. Wodehouse, JEEVES AND THE UNBIDDEN GUEST

OBITUARY

10 She [Margot Asquith] had a great taste for writing obituaries and rarely missed an opportunity of doing so. Once when she was staying with Arthur Balfour he was surprised to find, written in Margot's hand on a sheet of paper, an unfinished opening: 'So Arthur Balfour is dead —'
Mark Bonham Carter, Introduction, Margot Asquith's AUTOBIOGRAPHY 1936

OBLIVION

11 There is only one thing that there isn't — and that's oblivion.
Jorge Luis Borges in an interview with Nicholas Shakespeare, The Times 6 Oct 1983

OBSCENITY

12 More to the point, would you allow your gamekeeper to read it?
Anon. Of Mervyn Griffiths Jones' remark during the Lady Chatterley trial

13 A vocabulary that would take the feathers off a hoody crow.
Lillian Beckwith, LIGHTLY POACHED

14 Obscenity is such a tiny kingdom that a single tour covers it completely.
Heywood Brown. Quoted Bennett Cerf, SHAKE WELL BEFORE USING 1948

265

1 I do not claim to be a literary critic, but I know dirt when I smell it and here it is in heaps — festering putrid heaps which smell to high heaven.
W. Charles Pilley, John Bull, review of WOMEN IN LOVE 17 *Sep* 1921

2 Obscenity is whatever happens to shock some elderly and ignorant magistrate.
Bertrand Russell, Look Magazine 23 Feb 1934

3 Obscenity can be found in every book except the telephone directory.
George Bernard Shaw

OBSCURITY

4 I am afraid of losing my obscurity. Genuineness only thrives in the dark. Like celery.
Aldous Huxley, THOSE BARREN LEAVES 1925

5 I'm never going to be famous. My name will never be writ large on the roster of Those Who Do Things. I don't do anything. Not a single thing. I used to bite my nails, but I don't even do that now.
Dorothy Parker, THE LITTLE HOURS

OBVIOUSNESS

6 I deal with the obvious. I present, reiterate and glorify the obvious — because the obvious is what people need to be told.
Dale Carnegie. Speech, New York Luncheon Club

7 Never be afraid of the deafeningly obvious. It is always news to somebody.
P. J. Kavanagh, A SONG AND DANCE

8 It requires a very unusual mind to undertake the analysis of the obvious.
A. N. Whitehead. SCIENCE AND THE MODERN WORLD 1925

ODOUR

9 He smelt like a rag used to wipe beer splashes from a bar.
Peter Townsend, HORSE'S NECK 1985

OLD AGE

10 Nobody hears old people complain because people think that's all old people do. And that's because old people are gnarled and sagged and twisted into the shape of a complaint.
Edward Albee, THE AMERICAN DREAM 1960

11 An old man looks permanent, as if he had been born an old man.
H. E. Bates, DEATH IN SPRING

12 Tidy the old into tall flats. Desolation at fourteen storeys becomes a view.
Alan Bennett, FORTY YEARS ON

13 While everything else physical and mental seems to diminish, the appreciation of beauty is on the increase. Landscapes, animals, men, women and children and all man-made things fascinate, delight and evoke my critical sense more and more.
Bernard Berenson (aged 85), SUNSET AND TWILIGHT 1960

14 Now all the world she knew is dead / In this small room she lives her days./ The washhand stand and single bed / Screened from the public gaze.
Sir John Betjeman, A FEW LATE CHRYSANTHEMUMS, *House of Rest*

15 Old age is . . . a lot of crossed off names in an address book.
Ronald Blythe, THE VIEW IN WINTER 1980

16 To be old is to be part of a huge and ordinary multitude . . . the reason why old age was venerated in the past was because it was extraordinary.
Ibid.

17 The robe of flesh wears thin, and with the years God shines through all things.
John Buchan, THE WISE YEARS

18 I smoke 10 to 15 cigars a day, at my age I have to hold on to something.
Comedian George Burns at 84

19 It is the misfortune of an old man that though he can put things out of his head he can't put them out of his feelings.
Joyce Cary, TO BE A PILGRIM 1942

1 Old age is the out-patients' department of purgatory.
Lord Hugh Cecil. Quoted David Cecil, THE CECILS OF HATFIELD HOUSE

2 Oh to be seventy again.
Georges Clemençeau on passing a pretty girl on the Champs Elysées on his eightieth birthday. Quoted James Agate, EGO 319 *Apr* 1938

3 When Winston Churchill became Prime Minister he was over sixty-five years old, already qualified for an old age pension.
John Colville, THE CHURCHILLIANS

4 The dusky p.m. of our common existence.
Leon Edel, HENRY JAMES, THE MASTER 1901–1906

5 An old man in a dry month.
T. S. Eliot, GERONTION

6 Very, very, very few / People die at ninety-two. / I suppose that I shall be / Safer still at ninety-three.
Willard Espy, ACTUARIAL REFLECTION

7 Simply because I have no seniors / The literati will raise the cry / Ewart's a genius.
Gavin Ewart, THE COLLECTED EWART

8 It is not becoming to lay to virtue the weariness of old age.
André Gide, JOURNALS 25 *Jul* 1934

9 The first sign of his approaching end was when my old aunts, while undressing him, removed a toe with one of his socks.
Graham Greene, TRAVELS WITH MY AUNT 1969

10 With the approach of death I care less and less about religious truth. One hasn't long to wait for revelation and darkness.
Graham Greene, A SORT OF LIFE

11 For the ageing person it is a duty and a necessity to give serious attention to himself.
Carl Jung, MODERN MAN IN SEARCH OF A SOUL 1933

12 The afternoon of a human life must have a significance of its own, and cannot be merely a pitiful appendage to life's morning.
Carl Jung, PSYCHOLOGICAL REFLECTIONS 1953

13 The ultimate indignity is to be given a bedpan by a stranger who calls you by your first name.
Maggie Kuhn, Observer 20 *Aug* 1978

14 Presently, I shall be introduced as 'this venerable old gentleman' and the axe will fall when they raise me to the degree of 'grand old man'. This means on our continent anyone with snow-white hair who has kept out of jail till eighty.
Stephen Leacock, THREE SCORE AND TEN

15 Will you still need me / Will you still feed me / When I'm sixty-four?
John Lennon and Paul McCartney, WHEN I'M SIXTY-FOUR *(song)*

16 You are beautiful and faded / Like an old opera tune / Played upon a harpsichord.
Amy Lowell, A LADY

17 They don't let me attend the board, but they allow me to come to lunch afternoons.
Harold Macmillan, at 85, in a speech at Merton College, referring to his position as president of the firm

18 Old Mr Neave felt that he was too old for spring.
Katherine Mansfield, THE GARDEN PARTY 1922

19 When you have loved as she has loved you grow old beautifully.
W. Somerset Maugham, THE CIRCLE 1921

20 Growing old is a bad habit which a busy man has no time to form.
André Maurois, THE AGEING AMERICAN

21 A ready means of being cherished by the English is to adopt the simple expedient of living a long time. I have little doubt that if, say, Oscar Wilde had lived into his nineties, instead of dying in his forties, he would have been considered a benign, distinguished figure suitable to preside at a school prize-giving or to instruct and exhort scout-masters at their jamborees. He might even have been knighted.
Malcolm Muggeridge, TREAD SOFTLY FOR YOU TREAD ON MY JOKES 1966

22 Oh dear! How age creeps up on one, slouch, slough, slop. Not like a winged chariot but like an old pedlar in snow-boots which are too big for him.
Harold Nicolson. Letter to Vita Sackville-West 12 *Jan* 1955

1 When one has reached 81 one likes to sit back and let the world turn by itself, without trying to push it.
Sean O'Casey, New York Times 25 Sep 1960

2 When you get to our age they miss out every other day.
Overheard. Quoted BBC Radio 4, Quote Unquote 28 Oct 1979

3 I'll dispose of my teeth as I think fit and after they've gone I'll get along. I started off living on gruel, and by God, I can always go back to it again.
S. J. Perelman, CRAZY LIKE A FOX 1944

4 One starts to get young at the age of sixty and then it is too late.
Pablo Picasso to Jean Cocteau. Quoted Derek Prouse, Sunday Times 20 Oct 1963

5 Growing old is like being increasingly penalised for a crime you haven't committed.
Anthony Powell, TEMPORARY KINGS

6 As the eighth decade gradually consumes itself, shadows lengthen, a masked and muffled figure loiters persistently at the back of every room as if waiting for a word at the most tactful moment, a presence more easily discerning than heretofore that exhales undoubted menace yet also extends persuasive charm of an enigmatic kind.
Anthony Powell, THE STRANGERS ALL ARE GONE 1982

7 Old men are dangerous; it doesn't matter to them what is going to happen to the world.
George Bernard Shaw, HEARTBREAK HOUSE 1920

8 The greatest problem about old age is the fear that it may go on too long.
A. J. P. Taylor, Observer, Sayings of the Week 1 Nov 1981

9 Old age should burn and rave at close of day; / Rage, rage against the dying of the light.
Dylan Thomas, DO NOT GO GENTLE INTO THAT GOOD NIGHT 1952

10 Old age is the most unexpected of all things to happen to a man.
Leon Trotsky, DIARY IN EXILE

11 My legs have become very ugly. But then, what use would beautiful legs be to a woman of 85?
Dame Rebecca West, in an interview with Frederic Raphael, Radio Times 28 Nov 1978

12 It is a terrible thing for an old woman to outlive her dogs.
Tennessee Williams, CAMINO REAL 1953

13 Your well beloved's hair has threads of grey / And little shadows come about her eyes.
W. B. Yeats, THE FOLLY OF BEING COMFORTED 1904

14 An aged man is but a paltry thing / A tattered coat upon a stick, unless / Soul clap its hands and sing.
W. B. Yeats, SAILING TO BYZANTIUM 1928

15 I pray — for fashion's word is out / And prayer comes round again — / That I may seem, though I die old, / A foolish passionate man.
W. B. Yeats, A PRAYER FOR OLD AGE

16 Withered old and skeleton-gaunt.
W. B. Yeats

OPERA

17 Opera is like a husband with a foreign title: expensive to support, hard to understand, and therefore a supreme social challenge.
Cleveland Amory, NBC TV 6 Apr 1960

18 I do not mind what language an opera is sung in so long as it is a language I do not understand.
Sir Edward Appleton. Quoted Observer 28 Jul 1955

19 No good opera plot can be sensible, for people do not sing when they are feeling sensible.
W. H. Auden, Time 29 Dec 1961

20 Wagner has done undeniably good work in humbling the singer.
Max Beerbohm. Quoted, THE FRANK MUIR BOOK

21 Opera has no business making money.
Sir Rudolf Bing, New York Times 15 Nov 1959

1 The absurdity of opera lies in the fact that rational elements are used and three-dimensional reality is aimed at while at the same time everything is neutralised by the music.
Bertolt Brecht, THE MODERN THEATRE IS THE EPIC THEATRE 1930

2 Opera, next to Gothic architecture, is one of the strangest inventions of modern man. It could not have been foreseen by any logical process.
Kenneth, Lord Clark, CIVILISATION 1969

3 People are wrong when they say the opera isn't what it used to be. It is what it used to be. That's what's wrong with it.
Noël Coward, DESIGN FOR LIVING 1933

4 *Blanche*: (genially) I think we've slept together once.
Adrian: I don't remember.
Blanche: At the opera, during *Bérénice*.
Ronald Firbank, THE PRINCESS ZOUBAROFF

5 Nobody really sings in opera. They just make loud noises.
Amelia Galli-Curci. Quoted, THE FRANK MUIR BOOK

6 Opera is when a guy gets stabbed in the back and instead of bleeding he sings.
Ed Gardener on American radio show, Duffy's Tavern

7 God in his Almighty Wisdom and Fairness has not always given the greatest voices to the persons with the greatest intellect or the best education, or to the most beautiful of His Creatures.
Tyrone Guthrie, A LIFE IN THE THEATRE

8 Opera is like an oyster. It must be swallowed whole or not at all.
Spike Hughes and Barbara McFadgen, NIGHTS AT THE OPERA 1948

9 Opera in English is, in the main, just about as sensible as baseball in Italian.
H. L. Mencken. Quoted, THE FRANK MUIR BOOK

10 The opera is to music what a bawdy house is to a castle.
H. L. Mencken, letter to Isaac Goldberg 6 *May* 1925

11 Any subject is good for opera if the composer feels it so intensely that he must sing it out.
Gian-Carlo Menotti, Time 1 *May* 1950

12 Bel canto is to opera what pole vaulting is to ballet, the glorification of a performer's prowess and not a creator's imagination.
Ned Rorem, The New Republic 3 *Jun* 1972

13 His vocal cords were kissed by God.
Harold Schoenberg, of Luciano Pavarotti. Quoted John Heilpern, The Times 30 *Jun* 1981

OPINION

14 A man's opinion on tramcars matters; his opinion on Botticelli matters; his opinion on all things does not matter.
G. K. Chesterton, HERETICS 1905

15 I suggest we worry less about the opinion that annoys, and more about those that remain unspoken.
William Hardcastle, Punch 12 *Jan* 1972

16 The trouble with success is that a man may be perfectly sound on the short story but not very good about the atomic bomb. They always ask your opinion about things. I don't like to give it.
Richard Hughes. Quoted Mary Kay Wilmers, Radio Times 12 *Jun* 1979

17 Opinions cannot survive if one has no chance to fight for them.
Thomas Mann, THE MAGIC MOUNTAIN 1924

18 It's not that I don't have opinions, rather that I'm paid not to think aloud.
President Yitzhak Navon of Israel. Quoted Observer, Sayings of the Week 9 *Jan* 1983

19 Refusing to have an opinion is a way of having one, isn't it?
Luigi Pirandello, EACH IN HIS OWN WAY

20 The average man's opinions are much less foolish than they would be if he thought for himself.
Bertrand Russell, AUTOBIOGRAPHY 1967

1 The fact that an opinion has been widely held is no evidence whatever that it is not utterly absurd.
Bertrand Russell, MARRIAGE AND MORALS 1929

2 It is difficult, if not impossible for most people to think otherwise than in the fashion of their own opinion.
George Bernard Shaw, SAINT JOAN, *Preface* 1927

3 The danger which faces so many people is to have no considered opinions on any subject . . . in most cases means an inability to distinguish between good and bad. There are still things which are worth fighting *against.*
Evelyn Waugh, A LITTLE ORDER

4 It is just when opinions universally prevail and we have added lip service to their authority that we become sometimes most keenly conscious that we do not believe a word that we are saying.
Virginia Woolf, THE COMMON READER 1925

5 People are responsible for their opinions but Providence is responsible for their morals.
W. B. Yeats. Quoted Christopher Hassall, EDWARD MARSH

OPINION POLL

6 A survey which claims to show what voters are thinking but which only succeeds in changing their minds.
Miles Kington, The Times 10 *May* 1983

OPPONENT

7 I respect only those who resist me; but I cannot tolerate them.
Gen. Charles de Gaulle. Quoted New York Times Magazine 12 *May* 1966

OPPORTUNISM

8 The time to repair the roof is when the sun is shining.
John F. Kennedy, State of Union Message 11 *Jan* 1962

270

9 Just enjoy your ice-cream while it's on your plate — that's my philosophy.
Thornton Wilder, THE SKIN OF OUR TEETH 1942

OPPORTUNITY

10 Opportunities are usually disguised as hard work, so most people don't recognise them.
Ann Landers. Quoted Barbara Rowe, A BOOK OF QUOTES

11 One can present people with opportunities. One cannot make them equal to them.
Rosamond Lehmann, THE BALLAD AND THE SOURCE 1945

12 There is no security in this life. There is only opportunity.
Gen. Douglas MacArthur. Quoted Courtney Whitney, MACARTHUR, HIS RENDEZVOUS WITH HISTORY

13 Equality of opportunity means equal opportunity to be unequal.
Iain MacLeod. Quoted John Boyd Carpenter, WAY OF LIFE

14 Grab a chance and you won't be sorry for a might have been.
Arthur Ransome, WE DIDN'T MEAN TO GO TO SEA

OPPOSITION

15 One fifth of the people are against everything all the time.
Robert Kennedy. Quoted Punch 16 *Feb* 1972

OPTIMISM

16 The pessimist is the man who believes things couldn't possibly be worse, to which the optimist replies 'Oh yes they could.'
Vladimir Bukovsky, Guardian Weekly 10 *Jul* 1977

17 The optimist proclaims that we live in the best of all possible worlds; the pessimist fears that this is true.
J. B. Cabell, THE SILVER STALLION 1926

18 The place where optimism most flourishes is the lunatic asylum.
Havelock Ellis, THE DANCE OF LIFE 1923

1 Optimism is the content of small men in high
  places.
  F. Scott Fitzgerald, THE CRACK-UP 1936

2 Optimism is a kind of heart stimulus — the
  digitalis of failure.
  Elbert Hubbard, A THOUSAND AND ONE
  EPIGRAMS 1927

3 An optimist is a guy that never had much
  experience.
  Don Marquis, ARCHY AND
  MEHITABEL 1926

4 I'm an optimist, but I'm an optimist who
  carries a raincoat.
  Sir Harold Wilson. Quoted Nigel Rees,
  QUOTE UNQUOTE

ORATORIO

5 If I had the power I would insist on all
  oratorios being sung in the costume of the
  period — with a possible exception in the
  case of the *Creation*.
  Sir Ernest Newman, New York Post 1924

ORATORY

6 In private conversation he tries on speeches
  like a man trying on ties in his bedroom to
  see how he would look in them.
  *Lionel Curtis of Winston Churchill in a letter
  to Nancy Astor* 1912

7 The finest eloquence is that which gets
  things done; the worst is that which delays
  them.
  *David Lloyd George. Speech, Paris Peace
  Conference, Jan* 1919

8 His speeches leave the impression of an
  army of pompous phrases moving over the
  landscape in search of an idea.
  *Senator William McAdoo. Quoted Leon
  Harris*, THE FINE ART OF POLITICAL WIT

9 Oratory is just like prostitution; you must
  have little tricks.
  Vittorio Emanuele Orlando, Time 8 Dec
  1952

ORCHESTRA

10 You know why conductors live so long?
   Because we perspire so much.
   Sir John Barbirolli. Quoted Nat Shapiro,
   ENCYCLOPEDIA OF QUOTATIONS ABOUT
   MUSIC

11 For a fine performance only two things are
   absolutely necessary; the maximum of
   virility coupled with the maximum of
   delicacy.
   *Sir Thomas Beecham. Quoted Humphrey
   Proctor-Gregg*, BEECHAM REMEMBERED

12 We do not expect you to follow us all the
   time, but if you would have the goodness to
   keep in touch with us occasionally . . .
   *Sir Thomas Beecham. Quoted Harold C.
   Schonberg*, THE GREAT CONDUCTORS 1967

13 I am not the greatest conductor in this
   country. On the other hand I am better than
   any damned foreigner.
   *Sir Thomas Beecham. Quoted Noël
   Goodwick, Daily Express* 9 Mar 1961

14 Having an exaggerated sense of chivalry I
   am not over-fond of women in my orchestras
   because I find it embarassing to rebuke
   them.
   *Sir Thomas Beecham. Speech, the Savoy, on
   the re-forming of the Royal Philharmonic
   Orchestra, Aug* 1948

15 The conductor has the advantage of not
   seeing the audience.
   André Kostelanitz. Quoted Nat Shapiro,
   ENCYCLOPEDIA OF QUOTATIONS ABOUT
   MUSIC

16 A conductor should reconcile himself to the
   realisation that regardless of his approach or
   temperament the eventual result is the
   same. The orchestra will hate him.
   Oscar Levant, A SMATTERING OF
   IGNORANCE 1940

17 Show me an orchestra that likes its conduc-
   tor and I'll show you a lousy orchestra.
   *Goddard Lieberson. Quoted Hubert
   Kupferberg*, THOSE FABULOUS
   PHILADELPHIANS 1969

18 I just don't think women should be in an
   orchestra. They become men. Men treat
   them as equals; they even change their pants
   in front of them. I think it is terrible.
   Zubin Mehta, New York Times 18 Oct 1970

1 I never use a score when conducting my orchestra . . . Does a lion tamer enter a cage with a book on how to tame a lion?
Dimitri Mitropoulos. Quoted Nat Shapiro, ENCYCLOPEDIA OF QUOTATIONS ABOUT MUSIC

ORGY

2 An orgy looks particularly alluring when seen through the mists of righteous indignation.
Malcolm Muggeridge, TREAD SOFTLY FOR YOU TREAD ON MY JOKES 1966

3 Home is heaven and orgies are vile / But you need an orgy once in a while.
Ogden Nash, HOME SWEET HOME

OXFORD

4 Not that I had any special reason for hating school. Strange as it may seem to my readers, I was not unpopular there. I was a modest, good-humoured boy. It is Oxford that has made me insufferable.
Max Beerbohm, GOING BACK TO SCHOOL

5 Americans have a perfect right to exist. But he did often find himself wishing Mr Rhodes had not enabled them to exercise that right at Oxford.
Max Beerbohm, ZULEIKA DOBSON 1911

6 Balliol made me, Balliol fed me / Whatever I had she gave me again / And the best of Balliol loved and led me / God be with you, Balliol men.
Hilaire Belloc, TO THE BALLIOL MEN STILL IN AFRICA

7 There are few greater temptations on earth than to stay permanently in Oxford and read all the books in the Bodleian.
Hilaire Belloc. Quoted Robert Speaight, LIFE OF HILAIRE BELLOC 1957

8 Christchurch undergraduates give the impression of having dropped in at Oxford on their way to a seat in the House of Lords.
Sir John Betjeman, MY OXFORD

9 Noon strikes in England, noon on Oxford town / Beauty she was statue cold — there's blood upon her gown / Noon of my dreams, O noon! / Proud and godly kings had built her long ago / With her towers and tombs and statues all around / With her fair and floral air, and the love that lingers there / And the streets where the dead men go.
James Elroy Flecker, THE DYING PATRIOT

10 The clever men at Oxford / Know all that there is to be knowed / But none of them know one half as much / As intelligent Mr Toad.
Kenneth Grahame, WIND IN THE WILLOWS 1908

11 Oxford at least taught me to drink pint by pint with any man.
Graham Greene, A SORT OF LIFE

12 Cambridge sees Oxford as the Latin quarter of Cowley.
Marjorie Knight, letter to Daily Telegraph 15 *Aug* 1979

13 We think of Cambridge as a little town and Oxford as a hive of industry, but they aren't that different.
Katherine Whitehorn, Observer 14 *Jan* 1979

P

PACIFISM

1 My pacifism is not based on any intellectual theory but on a deep antipathy to every form of cruelty and hatred.
Albert Einstein on outbreak of 1914 *war*

PAIN

2 People will not readily bear pain unless there is hope.
Sir Michael Edwardes. Speech 2 *Jul* 1980

3 As painful as a grapestone under a dental plate.
George Orwell. Quoted from his notebooks by Bernard Crick, GEORGE ORWELL: A LIFE

PAINTING

4 *Painting, n.* The art of protecting flat surfaces from the weather and exposing them to the critic.
Ambrose Bierce, THE DEVIL'S DICTIONARY 1906

5 Once an object has been incorporated in a picture it accepts a new destiny.
Georges Braque. Quoted in his obituary The Times 21 *Sep* 1963

6 One needs a certain time to realise that the faces in the Italian primitives are those one meets daily on the streets. We have lost the habit of seeing what is really important in a face.
Albert Camus, NOTEBOOKS 1935–1942

7 The day is coming when a single carrot, freshly observed, will set off a revolution.
Paul Cézanne. Quoted Joachim Gasquet, PAUL CÉZANNE

8 Treat nature in terms of the cylinder, the sphere, the cone, all in perspective.
Paul Cézanne. Quoted Emile Bernard, PAUL CÉZANNE

9 The famous soft watches are nothing else than the tender, extravagant, solitary paranoiac-critical camembert of time and space.
Salvador Dali, CONQUEST OF THE IRRATIONAL

10 I do not paint a portrait to look like the subject, rather does the person grow to look like his portrait.
Salvador Dali. Quoted Evan Esar, TREASURY OF HUMOROUS QUOTATIONS

11 The big artist does not sit down monkey-like and copy a coal scuttle or an ugly woman like some Dutch painters have done, nor a dung pile, but he keeps a sharp eye on Nature and steals her roots.
Thomas Eakins. Quoted Gordon Hendricks, THE LIFE AND WORK OF THOMAS EAKINS

12 I'm sorry you had such bad weather, Mr Piper.
George VI on looking at John Piper's gloomy painting of Windsor Castle

13 Never put more than two waves in a picture; it's fussy.
Winslow Homer. Quoted Lloyd Goodrich, WINSLOW HOMER

14 Every good painter invents a new way of painting.
Aldous Huxley, COLLECTED ESSAYS 1960

15 A seventeenth-century painting can be 'modern' because the living eye finds it fresh and new. A 'modern' painting can be outdated because it was a product of the moment and not of time.
Marya Mannes, MORE IN ANGER 1954

16 I try to apply colours like words that shape poems, like notes that shape music.
Joan Miró. Quoted John Gruen, CLOSE-UP

1 Everyone wants to understand painting. Why don't they try to understand the singing of birds? People love the night, a flower, everything which surrounds them without trying to understand them. But painting — that they *must* understand.
Pablo Picasso. Quoted Gerald Brenan,
THOUGHTS IN A DRY SEASON 1979

2 I paint objects as I think them, not as I see them.
Pablo Picasso. Quoted John Golding,
CUBISM

3 'How can you remember which paintings are yours?'
'If I like it, I say it's mine. If I don't I say it's a fake.'
Pablo Picasso. Quoted Sunday Times 10 Oct 1965

4 Abstract painting is abstract. It confronts you. There was a reviewer a while back who wrote that my pictures didn't have any beginning or any end. He didn't mean it as a compliment but it was. It was a fine compliment.
Jackson Pollock. Quoted Francis V. O'Connor, JACKSON POLLOCK

5 A painter is not intellectual when, having painted a nude woman, he leaves in our minds the idea that she is going to get dressed again right away.
Odilon Rédon. Quoted R. Goldwater and M. Treves, ARTISTS ON ART

6 In a few generations you can breed a racehorse. The recipe for making a man like Delacroix is less well known.
Auguste Pierre Renoir. Quoted Jean Renoir, RENOIR, MY FATHER

7 I have a predilection for painting that lends joyousness to a wall.
Auguste Pierre Renoir. Quoted Ambrose Vollard, RENOIR

8 An Orpen or a Sargent can begin a portrait with a dab on the canvas which shall stand for the highlight on the nose: but a tyro will find it safer to begin by drawing the outline of the head.
Frank Rutter, TP's Weekly 17 Mar 1928

9 Mr Lewis's [(Percy) Wyndham Lewis] pictures appeared, as a very great painter said to me, to have been painted by a mailed fist in a cotton glove.
Edith Sitwell, TAKEN CARE OF

10 A painter should not paint what he sees, but what will be seen.
Paul Valéry, MAUVAISES PENSÉES ET AUTRES 1941

11 Give a painter money and see what he'll do. If he does not paint, his work is well lost to the world.
J. M. Whistler. Quoted Hesketh Pearson, THE MAN WHISTLER

PAKISTAN

12 We eat dust, breathe dust and think dust.
T. E. Lawrence, describing Karachi. Quoted Jean B. Villars, T. E. LAWRENCE: THE SEARCH FOR THE ABSOLUTE

PANTOMIME

13 Words can be deceitful, but pantomime necessarily is simple, clear and direct.
Marcel Marceau, Theatre Arts Magazine, Mar 1958

PARADISE

14 The longing for paradise is paradise itself.
Kahil Gibran, SPIRITUAL SAYINGS 1963

15 Even the paradise of fools is not an unpleasant abode while it is inhabitable.
W. R. Inge (Dean of St Pauls)

PARADOX

16 Paradoxes are useful to attract attention to ideas.
Mandell Creighton, LIFE AND LETTERS 1904

17 He who confronts the paradoxical exposes himself to reality.
Friedrich Dürrenmatt, THE PHYSICISTS 1962

PARANOIA

18 I wouldn't be paranoid if people didn't pick on me.
Graffito. Quoted Nigel Rees, GRAFFITI LIVES OK

PARENTS

1 I was born in 1896 and my parents were married in 1919.
J. R. Ackerley, opening words of MY FATHER AND MYSELF

2 Parents exist to teach the child, but also they must learn what the child has to teach them; and the child has a great deal to teach them.
Arnold Bennett, HOW TO MAKE THE BEST OF LIFE

3 If one is not going to take the necessary precautions to avoid having parents one must undertake to bring them up.
Quentin Crisp, THE NAKED CIVIL SERVANT

4 There are times when parenthood seems nothing but feeding the mouth that bites you.
Peter De Vries, TUNNEL OF LOVE 1954

5 Possessive parents rarely live long enough to see the fruits of their selfishness.
Alan Garner, epigraph to THE OWL SERVICE 1967

6 My father was frightened of his mother. I was frightened of my father, and I'm damned well going to make sure that my children are frightened of me.
George V. Quoted Randolph Churchill, LIFE OF THE EARL OF DERBY

7 You are the bows from which your children as living arrows are sent forth.
Kahil Gibran, THE PROPHET 1923

8 The real menace in dealing with a five-year-old is that in no time at all you begin to sound like a five-year-old.
Jean Kerr, PLEASE DON'T EAT THE DAISIES

9 The parent who could see his boy as he really is would shake his head and say 'Willie is no good. I'll sell him.'
Stephen Leacock, LITERARY LAPSES 1910

10 He is too experienced a parent ever to make positive promises.
Christopher Morley, THUNDER ON THE LEFT 1925

11 Children aren't happy with nothing to ignore / And that's what parents were created for.
Ogden Nash, THE PARENT

12 The worst misfortune that can happen to an ordinary man is to have an extraordinary father.
Austen O'Malley

13 What a relief it is when you find that you've actually brought up a reasonable and civilised human being.
Philip, Duke of Edinburgh. Quoted Peter Lane, OUR FUTURE KING

14 Parents are sometimes a bit of a disappointment to their children. They don't fulfil the promise of their early years.
Anthony Powell, A BUYER'S MARKET 1952

15 Parents lend children their experience and a vicarious memory; children endow their parents with a vicarious immortality.
George Santayana, THE LIFE OF REASON 1906

16 Parentage is a very important profession; but no test of fitness for it is ever imposed in the interest of the children.
George Bernard Shaw, EVERYBODY'S POLITICAL WHAT'S WHAT 1944

17 The natural term of the affection of the human animal for its offspring is six years.
George Bernard Shaw, HEARTBREAK HOUSE 1920

18 Parents learn a lot from their children about coping with life.
Muriel Spark, THE COMFORTERS 1957

19 The more people have studied different methods of bringing up children the more they have come to the conclusion that what good mothers and fathers instinctively feel like doing for their babies is best after all.
Dr Benjamin Spock, THE COMMONSENSE BOOK OF BABY AND CHILD CARE 1946

20 I like children. I never gave them a second thought when I was making them, but I like them very much.
Jake Thackeray in an interview with Frank Kempe, North Devon Herald 6 Sep 1979

21 Maternity is a matter of fact; paternity is a matter of opinion.
Sir Miles Thomas. Speech, Association of Supervisory Electrical Engineers, Connaught Rooms, London 2 Apr 1953

1 Parents are the bones on which children sharpen their teeth.
Peter Ustinov, DEAR ME 1977

2 'Parents are strange,' said Amy, 'for their age.'
Amanda Vail, LOVE ME LITTLE

3 Don't hold your parents up to contempt. After all, you are their son, and it is just possible that you may take after them.
Evelyn Waugh, Tablet 9 *May* 1951

4 Fatherhood ought to be emphasised as much as motherhood. The idea that women are solely responsible for deciding whether or not to have babies leads on to the idea that they are also responsible for bringing the children up.
Shirley Williams, Observer, Interview with Miriam Gross 22 *Mar* 1981

5 The thing that impresses me most about America is the way parents obey their children.
Duke of Windsor, Look Magazine 5 *Mar* 1957

PARIS

6 The Eyefull Tower is devine.
Anita Loos, GENTLEMEN PREFER BLONDES 1925

7 Old crumbling walls and the pleasant sound of water running in the urinals.
Henry Miller, TROPIC OF CANCER 1934

PARLIAMENT

8 The House of Lords is like a glass of champagne that has stood for five days.
Clement Attlee. Quoted Leon Harris, THE FINE ART OF POLITICAL WIT

9 The House of Lords is the British Outer Mongolia for retired politicians.
Tony Benn. Speech 11 *Feb* 1962

10 Like many other anachronisms in British public life, the House of Lords has one supreme merit. It works.
Lord Boothby. Quoted Leon Harris, THE FINE ART OF POLITICAL WIT

11 Most of us in the Lords are Mods. Those in the House of Commons are Rockers.
Duke of Devonshire, Observer, Sayings of the Year 1964

12 The House of Lords is a model of how to care for the elderly.
Frank Field MP. Quoted Observer 24 *May* 1981

13 The State Opening of Parliament is a bit like one of those pretentious *nouvelle cuisine* restaurants where the *patron* insists on talking through the menu in finger-licking detail. So the Sword of State is carried in as reverently as the carving knife at Simpson's and the Lord Chamberlain totters about like a doddering old waiter who should have been pensioned off years ago, with the customers holding their breath in case he drops something . . . the cook, or Prime Minister, is allowed up into the restaurant on this one day of the year, provided she stands at the back with the rest of the staff.
Philip Howard, The Times 7 *Nov* 1985

14 The House of Lords is not the watchdog of the constitution; it is Mr Balfour's poodle. It fetches and carries for him. It barks for him. It bites anyone that he sets it on to.
David Lloyd George. Speech, House of Commons 21 *Dec* 1908

15 If, like me, you are over 90, frail, on two sticks, half deaf and half blind, you stick out like a sore thumb in most places, but not in the House of Lords. Besides, they seem to have a bar and a loo within 30 yards in any direction.
Harold Macmillan (Lord Stockton), Observer 19 *May* 1985

16 The House of Lords must be the only institution in the world which is kept efficient by the persistent absenteeism of most of its members.
Viscount Samuel. Quoted News Review 5 *Feb* 1948

17 One does wish that there were a few more women in parliament. Then one could be less conspicuous oneself.
Margaret Thatcher. Quoted Observer 6 *May* 1979

18 The House of Commons is not so much a gentleman's club as a boy's boarding school.
Shirley Williams, Granada TV 30 *Jul* 1985

PARTING

1 Goodbyes breed a sort of distaste for whomever you say goodbye to; this hurts, you feel; this must not happen again.
Elizabeth Bowen, THE HOUSE IN PARIS 1935

PARTY

2 I'd rather be a host than a guest. As Beerbohm wonderfully observed, a happy host makes a sad guest.
Harold Acton, The Times 18 *Apr* 1970

3 Elyot: Delightful parties Lady Bundle always gives, doesn't she?
Amanda: Entrancing. Such a dear old lady.
Elyot: And so gay. Did you notice her at supper blowing all those shrimps through her ear trumpet?
Noël Coward, PRIVATE LIVES 1930

4 The best number for a dinner party is two — myself and a dam' good head waiter.
Nubar Gulbenkian

5 At a dinner party one should eat wisely, but not too well, and talk well but not too wisely.
W. Somerset Maugham, A WRITER'S NOTEBOOK 1949

6 It was a fête worse than death.
Barbara Stanwyck. Quoted columnist Harrison Carroll

7 The final ritual for gentlemen before they rejoin the ladies is for their host to lead them outside to urinate in the garden. The resultant patches of dead grass on the lawn are put down to wireworm and the blighted roses are blamed on the damned greenfly.
Douglas Sutherland, THE ENGLISH GENTLEMAN 1978

8 'So like one's first parties,' said Miss Runcible 'being sick with other people singing.'
Evelyn Waugh, VILE BODIES 1930

9 The main purpose of children's parties is to remind you that there are children more awful than your own.
Katherine Whitehorn, HOW TO SURVIVE CHILDREN

10 He would give them his every imitation from 'Eton and Oxford' to the flushing of the lavatory cistern, and so, perhaps, carry the evening through.
Angus Wilson, A BIT OFF THE MAP 1957

11 What with excellent browsing and sluicing and cheery conversation and what-not, the afternoon passed quite happily.
P. G. Wodehouse, JEEVES AND THE UNBIDDEN GUEST

PASSION

12 Bernard placed one arm tightly round her. When will you marry me Ethel he uttered you must be my wife it has come to that I love you so intensely that if you say no I shall perforce dash my body to the brink of yon muddy river he panted wildly.
O don't do that implored Ethel breathing rather hard.
Daisy Ashford (aged 9), THE YOUNG VISITERS 1919

13 Oh Bernard she sighed fervently I certainly love you madly you are to me like a Heathen god she cried, looking at his manly form and flashing face I will indeed marry you.
Ibid.

14 The man who is master of his passions is Reason's slave.
Cyril Connolly. Quoted V. S. Pritchett, TURNSTILE ONE

15 Violent physical passions do not, in themselves, separate men from each other, but rather tend to reduce them to the same state.
T. S. Eliot, AFTER STRANGE GODS

16 A madness of tender caressing seized her. She purred as a tiger might have done, while she undulated like a snake.
Elinor Glyn, THREE WEEKS 1907

17 A man who has not passed through the inferno of his passions has never overcome them.
Carl Jung, MEMORIES, DREAMS, REFLECTIONS

18 Mortal lovers must not try to remain at the first step; for lasting passion is the dream of a harlot and from it we can wake in despair.
C. S. Lewis, THE PILGRIM'S REGRESS

19 It is only with the passions of others that we are ever really familiar, and what we come to find out about our own can be no more than what other people have shown us.
Marcel Proust, REMEMBRANCE OF THINGS PAST 1913–1927

1 The worst sin — perhaps the only sin —
passion can commit is to be joyless.
Dorothy L. Sayers, GAUDY NIGHT

2 'Mr Little is certainly warm-hearted, sir.'
'Warm hearted! I should think he has to
wear asbestos vests.'
P. G. Wodehouse, BINGO AND THE LITTLE
WOMAN

PAST

3 Man is a history-making creature who can
neither repeat his past nor leave it behind.
W. H. Auden, THE DYER'S HAND 1963

4 The past is always being changed.
*Jorge Luis Borges in an interview with
Nicholas Shakespeare, The Times* 6 Oct 1983

5 It is unhealthy and undesirable to live so
much in the past, and yet, God forgive me,
how I do it. And one cannot bring it back
and one would probably not like it, if one
could.
Gamaliel Bradford, LETTERS

6 The world broke in two in 1922 or there-
abouts and all that went before belongs with
yesterday's seven thousand years.
Willa Cather, NOT UNDER FORTY, *Prefatory
note*

7 The past is a foreign country. They do things
differently there.
L. P. Hartley, THE GO-BETWEEN 1953

8 I learnt to hate and fear the past because it
threatened my future.
Christopher Isherwood, KATHLEEN AND
FRANK

9 Why doesn't the past decently bury itself,
instead of sitting and waiting to be admitted
by the present?
D. H. Lawrence, ST MAWR 1925

10 The earth is about five thousand million
years old at least. Who can afford to live in
the past?
Harold Pinter, THE HOMECOMING

11 Keep off your thoughts of things that are
past and done / For thinking of the past
wakes regret and pain.
Arthur Waley, RESIGNATION

12 We are tomorrow's past.
Mary Webb, PRECIOUS BANE 1925

13 Each has his past shut in him like the leaves
of a book known to him by heart and his
friends can only read the title.
Virginia Woolf, JACOB'S ROOM 1922

PASTIME

14 I say, let's banish bridge; let's find some
pleasanter way of being miserable together.
Don Herold

15 Children make the most desirable opponents in Scrabble as they are both easy to
beat and fun to cheat.
Fran Lebowitz. Quoted Frank Muir, ON
CHILDREN

16 A man who wants to play billiards must have
no other ambitions. Billiards is all.
E. V. Lucas, CHARACTER AND COMEDY

17 I hate people who play bridge as though they
were at a funeral and knew their feet were
getting wet.
W. Somerset Maugham, THE CIRCLE 1921

18 To play billiards well is a sign of a mis-spent
youth.
Attr. Herbert Spencer

PATIENCE

19 Always remember that the future comes one
day at a time.
Dean Acheson, SKETCHES FROM LIFE

20 A minor form of despair disguised as a
virtue.
Ambrose Bierce, THE DEVIL'S
DICTIONARY 1906

21 Suffer us not to mock ourselves with
falsehood / Teach us to care and not to
care / Teach us to sit still.
T. S. Eliot, ASH WEDNESDAY 1930

22 'Sir, you try my patience.'
'I don't mind if I do. You must come over
and try mine some time.'
Groucho Marx, DUCK SOUP

PATRIOTISM

1 Patriotism is a lively sense of collective responsibility. Nationalism is a silly cock crowing on its own dung hill.
Richard Aldington, THE COLONEL'S DAUGHTER 1931

2 I regret that I have only one life to give for my country — I'd feel safer if I had two.
Anon. soldier at D-Day landings

3 I realise that patriotism is not enough. I must have no hatred or bitterness towards anyone.
Edith Cavell, last words, reported in The Times 23 Oct 1915

4 'My country right or wrong' is a thing that no patriot would think of saying except in a desperate case. It is like saying, 'My mother, drunk or sober.'
G. K. Chesterton, THE DEFENDANT 1911

5 A man who says that no patriot should attack the war until it is over is not worth answering intellligently; he is saying that no good son should warn his mother off a cliff until she has fallen over it.
G. K. Chesterton, ORTHODOXY 1908

6 Patriotism is easy to understand in America; it means looking out for yourself while looking out for your country.
Calvin Coolidge. Quoted Evan Esar, TREASURY OF HUMOROUS QUOTATIONS

7 The *Daily Mirror* does not believe that patriotism had to be proved in blood. Especially someone else's blood.
Daily Mirror leader on the Falkland War, Apr 1982

8 We prefer the less bad to the more bad and so become patriots, while keeping our brains and hearts intact.
E. M. Forster, TWO CHEERS FOR DEMOCRACY 1951

9 Originality and initiative are what I ask for my country.
Robert Frost, THE FIGURE A POEM MAKES

10 I have never understood why one's affections must be confined, as once with women, to a single country.
J. K. Galbraith, A LIFE IN OUR TIMES 1981

11 One of the great attractions of patriotism — it fulfils our worst wishes. In the person of our nation we are able, vicariously, to bully and to cheat. Bully and cheat, what's more, with a feeling that we are profoundly virtuous.
Aldous Huxley, EYELESS IN GAZA 1936

12 Those only can care intelligently for the future of England to whom the past is dear.
W. R. Inge (Dean of St Pauls), ASSESSMENTS AND ANTICIPATIONS

13 Ask not what your country can do for you. Ask what you can do for your country.
John F. Kennedy. Inaugural address 20 Jan 1961

14 Is it an offence, is it a mistake, is it a crime to take a hopeful view of the prospects of your own country? Why should it be? Why should patriotism and pessimism be identical? Hope is the mainspring of patriotism.
David Lloyd George, House of Commons 30 Oct 1919

15 Duty and patriotism clad in glittering white; the great pinnacle of sacrifice pointing like a pinnacle to heaven.
David Lloyd George. Speech, Queens Hall, London 19 Sep 1914

16 Patriotism is often an arbitrary veneration of real estate above principles.
G. J. Nathan, TESTAMENT OF A CRITIC

17 When Ghana gained its independence in 1957 the country's *Daily Graphic* proudly announced Ghana's first set of traffic lights 'in the national colours, red, yellow and green'.
Peterborough, Daily Telegraph 4 Oct 1983

18 Patriots always talk of dying for their country and never of killing for their country.
Bertrand Russell, AUTOBIOGRAPHY 1967

19 [Today] anyone standing to attention in a cinema during the playing of 'God Save the Queen' is either the producer of the little film of Her Majesty that goes with it or he has inadvertently tied his bootlaces together.
Harry Secombe, Punch 10 May 1972

1 The national anthem belongs to the eighteenth century. In it you find us ordering God about to do our dirty work.
George Bernard Shaw, THE ADVENTURES OF THE BLACK GIRL IN HER SEARCH FOR GOD

2 You'll never have a quiet world till you knock the patriotism out of the human race.
George Bernard Shaw, O'FLAHERTY VC

3 Patriotism is your conviction that this country is superior to all other countries because you were born in it.
George Bernard Shaw

4 To strike freedom of the mind with the fist of patriotism is an old and ugly subtlety.
Adlai Stevenson. Speech, American Legion Convention 30 *Aug* 1952

5 He was inordinately proud of England and he abused her incessantly.
H. G. Wells, MR BRITLING SEES IT THROUGH 1916

6 Patriotism has become a mere national self assertion, a sentimentality of flag-cheering with no constructive duties.
H. G. Wells, THE FUTURE IN AMERICA

PATRONAGE

7 British Prime Ministers have more absolute authority than medieval monarchs and they control huge patronage. Prime Ministers have made 640 peers in seven years and it takes 40 million people to elect 640 legislators to parliament.
Tony Benn. Quoted John Mortimer, IN CHARACTER 1983

8 He liked to patronise coloured people and treated them as equals because he was quite sure they were not.
Bertrand Russell, AUTOBIOGRAPHY VOL 4 1967

9 Getting patronage is the whole art of life. A man cannot have a career without it.
George Bernard Shaw, CAPTAIN BRASSBOUND'S CONVERSION 1900

PEACE

10 In international affairs, a period of cheating between two periods of fighting.
Ambrose Bierce, THE DEVIL'S DICTIONARY 1906

11 What they could do with round here is a good war . . . You know what the trouble with peace is? No organisation.
Bertolt Brecht, MOTHER COURAGE AND HER CHILDREN 1939

12 Peace with honour. I believe it is peace in our time.
Neville Chamberlain after the Munich Agreement 30 *Sep* 1938

13 The Bomb brought peace but man alone can keep that peace.
Winston Churchill. Speech, House of Commons 16 *Aug* 1945

14 It is far easier to make war than to make peace.
Georges Clemençeau. Speech, Verdun 14 *Jul* 1919

15 Peace cannot be kept by force. It can only be achieved by understanding.
Albert Einstein, NOTES ON PACIFISM

16 The mere absence of war is not peace.
John F. Kennedy. State of the Union Message 14 *Jan* 1963

17 The peaceful two [John Lennon and Yoko] argued, reasonably enough, that if everyone stayed in bed, occupying themselves in growing their hair, there would be no wars.
Bernard Levin, THE PENDULUM YEARS 1976

18 Peace is indivisible.
Maxim Litvinov. Speech to League of Nations 1 *Jul* 1936

19 Peace is not only better than war, but infinitely more arduous.
George Bernard Shaw, HEARTBREAK HOUSE, *Preface* 1920

20 In the arts of peace, Man is a bungler.
George Bernard Shaw, MAN AND SUPERMAN 1905

PEDANTRY

21 Pedantry is the dotage of knowledge.
Holebrook Jackson, THE ANATOMY OF BIBLIOMANIA 1930

22 An artist may visit a museum, but only a pedant can live there.
George Santayana, THE LIFE OF REASON 1906

PEERAGE

1 I was obviously destined to go down and down when in 1958 my father and brother died within ten days of each other and I became an Earl . . . Life is much easier, being an Earl. It has changed me a lot. I'm much nastier now.
Earl of Arran [formerly Arthur Gore],
Sunday Times 15 *Jan* 1967

2 Accepting a peerage in 1916 was my greatest mistake.
Lord Beaverbrook quoted BBC 2 TV,
Reputations 28 *Jun* 1981

3 I did have a coronet, until another duke borrowed the thing and lost it.
Duke of Bedford (John Robert Russell), on
American TV

4 It was but a few weeks since he had taken his seat in the Lords; and this afternoon, for want of something better to do, he strayed in.
Max Beerbohm, ZULEIKA DOBSON 1906

5 The nobility of England, my lord, would have snored through the Sermon on the Mount.
Robert Bolt, A MAN FOR ALL SEASONS 1961

6 Who can fathom the mind of one suddenly raised to the peerage?
Edward Bond, RESTORATION

7 If one knows how to use a knife and fork, and has a title, one will never go hungry.
Lord Kingsdale, Observer, Sayings of the
Week 7 *Oct* 1984

8 There are no credentials. They do not even need a medical certificate. They need not be sound either in body or mind. They only require a certificate of birth — just to prove that they are first of the litter. You would not choose a spaniel on these principles.
David Lloyd George. Budget speech 1909

9 Most of the hereditary peers are so unspeakably middle class.
Harold Macmillan. Quoted Simon
Winchester, THEIR NOBLE LORDSHIPS 1981

10 When I want a peerage I shall buy one like an honest man.
Lord Northcliffe. Quoted Hannen Swaffer

11 A person seeking a quiet life is greatly helped by not having a title.
Captain Mark Phillips, explaining why he
wished to remain a commoner

12 The hereditary system is the only method of selecting a body of people which is completely unbiased. Every other method, except perhaps lottery, must depend on someone's opinion.
Lord Saye and Sele. Maiden speech in House
of Lords, reported in The Times

13 A life peer is like a mule — no pride of ancestry, no hope of posterity.
Lord Shackleton, himself a life peer

14 Only through the accident of being a hereditary peer can anyone, in these days of votes for Everybody, get into parliament if handicapped by serious modern cultural equipment.
George Bernard Shaw, HEARTBREAK
HOUSE, *Preface* 1920

15 Titles distinguish the mediocre, embarrass the superior, and are disgraced by the inferior.
George Bernard Shaw, MAN AND
SUPERMAN 1905

16 I don't mind what I'm called, as long as I'm called for breakfast.
George Thomas, a former speaker, on being
made a viscount, BBC Radio 4, *World at*
One 1 *July* 1983

17 I'm still the same shape in my bath.
Ibid.

18 One way a peer can make a bit of extra money is by letting the public into his house. Another way is by letting the public into his head. Either way, the dottier the contents the better.
Sunday Times, on the Earl of Arran's
column in the Evening News 15 *Jan* 1967

19 The House of Lords has lost, at the age of 91, one of its most picturesque personalities in the Earl of Morton. He had a great gift for silence, and during all the years that he attended at Westminster as a Scottish representative peer his voice was never heard in debate.
The Times obituary

1 I have heard it said of the 'backwoods' peer that he had three qualities. He knew how to kill a fox, he knew how to get rid of a bad tenant, and he knew how to discard an unwanted mistress. A man who possesses these three qualities would certainly have something to contribute to the work of the House.
Lord Winster. Speech, House of Lords

PELICAN

2 A wonderful bird is the pelican / His bill will hold more than his belican / He can take in his beak / Food enough for a week / But I'm damned if I see how the helican.
Dixon Lanier Merritt, THE PELICAN

PERFECTION

3 American women expect to find in their husbands a perfection that English women only hope to find in their butlers.
W. Somerset Maugham, A WRITER'S NOTEBOOK 1949

4 Perfection has one grave defect; it is apt to be dull.
W. Somerset Maugham, THE SUMMING UP 1938

5 People are willing to devise and praise Utopias but not to live in them.
David Pryce-Jones, The Times 20 Mar 1972

6 Humanity will ever seek but never attain perfection. Let us at least survive and go on trying.
Dora Russell, THE RELIGION OF THE MACHINE AGE 1983

7 In anything at all, perfection is finally attained not when there is no longer anything to add, but when there is no longer anything to take away.
Antoine de Saint-Exupéry, WIND, SAND AND STARS 1939

PERMISSIVENESS

8 The terrible trouble nowadays is that they [youth] have lost the chance to disobey. That is what all children and all artists need. Today the rule is, do what you like.
Jean Cocteau in an interview with Derek Prouse, Sunday Times 20 Oct 1963

9 As he [Aldous Huxley] speaks a look of anxiety comes on the faces of the women present as though they would be unspeakably shocked if any thought they could possibly be shocked by anything.
William Gerhardie, MEMOIRS OF A POLYGLOT 1925

10 Take all the sexual pleasures you can but be very careful about the Pox.
Llewelyn Powys. Quoted Richard Perceval Graves, THE BROTHERS POWYS 1983

11 Love as a relation between men and women was ruined by the desire to make sure of the legitimacy of the children.
Bertrand Russell, MARRIAGE AND MORALS 1929

PERSEVERANCE

12 U-turn if you want to. The lady's not for turning.
Margaret Thatcher. Conservative Party Conference 11 Oct 1980

PESSIMISM

13 Pessimism does win us some great moments.
Max Beerbohm, AND EVEN NOW, *Hosts and Guests* 1920

14 Pessimism, when you get used to it, is just as agreeable as optimism.
Arnold Bennett, THINGS THAT HAVE INTERESTED ME

15 Scratch a pessimist and you find often a defender of privilege.
Lord Beveridge. Quoted Observer 17 Oct 1943

16 Only the man who finds everything wrong and expects it to get worse is thought to have a clear brain.
J. K. Galbraith, THE AGE OF UNCERTAINTY 1977

17 A bilious philosopher's opinion of the world can only be accepted with a pinch of salt, of Epsom salt for preference.
Aldous Huxley, PROPER STUDIES 1927

18 Nothing makes me more pessimistic than the obligation not to be pessimistic.
Eugene Ionesco. Quoted Martin Esslin, THE THEATRE OF THE ABSURD

1 If we see light at the end of the tunnel it is the light of an oncoming train.
Robert Lowell, DAY BY DAY. *Quoted BBC Radio 4, Quote Unquote 21 Jul 1980*

2 A pessimist is a man who looks both ways before crossing a one-way street.
Laurence J. Peter, PETER'S QUOTATIONS

3 In my next life I would like to be a pessimist. And then other people could spend all their time cheering me up.
Katherine Whitehorn, VIEW FROM A COLUMN 1981

PET

4 A British home is nothing without a pet.
Yvonne Arnaud, *News Review 8 Apr* 1948

5 The woman who is really kind to dogs is always one who has failed to inspire sympathy in men.
Max Beerbohm, ZULEIKA DOBSON 1911

6 George V hated to be parted from his pet parrot Charlotte. At Sandringham he would come to breakfast with the bird perched on his finger, then let it forage over the table. If Charlotte disgraced herself by making a mess the king would slide a mustard pot over it so that the Queen should not see.
Kenneth Rose, KINGS, QUEENS AND COURTIERS 1985

7 I prefer cats to dogs because they are not so loud and clumsy, nor so overtly masculine. They have a feminine grace.
A. L. Rowse, THREE CORNISH CATS

8 If a dog jumps onto your lap it is because he is fond of you; but if a cat does the same thing it is because your lap is warmer.
A. N. Whitehead, DIALOGUES 1953

PHILANTHROPIST

9 Suspicion of one's own motives is especially necessary for the philanthropist.
Bertrand Russell, THE CONQUEST OF HAPPINESS 1930

PHILIP, DUKE OF EDINBURGH

10 A man attractive to women, envied by men, a bit vicious on the polo-field, autocratic, something of a ham actor — and in the red. He lives a good life but he has to pay for it. He has never been rich.
Andrew Duncan. Quoted Philip Howard, The Times, Profile of the Duke of Edinburgh 26 Apr 1982

11 With his great (and carefully calculated) talent for putting his foot in it, we might consider Prince Philip to be the most eloquent, literate and classless member of the Royal Family.
Willie Hamilton. Quoted Philip Howard, The Times, Profile of the Duke of Edinburgh 26 Apr 1982

12 No one has a kinder heart or takes more trouble to conceal it.
Michael Parker. Quoted Basil Boothroyd in his official biography of Prince Philip 1971

13 Whatever happens to him in his present capacity as royal poor relation can't do him much good in the long run. My advice to him would be — give up being a royal personage, stick to the sea, learn a trade and find an anchorage with an average good wife.
Daily Worker 12 Dec 1946

PHILOSOPHY

14 The dictionary definition of philosophical as meaning 'calm and temperate'. That is rubbish. I don't believe there is such a thing as a calm philosopher. Bertrand Russell, in my opinion the greatest, certainly isn't.
A. J. Ayer, The Times 28 Aug 1968

15 Truth is the object of philosophy, but not always of philosophers.
John Churton Collins. Quoted Logan Pearsall Smith, TREASURY OF ENGLISH APHORISMS

16 In philosophy it is not the attainment of the goal that matters, it is the things that are met with by the way.
Havelock Ellis, THE DANCE OF LIFE 1923

17 There is no such person as a philosopher; no one is detached; the observer, like the observed, is in chains.
E. M. Forster, TWO CHEERS FOR DEMOCRACY, The Menace to Freedom 1951

1 You can't do without philosophy, since everything has its hidden meaning which we must know.
Maxim Gorky, THE ZYKOVS 1914

2 The object of studying philosophy is to know one's own mind, not other people's.
W. R. Inge (Dean of St Pauls), OUTSPOKEN ESSAYS 1919

3 When philosophers try to be politicians they generally cease to be philosophers.
Walter Lippmann, A PREFACE TO POLITICS, *The Changing Focus* 1914

4 Most philosophical treatises show the human cerebrum loaded far beyond its Plimsoll mark.
H. L. Mencken, PREJUDICES 1924

5 Any genuine philosophy leads to action and from action back to wonder, to the enduring of mystery.
Henry Miller, THE WISDOM OF THE HEART 1941

6 Who could fathom Plato's mind? Unless one is a genius Philosophy is a mug's game.
Iris Murdoch, THE PHILOSOPHER'S PUPIL 1983

7 None can call himself a philosopher whose own days are not made more intense and dramatic by his philosophising. Even if his vision of things be bitter and grim, his world is made more interesting by his pondering on it, not more commonplace or tedious.
John Cowper Powys, THE MEANING OF CULTURE 1930

8 Nowadays there are no serious philosophers who are not looking forward to the pension to which their involvement with the subject entitles them.
Anthony Quinton, THOUGHTS AND THINKERS

9 To teach how to live without certainty and yet without being paralysed by hesitation is perhaps the chief thing that philosophy, in our age, can do for those who study it.
Bertrand Russell, HISTORY OF WESTERN PHILOSOPHY 1945

10 The point of philosophy is to start with something so simple as to seem not worth stating, and to end with something so paradoxical that no one will believe it.
Bertrand Russell, LOGIC AND KNOWLEDGE

11 For the learning of every virtue there is an appropriate discipline, and for this learning of suspended judgment the best discipline is philosophy.
Bertrand Russell, UNPOPULAR ESSAYS, *Philosophy for Laymen* 1950

12 My doctor said to me afterwards, 'When you were ill you behaved like a true philosopher. Every time you came to yourself you made a joke.' I never had a compliment that pleased me more.
Bertrand Russell, after a bout of pneumonia, in a letter to Jean Nichol 2 Oct 1921

13 Philosophy is the replacement of category habits by category disciplines.
Gilbert Ryle, THE CONCEPT OF MIND

14 Philosophers are as jealous as women. Each wants a monopoly of praise.
George Santayana, DIALOGUES IN LIMBO

15 The philosopher is Nature's pilot. And there you have our difference; to be in hell is to drift; to be in heaven is to steer.
George Bernard Shaw, MAN AND SUPERMAN 1905

16 The greater the philosopher, the harder it is for him to answer the questions of the average man.
Henryk Sienkiewicz

17 A philosopher of imposing stature doesn't think in a vacuum. Even his most abstract ideas are, to some extent, conditioned by what is or what is not known in the time when he lives.
A. N. Whitehead, DIALOGUES 1953

18 Philosophy is the product of wonder.
A. N. Whitehead, NATURE AND LIFE

19 The safest general characterization of the European philosophical tradition is that it consists of a series of footnotes to Plato.
A. N. Whitehead, PROCESS AND REALITY 1929

PHOTOGRAPHY

20 Tony made my nose look wonderful, but everyone thought I'd had it fixed by plastic surgery.
Princess Alexandra, of a portrait by Lord Snowdon

1 The virtue of the camera is not the power it has to transform the photographer into an artist, but the impulse it gives him to keep on looking.
Brooks Anderson, ONCE AROUND THE SUN 1951

PHYSICS

2 The content of physics is the concern of physicists, its effect the concern of all men.
Friedrich Dürrenmatt, THE PHYSICISTS, 21 *Points*

3 Physical concepts are free creations of the human mind and are not, however it may seem, uniquely determined by the external world.
Albert Einstein, EVOLUTION OF PHYSICS

4 We have no right to assume that any physical laws exist, or if they have existed up to now, that they will continue to exist in a similar manner in the future.
Max Planck, THE UNIVERSE IN THE LIGHT OF MODERN PHYSICS

PIANO

5 A pianist needs three things — muscles, a brain and a heart.
Bernard d'Ascoli, Observer 31 *Jan* 1982

6 They laughed when I sat down at the piano — but when I began to play!
John Caples, advertising slogan 1925

7 If there is time left over I fill in with a lot of runs up and down the keyboard.
Liberace. Quoted Stuart Hall and Paddy Whannel, THE POPULAR ARTS

8 Piano playing is more difficult than statesmanship. It is harder to waken emotions in ivory keys than it is in human beings.
Ignacy Paderewski. Quoted Nat Shapiro, ENCYCLOPEDIA OF QUOTATIONS ABOUT MUSIC

9 The notes I handle no better than many pianists. But the pauses between the notes — ah that is where the art resides.
Artur Schnabel. Quoted Chicago Daily News 11 *Jun* 1958

10 The kid that handles the music box was hitting a rag-time tune.
R. W. Service, THE SHOOTING OF DAN MAGRUE 1907

11 I wish the Government would put a tax on pianos for the incompetent.
Edith Sitwell, LETTERS 1916–1964

PABLO PICASSO

12 A Catalan wizard who fools with shapes.
Bernard Berenson. Quoted Sylvan Sprigge, BERENSON: A BIOGRAPHY

13 Nothing unites the English like war. Nothing divides them like Picasso.
Hugh Mills, PRUDENCE AND THE PILL

14 Many painters and writers have made beautiful works out of repulsive subjects: Picasso enjoys making repulsive works out of beautiful subjects.
Raymond Mortimer, TRY ANYTHING ONCE

15 Picasso had a whim of iron.
John Richardson, PICASSO IN PRIVATE

PIETY

16 Bernard always had a few prayers in the hall and some whiskey afterwards as he was rather pious.
Daisy Ashford (aged 9), THE YOUNG VISITERS 1919

17 All great harlots become pious in their old age, as if faith could take the place of love.
Louis Bromfield, THE STRANGE CASE OF MISS ANNIE SPRAGG 1928

PIG

18 One disadvantage of being a hog is that at any moment some bleeding fool may try to make a silk purse out of your wife's ear.
Beachcomber (J. B. Morton), Daily Express, By the Way

PIGEON

19 Pigeons walking up and down the roof with their hands behind their backs.
Jean Cocteau.

1 No bird sits a tree more proudly than a pigeon. It looks as though placed there by the Lord.
Katherine Mansfield, JOURNAL 1954

2 The lovesick woodpigeons mooning in bed.
Dylan Thomas, UNDER MILK WOOD 1954

PITY

3 We have only one thing to keep us sane, pity; and the man without pity is mad.
Edward Bond, LEAR

4 When Man evolved Pity, he did a queer thing — deprived himself of the power of living life as it is without wishing it to become something different.
John Galsworthy, letter to Thomas Hardy 27 Mar 1910

5 Pity is a corroding thing.
Martha Graham. Quoted Robin Stringer, Daily Telegraph 23 Jul 1979

6 Contempt for pain soon becomes a contempt for pity.
Francis Hackett, HENRY VIII 1929

7 The sparrow is sorry for the peacock at the burden of its tail.
Rabindranath Tagore, STRAY BIRDS 1916

PLAGIARISM

8 . . . the bubonic plagiarist.
Jonathan Miller of David Frost. Quoted, FROM FRINGE TO FLYING CIRCUS 1981

9 I would like to thank Beethoven, Brahms, Wagner, Strauss, Rimsky-Korsakov . . .
Dimitry Tiomkin. Speech accepting Academy Award for the best original dramatic score composed for THE HIGH AND THE MIGHTY 1955

PLATITUDE

10 The man who has the courage of his platitudes is always a successful man.
Van Wyck Brooks, A CHILMARK MISCELLANY

11 The banalities of a great man pass for wit.
Alexander Chase, PERSPECTIVES 1966

12 The Republicans stroke platitudes until they purr like epigrams.
Adlai Stevenson. Quoted Leon Harris, THE FINE ART OF POLITICAL WIT

13 His public utterances are sensible but never arresting. Even a platitude dropped from a sufficiently great height can sound like a brick.
Peregrine Worsthorne of Bernard Baruch, Daily Telegraph 14 Apr 1958

PLEASURE

14 I have finished my novel. What am I to do? There is pleasure, of course, but I like it only when it is stolen from my hours of work. When it is just a way of filling in leisure it no longer amuses me.
Julian Green, DIARY 1928–1957

15 Are creature comforts more demoralizing when consciously enjoyed or when taken for granted?
Ronald Knox, PENSÉES

16 There is no more lamentable pursuit than a life of pleasure.
W. Somerset Maugham, THE CIRCLE 1921

17 Surely a king who loves pleasure is less dangerous than one who loves glory.
Nancy Mitford, THE WATER BEETLE

18 A life of pleasure requires an aristocratic setting to make it interesting.
George Santayana, LIFE OF REASON, *Reason in Society* 1905

19 The most intolerable pain is produced by prolonging the keenest pleasures.
George Bernard Shaw, MAN AND SUPERMAN 1905

20 I take it as a prime cause of the present confusion of society that it is too sickly and too doubtful to use pleasure frankly as a test of value.
Rebecca West. Quoted Dr Karl Menninger, A PSYCHIATRIST'S WORLD

POET AND POETRY

21 Poetry is the stuff in books that doesn't quite reach the margins.
Anonymous child's essay

1 When one thinks of the attention that a great poem demands there is something frivolous about the idea of spending every day with one. Masterpieces should be kept for High Days of the Spirit.
W. H. Auden, THE DYER'S HAND 1963

2 A verbal art like poetry is reflective. It stops to think. Music is immediate; it goes on to become.
W. H. Auden. Quoted Aaron Copland, MUSIC AND IMAGINATION 1952

3 Poetry makes nothing happen, it survives / In the valley of its saying.
W. H. Auden, ANOTHER TIME, *In Memory of W. B. Yeats* 1940

4 A poet is, before anything else, a person who is passionately in love with language.
W. H. Auden, New York Times 9 *Oct* 1960

5 It is not possible for a poet to be a professional. Poetry is essentially an amateur activity.
Viscount Barrington, House of Lords 23 *Nov* 1978

6 I agree with one of your reputable critics that a taste for drawing rooms has spoiled more poets than ever did a taste for gutters.
Thomas Beer, THE MAUVE DECADE 1926

7 Poetry is as much a part of the universe as mathematics and physics. It is not a cleverer device or recreation, unless the Eternal is clever.
Edmund Blunden on being elected Professor of Poetry at Oxford University 5 *Feb* 1966

8 I have nothing to say and I'm saying it and that is poetry.
John Cage, SILENCE 1961

9 Lyricism cannot exist without rules, and it is essential that they should be strict. Otherwise there is only a faculty for lyricism, and that exists everywhere.
Charles Albert Cingria. Quoted Igor Stravinsky, AN AUTOBIOGRAPHY 1936

10 A poet's technique is not something that should ever call attention to itself; technique can kill freshness.
Jean Cocteau in an interview with Derek Prouse, Sunday Times 20 *Oct* 1903

11 You don't make a poem with thoughts; you must make it with words.
Ibid.

12 Poetry does not necessarily have to be beautiful to stick in the depths of our memory.
Colette, EARTHLY PARADISE, *Under the Blue Lantern* 1960

13 Everyone writes so well nowadays that it is hardly worth while for any new poet to write well. All can raise the flower because all have got the seed.
Hubert Cornish. Quoted Maurice Baring, THE PUPPET SHOW OF MEMORY 1922

14 My mind has thunderstorms / That brood for heavy hours; / Until they rain me words / My thoughts are drooping flowers / And sucking silent birds.
W. H. Davies, COLLECTED POEMS 1943

15 A poet in history is divine, but a poet in the next room is a joke.
Max Eastman. Quoted Evan Esar, TREASURY OF HUMOROUS QUOTATIONS

16 Genuine poetry can communicate before it is understood.
T. S. Eliot, DANTE 1929

17 Immature poets imitate; mature poets steal.
T. S. Eliot, PHILIP MASSINGER 1920

18 The ordinary man falls in love, or reads Spinoza, and these two experiences have nothing to do with each other, or with the noise of the typewriter or the smell of cooking; in the mind of the poet these experiences are always forming new wholes.
T. S. Eliot, THE METAPHYSICAL POETS 1921

19 The majority of poems one outgrows and outlives, as one outgrows and outlives the majority of human passions.
T. S. Eliot, SELECTED ESSAYS

20 Poetry is not a turning loose of emotion but an escape from emotion; it is not the expression of personality, but an escape from personality. But of course, only those who have personality and emotions know what it means to escape from these things.
T. S. Eliot, TRADITION AND THE INDIVIDUAL TALENT 1919

21 Poetry is not a career, but a mug's game. No honest poet can ever feel quite sure of the permanent value of what he has written, he may have wasted his time and messed up his life for nothing.
T. S. Eliot, THE USE OF POETRY AND THE USE OF CRITICISM 1932

1 I can understand you wanting to write poems. But I don't know what you mean by 'being a poet'.
T. S. Eliot. Quoted Stephen Spender,
WORLD WITHIN WORLD

2 We all write poems; it is simply that poets are the ones who write in words.
John Fowles, THE FRENCH LIEUTENANT'S WOMAN

3 Like a piece of ice on a hot stove, the poem must ride on its own melting.
Robert Frost, COLLECTED WORKS, *Preface* 1951

4 Poetry is the language in which man explores his own amazement.
Christopher Fry, Time 3 Apr 1950

5 Poets should never marry. The world should thank me for not marrying you.
Maud Gonne to W. B. Yeats. Quoted Nancy Cardozo, MAUD GONNE

6 Most poets are dead by their late twenties.
Robert Graves. Quoted Observer 11 Nov 1962

7 It's hard to say why writing verse / Should terminate in drink or worse.
A. P. Herbert, Punch, Lines For a Worldly Person

8 Literature is a state of culture, poetry a state of grace, before and after culture.
Juan Ramon Jimenez, POETRY AND LITERATURE 1957

9 When power narrows the areas of man's concern, poetry reminds him of the richness and diversity of his existence. When power corrupts, poetry cleanses.
John F. Kennedy. Speech at dedication of Robert Frost Library, Nov 1962

10 A language not thoroughly recorded by poetry would become so discredited and stripped of meaning that a threat would arise to meaning itself.
Lord Kilmarnock, House of Lords 22 Nov 1978

11 I rather think poetry has given me up, which is a great sorrow to me, but not an enormous, crushing sorrow. It's rather like going bald.
Philip Larkin, Observer, Saying of the Week 15 Apr 1984

12 I think more of a bird with broad wings flying and lapsing through the air than anything when I think of metre.
D. H. Lawrence, letter to Edward Marsh, Nov 1913

13 Poetry can communicate the actual quality of experience with a subtlety and precision unapproachable by any other means.
F. R. Leavis, NEW BEARINGS IN ENGLISH POETRY 1932

14 Verse libre; a device for making poetry easier to read and harder to write.
H. L. Mencken, A BOOK OF BURLESQUES 1916

15 When one hears of a poet past thirty-five he seems somehow unnatural and obscene.
H. L. Mencken, PREJUDICES 1919

16 Poetry is a comforting piece of fiction set to more or less lascivious music.
H. L. Mencken, PREJUDICES (*3rd series*) 1922

17 The poem is the dream made flesh, in a two-fold sense as a work of art, and as life which is a work of art.
Henry Miller, THE WISDOM OF THE HEART, *Creative Death* 1941

18 The courage of the poet is to keep ajar the door that leads to madness.
Christopher Morley, INWARD HO 1923

19 A poet, any real poet, is simply an alchemist who transmutes his cynicism regarding human beings into an optimism regarding the moon, the stars, the heavens and the flowers to say nothing of Spring, love, and dogs.
George Jean Nathan, MONKS ARE MONKS, *Poet* 1929

20 It is needful for a serious writer to try to measure his own limitations . . . Much verse . . . is deformed by the inability of its authors to harmonise what they intend to say with the way they are saying it, or to convince even the well-disposed reader that it is worth saying.
William Plomer, London Magazine, Mar 1956

21 I am at work on a cryselephantine poem of immeasurable length which will occupy one for the next four decades unless it becomes a bore.
Ezra Pound, of the CANTOS *in a letter to Milton Bronner 21 Sep* 1915

1 Poetry is a perfectly reasonable means of overcoming chaos.
I. A. Richards, SCIENCE AND POETRY

2 More often than prose or mathematics, poetry is received in a hostile spirit as if its publication were an affront to the reader.
Michael Roberts, Introduction to FABER BOOK OF MODERN VERSE

3 Poetry has too strong a tradition to acquire a vigorous modern life. With few exceptions nothing can be mentioned in poetry which was not known in the time of Shakespeare.
Bertrand Russell, FORTNIGHTLY REVIEW, *May* 1928

4 Poetry is the achievement of the synthesis of hyacinths and biscuits.
Carl Sandburg, Atlantic Monthly, Poetry Considered, Mar 1923

5 Poetry is the opening and closing of a door, leaving those who look through to guess about what is seen during a moment.
Carl Sandburg, TENTATIVE (FIRST MODEL), *Definitions of Poetry* 1950

6 Ordering a man to write a poem is like commanding a pregnant woman to give birth to a red-headed child. You can't do it — it's an act of God.
Carl Sandburg. Quoted Reader's Digest, Dec 1938

7 Popular poets are the parish priests of the Muse, retailing her ancient divinations to a long since converted public.
George Santayana, THE LIFE OF REASON, *Reason in Art* 1906

8 The truth, which is a standard for the naturalist, for the poet is only a stimulus.
George Santayana, SOLILOQUIES IN ENGLAND 1922

9 All poets' wives have rotten lives / Their husbands look at them like knives.
Delmore Schwartz. Quoted James Atlas in his biography, DELMORE SCHWARTZ: THE LIFE OF AN AMERICAN POET

10 It is as unseeing to ask what is the *use* of poetry as it would be to ask what is the use of religion.
Edith Sitwell, THE OUTCASTS, *Preface*

11 The poet speaks to all men of that other life of theirs that they have smothered and forgotten.
Edith Sitwell, RHYME AND REASON

12 One of the purposes of poetry is to show the dimensions of man that are, as Sir Arthur Eddington said 'midway in scale between the atom and the star.'
Ibid.

13 Poetry ennobles the heart and the eyes and unveils the meaning of things upon which the heart and the eyes dwell.
Ibid.

14 As far as the public goes, poetry might be one of those branch lines scheduled for closing.
Stevie Smith. Quoted Jack Barbera and William MacBrien, STEVIE 1985

15 The poet is the priest of the invisible.
Wallace Stevens, OPUS POSTHUMOUS, *Adagio* 1957

16 Re-write the thrice re-written. Strive to say / Some older nothing in some newer way.
John St Leo Strachey, THE POETASTER

17 A good poem is a contribution to reality. The world is never the same once a good poem has been added to it.
Dylan Thomas, QUITE EARLY ONE MORNING, *On Poetry* 1960

18 There is only one object: the removing of veils from your soul and scabs from your body.
Dylan Thomas. Quoted Andrew Sinclair, DYLAN THOMAS: POET OF HIS PEOPLE

19 To hell with everything except the inner necessity for expression and the medium of expression, everything except the great need of forever striving after this mystery and meaning I moan about.
Dylan Thomas at 18. *Quoted Ibid.*

20 I hold a beast, an angel and a madman in me, and my enquiry is as to their working, and my problem is their subjugation and victory, downthrow and upheaval, and my effort is their self expression.
Dylan Thomas, letter to Henry Treece

21 The poet may be used as the barometer, but let us not forget he is also part of the weather.
Lionel Trilling, THE LIBERAL IMAGINATION, *The Sense of Past* 1950

1 There are no poetic ideas; only poetic utterances.
Evelyn Waugh, BOOKS ON TRIAL

2 The poet produces the beautiful by fixing his attention on something real.
Simone Weil, GRAVITY AND GRACE 1947

3 All poets who when reading from their own works experience a choking feeling are major. For that matter, all poets who read from their own works are major, whether they choke or not.
E. B. White, HOW TO TELL A MAJOR POET FROM A MINOR POET 1939

4 You cannot lecture on really pure poetry any more than you can talk about the ingredients of pure water — it is adulterated, methylated, sanded poetry that makes the best lectures.
Virginia Woolf of Christina G. Rossetti, SECOND COMMON READER 1932

5 'How are you?' / 'Not very well. I can only write prose today.'
W. B. Yeats in conversation

6 Too true, too sincere. The Muse prefers the liars, the gay and warty lads.
W. B. Yeats on the poetry of James Reed.
Quoted Robert Graves and Alan Hodge, THE LONG WEEK END 1940

POLICE

7 I have never seen a situation so dismal that a policeman couldn't make it worse.
Brendan Behan. Quoted Barbara Rowe, A BOOK OF QUOTES

8 I like to see policemen about the place, preferably large ones who have been at it long enough not to look embarrassed by their hats.
H. F. Ellis, Punch 12 Sep 1962

9 I didn't like the police helmet. That's why I was hoping to get into the motor squad where I could have worn a flat cap.
Gilbert Harding to John Freeman, BBC TV, Face to Face

10 For the middle-class, the police protect property, give directions, and help old ladies. For the urban poor the police are those who arrest you.
Michael Harrington, THE OTHER AMERICA 1962

11 The general conclusion seems to be that police are not very popular but that they never have been. I suspect this is true and that the main difference between our times and Victorian times is that in Victorian times the classes that had most reasons for disliking the police had least facilities for expressing their opinions in print.
Christopher Hollis, Punch 1 Aug 1962

12 Why can't the police be equipped with fast-acting tranquilliser darts or pellets? If it works with rhinos, why not with robbers?
U. Light in a letter to Observer 21 Jan 1979

13 Policemen, like red squirrels, must be protected.
Joe Orton, LOOT

14 They stick people in dustbins and then ask us to sit on the lid.
A police constable in a TV interview. Quoted Albert Hunt, Radio Times 17 Feb 1979

15 The South African police would leave no stone unturned to see that nothing disturbed the even terror of their lives.
Tom Sharpe, INDECENT EXPOSURE

16 PC Attila Rees, ox-broad, barge-booted, stamping out of Handcuff House in a heavy, beef-red huff, blackbrowed under his damp helmet . . . and lumbering down towards the strand to see that the sea is still there.
Dylan Thomas, UNDER MILK WOOD 1954

17 The tragedy of the Police State is that it always regards all opposition as a crime, and there are no degrees.
Lord Vansittart, House of Lords, Jun 1947

POLITENESS

18 Being polite is when you eat sandwiches without looking inside first.
Caption to cartoon, TV Times, Kidstuff 5 Mar 1979

19 Politeness is only one half good manners and the other half good lying.
Mary Wilson Little. Quoted Evan Esar, TREASURY OF HUMOROUS QUOTATIONS

20 If we treat people too long with that pretended liking called politeness, we shall find it hard not to like them in the end.
Logan Pearsall Smith, ALL TRIVIA, *Afterthoughts* 1931

1 Politeness is organised indifference.
Paul Valéry, TEL QUEL 1943

POLITICS

2 When the political columnists say 'Every thinking man' they mean themselves and when the candidates appeal to 'Every intelligent voter' they mean everybody who is going to vote for them.
Franklin P. Adams, NODS AND BECKS 1944

3 Politics, as a practice, whatever its professions, has always been the systematic organisation of hatreds.
Henry Brooks Adams, THE EDUCATION OF HENRY ADAMS 1907

4 Knowledge of human nature is the beginning and end of political education.
Ibid.

5 Practical politics consists in ignoring facts.
Ibid.

6 Political economy: two words that should be divorced on grounds of incompatibility.
Anon., Wall Street Journal. Quoted Reader's Digest, Jul 1981

7 As the intelligent are liberals, I am on the side of the idiots.
Maurice Baring, quoting his friend Brewster in THE PUPPET SHOW OF MEMORY 1922

8 Who — except a freakish intellectual — has ever been argued into giving up political power when he doesn't have to; and to give it up, moreover, for the sake of an abstraction, a principle? The idea is ludicrous!
Julian Barnes, Observer 6 May 1979

9 The connection between humbug and politics is too long established to be challenged.
Ronald Bell, MP for Beaconsfield, House of Commons 5 Dec 1979

10 Every Briton is at heart a Tory — especially every British Liberal.
Arnold Bennett, JOURNAL

11 We know what happens to people who stay in the middle of the road. They get run over.
Aneurin Bevan in a speech. Reported Observer 9 Dec 1953

12 I have never regarded politics as the arena of morals. It is the arena of interests.
Aneurin Bevan. Quoted Michael Foot, ANEURIN BEVAN 1897–1945

13 So far as I am concerned the Tory Party are lower than vermin.
Aneurin Bevan. Speech, Manchester 4 Jul 1949

14 Politics is a blood sport.
Aneurin Bevan. Quoted Jennie Lee, MY LIFE WITH NYE

15 Politics are not the task of a Christian.
Dietrich Bonhoeffer, NO RUSTY SWORDS

16 In politics it is immensely important to know what it *feels* like to be someone else . . . Human beings are not islands, least of all politicians.
Sir Edward Boyle. Quoted Susan Barnes, Sunday Express 25 Aug 1963

17 Politics, and the fate of mankind, are shaped by men without ideals and without greatness. Men who have greatness within them don't go in for politics.
Albert Camus, NOTEBOOKS 1935–1942

18 I am not made for politics because I am incapable of wishing for, or accepting the death of my adversary.
Albert Camus, THE REBEL 1951

19 No wonder Harold is back in form — every Labour politician feels more at home attacking his own party's politics.
Cartoon caption, Punch 31 Jan 1973

20 Every politician is emphatically a promising politician.
G. K. Chesterton, THE RED MOON OF MERU

21 It has been said that success in politics cannot be won without a conviction that one's opponents are not only wrong but damned.
Colin R. Coote, Daily Telegraph 7 Mar 1963

22 The only safe pleasure for a parliamentarian is a bag of boiled sweets.
Julian Critchley MP, Observer 13 Jun 1982

23 a politician is an arse upon / which everyone has sat except a man.
e. e. cummings, ONE TIMES ONE, *a politician* 1944

1 To sacrifice one's honour to one's party is so unselfish an act that our most generous statesmen have not hesitated to do it.
Charles John (Justice) Darling, SCINTILLAE JURIS

2 My family would hardly approve of my marrying a politician.
Actress Joan Fontaine to Adlai Stevenson, recorded in her autobiography, NO BED OF ROSES

3 You can't just read blue books. It's like having straw for breakfast.
Michael Foot. Quoted John Mortimer, Sunday Times, Foot at Bay 19 Sep 1982

4 Few things are as immutable as the addiction of political groups to the ideas by which they have once won office.
J. K. Galbraith, THE AFFLUENT SOCIETY 1958

5 Politics consists in choosing between the disastrous and the unpalatable.
J. K. Galbraith, LIFE IN OUR TIMES 1981

6 There is just one rule for politicians all over the world. Don't say in Power what you say in Opposition: if you do you only have to carry out what the other fellows have found impossible.
John Galsworthy, MAID IN WAITING

7 Since a politician never believes what he says, he is surprised when others believe him.
Gen. Charles de Gaulle, Newsweek 1 Oct 1962

8 Politics is too serious a matter to be left to the politicians.
Gen. Charles de Gaulle

9 Most British statesmen have either drunk too much or womanised too much. I never fell into the second category.
Lord George-Brown

10 There are too many men in politics and not enough elsewhere.
Hermione Gingold. Quoted Observer 2 Oct 1958

11 One political party is very much like another, especially in office.
Norman Ginsbury, VICEROY SARAH

12 If Labour is the answer it must have been a bloody silly question.
Graffito, reported in the Daily Telegraph 25 Jan 1979

13 The thing about a politician is that you have to take the smooth with the smooth.
Susan Hill, BBC Radio 4, Quote Unquote 29 Aug 1980

14 Never judge a country by its politics. After all, we English are quite honest by nature, aren't we?
Alfred Hitchcock, THE LADY VANISHES

15 You can't adopt politics as a profession and remain honest.
Louis McHenry Howe, F. D. Roosevelt's secretary. Speech, Columbia University School of Journalism 17 Jan 1933

16 A politician rises on the backs of his friends . . . but it is through his enemies he will have to govern afterwards.
Richard Hughes, THE FOX IN THE ATTIC 1961

17 We should always tell the Press, freely and frankly, anything they could find out in some other way.
Anthony Jay and Jonathan Lynn, BBC 2 TV, Yes, Prime Minister 9 Jan 1986

18 All that politicians are required to do is to look plausible, stay sober, and say the lines they are given.
Ibid. 13 Feb 1986

19 MPs are only human — give or take the occasional vampire or Martian.
Frank Johnson, Daily Telegraph 20 Mar 1979

20 Mothers all want their sons to grow up to become president, but they don't want them to become politicians in the process.
John F. Kennedy. Quoted Barbara Rowe, A BOOK OF QUOTES

21 Politicians are the same everywhere. They promise to build bridges even where there are no rivers.
Nikita Khrushchev to American reporters, Oct 1960

22 We demand of our political life greater certainty and greater perfection than we demand of our personal life.
Max Lerner, ACTIONS AND PASSIONS 1946

1 The acting abilities of Mr Wilson and Mr Macmillan were such that either could have earned a substantial living and devoted following on the stage of the theatre had he not been called instead to the drama of politics.
Bernard Levin, THE PENDULUM YEARS 1976

2 Politicians tend to live *in character* and many a public figure has come to imitate the journalism which describes him.
Walter Lippmann, A PREFACE TO POLITICS 1914

3 The man who raises new issues has always been distasteful to politicians. He messes up what has been so tidily arranged.
Ibid.

4 What do you want to be a sailor for? There are greater storms in politics than you'll ever find at sea. Piracy, broadsides, blood on the deck — you'll find them all in politics.
David Lloyd George to Julian Amery.
Quoted Observer, Buccaneer of the Right 2 *Jan* 1966

5 A politician is a person with whose politics you don't agree; if you agree with him he is a statesman.
David Lloyd George

6 When you're abroad you're a statesman. When you're at home you're just a politician.
Harold Macmillan. Speech 1958

7 A candidate for office can have no greater advantage than muddled syntax; no greater liability than a command of language.
Marya Mannes, MORE IN ANGER 1958

8 It is very unfair to expect a politician to live in private up to the statements he makes in public.
W. Somerset Maugham, THE CIRCLE 1921

9 Porteous: Shouldn't I have been Prime Minister, Clare?
Lady Kitty: Prime Minister? You haven't the brain, you haven't the character.
Champion-Cheny: Cheek, push and a gift of the gab will serve very well instead, you know.
Ibid.

10 One has to be a lowbrow, a bit of a murderer, to be a politician, ready and willing to see people sacrificed, slaughtered for the sake of an idea, whether a good one or a bad one.
Henry Miller, WRITERS AT WORK

11 The proper memory for a politician is one that knows when to remember and when to forget.
John Morley, RECOLLECTIONS 1917

12 Any party which takes credit for the rain must not be surprised if its opponents blame it for the drought.
Dwight W. Morrow. Campaign speech, Oct 1930

13 The misfortune of high-minded intellectuals [in politics] is that, until it is too late, they remain as unaware of the sudden waves of emotion by which the majority can be swayed as they do of the shabby secret stratagems of ambitious men.
Harold Nicolson, Observer 12 *Oct* 1958

14 I'll speak for the man, or against him, whichever will do him most good.
President Richard Nixon, when agreeing to support a politician

15 A politician is like quicksilver. If you try to put your finger on him you will find nothing under it.
Austin O'Malley

16 Political language — and with variations this is true of all political parties from Conservatives to Anarchists – is designed to make lies sound truthful, a murder respectable, and to give an appearance of solidity to pure wind.
George Orwell, SHOOTING AN ELEPHANT 1950

17 I gave up politics when I discovered that I would rather be a poet than a prime minister.
John Pardoe, BBC Radio 4 2 *Apr* 1980

18 Let us suppose that the post to be filled is that of Prime Minister. The modern method is to trust in various methods of election, with results that are almost invariably disastrous.
C. Northcote Parkinson, PARKINSON'S LAW 1957

19 It rarely pays in politics to be wise before the event.
Christopher Patten, The Times, The artist of the possible 23 *Apr* 1981

1 All political lives, unless they are cut off in mid-stream at a happy juncture, end in failure.
Enoch Powell in a Sunday Times interview
6 *Nov* 1977

2 The amateur in politics is the person who is always sure he knows the result of the next General Election.
Enoch Powell. Speech 3 *Feb* 1981

3 The rule of practice for serious politicians is 'Read, read, read'. One can never read enough.
Enoch Powell. Quoted Observer, Sayings of the Week 9 *Jan* 1983

4 I used to say that politics was the second lowest profession and I have come to know that it bears a great similarity to the first.
Ronald Reagan. Quoted Observer 3 *May* 1979

5 Political campaigns are designedly made into emotional orgies which endeavour to distract attention from the real issues involved, and they actually paralyse what slight powers of cerebration man can normally master.
James Harvey Robinson, THE HUMAN COMEDY

6 The more you read about politics, you got to admit that each party is worse than the other.
Will Rogers, A ROGERS' THESAURUS

7 I am reminded of four definitions. A radical is a man with both feet firmly planted — in the air; a conservative is a man with two perfectly good legs who, however, has never learned to walk; a reactionary is a somnambulist walking backwards; a liberal is a man who uses his legs and his hands at the behest of his head.
Franklin D. Roosevelt. Radio broadcast 26 *Oct* 1939

8 I have seen too many people drop dead or become alcoholics because they can't get away from the glamour that seems to pervade being an MP.
Paul Rose MP for Manchester Blackley, explaining his reasons for giving up politics
22 *Feb* 1979

9 This evil-smelling bog.
Lord Rosebery. Quoted Winston Churchill, GREAT CONTEMPORARIES 1937

10 Revolutionary spirits of my father's generation waited for Lefty. Existentialist heroes of my youth waited for Godot. Neither showed up.
Theodore Roszak, UNFINISHED ANIMAL

11 Our great democracies still tend to think that a stupid man is more likely to be honest than a clever man, and our politicians take advantage of this prejudice by pretending to be even more stupid than nature has made them.
Bertrand Russell, NEW HOPES FOR A CHANGING WORLD 1951

12 An Englishman has to have a Party, just as he has to have trousers.
Bertrand Russell in a letter to Maurice Amos MP 16 *Jun* 1936

13 A remark once made to me by the late Philip Guedella was to the effect that voting papers should be made so complicated that only the most highly educated Liberals could understand them.
Mrs Jean V. Saunders, letter to Daily Telegraph 21 *Mar* 1979

14 The politician who once had to learn how to flatter kings has now to learn how to fascinate, amuse, coax, humbug, frighten or otherwise strike the fancy of the electorate.
George Bernard Shaw, MAN AND SUPERMAN 1905

15 He knows nothing and thinks he knows everything. That points clearly to a political career.
George Bernard Shaw, MAJOR BARBARA 1905

16 A politician is a statesman who approaches every question with an open mouth.
Adlai Stevenson. Quoted L. Harris, THE FINE ART OF POLITICAL WIT 1966

17 An independent is a guy who wants to take the politics out of politics.
Adlai Stevenson, THE ART OF POLITICS

18 A particular feature of British politics is 'the indispensable man'. He is the one who undertakes the awkward tasks that no one else wants to bother with. He gets down to work, solves most of the difficult problems and then trips up over one of them. On this he is cast out of office with a few words of regret.
A. J. P. Taylor, Observer, Doing the donkey work, review of *J. A. Cross's* LORD SWINTON 9 *Jan* 1983

1 Some of our best politicians are unable to form a grammatical sentence of more than ten words.
Daily Telegraph, leader 19 *Feb* 1983

2 In politics, if you want anything said, ask a man; if you want anything done, ask a woman.
Margaret Thatcher, in 1965. *Quoted Anthony Sampson,* THE CHANGING ANATOMY OF BRITAIN 1982

3 The Prime Minister is stealing our clothes but he is going to look pretty ridiculous walking around in mine.
Margaret Thatcher of James Callaghan 1973

4 I can trust my husband not to fall asleep on a public platform and he usually claps in the right places.
Margaret Thatcher, Observer 20 *Aug* 1978

5 You've got to accept it. Politicians can plait sawdust.
A trade union official. Quoted Sunday Times 2 *Jul* 1967

6 Politics is the art of preventing people from taking part in affairs which properly concern them.
Paul Valéry, TEL QUEL 1943

7 Politicians can forgive almost anything in the way of abuse; they can forgive subversion, revolution, being contradicted, exposed as liars, even ridiculed, but they can never forgive being ignored.
Auberon Waugh, Observer, How Wodehouse Had the Last Laugh 11 *Oct* 1981

8 Margaret Thatcher's great strength seems to be the better people know her, the better they like her. But, of course, she has one great disadvantage — she is a daughter of the people and looks trim, as the daughters of the people desire to be. Shirley Williams has such an advantage over her because she's a member of the upper middle-class and can achieve that distraught kitchen-sink-revolutionary look that one cannot get unless one's been to a really good school.
Dame Rebecca West at age 83 *in an interview with Jilly Cooper*

9 A week is a long time in politics.
Sir Harold Wilson

10 A constant effort to keep his party together, without sacrificing either principle or the

essentials of basic strategy, is the very stuff of political leadership. Macmillan was canonised for it.
Sir Harold Wilson, FINAL TERM: THE LABOUR GOVERNMENT 1974—76

11 The Labour party is like a stage-coach. If you rattle along at great speed everybody inside is too exhilarated or too seasick to cause any trouble. But if you stop everybody gets out and argues about where to go next.
Sir Harold Wilson. Quoted Leslie Smith, HAROLD WILSON, THE AUTHENTIC PORTRAIT

12 For socialists, going to bed with the Liberals is like having oral sex with a shark.
Larry Zolf

POLLUTION

13 The quality of Mersey is not strained.
Anon., Sunday Graphic 14 *Aug* 1932

14 The crowd has found the door into the secret garden. Now they will tear up the flowers by the roots, strip the borders and strew them with paper and broken bottles.
Alan Bennett, FORTY YEARS ON

15 Do no dishonour to the earth, lest you dishonour the spirit of man.
Henry Besson, THE OUTERMOST HOUSE

16 They [seaside resorts] improvidentially piped growing volumes of sewage into the sea, the healing virtues of which were advertised on every railway station.
Robert Cecil, LIFE IN EDWARDIAN ENGLAND 1969

17 Our Georgian forerunners . . . ignored the natural smells of sweat and dung and dirt as we ignore the artificial smells of petrol fumes and industrial effluents.
John Gloag, GEORGIAN GRACE

18 Many people live in ugly wastelands but in the absence of imaginative standards most of them do not even know it.
C. Wright Mills, POWER POLITICS AND PEOPLE 1963

19 Unless man can make new and original adaptations to his environment as rapidly as his science can change the environment, our culture will perish.
Carl R. Rogers, ON BECOMING A PERSON

1 The emergence of intelligence, I am convinced, tends to unbalance the ecology. In other words, intelligence is the great polluter. It is not until a creature begins to manage its environment that nature is thrown into disorder.
Clifford D. Simak, SHAKESPEARE'S PLANET

POPULARITY

2 Everybody hates me because I'm so universally liked.
Peter De Vries, THE VALE OF LAUGHTER 1968

POPULATION

3 The command 'Be fruitful and multiply' was promulgated according to our authorities, when the population of the world consisted of two people.
W. R. Inge (Dean of St Pauls), MORE LAY THOUGHTS OF A DEAN

4 The purpose of population is not ultimately peopling earth. It is to fill heaven.
Dr Graham Leonard (Bishop of London), CHURCH OF ENGLAND SYNOD, *Church and Bomb debate* 10 *Feb* 1983

PORNOGRAPHY

5 Oh Calcutta is the sort of show that gives pornography a bad name.
Clive Barnes. Quoted, THE FRANK MUIR BOOK

6 It is not good enough to spend time and ink in describing the penultimate sensations and physical movements of people getting into a state of rut, we all know them too well.
John Galsworthy of D. H. Lawrence's SONS AND LOVERS, *in a letter to Edward Garnett* 13 *Apr* 1914

7 It is just possible that those who are most vocally concerned about pornography are really pre-occupied with their own hang-ups.
William Hardcastle, Punch 1 *Dec* 1972

8 If pornography were the only evil in society we'd be extremely lucky.
Roy Jenkins. Quoted John Mortimer, IN CHARACTER 1983

9 Why are pornographic films labelled 'adult'?
Miles Kington, The Times, Great Mysteries of our time 9 *Aug* 1983

10 Pornography is the attempt to insult sex, to do dirt on it.
D. H. Lawrence, PHOENIX 1936

11 It is heartless and it is mindless and it is a lie.
John McGahern, THE PORNOGRAPHER

12 Inside every pornographer there is an infant screaming for the breast from which it has been torn. Pornography represents an endless and infinitely repeated effort to recapture that breast, and the bliss it offered.
Steven Marcus, THE OTHER VICTORIANS

13 Laughter serves to neutralise pornography and is therefore anathema to pornographers. A man I know was thrown out of a Marseilles brothel for laughing at a pornographic film which was being shown there to stimulate business.
Malcolm Muggeridge, TREAD SOFTLY FOR YOU TREAD ON MY JOKES 1966

14 Its avowed purpose is to excite sexual desire, which, I should have thought, is unnecessary in the case of the young, inconvenient in the case of the middle aged, and unseemly in the old.
Ibid.

15 Nine tenths of the appeal of pornography is due to the indecent feelings concerning sex which moralists inculcate in the young. The other tenth is physiological, and will occur in one way or another whatever the state of the law may be.
Bertrand Russell, MARRIAGE AND MORALS 1929

16 Many women, and I agree with them, think there is some connection between the rising tide of sexual crime and Page Three.
Clare Short, House of Commons 14 *Mar* 1986

17 Don't be daft. You don't get pornography on there, not on the telly. You get filth, that's all. The only place you get pornography is in yer Sunday papers.
Johnny Speight, BBC 1 *TV, Till Death Us Do Part*

1 Dirty old men are incapable of being corrupted any further, and as long as they make up the majority of regular customers a bookseller does not break the law in selling dirty books to them, two High Court judges decided yesterday.
Daily Telegraph. Quoted Alan Coren, Punch 23 Feb 1972

2 I have never heard of a girl being seduced by a book.
James J. Walker, Mayor of New York. Quoted J. K. Galbraith, THE AGE OF UNCERTAINTY 1977

PORTRAIT

3 It's an outrage — but it's a masterpiece.
Lord Beaverbrook, on first seeing Graham Sutherland's portrait of him

4 It seems to be a law of nature that no man ever is loth to sit for his portrait.
Max Beerbohm, QUIA IMPERFECTUM

5 This portrait is a remarkable example of modern art. It certainly combines force with candour.
Winston Churchill on Graham Sutherland's portrait of him.

6 It makes me look as if I was straining at stool.
Ibid.

7 You have no idea what portrait painters suffer from the vanity of their sitters.
Kenneth, Lord Clark. Quoted Observer 29 Mar 1959

8 Mr Fildes, to whom I am sitting for my portrait, is under the impression that I am a short, stout man.
Edward VII. Quoted L. V. Fildes, LUKE FILDES: A VICTORIAN PAINTER

9 The painter does not copy the expression a face may have shown, he divines and paints the expression the face must have shown had the man fully revealed himself.
Edward Howard Griggs, A BOOK OF MEDITATIONS

10 I think it's marvellous. I do so love sitting still while other people work.
Robert Morley, on having his portrait painted, The Times 21 Dec 1981

11 To have one's portrait painted is such good value for the ego in these troubled times. It is a pity the poor artist makes so little out of it. They have to buy all the paints, you know.
Ibid.

12 The person portrayed and the portrait are two entirely different things.
José Ortega y Gasset, THE DEHUMANISATION OF ART

13 Few persons who ever sat for a portrait can have felt anything but inferior while the process is going on.
Anthony Powell. Quoted Observer 9 Jan 1983

14 Every time I paint a portrait I lose a friend.
John Singer Sargent. Quoted Richard Ormond, JOHN SINGER SARGENT

15 More and more people are having their portraits painted. Once a company has set a precedent no chairman will miss his chance, whatever the cost, to hang on the boardroom wall with the rest of them, even though many regard the sittings in the same light as going to the dentist.
Carl De Winter, The Times 21 Dec 1981

POSSIBILITY

16 The only way of finding the limits of the possible is by going beyond them into the impossible.
Arthur C. Clarke, THE LOST WORLDS OF 2001

17 Knowledge of what is possible is the beginning of happiness.
George Santayana, LITTLE ESSAYS 1920

POSTERITY

18 Posterity is as likely to be wrong as anybody else.
Heywood Brown, SITTING ON THE WORLD

POTATO

19 What I say is that, if a fellow really likes potatoes, he must be a pretty decent sort of fellow.
A. A. Milne, NOT THAT IT MATTERS

EZRA POUND

1 I remember only one thing about Pound. He
had a beard, and it looked false.
*Anonymous critic in Times Literary
Supplement. Quoted Anthony Burgess,
Observer, Mad About Writing 13 Mar 1983*

2 A genine naif, a sort of revolutionary
simpleton.
*Wyndham Lewis. Quoted Humphrey
Carpenter, Observer 12 May 1985*

POVERTY

3 What fun it would be to be poor, as long as
one was *excessively* poor. Anything in
excess is most exhilarating.
Jean Anouilh, THE REHEARSAL 1950

4 Nothing is sadder than having worldly
standards without worldly means.
*Van Wyck Brooks, A CHILMARK
MISCELLANY*

5 When you have learnt all that Oxford can
teach you, go and discover why, with so
much wealth in Britain, there continues to
be so much poverty, and how poverty can be
cured.
*Edward Caird, Master of Balliol to William,
Lord Beveridge*

6 People don't resent having nothing nearly as
much as too little.
*Ivy Compton-Burnett, A FAMILY AND A
FORTUNE 1934*

7 The very poor are unthinkable and only to
be approached by the statistician and the
poet.
E. M. Forster, HOWARDS END 1910

8 The arithmetic of modern politics makes it
tempting to overlook the very poor, because
they are an inarticulate minority.
*J. K. Galbraith. Quoted Lyndon B.
Johnson, THE VANTAGE POINT*

9 For every talent that poverty has stimulated,
it has blighted a hundred.
John W. Gardner, EXCELLENCE 1961

10 That is one of the bitter curses of poverty, it
leaves no right to be generous.
*George Gissing, THE PRIVATE PAPERS OF
HENRY RYECROFT 1903*

11 People who are much too sensitive to
demand of cripples that they run races ask of
the poor that they get up and act just like
everyone else in society.
*Michael Harrington, THE OTHER
AMERICA 1962*

12 If a free society cannot help the many who
are poor it cannot save the few who are rich.
John F. Kennedy. Speech 20 Jan 1961

13 The trouble with being poor is that it takes
up all your time.
*William de Kooning. Quoted Barbara
Rowe, A BOOK OF QUOTES*

14 The poor insist on being buried. It's usually
the only way they can ensure of getting a
garden of their own.
Derek Marlowe, A DANDY IN ASPIC 1966

15 We shall never solve the paradox of want in
the midst of plenty by doing away with
plenty.
Ogden Mills. Speech, New York 21 Mar 1934

16 Poverty is the great reality. That is why the
artist seeks it.
Anaïs Nin, DIARY, Summer 1937

17 Poverty keeps together more homes than it
breaks up.
*Saki, THE CHRONICLES OF CLOVIS,
Esme 1912*

18 I have been a common man and a poor man,
and it has no romance for me.
*George Bernard Shaw, MAJOR
BARBARA 1905*

19 It is very good, sometimes, to have nothing.
I want society, not me, to have places to sit
in and beds to lie in; and who wants a
hatstand of his very own?
*Dylan Thomas. Quoted Andrew Sinclair,
DYLAN THOMAS: POET OF HIS PEOPLE*

20 I have achieved poverty with distinction, but
never poverty with dignity; the best I can
manage is dignity with poverty.
Dylan Thomas, Letter to Henry Treece

21 A society of *poor* gentlemen, upon whose
hands time lies heavy, is absolutely necessary to art and literature.
*Jack B. Yeats in a letter. Quoted William
Plomer, ELECTRIC DELIGHTS*

POWER

1 A friend in power is a friend lost.
Henry Brooks Adams, THE EDUCATION OF
HENRY ADAMS 1907

2 One man can change the world with a bullet
in the right place.
*Lindsay Anderson's 'IF . . .' (film), script by
David Sherwin* 1968

3 Power without responsibility has been the
privilege of the harlot throughout the ages.
*Stanley Baldwin, of Beaverbrook's
newspapers, in a by-election speech* 1931

4 If you are the summit of a volcano the least
you can do is smoke.
Winston Churchill, GREAT
CONTEMPORARIES, *The Ex-Kaiser* 1937

5 To be a great autocrat you must be a great
barbarian.
Joseph Conrad,

6 Men of power have not time to read; yet
men who do not read are unfit for power.
Michael Foot, DEBTS OF HONOUR

7 'Power' tends to be something believed in by
those who have never worked near the
putative centre of it.
Douglas Jay, CHANGES AND FORTUNE 1980

8 Power is the ultimate aphrodisiac.
Henry Kissinger. Quoted Guardian 28 *Nov*
1976

9 Political power grows out of the barrel of a
gun.
Mao Tse-Tung, THE THOUGHTS OF
CHAIRMAN MAO

10 The men who really wield, retain and covet
power are the kind who answer bedside
telephones while making love.
Nicholas Pileggi. Quoted Barbara Rowe, A
BOOK OF QUOTES

11 Religions, which condemn the pleasures of
sense, drive men to seek the pleasures of
power. Throughout history power has been
the vice of the ascetic.
*Bertrand Russell, New York Herald-Tribune
Magazine* 6 *May* 1938

12 The poor don't know that their function in
life is to exercise our generosity.
Jean-Paul Sartre, THE WORDS 1964

13 The wrong sort of people are always in
power because they would not be in power if
they were not the wrong sort of people.
*Jon Wynne Tyson, Times Literary
Supplement*

14 Looking about me at certain prefects, a few
masters, I could see that if power, as Marx
claimed, was a responsibility it was also an
appetite.
Peter Vansittart, PATHS FROM A WHITE
HORSE 1985

15 Cheerful, irresponsible people are
rewarded for possessing some knack such as
being able to hit a golf-ball accurately or
play records on the wireless in a winning
manner . . . It is all wrong. There is too
much grit in the money-machine. When
money is the key to power some of the
power will get into the wrong hands.
John Wain, Punch 28 *Sep* 1960

PRACTICE

16 That practice makes perfect is not neces-
sarily so. Practice makes permanent . . .
Incorrect practice, bad practice, will even-
tually produce permanent bad habits.
Charles Hughes, THE FA COACHING BOOK
OF SOCCER TACTICS AND SKILLS

17 If I go a week without practice the audience
notices it. If I go a day without practice, I
notice it.
*Artur Rubenstein. Quoted Alistair Cooke
BBC* 4, *Letter From America* 31 *May* 1974

PRAISE

18 Praise out of season or tactlessly bestowed
can freeze the heart as much as blame.
Pearl S. Buck, TO MY DAUGHTERS, WITH
LOVE 1916

19 Watch how a man takes praise and there you
have the measure of him.
*Thomas Burke, TP's Weekly, Talks With
Theodore Dreiser* 8 *Jun* 1928

20 From the moment I picked up your book
until I laid it down, I was convulsed with
laughter. Some day I intend reading it.
*Groucho Marx to S. J. Perelman. Quoted
Perelman,* THE LAST LAUGH

1 People ask you for criticism, but they only want praise.
W. Somerset Maugham, OF HUMAN BONDAGE 1915

2 In recommending a book to a friend the less said the better. The moment you praise a book too highly you awaken resistance in your listener.
Henry Miller, THE BOOKS IN MY LIFE 1952

3 The highest term of praise that many English people ever use is 'Not bad'.
Bertrand Russell, *Saturday Evening Post* 3 *Jun* 1956

4 Praise shames me, for I secretly beg for it.
Rabindranath Tagore, STRAY BIRDS 1916

PRAYER

5 Even if there were no ear for them but the void our prayers would be the only things that sanctify our existence.
William Barrett, THE ILLUSION OF TECHNIQUE

6 The wish to pray is a prayer in itself.
George Bernanos, DIARY OF A COUNTRY PRIEST 1936

7 *Pray, v.* To ask that the rules of the universe be annulled on behalf of a single petitioner, confessedly unworthy.
Ambrose Bierce, THE DEVIL'S DICTIONARY 1906

8 'Does God always answer prayer?' the cardinal was asked. 'Yes' he said. 'And sometimes the answer is — "No" '
Alistair Cooke, BBC Radio 4, Letter from America 8 *Mar* 1981

9 The most odious of concealed narcissisms — prayer.
John Fowles, THE ARISTOS

10 Lord forgive me all the little tricks I play on you and I'll forgive the great big one you played on me.
Robert Frost

11 Prayer is not an old woman's idle amusement. Properly understood and applied it is the most potent instrument of action.
Mahatma Gandhi, NON-VIOLENCE IN PEACE AND WAR 1948

12 You pray in your distress and in your need; would that you might pray also in the fullness of your joy and in your days of abundance.
Kahil Gibran, THE PROPHET 1926

13 Your cravings as a human animal do not become a prayer just because it is God whom you must ask to attend to them.
Dag Hammarskjöld, MARKINGS 1964

14 Work is prayer. Work is also stink. Therefore stink is prayer.
Aldous Huxley, JESTING PILATE 1926

15 Prayer is more than meditation. In meditation the source of strength is one's self. When one prays he goes to a source of strength greater than his own.
Mme Chiang Kai-shek, I CONFESS MY FAITH

16 A child's prayer: Please make the bad people good, and the good people nice.
Marwood (Devon), Parish Magazine, Nov 1984

17 Our dourest parsons, who followed the nonconformist fashion of long extemporary prayers, always seemed to me to be bent on bullying God. After a few 'beseech thees' as a mere politeness, they adopted a sterner tone and told Him what they expected from Him and more than hinted He must attend to His work.
J. B. Priestley, OUTCRIES AND ASIDES

18 Common people do not pray; they only beg.
George Bernard Shaw, MISALLIANCE 1910

19 And here's to you, Mrs Robinson / Jesus loves you more than you will know. / God bless you please, Mrs Robinson / Heaven holds a place for those who pray.
Paul Simon, MRS ROBINSON

20 I don't want to bore God.
Orson Welles, explaining why he did not pray, Observer, Sayings of the Week 28 *Mar* 1982

21 Prayers for the condemned man will be offered on an adding machine. Numbers constitute the only universal language.
Nathanael West, MISS LONELY HEARTS 1933

PREACHING

1 Preaching to some people is like eating custard with a fork. It goes in one ear and out the other.
Anonymous curate. Quoted BBC Radio 4, Quote Unquote 2 Feb 1982

2 Ah, sir, you should have heard him throw down Jezebel.
Anthony C. Deane, quoting a verger, in TIME REMEMBERED

3 He [Adam Starkadder] paused and drew a long breath, then thundered at the top of his voice 'Ye're all damned!'
An expression of lively interest and satisfaction passed over the faces of the Brethren, and there was a general rearranging of arms and legs as though they wanted to sit as comfortably as possible while listening to the bad news.
Stella Gibbons, COLD COMFORT FARM 1932

4 Only the sinner has the right to preach.
Robert Morley

5 The British churchgoer prefers a severe preacher because he thinks a few home truths will do his neighbours no harm.
George Bernard Shaw

PRECAUTION

6 I hate to depress you, but you'll hate the day you ever took this assignment. This is an ordeal by fire. Make sure you wear asbestos pants.
Hermann Mankiewicz, advice to S. J. Perelman on working for the Marx Brothers. Quoted S. J. Perelman, THE LAST LAUGH 1982

7 Reading and smoking in bed are the sort of faults of which wives complain, and they are the sort of things they could and should have found out before they got married.
Letter to Daily Mirror. Quoted News Review 15 Apr 1948

8 In baiting a mouse-trap with cheese always leave room for the mouse.
Saki, THE SQUARE EGG, *The Infernal Parliament* 1924

PREJUDICE

9 Mother is far too clever to understand anything she does not like.
Arnold Bennett, THE TITLE 1918

10 Prejudice is a vagrant opinion without visible means of support.
Ambrose Bierce, THE DEVIL'S DICTIONARY 1906

11 I am free of all prejudice. I hate everyone equally.
W. C. Fields. Quoted Jerome Beatty, Saturday Review 28 Jan 1967

12 Prejudices are the props of civilisation.
André Gide, THE COUNTERFEITERS 1926

13 Nobody outside of a baby carriage or a judge's chamber believes in an unprejudiced point of view.
Lillian Hellman. Quoted Barbara Rowe, A BOOK OF QUOTES

14 There is a tendency to judge a race, a nation, or a distinct group by its least worthy members.
Eric Hoffer, THE TRUE BELIEVER 1951

15 A great many people think they are thinking when they are merely rearranging their prejudices.
William James. Quoted A. A. Andrews, QUOTATIONS FOR SPEAKERS AND WRITERS. *Also attr. Ed Murrow,* AMERICAN BROADCASTER *and to Adlai Stevenson by Leon Harris in* THE FINE ART OF POLITICAL WIT

16 The tendency of the casual mind is to pick out or stumble upon a sample which supports or defines its prejudices, and then to make it representative of a whole class.
Walter Lippmann, PUBLIC OPINIONS 1929

17 One may no more live in the world without picking up the moral prejudice of the world than one will be able to go to hell without perspiring.
H. L. Mencken, PREJUDICES 1921

18 Everyone is a prisoner of his own experiences. No one can eliminate prejudices — just recognise them.
Ed Murrow, broadcast 31 Dec 1955

1 The collection of prejudices which is called political philosophy is useful provided it is not called philosophy.
Bertrand Russell, AUTOBIOGRAPHY 1967

PRESENT

2 The now, the here, through which all future plunges to the past.
James Joyce, ULYSSES 1922

3 The future will one day be the present and will seem as unimportant as the present does now.
W. Somerset Maugham, THE SUMMING UP 1938

4 The passing moment is all we can be sure of; it is only common sense to extract the utmost value from it.
Ibid.

5 The word 'now' is like a bomb through the window, and it ticks.
Arthur Miller, AFTER THE FALL 1964

6 The only living life is in the past and future — the present is an interlude — strange interlude in which we call on past and future to bear witness that we are living.
Eugene O'Neill, STRANGE INTERLUDE 1928

PRETENTIOUSNESS

7 Last year the sanitary engineers suggested that they should be known as Public Health Officers. We should be lucky they did not want to call themselves Privy Counsellors.
Lord Mancroft. Speech to Auctioneers and Estate Agents, Dorchester Hotel 31 *Oct* 1957

8 [He] is always called a nerve specialist because it sounds better, but everyone knows he's a sort of janitor in a looney bin.
P. G. Wodehouse, THE INIMITABLE JEEVES 1924

PRIDE

9 Don't think yourself so pretty. Even if a man on a galloping horse did carry you off one dark night he would drop you off at the first lighted lamp post.
Sir Hugh Casson and Joyce Grenfell, NANNY SAYS 1972

10 The virtue of pride, which was once the beauty of mankind, has given place to that fount of all ugliness, Christian humility.
Max Ernst. Quoted John Russell, MAX ERNST

11 Many a man is praised for his reserve and so-called shyness when he is simply too proud to risk making a fool of himself. The vain man will cut capers in order to obtain notice and applause. The proud man asks for notice and applause without being willing to cut the capers, while the very proud man does not even want the applause.
J. B. Priestley, ALL ABOUT OURSELVES

12 A confessional passage has probably never been written that didn't stink a little of the writer's pride in having given up pride.
J. D. Salinger, SEYMOUR: AN INTRODUCTION 1963

13 Don't let that chip on your shoulder be your only reason for walking erect.
James Thurber, LANTERNS AND LANCES, *Midnight at Tim's Place* 1962

PRIEST

14 I always like to associate with a lot of priests because it makes me understand anti-clerical things so well.
Hilaire Belloc, letter to E.S.P. Haynes 9 *Nov* 1909

15 A priest is a man who is called Father by everyone except his own children who are obliged to call him Uncle.
Italian saying. Quoted Rupert Hart-Davis, THE LYTTELTON HART-DAVIS LETTERS 15 *Jul* 1956

PRINCIPLE

16 You can't learn too soon that the most useful thing about a principle is that it can always be sacrificed to an expediency.
W. Somerset Maugham, THE CIRCLE 1921

17 It is often easier to fight for principles than to live up to them.
Adlai Stevenson. Speech, New York 27 *Aug* 1952

PRISON

1 Half the people in prison should never be there at all, although the other half should never be let out.
James Anderton, Chief Constable of Greater Manchester. Quoted John Mortimer, IN CHARACTER 1983

2 In prison they give you a green billiard ball and tell you it is an apple. If you try to cat it, they put you in the mailbag shop.
Anonymous prison inmate, BBC 1 *TV, Strangeways* 29 *Oct* 1980

3 All prisons are brimming over with innocence. It is those who cram their fellows into them, in the name of empty ideas, who are the only guilty ones.
Jean Anouilh, CATCH AS CATCH CAN 1960

4 The same skills needed to be a successful criminal are needed to survive in prison.
Robert Chesshyre, Observer, This Is Your Life 9 *Aug* 1981

5 In prison those things withheld from and denied the prisoner become precisely what he wants most of all.
Eldridge Cleaver, SOUL ON ICE, *On Becoming* 1968

6 The most efficient way for a man to survive in Britain is to be almost half-witted, completely irresponsible and spend a lot of time in prison, where his health is far better looked after than outside.
Charles Galton Darwin, THE NEXT MILLION YEARS

7 In the vocational training section prisoners were being taught the art of copper beating, and I saw some examples of excellent craftsmanship.
High Sheriff of Essex, letter to The Times. Quoted, PRIVATE EYE BUMPER BOOK OF BOOBS

8 The only thing I really mind about going to prison is the thought of Lord Longford coming to visit me.
Richard Ingrams, editor of Private Eye

9 It feels like being in hospital without the fear of pain or in the army without fear of war.
Lord Kagan to reporters, on being released from prison 24 *Jun* 1981

10 It was better to be in a jail where you could bang the walls than in a jail you could not see.
Carson McCullers, THE MEMBER OF THE WEDDING 1946

11 We do not want our prisons to become dustbins.
Patrick Mayhew MP, House of Commons 26 *Nov* 1981

12 A prisoner has no sex. He is God's own eunuch.
Henry Miller, THE AIR-CONDITIONED NIGHTMARE 1945

13 There can be few places where false gods are more frequently found or more diligently followed than in the exercise yard of a large prison.
Sir Alexander Paterson, News Review 16 *Jan* 1947

14 Prison will not work until we start sending a better class of people there.
Laurence J. Peter

15 My fellow-prisoners seemed to me in no way morally inferior to the rest of the population though they were on the whole slightly below the usual level of intelligence, as was shown by their having been caught.
Bertrand Russell, AUTOBIOGRAPHY 1967

16 Here I have not a care in the world; the rest to nerves and will is heavenly. One is free from the torturing question: what more might I be doing? . . . Prison has some of the advantages of the Catholic Church.
Bertrand Russell, letter from prison to Frank Russell, May 1918

17 Prison is not a mere physical horror. It is using a pickaxe to no purpose that makes a prison.
Antoine de Saint-Exupéry, WIND SAND AND STARS 1939

18 The most anxious man in a prison is the warden.
George Bernard Shaw

19 Anyone who has been to an English public school will always feel comparatively at home in prison. It is the people brought up in the gay intimacy of the slums who find prison so soul-destroying.
Evelyn Waugh, DECLINE AND FALL 1928

PRIVACY

1 It is when we pass our own private gate, and open our own secret door, that we step into the land of the giants.
G. K. Chesterton, CHARLES DICKENS 1906

2 The human animal needs a privacy seldom mentioned, freedom from intrusion. He needs a little privacy quite as much as he wants understanding or vitamins or exercise or praise.
Phyllis McGinley, THE PROVINCE OF THE HEART, *A Lost Privilege* 1959

3 I might have been a goldfish in a glass bowl for all the privacy I got.
Saki, THE INNOCENCE OF REGINALD 1904

PRIVILEGE

4 People of privilege will always risk their complete destruction rather than surrender any material part of their advantage.
J. K. Galbraith. Quoted Barbara Rowe, A BOOK OF QUOTES

5 One of the privileges of the great is to witness catastrophes from a terrace.
Jean Giraudoux, TIGER AT THE GATES 1935

6 What men value in this world is not rights but privileges.
H. L. Mencken, MINORITY REPORT

7 Privilege is privilege, whether it is due to money or intellect or whether you have six toes.
Philip, Duke of Edinburgh. Quoted Noël St George, ROYAL QUOTES

8 Privilege is not difficult to defend because even the most egalitarian societies have always recognised that it must be admitted to some extent.
John Wain, Punch 28 Sep 1960

PRIZE

9 The world continues to offer glittering prizes to those who have stout hearts and sharp swords.
Lord Birkenhead, COLLECTED SPEECHES

10 Not only should you not accept a prize. You should not try to deserve one either.
Jean Cocteau. Quoted Geoffrey Grigson, Sunday Times 23 Jan 1973

11 The real object of giving prizes in schools is to encourage the children to give as little trouble as possible.
George Bernard Shaw. Quoted Hesketh Pearson, BERNARD SHAW 1942

PROBLEM

12 I do not believe in final solutions. Even if you solve some problem the solution will always give rise to another problem.
Isaiah Berlin, CONCEPTS AND CATEGORIES

13 Few [problems] are difficult of solution. The difficulty, all but invariably, is in confronting them. We know what needs to be done; for reasons of inertia, pecuniary interest, passion or ignorance, we do not wish to say so.
J. K. Galbraith, THE AGE OF UNCERTAINTY 1977

14 The worst thing you can do to an important problem is discuss it.
Simon Gray, OTHERWISE ENGAGED *(play)*

15 You do not have to ignore problems in order to be happy, but you need to remind yourself constantly that the insurmountable difficulties of today are the solved problems of tomorrow.
Cardinal Heenan, THROUGH THE YEAR WITH CARDINAL HEENAN

16 Problems are only opportunities in work clothes.
Henry J. Kaiser. A favourite maxim, often quoted by him

17 Our problems are man-made, therefore they may be solved by man. And man can be as big as he wants. No problem of human destiny is beyond human beings.
John F. Kennedy. Speech, Washington University 10 Jan 1963

18 All progress is precarious, and the solution of one problem brings us face to face with another problem.
Martin Luther King, STRENGTH TO LIVE 1963

19 She probably laboured under the common delusion that you made things better by talking about them.
Rose Macaulay, CREWE TRAIN 1926

1 The man who is forever disturbed about the condition of humanity either has no problems of his own or has refused to face them.
Henry Miller, SUNDAY AFTER THE WAR 1944

2 The chief cause of problems is solutions.
Sevareid's Rule. Quoted Peter Dickson, THE OFFICIAL RULES

3 A problem left to itself dries up or goes rotten. But fertilise a problem with a solution — you'll hatch out a dozen others.
N. F. Simpson, A RESOUNDING TINKLE

4 No problem is insoluble given a big enough plastic bag.
Tom Stoppard, JUMPERS

PROCRASTINATION

5 Procrastination is the art of keeping up with yesterday.
Don Marquis, ARCHY AND MEHITABEL, *certain maxims of archy* 1927

6 Make me a beautiful word for doing things tomorrow, for that surely is a great and blessed invention.
George Bernard Shaw, BACK TO METHUSELAH 1922

7 In England we have come to rely upon a comfortable time lag of fifty years or a century intervening between the perception that something ought to be done and a serious attempt to do it.
H. G. Wells, THE WORK, WEALTH AND HAPPINESS OF MANKIND 1932

PRODIGY

8 *Prodigy:* A child who plays the piano when he ought to be asleep in bed.
Beachcomber (J. B. Morton)

PROFANITY

9 Pa's out and ma's out, let's talk dirt / Pee-poh-belly-bottom-drawers.
Children's rhyme. Quoted Robert Graves, OCCUPATION WRITER

10 How easy to swear if you're properly educated.
Christopher Fry, A PHOENIX TOO FREQUENT 1949

11 The word 'bloody' as we now use it is almost a term of affection.
Judge Rawlins, at Clerkenwell Court. Quoted News Review 20 May 1948

12 A foreign swear word is practically inoffensive except to the person who has learnt it early in life and knows its social limits.
Paul Theroux, THE GREAT RAILWAY BAZAAR

PROFESSOR

13 Our American professors like their literature clear, cold, pure and very dead.
Sinclair Lewis. Address, Swedish Academy 12 Dec 1930

PROFIT

14 It is a socialist idea that making profits is a vice. I consider the real vice is making losses.
Winston Churchill. Quoted Evan Esar, TREASURY OF HUMOROUS QUOTATIONS

15 The trouble with the profit system has always been that it was highly unprofitable to most people.
E. B. White, ONE MAN'S MEAT 1944

PROGRESS

16 All progress is based upon a universal innate desire on the part of every organism to live beyond its income.
Samuel Butler, NOTEBOOKS, *Life* 1912

17 Change is certain. Progress is not.
E. H. Carr, FROM NAPOLEON TO STALIN, AND OTHER ESSAYS

18 Unfortunately movement cannot be equated with progress.
Leslie Chapman, WASTE AWAY

19 Humanity has a naïve faith in progress. We are progressing, no doubt about that, but so were the Gadarene swine.
Bishop of Chelmsford, Courier Vol. 3 No. 2 1943

20 As enunciated today 'progress' is simply a comparative of which we have no settled superlative.
G. K. Chesterton, HERETICS 1905

1 Progress is merely a metaphor for walking along a road – very likely the wrong road.
G. K. Chesterton, ORTHODOXY 1908

2 pity this busy monster manunkind / not.
Progress is a comfortable disease.
e. e. cummings, ONE TIMES ONE 1944

3 What we call progress is the exchange of one nuisance for another nuisance.
Havelock Ellis

4 What progress we are making. In the Middle Ages they would have burned me. Now they are content with burning my books.
Sigmund Freud, in a letter to Ernest Jones on the public burning of his books in Berlin 1933

5 They say you can't stop progress. But what is progress if it's just destroying everything?
Thor Heyerdahl, Radio Times, interview with Tim Heald 16 Feb 1979

6 The reason that men oppose progress is not that they hate progress but that they love inertia.
Elbert Hubbard, THE NOTEBOOK 1927

7 The world is moving so fast these days that the man who says it can't be done is generally interrupted by someone doing it.
Ibid.

8 Spiritual progress is our one ultimate aim. It may be towards the dateless and irrevocable, but it is inevitably dependent upon progress intellectual, moral and physical – progress in this changing, revolving world of dated events.
Julian Huxley, ESSAYS OF A BIOLOGIST 1923

9 The trouble with progress is that it can progress in any direction.
W. A. Ireland, Saturday Evening Post 26 Apr 1952

10 Progress is a nice word. But change is its motivator and change has its enemies.
Robert F. Kennedy, THE PURSUIT OF JUSTICE 1964

11 The notion of progress in a single line without goal or limit seems perhaps the most parochial notion of a very parochial century.
Lewis Mumford, TECHNICS AND CIVILISATION 1934

12 In every age the great human civilisations have depended far more upon emotional inspiration than upon the standard of plumbing.
Philip, Duke of Edinburgh, A QUESTION OF BALANCE

13 If anyone has a new idea in this country there are twice as many people who advocate putting a red flag in front of it.
Ibid.

14 To put it crudely, progress gives us better medical science, but it also gives us better bombs.
Philip, Duke of Edinburgh. Address to the Coal Industry Society

15 The test of our progress is not whether we add more to the abundance of those who have much; it is whether we provide enough for those who have too little.
F. D. Roosevelt. Second Inaugural Address 20 Jan 1937

16 Organic life has developed gradually from the protozoon to the philosopher and this development, we are assured, is indubitably an advancement. Unfortunately it is the philosopher, not the protozoon, who gives this assurance.
Bertrand Russell, MYSTICISM AND LOGIC 1917

17 'Change' is scientific, 'progress' is ethical. Change is indubitable, whereas progress is a matter of controversy.
Bertrand Russell, UNPOPULAR ESSAYS 1950

18 Man's 'progress' is but a gradual discovery that his questions have no meaning.
Antoine Saint-Exupéry, THE WISDOM OF THE SANDS 1948

19 Three kinds of progress are significant; progress in knowledge and technology, progress in the socialisation of man, progress in spirituality. The last is the most important.
Albert Schweitzer, THE TEACHING OF REVERENCE FOR LIFE

20 In America getting on in the world means getting out of the world we have known before.
Ellery Sedgwick, THE HAPPY PROFESSION 1946

1 All progress means war with Society.
George Bernard Shaw, GETTING
MARRIED 1911

2 When people shake their heads because we
are living in a restless age, ask them how
they would like to live in a stationary one
and do without change.
George Bernard Shaw, INTELLIGENT
WOMAN'S GUIDE TO SOCIALISM AND
CAPITALISM 1928

3 The reasonable man adapts himself to the
world; the unreasonable one persists in
trying to adapt the world to himself.
Therefore all progress depends on the
unreasonable man.
George Bernard Shaw, MAN AND
SUPERMAN 1905

4 Life means progress, and progress means
suffering.
H. W. Van Loon, TOLERANCE

5 We are about to enter the age of flight
before we've even developed a chair that a
man can sit in comfortably.
Philip Wylie

PROHIBITION

6 Prohibition has made nothing but trouble.
*Al Capone, gangster, in a newspaper
interview*

7 A great social and economic experiment,
noble in motive and far-reaching in purpose.
*President Herbert Hoover on the
introduction of prohibition*

8 Prohibition more than almost any human
edict this century, proved that all extremes
are wrong, and that bad extremes, pursued
for ostensibly good ends, are worst of all.
Richard Last, Daily Telegraph 19 Aug 1981

9 Prohibition is going to be recorded as one of
the results of the European War, foreseen
by nobody.
Stephen Leacock, THE WOMAN QUESTION

10 The prohibition law, written for weaklings
and derelicts, has divided the nation, like
Gaul, into three parts — wets, drys and
hypocrites.
Pauline Morton Sabu. Speech 9 Mar 1931

11 When by mere legislation, man can stop
fruit from fermenting of its own accord after
it falls to the ground he can talk about a law
of prohibition. The very word destroys its
meaning. You can't prohibit nature.
E. Temple Thurston, MR BOTTLEBY DOES
SOMETHING

PROMISCUITY

12 She thrived on advances — financial and
sexual. She had four husbands and a
regiment of lovers, and she could have had
more if she hadn't been occupied with
writing. She stopped being a *femme fatale*
when she was 87 as the result of a series of
strokes.
*Paul Bailey, of Katherine Anne Porter,
Observer, Callie the Incredible 13 Mar 1983*

13 Like the bee its sting, the promiscuous leave
behind in each encounter something of
themselves by which they are made to
suffer.
Cyril Connolly, THE UNQUIET GRAVE 1945

14 She's the original good time that was had by
all.
*Bette Davis of a rival actress. Quoted Leslie
Halliwell*, FILMGOER'S BOOK OF QUOTES

15 Elspeth had had so many men. Two of her
sisters rode, so to speak, her discarded
mounts.
F. Scott Fitzgerald, THE CRACK-UP 1936

16 If I'd been a ranch, they'd have named me
the Bar Nothing.
Rita Hayworth, lines spoken in the film
GILDA

17 The promiscuous world goes with thinking
that you don't have any value. It can
represent a kind of despair.
*Iris Murdoch. Quoted Adam Mars-Jones,
Sunday Times 29 Sep 1985*

18 You were born with your legs apart. They'll
send you to your grave in a Y-shaped coffin.
Joe Orton, WHAT THE BUTLER SAW *(play)*

19 That girl speaks eighteen languages and
can't say no in any of them.
*Dorothy Parker, of a film star. Quoted Leslie
Halliwell*, FILMGOER'S BOOK OF QUOTES

1 For Ian, women were like fishcakes. Mind you, he was very fond of fishcakes, but he never pretended that there was any great mystique about eating them.
John Pearson, quoting one of Ian Fleming's girl friends, LIFE OF IAN FLEMING 1966

2 I have been so misused by chaste men with one wife / That I would live with satyrs all my life.
Anna Wickham, SHIP NEAR SHOALS

doesn't it? Gibberish. It's where we get babble from.'
'That's a fabble," said Noël.
William Merchant, THE PRIVILEGE OF HIS COMPANY

11 To correct an Englishman's pronunciation is to imply that he is not quite a gentleman.
George Bernard Shaw, when chairman of the BBC's committee on standard pronunciation

PROMISE

3 If you won't give me your word of honour, will you give me your promise?
Sam Goldwyn. Quoted Alva Johnson, THE GREAT GOLDWYN

4 Since election promises are all the fashion, I challenge Mr Gaitskell to meet this one; I promise you it'll rain on October 9th.
Harold Macmillan during election campaign, Sep 1959

5 A promise to men in grief is lightly broken.
John Masefield, THE WILD SWAN

6 A promise made is a debt unpaid.
Robert W. Service, THE SPELL OF THE YUKON 1907

PRONUNCIATION

7 'There's a moose loose.'
'Are you English or Scots?'
Caption to cartoon, Punch

8 Everybody has the right to pronounce foreign names as he chooses.
Winston Churchill, Observer, Sayings of the Week 5 Aug 1951

9 Fine ear for the haspirate, that's what my darter Maria 'ave and what I, for one, 'ave not.
H. G. Hutchinson, Punch 29 Jan 1929

10 Elaine [Stritch] began to sing 'When the tower of Babel fell' . . . and pronounced it to rhyme with scrabble.
Noël [Coward] stopped her and said 'It's bayble Stritch.'
'I've always said babble. Everyone says babble. It means mixed-up language,

PROPAGANDA

12 Propaganda is a soft weapon; hold it in your hands too long, and it will move about like a snake, and strike the other way.
Jean Anouilh, THE LARK 1953

13 The greater the lie, the greater the chance that it will be believed.
Adolf Hitler, MEIN KAMPF 1924

14 The greatest triumphs of propaganda have been accomplished, not by doing something, but by refraining from doing. Great is truth, but still greater from a practical point of view, is silence about truth.
Aldous Huxley, BRAVE NEW WORLD, *Foreword 1932*

15 The propagandist's purpose is to make one set of people forget that certain other sets of people are human.
Aldous Huxley, THE OLIVE TREE 1937

16 The first casualty when war comes is truth.
Hiram Johnson, US senator. Speech quoted Burton Stevenson, HOME BOOK OF QUOTATIONS

17 In our own day it would not be an unfair description of education to define it as the art which teaches men to be deceived by the printed word.
Prof. H. J. Laski, LIBERTY IN THE MODERN STATE

18 I give you bitter pills in sugar coating. The pills are harmless, the poison is in the sugar.
Stanislaw Lec, UNKEMPT THOUGHTS 1962

19 Nobody has ever succeeded in keeping nations at war except by lies.
Salvador de Madariaga. Quoted Burton Stevenson, THE HOME BOOK OF QUOTATIONS

1 Why is propaganda so much more successful when it stirs up hatred than when it tries to stir up friendly feeling?
Bertrand Russell, THE CONQUEST OF HAPPINESS 1936

PROPERTY

2 Property is necessary, but it is not necessary that it should remain for ever in the same hands.
Rémy de Gourmont

3 Property is organised robbery.
George Bernard Shaw, MAJOR BARBARA, *Preface* 1905

4 Gambling promises the poor what property performs for the rich — something for nothing.
George Bernard Shaw, MAJOR BARBARA 1905

PROPHECY

5 A hopeful disposition is not the sole qualification to be a prophet.
Winston Churchill, House of Commons 10 *Apr* 1927

6 There is no future, no present, in prophecy.
Alistair Cooke, BBC Radio 4, *Letter from America* 14 *Feb* 1982

7 The prophet himself stands under the judgment which he preaches. If he does not know that, he is a false prophet.
Reinhold Niebuhr, BEYOND TRAGEDY

8 It will be years — and not in my time — before a woman will lead the party or become Prime Minister.
Margaret Thatcher. Speech in 1974. *Quoted Observer* 8 *May* 1979

PROPRIETY

9 There can be no salacious or improper significance in applying the word 'Oomph' to women's footware.
Mr Justice Evershed, giving judgment in the High Court 14 *Oct* 1946

PROSPERITY

10 Prosperity is only an instrument to be used, not a deity to be worshipped.
President Calvin Coolidge. Speech, Boston 11 *Jun* 1928

11 Armaments, universal debt and planned obsolescence — those are the three pillars of Western prosperity.
Aldous Huxley, ISLAND

12 The American economy is not going to be able to prosper unless Americans regard as necessities what other people look on as luxuries.
Wendell Wilkie, ONE WORLD

PROSTITUTION

13 Take the courtesan. It is inconceivable to Jack [J. B. Priestley] that a courtesan best expresses herself by being a courtesan. To him, an unfortunate is a woman who has been abused.
James Agate on J. B. Priestley's MUSIC AT NIGHT, EGO 4 11 *Oct* 1939

14 Even if you're a pro you've got to *look* like you're an amacher otherwise the kids are going to think you're doing something they couldn't do. That way you'd scare 'em.
Alex Atkinson, THE BIG CITY

15 If brothels were nationalised instead of merely legalised, prostitution would inevitably die out.
Brigit Batlow, letter to Daily Telegraph 19 *Sep* 1979

16 Men of good taste have complicated me on that carpet.
Brendan Behan, THE HOSTAGE 1958

17 It is accepted by psychiatrists that prostitutes have a great therapeutic value in society and are practitioners of professional therapy.
Mrs Maureen Colquhoun, MP for Northants N., House of Commons 6 *Mar* 1979

18 Prostitution gives her an opportunity to meet people. It provides fresh air and wholesome exercise, and it keeps her out of trouble.
Joseph Heller, CATCH 22 1961

1 An epoch which is not an age of promiscuity is necessarily an age of prostitution.
James Laver, TASTE AND FASHION FROM THE FRENCH REVOLUTION UNTIL TODAY

2 If you want to buy my wares / Follow me and climb the stairs / Love for Sale.
Cole Porter, NEW YORKER *(musical), Love For Sale*

3 I am notorious. I will go down in history as another Lady Hamilton.
Mandy Rice-Davis in an interview after the Profumo affair

4 There is something utterly nauseating about a system of society which pays a harlot twenty-five times as much as it pays its Prime Minister.
Harold Wilson, referring to the Christine Keeler case in a speech, House of Commons 1963

PROTEST

5 The protest march has replaced the queue as Britain's favourite communal activity. It's lively, it's an outlet for aggressive instincts, and it gives one something to do on a rainy day. Not least, it's a good way of meeting the opposite sex. Hyde Park rallies, in particular, are noted for being a more than satisfactory substitute for the old *Palais de danse*.
William Davis, *Punch* 16 Feb 1972

6 Idealism is no excuse for irrational behaviour.
Sunday Telegraph of the anti-apartheid riots in New Zealand 26 *Jul* 1981

7 If you mean merely that noisiness and hysteria are proofs of unfitness for public life then every Parliament in the world should close, every election meeting be prohibited, every sex be disfranchised. Did Englishmen ever get their voting right save by noisiness and hysteria?
Israel Zangwill (on the suffragette movement), letter to The Times 29 *Oct* 1906

PROVERB

8 Proverbs are always platitudes until you have personally experienced the truth of them.
Aldous Huxley, JESTING PILATE 1926

9 Proverbs contradict each other. That is the wisdom of a nation.
Stanislaw Lec, UNKEMPT THOUGHTS 1962

PROVIDENCE

10 There is nothing more agreeable than to find providence dislikes the same people that we do. It adds to our good opinion of providence.
Frank Moore Colby, THE COLBY ESSAYS 1926

PRUDERY

11 Parsons always seem to be specially horrified about things like sunbathing and naked bodies. They don't mind poverty and misery and cruelty to animals nearly as much.
Susan Ertz, JULIAN PROBERT

PSYCHIATRY AND PSYCHOANALYSIS

12 Psychiatry's chief contribution to philosophy is the discovery that the toilet is the seat of the soul.
Alexander Chase, PERSPECTIVES 1966

13 It might be said of psychoanalysis that if you give it your little finger it will soon have your whole hand.
Sigmund Freud, INTRODUCTORY LECTURES IN PSYCHOANALYSIS 1932

14 I do not think our successes can compete wih those at Lourdes. There are so many more people who believe in the miracles of the Blessed Virgin than in the existence of the unconscious.
Ibid.

15 Anyone who goes to a psychiatrist ought to have his head examined.
Sam Goldwyn. Quoted Alva Johnson, THE GREAT GOLDWYN

16 Freud is the father of psychoanalysis. It has no mother.
Germaine Greer, THE FEMALE EUNUCH

17 Fortunately psycho-analysis is not the only way to resolve inner conflicts. Life itself still remains a very effective therapist.
Karen Horney, OUR INNER CONFLICTS

1 So then Dr Froyd said all I needed was to cultivate some inhibitions and get some sleep.
Anita Loos, GENTLEMEN PREFER BLONDES 1925

2 Psychoanalysis has terrified educated parents with the fear of the harm they may unwittingly do their children.
Bertrand Russell, THE CONQUEST OF HAPPINESS 1930

3 A psychiatrist is a man who goes to the Folies Bergères to look at the audience.
Mervyn Stockwood (Bishop of Southwark), Observer 15 *Jun* 1961

4 Psychiatrists classify a person as a neurotic if he suffers from his problems in living, and as psychotic if he makes others suffer.
Thomas Szasz, THE SECOND SIN, PSYCHIATRY

5 Psychoanalysts believe that the only 'normal' people are those who cause no trouble either to themselves or anyone else.
A. J. P. Taylor, THE TROUBLE MAKERS 1957

6 A child's incessant weeping, at first variously attributed by her worried custodians to an incest-complex, a mother-fixation or a malfunctioning gland, was eventually traced (to her mother's surprise) to wearing shoes two sizes too small.
Peter Vansittart, PATHS FROM A WHITE HORSE 1985

PSYCHOLOGY

7 Behavioural psychology is the science of pulling habits out of rats.
Dr Douglas Busch

8 The subtle man is infinitely more easy to understand than the natural man.
G. K. Chesterton, ROBERT BROWNING 1903

9 Psychology has a long past, but only a short history.
Hermann Ebbinghaus, SUMMARY OF PSYCHOLOGY

10 The psychic development of the individual is a short repetition of the course of development of the race.
Sigmund Freud, LEONARDO DA VINCI

11 The British have never accepted the word psychology as relevant to their own lives . . . only in Britain do people need reminding that it is not just about rats, mental illness or Freud.
Beverley Hayne, Observer 25 *Feb* 1979

12 In certain persons, at least, the total possible consciousness may be split into parts which co-exist but mutually ignore each other, and share the objects of knowledge between them.
William James, THE PRINCIPLES OF PSYCHOLOGY

13 Freud was a hero. He descended to the 'Underworld' and met there stark terrors. He carried with him his theory as a Medusa's head which turned these terrors to stone.
R. D. Laing, THE DIVIDED SELF

14 Thousands of American women know far more about the subconscious than they do about sewing.
H. L. Mencken, PREJUDICES 1919

15 *Morgan:* Did you hear what the white rat said to the other white rat:
Analyst: What?
Morgan: I've got that psychologist so well trained that every time I ring the bell he brings me something to eat.
David Mercer, A SUITABLE CASE FOR TREATMENT (*TV play*)

16 Psychology which explains everything / Explains nothing / And we are still in doubt.
Marianne Moore, COLLECTED POEMS, *Marriage* 1951

17 The purpose of psychology is to give us a completely different idea of the things we know best.
Paul Valéry, TEL QUEL 1945

18 Psychology as the behaviourist views it is a purely objective experimental branch of natural science.
J. B. Watson. Quoted David Cohen, THE FOUNDER OF BEHAVIOURISM

PUBLICITY

19 All publicity is good, except an obituary notice.
Brendan Behan. Quoted Robert Pitman, Sunday Express 5 *Jan* 1964

1 Formerly a public man needed a *private* secretary for a barrier between himself and the public. Nowadays he has a *press* secretary to keep him properly in the public eye.
Daniel J. Boorstin, THE IMAGE 1962

2 It is a major story when an attractive young woman throws ink all over the Prime Minister or someone tries to blow up the Post Office Tower. The very fact that such acts guarantee vast publicity is a powerful incentive to commit them.
William Davis, Punch 9 Feb 1972

3 I want it so that you can't wipe your ass on a piece of paper that hasn't got my picture on it.
*Lyndon B. Johnson to his press agents.
Quoted Robert A. Caro*, THE PATH TO POWER 1983

4 To have news value is to have a tin can tied to one's tail.
T. E. Lawrence, letter to Sir Evelyn Wrench, Mar 1935

5 Reviews matter very little in the case of a novel. The important thing is to make people talk about it. You can do this by forcing yourself into the newspaper in some other way. Attempt to swim the Channel, get unjustly arrested in a public park, disappear. There are innumerable means of attracting public notice.
Evelyn Waugh, Passing Show 2 *Feb 1929*

PUBLIC OPINION

6 Public opinion, a vulgar, impertinent, anonymous tyrant who deliberately makes life unpleasant for anyone who is not content to be the average man.
W. R. Inge (Dean of St Pauls), OUTSPOKEN ESSAYS, *Our Present Discontents* 1919

PUBLIC SCHOOL

7 They had the Eton something or the Harrow something. I felt I was nearer to grasping what the something is than ever before. It is a sleek happiness that comes of a shininess which only Eton — or Harrow — can import. The nearest thing to it must be boot polish.
J. M. Barrie, letter to Lady Cynthia Asquith 10 *Jul* 1920

8 A public schoolboy must be acceptable at a dance, and invaluable in a shipwreck.
Alan Bennett, FORTY YEARS ON

9 His English education at one of the great public schools had preserved his intellect perfectly and permanently at the stage of boyhood.
G. K. Chesterton, THE MAN WHO KNEW TOO MUCH 1922

10 The ape-like virtues without which no one can enjoy a public school.
Cyril Connolly, ENEMIES OF PROMISE 1938

11 A mildewy scriptural odour pervaded the institution — it reeked of Jeroboam and Jesus; the masters struck me as supercilious humbugs; the food was so vile that for the first day or two after returning from holidays I could not get it down. The only good which ever came out of the place was cheese from the neighbouring Stilton, and that of course, they never gave us.
Norman Douglas, LOOKING BACK 1933

12 It is not that the Englishman can't feel, it is that he is afraid to feel. He has been taught at his public school that feeling is bad form.
E. M. Forster, ABINGER HARVEST 1936

13 It is hardly surprising if judges who have been to Eton or Winchester have few qualms about sending lower-class young men to Parkhurst or Wormwood Scrubs.
David Frost and Anthony Jay, TO ENGLAND WITH LOVE

14 By virtue of his [Public School] training he kept his pores open and his mouth shut.
Rudyard Kipling, THE BRUSHWOOD BOY

15 There's nothing like a public school for hiding your true feelings; it must have been a wonderful training ground for a spy.
Julian Mitchell in an interview with Sheridan Morley, The Times 29 *Oct* 1981

16 You can't expect a boy to be depraved until he has been to a good school.
Saki, A BAKER'S DOZEN

17 'Which do you consider to be public schools?'
'Well, Eton — and Harrow.'
'Rugby?'
'No, that's a railway junction.'
Dorothy L. Sayers, MURDER MUST ADVERTISE 1933

1 Having been to Westminster is like being able to waggle your ears. It's a facility you will have all your life, but the value of it isn't quite clear.
A pupil named Simon Target, BBC 1 TV, Public School 14 Sep 1979

2 There at Westminster School I was given the clothes of an undertaker, together with a furled umbrella, in order, we were told, to distinguish the boys from City of London bank messengers.
Peter Ustinov, DEAR ME 1977

3 The whole purpose of a public school education is to teach a chap to accept injustice like a man; it should leave no mark on him beyond a certain resolve to get his own back on the next generation.
Auberon Waugh, Spectator 3 Nov 1984

4 Anyone who has been to an English public school will feel comparatively at home in prison.
Evelyn Waugh, DECLINE AND FALL 1928

5 You send a boy to school in order to make friends — the right sort.
Virginia Woolf, in her diary. Quoting Countess of Cromer

PUBLIC SPEAKING

6 It's not the way people in my audience start looking at their watch that worries me — it's when they keep tapping them to see if they have stopped.
Lady Barnett in a radio interview

7 I do not object to people looking at their watches when I am speaking — but I strongly object when they start shaking them to make certain they are still going.
Lord Birkett, New York Times 13 Nov 1960

8 An after-dinner speech should be like a lady's dress — long enough to cover the subject and short enough to be interesting.
R. A. Butler, Anglo-Jewish Association dinner, Dorchester Hotel 1 Jun 1957

9 Oratory is the art of making a loud noise sound like a deep thought.
Bennett Cerf, LAUGHING STOCK 1952

10 Haven't you learned yet that I put something more than whisky into my speeches?
Winston Churchill to his son Randolph

11 He is one of those orators of whom it was well said 'Before they get up they do not know what they are going to say; when they are speaking they do not know what they are saying; and when they sit down they do not know what they have said.'
Winston Churchill of Lord Charles Beresford, House of Commons 20 Dec 1912

12 A good rule is to resist the temptation to say '. . . and finally' unless you have actually reached your penultimate sentence.
Paul Johnson, Daily Telegraph, Sending for a Phrase 21 Jul 1979

13 I have heard, on Xmas Day, in the First Lesson, 'Wonderful, Counsellor, Prince of Peace' etc. read as if they were the names of stations on the Underground. The truth, of course, is that the path between too little expression and too much is a very narrow one.
G. W. Lyttelton, THE LYTTELTON HART-DAVIS LETTERS 2 *May* 1956

14 I listen to my own speeches with keen interest and extreme pleasure. I have seldom listened to a speech of mine without learning something.
Bonar Thompson, Hyde Park orator, THE BLACK HAT

15 If you want me to talk for ten minutes I'll come next week. If you want me to talk for an hour I'll come tonight.
Woodrow Wilson, answering an invitation to make a speech. Quoted Adlai Stevenson to Leon Harris, THE FINE ART OF POLITICAL WIT

PUBLISHING

16 Editors have to be able to spell; publishers can be illiterate.
Anthony Blond, THE BOOK BOOK 1985

17 There is probably no hell for authors in the next world — they suffer too much from critics and publishers in this.
Christian Nastell Boyce, SUMMARIES OF THOUGHT

18 As repressed sadists are said to become policemen or butchers so those with an irrational fear of life become publishers.
Cyril Connolly, ENEMIES OF PROMISE 1938

1 Great editors do not discover nor produce great authors, great authors create and produce great publishers.
John Farrar, WHAT HAPPENS IN BOOK PUBLISHING 1957

2 I have never been rich in anything but unsold books and of them I have warehouses full.
Rupert Hart-Davis, THE LYTTELTON HART-DAVIS LETTERS 20 *Nov* 1955

3 Some say the reason for these [misprints] is the increasingly liberal attitude of the Church of England. Not enough parsons are unfrocked these days. The unfortunates of earlier days were often happy to find themselves employment in printing houses, correcting proofs.
David Holloway, Daily Telegraph 21 *Apr* 1979

4 Curse the blasted, jelly-boned swines, the slimy, the belly-wriggling invertebrates, the miserable sodding rutters, the flaming sods, the snivelling, dribbling, dithering, palsied, pulse-less lot that make up England today. They've got white of egg in their veins and their spunk is that watery it's a marvel they can breed.
D. H. Lawrence to Edward Garnet on Heinemann's rejection of SONS AND LOVERS

5 The unpublished manuscript is like an unconfessed sin that festers in the soul, corrupting and contaminating it.
Antonio Machado, JUAN DE MAIRENA 1943

6 Publishing a volume of poetry is like dropping a rose petal down the Grand Canyon and waiting for the echo.
Don Marquis, THE SUN DIAL

7 A person who publishes a book wilfully appears before the public with his pants down.
Edna St Vincent Millay, LETTERS 1952

8 They [publishers] are like Methodists. They love to keep the Sabbath and everything else they can lay their hands on.
Amanda Ros, letter to Lord Ponsonby 1910

9 The trouble with you, my dear Rupert, is that you will persist in seeing me 'in book form.'
G. M. Young to Rupert Hart-Davis. Quoted THE LYTTELTON HART-DAVIS LETTERS 20 *Nov* 1955

10 Being published by the OUP is rather like being married to a duchess; the honour is almost greater than the pleasure.
Ibid. 29 *Nov* 1956

PUNCTUALITY

11 We are not saints but we have kept our appointment. How many people can boast as much?
Samuel Beckett, WAITING FOR GODOT 1952

12 I would rather arrive on time with a sergeant-pilot than late with an Old Etonian.
Air Vice-Marshal Fielden, Captain of the King's Flight. Quoted Kenneth Rose, KINGS, QUEENS AND COURTIERS 1985

13 I am a believer in punctuality, though it makes me lonely.
E. V. Lucas, READING, WRITING AND REMEMBERING

14 I have noticed that the people who are late are often so much jollier than the people who have to wait for them.
Ibid.

15 'Twenty-three and a quarter minutes past', Uncle Matthew was saying furiously, 'in precisely six and three-quarter minutes the damned fella will be late.'
Nancy Mitford, LOVE IN A COLD CLIMATE

16 I make unpunctuality an art. The only time I am conscious of the time is when I am on time. Then I am frankly astonished.
George Sava, TWICE THE CLOCK ROUND

17 W. H. Auden could not tolerate unpunctuality and not sticking to time-tables. He had an open mind about sex but a closed one about clocks.
Sir Stephen Spender, JOURNALS 1985

18 A gentleman is punctual to a fault. He sits down to his meals exactly at the appointed hour and expects to be served even if there has been a power cut or the cook has run off with the second footman.
Douglas Sutherland, THE ENGLISH GENTLEMAN 1978

19 If you're there before it's over, you're on time.
James J. Walker, Mayor of New York

1 Punctuality is the virtue of the bored.
Evelyn Waugh, DIARIES 26 *Mar* 1962

PUNCTUATION

2 Cut out all those exclamation marks. An exclamation mark is like laughing at your own joke.
F. Scott Fitzgerald. Quoted Sheila Graham and Gerald Frank, BELOVED INFIDEL

3 I expect to be, quite soon, the last living man to know the difference between a colon and a semicolon.
Bernard Levin, ENTHUSIASMS 1983

PUNISHMENT

4 Guilt always hurries towards its complement, punishment; only there does its satisfaction lie.
Lawrence Durrell, JUSTINE 1957

5 The use of the birch is not to be deplored. All the best men in the country have been beaten, archbishops, bishops and even deans. Without sensible correction they could not be the men they are today.
Dean Ely, reported in the Manchester Guardian

6 The refined punishments of the spiritual minds are usually much more indecent and dangerous than a good smack.
D. H. Lawrence, FANTASIA OF THE UNCONSCIOUS 1922

7 My father believed in smiting sin wherever he found it; what I complained of was that he always seemed to find it in the same place.
Saki and Charles Maude, THE WATCHED POT

8 If you strike a child take care that you strike it in anger, even at the risk of maiming it for life. A blow in cold blood neither can nor should be forgiven.
George Bernard Shaw, MAN AND SUPERMAN 1905

9 Every child should have an occasional pat on the back, as long as it is applied low enough, and hard enough.
Bishop Fulton J. Sheen. Quoted Frank Muir, ON CHILDREN

PUPIL

10 He was his pupil, so now he is his enemy.
Bertolt Brecht, GALILEO 1939

PURITY

11 To the puritan all things are impure.
D. H. Lawrence, ETRUSCAN PLACES 1927

12 I was surprised when I learnt that Mrs Hicks had a mother — she was so pure I thought she had come to life out of the house-dress section of the Sears Roebuck catalogue.
Betty MacDonald, THE EGG AND I 1946

13 The impurity of those to whom all things pertaining to themselves are pure.
Muriel Spark, THE GO-AWAY BIRD

14 Purity is the ability to contemplate defilement.
Simone Weil, GRAVITY AND GRACE 1914

PURPOSE

15 If after all, men cannot always make history have a meaning, they can always act so that their own lives have one.
Albert Camus, RESISTANCE, REBELLION AND DEATH 1961

16 There must be more to life than having everything.
Maurice Sendak, HIGGLETY PIGGLETY POP

Q

QUESTION

1 To ask the hard question is simple.
W. H. Auden, THE QUESTION

2 We have found all the questions that can be found. It is time we gave up looking for questions and began looking for answers.
G. K. Chesterton, ORTHODOXY 1908

QUOTATION

3 The surest way of making a monkey out of a man is to quote him.
Robert Benchley, QUICK QUOTATIONS

4 Some men have a mania for Greek and Latin quotations. This is to be avoided. It is like pulling up the stones from a tomb to kill the living.
Michael Brett, THINGS A GENTLEMAN WOULD LIKE TO KNOW CONCERNING THE SOCIAL GRACES

5 It is a good thing for an uneducated man to read books of quotations.
Winston Churchill, MY EARLY LIFE 1930

6 It would be nice if sometimes the kind things I say were considered worthy of quotation. It isn't difficult, you know, to be witty or amusing when one has something to say that is destructive, but damned hard to be clever and quotable when you are singing someone's praises.
Noël Coward. Quoted William Marchant, THE PLEASURE OF HIS COMPANY 1981

7 Sometimes it seems the only accomplishment my education ever bestowed on me was the ability to think in quotations.
Margaret Drabble, A SUMMER BIRDCAGE

8 In England only uneducated people show off their knowledge; nobody quotes Latin or Greek authors in the course of conversation, unless he has never read them.
George Mikes, HOW TO BE AN ALIEN 1946

9 To be amused by what you read — that is the great spring of happy quotations.
C. E. Montague, A WRITER'S NOTES ON HIS TRADE 1930

10 I might repeat to myself, slowly and soothingly, a list of quotations beautiful from minds profound; if I can remember any of the damn things.
Dorothy Parker, THE LITTLE HOUR

11 If with the literate I am / Impelled to try an epigram / I never seek to take the credit / We all assume that Oscar said it.
Dorothy Parker, OSCAR WILDE

12 Misquotation is the pride and privilege of the learned.
Hesketh Pearson. Quoted BBC Radio 4, Quote Unquote 24 Apr 1980

13 A man can be forgiven a lot if he can quote Shakespeare in an economic crisis.
Philip, Duke of Edinburgh, of Karl Marx

14 The quotation of two or three lines of a stanza from Spenser's *Faery Queen* is probably as good an all-round silencer as anything.
Stephen Potter, LIFEMANSHIP 1950

15 To say that anything was a quotation was an excellent method, in Eleanor's eyes, for withdrawing it from discussion.
Saki, THE JESTING OF ARLINGTON STRINGHAM

16 I often quote myself. It adds spice to my conversation.
George Bernard Shaw. Quoted Reader's Digest, Jun 1943

17 Famous remarks are seldom quoted correctly.
Simeon Strunksy, NO MEAN CITY

1 In the dying world I come from, quotation is a national vice. It used to be the classics, now it's lyric verse.
Evelyn Waugh, THE LOVED ONE 1948

2 One has to secrete a jelly in which to slip quotations down people's throats and one always secretes too much jelly.
Virginia Woolf, LEAVE THE LETTERS TILL WE ARE DEAD 1981

3 There are almost as many quotations in P. G. Wodehouse as there are in Shakespeare.
Woodrow Wyatt, The Times 24 *Nov* 1983

R

RACE RELATIONS

1 It is a great shock at the age of five or six to find that in a world of Gary Coopers you are the Indian.
James Baldwin. Speech, Cambridge Union 17 Feb 1965

2 to like an individual because he's black is just as insulting as to dislike him because he isn't white.
e. e. cummings. Quoted Barbara Rowe, A BOOK OF QUOTES

3 When people like me, they tell me it is in spite of my colour. When they dislike me they point out it is not because of my colour.
Frantz Fanon, BLACK SKIN WHITE MASKS

4 What we need is hatred. From it are our ideas born.
Jean Genet, THE NEGROES

5 My heart is as black as yours.
Malcolm Gluck. Quoting white politician to Harlem audience, Punch 18 Aug 1976

6 Racial Prejudice is a pigment of the imagination.
Graffito. Quoted Nigel Rees, GRAFFITI LIVES OK.

7 Can you explain why black Englishmen and women who win Olympic medals and excel at games are described as 'English', while those who riot and throw petrol bombs are almost invariably 'West Indian'?
Edward Hughes. Letter to Daily Telegraph 13 Sep 1985

8 An English anti-semitic seeing a Jew in his club does not throw him out. He leaves the club himself.
Lord Kagan. Quoted Observer 24 Dec 1979

9 There are no 'white' or 'coloured' signs on the fox holes or graveyards of battles.
John F. Kennedy. Message to Congress on Civil Rights 19 Jan 1963

10 I wouldn't trust an Aryan with my great-grandmother.
V. S. Naipaul, A HOUSE FOR MR BISWAS 1961

11 If you want to make beautiful music you must play the black and the white notes together.
Richard Nixon. Quoted Barbara Rowe, A BOOK OF QUOTES, but probably not original

12 He's really awfully fond of coloured people. Well, he says himself, he wouldn't have white servants.
Dorothy Parker, ARRANGEMENTS IN BLACK AND WHITE

RAILWAY

13 This is the night mail crossing the border / Bringing the cheque and the postal order.
W. H. Auden, The Night Mail 1935

14 Rumbling under blackened girders Midland bound for Cricklewood / Puffed its sulphur to the sunset where that land of laundries stood.
Sir John Betjeman, PARLIAMENT HILL FIELDS

15 People's back yards are much more interesting than their front gardens, and houses that back on to railways are public benefactors.
Sir John Betjeman. Quoted Janet Watts, Observer magazine, The Time of His Life 13 Mar 1983

16 A third-class carriage is a community, while a first-class carriage is a place of wild hermits.
G. K. Chesterton, HERETICS 1905

17 God set a limit to man's locomotive ambition in the construction of his body. Man immediately proceeded to discover means of over-riding the limit . . . Railways are a most dangerous institution.
Mahatma Gandhi. Quoted This and That 25 Jan 1930

1 Here at the wayside station, as many a morning / I watch the smoke torn from the fumy engine / Crawling across the fields in serpent sorrow.
Edwin Muir, THE WAYSIDE STATION

2 We like a tidy station and passengers make it untidy.
Official explanation for not providing seats at Euston station. Quoted Bernard Levin, THE PENDULUM YEARS 1976

RAIN

3 I love the rain. I want the feeling of it on my face.
Katherine Mansfield, last words

4 Still falls the Rain / Dark as the world of man, black as our loss — / Blind as the nineteen hundred and forty nails / Upon the Cross.
Edith Sitwell, STILL FALLS THE RAIN

READING

5 The middle brows like [John Henry] O'Hara because his books remind them of the lives they imagine themselves to be leading.
John W. Aldridge, TIME TO MURDER AND CREATE

6 He has only half learned the art of reading who has not added to it the even more refined accomplishments of skipping and skimming.
A. J. Balfour. Quoted E. T. Raymond, MR BALFOUR

7 The test of a first-rate work, and a test of your sincerity in calling it a first-rate work, is that you finish it.
Arnold Bennett, THINGS THAT HAVE INTERESTED ME

8 It is impossible to read properly without using all one's engine power. If we are not tired after reading, commonsense is not in us.
Ibid.

9 Of all odd crazes, the craze to be forever reading new books is one of the oddest.
Augustine Birrell, ESSAYS, *Books Old and New* 1922

10 I read books like mad, but I am careful not to let anything I read influence me.
Michael Caine, Woman's Own

11 When one can read, can penetrate the enchanting world of books, why write?
Colette, EARTHLY PARADISE 1966

12 Reading after a certain age diverts the mind too much from its creative pursuits. Any man who reads too much and uses his own brain too little falls into lazy habits of thinking.
Albert Einstein. Quoted Edwin Muller, EINSTEIN: A STUDY IN SIMPLICITY

13 One always tends to overpraise a long book because one has got through it.
E. M. Forster, ASPECTS OF THE NOVEL 1927

14 We can never know that a piece of writing is bad unless we have begun by trying to read it as if it was very good and ended by discovering that we were paying the author an undeserved compliment.
C. S. Lewis, AN EXPERIMENT IN CRITICISM 1961

15 The pleasure of all reading is doubled when one lives with another who shares the same books.
Katherine Mansfield, LETTERS 1928

16 I would sooner read a time-table or a catalogue than nothing at all. They are much more entertaining than half the novels that are written.
W. Somerset Maugham, THE SUMMING UP 1938

17 All my good reading, you might say, was done in the toilet.
Henry Miller, BLACK SPRING 1936

18 I have only read one book in my life and that is *White Fang*. It's so frightfully good I've never bothered to read another.
Nancy Mitford, THE PURSUIT OF LOVE 1945

19 Have you read any good books lately?
Catch phrase used by Richard Murdoch in BBC Radio, Much Binding in the Marsh

20 I'm quite illiterate, but I read a lot.
J. D. Salinger, THE CATCHER IN THE RYE 1951

1 We shouldn't teach great books; we should
teach a love of reading.
B. F. Skinner. Quoted R. Evans, B. F.
SKINNER: THE MAN AND HIS IDEALS

2 People say that life is the thing, but I prefer
reading.
Logan Pearsall Smith,
AFTERTHOUGHTS 1931

3 I read a good deal of criticism, but only as a
vice, not so good as reading science fiction,
rather better than reading mystery stories.
Gore Vidal, BEHIND THE SCENES

4 As in the sexual experience, there are never
more than two persons present in the act of
reading — the writer who is the impregnator
and the reader who is the respondent.
E. B. White, THE SECOND TREE FROM THE
CORNER 1954

RONALD REAGAN

5 That youthful sparkle in his eye is caused by
his contact lenses, which he keeps highly
polished.
Sheila Graham, The Times 22 Aug 1981

6 I have a strange feeling that he will wake up
one day and ask 'What movie am I in?'
Ibid.

7 He is the first man for twenty years to make
the Presidency a part-time job, a means of
filling up a few of the otherwise blank days
of retirement.
Simon Hoggart, Observer 21 Jun 1981

8 In a disastrous fire in President Reagan's
library both books were destroyed. And the
real tragedy is that he hadn't finished
colouring one.
Jonathan Hunt, Observer, Public Eye 30
Aug 1981

9 Ronnie is a very soft touch, and I don't want
anyone taking advantage of him.
*Nancy Reagan, Observer, Sayings of the
Week* 25 Nov 1984

10 Everybody should have a Ronald Reagan in
their lives.
Ibid. 9 Feb 1986

11 As the age of television progresses the
Reagans will be the rule, not the exception.

To be perfect for television is all a President
has to be these days.
Gore Vidal. Quoted Martin Amis, Observer
7 Feb 1982

12 A triumph of the embalmer's art.
Gore Vidal. Quoted John Heilpern,
Observer 26 Apr 1981

13 What's really worrying about Reagan is that
he always seems to be waiting for someone
to say 'Cut' and has no idea how they've
decided the script should end.
*Katherine Whitehorn, Observer, Act Your
Self* 4 Dec 1983

14 Ask him the time and he'll tell you how the
watch was made.
*Jane Wyman (Ronald Reagan's first wife).
Quoted Sheila Graham The Times* 22 Aug
1981

REALITY

15 I like reality. It tastes of bread.
Jean Anouilh, CATCH AS CATCH CAN 1960

16 An independent reality in the ordinary
physical sense can neither be ascribed to the
phenomenon nor to the agencies of observa-
tion.
Niels Bohr 1927

17 Reality only reveals itself when it is illumin-
ated by a ray of poetry.
*Georges Braque. Quoted in his obituary,
The Times* 2 Sep 1963

18 Everything is a dangerous drug except
reality, which is unendurable.
Cyril Connolly, THE UNQUIET GRAVE 1945

19 I am afraid of this word Reality, not
connoting an ordinary definable characteristic of the things it is applied to, but used as
though it were some kind of celestial halo.
Sir Arthur Eddington, THE NATURE OF THE
PHYSICAL WORLD 1928

20 Human kind / Cannot bear much reality.
T. S. Eliot, BURNT NORTON 1935

21 There is no reality except the one contained
within us. That is why so many people live
such an unreal life. They take the images
outside them for reality and never allow the
world within to assert itself.
Hermann Hesse, DAMIAN 1919

1 The horror, no less than the charm of real life, consists precisely in the recurrent actualisation of the inconceivable.
Aldous Huxley, THEME AND VARIATIONS 1930

2 We live in a fantasy world, a world of illusion. The great task in life is to find reality.
Iris Murdoch. Quoted Rachel Billington, The Times, Profile: Iris Murdoch 15 Apr 1983

3 Reality is a staircase going neither up nor down, we don't move, today is today, always is today.
Octavio Paz, MODERN EUROPEAN POETRY, *The Endless Instant* 1966

4 Reality is pretty brutal, pretty filthy, when you come to grips with it. Yet it's glorious all the same. It's so real and satisfactory.
George Bernard Shaw, FANNY'S FIRST PLAY 1912

5 A test of what is real is that it is hard and rough. Joys are found in it, not pleasures. What is pleasant belongs to dreams.
Simone Weil, GRAVITY AND GRACE 1947

REASON

6 Men do not live by reason, but are merely controlled by it. Otherwise why do they fall in love and practise the arts?
Gerald Brenan, THOUGHTS IN A DRY SEASON 1979

7 Human reason needs only to will more strongly than fate, and she *is* fate.
Thomas Mann, THE MAGIC MOUNTAIN 1924

8 The man who listens to Reason is lost; Reason enslaves all whose minds are not strong enough to master her.
George Bernard Shaw, MAN AND SUPERMAN, *Maxims for Revolutionists* 1905

REBELLION

9 Every act of rebelling expresses a nostalgia for innocence and an appeal to the essence of being.
Albert Camus, THE REBEL 1951

10 No one can go on being a rebel too long without turning into an autocrat.
Laurence Durrell, BALTHAZAR 1958

REFORM

11 It is simply impertinence for any man, or any body of men, to begin, or contemplate, reform of the whole world. To attempt to do so by means of highly artificial and speedy locomotion is to attempt the impossible.
Mahatma Gandhi. Quoted in his obituary, News Chronicle 31 Jan 1948

12 Reform must come from within, not from without. You cannot legislate for virtue.
Cardinal Gibbons. Speech, Baltimore 13 Sep 1909

13 Unless the reformer can invent something which substitutes attractive virtues for attractive vices he will fail.
Walter Lippmann, A PREFACE TO POLITICS, *The Taboo* 1914

14 Every reform movement has a lunatic fringe.
Theodore Roosevelt. Speech 1913

15 There are too many people trying to change this world who could not change a fuse.
Nicholas Shakespeare, The Times, Critic's Choice 4 Dec 1982

16 A reformer is a guy who rides through a sewer in a glass-bottomed boat.
James J. Walker, Mayor of New York, in a speech 1928

REGRET

17 Sighs for follys said and done / Twist our narrow days
W. H. Auden, FISH IN THE UNRUFFLED LAKE 1936

18 What I regret, on behalf of myself of long ago, is not the overweeningness, but the playing it safe.
Elizabeth Bowen. Quoted Reader's Digest, Nov 1946

19 *Victor:* It's easy enough to be sorry.
Elyot: On the contrary. I find it exceedingly difficult. I seldom regret anything. This is a very rare and notable exception, a sort of red letter day. We must all make the most of it.
Noël Coward, PRIVATE LIVES 1930

1 Only with beauty wake wild memories — /
Sorrow for where you are, for where you
would be.
Walter De La Mare, THE CAGE

2 Never regret and never look back. Regret is
an appalling waste of energy; you can't build
on it; it is only good for wallowing in.
Katherine Mansfield, BLISS 1920

3 Miss Otis regrets she is unable to lunch
today.
Cole Porter, first line of lyric

4 Regrets are idle, yet history is one long
regret. Everything might have turned out so
differently.
Charles Dudley Warner, MY SUMMER IN A
GARDEN

REINCARNATION

5 I hold that when a person dies / His soul
returns again to earth; / Arrayed in some
new flesh-disguise / Another mother gives
him birth / With sturdier limbs and brighter
brain / The old soul takes the roads again.
John Masefield, A CREED

6 Sex is one of the nine reasons for reincarna-
tion — the other eight are unimportant.
Henry Miller, BIG SIR AND THE ORANGES OF
HIERONYMUS BOSCH 1957

SIR JOHN REITH

7 Dante without the poetry, Irving without
the mystery, Mephistopheles without the
fun.
*Alan Dent's characterisation. Quoted James
Agate*, EGO 4 17 *Apr* 1939

REJECTION

8 In order to be rejected you must first be
considered.
*Rev. Jesse Jackson, Observer, Sayings of the
Week* 15 *Jul* 1984

9 'It's not twenty-four hours since she turned
me down.'
'Turned you down?'
'Like a bedspread. In this very garden.'
P. G. Wodehouse, RIGHT HO JEEVES

REJUVENATION

10 In Vienna you can see whole rows of
decrepit old rats carrying on like Tiller girls.
Noël Coward, PRIVATE LIVES 1930

RELATIVITY

11 When you are courting a nice girl an hour
seems like a second. When you sit on a
red-hot cinder a second seems like an hour.
That's relativity.
Albert Einstein. Quoted Ritchie Calder,
News Chronicle 14 *Mar* 1949

12 I believe my theory of relativity to be true.
But it will only be proved for certain in 1981,
when I am dead.
Albert Einstein. Quoted Edwin Miller,
EINSTEIN: A STUDY IN SIMPLICITY 1938

13 Going to work for a large company is like
getting on a train. Are you going sixty miles
an hour or is the train going sixty miles an
hour and you're just sitting still?
J. Paul Getty. Quoted Barbara Rowe, A
BOOK OF QUOTES

RELEVANCE

14 What does my hair-do have to do with my
husband's ability to be president?
*Jacqueline Kennedy. Quoted Barbara
Rowe*, BOOK OF QUOTES

RELIGION

15 He was of the faith chiefly in the sense that
the church he currently did not attend was
Catholic.
Kingsley Amis, ONE FAT ENGLISHMAN 1963

16 Religion is not proficiency in the fine art of
mystical knowledge, but just the love of God
and our neighbour.
Father Andrew, LIFE AND LETTERS

17 An American girl who spoke scoldingly of
the Ten Commandments said 'They don't
tell you what you ought to do and only put
ideas into your head.'
Herbert Henry Asquith Earl of Oxford

18 I'm a Communist by day and a Catholic as
soon as it gets dark.
Brendan Behan

1 The children of dogmatic atheists tend to become Wesleyan missionaries.
Gerald Brenan, THOUGHTS IN A DRY SEASON 1979

2 Every day people are straying away from the church and going back to God.
Lenny Bruce, THE ESSENTIAL LENNY BRUCE

3 A cosmic philosophy is not constructed to fit a man, a cosmic philosophy is constructed to fit a cosmos. A man can no more possess a private religion than he can possess a private sun or moon.
G. K. Chesterton, THE BOOK OF JOB 1929

4 In my religion there would be no exclusive doctrine; all would be love, poetry and doubt.
Cyril Connolly, THE UNQUIET GRAVE 1945

5 Science without religion is lame; religion without science is blind.
Albert Einstein. Quoted Reader's Digest, Nov 1973

6 If one purges Judaism of the Prophets and Christianity as Jesus Christ taught it of all subsequent additions, especially those of priests, one is left with a teaching which is capable of curing all the social ills of humanity.
Albert Einstein, THE WORLD AS I SEE IT 1934

7 To know that what is impenetrable to us really exists . . . is at the centre of true religiousness. In this sense, and in this sense only, I belong to the ranks of the devoutly religious men.
Albert Einstein, WHAT I BELIEVE

8 The whole religious complexion of the modern world is due to the absence from Jerusalem of a lunatic asylum.
Havelock Ellis, IMPRESSIONS AND COMMENTS

9 A refusal to come to an unjustified conclusion is an element of an honest man's religion.
Bergen Evans, THE NATURAL HISTORY OF NONSENSE

10 Religion is far more acute than science, and if it only added judgment to insight, would be the greatest thing in the world.
E. M. Forster, MAURICE

11 Ronnie approved of religion as long as it endorsed the National Anthem, but he objected when it attempted to influence his life.
E. M. Forster, A PASSAGE TO INDIA 1924

12 Religion is an attempt to get control over the sensory world . . . by means of the wish world which we have developed inside us as a result of biological and psychological necessities.
Sigmund Freud, LECTURES IN PSYCHOANALYSIS, *A Philosophy of Life* 1932

13 Religion is an illusion and it derives its strength from the fact that it falls in with our instinctual desires.
Ibid.

14 If the truth of religious doctrines is dependent on an inner experience that bears witness to that truth, what is one to make of the many people who do not have that experience?
Sigmund Freud, THE FUTURE OF AN ILLUSION

15 Religion is comparable to a childhood neurosis.
Ibid.

16 Religions revolve madly round sexual questions.
Rémy de Gourmont

17 Formal religion was organised for slaves; it offered them consolation which earth did not provide.
Elbert Hubbard, Philistine, Vol. 25

18 [My father] considered a walk among the mountains as the equivalent of church-going.
Aldous Huxley, BARREN LEAVES 1925

19 You never see animals going through the absurd and often horrible fooleries of magic and religion . . . It is the price [man] has to pay for being intelligent, but not, as yet, intelligent enough.
Aldous Huxley, BRIEF CANDLES

20 For English Catholics, sacraments are the psychological equivalent of tractors in Russia.
Aldous Huxley, EYELESS IN GAZA 1936

1 Nobody can have the consolations of religion or philosophy unless he has first experienced their desolations.
Aldous Huxley, THEME AND VARIATIONS, *Variations on a Baroque Tomb* 1950

2 Religion is caught, not taught.
W. R. Inge (Dean of St Pauls)

3 Religion is what the individual does with his own solitude. If you are never solitary you are never religious.
Ibid.

4 It is difficult to accept a position that gives only atheism the right of citizenship in public and social life while believers are, as though by principle, barely tolerated or are treated as second-class citizens.
Pope John Paul II, ENCYCLICAL: THE REDEEMER OF MAN

5 The idea of Christ as a political figure, a revolutionary, as the subversive man from Nazareth does not tally with the Church's catechesis.
Pope John Paul II during a visit to Mexico 1 *Feb* 1979

6 Among all my patients in the second half of life — that is to say over thirty-five — there has not been one whose problem in the last resort was not that of finding a religious outlook on life.
Carl Jung, MODERN MAN IN SEARCH OF HIS SOUL

7 Religion is the tendency to prefer God to the government, most commonly found in Communist countries.
Miles Kington, *The Times, A Guide to Real Meanings* 2 *Jul* 1982

8 Religion is the frozen thought of men, out of which they build temples.
Krishnamurti, Observer, Sayings of the Week 22 *Apr* 1928

9 Jehovah's Witnesses, awaiting the Last Day with the quiet kind of satisfaction that a man gets in a dry season when he knows his neighbour's house is not insured against fire.
Bernard Levin, THE PENDULUM YEARS 1976

10 'You must never forget, Laurie, that dissenters are often excellent Christian people. You must never be narrow minded.'

I promised that I never would.
'Though of course' my aunt added, 'you must always remember that *we* are always right.'
I promised that I always would.
Rose Macaulay, THE TOWERS OF TREBIZOND 1956

11 What mean and cruel things men do for the love of God.
W. Somerset Maugham, A WRITER'S NOTEBOOK 1945

12 Religion is always revolutionary, far more revolutionary than bread-and-butter philosophies.
Henry Miller, THE AIR CONDITIONED NIGHTMARE 1943

13 Of course Low Churches are very holy, but they do so treat God like their first cousin.
Nancy Mitford quoting her grandmother in a letter to Mark Ogilvie-Grant 30 *Dec* 1929

14 I want nothing to do with any religion concerned with keeping the masses satisfied to live in hunger, filth and ignorance. I want nothing to do with any order, religious or otherwise, which does not teach people that they are capable of becoming happier and more civilised.
Jawaharlal Nehru. Quoted Edgar Snow, JOURNEY TO THE BEGINNING

15 I've taken up the Bible again somewhat in the spirit of W. C. Fields — looking for loopholes.
David Niven. Quoted Observer 24 *Dec* 1978

16 You are not an agnostic, Paddy. You are just a fat slob who is too lazy to go to Mass.
Conor Cruise O'Brien, quoting an Irish parish priest, Observer 4 *Feb* 1979

17 We ought to have as great a regard for religion as we can, so as to keep it out of as many things as possible.
Sean O'Casey, THE PLOUGH AND THE STARS 1926

18 One cannot really be a Catholic and grown-up.
George Orwell, COLLECTED ESSAYS, *Manuscript Notebook* 1965

19 The truth of religion is in its ritual and the truth of dogma is in its poetry.
John Cowper Powys, THE COMPLEX VISION

1 A church which starves itself and its members in the contemplative life deserves whatever spiritual leanness it may experience.
Michael Ramsey, CANTERBURY PILGRIM

2 Religious terms towards the end of the book have been rearranged so that dissenters and nonconformists are no longer grouped with idolaters, fire-worshippers and other heathens.
Introduction to Everyman edition of
ROGET'S THESAURUS

3 I think the most important quality in a person concerned with religion is absolute devotion to truth.
Albert Schweitzer, OUT OF MY LIFE AND THOUGHT 1932

4 Good-natured unambitious men are cowards when they have no religion.
George Bernard Shaw, BACK TO METHUSELAH, *Preface* 1921

5 I am a sort of collector of religions, and the curious thing is I find I can believe in them all.
George Bernard Shaw, MAJOR BARBARA 1905

6 I judge the character of a man of the Church not by the reason they find for things, but by the things they find reasons for.
George Bernard Shaw, letter to William Temple, Archbishop of Canterbury

7 We must disentangle what is Christian from what is middle class.
Rev. Chris Smith. Quoted Alan Road, Observer Magazine 8 Mar 1974

8 Extreme happiness invites religion almost as much as extreme misery.
Dodie Smith, I CAPTURE THE CASTLE 1948

9 The one certain way for a woman to hold a man is to leave him for religion.
Muriel Spark, THE COMFORTERS 1957

10 I know that a community of God-seekers is a great shelter for man. But directly this grows into an Institution it is apt to give ready access to the Devil by its back door.
Rabindranath Tagore, LETTERS TO A FRIEND

11 Why do born-again people make you wish they had never been born in the first place?
Katherine Whitehorn, VIEW FROM A COLUMN 1981

12 I haven't been to mass for years. I've got every mortal sin on my conscience, but I know when I'm doing wrong. I'm still a Catholic.
Angus Wilson, THE WRONG SET

13 I would rather think of my religion as a gamble than think of it as an insurance policy.
Stephen Samuel Wise. Quoted Justin Wintle and Richard Kenin, DICTIONARY OF BIOGRAPHICAL QUOTATIONS.

REMEDY

14 There is no doubt that Jeeves' pick-me-up will produce immediate results in anything short of an Egyptian mummy.
P. G. Wodehouse, THE INIMITABLE JEEVES 1924

REMEMBRANCE

15 At the going down of the sun and in the morning we will remember them.
Laurence Binyon, FOR THE FALLEN

16 Rejoice ye dead, where'er your spirits dwell / Rejoice that yet on earth your fame is bright / And that your names, remembered day and night / Live on the lips of those who love you well.
Robert Bridges, ODE TO MUSIC

17 Who will remember, passing through this gate / The unheroic dead who fed the guns? / Who shall absolve the foulness of their fate — / Those doomed, conscripted, unvictorious ones?
Siegfried Sassoon, ON PASSING THE NEW MENIN GATE 1918

REMORSE

18 Chronic remorse is a most undesirable sentiment . . . Rolling in the muck is not the best way of getting clean.
Aldous Huxley, BRAVE NEW WORLD 1932

19 Remorse is pride's *ersatz* for repentance.
Aldous Huxley, TIME MUST HAVE A STOP 1944

20 Remorse is impotence, it will sin again. Only repentance is strong, it can end everything.
Henry Miller, THE WISDOM OF THE HEART 1941

1 There are people who are very resourceful /
At being remorseful / And who apparently
feel the best way to make friends / Is to do
something terrible and then make amends.
Ogden Nash, MANY LONG YEARS AGO,
Hearts of Gold 1945

REPENTANCE

2 American people like to have you repent,
then they are generous.
Will Rogers, THE ILLITERATE DIGEST, *One
Oil Lawyer per Barrel* 1924

REPETITION

3 Repetition does not transform a lie into a
truth.
*Franklin D. Roosevelt, Radio Fireside
Chat 26 Oct* 1939

4 Repetition is the only form of permanence
that nature can achieve.
George Santayana, SOLILOQUIES IN
ENGLAND, *A version From Platonism* 1922

5 After people have repeated a phrase a great
many times they begin to realise it has
meaning and may even be true.
H. G. Wells, THE HAPPY JOURNEY 1946

6 Repetition is the death of art.
A. N. Whitehead, DIALOGUES 1953

REPRESSION

7 Stalin when he killed off his egg-heads like
Bukharin, was only establishing a sound and
stable government. In this country the
victims would have been given the OM and
sent to the House of Lords, but the end
result would have been the same.
Malcolm Muggeridge, TREAD SOFTLY FOR
YOU TREAD ON MY JOKES 1966

REPRISAL

8 When Lady Cunard was displeased by a
horse introduced into a picture she had
commissioned, Marie Laurencin painted
her on a camel.
René Gimpel, DIARY OF AN ART DEALER

REPUTATION

9 The reputation through a thousand years
may depend upon the conduct through a
single moment.
Ernest Bramah, KAI LUNG UNROLLS HIS
MAT 1928

10 The easiest way to get a reputation is to go
outside the fold, shout around for a few
years as a violent atheist or a dangerous
radical and then crawl back to shelter.
F. Scott Fitzgerald, NOTEBOOKS

11 Worldly wisdom teaches us that it is better
for the reputation that one should fail
conventionally than to succeed unconven-
tionally.
J. M. Keynes, GENERAL THEORY OF
EMPLOYMENT 1936

12 The Englishman wants to be recognised as a
gentleman, or as some other suitable species
of human being; the American wants to be
considered a good guy.
Louis Kronenberger, COMPANY
MANNERS 1954

13 My reputation grew with every failure.
*George Bernard Shaw of his unsuccessful
early novels. Quoted Hesketh Pearson,*
BERNARD SHAW 1942

RESEARCH

14 Basic research is what I am doing when I
don't know what I am doing.
Wernher von Braun. Quoted Barbara Rowe,
BOOK OF QUOTES

15 There is only one proved method of assisting
the advancement of pure science — that of
picking men of genius, backing them heavi-
ly, and leaving them to direct themselves.
*J. B. Conant, letter to New York Times 13
Aug* 1945

16 In science the credit goes to the man who
convinces the world not to the man to whom
the idea first occurred.
*Sir Francis Darwin. Galton Lecture to
Eugenics Society* 1914

17 When Dr Watson watches rats in mazes,
what he knows, apart from difficult infer-
ences, are certain events in himself.
Sir Arthur Eddington, SCIENCE AND THE
UNSEEN WORLD

1 It is a very great mistake to think that the enjoyment of seeing and searching can be promoted by means of coercion and a sense of duty.
Albert Einstein, AUTOBIOGRAPHY

2 I want to know how God created the world. I'm not interested in this or that phenomenon. I want to know his thoughts, the rest are details.
Albert Einstein. Quoted Ronald W. Clark, EINSTEIN: HIS LIFE AND TIMES

3 The cosmic religious experience is the strongest and noblest driving force behind scientific research.
Albert Einstein. Quoted in an obituary 19 Apr 1955

4 It is a good morning exercise for a research scientist to discard a pet hypothesis every day before breakfast. It keeps him young.
Konrad Lorenz, ON AGGRESSION

RESPECT

5 His indolence was qualified with enough basic bad temper to ensure the respect of those about him.
Evelyn Waugh, PUT OUT MORE FLAGS 1942

RESPECTABILITY

6 A respectable girl is one who doesn't want to go to bed with anyone.
Mervyn Griffith-Jones during the Stephen Ward trial

7 Men have to do some awfully mean things to keep up their respectability.
George Bernard Shaw, FANNY'S FIRST PLAY 1912

8 The more things a man is ashamed of, the more respectable he is.
George Bernard Shaw, MAN AND SUPERMAN 1905

RESPONSIBILITY

9 We take no responsibility, like the owners of umbrella stands in hotels.
Malcolm Bradbury, STEPPING WESTWARD

10 A wrong decision can make me very miserable. But I have trust in God. If you have this trust you don't have to worry, as you don't have sole responsibility.
Lord Denning, longest serving judge, on retiring at the age of 83, *Sep* 1982

11 Man's responsibility increases as that of God's decreases.
André Gide, JOURNALS 27 *Sep* 1940

12 No snowflake in an avalanche ever feels responsible.
Stanislaw Lec, MORE UNKEMPT THOUGHTS 1962

13 Life has no meaning except in terms of responsibility.
Reinhold Neibuhr, FAITH AND HISTORY

14 To be a man is, precisely, to be responsible.
Antoine de Saint-Exupéry, WIND, SAND AND STARS 1939

15 The buck stops here.
Harry S Truman, sign on his presidential desk

16 Every man who takes office in Washington either grows or swells, and when I give a man office I watch him carefully to see whether he is growing or swelling.
Woodrow Wilson. Speech 15 *May* 1916

RESURRECTION

17 . . . those coming out of church / Spread all over the churchyard. They scan / The crowd, recognise, smile and shake hands / By each tombstone a well-dressed person stands / It looks just like the / Resurrection.
Patricia Beer, CONCERT AT LONG MELFORD CHURCH

18 I think the resurrection of the body, unless much improved in construction, a mistake.
Evelyn Underhill, LETTERS

RETALIATION

19 If you kick a man he kicks you back again. Therefore never be too eager to engage in combat.
Bertolt Brecht, THE THREEPENNY OPERA 1928

327

1 If you start throwing hedgehogs under me I shall throw two porcupines under you.
Nikita Khrushchev. Quoted Observer 10 *Nov* 1963

RETICENCE

2 He [Alexander of Tunis] believed that reticence increases a soldier's authority. It was his nature. A gentleman does not utter everything he thinks.
Harold Nicolson, ALEX: THE LIFE OF FIELD MARSHAL EARL ALEXANDER OF TUNIS

RETIREMENT

3 We mean to live quietly, seeing only the King and a few friends.
Margot Asquith. Quoted Lord David Cecil, Observer, Staying With Margot 20 *Dec* 1981

4 I must adjust myself to private life and try to grow old gracefully without being a nuisance to anyone.
Stanley Baldwin. Speech to Federation of British Industries 13 *Apr* 1937

5 Lady Bancroft and I have eighty thousand golden reasons for retiring and every one lodged in the bank.
Squire Bancroft, AUTOBIOGRAPHY

6 Retirement at sixty-five is ridiculous. When I was sixty-five I still had pimples.
George Burns. Quoted Barbara Rowe, A BOOK OF QUOTES

7 To forge a fixed and arbitrary rule in terms of years as the limit of a man's usefulness of human service would only be to behead a large portion of the world's intellectual and moral leadership and thereby impoverish mankind.
Dr Nicholas Murray Butler. Address to Columbia University 1 *Jun* 1937

8 Queen Victoria in her eighties was more known, more revered and a more important part of the life of the country than she had ever been. Retirement, for a monarch, is not a good idea.
Charles, Prince of Wales. Speech 1974

9 I want to retire at 50. I want to play cricket in the summer and geriatric football in the winter, and sing in the choir.
Neil Kinnock MP, The Times 28 *Jul* 1980

10 Have you ever been out for a late autumn walk in the closing part of the afternoon and suddenly looked up to realise that the leaves have practically all gone? And the sun has set and the day gone before you knew it — and with that a cold wind blows across the landscape? That's retirement.
Stephen Leacock, TOO MUCH COLLEGE

11 Few men of action have been able to make a graceful exit at the appropriate time.
Malcolm Muggeridge, CHRONICLES OF WASTED TIME 1972

12 We know how to make our predecessors retire. When it comes to forcing us to retire our successors must find some method of their own.
C. Northcote Parkinson, PARKINSON'S LAW 1957

RETRIBUTION

13 Don't wait for the Last Judgement. It takes place every day.
Albert Camus, THE FALL 1956

REVENGE

14 She wrote a polite refusal to the wedding to which she had not been asked on the grounds that she had a prior engagement, and sent a richly wrapped parcel bearing the name of a top people's shop. When opened it was found to contain a can of a well-known deodorant.
Douglas Sutherland, THE ENGLISH GENTLEMAN'S WIFE 1979

REVOLUTION

15 All modern revolutions have ended in a reinforcement of the power of the State.
Albert Camus, THE REBEL 1951

16 The slave begins by demanding justice and ends by wanting to wear a crown. He must be dominated in his turn.
Ibid.

17 The overwhelming pressure of mediocrity, sluggish and indomitable as a glacier, will mitigate the most violent, and depress the most exalted revolution.
T. S. Eliot, THE IDEA OF A CHRISTIAN SOCIETY 1939

1 The violence of revolution is the violence of men who charge into a vacuum.
J. K. Galbraith, THE AGE OF UNCERTAINTY 1977

2 All successful revolutions are the kicking in of a rotten door.
Ibid.

3 A non-violent revolution is not a programme of seizure of power. It is a programme of transformation of relationships, ending in a peaceful transfer of power.
Mahatma Gandhi, NON-VIOLENCE IN PEACE AND WAR 1948

4 It wasn't a revolution that would have led anywhere. Kerensky's rather than Lenin's.
Bamber Gascoigne, FROM FRINGE TO FLYING CIRCUS, *Preface* 1980

5 Though a revolution may call itself *national* it always works the victory of a single party.
André Gide, JOURNALS 17 *Oct* 1941

6 We used to think that revolutions are the cause of change. Actually it is the other way round; change prepares the ground for revolution.
Eric Hoffer, THE TEMPER OF OUR TIME, *A Time of Juveniles* 1967

7 Revolution is delightful in the preliminary stages. So long as it's a question of getting rid of the people at the top.
Aldous Huxley, EYELESS IN GAZA 1936

8 Every revolution evaporates, leaving behind only the slime of a new bureaucracy.
Franz Kafka

9 It has all been tried before. The older Puritans took away the maypoles and the mince pies, but they did not bring in the millennium, they only brought in the Restoration.
C. S. Lewis, A PREFACE TO PARADISE LOST, *being the Ballard Matthews Lectures, delivered at University College, North Wales* 1941

10 'There won't be any revolution in America,' said Isodore. 'The people are too clean. They spend all their time changing their shirts and washing themselves. You can't feel fierce and revolutionary in a bathroom.'
Eric Linklater, JUAN IN AMERICA 1931

11 A revolution only remains victorious through methods which are alien to those who made it.
André Malraux. Quoted Fitzroy McLean, BACK TO BOKHARA

12 Revolution is the proper occupation of the masses.
Mao Tse Tung. Quoted Dennis Bloodworth, THE MESSIAH AND THE MANDARINS 1983

13 It was not Napoleon who made the French Revolution; but Rousseau, a crazy Swiss who took to knitting and dressing up in Armenian costume, had a lot to do with it.
Malcolm Muggeridge, TREAD SOFTLY FOR YOU TREAD ON MY JOKES 1966

14 Those countries which choose tyrannies for themselves must be left to get on with it. They created their revolutions.
V. S. Naipaul, Radio Times 24 *Mar* 1979

15 A revolution only lasts fifteen years, a period which coincides with the effectiveness of a generation.
José Ortega y Gasset, THE REVOLT OF THE MASSES 1930

16 The revolution eats its own. Capitalism re-creates itself.
Mordecai Richter, COCKSURE

17 You can jail a revolutionary but you cannot jail the revolution.
Bobby Seale, Chairman of the Black Panthers

18 Hot water is the revolutionist's element. You clean men as you clean milk-pans, by scalding them.
George Bernard Shaw, MAN AND SUPERMAN 1905

19 The export of revolution is nonsense. Every country makes its own revolution if it wants to, and if it does not want to there will be no revolution.
Joseph Stalin, in an interview 1936

20 Revolution is a trivial shift in the emphasis of suffering.
Tom Stoppard, Quoted Barbara Rowe, A BOOK OF QUOTES

21 Insurrection is an art, and like all arts it has its laws.
Leon Trotsky, HISTORY OF THE RUSSIAN REVOLUTION

1 Power fell into the street.
Leon Trotsky, MY LIFE

RHYME

2 'I have spent uncomfortable week-ends looking for a rhyme for Balenciaga.'
I looked a question.
'Forsyte Saga' he [Noel Coward] said.
William Marchant, THE PRIVILEGE OF HIS COMPANY 1981

3 I can think of no rhyme to Stella but umbrella.
George Bernard Shaw, letter to Mrs Pat Campbell

RISK

4 Take calculated risks. That is quite different from being rash.
Gen. George Smith Patton, letter to Cadet G. S. Patton IV 6 Jun 1944

5 The only way to be absolutely safe is never to try anything for the first time.
Dr Magnus Pyke, BBC Radio 17 Mar 1979

RIVER

6 I do not know much about gods, but I / Think that the river / Is a strong brown god.
T. S. Eliot, FOUR QUARTETS, *The Dry Salvages 1941*

7 Ol' man river, dat ol' man river / He must know sumpen but don't say nothin' / He just keeps rollin', he just keeps on rollin' along.
Oscar Hammerstein II, OL' MAN RIVER 1927

8 Riveruns, past Eve and Adam's, from swerve of shore to bend of bay, brings us by a commodius vicus of recirculation back to Howth Castle and Environs.
James Joyce, FINNEGANS WAKE, *opening words 1939*

ROMANCE

9 Do I remember when I first met your mother, you ask? Ah, as if I could ever forget. A beautiful June night, a garden party, a full moon, Japanese lanterns glimmering softly in the trees, a Strauss waltz playing. Then, to make the evening complete, this sublime creature appeared — no wait a minute, that was the night I met Alice Fletcher. Let me see, where did I first meet your mother?
Father to child, cartoon caption by Follette, Saturday Evening Post Feb 1950

10 Is not this the true romantic feeling — not to desire to escape life, but to prevent life from escaping you?
Thomas Wolfe. Quoted Andrew Turnbull, THOMAS WOLFE

ROOM

11 A room is a place where you hide from the wolves outside and that's all any room is.
Jean Rhys, GOOD MORNING, MIDNIGHT 1939

FRANKLIN D. ROOSEVELT

12 The best newspaperman who has ever been President of the United States.
Heywood Brown. Quoted D. Boorstin, THE IMAGE

13 Restless and mercurial in his thinking, a connoisseur of theories but impatient with people who took theories seriously, he trusted no system except the system of endless experimentation.
Earl Goldman, RENDEZVOUS WITH DESTINY

14 A chameleon on plaid.
Herbert Hoover. Quoted James MacGregor Burns, ROOSEVELT: THE LION AND THE FOX

15 He [Roosevelt] would rather follow public opinion than lead it.
Harry Hopkins. Quoted G. Wolfskill and J. A. Hudson, ALL BUT THE PEOPLE: F. D. ROOSEVELT AND HIS CRITICS

16 The man who started more creations than were ever begun since Genesis — and finished none.
Hugh Johnson. Ibid.

17 If he became convinced tomorrow that coming out for cannibalism would get him the votes he so sorely needs, he would begin fattening a missionary on the White House backyard come Wednesday.
H. L. Mencken, FRANKLIN D. ROOSEVELT, A PROFILE *(ed. W. E. Leuchtenburg)*

ROYALTY

1 The Royal Family are as complicated a thesis as only a sophisticated nation like Great Britain could invent. They are as full of paradoxes as cricket. Only the British really understand them and then more by instinct than by rule of law.
Anon. Topic Magazine. Quoted Noël St George, ROYAL QUOTES

2 The British Royal Family is an adman's dream, a unique selling proposition with a pliable market strongly predisposed towards the product.
Andrew Duncan, THE REALITY OF MONARCHY

3 Royalty must think the whole country always smells of fresh paint.
Elizabeth Dunn, Sunday Times

4 The absurd thing about being a duke or a prince is that you are a professional ignoramus.
Duke of Gloucester. Speech, Jun 1984

5 Like Royalty, I simply do not complain.
Mandy Rice-Davies, MANDY 1980

RUDENESS

6 'You are extremely rude, young man.'
'As a matter of fact, we both are; the only difference being that I am trying to be, and you can't help it.'
Lord Birkenhead (F. E. Smith) to Judge Willis. Quoted by his son and biographer, The Second Lord Birkenhead

7 It's not a slam at *you* when people are rude — it's a slam at the people they've met before.
F. Scott Fitzgerald, THE LAST TYCOON 1941

BERTRAND RUSSELL

8 I told D. H. Lawrence how enchanted I had been by the lucidity, the suppleness and pliability of Bertrand Russell's mind. He sniffed. 'Have you ever seen him in a bathing dress?' he asked 'Poor Bertie Russell! He is all Disembodied Mind.'
William Gerhardie, MEMOIRS OF A POLYGLOT

9 To me he was exactly like the mad hatter.
Dora Russell, THE TAMARISK TREE VOL 3 1985

RUSSIA

10 Don't you forget what's divine in the Russian soul — and that's resignation.
Joseph Conrad, UNDER WESTERN EYES 1911

11 One Russian is an anarchist / Two Russians are a chess game / Three Russians are a revolution / Four Russians are the Budapest String Quartet.
Jascha Heifetz. Quoted Nat Shapiro, ENCYCLOPEDIA OF QUOTATIONS ABOUT MUSIC

12 I have been there. It's a paradise. No ladies and gentlemen.
George Bernard Shaw, letter to Alfred Douglas

13 I resigned after four premierships in the week I became 60. In Moscow that would be the age of a ministerial trainee.
Harold Wilson

RUTHLESSNESS

14 You can only help one of your luckless brothers / By trampling down a dozen others.
Bertolt Brecht, THE GOOD WOMAN OF SETZUAN 1940

15 Never fight fair with a stranger, boy. You'll never get out the jungle that way.
Arthur Miller, DEATH OF A SALESMAN 1947

S

SACRIFICE

1 Sacrificers are not the ones to pity, the ones to pity are those they sacrifice.
Elizabeth Bowen, THE DEATH OF THE HEART 1938

2 No sacrifice is worth the name unless it is a joy. Sacrifice and a long face go ill together.
Mahatma Gandhi

3 If a man hasn't discovered something that he would die for, he isn't fit to live.
Martin Luther King. Speech, Detroit 23 Jun 1963

4 Too long a sacrifice / Can make a stone of the heart.
W. B. Yeats, EASTER 1916

SADNESS

5 Sadness is almost never anything but a form of fatigue.
André Gide, JOURNALS 1922

6 Sadness is a communicable disease.
Martha Graham. Quoted Robin Stringer, Daily Telegraph 23 Jul 1979

SAINT

7 Saintliness is also a temptation.
Jean Anouilh, BECKET 1959

8 *Saint, n.* a dead sinner, revised and edited.
Ambrose Bierce, THE DEVIL'S DICTIONARY 1906

9 *More:* You are either idiots or children.
Chapuys: Or saints, my lord.
Robert Bolt, A MAN FOR ALL SEASONS 1961

10 Can one be a saint if God does not exist? That is the only concrete problem I know of today.
Albert Camus, THE PLAGUE 1947

11 It is easier to make a saint out of a libertine than out of a prig.
George Santayana, THE LIFE OF REASON 1905

12 I don't believe in God, but I do believe in his saints.
Edith Wharton. Quoted Percy Lubbock, PORTRAIT OF EDITH WHARTON

SALESMANSHIP

13 He's a man way out there in the blue, riding on a smile and a shoeshine.
Arthur Miller, DEATH OF A SALESMAN 1949

14 A salesman is got to dream, boy. It comes with the territory.
Ibid.

SALVATION

15 Human salvation lies in the hands of the creatively maladjusted.
Martin Luther King, STRENGTH TO LOVE 1963

16 I always claim the mission workers came out too early to catch any sinners on this part of Broadway. At such an hour the sinners are in bed resting up from their sinning of the night before, so they will be in good shape for more sinning a little later on.
Damon Runyon, GUYS AND DOLLS 1932

17 Mrs Ape, as was her invariable rule, took round the hat and collected nearly two pounds. 'Salvation doesn't do them the same good if they think it's free' was her favourite axiom.
Evelyn Waugh, VILE BODIES 1930

SANCTIMONIOUSNESS

1 Sophia wished that Florence would not talk
about the Almighty as if his real name was
Godfrey, and God was just Florence's
nickname for him.
Nancy Mitford, PIGEON PIE

SAUSAGE

2 Breadcrumbs in battledress.
Tommy Handley, BBC Radio, ITMA 1942

DOROTHY L. SAYERS

3 An enormously definite person.
John Gielgud. Quoted BBC Radio 4 31 *Jan*
1982

SCEPTICISM

4 She believed in nothing; only her scepticism
kept her from being an atheist.
Jean-Paul Sartre, WORDS

SCHIZOPHRENIA

5 Schizophrenic behaviour is a special
strategy that a person invents in order to live
in an unlivable situation.
R. D. Laing, THE POLITICS OF EXPERIENCE

SCHOOL

6 The dread of beatings, / Dread of Being
Late / And greatest dread of all, the dread of
games.
Sir John Betjeman, SUMMONED BY
BELLS 1960

7 Headmasters have powers at their disposal
with which Prime Ministers have never yet
been invested.
Winston Churchill, MY EARLY LIFE 1930

8 When I was a boy at school I never minded
the lessons. I just resented having to work
terribly hard at playing.
John Mortimer, A VOYAGE ROUND MY
FATHER

9 There is nothing on earth intended for
innocent people so horrible as a school. It is
in some respects more cruel than a prison. In
a prison, for example, you are not forced to
read books written by the warders and the
governor.
George Bernard Shaw, PARENTS AND
CHILDREN

10 School is where you go between when your
parents can't take you and industry can't
take you.
John Updike, THE CENTAUR 1963

11 We class schools, you see, into four grades;
Leading School, First-Rate School, Good
School, and School.
Evelyn Waugh, DECLINE AND FALL 1928

SCHOOLTEACHER

12 Whenever I look in the glass or see a
photograph of myself, I am reminded of
Petrarch's simple statement 'Nothing is
more hideous than an old schoolmaster'!
G. W. Lyttelton, THE LYTTELTON HART-
DAVIS LETTERS 11 *Apr* 1956

13 Every schoolmaster after the age of 49 is
inclined to flatulence, is apt to swallow
frequently, and to puff.
Harold Nicolson, THE OLD SCHOOL

14 The schoolteacher is certainly underpaid as
a child minder, but ludicrously overpaid as a
teacher.
*John Osborne, Observer, Sayings of the
Week* 21 *Jul* 1985

15 I expect you'll be becoming a schoolmaster,
sir. That's what most of the young gentlemen does, sir, that gets sent down for
indecent behaviour.
Evelyn Waugh, DECLINE AND FALL 1928

16 Assistant masters came and went. Some
liked little boys too little and some too
much.
Evelyn Waugh, A LITTLE LEARNING

SCIENCE

17 When I find myself in the company of
scientists I feel like a shabby curate who has
strayed by mistake into a drawing-room full
of dukes.
W. H. Auden, THE DYER'S HAND 1962

333

1 And the continuity of our science has not been affected by all these turbulent happenings, as the older theories have always been included as limiting cases in the new ones.
Max Born, PHYSICS IN THE LAST FIFTY YEARS 1951

2 That is the essence of science; ask an impertinent question and you are on the way to a pertinent answer.
J. Bronowski, THE ASCENT OF MAN 1973

3 When a distinguished elderly scientist says something is possible, he is probably right; when he says something is impossible he is probably wrong.
Arthur C. Clarke

4 Man is slightly nearer to the atom than the stars. From his central position he can survey the grandest works of Nature with the astronomer, or the minutest works with the physicist.
Sir Arthur Eddington, STARS AND ATOMS

5 The whole of science is nothing more than a refinement of everyday thinking.
Albert Einstein, OUT OF MY LATER YEARS

6 Science has 'explained' nothing; the more we know the more fantastic the world becomes and the profounder the surrounding darkness.
Aldous Huxley, VIEWS OF HOLLAND

7 The wallpaper with which the men of science have covered the world of reality is falling to tatters.
Henry Miller, TROPIC OF CANCER 1934

8 Science has replaced the church as the constitutional bedfellow of the State. Our passive acceptance of the admonitions of anyone claiming scientific status mirrors the servility of medieval peasants towards anyone claiming divine authority.
John Naughton, Observer, The Menace of Expertise 8 Apr 1979

9 Science may be described as the art of systematic over-simplification.
Karl Popper, Observer, Sayings of the Week 1 Aug 1982

10 Science may well be converging ultimately to a unique truth.
H. R. Post, Stud. Hist. Phil. Sci. 2 (1971)

11 Science in itself appears to be neutral. It increases men's power whether for good or evil. An appreciation of the ends of life is something that must be superadded to science if it is to bring happiness.
Bertrand Russell, Letter to W. W. Norton 27 Jan 1931

12 A good scientific theory should be explicable to a barmaid.
Ernest Rutherford. Quoted Ronald W. Clark, THE GREATEST POWER ON EARTH

13 Classical physics has been superseded by quantum theory: quantum theory is verified by experiments. Experiments must be described in terms of classical physics.
C. F. von Weizsäcker

14 If we could all agree where science was going, everything would be solved and we would have no recourse but to be engineers or doctors.
Maurice Wilkins. Quoted James D. Watson, THE DOUBLE HELIX

SCOT

15 Join a Highland regiment, me boy. The kilt is an unrivalled garment for fornication and diarrhoea.
John Masters, BUGLES AND A TIGER

16 Is anything worn beneath the kilt? No, it's all in perfect working order.
Spike Milligan, THE GREAT MCGONAGALL SCRAPBOOK

17 It is never difficult to distinguish between a Scotsman with a grievance and a ray of sunshine.
P. G. Wodehouse. Quoted R. Usborne, WODEHOUSE AT WORK 1961

SCULPTURE

18 A lot was lost when colour was abandoned in sculpture. It's a lovely sensation painting on terra-cotta and no one has done it for 600 years.
Quentin Bell in an interview with Sarah Howell, Observer Magazine 18 Mar 1979

19 I always liked big women. I suppose I was meant to be a sculptor.
Joyce Cary, THE HORSE'S MOUTH 1944

1 I'm having a bust made of my wife's hands.
Sam Goldwyn. Quoted Alva Johnson, THE
GREAT GOLDWYN

SEA

2 I've never seen the point of the sea, except
where it meets the land. The shore has
point. The sea has none.
Alan Bennett, THE OLD COUNTRY

3 There is nothing more enticing, disenchant-
ing and enslaving, than the life of the sea.
Joseph Conrad, LORD JIM 1900

4 The sea has never been friendly to man. At
most it has been the accomplice of human
restlessness.
Joseph Conrad, THE MIRROR OF THE
SEA 1906

5 The sea never changes and its works, for all
the talk of men, are wrapped in mystery.
Joseph Conrad, TYPHOON 1903

6 The snotgreen sea. The scrotumtightening
sea.
James Joyce, ULYSSES

7 The sea hates a coward.
Eugene O'Neill, MOURNING BECOMES
ELECTRA 1931

8 A man who is not afraid of the sea will soon
be drowned.
J. M. Synge, THE ARAN ISLANDS 1907

9 The sloe-black, slow black, crow black,
fishing-boat bobbing sea.
Dylan Thomas, UNDER MILK WOOD 1954

SEASIDE

10 There's sand in the porridge and sand in the
bed / And if this is pleasure we'd rather be
dead.
Noël Coward, THE ENGLISH LIDO

SECRET

11 I have other irons in the fire, but I'm keeping
them close to my chest.
*John Bond, on leaving Manchester City FC
as manager* 1983

12 There are no secrets except the secrets that
keep themselves.
George Bernard Shaw, BACK TO
METHUSELAH 1922

SEDUCTION

13 Older women are best because they always
think they may be doing it for the last time.
*Ian Fleming, from his private notebooks.
Quoted John Pearson,* LIFE OF IAN
FLEMING 1966

14 Candy / Is dandy / But liquor / Is quicker.
Ogden Nash, VERSUS, *Reflections on Ice-
Breaking* 1949

15 Men seldom make passes / At girls who
wear glasses / But a girl on a sofa / Is easily
won ofa.
Dorothy Parker, ENOUGH ROPE 1927

SEDUCTIVENESS

16 When she raises her eyelids it's as if she were
taking off all her clothes.
Colette, CLAUDINE AND ANNIE

SELF-INDULGENCE

17 My problem lies in reconciling my gross
habits with my net income.
Errol Flynn. Quoted Jane Mercer, GREAT
LOVERS OF THE MOVIES

SELF-RESPECT

18 Self-respect — the secure feeling that no
one, as yet, is suspicious.
H. L. Mencken, A MENCKEN
CHRESTOMATHY 1949

SELF-SACRIFICE

19 Self-sacrifice enables us to sacrifice / Other
people without blushing.
George Bernard Shaw, MAN AND
SUPERMAN 1905

SENTIMENTALITY

1 Sentimentality is the emotional promiscuity of those who have no sentiment.
Norman Mailer, CANNIBALS AND CHRISTIANS, *Lambs* 1966

SERVANT

2 There are only two kinds of people in the world. Those who are nice to their servants and those who aren't.
Duke of Argyll. Quoted Art Buchwald, I CHOSE CAVIAR

3 His lordship may compel us to be equal upstairs, but there will never be equality in the servants' hall.
J. M. Barrie, THE ADMIRABLE CRICHTON 1902

4 Servants should not be ill. We have quite enough illnesses of our own without them adding to the symptoms.
Lady Diana Cooper. Quoted Philip Ziegler, DIANA COOPER

5 I am aware of the damp souls of housemaids / Sprouting despondently at area gates.
T. S. Eliot, MORNING AT THE WINDOW 1917

6 He was caught / Red-handed with the silver and his Grace / Being short of staff at the time asked him to stay / And clean it.
Christopher Fry, VENUS OBSERVED 1950

7 Servants must not be spoiled.
Aldous Huxley, VULGARITY IN LITERATURE

8 On a raw Wednesday morning, in a few ill-chosen words, she told the cook that she drank. She remembered the scene afterwards as vividly as though it had been painted in her mind by Abbey. The cook was a good cook, as cooks go; and as cooks go she went.
Saki, REGINALD ON BESETTING SINS 1901

9 Nannies never retire but continue to live, long after their charges have married and had children of their own, in 'nanny's room'. There they sit all day long, surrounded by eyeless teddy bears and broken toys, knitting endless socks and sewing on trouser buttons.
Douglas Sutherland, THE ENGLISH GENTLEMAN 1978

SEX

10 Is sex dirty? Only when it is being done right.
Woody Allen, ALL YOU'VE EVER WANTED TO KNOW ABOUT SEX *(film)*

11 In the old days a lot of people, men as well as women, didn't quite know what to expect from sex so they didn't worry when it didn't work too well
Kingsley Amis, JAKE'S THING

12 It isn't the ecstatic leap across that I deplore, it's the weary trudge home.
Anon, comment on single beds

13 He said it was artificial respiration but now I find I'm to have his child.
Anthony Burgess, INSIDE MR ENDERBY 1966

14 There is more difference within the sexes than between them.
Ivy Compton-Burnett, MOTHER AND SON 1955

15 It would take a far more concentrated woman than Amanda to be unfaithful every five minutes.
Noël Coward, PRIVATE LIVES 1930

16 What happens is that, as with drugs, one needs a stronger shot each time, and women are just women. The consumption of one woman is the consumption of all. You can't double the dose.
Ian Fleming. Quoted John Pearson, LIFE OF IAN FLEMING 1960

17 Life to him was identified with the intimate charm of the feminine form in its greatest variety: and so he spent his days in quest of the red light.
William Gerhardie, THE POLYGLOTS 1925

18 Sex is bad for one — but it's good for two.
Graffito. Quoted BBC Radio 4, *Quote Unquote*

19 To succeed with the opposite sex, tell her you're impotent. She can't wait to disprove it.
Cary Grant, at the age of 72

20 Mr Mercaptan went on to preach a brilliant sermon on that melancholy sexual perversion known as continence.
Aldous Huxley, ANTIC HAY 1923

1 There is no more immorality in the enjoy-
ment of sexual intercourse than in the
enjoyment of mince pies.
*Letter from Dr George Jones to Marie
Stopes. Quoted Ruth Hall,* DEAR DR STOPES:
SEX IN THE 1920s 1978

2 I don't see so much of Alfred any more since
he got so interested in sex.
Mrs Alfred Kinsey, wife of the author of THE
KINSEY REPORT ON SEXUAL BEHAVIOUR

3 No sex without responsibility.
Lord Longford, Observer 3 *May* 1964

4 How alike are the groans of love to those of
the dying.
Malcolm Lowry, UNDER THE
VOLCANO 1947

5 We have long passed the Victorian Era
when asterisks were followed after a certain
interval by a baby.
W. Somerset Maugham, THE CONSTANT
WIFE 1926

6 Continental people have sex-life; the English have hot-water bottles.
George Mikes, HOW TO BE AN ALIEN 1946

7 Sex is one of the nine reasons for reincarna-
tion. The other eight aren't important.
Henry Miller, BIG SIR AND THE ORANGES OF
HIERONYMUS BOSCH 1957

8 When she saw the sign 'Members Only' she
thought of him.
Spike Milligan, PUCKOON

9 I thought oral contraception was when you
talked your way out of it.
*Overheard. Quoted Peterborough, Daily
Telegraph* 12 *Feb* 1970

10 I've been the whole hog plenty of times.
Sometimes you can be happy and not go the
whole hog. Now and again you can be happy
without going any hog.
Harold Pinter, HOMECOMING 1965

11 On a sofa upholstered in panther skin /
Mona did researches in original sin.
William Plomer, MEWS FLAT MONA

12 There is nothing like desire for preventing
the thing one says from bearing any
resemblance to what one has in mind.
Marcel Proust, REMEMBRANCE OF THINGS
PAST 1913—1927

13 The Christian view of sex is that it is, indeed,
a form of holy communion.
*John Robinson (Bishop of Woolwich),
giving evidence for the defence in the* LADY
CHATTERLEY'S LOVER *case* 1960

14 Even people who think themselves quite
advanced believe that only the sexually
starved can exert a wholesome moral
influence.
Bertrand Russell in a letter to A. S. Neill
31 *Jan* 1931

15 I keep making up these sex rules for myself
and then I break them right away.
J. D. Salinger, THE CATCHER IN THE
RYE 1951

16 All this fuss about sleeping together. For
physical pleasure I'd sooner go to my dentist
any day.
Evelyn Waugh, VILE BODIES 1930

17 Being a sex symbol is rather like being a
convict.
Raquel Welch. Quoted Observer 25 *Feb* 1979

18 It's not the men in my life that count; it's the
life in my men.
Mae West

SHARK

19 Oh the shark has pretty teeth dear / And he
shows them pearly white.
Bertolt Brecht, THE THREEPENNY OPERA,
The Ballad of Mack the Knife 1928

GEORGE BERNARD SHAW

20 Shaw was charming with one person, fidgety
with two, and stood on his head with four.
Stanley Baldwin. Quoted G. W. Lyttelton,
THE LYTTELTON HART-DAVIS LETTERS 18
Jul 1956

21 I really enjoy only his stage directions; the
dialogue is vortical, and, I find, fatiguing. It
is like being harangued . . . He uses the
English language like a truncheon.
Max Beerbohm. Quoted S. N. Behrens,
CONVERSATION WITH MAX 1960

22 This astonishing Mr Shaw has been greater
than anything even he has ever written.
John Mason Brown

1 Shaw, one day you will eat a pork chop and
then God help all women.
Mrs Pat Campbell

2 Mr Shaw is (I suspect) the only man on earth
who has never written any poetry.
G. K. Chesterton, ORTHODOXY 1908

3 Shaw's works make me admire the magnificent tolerance and broadmindedness of the
English.
James Joyce. Quoted Gerald Griffin, THE
WILD GEESE

4 He is a good man fallen among Fabians.
V. I. Lenin

5 He writes like a Pakistani who has learned
English when he was twelve years old in
order to become a chartered accountant.
John Osborne

6 Shaw is the most fraudulent, inept writer of
Victorian melodramas ever to gull a timid
critic or fool a dull public.
Ibid.

7 I remember coming across him at the Grand
Canyon and finding him peevish, refusing to
admire it or even look at it properly. He was
jealous of it.
J. B. Priestley, THOUGHTS IN THE
WILDERNESS

8 The absence of fine shades and atmosphere
explains why repertory companies in a hurry
so often choose a Shaw play. You have only
to learn the lines, slam them across, and the
piece comes to life.
Ibid.

9 I am a disciple of Bernard Shaw.
George Bernard Shaw, THE DOCTOR'S
DILEMMA 1906

10 He is an idiot child screaming in a hospital.
H. G. Wells, Daily Chronicle 1914

11 At 83 Shaw's mind was perhaps not quite as
good as it used to be. It was still better than
anyone else's.
Alexander Woollcott, WHILE ROME
BURNS 1934

SHIP

12 *First Mate*: There are four stowaways in the
forward hatch.

Captain: How do you know there are four?
First Mate: They keep singing 'Sweet
Adeline'.
Marx Brothers, MONKEY BUSINESS

SHOCK

13 I can still remember the day when I
encountered my first Conservative, a shock
all the greater in that it coincided with the
crisis of puberty.
*Prof. Gwyn Williams, Observer, Sayings of
the Week* 30 *Aug* 1981

SHOOTING

14 He [Godfrey Webb] went out duck shooting. He was asked afterwards whether he
had shot many. 'Not even a Mallard
imaginaire' was his answer.
Maurice Baring, THE PUPPET SHOW OF
MEMORY 1922

15 To a complaint that one of the churchyards
on his estate was disgracefully overgrown
the 3rd Earl of Leicester replied, 'Nonsense.
Best breeding ground for partridges in
England'.
Kenneth Rose, KINGS, QUEENS AND
COURTIERS 1985

SHOP

16 It is very difficult to spend less than £200 a
morning when one goes shopping.
Sir Henry Channon, DIARY 27 *Sep* 1935

17 Pile it high, sell it cheap.
*Motto of Sir John Cohen, founder of Tesco
supermarkets*

18 All English shop assistants are Miltonists.
All Miltonists firmly believe that 'they also
serve who only stand and wait.'
George Mikes, HOW TO BE INIMITABLE 1960

SHYNESS

19 I have all the shyness of the very vain.
V. S. Naipaul, Radio Times 24 *Mar* 1979

SILENCE

1 Silence is the best substitute for brains ever invented.
Senator Henry F. Ashurst. Quoted Leon Harris, THE FINE ART OF POLITICAL WIT 1966

2 Silences have a climax, when you have to speak.
Elizabeth Bowen, THE HOUSE IN PARIS 1935

3 Silence is the most perfect expression of scorn.
George Bernard Shaw, BACK TO METHUSELAH 1922

4 My personal hobbies are reading, listening to music, and silence.
Edith Sitwell

5 God is the friend of silence. Trees, flowers, grass grow in silence. See the stars, moon and sun, how they move in silence.
Mother Teresa, FOR THE BROTHERHOOD OF MAN 1981

SIR JOHN SIMON

6 The Right Honourable and Learned gentleman has twice crossed the floor of this House, each time leaving behind him a trail of slime.
David Lloyd George, House of Commons 1931

SIMPLICITY

7 The ability to simplify means to eliminate the unnecessary so that the necessary may speak.
Hans Hofmann, SEARCH FOR THE REAL 1967

SIN

8 All sins are attempts to fill voids.
W. H. Auden, A CERTAIN WORLD 1971

9 There are different kinds of wrong. The people sinned against are not always the best.
Ivy Compton-Burnett, THE MIGHTY AND THEIR FALL 1962

10 It is right to hate sin, but not to hate the sinner.
Giovanni Guareschi, THE LITTLE WORLD OF DON CAMILLO

11 There is but one thing more dangerous than sin — the murder of a man's sense of sin.
Pope John Paul II. Quoted Observer 8 *Apr* 1979

12 The only people who should really sin / Are the people who can sin with a grin.
Ogden Nash, I'M A STRANGER HERE MYSELF, *Inter-Office Memorandum* 1938

13 Sin cannot be undone, only forgiven.
Igor Stravinsky, CONVERSATIONS WITH STRAVINSKY 1959

14 Sin is the preference of an immediately satisfying experience to the declared pattern of the universe.
Charles Williams, HE CAME DOWN FROM HEAVEN 1938

SINCERITY

15 Sincerity is all that counts. It's a widespread modern heresy. Think again. Bolsheviks are sincere. Fascists are sincere. Lunatics are sincere. People who believe the earth is flat are sincere. They can't all be right. Better make certain first you've got something to be sincere about and with.
Tom Driberg, Daily Express 1937

16 It is dangerous to be sincere unless you are also stupid.
George Bernard Shaw, MAN AND SUPERMAN 1905

SINGING

17 Her singing reminds me of a cart coming downhill with the brake on.
Sir Thomas Beecham of a soprano in DIE WALKÜRE. *Quoted Harold Atkins and Archie Newman,* BEECHAM STORIES 1978

18 Most sopranos sound as if they live on seaweed.
Sir Thomas Beecham, Newsweek 3 *Apr* 1956

19 He made a mistake — he thinks he's the bull instead of the toreador.
Sir Thomas Beecham, auditioning a baritone for CARMEN. *Quoted Harold Atkin and Archie Newman,* BEECHAM STORIES 1978

1 To be a great singer you need a big chest, a big mouth, 90 per cent memory, 10 per cent intelligence, lots of hard work and something in the heart.
Enrico Caruso. Quoted Dorothy Caruso,
ENRICO CARUSO

2 All the intelligence and talent in the world can't make a singer. The voice is a wild thing. It can't be bred in captivity.
Willa Cather, THE SONG OF THE LARK 1915

3 She was a singer who had to take any note above A with her eyebrows.
Montague Glass. Quoted Frank Muir, THE FRANK MUIR BOOK

4 I can't stand to sing the same song the same way two nights in succession. If you can, then it ain't music, it's close order drill, or exercise or yodelling or something, not music.
Billie Holiday, LADY SINGS THE BLUES 1956

5 There are few moments during her [Margaret Truman's] recital when one can relax and feel confident that she will make her goal, which is the end of the song.
Paul Hume, Washington Post

6 The Italian language is peculiarly suitable for singing, having no awkward diphthongs and virtually no final consonants.
Frank Muir, THE FRANK MUIR BOOK

7 My own objection to the prima donna is that, as a rule, she represents merely tone and technique without intelligence.
Sir Ernest Newman, A MUSICAL MOTLEY 1919

8 My arias made me take off as if I was on a trampoline.
Jessye Norman, Radio Times 24 Oct 1981

9 A prima donna, you know, should always sing with her vowels open.
Arthur Wimperis to Luella Paikin. Quoted Reginald Pound, THEIR MOODS AND MINE 1935

EDITH SITWELL

10 Then Edith Sitwell appeared, her nose longer than an anteater's, and read some of her absurd stuff.
Lytton Strachey, of an evening with Arnold Bennett, in a letter to Dora Carrington 28 Jun 1921

11 So you've been reviewing Edith Sitwell's latest piece of virgin dung, have you? Isn't she a poisonous thing of a woman, lying, concealing, flipping, plagiarising, misquoting, and being as clever a literary publicist as ever.
Dylan Thomas, letter to Glyn Jones 1934

12 I am as appreciatively indifferent to Edith Sitwell as I am to the quaint patterns of old chintzes, the designs on dinner plates, or the charm of nursery rhymes.
H. G. Wells, EXPERIMENT IN AUTOBIOGRAPHY 1934

SKY

13 For rich people, the sky is just an extra, a gift of nature. The poor, on the other hand, can see it as it is, a gift of infinite grace.
Albert Camus, NOTEBOOKS 1935–1942

SLANG

14 I know only two words of American slang, 'swell' and 'lousy'. I think 'swell' is lousy, but 'lousy' is swell.
J. B. Priestley when interviewed on American radio

SLAVERY

15 The slave clings to his chains and he must have them struck from him.
Mahatma Gandhi. Quoted Woodrow Wyatt, CONFESSIONS OF AN OPTIMIST 1985

16 Death is a slave's freedom.
Nikki Giovanni at the funeral of Martin Luther King 1968

SLEEP

17 I like heat without weight. Henry likes weight without heat. I sleep under a couple of Shetland shawls. Henry would be happy stark naked under a grand piano.
Margot Asquith, AUTOBIOGRAPHY 1936

18 By day she never looked old. She grew up in sleep. Then a map of unwilling adult-awareness lines, tensions and hollows — appeared in her exposed face.
Elizabeth Bowen, A LOVE STORY

1 Laugh and the world laughs with you; snore and you sleep alone.
Anthony Burgess, INSIDE MR ENDERBY 1966

2 Exhausted socially and mentally I slept for two hours this afternoon in the Library of the House of Commons. A deep House of Commons sleep. There is no sleep to compare with it — rich, deep and guilty.
Sir Henry Channon, DIARY 15 Jul 1935

3 Sleep is when all the unsorted stuff comes flying out as from a dustbin upset in a high wind.
William Golding, PINCHER MARTIN 1956

4 That we are not much sicker and much madder than we are is due exclusively to that most blessed and blessing of natural graces, sleep.
Aldous Huxley, THEME AND VARIATIONS 1950

5 Sleep, whom the old writers called the brother of Death.
Louis MacNeice, NOW THAT THE SHAPES OF MIST

6 Just begin a story with such a phrase as 'I remember Disraeli — poor old Dizzy! — once saying to me, in answer to my poke in the eye,' and you will find me and Morpheus off in a corner, necking.
Dorothy Parker (Constant Reader) of Margot Asquith's autobiography, The New Yorker 22 Oct 1927

7 I can't be expected to drop everything and start counting sheep at my age. I hate sheep.
Dorothy Parker, THE LITTLE HOURS

8 Those no-sooner-have-I-touched-the-pillow people are past my comprehension. There is something bovine about them.
J. B. Priestley, ALL ABOUT OURSELVES

9 I have come to the borders of sleep / The unfathomable deep / Forest where all must lose / Their way, however straight / Or winding, soon or late; / They cannot choose.
Edward Thomas, LIGHTS OUT

10 I haven't been to sleep for over a year. That's why I go to bed early. One needs more rest if one doesn't sleep.
Evelyn Waugh, DECLINE AND FALL 1928

SLOUGH

11 Come friendly bombs and fall on Slough / It isn't fit for humans now / There isn't grass to graze a cow / Swarm over, Death.
Sir John Betjeman, SLOUGH

SMELL

12 To me, smells are like music; they have an aching familiar power to evoke the past. A good strong whiff can stab you to the heart with longing and remembrance.
Ray Bolitho, Daily Telegraph 20 Dec 1978

13 I love the people with their straightforward minds. It's just that their smell brings on my migraine.
Bertolt Brecht, THE CAUCASIAN CHALK CIRCLE 1945

14 A police officer could have confused the smell of cannabis with that of smelly feet, a defendant claimed at Beaconsfield on Tuesday.
Bucks Free Press. Quoted Punch 16 May 1973

15 'The lotuses smell like pineapples.' 'Everything smells like something else. It's so dreadfully confusing.'
Noël Coward, SHADOW PLAY

SMILE

16 She gave me a smile I could feel in my hip pocket.
Raymond Chandler, FAREWELL MY LOVELY 1940

17 A smile that snapped back after using, like a stretched rubber band.
Sinclair Lewis. Quoted Reader's Digest, Aug 1941

18 Smiling encouragement like a clumsy dentist.
Katherine Mansfield, BANK HOLIDAY

19 A smile that floated without support, in the air.
Marcel Proust, REMEMBRANCE OF THINGS PAST, *Cities of the Plain* 1921—2

20 He had a smile like a razor-blade.
Anthony Sampson, of Moss Evans, THE CHANGING ANATOMY OF BRITAIN 1982

1 He smiled, bunching his fat cheeks like twin
   rolls of smooth pink toilet paper.
   Nathanael West, MISS LONELYHEARTS 1933

SMOKING

2 'You won't object if I smoke?'
   'Certainly not — if you don't object if I'm
   sick.'
   *Sir Thomas Beecham replying to a woman in
   a non-smoking railway compartment*

3 Men have always smoked. With women it's
   just a habit.
   *Letter to Bradford Telegraph and Argus.
   Quoted Michael Bateman*, THIS ENGLAND

4 Smokers, male and female, inject and
   excuse idleness in their lives every time they
   light a cigarette.
   Colette, EARTHLY PARADISE,
   Freedom 1966

5 Orson Welles once said that he made movies
   in order to be able to smoke cigars gratis.
   'That's why I wrote so many cigar-smoking
   heroes, and villains who chomp their
   cigars', he once said. 'Cigars are my
   inspiration.'
   G. Cabrera Infante, HOLY SMOKE 1985

DAME ETHEL SMYTHE

6 Nobody ever managed to kiss Ethel.
   Sir Thomas Beecham

7 She would be like Richard Wagner, if only
   she looked a bit more feminine.
   Osbert Sitwell. Quoted Elizabeth Lutyens, A
   GOLDFISH BOWL

SNOBBERY

8 In our way we were both snobs, and no snob
   welcomes another who has risen with him.
   Cecil Beaton of Evelyn Waugh

9 The Hon. Mrs Ronald Greville was a
   galumphing, greedy, snobbish old toad who
   watered at the chops at the sight of royalty.
   Cecil Beaton, DIARY

10 One of those refined people who go out to
   sew for the rich because they cannot bear
   contact with the poor.
   Colette, THE OTHER ONE

11 Marie Laurencin loves princes. She lunched
   with the King and Queen of the Belgians but
   was disillusioned on learning that Belgium
   was so small.
   René Gimpel, DIARY OF AN ART DEALER

12 Dukes and dustmen are generally not snobs
   as both are devoid of social pretension.
   Neil Mackwood, IN AND OUT

13 His hatred of snobs was a derivative of his
   snobbishness, but made the simpletons (in
   other words, everyone) believe that he was
   immune from snobbishness.
   Marcel Proust, REMEMBRANCE OF THINGS
   PAST 1913—1927

14 The English have no respect for their
   language. It is impossible for an Englishman
   to open his mouth without making some
   other Englishman despise him.
   George Bernard Shaw, PYGMALION 1913

15 I mustn't go on singling out names. One
   must not be a name-dropper, as Her
   Majesty remarked to me yesterday.
   *Norman St John Stevas. Speech at Museum
   of the Year luncheon 20 Jun 1979*

16 This water strike is making our water taste
   like Fulham's.
   *The Times Diary. Remark overheard in
   Chelsea 14 Feb 1983*

SNOW

17 His soul swooned slowly as he heard the
   snow falling faintly through the universe and
   faintly falling, like the descent of their last
   end, upon all the living and the dead.
   James Joyce, DUBLINERS, *The Dead* 1914

18 The first fall of snow is not only an event, it is
   a magical event. You go to bed in one kind
   of world and wake up in another quite
   different, and if this is not enchantment then
   where is it to be found?
   J. B. Priestley, APES AND ANGELS

SOCIALISM

19 What a genius the Labour Party has for
   cutting itself in half and letting the two parts
   writhe in public.
   *Cassandra (Sir William Connor), Daily
   Mirror*

1 The disastrous element in the Labour party
is its intellectuals.
G. N. Clark. Quoted A. L. Rowse, A MAN OF
THE THIRTIES

2 We need less *egalité* and more *fraternité*.
John Fowles, THE ARISTOS

3 As with the Christian religion, the worst
advertisement for Socialism is its adherents.
George Orwell, THE ROAD TO WIGAN
PIER 1937

4 I am a socialist — and I only wish the Labour
Party was.
Rev. Donald Soper, BBC Radio 4, *Any
Questions* 11 *May* 1979

SOCIETY

5 Britain is the society where the ruling class
does not rule, the working class does not
work and the middle class is not in the
middle.
George Mikes, ENGLISH HUMOUR FOR
BEGINNERS 1983

6 British society these days is governed by
three things; thuggery, muggery — and I've
written a book about the other one.
*A. L. Rowse. Quoted Alan Hamilton, The
Times Profile* 7 *Mar* 1983

7 There are two classes in good society in
England. The equestrian classes and the
neurotic classes.
George Bernard Shaw, HEARTBREAK
HOUSE 1920

SOCIOLOGY

8 Sociology is the science with the greatest
number of methods and the least results.
J. H. Poincaré. Quoted Bertrand Russell,
SCIENCE AND METHOD

9 Those terrible sociologists who are the
astrologers and alchemists of our twentieth
century.
Miguel de Unamuno, FANATICAL
SCEPTICISM

SOLDIER

10 O what is that sound which so thrills the
ear / Down in the valley, drumming,

drumming? / Only the scarlet soldiers,
dear / The soldiers coming.
W. H. Auden, O WHAT IS THAT SOUND?

11 It must have been a little trying to the
colonel who came up to him [Osbert Sitwell]
and asked him if he was fond of horses to be
told 'No but I adore giraffes.'
Beverley Nichols, TWENTY FIVE 1926

12 The soldier's body becomes a stock of
accessories that are not his property.
Antoine de Saint-Exupéry, FLIGHT TO
ARRAS 1942

13 Soldiers are citizens of death's grey land /
Drawing no dividend from time's tomor-
row.
Siegfried Sassoon, DREAMER 1918

14 The British soldier can stand up to anything
except the British War Office.
George Bernard Shaw, THE DEVIL'S
DISCIPLE 1900

15 I never expect a soldier to think.
Ibid.

16 He [the recruiting officer] asked me 'Why
tanks?' I replied that I preferred to go into
battle sitting down.
Peter Ustinov, DEAR ME 1977

SOLITUDE

17 Bold gnats that revel round my solitude.
Edmund Blunden, POEMS 1911–1930

18 Solitude, a luxury of the rich.
Albert Camus, NOTEBOOKS 1935–1942

19 Only solitary men know the full joys of
friendship. Others have their family — but
to a solitary and an exile his friends are
everything.
Willa Cather, SHADOWS ON THE ROCK 1931

20 There are days when solitude is a heady
wine that intoxicates you with freedom,
others when it is a bitter tonic, and still
others when it is a poison that makes you
beat your head against the wall.
Colette, EARTHLY PARADISE,
Freedom 1966

21 I want to be alone.
*Popularly attr. to Greta Garbo, although she
frequently denied ever having said it*

1 Solitude, as death proves, is our natural state.
Ernest Hemingway. Quoted Anthony Burgess, HEMINGWAY AND HIS WORLD 1978

2 The more powerful and original a mind, the more it will incline towards the religion of solitude.
Aldous Huxley, PROPER STUDIES 1927

3 People could with advantage be compelled to remain alone for several hours a day; and a week's solitary confinement would be an excellent provision.
(Percy) Wyndham Lewis, TIME AND WESTERN MAN 1927

4 Solitude gives birth to the original in us: to beauty unfamiliar and perilous — to poetry. But also it gives birth to the opposite, to the perverse, the illicit, the absurd.
Thomas Mann, DEATH IN VENICE 1913

5 Solitude is the playfield of Satan.
Vladimir Nabokov, PALE FIRE 1962

6 Life is for each man a solitary cell whose walls are mirrors.
Eugene O'Neill, LAZARUS LAUGHED 1927

SONG

7 It is the best of all trades to make songs, and the second best to sing them.
Hilaire Belloc, ON EVERYTHING, *On Song* 1909

8 Song: the licensed medium for bawling in public things too silly or too sacred to be uttered in ordinary speech.
Oliver Herford. Quoted Nat Shapiro, ENCYCLOPEDIA OF QUOTATIONS ABOUT MUSIC

9 Why 'words for music' are almost invariably trash now, though the words of Elizabethan songs are better than any music, is a gloomy and difficult question.
Andrew Lang, ESSAY ON T. H. BAYLY

10 Cheap music set to noble words exposes the cheapness of the music; beautiful and profound music set to insignificant words still communicates the beauty of the music.
Artur Schnabel, MUSIC AND THE LINE OF MOST RESISTANCE 1947

11 Some of the songs making the rounds now will be popular when Bach, Beethoven and Wagner are forgotten – but not before.
Louis Sobel. Quoted Nat Shapiro, ENCYCLOPEDIA OF QUOTATIONS ABOUT MUSIC

12 Having verse set to music is like looking at a painting through a stained glass window.
Paul Valéry. Ibid.

SORROW

13 Sorrow is tranquillity remembered in emotion.
Dorothy Parker, SENTIMENT

SOUVENIR

14 I don't have a photograph, but you can have my footprints. They are upstairs in my socks.
Groucho Marx, A NIGHT AT THE OPERA

15 Over the chimney-piece . . . hangs an entrenching tool with which, in 1915, Uncle Matthew had whacked to death eight Germans one by one as they crawled out of a dug-out. It is still covered in blood and hairs, an object of fascination to us children.
Nancy Mitford, THE PURSUIT OF LOVE 1945

SPACE-RESEARCH

16 One small step for man, one giant leap for mankind.
Neil Armstrong, first man on the moon 21 Jul 1969

17 Outer space is no place for a person of breeding.
Lady Violet Bonham Carter. Quoted B. G., *New Yorker* 11 Jun 1979

18 Today we can no more predict what use mankind may make of the Moon than could Columbus have imagined the future of the continent he had discovered.
Arthur C. Clarke, THE EXPLORATION OF SPACE

19 Space isn't remote at all. It's only an hour's drive away if your car could go straight upwards.
Sir Fred Hoyle, *Observer* 9 Sep 1979

1 Treading the soil of the moon, palpating its pebbles, tasting the panic and splendour of the event, feeling in the pit of one's stomach the separation from terra — these form the most romantic sensation an explorer has ever known.
Vladimir Nabokov, New York Times 21 *Jul* 1969

2 This is the greatest week in the history of the world since the creation.
Richard Nixon of the moon landing 24 *Jul* 1969

3 Because of what you have done the heavens have become part of man's world. And as you talk to us from the Sea of Tranquillity it inspires us to redouble our efforts to bring peace and tranquillity to earth.
Richard Nixon, Radio message to astronauts on the moon 20 *Jul* 1969

4 For years politicians have promised the moon. I'm the first one to be able to deliver it.
Ibid.

5 The astronauts . . . Rotarians in outer space.
Gore Vidal, TWO SISTERS 1970

SPEECH

6 Words fluttered from him like swallows leaving a barn at daylight.
O. Henry

7 It is a mysterious fact that no animal has ever been discovered that had the power of speech, nor any human society on earth that was without a language.
Margaret Lane, Daily Telegraph 22 *Feb* 1985

8 Speech is civilisation itself. The word, even the most contradictory word, preserves contact — it is silence which isolates.
Thomas Mann, THE MAGIC MOUNTAIN 1924

9 I don't want to talk grammar. I want to talk like a lady.
George Bernard Shaw, PYGMALION 1913

10 Remember that you are a human being with the divine gift of articulate speech; that your native language is the language of Shakespeare and Milton and the Bible; and don't sit there crooning like a bilious pigeon.
Ibid.

SPEED

11 Speed provides the one genuinely modern pleasure.
Aldous Huxley, MUSIC AT NIGHT, *Wanted, a New Pleasure* 1931

12 In the past human life was lived in a bullock cart, in the future it will be lived in an aeroplane, and the change in speed amounts to a difference in quality.
A. N. Whitehead, SCIENCE AND THE MODERN WORLD 1925

SPINSTER

13 Being an old maid is like death by drowning, a really delightful sensation after you cease to struggle.
Edna Ferber, A PECULIAR TREASURE 1939

SPORT

14 I went skiing and broke a leg. Fortunately it wasn't mine.
Anon. Quoted Daily Telegraph

15 It is international sport that helps to kick the world downhill. Started by foolish athletes, who thought it would promote 'understanding' it is supported today by the desire for political prestige and by the interests involved in gate monies. It is completely harmful.
E. M. Forster, TWO CHEERS FOR DEMOCRACY 1957

SPRING

16 Now Spring, sweet laxative of Georgian strains / Quickens the ink in literary veins.
Roy Campbell, THE GEORGIAD 1930

17 Every year, back Spring comes, with nasty little birds, yapping their fool heads off, and the ground all mucked up with arbutus.
Dorothy Parker. Quoted Robert N. Linscott, AN OMNIBUS OF AMERICAN HUMOUR

18 In the spring your lovely Chloe lightly turns one mass of spots.
Ronald Searle and Timothy Sly, THE TERROR OF ST TRINIANS

1 Spring makes everything look filthy.
   Katherine Whitehorn, Observer, Wonder
   Shirkers 24 Feb 1980

SPY

2 The members of our secret service have
   apparently spent so much time looking
   under the beds for Communists, they
   haven't had time to look in the bed.
   Michael Foot, at the time of the Profumo
   affair

JOSEPH STALIN

3 My father died a difficult and terrible
   death . . . God grants an easy death only to
   the just.
   Svetlana Alliluyeva, Stalin's daughter,
   TWENTY LETTERS TO A FRIEND

4 I like old Joe Stalin. He's a good fellow but
   he's a prisoner of the Politburo. He would
   make certain agreements but they won't let
   him keep them.
   Harry S Truman. Speech. Quoted News
   Review 24 Jun 1948

STATELY HOME

5 An extraordinary aspect of running a stately
   home is that much of its success depends,
   not on how many Van Dycks you have, but
   how many loos. No amount of beautiful
   objects can compensate a visitor who is kept
   queuing in the cold.
   Duchess of Bedford, NICOLE NOBODY

6 The Stately Homes of England open their
   doors / To piping Nancy boys and crashing
   bores.
   Roy Campbell, THE GEORGIAD 1930

7 I am told you can even smell the people who
   come round.
   Lord Radnor, refusing to open his castle to
   the public. Quoted Simon Winchester, THEIR
   NOBLE LORDSHIPS 1981

8 These comfortably padded lunatic asylums
   which are known, euphemistically, as the
   stately homes of England.
   Virginia Woolf, THE COMMON
   READER 1925

STATESMAN

9 He therefore was at strenuous pains / To
   atrophy his puny brains / And registered
   success in this / Beyond the dreams of
   avarice. / Till when he had at last become /
   Blind, paralytic, deaf and dumb / Insensible
   and cretinous / He was admitted ONE OF
   US.
   Hilaire Belloc, THE STATESMAN

10 When statesmen forsake their own private
    conscience for the sake of their public duties
    they lead their country by a short route to
    chaos.
    Robert Bolt, A MAN FOR ALL SEASONS 1961

11 The difference between being an elder
    statesman / And posing successfully as an
    elder statesman / Is practically negligible.
    T. S. Eliot, THE ELDER STATESMAN

12 A statesman is a politician when he has been
    dead ten years.
    Harry S Truman, interview, New York
    World Telegram 12 Apr 1958

STATISTICS

13 Nearly half of Northern Ireland's sub-
    postmistresses are women.
    Journal of the Federation of Sub-
    Postmasters

14 He uses statistics as a drunken man uses
    lamp-posts — for support rather than
    illumination.
    Andrew Lang. Quoted A. L. Mackay,
    HARVEST OF A QUIET EYE

15 Statistical figures referring to economic
    events are historical data. They tell us what
    happened in a non-repeatable historical
    case.
    Ludwig Elder von Mises, HUMAN ACTION

16 Statistics will prove anything, even the
    truth.
    Lord Moynihan. Quoted Lore and Maurice
    Cowen, THE WIT OF MEDICINE

17 A single death is a tragedy; a million is a
    statistic.
    Joseph Stalin. Quoted John Bartlett,
    FAMILIAR QUOTATIONS

18 Statistics are mendacious truths.
    Lionel Strachey

STATUS

1 There is a lot to be said in schools and in communities generally for seeing that nobody is below the rank of lance-corporal.
Rhodes Boyson, Observer 23 Nov 1980

2 A man's name, title and rank are artificial and impermanent; they do nothing to reveal what he really is, even to himself.
Jean Giraudoux, SIEGFRIED 1928

3 A society person who is enthusiastic about modern painting or Truman Capote is already half a traitor to his class. It is only middle-class people who, quite mistakenly, imagine that a lively pursuit of the latest in reading or painting will advance their status in the world.
Mary McCarthy, ON THE CONTRARY 1961

GERTRUDE STEIN

4 Reading Gertrude Stein at length is not unlike making one's way through an interminable and badly printed game book.
Richard Bridgeman, GERTRUDE STEIN IN PIECES

5 While she believed that most writers failed to allow writing to express all that it could, in her own practice she scrupulously saw to it that writing expressed less than it would.
John Malcolm Brinnin, THE THIRD ROSE 1959

6 Gertrude Stein is the mama of dada.
Clifton Fadiman

7 Gertrude Stein's prose song is a cold, black suet-pudding. We can represent it as a cold suet roll of fabulously reptilian length. Cut it at any point, it is the same thing; the same heavy, sticky, opaque mass all through, and all along . . . it is mournful and monstrous, composed of dead and inanimate material.
(Percy) Wyndham Lewis.

NORMAN ST JOHN STEVAS

8 A Catholic layman who has never been averse to giving advice to the Pope, or indeed anybody else who he thought might be in need of it.
Bernard Levin, THE PENDULUM YEARS 1976

LYTTON STRACHEY

9 Strachey had recently published *Eminent Victorians,* and *Queen Victoria.* Someone incautiously asked him who would be the subject of his next biography. At the top of his small, weak, but piercing voice he shouted 'God'.
Jacques-Emile Blanche, MORE PORTRAITS OF A LIFETIME 1918–1938

IGOR STRAVINSKY

10 His music used to be original. Now it is aboriginal.
Sir Ernest Newman, Musical Times, Jul 1921

STRENGTH

11 Ettie (Lady Desborough) is so strong she will be made into Bovril when she dies.
Margot Asquith. Quoted Lord David Cecil, Observer, Staying with Margot 20 Dec 1981

12 The awareness of our own strength makes us modest.
Paul Cézanne, LETTERS 1937

STRIKE

13 It is difficult to go on strike if there is no work in the first place.
Lord George-Brown, Observer 24 Feb 1980

STUPIDITY

14 Just as the results of inebriety are most painful to the habitually sober, and just as the greatest saints have often been the greatest sinners, so, when the first class brain does something stupid, the stupidity of that occasion is colossal.
Stanley Baldwin, House of Commons 13 May 1924

15 He's the kind of guy who, if you say 'Hiya Clark, how are yah?' is stuck for an answer.
Ava Gardner, of Clark Gable. Quoted Donald Sinden, A TOUCH OF THE MEMOIRS 1982

16 Nothing in the world is more dangerous than sincere ignorance and conscientious stupidity.
Martin Luther King, STRENGTH TO LOVE 1963

1 'How can you be so stupid?'
'I can do anything if I apply my mind to it.'
Simon Moss, COCK UPS *(Play. First
presented at Edinburgh Festival, Aug* 1981)

2 'I simply cannot *bear* fools.'
'Apparently your mother did not have the
same difficulty.'
Dorothy Parker. Quoted Bennett Cerf, TRY
AND STOP ME 1947

3 A routine of port and a fall on his head once
a week kept him in that state of chronic,
numbing confusion which was then the aim
of every cavalry officer.
Osbert Sitwell, GREAT MORNING 1947

4 'Dyall, you're a perfect idiot.'
'Oh no, sir. I wouldn't say that. No one is
perfect.'
Hal Wilton, ROCKFIST ROGAN

5 He was in many ways one of the most
pronounced fatheads that ever pulled on a
suit of gent's underwear.
P. G. Wodehouse, MY MAN JEEVES 1919

STYLE

6 Swinburne mastered his technique, which is
a great deal, but he did not make it to the
extent of being able to take liberties with it,
which is everything.
T. S. Eliot, REFLECTIONS ON VERS LIBRE

7 Properly understood style is not a seductive
decoration added to a functional structure;
it is of the essence of a work of art.
Evelyn Waugh, BOOKS ON TRIAL

8 Bruce Cabot and Myrna Loy make a crash
landing in the jungle and crawl out of the
wreckage in their Abercrombie & Fitch
white safari blouses and tan gabardine
jodhpurs and stagger into a clearing.
Tom Wolfe, FROM BAUHAUS TO OUR HOUSE

SUCCESS

9 The penalty of success is to be bored by
people who used to snub you.
*Lady Astor. Quoted Geoffrey Bocca,
Sunday Express* 12 Jan 1956 *(also attr. to
Mary Wilson Little)*

10 The toughest thing about success is that
you've got to keep on being a success.
Talent is only a starting point in this
business.
Irving Berlin, Theatre Arts, Feb 1958

11 Success is like knowledge; where is the fun if
everybody's got it?
Basil Boothroyd, Punch 10 *May* 1972

12 Success is relative. It is what we can make of
the mess we have made of things.
T. S. Eliot, THE FAMILY REUNION 1939

13 The compensation of very early success is a
conviction that life is a romantic matter. In
the best sense one stays young.
F. Scott Fitzgerald, THE CRACK-UP 1936

14 Gentlemen, I have invented a new slogan —
Goldwyn pictures griddle the earth.
Sam Goldwyn. Quoted Alva Johnson, THE
GREAT GOLDWYN

15 There are two reasons why I am successful in
show business and I am standing on both of
them.
Betty Grable

16 Success is always temporary; success is only
delayed failure.
Graham Greene, A SORT OF LIFE 1971

17 I've never consciously striven for success.
But once I was aware I had it I must say I was
terrified of losing it.
*Gilbert Harding to John Freeman on BBC
TV, Face to Face*

18 Success — 'the bitch-goddess Success' in
William James' phrase — demands strange
sacrifices from those who worship her.
Aldous Huxley, PROPER STUDIES 1927

19 Unless a man has been taught what to do
with success after getting it, the achievement
of it must inevitably leave him prey to
boredom.
Bertrand Russell, THE CONQUEST OF
HAPPINESS 1930

20 The only way to succeed is to make people
hate you. That way, they remember you.
Joseph von Sternberg, AUTOBIOGRAPHY

21 There are no gains without pains.
Adlai Stevenson. Nomination address 1952

1 Success to me is having ten honeydew melons and eating only the top half of each slice.
Barbra Streisand, Life 20 *Sep* 1963

2 To succeed in life it is not enough to be stupid. One must be well mannered as well.
Bonar Thompson (Hyde Park orator), THE BLACK HAT

3 The best thing that can come with success is the knowledge that it is nothing to long for.
Liv Ullmann, CHANGING MASKS

4 Whenever a friend succeeds, a little something in me dies.
Gore Vidal. Quoted Susan Barnes, BEHIND THE IMAGE

5 It is not enough to succeed. Others must fail.
Gore Vidal, BBC Radio 4, *Quote Unquote* 5 *Jun* 1980. *Also attr. to David Merrick in Barbara Rowe,* A BOOK OF QUOTES

SUFFERING

6 [Suffering is] a form of gratitude to experience or an opportunity to experience evil and change it into good.
Saul Bellow, HERZOG 1964

7 A cause is like champagne and high heels — one must be prepared to suffer for it.
Arnold Bennett, THE TITLE 1918

8 If you are convinced of your despair, you must either act as if you did hope after all — or kill yourself. Suffering gives no rights.
Albert Camus, NOTEBOOKS 1935–1942

9 Every now and then people have preferred sorrow to joy and asserted that wisdom and creation can only result from suffering.
E. M. Forster, TWO CHEERS FOR DEMOCRACY

10 Few can believe that suffering, especially by others, is in vain. Anything that is disagreeable must surely have beneficial economic effects.
J. K. Galbraith, THE AGE OF UNCERTAINTY 1977

11 We are healed of a suffering only by experiencing it to the full.
Marcel Proust, REMEMBRANCE OF THINGS PAST, *The Fugitive* 1925

12 There is also a cup of pain for you to drink all up / Or setting it aside for sweeter drink / Thirst ever more.
Stevie Smith, AND SO TO FATNESS COME

13 He groaned slightly, and winced, like Prometheus watching his vulture dropping in for lunch.
P. G. Wodehouse. Quoted Richard Usborne, WODEHOUSE AT WORK 1961

SUICIDE

14 If I had the use of my body I would throw it out of the window.
Samuel Beckett, MALONE DIES 1956

15 There is but one truly serious philosophical problem, and that is suicide. Judging whether life is, or is not worth living amounts to answering the fundamental question of philosophy.
Albert Camus, THE MYTH OF SISYPHUS

16 Not only is suicide a sin, it is the sin. It is the ultimate and absolute evil, the refusal to take the oath of loyalty to life. The man who kills a man, kills a man. The man who kills himself kills all men; as far as he is concerned he wipes out the world.
G. K. Chesterton, ORTHODOXY 1908

17 There are many who dare not kill themselves for fear of what the neighbours might say.
Cyril Connolly, THE UNQUIET GRAVE 1945

18 My work is done. Why wait?
George Eastman. Suicide note

19 Doesn't it seem a little like going where you haven't been invited?
Richard Eberhart, HOW IT IS

20 Last night I would have put my head in the gas oven if I was not too frightened of the cook to go into the kitchen.
Ann Fleming, LETTERS 1985

21 No neurotic harbours thoughts of suicide which are not murderous impulses against others redirected upon himself.
Sigmund Freud, TOTEM AND TABOO 1918

22 Razors pain you / Rivers are damp / Acids stain you / And drugs cause cramp / Guns aren't lawful / Nooses give / Gas smells awful, / You might as well live.
Dorothy Parker, ENOUGH ROPE, *Résumé* 1927

1 When you're between any sort of devil and the deep blue sea, the deep blue sea sometimes looks very inviting.
Terence Rattigan, THE DEEP BLUE SEA 1952

2 'It is against the law to commit suicide in this man's town' I say, 'although what the law can do to a guy who commits suicide I am never able to figure out.'
Damon Runyon, GUYS AND DOLLS 1932

3 Suicide . . . is about life, being in fact the sincerest criticism life gets.
Wilfrid Sheed, THE GOOD WORD

4 The body of Pipkin lay spreadeagled on the roof of an Austin Princess, the owner of which was surveying it with the weary distaste he normally reserved for pigeon droppings.
E. S. Turner, Punch 10 May 1973

5 I am the only man in the world who cannot commit suicide.
Rev. Chad Varah (founder of the Samaritans)

SUMMER

6 Summer has filled her veins with light / And her warm heart is washed with noon.
C. Day Lewis, FROM FEATHERS TO IRON

7 In Cornwall I overheard the following; 'You can tell it's summer. The rain is warmer.'
Mervyn Madge. Letter to Daily Telegraph 10 Aug 1985

8 Last summer — that is, three years ago.
Spike Milligan. Quoted Miles Kington, The Times 12 Aug 1985

9 The dynamo hum of summer running down.
Reginald Pound, THEIR MOODS AND MINE 1937

10 Summer makes a silence after spring.
Vita Sackville-West, THE LAND 1926

11 In this noble country of ours there is no such thing as summer weather or summer clothing. There are simply different kinds of temperature and different kinds of garments appropriate to them. As a guide the calendar is a monstrous fraud.
Times leader. Quoted News Review 17 Jul 1947

SUN

12 O praise / With lion-music such as that heard in the air / When the roaring golden lion that roams the heavens / Devours the dark, and multitudes and magnitudes respond.
Edith Sitwell, THE OUTCASTS, *Praise We Great Men*

13 Thank heavens the sun has gone in and I don't have to go out and enjoy it.
Logan Pearsall Smith, last words

SUNDAY

14 The boredom of Sunday afternoon, which drove De Quincey to opium also gave birth to surrealism; hours propitious to making bombs.
Cyril Connolly, THE UNQUIET GRAVE 1945

15 The feeling of Sunday is the same everywhere, heavy, melancholy, standing still. Like when they say 'As it was in the beginning, is now, and ever shall be, world without end.'
Jean Rhys, VOYAGE IN THE DARK 1934

16 Do not take a bath in Jordan / Gordon / On the Holy Sabbath, on the peaceful day!
Edith Sitwell, SCOTCH RHAPSODY

17 And the sabbath rang slowly / In the pebbles of the holy streams.
Dylan Thomas, FERN HILL 1952

18 Sunday is not for sale.
George Thomas, Viscount Tonypandy. Speech, House of Lords, opposing repeal of the Sunday Act 2 Dec 1985

SUNSET

19 Shipwrecked, the sun sinks down harbours / of a sky, unloads its liquid cargo / of marigolds.
Dannie Abse, WALKING UNDER WATER, *Epithalamion*

20 There is nothing more musical than a sunset.
Claude Debussy. Quoted Nat Shapiro, ENCYCLOPEDIA OF QUOTATIONS ABOUT MUSIC

21 Or autumn sunsets exquisitely dying.
Aldous Huxley, THE NORTH PHILOSOPHER'S SONG

1 I have a horror of sunsets. They are so romantic, so operatic.
Marcel Proust, REMEMBRANCE OF THINGS PAST, *Cities of the Plain* 1921–2

2 A large red drop of sun lingered on the horizon, then dipped over and was gone.
John Steinbeck, THE GRAPES OF WRATH 1939

SUPERFLUITY

3 When struck by a thunderbolt it is unnecessary to consult the Book of Rules as to the precise meaning of the omen.
Ernest Bramah, THE WALLET OF KAI LUNG 1920

4 Life is too short to stuff a mushroom.
Shirley Conran, SUPERWOMAN

5 As superfluous as a Gideon Bible in the Ritz.
F. Scott Fitzgerald, THE CRACK-UP 1936

SUPERIORITY

6 He was not brought by the stork; he was delivered by a man from the Audubon Society personally.
Fred Allen, *American radio comedian*

7 He lies below, correct in cypress wood / And entertains the most exclusive worms.
Dorothy Parker, EPITAPH FOR A VERY RICH MAN

SUPERNATURAL

8 Religion / Has made an honest woman of the supernatural.
Christopher Fry, THE LADY'S NOT FOR BURNING 1949

SUPERSTITION

9 I miss my daily Mass, and have a superstitious feeling that anything may happen on the days I don't go. However, nothing in particular has.
Rose Macaulay, LETTERS TO A FRIEND 1961

SURGERY

10 A man will bleed to death from a severed carotid artery in three minutes. You can tie his artery in two minutes *if you are not in a hurry.*
Anon. Variously attrib

11 The greatest discoveries of surgery are anaesthesia, asepsis and roentonology — and none was discovered by a surgeon.
Martin Henry Fisher

SURPRISE

12 The thing startled poor old Bully considerably. He rose from his seat like a rocketing pheasant.
P. G. Wodehouse, JEEVES AND THE HARD BOILED EGG

13 Captain Biggar's strong jaw fell like an unsupported stick of asparagus.
P. G. Wodehouse, THE RETURN OF JEEVES

SURREALISM

14 To them, chaos is the shape and order. This seems to me to be exceedingly presumptuous; the Surrealists imagine that whatever they dredge up from their sub-conscious selves and put down in paint or words must essentially be of some value. I deny this.
Dylan Thomas. Quoted Andrew Sinclair, DYLAN THOMAS, POET OF HIS PEOPLE

SURVIVAL

15 It isn't important to come out on top; what matters is to come out alive.
Bertolt Brecht, JUNGLE OF CITIES 1924

16 People are inexterminable — like flies and bed-bugs. There will always be some that survive in cracks and crevices — that's us.
Robert Frost. Quoted Observer 29 Mar 1959

17 He was as fitted to survival in this modern world as a tapeworm in an intestine.
William Golding, FREE FALL 1959

18 We can survive if we dig enough holes.
T. K. Jones, a Reagan aide. Quoted BBC Radio 4, World Tonight, Nov 1982

1 The supreme reality of our time is . . . the vulnerability of this planet.
John F. Kennedy. Speech, Dublin 28 Jun 1963

2 Building up arms is not a substitute for diplomacy.
Samuel Pisar, OF BLOOD AND HOPE

3 When you get to the end of your rope, tie a knot and hang on.
Franklin D. Roosevelt

SUSPICION

4 Suspicion is a thing very few people can entertain without letting the hypothesis turn, in their minds, to fact.
David Cort, SOCIAL ASTONISHMENTS

5 He had the sort of convoluted mind that could attribute evil and devious motives to a bee-keeper offering him a pot of honey as a gift.
Hugh Cudlipp, of H. G. Bartholomew, editor of the Daily Mirror; WALKING ON THE WATER

6 I found a long grey hair on Kevin's jacket last night — If it's another woman's I'll kill him. If it's mine I'll kill myself.
Neil Simon, IT HURTS ONLY WHEN I LAUGH *(play)*

7 We have to distrust each other. It is our only defence against betrayal.
Tennessee Williams, CAMINO REAL 1953

SWEARING

8 Ordinary men . . . / Put up a barrage of common sense to baulk / Intimacy, but by mistake interpolate / Swear-words like roses in their talk.
Louis MacNeice, CONVERSATION 1929

SWITZERLAND

9 The Swiss are not a people so much as a neat, clean, quite solvent business.
William Faulkner, INTRUDER IN THE DUST 1948

10 In Italy for thirty years under the Borgias they had warfare, terror, murder, bloodshed and they produced Michelangelo, Leonardo da Vinci and the Renaissance. In Switzerland they had brotherly love, five hundred years of democracy and peace and what did they produce? The cuckoo clock.
Orson Welles, added by him to the script of his film The Third Man

SYCOPHANCY

11 I see her as one great stampede of lips directed at the nearest derrière.
Noël Coward of a newspaper columnist. Quoted William Marchant, THE PRIVILEGE OF HIS COMPANY 1980

12 Don't say 'Yes' until I finish talking.
Attrib. Darryl F. Zanuck. Quoted in his obituary, Daily Telegraph 24 Dec 1979

SYMBOLISM

13 In so far as a symbol is a living thing, it is the expression of a thing not to be characterised in any other way. The symbol is alive in so far as it is pregnant with meaning.
Carl Jung

SYMPATHY

14 To be sympathetic without discrimination is so very debilitating.
Ronald Firbank, PRANCING NIGGER 1924

15 She was a machine gun, riddling her hostess with sympathy.
Aldous Huxley, THE GIOCONDA SMILE

T

TACT

1 My advice was delicately poised between the cliché and the indiscretion.
Robert Runcie (Archbishop of Canterbury) to the press concerning his advice to the Prince of Wales and Lady Diana Spencer on their approaching wedding 13 Jul 1981

TACTLESSNESS

2 Although there exist many thousand subjects for elegant conversation, there are persons who cannot meet a cripple without talking about feet.
Ernest Bramah, THE WALLET OF KAI LUNG 1920

3 Never speak of rope in the house of a man who has been hanged.
Franklin D. Roosevelt. Campaign speech, Washington 23 Sep 1944

TALENT

4 In this world people have to pay an extortionate price for any exceptional gift whatever.
Willa Cather, THE OLD BEAUTY AND OTHERS   1948

5 Middle age snuffs out more talent than ever wars or sudden deaths do.
Richard Hughes, THE FOX IN THE ATTIC 1961

TASTE

6 Between friends differences in taste or opinions are irritating in direct proportion to their triviality.
W. H. Auden, THE DYER'S HAND 1962

7 People care more about being thought to have taste than about being thought either good, clever or amiable.
Samuel Butler, NOTEBOOKS 1912

8 The kind of people who always go on about whether a thing is in good taste invariably have very bad taste.
Joe Orton, BEHIND THE SCENES *(edited by Joseph F. McCrindle)*

9 We talk of acquired taste, but all tastes are really acquired, and it is doubtful whether we are any better off for having acquired them, better in the sense that through them our enjoyment of life is rendered any more intense.
Alec Waugh, ON DOING WHAT ONE LIKES

TAXATION

10 When they fire a rocket at Cape Canaveral, I feel as if I own it.
William Holden. Quoted Robert Ottaway, TV Times 24 Aug 1972

11 The taxpayer is someone who works for the federal government but doesn't have to take a civil service examination.
Ronald Reagan. Quoted Barbara Rowe, A BOOK OF QUOTES

ELIZABETH TAYLOR

12 Miss Taylor lists about, her hands fluttering idly like a wind-up doll in need of a new mainspring.
New York Times, of her performance in PRIVATE LIVES 9 *May* 1983

13 Just how garish her commonplace accent, her squeakily shrill voice, and the childish petulance with which she delivers her lines are, my pen is neither scratchy nor leaky enough to convey.
John Simon, of Elizabeth Taylor's performance in THE TAMING OF THE SHREW

TEA

1 If I had known there was no Latin word for
tea I would have let the vulgar stuff alone.
Hilaire Belloc. Quoted Frank Muir, THE
FRANK MUIR BOOK

2 The best thing to do when you've got a dead
body and it's your husband's, on the kitchen
floor, and you don't know what to do about
it, is to make a cup of tea.
Anthony Burgess, ONE HAND CLAPPING

3 I like a nice cup of tea in the morning / For to
start the day you see / And at half-past
eleven / Well my idea of Heaven / Is a nice
cup of tea / I like a nice cup of tea with my
dinner / And a nice cup of tea with my tea /
And when it's time for bed / There's a lot to
be said / For a nice cup of tea.
A. P. Herbert, the Cochran revue, HOME
AND BEAUTY

4 When I makes tea I makes tea as old mother
Grogan said. And when I makes water I
makes water.
James Joyce, ULYSSES 1922

TEACHING

5 It is nothing short of a miracle that the
modern methods of instruction have not
entirely strangled the holy curiosity of
enquiry.
*Albert Einstein. Quoted George B.
Leonard,* EDUCATION AND ECSTASY

6 You sought the last resort of feeble minds
with classical educations. You became a
schoolmaster.
Aldous Huxley, ANTIC HAY 1923

TECHNOLOGY

7 Any sufficiently advanced technology is
indistinguishable from magic.
Arthur C. Clarke, THE LOST WORLDS OF
2001

TEETH

8 Now Albert's coming back, make yourself a
bit smart / He'll want to know what you
done with that money he gave you / To get
yourself some teeth. He did, I was there /
You have them all out, Lil, and get a nice
set / He said, I swear, I can't bear to look at
you.
T. S. Eliot, THE WASTE LAND 1922

TELEPHONE

9 I never pass an empty telephone box without
pressing Button B. Button B has often been
kind to me.
Joyce Cary, THE HORSE'S MOUTH 1942

10 *Witness:* I went to the Elephant to make a
telephone call.
Lord Darling· A trunk call, no doubt.
Lord Darling. Quoted Edward Bell, THESE
MEDDLESOME ATTORNEYS

11 She bellowed into the mouthpiece as if it
were a cave in whose depths children
missing for several days might have taken
shelter.
Clive James, BRILLIANT CREATURES 1983

TELEVISION

12 Three quarters of television is for half-wits.
The boxing's all right.
*Sir Thomas Beecham. Quoted Harold
Atkins and Archie Newman,* BEECHAM
STORIES

13 All the music I have ever seen on television
looks grotesque . . . You see right down the
larynx, almost into the tummy, the eyes go
this way, the nose goes that way, and the
mouth is twisted round. The whole thing is
revolting. That's television, so far as music is
concerned.
*Sir Thomas Beecham. Quoted Lord
Boothby,* MY YESTERDAY YOUR
TOMORROW

14 Why should people go out and pay to see
bad films when they can stay at home and
see bad television for nothing?
Sam Goldwyn. Quoted Observer 9 Sep 1956

15 I'll believe in colour television when I see it
in black and white.
*Sam Goldwyn. Quoted Benny Green, Radio
Times 17 Feb 1979*

16 Television seems such a silly thing to make
him famous.
*Gilbert Harding's mother. Quoted Wallace
Rayburn,* GILBERT HARDING: A CANDID
PORTRAIT 1979

17 Television won't matter in your lifetime or
mine.
Rex Lambert, The Listener 1936

1 Television brought the brutality of war into the comfort of the living room. Vietnam was lost in the living rooms of America, not on the battlefields of Vietnam.
Marshall McLuhan, Montreal Gazette 16 *May* 1975

2 He doesn't suit daylight does he?
Elderly lady's comment on Michael Parkinson. Quoted Russell Harty, Observer 4 *Nov* 1979

3 Television? No good will come of this new device. The word is half Greek and half Latin.
C. P. Scott, Manchester Guardian

4 I'm still big. It's the pictures that got small.
Gloria Swanson, SWANSON ON SWANSON 1981

5 Marietta . . . knows all the right questions. Unfortunately she is driven to give wrong answers. She is very effective on television panel programmes.
Gore Vidal, TWO SISTERS

6 The television screen is the finest medium ever devised for showing old films.
Keith Waterhouse, Radio Times 17 *Mar* 1979

7 The camera brings out exhibitionist streaks in the quietest people.
Viscount Weymouth, BBC 2 TV, A Year in the Life of 1 *Oct* 1981

8 Chewing-gum for the eyes.
Attr. Frank Lloyd Wright and, by J. B. Simpson, to John Mason Brown

TEMPTATION

9 The Devil, having nothing else to do / Went off to tempt my Lady Poltagrue / My Lady, tempted by a private whim / To his annoyance tempted him.
Hilaire Belloc, EPIGRAMS

10 She's not so pretty anyone would want to ruin her.
Bertolt Brecht, MOTHER COURAGE AND HER CHILDREN 1939

11 No temptation can ever be measured by the value of its object.
Colette, EARTHLY PARADISE, *Human Nature* 1966

12 In this new experience you may find temptations both in wine and women. You must entirely resist both temptations, and while treating all women with perfect courtesy, you should avoid any intimacy.
Lord Kitchener. Message in soldier's pay books 1914—18 *war*

13 Better to enjoy and suffer than sit around with folded arms. You know the only true prayer? Please God, lead me into temptation.
Jennie Lee, MY LIFE WITH NYE

14 We cannot go about, unfortunately, telling everybody about the temptations we have resisted. As a result people judge us exclusively by the temptations to which we yield.
Robert Lynd, THE PEAL OF BELLS

15 I never resist temptation because I have found that things that are bad for me never tempt me.
George Bernard Shaw, THE APPLE CART 1929

16 I have always despised Adam because he had to be tempted by the woman, as she was by the serpent, before he could be induced to pluck the apple from the tree of knowledge. I should have swallowed every apple on the tree the moment the owner's back was turned.
George Bernard Shaw. Quoted Hesketh Pearson, BERNARD SHAW 1942

17 She had no use for morals and always omitted 'Lead us not into temptation' from the Lord's Prayer. 'It's no business of His' she proclaimed.
Philip Ziegler, DIANA COOPER

TENNIS

18 Pam, I adore you, Pam, you great big mountainous sports girl, / Whizzing them over the net, full of the strength of five.
Sir John Betjeman, POT POURRI FROM A SURREY GARDEN

19 'If you can't volley, wear velvet socks' one Old Gamesman used to say.
Stephen Potter, GAMESMANSHIP 1947

1 Players must provide their own rackets and must wear shoes without heels. Balls for practice may be obtained on application to the gardener.
Rules for the first tennis competition at Wimbledon. Quoted A. Wallis Myers,
MEMORY'S PARADE

TERRORISM

2 It's too bad that blood is involved, otherwise one might almost say that terrorism is a good thing.
Ken Glass, BBC Radio 3, Terror 19 Aug 1981

TESTIMONIAL

3 He coxed his college boat at Oxford — and I'm told he sings Gilbert and Sullivan in his bath, which immediately makes us take him to our hearts.
Alec Douglas-Home, of the Pakistan Prime Minister, Evening Standard. Quoted Michael Bateman, THIS ENGLAND

THAMES

4 Sweet Thames run softly till I end my song.
T. S. Eliot, THE WASTE LAND 1922

MARGARET THATCHER

5 She is trying to wear the trousers of Winston Churchill.
Leonid Brezhnev. Speech 1979

6 She is clearly the best man among them.
Barbara Castle, DIARIES

7 Politicians are either warriors or healers. Margaret Thatcher is a healer.
Patrick Cosgrave, BIOGRAPHY OF MARGARET THATCHER

8 She has been beastly to the Bank of England, has demanded that the BBC 'set its house in order', and tends to believe the worst of the Foreign and Commonwealth Office. She cannot see an institution without hitting it with her handbag.
Julian Critchley, The Times profile, Margaret Thatcher 21 Jun 1982

9 The improbable PM; she seems *totally* humourless, with the nervous system usually attributed to fishes. Surely she has never read a book or looked at a picture?
Ann Fleming, LETTERS 1985

10 She has no imagination, and that means no compassion.
Michael Foot. Quoted John Mortimer, Sunday Times, Foot at Bay 19 Sep 1982

11 Attila the Hen.
Clement Freud, BBC Radio 4, News Quiz 26 Oct 1979

12 She approaches the problem of our country with all the one-dimensional subtlety of a comic strip.
Denis Healey, House of Commons 22 May 1979

13 Mrs Thatcher is doing for monetarism what the Boston Strangler did for door-to-door salesmen.
Ibid. 15 Dec 1977

14 For the past few months she has been charging about like some bargain-basement Boadicea.
Denis Healey, Observer, Sayings of the Week 7 Nov 1982

15 She is the Enid Blyton of economics. Nothing must be allowed to spoil her simple plots.
Richard Holme. Speech, Liberal Party Conference 10 Sep 1980

16 She sounded like the book of Revelations read out over a railway station public address system by a headmistress of a certain age wearing calico knickers.
Clive James, of Margaret Thatcher on television, Observer 1979

17 She is a very ordinary woman, occupying a position where ordinary virtues are not enough.
Paul Johnson, Observer 20 Nov 1983

18 I am a great admirer of Mrs Thatcher — one of the most splendid headmistresses there has ever been.
Arthur Marshall, BBC Radio 4, Any Questions 22 Jan 1982

1 I think I'm thoroughly in favour of Mrs Thatcher's visit to the Falklands. I find a bit of hesitation, though, about her coming back.
John Mortimer, BBC Radio 4, Any Questions? 1983

2 Mrs Thatcher has taken to power the way others take to the air of Colwyn Bay. It braces her. She is invigorated. She knocks people down.
Edward Pearce, Daily Telegraph 27 Jun 1979

3 She is the best man in England.
Ronald Reagan to reporters 7 Jan 1983

4 This woman is headstrong, obstinate and dangerously self-opinionated.
Report on Margaret Thatcher by personnel officer at ICI when rejecting her for a job in 1948

5 Margaret Thatcher is David Owen in drag.
Rhodesia Herald 8 Aug 1979

6 I am extraordinarily patient, provided I get my own way in the end.
Margaret Thatcher. Quoted Observer, Sayings of the Year 2 Jan 1983

7 Don't forget Denis (her husband) when you're considering the influences on her. He sees her every morning at breakfast — far more often than any of us.
A Tory MP on Mrs Thatcher becoming Prime Minister. Quoted Laurence Marks, Observer 6 May 1979

8 Plunder Woman.
Harry Unwin. Trades Union Congress, Brighton 6 Sep 1980

9 Mrs Thatcher plays, I suspect, to an unseen gallery of headmistresses, economists and the Madame Tussaud version of Winston Churchill.
Katherine Whitehorn, Observer, Act Your Self 4 Dec 1983

10 You need a thug to fight her, and the Labour Party didn't have one.
Harold Wilson, Woman's Own 15 Mar 1986

THEATRE

11 The reason why Absurdist plays take place in No Man's Land with only two characters is mainly financial.
Arthur Adamov. Speech, Edinburgh 13 Sep 1962

12 Some of my plays peter out, and some pan out.
J. M. Barrie. Quoted Leonard Rossiter, LOWEST FORM OF WIT

13 It was one of those plays in which all the actors unfortunately enunciated very clearly.
Robert Benchley, CHIPS OFF THE OLD BENCHLEY 1949

14 My companion had a point when, listening to one of the bursts of noise off stage from time to time, she remarked that there was obviously a better play going on back stage.
Katherine Brisbane of a performance of OTHELLO, Australian 10 Oct 1967

15 I go to the theatre to be entertained. I don't want to see plays about rape, sodomy and drug addiction – I can get all that at home.
Cartoon caption in Observer 8 Jul 1962

16 The play was a success but the audience was a failure.
William Collier. Quoted Bennett Cerf, TRY AND STOP ME 1947

17 Don't put your daughter on the stage, Mrs Worthington.
Noël Coward, song title

18 Don't whatever you do, be nervous on the opening night. It's *such* a waste of time and spoils most of the fun.
Noël Coward. Quoted William Marchant, THE PRIVILEGE OF HIS COMPANY 1980

19 Generally speaking, the American theatre is the aspirin of the middle classes.
Wolcott Gibbs, MORE IN SORROW, Shakespeare, Here's Your Hat

20 No good play is a success; fine writing and high morals are useless on the stage. I have been scribbling twaddle for thirty-five years to suit the public taste, and I should know.
W. S. Gilbert. Quoted Isaac Goldberg, THE STORY OF GILBERT AND SULLIVAN

21 The Twenties did indeed temporarily raise the mental age of the average theatre-goer from fourteen to seventeen.
Robert Graves and Alan Hodge, THE LONG WEEKEND 1940

1 All that Russian gloom and doom, and people shooting themselves from loneliness and depression and that sort of thing. But then, mother says I don't understand comedy. I expect she's right.
Simon Gray, QUARTERMAINE'S TERMS *(play)*

2 I have knocked everything except the knees of the chorus girls. Nature anticipated us there.
Percy Hammond. Quoted Frank Muir, THE FRANK MUIR BOOK

3 Watching my plays performed in London is like seeing them in translation.
Lillian Helman. Quoted The Times obituary 2 Jul 1984

4 Characters in a play don't always have to be bigger fools than in everyday life.
Eugene Ionesco, FOURSOME

5 I thought the play was frightful but I saw it under particularly unfortunate circumstances. The curtain was up.
George Kaufman. Quoted Bennett Cerf, SATURDAY REVIEW OF LITERATURE

6 Coughing in the theatre is not a respiratory ailment. It is a criticism.
Alan Jay Lerner, THE STREET WHERE I LIVE

7 When I go to the theatre I like the curtain to rise to reveal a smart maid at the telephone saying 'I am afraid her ladyship isn't back yet!' And through the window a view of Sloane Square may be seen.
Arthur Marshall, Radio Times 23 Jul 1977

8 How can you write a play of which the ideas are so significant that they will make the critic of *The Times* get up in his stall and at the same time induce the shop girl in the gallery to forget the young man who is holding her hand?
W. Somerset Maugham, CAKES AND ALE 1930

9 I hate harrowing plays. *Love on the Dole* made me cry with rage — to think that one of the greatest of the arts had been used to upset people so.
Evelyn Millard, THE ERA

10 Theatre is what *works* even with an audience of a dozen pensioners . . . not a matter of higher aesthetics.
John Osborne, A BETTER CLASS OF PERSON 1981

11 *The House Beautiful* is the play lousy.
Dorothy Parker, Life

12 Depending upon shock tactics is easy, whereas writing a good play is difficult. Pubic hair is no substitute for wit.
J. B. Priestley, OUTCRIES AND ASIDES

13 A novelist may lose his readers for a few pages; a playwright never dares lose his audience for a minute.
Terence Rattigan, New York Journal American 29 Oct 1956

14 *Peter Pan* is a charming play for children. It is not a rule of conduct for a great nation.
Edith Shackleton. Quoted James Agate, EGO 3, 4 Dec 1936

15 A novel is a static thing that one moves through: a play is a dynamic thing that moves past one.
Kenneth Tynan, CURTAINS

16 A good many inconveniences attend playgoing in any large city, but the greatest of them is usually the play itself.
Kenneth Tynan, New York Herald Tribune 17 Feb 1957

17 What a pity it is that there are so few of you and so many of me.
Orson Welles, when facing a tiny audience in Wisconsin

18 One of the best tips for writing a play is 'Never let them sit down'. Keep the characters buzzing about without a pause.
P. G. Wodehouse, PERFORMING FLEA 1953

19 The play left a taste of lukewarm parsnip juice.
Alexander Woollcott. Quoted Howard Techmann, SMART ALEX 1976

THEOLOGY

20 Only a minority of the religions of the world have a theology. There was no systematic series of statements which the Greeks agreed in believing about Zeus.
C. S. Lewis, IS THEOLOGY POETRY?

21 All your Western theologies, the whole mythology of them are based on the concept of God as a senile delinquent.
Tennessee Williams, THE NIGHT OF THE IGUANA 1961

THEORY

1 Factual evidence can never 'prove' a
hypothesis; it can only fail to disprove it,
which is what we generally mean when we
say, somewhat inexactly, that the hypothesis is 'confirmed' by experience.
Milton Friedman, ESSAYS IN POSITIVE
ECONOMICS

2 No theory is good except on condition that
one uses it to go beyond.
André Gide, JOURNALS 1918

3 A first rate theory predicts; a second rate
theory forbids, and a third rate theory
explains after the event.
A. I. Kitaigorodskii. Quoted A. L. Mackay,
HARVEST OF A QUIET EYE

4 Theory, glamorous mother of the drudge
experiment.
Harlan Mayer Jr. Quoted Eric M. Rogers,
PHYSICS FOR THE INQUIRING MIND 1949

DYLAN THOMAS

5 The fear of being unable to write was nearer
the root of his troubles than the fear of not
being able to pay the grocer.
Anon. New Yorker 21 *Nov* 1977

6 The crabbed and dark-eyed Welshman,
Dylan Thomas, whose poems were strewn
with wild, organic, telescoped images
underneath which, perhaps, ran a sub-
merged stream of poetic thought.
Robert Graves and Alan Hodge, THE LONG
WEEKEND 1940

7 He was a detestable man. Men pressed
money on him, and women their bodies.
Dylan took both with equal contempt. His
great pleasure was to humiliate people.
A. J. P. Taylor, A PERSONAL HISTORY 1983

THOUGHT

8 As soon as you can say what you think and
not what some other person has thought for
you, you are on your way to being a
remarkable man.
J. M. Barrie, TOMMY AND GRIZEL 1900

9 He can't think without his hat.
Samuel Beckett, WAITING FOR GODOT 1952

10 What was once thought can never be
unthought.
Friedrich Durrenmatt, THE PHYSICISTS 1960

11 Thinking is a momentary dismissal of
irrelevances.
R. Buckminster Fuller, UTOPIA OR
OBLIVION

12 Thinking does not bring knowledge as do
the sciences.
Martin Heidegger. Quoted Hannah Arendt,
New Yorker 21 *Nov* 1977

13 A thing in itself never expresses anything. It
is the relation between things that gives
meaning to them and that formulates a
thought. A thought functions only as a
fragmentary part in the formulation of an
idea.
Hans Hoffman, SEARCH FOR THE REAL

14 How can I know what I think until I have
heard what I have said?
Christopher Hollis (Conservative MP for
Devizes). Quoted News Review 12 *Dec* 1946

15 Most of one's life is a prolonged effort to
avoid thinking.
Aldous Huxley, GREEN TUNNELS

16 Sooner or later false thinking brings wrong
conduct.
Julian Huxley, ESSAYS OF A BIOLOGIST 1923

17 One has to multiply thoughts to the point
where there aren't enough policemen to
control them.
Stanislaw Lec, UNKEMPT THOUGHTS 1962

18 If you make people think they're thinking,
they'll love you: but if you really make them
think, they'll hate you.
Don Marquis, ARCHY AND
MEHITABEL 1927

19 My thought is *one.* That is why I cannot stop.
I exist by what I think.
Jean-Paul Sartre, NAUSEA 1938

20 As soon as man does not take his existence
for granted, but beholds it as something
unfathomably mysterious, thought begins.
Albert Schweitzer, THE TEACHING OF
REVERENCE FOR LIFE

21 You can't think of nothing.
Subtitle of THE AVIATOR'S WIFE *(film)*

THRIFT

1 The man who tips a shilling every time he stops for petrol is giving away annually the cost of lubricating his car.
J. Paul Getty. Quoted Barbara Rowe, A BOOK OF QUOTES

2 Whenever you save five shillings you put a man out of work for a day.
J. M. Keynes, TREATISE ON MONEY 1931

3 The woman who can sacrifice a clean unspoiled penny stamp is probably unborn.
Saki, THE UNBEARABLE BASSINGTON 1912

THUNDER

4 Dry sterile thunder without rain.
T. S. Eliot, THE WASTE LAND 1922

TIDINESS

5 Keep London tidy — eat a pigeon a day.
Graffito. Quoted BBC Radio 4, Quote Unquote 7 Jun 1979

TIME

6 'Well, that's passed the time.'
'It would have passed in any case.'
Samuel Beckett, WAITING FOR GODOT 1952

7 I have not found out why we humans think of time as a line going from backwards, forwards, whilst it must be in all directions like everything else in the system of the world.
Ferruccio Busoni, BUSONI'S LETTERS TO HIS WIFE

8 It is so interminable and exasperating to watch the hand turn for five minutes on a clock that it is almost impossible to do so.
Albert Camus, NOTEBOOKS 1935–1942

9 Time present and time past / Are both perhaps present in time future / And time future contained in time past.
T. S. Eliot, FOUR QUARTETS, *Burnt Norton* 1936

10 We have all passed a lot of water since then.
Sam Goldwyn

11 In theory one is aware that the earth revolves but in practice one does not perceive it, the ground upon which one treads seems not to move, and one can live undisturbed. So it is with Time in one's life.
Marcel Proust, REMEMBRANCE OF THINGS PAST, *Within a Budding Grove* 1919

12 The necessity of not missing a train has taught us to account for minutes whereas among ancient Romans . . . the notion not of minutes but even of fixed hours barely existed.
Marcel Proust, REMEMBRANCE OF THINGS PAST, *Cities of the Plain* 1921–2

13 They do that to pass the time, nothing more. But Time is too large, it refuses to let itself be filled up.
Jean-Paul Sartre, NAUSEA 1938

14 Three o'clock is always too late or too early for anything you want to do.
Ibid.

15 Ah! The clock is always slow; / It is later than you think.
Robert W. Service, SONGS OF A SOURDOUGH 1907

16 The last years of his life had become so precious to him that, as he said, he would willingly stand at street corners hat in hand, begging passers-by to drop their unused minutes into it.
John Walker, of Bernard Berenson, THE BERNARD BERENSON TREASURY

TIMIDITY

17 I'm really a timid person — I was beaten up by Quakers.
Woody Allen and Marshall Brickman, SLEEPER *(film)*

18 People wish to learn to swim and at the same time to keep one foot on the ground.
Marcel Proust, REMEMBRANCE OF THINGS PAST, *The Fugitive* 1925

TOLERANCE

19 More and more people care about religious tolerance as fewer and fewer care about religion.
Alexander Chase, PERSPECTIVES 1966

1 Tolerance is a very dull virtue. It is boring. Unlike love, it has always had a bad press. It is negative. It merely means putting up with people, being able to stand things.
E. M. Forster, TWO CHEERS FOR DEMOCRACY, *Tolerance* 1951

2 If you don't like people, put up with them as well as you can. Don't try to love them; you can't, you'll only strain yourself.
Ibid.

3 We tolerate shapes in human beings that would horrify us if we saw them in a horse.
W. R. Inge (Dean of St Pauls). Quoted J. M. and M. J. Cohen, PENGUIN DICTIONARY OF MODERN QUOTATIONS

4 Once lead this people into war and they'll forget there ever was such a thing as tolerance.
President Woodrow Wilson. Quoted John Dos Passos, MR WILSON'S WAR

TOWN

5 Parks are but pavements disguised with a growth of grass.
George Gissing, THE PRIVATE PAPERS OF HENRY RYECROFT 1903

TRADE UNION

6 I thought the miners' leaders were the stupidest body of men in the world — until I met the mine owners.
Lord Birkenhead on the General Strike 1926

7 There are those who collect the refuse of the public streets, but in order to be received into the band it is necessary to have been born one of the Hereditary Confederacy of Superfluity Removers and Abandoned Oddment Gatherers.
Ernest Bramah, KAI LUNG UNROLLS HIS MAT 1928

8 There are only two good unions. The Mothers Union and Rugby Union.
Graffito. Quoted Daily Telegraph 3 Feb 1979

9 We are very good at stopping what we do not like, but not at starting anything.
Len Murray, in 1976. Quoted Robert Taylor, THE FIFTH ESTATE 1978

TRADITION

10 Tradition becomes our security, and when the mind is secure it is in decay.
Krishnamurti, THE PENGUIN KRISHNAMURTI READER

TRAFFIC

11 *Rush hour:* that hour when traffic is almost at a standstill.
Beachcomber (J. B. Morton), MORTON'S FOLLY

12 Horsedrawn carriages used to average 11½ miles an hour in New York's midtown traffic; the average speed of automobiles is a bare six miles an hour.
Norman B. Geddes, MAGIC MOTORWAYS

TRAGEDY

13 Tragedy is restful and the reason is that hope, that foul, deceitful thing, has no part in it.
Jean Anouilh, ANTIGONE 1942

14 The bad end unhappily, the good unluckily. That is what tragedy means.
Tom Stoppard, ROSENCRANTZ AND GUILDENSTERN ARE DEAD 1966

15 We begin to live when we have conceived life as a tragedy.
W. B. Yeats, AUTOBIOGRAPHY 1926

TRANSLATION

16 There are a number of mistranslations of that famous motto *'Honi Soit Qui Mal Y Pense'*, the latest I have heard is 'I honestly think I am going to be sick'.
Philip, Duke of Edinburgh. Speech to French Chamber of Commerce in Great Britain 1963

17 She has ideas above her station. How could you say that in French? You can't say au-dessus de sa gare. It isn't the same station.
Terence Rattigan, FRENCH WITHOUT TEARS 1936

18 A translation is no translation unless it will give you the music of a poem along with the words of it.
J. M. Synge, THE ARAN ISLANDS 1902

1 An idea does not pass from one language to another without change.
Miguel de Unamuno, TRAGIC SENSE OF LIFE 1913

2 Humour is the first of the gifts to perish in a foreign tongue.
Virginia Woolf, THE COMMON READER 1925

TRAVEL

3 The time to enjoy a European tour is about three weeks after you unpack.
George Ade, FORTY MODERN FABLES, *The Hungry Man From the Bird Centre* 1901

4 You'd think, with all these tourists about, they would build an elevator.
American lady climbing the Parthenon

5 I have recently been all round the world and have formed a very poor opinion of it.
Sir Thomas Beecham. Speech at the Savoy. Quoted News Review 22 Aug 1946

6 The longer the cruise the older the passengers.
Peg Bracken, BUT I WOULDN'T HAVE MISSED IT FOR THE WORLD

7 It is easier to find a travelling companion than to get rid of one.
Ibid.

8 One of the main troubles about going to Europe is that no one wants to hear about your trip when you get back home. Your friends and relatives are rife with jealousy, and are not only sorry that you went to Europe, but deeply regret that you came back.
Art Buchwald, Vogue 1 Apr 1954

9 There is no pleasure in travelling and I look upon it more as an occasion for spiritual testing.
Albert Camus, NOTEBOOKS 1939–1942

10 Henry wants me to take a trip around the world, but I'd rather go somewhere else.
Cartoon caption in New Yorker 1938

11 Men travel faster now, but I do not know if they go to better things.
Willa Cather, DEATH COMES FOR THE ARCHBISHOP 1927

12 It is a pity that people travel in foreign countries; it narrows their minds so much.
G. K. Chesterton

13 [Railway stations] are our gates to the glorious and the unknown. Through them we pass out into adventure and sunshine, and to them, alas, we return.
E. M. Forster, HOWARDS END 1910

14 If you put to sea in a wooden raft, with a parrot and five companions, it is inevitable that sooner or later you will wake up one morning out at sea, perhaps a little better rested than ordinarily, and begin to think about it.
Thor Heyerdahl, THE KONTIKI EXPEDITION

15 The best travel books are the ones that go the shortest distances. The best one of all is about a man who stayed where he was the whole time, Robinson Crusoe.
Miles Kington, The Times, I feel a journey coming on 15 Sep 1983

16 Americans are people who prefer the Continent to their own country but refuse to learn its languages.
E. V. Lucas, WANDERINGS AND DIVERSIONS

17 The great and recurrent question about abroad is, is it worth getting there?
Rose Macaulay. Quoted J. M. and M. J. Cohen, PENGUIN DICTIONARY OF MODERN QUOTATIONS

18 Travelling together is a great test, which has damaged many friendships and even honeymoons.
Rose Macaulay, THE TOWERS OF TREBIZOND 1956

19 [Everyone] hoped silently that the sense of being imprisoned in a decaying hotwater bottle would pass away in the fresh Atlantic breezes.
Compton Mackenzie, POOR RELATIONS

20 Whenever I prepare for a journey I prepare as though for death. Should I never return, all is in order. That is what life has taught me.
Katherine Mansfield, JOURNAL 1922

21 The only places John likes on the continent are those in which it is only by an effort of the imagination that you can tell you're not in England.
W. Somerset Maugham, THE CONSTANT WIFE 1926

1 *Seagoon:* I want you to accompany me on the safari.
Bloodnock: Gad sir, I'm sorry, I've never played one.
Spike Milligan, BBC Radio, The Goon Show

2 Only on the third class tourist class passengers' deck was it a sultry overcast morning, but then if you do things on the cheap you must expect these things.
Spike Milligan, A DUSTBIN OF MILLIGAN

3 There are only two rules. One is E. M. Forster's guide to Alexandria; the best way to know Alexandria is to wander aimlessly. The second is from the Psalms; grin like a dog and run about through the city.
Jan Morris, DESTINATIONS

4 All journeys begin in the same way. All travel is a form of gradual self-extinction.
Shiva Naipaul, NOTEBOOKS 1985

5 Travel is glamorous only in retrospect.
Paul Theroux. Quoted Observer 7 Oct 1979

6 He travelled in order to come home.
William Trevor, MATILDA'S ENGLAND (BBC play)

7 I have travelled so much because travel has enabled me to arrive at unknown places within my clouded self.
Laurens Van Der Post

8 One of the great things about travelling is you find out how many good, kind people there are.
William Wharton, DAD 1981

TREE

9 The boughs of the oak are roaring / inside the acorn shell.
Charles Tomlinson, A SENSE OF DISTANCE

TROUBLE

10 I see the President of Romania's mother is dead — there's always trouble for somebody.
Alan Bennett.

11 A trouble shared is a trouble dragged out till bedtime.
Victoria Wood, HAPPY SINCE I MET YOU, Granada TV play 8 Aug 1981

TRUTH

12 — three fundamental truths without a recognition of which there can be no effective liberty; that what we believe is not necessarily true; that what we like is not necessarily good; and that all questions are open.
Clive Bell, CIVILISATIONS 1928

13 Truth is so precious that it must be protected by a bodyguard of lies.
Winston Churchill. Quoted Leo Rosten, THE POWER OF POSITIVE NONSENSE

14 'I am wedded to the truth My Lord'
'How long have you been a widower?'
Lord Darling to a witness. Quoted Derek Walker-Smith, LIFE OF LORD DARLING

15 Ethical axioms are found and tested not very differently from the axioms of science. Truth is what stands the test of experience.
Albert Einstein, OUT OF MY LATER YEARS 1950

16 A truth is something that everyone can be shown to know and to have known, as people say, all along.
Mary McCarthy, ON THE CONTRARY 1961

17 It is hard to believe that a man is telling the truth when you know that you would lie if you were in his place.
H. L. Mencken, PREJUDICES 1919

18 We find so many who think truth is on their side but precious few who are 'on the side of truth'.
Sir William Oder. Quoted Lore and Maurice Cowan, THE WIT OF MEDICINE

19 Truths that become old become decrepit and unreliable and sometimes they may be kept going for a certain length of time but there is no life in them.
P. D. Ouspensky, A NEW MODEL OF THE UNIVERSE

20 Truth is stranger than fiction; fiction has to make sense.
Leo Rosten, THE POWER OF POSITIVE NONSENSE

21 Truth is not that which is demonstrable, but that which is ineluctable.
Antoine de Saint-Exupéry, WIND, SAND AND STARS 1939

1 Truth has no special time of its own. Its hour is now — always.
Albert Schweitzer, OUT OF MY LIFE AND THOUGHT

2 Truth telling is not compatible with the defence of the realm.
George Bernard Shaw, HEARTBREAK HOUSE 1920

3 Mr Mencken talks about truth as if she were his mistress, but he handles her like an iceman.
Stuart P. Sherman

4 When truth is discovered by someone else it loses some of its attractiveness.
Alexander Solzhenitsyn, CANDLE IN THE WIND

5 I never give them hell. I just tell the truth and they think it is hell.
Harry S Truman, *Look* 3 *Apr* 1956

6 The only truths which are universal are those gross enough to be thought so.
Paul Valéry, MAUVAISES PENSÉES 1942

7 Truth can be the worst destroyer of all.
Patrick White, FLAWS IN THE GRASS 1978

TYRANNY

8 Under conditions of tyranny it is easier to act than to think.
Hannah Arendt. Quoted W. H. Auden, A CERTAIN WORLD

9 The slave begins by demanding justice and ends by wanting to wear a crown. He must dominate in his turn.
Albert Camus, THE REBEL, *Metaphysical Rebellion* 1951

10 Tyranny is always better organised than freedom.
Charles Péguy, BASIC VIRTUES, *War and Peace*

11 People will endure their tyrants for years but they tear their deliverers to pieces if a millennium is not created immediately.
President Woodrow Wilson. Quoted John Dos Passos, MR WILSON'S WAR 1963

U

UGLINESS

1 It's nothing to be born ugly. Sensibly, the ugly woman comes to terms with her ugliness and exploits it as a grace of nature.
Colette, JOURNEY FOR MYSELF

2 The secret of my success is that no woman has ever been jealous of me.
Elsa Maxwell. Quoted Noël Barber, THE NATIVES WERE FRIENDLY

UNCERTAINTY

3 We are not certain, we are never certain. If we were we could reach some conclusions, and we could, at last, make others take us seriously.
Albert Camus, THE FALL 1956

4 Without measureless and perpetual uncertainty the drama of human life would be destroyed.
Winston Churchill, THE GATHERING STORM 1948

UNDERSTANDING

5 Between / Our birth and death we may touch understanding / As a moth brushes a window with its wing.
Christopher Fry, THE BOY WITH A CART 1925

6 Understanding is the beginning of approving.
André Gide, JOURNALS 1902

UNDERTAKER

7 Evan the Death presses hard with black gloves on the coffin of his breast in case his heart jumps out.
Dylan Thomas, UNDER MILK WOOD 1957

UNEMPLOYMENT

8 As post-war Chancellor of the Exchequer I turned on the apostles of old-style economics and said that 'those who talked about creating pools of unemployment should be thrown in them and made to swim'.
Lord Butler, THE ART OF THE POSSIBLE 1971

9 Giz a job.
Yosser Hughes in Alan Bleasdale's BOYS FROM THE BLACKSTUFF, *BBC TV 1982*

10 When a great many people are unable to find work, unemployment results.
Calvin Coolidge, in a syndicated newspaper column. Quoted Stanley Walker, CITY EDITOR

11 A lot of fellows nowadays have a BA, MD or PhD. Unfortunately they don't have a JOB.
Fats Domino. Quoted Barbara Rowe, A BOOK OF QUOTES

UNHAPPINESS

12 I have the true feeling of myself only when I am unbearably unhappy.
Franz Kafka, DIARIES 1914–1923

13 He has simply got the instinct for being unhappy highly developed.
Saki, THE CHRONICLES OF CLOVIS 1912

14 Those who are unhappy have no need for anything in this world but people capable of giving them their attention.
Simone Weil, WAITING FOR GOD 1950

UNITED STATES OF AMERICA

15 Americans have a perfect right to exist.
Max Beerbohm, ZULEIKA DOBSON 1911

1 America is the only nation in history which, miraculously, has gone directly from barbarism to degeneration without the usual interval of civilisation.
Georges Clemenceau

2 The business of America is business.
Calvin Coolidge. Speech 17 Jan 1923

3 When I was a boy I was told that anybody could become President of the United States. I am beginning to believe it.
Clarence Darrow

4 I went to Philadelphia one Sunday. The place was closed.
W. C. Fields

5 The Americans cannot build aeroplanes. They are very good at refrigerators and razor blades.
Hermann Goering's assurances to Hitler. Quoted Alistair Cooke, AMERICA

6 Everything about the behaviour of American society reveals that it is half judaised and half negrified. How can one expect a state like that to hold together.
Adolf Hitler at a secret conference

7 The American character looks always as if it had just had a rather bad haircut, which gives it, in our eyes at least, a greater humanity than the European, which even among its beggars gives it an all too professional air.
Mary McCarthy, ON THE CONTRARY 1961

8 American women expect to find in their husbands the perfection that English women only hope to find in their butlers.
W. Somerset Maugham

9 When you become used to never being alone you may consider yourself Americanised.
André Maurois

10 A nation which does not appreciate that the simple elocution exercise 'Merry Mary married hairy Harry' contains not one but *three* vowel sounds.
Jessica Mitford. Quoted Sue Arnold, Observer magazine 25 Feb 1979

11 America . . . where law and customs alike are based on the dreams of spinsters.
Bertrand Russell, MARRIAGE AND MORALS 1929

12 The reason American cities are prosperous is that there is no place to sit down.
Alfred J. Talley (American lawyer), on returning from a visit to Europe. Quoted Burton Stevenson, HOME BOOK OF QUOTATIONS

13 America is a large, friendly dog in a very small room. Every time it wags its tail it knocks over a chair.
Arnold Toynbee. Broadcast 14 Jul 1954

14 The thing that impresses me most about America is the way parents obey their children.
Duke of Windsor

UNIVERSE

15 There is no reason to assume that the universe has the slightest interest in intelligence — or even in life. Both may be random accidental by-products of its operations like the beautiful patterns on a butterfly's wings. The insect would fly just as well without them.
Arthur C. Clarke, THE LOST WORLDS OF 2001

16 listen; there's a hell of a good universe next door: let's go.
e.e. cummings, PITY THIS BUSY MONSTER, MANKIND

17 Universe is the aggregate of all humanity's consciously apprehended and communicated non-simultaneous and only partially overlapping experiences.
R. Buckminster Fuller, SYNERGETICS

18 The universe begins to look more like a great thought than like a great machine.
Sir James Jeans, THE MYSTERIOUS UNIVERSE 1930

19 In my youth I regarded the universe as an open book, printed in the language of physical equations, whereas now it appears to me as a text written in invisible ink, of which in our rare moments of grace we are able to decipher a small fragment.
Arthur Koestler, BRICKS TO BABEL, *Epilogue 1983*

1 Out of all possible universes, the only one which can exist, in the sense that it can be known, is simply the one which satisfies the narrow conditions necessary for the development of intelligent life.
Sir Bernard Lovell, IN THE CENTRE OF IMMENSITIES

2 If at that moment [one second after beginning to expand] the rate of expansion had been reduced by only a part in a thousand billion then the universe would have collapsed after a few million years.
Ibid.

3 I do not pretend to understand the universe. It is a great deal bigger than I am.
Tom Stoppard, LORD MALQUIST AND MR MOON

UNIVERSITY

4 If you feel that you have both feet planted on the ground then the university has failed you.
Robert Cohen, Time 23 *Jun* 1961

5 There are as many fools at university as elsewhere, but their folly has a certain stamp – the stamp of university training. It is a trained folly.
William Gerhardie, THE POLYGLOTS 1925

6 I find that the three major administrative problems on a campus are sex for the students, athletics for the alumni and parking for the faculty.
Clark Kerr (President of the University of California), Time 17 *Nov* 1958

7 Finals, the very name of which implies that nothing of importance can happen after it. The British postgraduate student is a lonely forlorn soul.
David Lodge, CHANGING PLACES

UNSELFISHNESS

8 There is nothing in Christianity or Buddhism that quite matches the sympathetic unselfishness of an oyster.
Saki, CHRONICLES OF CLOVIS 1912

V

VALUE

1 Nothing is intrinsically valuable; the value of everything is attributed to it, assigned to it from outside the thing itself, by people.
John Barth, THE FLOATING OPERA 1956

2 What we must decide is perhaps how we are valuable, rather than how valuable we are.
F. Scott Fitzgerald, THE CRACK-UP 1936

VANITY

3 Vanity is a great toughener.
Brendan Bracken, to Lord Beaverbrook, during the Suez crisis. Quoted David Carlton, ANTHONY EDEN

4 Vanity plays lurid tricks with our memory.
Joseph Conrad, LORD JIM 1900

5 Half of the harm that is done in this world / Is due to people who want to feel important.
T. S. Eliot, THE COCKTAIL PARTY 1949

6 It's always our touches of vanity / That manage to betray us.
Christopher Fry, THE LADY'S NOT FOR BURNING 1949

7 I have all the shyness of the very vain.
V. S. Naipaul, Radio Times 24 Mar 1979

8 Self-love seems so often unrequited.
Anthony Powell, THE ACCEPTANCE WORLD 1955

9 Whatever talents I possess may suddenly diminish or suddenly increase. I can with ease become an ordinary fool. I may be one now. But it doesn't do to upset one's own vanity.
Dylan Thomas, NOTEBOOKS

10 She keeps on being queenly in her own room with the door shut.
Edith Wharton, THE HOUSE OF MIRTH 1905

11 Vanity is so intimately associated with our spiritual identity that whatever hurts it, above all if it came from it, is more painful in the memory than serious sin.
W. B. Yeats, DRAMATIS PERSONAE

VASECTOMY

12 Vasectomy means never ever having to say 'Sorry'.
Larry Adler, BBC Radio 4, *Interview*

VEGETARIAN

13 Vegetarians have wicked, shifty eyes and laugh in a cold calculating manner. They pinch little children, steal stamps, drink water, favour beards.
Beachcomber (J.B. Morton), Daily Express, By the Way

14 I have known many meat-eaters to be far more non-violent than vegetarians.
Mahatma Gandhi, NON-VIOLENCE IN PEACE AND WAR 1948

15 Vegetarianism is harmless enough, though it is apt to fill a man with wind and self righteousness.
Sir Robert Hutchinson (President, Royal College of Physicians). Quoted Lore and Maurice Cowan, THE WIT OF MEDICINE

16 A man of my spiritual intensity does not eat corpses.
George Bernard Shaw. Quoted Hesketh Pearson, BERNARD SHAW 1942

17 There are millions of vegetarians in the world but only one Bernard Shaw. You do not obtain eminence quite so cheaply as by eating macaroni instead of mutton chops.
George Bernard Shaw, when, during the meat shortage of the 1914—18, *war, it was suggested he should be cited as an example of the advantages of vegetarianism*

VICE

1 It is the function of vice to keep virtue within reasonable bounds.
Samuel Butler, NOTEBOOKS 1912

2 Half the vices which the world condemns most loudly have seeds of good in them and require moderate use rather than total abstinence.
Samuel Butler, THE WAY OF ALL FLESH 1903

3 It is the restrictions placed on vice by our social code which makes its pursuit so peculiarly agreeable.
Kenneth Grahame, PAGAN PAPERS

4 Vice is waste of life. Poverty, obedience and celibacy are the canonical vices.
George Bernard Shaw, MAN AND SUPERMAN 1905

5 Never support two weaknesses at the same time. It's your combination sinners — your lecherous liars and your miserly drunkards — who dishonour the vices and bring them into disrepute.
Thornton Wilder, THE MATCHMAKER 1955

VICTIM

6 It takes two to make a murder. There are born victims, born to have their throats cut.
Aldous Huxley, POINT COUNTER POINT 1934

7 Every reformation must have its victims. You can't expect the fatted calf to show the enthusiasm of the angels over the prodigal's return.
Saki, REGINALD AND THE ACADEMY

VICTORY

8 Victory at all costs, victory in spite of all terror, victory however long and hard the road may be; for without victory there is no survival.
Winston Churchill. Speech, House of Commons 13 May 1940

9 The earth is still bursting with the dead bodies of the victors.
George Bernard Shaw, HEARTBREAK HOUSE, *Preface* 1920

VIETNAM WAR

10 To win in Vietnam we will have to exterminate a nation.
Dr Benjamin Spock, ON VIETNAM

VIEWPOINT

11 The loveliest face in all the world will not please you if you see it suddenly eye to eye, at a distance of half an inch from your own.
Max Beerbohm, ZULEIKA DOBSON 1911

12 Part of the reason for the ugliness of adults, in a child's eyes, is that the child is usually looking upwards, and few faces are at their best when seen from below.
George Orwell, ESSAYS 1946

13 What critics call dirty in our movies they call lusty in foreign films.
Billy Wilder. Quoted Leslie Halliwell, A FILMGOER'S BOOK OF QUOTES 1973

VIOLENCE

14 Keep violence in the mind where it belongs.
Brian Aldiss, BAREFOOT IN THE HEAD

15 A bit of shooting takes your mind off your troubles — it makes you forget the cost of living.
Brendan Behan, THE HOSTAGE 1958

16 Violence is the repartee of the illiterate.
Alan Brien, Punch 7 Feb 1973

17 It is better to be violent, if there is violence in our hearts, than to put on the cloak of non-violence to cover impotence.
Mahatma Gandhi, NON-VIOLENCE IN PEACE AND WAR 1948

18 It would surely be better for the Mods and Rockers, and for the community at large, if instead of breaking up Clacton and places like that, they all stayed at home and read a little light pornography.
Ian Gilmour, Observer, Sayings of the Year 1984

19 It is possible to disagree with someone about the ethics of non-violence without wanting to kick his teeth in.
Christopher Hampton, TREATS *(play)*

1 I went out and caught that boy and shook him until his freckles rattled.
O. Henry, THE RANSOM OF RED CHIEF

2 In violence we forget who we are.
Mary McCarthy, ON THE CONTRARY 1961

3 If someone puts his hand on you, send him to the cemetery.
Malcolm X, MALCOLM X SPEAKS 1965

4 Remove your pants before resorting to violence.
Yoko Ono. Quoted Bernard Levin, THE PENDULUM YEARS 1976

5 Today violence is the rhetoric of the period.
José Ortega y Gasset, THE REVOLT OF THE MASSES 1930

6 The argument of the broken pane of glass is the most valuable argument in modern politics.
Emmeline Pankhurst, VOTES FOR WOMEN 23 *Feb* 1912

7 I distrust the incommunicable. It is the source of all violence.
Jean-Paul Sartre, WHAT IS LITERATURE?

VIOLIN

8 *Fiddle, n.* An instrument to tickle human ears by function of a horse's tail on the entrails of a cat.
Ambrose Bierce, THE DEVIL'S DICTIONARY 1906

9 In respect to violins, I am polygamous.
Fritz Kreisler

VIRTUE

10 Righteous people terrify me . . . Virtue is its own punishment.
Aneurin Bevan. Quoted Michael Foot, ANEURIN BEVAN 1897—1945

11 Wolfgang Amadeus Mozart honoured his parents, loved his sister and adored his wife. In fact he was such a nice fellow it's a wonder he ever amounted to anything at all.
Victor Borge, MY FAVOURITE INTERVALS

12 Whenever there are tremendous virtues it's a sure sign something's wrong.
Bertolt Brecht, MOTHER COURAGE 1939

13 A virtue to be serviceable must, like gold, be alloyed with some commoner but more durable metal.
Samuel Butler, THE WAY OF ALL FLESH 1903

14 Virtue consisted in avoiding scandal and venereal disease.
Robert Cecil, LIFE IN EDWARDIAN ENGLAND 1969

15 My virtue's still far too small, I don't trot it out and about yet.
Colette, CLAUDINE AT SCHOOL

16 Our age is an age of moderate virtue.
T. S. Eliot

17 The absence of vices adds so little to the sum of one's virtues.
Antonio Machado, JUAN DE MAIRENO 1943

18 I am not impressed by external devices for the preservation of virtue in men or women. Marriage laws, the police, armies and navies are the mark of human incompetence.
Dora Russell, THE RIGHT TO BE HAPPY

VOCABULARY

19 William Nicholson, noticing that J. M. Barrie always ordered Brussels sprouts and never ate them, one day asked him why. J. M. B. replied 'I cannot resist ordering them. The words are so lovely to say.'
Anon. Sunday Referee 5 *Dec* 1927

20 All the artistic words have changed their meaning in California. *Book* means magazine, *music* means jazz, *act* means behaving, *picture* means a snapshot.
Stella Benson, THE POOR MAN 1922

21 The monstrous word 'electrocute' for kill by electricity is now of regular occurrence, and bids fair to become part of our language. When we have the legitimately formed word 'electrocide' at our service why should it not be adopted and so detestable a solecism as the word referred to be repudiated?
J. Churton Collins, letter to The Times 29 *Mar* 1906

22 It comes in three sizes, Large, Giant and Super. I gave you the small size — Large.
Shop assistant. Quoted by correspondent to Competitor's Journal

1 The four-letter words in *Lady Chatterley* are not likely to be included in the Oxford Dictionary as a result of the case. 'The legal judgment is irrelevant to our purpose' said Oxford University Press. 'We don't take into account anything but common usage.'
Daily Express. Quoted Michael Bateman, THIS ENGLAND

2 'Well' said the Owl, 'the customary procedure in such cases is as follows.'
'What does Crustimoney Proseedcake mean?' said Pooh. 'For I am a bear of Very Little Brain, and long words bother me.'
A. A. Milne, WINNIE THE POOH 1927

3 One forgets words as one forgets names. One's vocabulary needs constant fertilisation or it will die.
Evelyn Waugh, DIARIES

VOICE

4 A voice of plum-coloured velvet.
James Agate, of Ellen Terry

5 There was nothing wrong with her that a vasectomy of her vocal cords wouldn't fix.
Lisa Alther, KINFLICKS 1976

6 . . . a young man with so superior a voice that he might have been to Oxford twice.
Vernon Bartlett, AND NOW, TOMORROW

7 That voice! She sounds as if she thinks a crèche is something that happens on the M1.
Jeananne Crowley, Sunday Times

8 There was always something in her voice that made you think of lorgnettes.
O. Henry, THE DEFEAT OF THE CITY

9 A good voice has ruined more actors than whiskey.
Actor Joseph Jefferson. Quoted Gary Cooper, WELL, IT WAS THIS WAY 1956

10 The most remarkable thing about her was her voice, high, metallic . . . irritating to the nerves like the pitiless clamour of the pneumatic drill.
W. Somerset Maugham, RAIN 1922

11 The unique quality of his voice was the fact that it could reach higher and lower notes than have ever been reached by any other human being, some of which were so high that only bats, others so low that only

horses, could hear them.
Nancy Mitford, PIGEON PIE 1940

12 His [André Gide] voice so clear and true, like the bells of those little Swiss churches sounding out on a Sunday morning in the chill mountain air.
Malcolm Muggeridge, CHRONICLES OF WASTED TIME 1972

13 His voice was intimate as the rustle of sheets.
Dorothy Parker, DUSK BEFORE FIREWORKS

14 She possessed a voice that, like a mill, ground silence into its component parts.
Sir Osbert Sitwell, THE SCARLET TREE 1945

15 Mr [Michael] Foot sounded like an affronted peke.
Honor Tracy, Daily Telegraph 12 May 1979

16 He spoke with a certain what-is-it in his voice, and I could tell that, if not actually disgruntled, he was far from being gruntled.
P. G. Wodehouse, CODE OF THE WOOSTERS 1938

VOLUNTEER

17 To qualify as a member of the Women's Royal Voluntary Service you need to be able to wear a cardigan and jumper and a rope of pearls and to have had a hysterectomy.
Stella, Lady Reading, chairman of WRVS, in an address to members

VOTE

18 What's the point of having a vote if there is nobody worth voting for?
Sheila MacLeod, Sunday Times, Look 26 *Jul* 1981

19 Actually I vote Labour, but my butler's a Tory.
Lord Mountbatten, to a Tory canvasser during the 1945 *election*

20 It's not the voting that's democracy; it's the counting.
Tom Stoppard, JUMPERS

21 I shall not vote because I do not aspire to advise my sovereign on the choice of her servants.
Evelyn Waugh, A LITTLE ORDER

VULGARITY

1 The need to be right — the sign of a vulgar mind.
Albert Camus, NOTEBOOKS 1935–42

2 It is disgusting to pick your teeth. What is vulgar is to use a gold toothpick.
Louis Kronenberger, THE CAT AND THE HORSE

W

WALES

1 Welsh Wales, full of ugly chapels, of hidden money, psalm-singing and rain.
Norman Lewis, JACKDAW CAKE 1985

2 The land of my fathers. And my fathers can have it.
Dylan Thomas. Quoted in the biography of him by John Ackerman

3 There are still parts of Wales where the only concession to gaiety is a striped shroud.
Gwyn Thomas, Punch 18 Jan 1958

4 The girls of Blaenau Ffestiniog / Can be had for a penny (Welsh: *ceiniog*) / This I know for a fact / I was caught in the act / By Lord Hailsham (formerly Mr Quintiniog)
Wynford Vaughan Thomas. Quoted Alan Watkins, Observer 13 May 1979

5 We can trace almost all the disasters of English history to the influence of Wales.
Evelyn Waugh, DECLINE AND FALL 1928

WALKING

6 It is a fact that not once in all my life have I gone out for a walk. I have been taken out for walks; but that is another matter.
Sir Max Beerbohm, GOING OUT FOR A WALK 1918

7 I enjoy my legs crunching the pebbles under my feet — the way I used to enjoy crunching a crust of bread when I had teeth.
Bernard Berenson (at 90), SUNSET AND TWILIGHT

8 He walks as if balancing the family tree on his nose.
Raymond Morley

9 Walking is the favourite sport of the good and the wise.
A. L. Rowse, THE USE OF HISTORY

WILLIAM WALTON

10 Walton wrote 'Balshazzar's Feast' in that barn out there. He made such a frightful din on the piano we had to banish him from the house.
Sacheverell Sitwell. Quoted Alan Hamilton, The Times, profile 16 Nov 1982

WAR

11 What price Glory?
Maxwell Anderson, title of play 1924

12 The only defence is offence, which means that you have to kill more women and children more quickly than the enemy if you wish to save yourselves.
Stanley Baldwin, House of Commons, Nov 1932

13 It takes twenty years or more of peace to make a man, it takes only twenty seconds of war to destroy him.
King Baudouin of the Belgians, addressing US Congress 12 May 1959

14 I have never understood this liking for war. It panders to instincts already catered for within the scope of any respectable domestic establishment.
Alan Bennett, FORTY YEARS ON

15 I was not anxious to go.
Edmund Blunden, opening words of UNDERTONES OF WAR 1928

16 War is like love. It always finds a way.
Bertolt Brecht, MOTHER COURAGE AND HER CHILDREN 1939

17 Nothing on this earth is perfect — a war of which we could say it left nothing to be desired will probably never exist.
Ibid.

1 I wanted the experience of war. I thought there would be no more wars.
Joyce Cary, on being asked why he had gone to the Balkan War in 1912

2 Wars, conflict, it's all business. One murder makes a villain. Millions a hero. Numbers sanctify.
Charles Chaplin, MONSIEUR VERDOUX *(film)*

3 We must be careful not to assign to this deliverance (at Dunkirk) the attributes of a victory. Wars are not won by evacuations.
Winston Churchill, THEIR FINEST HOUR 1949

4 Be calm! Nobody is ever wounded twice on the same day.
Winston Churchill, shortly before his capture by Boers

5 The only time in his life he [Marshal Joffre] ever put up a fight was when we asked him for his resignation.
Georges Clemenceau. Quoted A. M. Thomson, HERE I LIE 1937

6 War is too important to be left to the generals.
Georges Clemenceau. Quoted J. M. Keynes, ESSAYS IN BIOGRAPHY

7 We are not at war with Egypt. We are in a state of armed conflict.
Anthony Eden, House of Commons 4 *Nov* 1956

8 There is nothing that war has ever achieved that we could not better achieve without it.
Havelock Ellis, THE PHILOSOPHY OF CONFLICT

9 The essence of war is surprise.
Lord Fisher. Quoted Lord Boothby, MY YESTERDAY, YOUR TOMORROW 1962

10 Moderation in war is imbecility.
Ibid.

11 Men love war because it allows them to look serious. Because it is the one thing that stops women laughing at them.
John Fowles, THE MAGUS 1965

12 Either man is obsolete, or war is.
R. Buckminster Fuller, I SEEM TO BE A VERB

13 The English do not treat very kindly the men who conduct their wars for them.
Joseph Goebbels, DIARIES

14 I'd like to see the government get out of war altogether and leave the whole feud to private industry.
Joseph Heller, CATCH 22

15 In starting and waging a war it is not right that matters but victory.
Adolf Hitler. Quoted W. L. Shirer, THE RISE AND FALL OF THE THIRD REICH

16 Old men declare war. But it is the youth that must fight and die.
Herbert C. Hoover. Speech 27 *Jun* 1944

17 The statistics of suicide show that, for non-combatants at least, life is more interesting in war than in peace.
W. R. Inge (Dean of St Pauls), THE END OF AN AGE 1918

18 War should belong to the tragic past, to history: it should find no place on humanity's agenda for the future.
Pope John Paul II, Coventry 1982

19 War alone brings up to their highest tension all human energies and imposes the stamp of nobility upon the peoples who have the courage to make it.
Benito Mussolini, ENCYCLOPEDIA ITALIANE 1932

20 The only alternative to co-existence is co-destruction.
Pandit Nehru. Quoted Observer 29 *Aug* 1954

21 The shrill demented choirs of wailing shells / And buglers calling for them from sad shires.
Wilfred Owen, ANTHEM FOR DOOMED YOUTH 1920

22 What passing bells for those who die as cattle? / Only the monstrous anger of the guns / Only the stuttering rifles' rapid rattle / Can patter out their hasty orisons.
Ibid.

23 Red lips are not so red / As the stained stones kissed by the English dead.
Wilfred Owen, GREATER LOVE 1920

1 All wars are planned by old men / In council rooms apart.
Grantland Rice, TWO SIDES OF WAR

2 I discovered to my amazement that average men and women were delighted at the prospect of war. I had fondly imagined what most pacifists contended, that wars were forced upon a reluctant population by despotic and Machiavellian governments.
Bertrand Russell, AUTOBIOGRAPHY 1967

3 War is not an adventure. It is a disease. It is like typhus.
Antoine de Saint-Exupéry, FLIGHT TO ARRAS 1942

4 Sometime they'll give a war and no one will come.
Carl Sandburg, THE PEOPLE, *Yes* 1936

5 When the rich wage war it is the poor who die.
Jean-Paul Sartre, THE DEVIL AND THE GOOD LORD 1951

6 All wars are popular for the first thirty days.
Arthur Schlesinger Jr. Quoted Barbara Rowe, A BOOK OF QUOTES

7 Wars come because not enough people are sufficiently afraid.
Hugh Schonfield, Peace News. Quoted News Review 26 *Feb* 1948

8 Nothing is ever done in this world until men are prepared to kill each other if it is not done.
George Bernard Shaw, MAJOR BARBARA 1905

9 They start bloody wars they can't afford. Chamberlain . . . didn't give a thought to the cost of it — didn't enter his head to get an estimate — soppy old sod.
Johnny Speight, BBC TV, Till Death Us Do Part

10 War is capitalism with the gloves off.
Tom Stoppard, TRAVESTIES

11 Butchery is not the mark of a good tactician.
Field-Marshal Wavell, telegram to Churchill who complained that, in evacuating Somaliland in World War II, his casualties were too light.

12 The military don't start wars. The politicians start wars.
Gen. William Westmorland. Quoted Barbara Rowe, A BOOK OF QUOTES

13 Bombs are unbelievable until they actually fall.
Patrick White, RIDERS IN THE CHARIOT

14 For Hon. Members opposite the deterrent is a phallic symbol. It convinces them that they are men.
George Wigg MP, House of Commons 1964

15 It takes only one gramme of explosive to kill a man, so why waste five tons?
Solly Zuckermann, FROM APES TO WARLORDS

WASTE

16 Nature is as wasteful of promising young men as she is of fish spawn.
Richard Hughes, THE FOX IN THE ATTIC 1961

17 Nothing is surely a waste of time when one enjoys the day.
Arthur Koestler. Quoted Observer, Sayings of the Week 8 *Oct* 1972

18 The biggest waste of water in the country by far is when you spend half a pint and flush two gallons.
Philip, Duke of Edinburgh in a speech 1965

EVELYN WAUGH

19 He had the sharp eye of a Hogarth alternating with that of the ancient mariner.
Harold Acton, ADAM

20 He drank port and put on weight, and attempted to behave in the manner of an Edwardian aristocrat . . . In fact Evelyn's abiding complex and the source of much of his misery was that he was not a six-foot tall extremely handsome and rich duke.
Cecil Beaton, THE STRENUOUS YEARS

21 The satire of Evelyn Waugh in his early books was derived from his ignorance of life. He found cruel things funny because he did not understand them and he was able to communicate that fun.
Cyril Connolly, ENEMIES OF PROMISE 1938

1 He is bored from morning till night and has
developed a personality he hates but cannot
escape from.
Ann Fleming, LETTERS 1985

2 A genius as a pure writer, but intellectually
infantile.
Ibid.

WEALTH

3 A rich man is one who isn't afraid to ask the
salesman to show him something cheaper.
Anon. Ladies Home Journal, Jan 1946

4 Lord Finchley tried to mend the electric
light / It struck him dead and serve him
right. / It is the business of the wealthy
man / To give employment to the artisan.
Hilaire Belloc, CAUTIONARY TALES 1907

5 The confidence inspired by the possession of
a well-filled vault of silver will last an
ordinary person a lifetime.
Ernest Bramah, KAI LUNG UNROLLS HIS
MAT 1928

6 The rich have fallen into bleak disapproval.
In the age of egalitarianism it is assumed
that no one should have very much more
than anyone else, unless he wins it in a
football pool.
William Davis, NO SIN TO BE RICH 1976

7 Wealth is not without its advantages and the
case to the contrary, although it has often
been made, has never proved widely persuasive.
J. K. Galbraith, THE AFFLUENT
SOCIETY 1958

8 I don't know how many millions I am worth.
If you can actually count your money you
are not a really rich man.
Paul Getty. Quoted Bernard Levin, THE
PENDULUM YEARS 1976

9 The rich hate signing cheques. Hence the
success of credit cards.
Graham Greene, DR FISCHER OF GENEVA

10 I have a prejudice against people with
money. I have known so many, and none
have escaped the corruption of power. In
this I am a purist. I love people motivated by
love and not by power. If you have money
and power, and are motivated by love, you
give it all away.
Anaïs Nin, DIARIES, VOL 4 1970

11 God shows his contempt for wealth by the
kind of person he selects to receive it.
Austin O'Malley

12 You can tell how wealthy they are. They
even have fruit on the sideboard when no
one is poorly.
*Contestant describing her employers to
Wilfred Pickles in radio show Have a Go*

13 I believe the power to make money is a gift
of God.
*J. D. Rockefeller. Quoted Matthew
Josephson,* THE ROBBER BARONS

14 I am a millionaire. That is my religion.
George Bernard Shaw, MAJOR
BARBARA 1905

15 If all the rich people in the world divided up
their money among themselves there
wouldn't be enough to go round.
Christina Stead, HOUSE OF ALL NATIONS

16 There is nothing sinful about being rich. My
fortune is as large as my credit rating is
limitless.
Lord Thomson of Fleet

17 Until the age of twelve I sincerely believed
that everybody had a house on Fifth
Avenue, a villa in Newport and a steam-
driven, ocean-going yacht.
Cornelius Vanderbilt Jr, FAREWELL TO
FIFTH AVENUE

18 People are seldom so harmlessly engaged as
when they are working to become rich. It is a
far less damaging occupation than the
pursuit of political power. The rich tend to
be ashamed of their riches, but politicians
are never ashamed of themselves, though
they should be.
Woodrow Wyatt, Observer 17 *Oct* 1976

WEAPON

19 Our scientific power has outrun our spiritual
power. We have guided missiles and mis-
guided men.
Martin Luther King, STRENGTH TO
LOVE 1963

20 A bayonet is a weapon with a worker at both
ends.
Pacifist slogan between the world wars

1 And this you can see is the bolt. The purpose of this / Is to open the breech, as you can see. We can slide it / Rapidly backwards and forwards; we call this / Easing the spring.
Herbert Reed, LESSONS OF THE WAR, Naming of Parts 1946

WEATHER

2 We regret we are unable to give you the weather. We rely on weather reports from the airport, which is closed because of the weather. Whether we are able to give you the weather tomorrow depends on the weather.
Arab News, Jan 1979. Quoted Stephen Pile, THE BOOK OF HEROIC FAILURES

WELFARE STATE

3 There is the fundamental paradox of the welfare state; that it is not built for the desperate, but for those who are already capable of helping themselves.
Michael Harrington, THE OTHER AMERICA

H. G. WELLS

4 He is the old maid among novelists; even the sex obsession that lay clotted on Ann Veronica and the New Machiavelli like cold white sauce was merely old maid's mania, the reaction towards the flesh of a mind too long absorbed in airships and colloids.
Rebecca West, reviewing ANN VERONICA for Freewoman 1912

MAE WEST

5 I've been in *Who's Who*, and I know what's what, but this is the first time I ever made the dictionary.
Mae West, on having a World War II life jacket named after her

6 She stole everything but the camera.
George Raft, after co-starring with her

WICKEDNESS

7 It takes a certain courage and a certain greatness even to be truly base.
Jean Anouilh, ARDELE 1948

8 The belief in a supernatural source of evil is not necessary, men alone are quite capable of every sort of wickedness.
Joseph Conrad, UNDER WESTERN EYES 1911

9 A good man can be stupid and still be good. But a bad man must have brains.
Maxim Gorky, THE LOWER DEPTHS

WIFE

10 Obviously a wife is worth something because she has attracted another man. Therefore she has some value, and must have had some value in the eyes of her husband.
Judge Essenhigh, in a divorce action. Quoted News Review 13 Feb 1947

11 Always see a fellow's weak point in his wife.
James Joyce, ULYSSES 1922

12 A loving wife will do anything for her husband except stop criticising and trying to improve him.
J. B. Priestley, RAIN ON GODSHILL

13 Marriage is for women the commonest mode of livelihood, and the total amount of undesired sex endured by women is probably greater in marriage than in prostitution.
Bertrand Russell, MARRIAGE AND MORALS, Prostitution 1929

HAROLD WILSON

14 Harold Wilson is not nearly so clever as we thought, but nicer.
Dora Gaitskell, Quoted Cecil King, DIARY 6 Dec 1968

15 I am probably one of the few Prime Ministers who cleans his own shoes.
Harold Wilson, Observer, Sayings of the Year, 1964

16 The biggest mistake I ever made was appointing George Brown as Foreign Secretary.
Harold Wilson, Woman's Own 15 Mar 1986

17 If Harold has a fault it is that he will smother everything with HP sauce.
Mrs Harold Wilson in an interview 1962

1 When Harold Wilson was forming his first government in 1964 I resented his being at No. 10. My distrust of him was the same as always. I felt he had weak principles, scarcely any that took precedence over his single-minded self interest. *Après moi le deluge* was his motto, and no provision for umbrellas.
Woodrow Wyatt, CONFESSIONS OF AN OPTIMIST 1985

WOODROW WILSON

2 A slim bespectacled man with a long jaw and the contained self-assurance of a bishop.
Alistair Cooke, AMERICA

3 Like Odysseus, he looked wiser when seated.
J. M. Keynes. Quoted Robert L. Heilbroner, THE WORLDLY PHILOSOPHERS

4 The air currents of the world never ventilated his mind.
Walter Hines Page. Quoted Patrick Devlin, TOO PROUD TO FIGHT, WOODROW WILSON'S NEUTRALITY

WIND

5 Wind moving through grass so that the grass quivers. This moves me with an emotion I don't even understand.
Katherine Mansfield, JOURNALS 1928

DUCHESS OF WINDSOR

6 Wallis is a very vulgar woman in gesture, she sticks her beautifully scented face within two inches and just asks to be kissed, only of course you don't do it.
Lord Eccles, BY SAFE HAND, LETTERS OF DAVID AND SYBIL ECCLES 1939—42, 1983

WINE

7 This wine is too good for toast-drinking, my dear. You don't want to mix emotions up with a wine like that. You lose the taste.
Ernest Hemingway, THE SUN ALSO RISES 1926

8 It's a Naive Domestic Burgundy, Without Any Breeding. But I think you'll be Amused by its Presumption.
James Thurber, cartoon caption, MEN, WOMEN AND DOGS 1943

WISDOM

9 *Judge:* I have read your case, Mr Smith, and am no wiser now than I was when I started.
F. E. Smith: Possibly not my Lord; but far better informed
Lord Birkenhead. Quoted Second Earl of Birkenhead, LIFE OF F. E. SMITH

10 If one is too lazy to think, too vain to do a thing badly, too cowardly to admit it, one will never attain wisdom.
Cyril Connolly, THE UNQUIET GRAVE 1945

11 Knowledge can be communicated but not wisdom.
Hermann Hesse, SIDDHARTHA 1923

12 God grant me the serenity to accept the things I cannnot change, courage to change the things I can, and wisdom always to tell the difference.
Kurt Vonnegut, SLAUGHTERHOUSE-FIVE 1969

13 He was gifted with the sly, sharp instinct for self-preservation that passes for wisdom among the rich.
Evelyn Waugh, SCOOP 1938

WIT

14 There's a hell of a distance between wisecracking and wit. Wit has truth in it; wisecracking is simply callisthenics with words.
Dorothy Parker, WRITERS AT WORK *(ed. Malcolm Cowley)* 1958

P. G. WODEHOUSE

15 Literature's performing flea.
Sean O'Casey

16 There is no suggestion that either club man or girl would recognise a double bed except as so much extra sweat to make an apple pie of.
Richard Usborne, WODEHOUSE AT WORK 1961

17 For Mr Wodehouse there has been no fall of man, no 'aboriginal calamity'. His characters have never tasted the forbidden fruit. They are still in Eden. The gardens of Blandings Castle are the original gardens from which we are all exiled.
Evelyn Waugh in a broadcast tribute to P. G. Wodehouse on his 80th birthday 1961

WOMAN

1 The sort of woman who, if accidentally
locked in alone in the National Gallery,
would start rearranging the pictures.
Anon.

2 One is not born a woman. One becomes
one.
Simone de Beauvoir, THE SECOND SEX 1949

3 Intimacies between women often go backwards, beginning in revelations and ending
in small talk without loss of esteem.
Elizabeth Bowen, THE DEATH OF THE
HEART 1938

4 Certain women should be struck regularly,
like gongs.
Noël Coward, PRIVATE LIVES 1930

5 Women never have young minds. They are
born three thousand years old.
Shelagh Delaney, A TASTE OF HONEY 1958

6 Women are most fascinating between the
ages of thirty-five and forty, after they have
won a few races and know how to pace
themselves. Since few women ever pass
forty, maximum fascination can continue
indefinitely.
Christian Dior, Colliers Magazine 10 *Jun*
1955

7 There are only three things to be done with a
woman. You can love her, you can suffer for
her, or you can turn her into literature.
Lawrence Durrell, JUSTINE 1957

8 All Berkshire women are very silly. I don't
know why women in Berkshire are more
silly than anywhere else.
*Judge Claude Duveen, Reading County
Court. Quoted Observer, Sayings of the
Week* 9 *Jul* 1972

9 As long as a woman's flesh is clean and
healthy what does it matter what shape she
is?
Ian Fleming, from his private notebooks

10 When a woman behaves like a man, why
doesn't she behave like a nice man?
Dame Edith Evans. Quoted Observer 30 *Sep*
1956

11 A woman should be an illusion.
Ian Fleming. Quoted John Pearson, LIFE OF
IAN FLEMING 1966

12 Women are equal because they are not
different any more.
Eric Fromm, THE ART OF LOVING 1956

13 If men knew how women pass their time
when they are alone, they'd never marry.
O. Henry, THE FOUR MILLION MEMOIRS OF A
YELLOW DOG 1906

14 The female of the species is more deadly
than the male.
Rudyard Kipling, THE FEMALE OF THE
SPECIES 1921

15 A woman should open everything to a man
except her mouth.
Derek Marlowe, A DANDY IN ASPIC 1966

16 The Professor of Gynaecology began his
course of lectures as follows: Gentlemen,
woman is an animal that micturates once a
day, defecates once a week, menstruates
once a month, parturates once a year and
copulates whenever she has the opportunity.
W. Somerset Maugham, A WRITER'S
NOTEBOOK 1949

17 There are two kinds of women; those who
want power in the world, and those who
want power in bed.
*Jacqueline Kennedy Onassis. Quoted
Barbara Rowe,* A BOOK OF QUOTES

18 Most good women are hidden treasures who
are only safe because nobody looks for
them.
*Dorothy Parker. Quoted in her obituary,
New York Times* 8 *Jun* 1967

19 There are two kinds of women — goddesses
and doormats.
Pablo Picasso. Quoted Barbara Rowe, A
BOOK OF QUOTES

20 Women are like dreams — they are never
the way you would like to have them.
Luigi Pirandello, EACH IN HIS OWN WAY

21 A woman is like a tea bag. Only when in hot
water do you realise how strong she is.
*Nancy Reagan, Observer, Sayings of the
Week* 29 *Mar* 1981

22 The doctors said at the time that she
couldn't live more than a fortnight, and she's
been trying ever since to see if she could.
Women are so opinionated.
Saki, REGINALD ON WOMEN

1 Women are not so completely enslaved as farm stock.
George Bernard Shaw, GETTING MARRIED 1908

2 This Englishwoman is so refined / She has no bosom and no behind.
Stevie Smith, THIS ENGLISHWOMAN

3 The great and almost only comfort about being a woman is that one can always pretend to be more stupid than one is, and no one is surprised.
Freya Stark, THE VALLEY OF THE ASSASSINS 1934

WONDER

4 To be surprised, to wonder, is to begin to understand.
José Ortega y Gasset, THE REVOLT OF THE MASSES 1930

VIRGINIA WOOLF

5 One of my *fears* — I don't think I was quite alone in this — was that one day she would speak to me (but she never did).
Hugo Dyson. Quoted Humphrey Carpenter, THE INKLINGS

6 I enjoyed talking to her, but thought *nothing* of her writing. I considered her 'a beautiful little knitter'.
Edith Sitwell, letter to G. Singleton 11 Jul 1955

WORDS

7 Words, as is well known, are great foes of reality.
Joseph Conrad, UNDER WESTERN EYES, *Prologue* 1911

8 It's strange that words are so inadequate / Yet, like the asthmatic struggling for breath, / so the lover must struggle for words.
T. S. Eliot, THE ELDER STATESMAN 1958

9 You can stroke people with words.
F. Scott Fitzgerald, THE CRACK-UP 1936

10 Words build bridges into unexplored regions.
Adolf Hitler. Quoted Alan Bullock, HITLER, A STUDY IN TYRANNY

11 Words are the dress of thoughts, which should no more be presented in rags, tatters and dirt than your person should.
Reggie Kray, Quoted James Fox, Observer Magazine 14 Mar 1986

12 Isn't everyone consoled when faced with a trouble or fact he doesn't understand, by a word, some simple word, which tells us nothing and yet calms us.
Luigi Pirandello, SIX CHARACTERS IN SEARCH OF AN AUTHOR 1921

WORK

13 *Rich:* Do you know how much I have to show for seven months' work?
More: Work?
Rich: Work! Waiting is work when you wait as I wait, Lord!
Robert Bolt, A MAN FOR ALL SEASONS 1961

14 Whether our work is art or science or the daily work of society, it is only the form in which we explore our experience that is different.
Jacob Bronowski, SCIENCE AND HUMAN VALUES, *The Sense of Human Dignity* 1956

15 There is dignity in work only when it is work freely accepted.
Albert Camus, NOTEBOOKS 1935—1942

16 Work is more fun than fun.
Noël Coward. Quoted Cole Leslie, NOËL COWARD AND HIS FRIENDS

17 One of the saddest things is that the only thing a man can do for eight hours a day, day after day, is work. You can't eat eight hours a day, nor drink for eight hours a day, nor make love for eight hours.
William Faulkner, WRITERS AT WORK 1958

18 The idea that to make a man work you've got to hold gold in front of his eyes is a growth, not an axiom. We've done that for so long that we've forgotten there's any other way.
F. Scott Fitzgerald, THIS SIDE OF PARADISE 1920

19 When work is a pleasure, life is a joy! When work is a duty, life is slavery.
Maxim Gorky, THE LOWER DEPTHS 1903

1 Work is the greatest thing in the world, so we should always save some for tomorrow.
Don Herold. Quoted Frank Muir, ON CHILDREN

2 I haven't had time to work in weeks.
Jack Kerouac, ON THE ROAD 1957

3 Why should I let the toad *work* / Squat on my life? / Can't I use my wit as a pitchfork / And drive the brute off?
Philip Larkin, TOADS

4 Work is the province of cattle.
Dorothy Parker

5 Work expands to fill the time available for its completion. General recognition of this fact is shown in the proverbial phrase 'It is the busiest man who has time to spare.'
C. Northcote Parkinson, PARKINSON'S LAW 1962

6 Work is necessary for man. Man invented the alarm clock.
Pablo Picasso. Quoted Barbara Rowe, A BOOK OF QUOTES

7 I should have worked just long enough to discover that I didn't like it.
Paul Theroux. Quoted Alan Road, Observer Magazine 1 Apr 1979

WORLD

8 The world is the mirror of myself dying.
Henry Miller, BLACK SPRING 1936

WRESTLING

9 Professional wrestling's most mystifying hold is on its audience.
Luke Neely, Saturday Evening Post 27 Nov 1953

WRITING

10 Writing comes more easily if you have something to say.
Sholem Asch, New York Herald Tribune 6 Nov 1955

11 As a rule, the sign that a beginner has genuine original talent is that he is more interested in playing with words than in saying something original.
W. H. Auden, THE DYER'S HAND AND OTHER ESSAYS 1962

12 Like the man who was complimented on the shortness of a speech and who remarked that he would have made it shorter if he'd had more time, I am a believer in economy of words.
Armiger Barclay (Countess Barcynska), TP's Weekly 15 Sep 1938

13 To give an accurate and exhaustive account of that period would need a far less brilliant pen than mine.
Max Beerbohm, DIMINUENDO

14 If you cannot say what you have to say in twenty minutes go away and write a book about it.
Lord Brabazon. Speech 1956

15 To write is to become disinterested. There is a certain renunciation in art.
Albert Camus, NOTEBOOKS 1935—1942

16 Writing has laws of perspective, of light and shade, just as painting does, or music. If you are born knowing them, fine. If not, learn them. Then rearrange the rules to suit yourself.
Truman Capote, WRITERS AT WORK 1958

17 When I split an infinitive, God damn it, I split it so that it will stay split, and when I interrupt the velvety smoothness of my more or less literate syntax with a few sudden words of bar-room vernacular that is done with the eyes wide open and the mind relaxed.
Raymond Chandler in a letter to his publisher. Quoted, RAYMOND CHANDLER SPEAKING

18 The health of a writer should not be too good, and perfect only in those periods of convalescence when he is not writing.
Cyril Connolly, ENEMIES OF PROMISE 1938

19 If, as Dr Johnson said, a man who is not married is only half a man, so a man who is very much married is only half a writer.
Ibid.

20 I feel his books are all written in hotels with the bed unmade at the back of the chair.
Ronald Firbank, THE FLOWER BENEATH THE FOOT 1923

21 Writers aren't exactly people, or, if they're any good, they're a whole lot of people trying so hard to be one person.
F. Scott Fitzgerald, THE LAST TYCOON 1941

1 All good writing is swimming under water and holding your breath.
F. Scott Fitzgerald, in a letter

2 If I had to give young writers advice I would say don't listen to writers talking about writing or themselves.
Lillian Hellman, New York Times 21 Feb 1960

3 Despite many disillusions I still cling obstinately to the belief that writing can be done with your left hand while your right is busy with something else.
Lillian Hellman. Quoted The Times obituary 2 Jul 1984

4 Writing, at its best, is a lonely life. Organisations for writers palliate his loneliness but I doubt if they improve his writing.
Ernest Hemingway, Nobel Prize Speech 10 Dec 1954

5 I always go to places *after* I've written about them. That stops me wanting to write about them any more.
Richard Hughes. Quoted Mary Jay Wilmers, Radio Times 12 Jun 1979

6 The fact that many people should be shocked by what he writes practically imposes it as a duty on a writer to go on shocking them.
Aldous Huxley, MUSIC AT NIGHT

7 A bad book is as much of a labour to write as a good one; it comes as sincerely from the author's soul.
Aldous Huxley, POINT COUNTER POINT 1928

8 So far as good writing goes, the use of the exclamation mark is a sign of failure. It is the literary equivalent of a man holding up a card reading LAUGHTER to a studio audience.
Miles Kington, Punch 18 Aug 1976

9 I like to write when I feel spiteful; it's like having a good sneeze.
D. H. Lawrence, letter to Cynthia Asquith, Nov 1913

10 All human activity to me is a way of avoiding writing. Thus, I sleep as much as possible or spend a hard day lying on the sofa.
Fran Lebowitz. Quoted in an interview with John Heilpern, Observer 21 Jan 1979

11 I stumbled on a form of writing that sets off recollections.
Laurie Lee in an interview with Philip Radcliffe, Observer 8 Jan 1979

12 It has been said that good prose should resemble the conversation of a well-bred man.
W. Somerset Maugham, THE SUMMING UP 1938

13 A writer is essentially a man who does not resign himself to loneliness.
François Mauriac, DIEU ET MAMMON 1929

14 Sin is the writer's element.
François Mauriac, SECOND THOUGHTS, *Literature and Sin* 1961

15 No man would set a word down on paper if he had the courage to live out what he believed in.
Henry Miller, SUNDAY AFTER THE WAR 1944

16 A writer is unfair to himself when he is unable to be hard on himself.
Marianne Moore, WRITERS AT WORK 1963

17 The writer is the Faust of modern society, the only surviving individualist in a mass age. To his orthodox contemporaries he seems a semi-madman.
Boris Pasternak, Observer 20 Dec 1959

18 'I do want you to meet Miss Leighton-Buzzard' said Mrs Bovey-Tracey, asking me to dinner the other day. 'She's such an interesting woman, and most unusual. She *doesn't write* you know.'
William Plomer, ELECTRIC DELIGHTS

19 Our passions shape our books, repose writes them in the intervals.
Marcel Proust, REMEMBRANCE OF THINGS PAST, *Time Regained* 1927

20 He [Laurie Lee] writes, as he has always done, in pencil. Not just any pencil, but a 3B. 'It doesn't make any noise', he says.
Philip Radcliffe, Observer 8 Jan 1979

21 Writing is not a profession but a vocation of unhappiness.
Georges Simenon, WRITERS AT WORK 1958

1 I found writing a book very strange because I'd never written one before. It was like starting on Everest when you hadn't climbed the Chilterns.
Mary Soames, on winning the Wolfson Literary Prize with Clementina Churchill in 1979

2 A born writer is born scrofulous; his career is an accident dictated by physical or circumstantial disabilities.
Dylan Thomas, letter to Pamela Hansford Johnson

3 You have to spend half your leisure in writing articles for the papers; the editors buy these because people buy your books, and people buy your books because they see your articles in the papers.
Evelyn Waugh, LABELS

4 I regard writing not as investigation of character but as an exercise in the use of language, and with this I am obsessed. I have no technical psychological interest. It is drama, speech and events that interest me.
Evelyn Waugh, PARIS REVIEW 1962

5 The fact that these books — two novels, a book of travel, a biography, a work of contemporary history — never got beyond the first ten thousand words was testimony to the resilience of his character.
Evelyn Waugh, PUT OUT MORE FLAGS 1942

6 I constantly rewrite — an incinerator is a writer's best friend.
Thornton Wilder, New York Times 6 Nov 1961

7 Literature is strewn with the wreckage of men who have minded beyond reason the opinion of others.
Virginia Woolf, A ROOM OF ONE'S OWN 1929

Y

W. B. YEATS

1 Earth, receive an honoured guest / William Yeats is laid to rest / Let the Irish vessel lie / Emptied of its poetry.
W. H. Auden, IN MEMORY OF W. B. YEATS 1940

2 I left him in my room to himself and at lunch time he told me he had done an excellent morning's work having written four lines and destroyed them.
John Drinkwater, DISCOVERY

3 I am too old for Yeats, just as I am too old to hear the cry of a bat.
G. W. Lyttelton, THE LYTTELTON HART-DAVIS LETTERS 20 Nov 1955

YOUTH

4 All evil comes from the old. They grow fat on ideas and young men die of them.
Jean Anouilh, CATCH AS CATCH CAN 1960

5 If age, which is certainly / As wicked as youth, looks any wiser / It is only that youth is still able to believe / It will get away with anything, while age / Knows only too well that it has got away with nothing.
W. H. Auden, THE SEA AND THE MIRROR 1945

6 The only thing I regret about my past life is the length of it. If I had my past life over again I'd make all the same mistakes — only sooner.
Talullah Bankhead. Quoted, The Times 28 Jul 1981

7 Americans began by loving youth and now, out of self-pity, they worship it.
Jacques Barzun, THE HOUSE OF INTELLECT 1959

8 Youth is like spring, an overpraised season.
Samuel Butler, THE WAY OF ALL FLESH 1903

9 It is typically the most sensitive and intelligent of the young who become revolutionaries, destroyers.
Joyce Cary, ART AND REALITY

10 If youth did not matter so much to itself it would never have the heart to go on.
Willa Cather, SONG OF THE LARK 1915

11 'And youth is cruel, and has no remorse / And smiles at situations which it cannot see.' / I smile of course, / And go on drinking tea.
T. S. Eliot, PORTRAIT OF A LADY 1917

12 Everybody's youth is a dream, a form of chemical madness.
F. Scott Fitzgerald, THE DIAMOND AS BIG AS THE RITZ

13 I never dared be radical when young, for fear it would make me conservative when old.
Robert Frost, PRECAUTION

14 The American ideal is youth – handsome, empty youth.
Henry Miller, THE WISDOM OF THE HEART, Raimu 1941

15 Youth is a malady of which one becomes cured a little every day.
Benito Mussolini, on his 50th birthday

16 Youth does not require reasons for living, only pretexts.
José Ortega y Gasset, THE REVOLT OF THE MASSES 1930

17 All that the young can do for the old [is] to shock them and keep them up to date.
George Bernard Shaw, FANNIE'S FIRST PLAY 1912

18 All youth is bound to be misspent, there is something in its very nature that makes it so, and that is why all men regret it.
Thomas Wolfe, OF TIME AND THE RIVER 1935

Z

ZEST

1 What hunger is in relation to food, zest is in relation to life.
Bertrand Russell, THE CONQUEST OF HAPPINESS 1930

ZOO

2 The sort of man who likes to spend his time watching a cage of monkeys chase one another, or a lizard catch flies, or a lion gnaw its tail, is precisely the sort of man whose mental weakness should be combatted at the public expense, and not fostered.
H. L. Mencken, New York Evening Mail 2 Feb 1918

Index of Authors

Quotation references are given by page, followed by the number of the quotation on that page. The latter appears in italics where the person indexed is being referred to in the quotation rather than quoting.

A

Abercrombie, Lascelles, 141:5
Ableman, Paul, 107:9, 263:18
Abrahams, Dr. Adolphe, 194:3
Abse, Dannie, 2:16, 34:3, 77:11, 172:18, 350:19
Acheson, Dean, 121:15, 212:2, 278:19
Ackerley, J.R., 202:4, 275:1
Ackroyd, Peter, 50:7, 150:3, 185:12
Acton, Harold, 26:5, 277:2, 375:19
Acton, Lord, 235:14
Adamov, Arthur, 357:11
Adams, Franklin P., 119:16, 291:2
Adams, Henry Brooks, 64:16, 153:12–13, 219:3, 222:16, 291:3–5, 299:1
Adamson, E., 41:1
Adcock, Sir Frank, 122:3
Ade, George, 90:13, 116:9, 142:1, 155:13, 362:3
Adler, Larry, 368:12
Admiralty classification of chamberpots, 64:10
Adrian, Max, 92:9
Advertisement, 41:2, 252:2
Agate, James, 7:1–2, 26:6, 36:13, 83:1, 118:4, 134:11, 160:6, 168:2, 201:7, 240:12, 309:13, 371:4
Agnew, Spiro, 206:7
Aitken, Jonathan, 147:5
Albee, Edward, 3:17, 191:1, 266:10
Aldington, Richard, 279:1
Aldiss, Brian, 369:14
Aldridge, John W., 319:5
Alexander, Herbert, 81:12
Alexandra, Princess, 284:20
Alexander of Tunis, Earl, 328:*2*
Alfonso XIII of Spain, 31:12, 236:16

Ali, Muhammad, 55:12, 55:*13*
Allen, Fred, 16:1, 60:1, 167:21, 351:6
Allen, Woody, 56:1, 97:8–11, 199:16, 336:10, 360:17
Alliluyeva, Svetlana, 346:3
Allingham, Margery, 65:4
Allington, Adrian, 90:14
Alsop, Joseph, 176:11
Alsop, Susan Mary, 136:10
Alther, Lisa, 12:4, 97:12, 371:5
Altrincham, Lord, 39:7
Alvarez, A, 107:10
American visitor, 362:4
Amery, Leo, 169:5
Amis, Kingsley, 21:10, 66:12, 111:13, 116:10, 175:3, 220:16, 322:15, 336:11
Amory, Cleveland, 268:17
Anderson, Brooks, 285:1
Anderson, Eddie, 240:9
Anderson, Lindsay, 299:2
Anderson, Maxwell, 373:11
Anderson, Sherwood, 124:19, 204:3, 262:2
Anderton, James, 303:1
Andrew, Elizabeth, 208:1
Andrew, Father, 69:14, 135:5, 199:17, 322:16
Andrews, Eamonn, 55:13
Andrews, Julie, 7:3, 8:6
Andrews, Lucilla, 204:10
Annan, Gabriele, 10:9
Annan, Lord, 100:20, 191:2
Anne, Princess, 71:9, 168:3, 184:1, 222:17
Anon, 4:5, 5:1, 7:3, 16:18, 16:19, 17:19, 21:11, 23:14, 31:7, 32:12, 35:4, 52:14, 76:17, 81:9, 96:1, 97:13, 120:9, 145:12, 166:1, 172:12, 180:5, 185:11, 192:14, 194:4, 212:5, 218:13, 220:17, 246:14, 248:9, 254:4–5, 255:18, 263:9, 265:12, 279:2, 286:21, 291:6, 295:13, 298:1, 301:1, 303:2,

331:1, 336:12, 345:14, 351:10, 355:2, 359:5, 370:19, 376:3, 379:1
Anouilh, Jean, 26:7, 79:16, 88:6, 166:3, 199:15, 219:4, 244:15, 261:15, 298:3, 303:3, 308:12, 320:15, 332:7, 361:13, 377:7, 384:4
Appleton, Sir Edward, 200:6, 268:18
Arab News, 377:2
Archibald, Steve, 150:4
Arendt, Hannah, 364:8
Argyll, Duke of, 336:2
Armour, Richard, 105:6
Armstrong, James Robertson, 48:16
Armstrong, Louis, 254:6
Armstrong, Neil, 344:16
Arnaud, Yvonne, 283:4
Arnell, Richard, 45:16
Arno, Peter, 221:17
Arnold, Sue, 32:6
Aron, Raymond, 33:4
Arp, Jean, 26:8
Arran (Arthur Gore), Earl of, 187:8, 191:3, 281:1, 281:*18*
Arrowsmith, Pat, 33:*8*, 141:*13*
Arthur, Lady Elizabeth, 51:11
Asch, Sholem, 150:16, 381:10
Ascherson, Neal, 212:6
Ascoli, Bernard d', 285:5
Ashford, Daisy, 43:7, 88:20, 131:9, 147:6, 165:9, 246:15, 277:12–13, 285:16
Ashurst, Senator Henry F., 339:1
Asquith, Lady Cynthia, 43:9, 48:5, 175:5
Asquith, The Hon. Sir Cyril, 26:9
Asquith (Earl of Oxford), H. H., 31:*3–6*, 201:*11*, 220:15, 246:*17*, 322:17, 340:*17*
Asquith (Countess of Oxford), Margot, 31:7–*11*,

Fisher, Martin Henry, 351:11
Fishlock, Trevor, 202:7
Fitzgerald, F. Scott, 3:6, 10:13,
    12:5, 17:16, 38:11, 43:16,
    72:3, 86:17, 89:2, 103:1,
    112:2, 131:18, 145:*14–16*,
    154:5, 168:1, 172:14, 185:18,
    189:1, 224:15, 240.11, 247.6,
    271:1, 307:15, 315:2, 326:10,
    331:7, 348:13, 351:5, 368:2,
    380:9, 380:18, 381:21, 382:1,
    384.12
Flanagan, Bud, 58:5, 124:8,
    188:8
Flecker, James Elroy, 60:16,
    98:9–10, 157:5, 272:9
Fleming, Sir Ambrose, 90:4
Fleming, Ann, 89:13, 349:20,
    356:9, 376:1–2
Fleming, Ian, 54:17, 101:4,
    146:7, 146:*8*, 147:*19*, 187:13,
    237:4, 308:1, 335:13, 336:16,
    379:9, 379:11
Fleming, Peter, 24:1, 46:4, 262:4
Flint, Rachel Heyhoe, 150:6
Flynn, Errol, 335:17
Follette, 330:9
Fonda, Jane, 8:1
Fontaine, Joan, 292:2
Foot, Michael, 49:5, 49:10, 89:3,
    150:2, 162:7, 169:16, 208:5,
    239:4, 252:15, 261:16, 292:3,
    299:6, 346:2, 356:10, 371:*15*
Foot, Paul, 213:1
Ford, Betty, 17:3
Ford, Ford Maddox, 131:*15*,
    227:20, 243:*13*
Ford, Gerald, 150:*14*
Ford, Henry, 59:10, 129:7,
    181:3–4, 248:21
Forder, H.P., 192:16
Forster, E.M., 43:17, 48:14,
    53:2, 86:15, 88:9, 98:11,
    122:15–16, 151:*6–7*, 151:15–
    16, 181:4–5, 196:16, 210:2,
    214:3, 231:10, 248:22, 256:2,
    279:8, 283:17, 298:7, 312:12,
    319:13, 323:10–11, 345:15,
    349:9, 361:1–2, 362:13, 363:*3*
Fosdick, Henry Emerson, 33:6
Fowles, John, 21:21, 113:10,
    201:4, 288:2, 300:9, 343:2,
    374:11
France, Anatole, 101:11, 225:6
Francis-Williams, Lord, 50:12
Franco, General, 151:*11*
Frank, Anne, 43:18
Frank, Waldo, 10:14
Fraser, Sir K., 209:3
Fraser, Lady Antonia, 85:11

Frayn, Michael, 90:5, 245:15
French War College report,
    161:1
Freud, Clement, 219:14, 356:11
Freud, Sigmund, 19:17, 72:*15*,
    84:3, 98:12, 121:3, 129:1,
    166:20, 175:8, 198:19–20,
    306:4, 310:13–14, 311:10,
    311:*13*, 323:12–15, 349:21
Frick, Henry, 199:12
Friedman, Milton, 61:11, 115:4,
    169:17, 359:1
Frisch, Max, 191:10
Frohman, Charles, 98:13
Fromm, Erich, 18:9, 84:4, 98:14,
    125:18, 379:12
Frost, David, 91:16, 286:*8*,
    312:13
Frost, Robert, 4:18, 46:5, 56:4,
    60:2, 64:13, 78:13, 98:15,
    103:3, 139:12, 151:1, 155:*11*,
    157:6, 166:21, 175:9, 184:20,
    202:16, 279:9, 288:3, 300:10,
    351:16, 384:13
Fry, Christopher, 63:4, 77:7,
    78:2, 98:16, 109:16, 125:19,
    130:4, 185:1, 204:12, 235:12,
    251:1, 260:14, 263:13, 288:4,
    305:10, 336:6, 351:8, 365:5,
    368:6
Fry, Roger, 27:18, 258:19
Fuller, Richard Buckminster,
    166:22, 359:11, 366:17,
    374:12
Fuller, Roy, 25:14, 103:8
Furlong, Monica, 2:1, 54:18,
    165:16
Fynn, 166:23–24

G

Gabor, Zsa-Zsa, 107:14, 132:2
Gaines, Steven, 43:4
Gaitskell, Dora, 377:14
Gaitskell, Hugh, 158:*2–5*,
    193:11, 308:*4*
Galbraith, J.K., 13:8–11, 15:6,
    49:14, 54:19, 60:10, 74:15,
    78:11, 105:9, 109:9, 115:5–10,
    116:19, 135:14, 139:2–3,
    151:12, 191:11, 203:12, 208:9,
    216:3, 217:8, 222:3–4, 239:5,
    249:1–2, 263:3, 279:10,
    282:16, 292:4–5, 298:8, 304:4,
    304:13, 329:1–2, 349:10,
    376:7
Gallagher, J., 154:6
Galland, Adolf, 40:3
Gallico, Paul, 4:10
Galli-Curci, Amelia, 269:5

Galsworthy, John, 48:6, 75:8,
    83:15, 84:11, 106:12, 125:16,
    143:11–13, 148:6, 158:6–7,
    211:19, 219:15, 221:2, 286:4,
    292:6, 296:6
Gandhi, Indira, 159:*13–15*
Gandhi, Mahatma, M.K., 15:7,
    73:22, 159:*16–17*, 160:*1–5*,
    166:25, 172:4, 186:9, 300:11,
    318:17, 321:11, 329:3, 332:2,
    340:15, 368:14
Garbo, Greta, 13:12, 160:*6–8*,
    343:21
Gardner, Ed, 269:6
Gardner, Ava, 37:18
Gardner, John W., 181:6, 298:9
Gardner, Richard, 209:17
Garel, Leo, 77:8
Garfield, Leon, 245:1
Garner, Alan, 275:5
Garnett, David, 130:5, 226:2
Gascoigne, Bamber, 8:2, 329:4
Gaulle, General Charles de,
    34:8, 66:5, 98:17, 154:*21*,
    160:*17*, 161:*1*, 270:7, 292:7–8
Geddes, Norman, B., 361:12
General Motors, 45:14
Genet, Jean, 120:7, 318:4
George V, King, 10:4, 52:13,
    164:*9–10*, 168:7, 247:16,
    275:6, 283:6, 328:3
George VI, King, 164:*11–13*,
    247:17, 257:9, 273:12
George-Brown, Lord, 292:9,
    347:13
Gerhardie, William, 282:9,
    331:8, 336:17, 367:5
Gershwin, George, 99:*14*
Getty, J. Paul, 165:2, 241:9,
    243:11, 322:13, 360:1, 376:8
Gibbons, Cardinal, 321:12
Gibbons, H.A., 158:11
Gibbons, Stella, 301:3
Gibbs, Wolcott, 357:19
Gibran, Kahil, 2:12, 25:2, 83:8,
    128:6, 178:16, 274:14, 275:7,
    300:12
Gide, André, 11:10, 12:18, 23:7,
    27:19, 80:3, 145:9, 166:26,
    174:14, 175:10, 200:14, 204:4,
    207:9, 227:21, 229:19, 245:8,
    247:7, 267:8, 301:12, 327:11,
    329:5, 332:5, 359:2, 365:6,
    371:*12*
Gielgud, Sir John, 38:12, 134:22,
    333:3
Gilbert, W.S., 357:20
Gill, Eric, 114:11, 171:11
Gilliat, Penelope, 21:15
Gilman, Charlotte P., 126:10

Wilkins, Maurice, 334:14
Willans, Geoffrey, 69:13
Willcocks, David, 47:16
Williams, Charles, 339:14
Williams, David, 158:7
Williams, Prof. Gwyn, 338:13
Williams, John Sharp, 171:2
Williams, Kenneth, 82:14
Williams, Ralph Vaughan,
258:7–8
Williams, Shirley, 2:8, 19:12,
70:11, 143:3, 276:3, 276:17,
295:8
Williams, Tennessee, 5:13,
19:13, 46:17, 100:15, 109:6,
128:5, 156:10, 209:14,
227:5–6, 242:21–22, 261:1,
268:12, 352:7, 358:21
Williamson, Henry, 45:15
Wilson, Angus, 277:10, 325:12
Wilson, A. N., 66:8
Wilson, Earl, 73:11
Wilson, Edmund, 42:12
Wilson, Sir Harold, 10:6, 48:2,
60:6–8, 113:1, 115:17, 150:13,
159:4, 171:3, 178:4, 185:8,
185:10, 204:2, 235:9, 248:8,
271:4, 293:1, 295:9–11, 310:4,
331:13, 357:10, 377:14–17,
378:1
Wilson, Mrs Harold, 377:17
Wilson, Sandy, 10:10, 24:14,
232:19
Wilson, Woodrow, 39:4,
102:17–18, 152:21, 155:7,
171:4, 176:9, 192:12, 199:14,
224:14, 313:15, 327:16, 361:4,
364:11, 378:2–4
Wilton, Hal, 250:6, 348:4
Wimperis, Arthur, 124:16, 340:9
Windsor, Duchess of, 19:14,
118:14, 129:18, 378:6
Windsor, Duke of, 164:10,
164:13, 247:13, 258:10, 276:4,
366:14

Winn, Godfrey, 64:9, 167:19,
Winster, Lord, 282:1
Winter, Carl de, 297:15
Winters, Shelley, 9:15
Wise, Stephen Samuel, 325:13
Withers, Googie, 37:7
Wittgenstein, Ludwig, 217:16,
259:3
Woddis, Roger, 48:12
Wodehouse, Leonora, 101:2
Wodehouse, P. G., 4:16, 15:18,
17:9, 17:13, 21:18, 22:13,
23:3–4, 24:15, 25:13,
37:12–16, 41:9, 54:15, 56:7,
56:12–13, 63:3, 100:18, 101:2,
103:6, 106:9, 121:9, 123:18,
163:7, 165:8, 189:6, 192:13,
193:8, 196:14, 215:4,
218:11–12, 227:7, 232:20,
238:16–18, 242:23–24,
245:7, 262:11, 265:9, 277:11,
278:2, 302:8, 317:3, 322:9,
325:14, 334:17, 348:5, 349:13,
351:12–13, 358:18, 371:16,
378:15–17
Wolf, Daniel, 82:15
Wolfe, Thomas, 200:11, 250:7,
262:12, 330:10, 348:8, 384:18
Woman and Beauty, 140:6
Wood, Victoria, 238:19, 363:11
Woodhouse, Barbara, 109:7
Woodward, Marcus, 5:14
Woolf, Leonard, 6:13, 106:15,
151:7, 206:6
Woolf, Virginia, 44:10, 104:1,
104:3–6, 144:17, 149:21,
155:8, 176:7, 186:7, 207:4,
229:2–3, 244:10, 262:17,
270:4, 278:13, 290:4, 313:5,
317:2, 346:8, 362:2, 380:5–6,
383:7
Woollcott, Alexander, 9:16,
37:8, 65:2, 85:9, 93:13, 109:8,
112:17, 141:3, 156:13, 250:8,
338:11, 358:19

Worsthorne, Peregrine, 286:13
Wright, Frank Lloyd, 24:16,
165:10, 235:2, 355:8
Wright, Laurence, 166:2
Wright, Wilbur and Orville,
146:16
Wyatt, Woodrow, 160:5, 317:3,
376:18, 378:1
Wylie, Philip, 198:6, 307:5
Wyman Jane, 320:14
Wynder, Ernest L., 241:2

Y
Yankwich, Judge Leon R.,
198:7
Yeatman, R. J., 55:18, 100: 16,
118:8–9, 128:11
Yeats, Jack B., 298:21
Yeats, W. B., 11:16, 74:13–14,
78:9, 96:16, 110:14, 121:10,
163:8, 164:7, 177:9–10,
202:8, 232:21, 247:8,
268:13–16, 270:5, 290:5–6,
332:4, 361:15, 368:11,
384:1–3
Yevtushenko, Yevgeny, 176:8
Yorkshire Post, 51:3
Yorkshire Telegraph and
Star, 140:7
Young, Andrew, 106:1
Young, G. M., 41:17, 314:9–10
Yourcenar, Margaret, 17:10
Yu, Cao, 31:1

Z
Zangwill, Israel, 54:13, 310:7
Zanuck, Darryl F., 352:12
Zanuck, Richard, 261:8
Ziegler, Philip, 168:14, 355:17
Zilliacus, Konni, 49:13
Zolf, Larry, 295:12
Zuckerman, Solly, 132:5, 375:15
Zukor, Adolph, 15:19